BEAUTIFUL SHADOW

BY PATRICIA HIGHSMITH

Novels

Strangers on a Train	1950
The Price of Salt (writing as Claire Morgan)	1952
(republished under her own name as *Carol* in 1990)	
The Blunderer	1954
The Talented Mr Ripley	1955
Deep Water	1957
A Game for the Living	1958
This Sweet Sickness	1960
The Cry of the Owl	1962
The Two Faces of January	1964
The Glass Cell	1964
A Suspension of Mercy	1965
(*The Story-Teller* in the US)	
Those Who Walk Away	1967
The Tremor of Forgery	1969
Ripley Under Ground	1970
A Dog's Ransom	1972
Ripley's Game	1974
Edith's Diary	1977
The Boy who Followed Ripley	1980
People who Knock on the Door	1983
Found in the Street	1986
Ripley Under Water	1991
Small g: a Summer Idyll	1995

Short-story collections

Eleven	1970
(*The Snail-Watcher and Other Stories* in the US)	
The Animal-Lover's Book of Beastly Murder	1975
Little Tales of Misogyny	1975
Slowly, Slowly in the Wind	1979
The Black House	1981
Mermaids on the Golf Course	1985
Tales of Natural and Unnatural Catastrophes	1987
The Selected Stories of Patricia Highsmith	2001
Nothing That Meets the Eye:	2002
The Uncollected Stories of Patricia Highsmith	

Non-fiction

Plotting and Writing Suspense Fiction	1966

For children (with Doris Sanders)

Miranda the Panda is on the Veranda	1958

BEAUTIFUL SHADOW

A LIFE OF PATRICIA HIGHSMITH

ANDREW WILSON

BLOOMSBURY

First published in Great Britain in 2003

Copyright © Andrew Wilson, 2003

Excerpts from unpublished and quotes from published material of Patricia Highsmith by kind
permission of the Literary Estate of Patricia Highsmith, Zurich and Diogenes Verlag, Zurich
Copyright © 1993 by Diogenes Verlag AG, Zürich

The moral right of the author has been asserted

Bloomsbury Publishing Plc, 38 Soho Square, London W1D 3HB

A CIP catalogue record for this book
is available from the British Library

ISBN 0 7475 6314 4

10 9 8 7 6 5 4 3 2

Typeset by Hewer Text Ltd, Edinburgh
Printed in Great Britain by Clays Ltd, St Ives plc

To
Kate Kingsley Skattebol
and
Charles Latimer
(1937–2002)

Contents

Introduction

'The individual has manifold shadows, all of which resemble him, and from time to time have equal claim to be the man himself.'

– Kierkegaard quoted in Highsmith's 1949 journal[1]

When Patricia Highsmith looked up at the luminous face of the clock at the entrance to Pennsylvania station, New York, she would have seen two stone-sculpted maidens flanking the extravagant timepiece. One figure stared out across Manhattan to signify day; the other, with eyes closed, symbolised night – an appropriate double image for Highsmith herself, a writer fascinated by the concept of split identity. On that particular day – 30 June 1950 – the twenty-nine-year-old novelist was in pursuit of her antithesis: a blonde, married woman she had cast as a mannequin in a romantic drama of her own creation. She was going in search of the woman who had, unwittingly, inspired her lesbian novel, *The Price of Salt*.

In December 1948 – a year and a half before Highsmith found herself walking through Pennsylvania station – she was working, temporarily, in the toy department of Bloomingdale's when into the store walked an elegant woman wearing a mink coat. That initial encounter lasted no longer than a few minutes, yet its effect on Highsmith was dramatic. After serving the woman, who bought a doll for one of her daughters, leaving her delivery details, Highsmith later confessed to feeling 'odd and swimmy in the head, near to fainting, yet at the same time uplifted, as if I had seen a vision'.[2] At the end of her shift, she went home and wrote the plot for *The Price of Salt*, published in 1952 under a pseudonym and, in 1990, re-issued under her own name as *Carol*. A few days after the meeting she came down with chickenpox; one of the runny-nosed children in the toy department must have passed on the germ, she said, 'but in a way the germ of a book too: fever is stimulating to the imagination'.[3]

The Bloomingdale's woman had done nothing more than buy a doll from a shop assistant in a department store, yet Highsmith had infused the encounter with greater significance. She could not forget the blonde woman and on that day in the summer of 1950 she walked through Pennsylvania station with the intention of catching a train to the woman's home in New Jersey. She was going to seek her out, to spy on her.

Highsmith recorded the incident – in almost photographic detail – in her diary. As she stepped on to the train bound for Ridgewood, she felt as guilty as a murderer in a novel and on arrival at the suburban station she had to drink two rye whiskeys in order to steady her nerves. At Ridgewood station, she climbed on board a 92 bus, but after a few minutes, worrying that she was going the wrong way, she asked the driver whether he had already passed by Murray Avenue, the woman's home. 'Murray Avenue?' said the other passengers, as they all started to shout the correct directions at her. Blushing, she stepped down from the bus and started walking through the neatly planned, suburban streets towards the woman's house.

When Highsmith reached North Murray Avenue, a small lane backing onto woodland, she felt so conspicuous and overwhelmed by guilt she decided to turn back. But then an aquamarine car eased its way out of a driveway and headed towards her. Inside was a woman with blonde hair, wearing a pale-blue dress and dark glasses. It was her.

Already fascinated by the intertwined motives of love and hate, Highsmith wrote in her journal: 'For the curious thing yesterday, I felt quite close to murder too, as I went to see the woman who almost made me love her when I saw her a moment in December, 1948. Murder is a kind of making love, a kind of possessing. (Is it not, too, a way of gaining complete and passionate attention, for a moment, from the object of one's attentions?) To arrest her suddenly, my hands upon her throat (which I should really like to kiss) as if I took a photograph, to make her in an instant cool and rigid as a statue.'[4]

On her return to New York she noticed that strangers eyed her with suspicion, as if they could see the traces of her guilt smeared across her face. Although the two women did not meet that day in Ridgewood, within six months Highsmith felt driven to try and see her again. In January 1951, as she was writing *The Price of Salt*, which details a love affair between two women – Therese, a shopgirl in a toy department and Carol, a customer, who is married with a child – Highsmith made another trip out to New Jersey. This time she noted how the woman's house, with its black turrets and greyish towers, looked like something out of a fairy tale. She closed her eyes and imprinted the image in her memory, before watching the woman's children at play, observing how little they resembled their mother. 'Yes, I am delighted my Beatrice lives in such a house,' she wrote in her diary.[5]

Highsmith projected a complex array of emotions onto the woman, so she became both the model for Carol in *The Price of Salt* and an externalised embodiment of past lovers, an incarnation of her drives, desires and frustrations. Highsmith could 'be called a balladeer of stalking,' wrote Susannah Clapp in *The New Yorker*. 'The fixation of one person on another – oscillating between attraction and antagonism – figures prominently in almost every Highsmith tale.'[6] Specifically, she used the women in her life – a quite dizzying parade of lovers – as muses, drawing upon her ambiguous responses to them and reworking these feelings into fiction.

Like many a romantic, she was, at times, promiscuous, but her bedhopping was an indicator, rather than a confutation, of her endless search for the ideal. To paraphrase Djuna Barnes' novel *Nightwood* – a book given to her by one of the women she worshipped – in Highsmith's heart lay the fossils of each of the women she loved, intaglios of their identities. 'All my life work will be an undedicated monument to a woman,' she wrote in her diary.[7] Highsmith herself recognised that these women held the key to understanding her personality and her fiction. 'O who am I?' she asked herself in the early 1950s. 'Reflections only in the eyes of those who love me.'[8]

Publicly, however, Highsmith was reluctant to talk about her writing, precisely because she knew its source was often so very close to home. 'She was the least forthcoming of authors, and hated talking about her work,' says Craig Brown, who interviewed her on a number of occasions.[9] 'She seems to favour two answers to journalistic questions,' wrote Janet Watts in the *Observer* in 1990. 'One is "true"; the other, "I don't understand the question." . . . She smiles, but her hand, when I shake it, feels like a reluctant paw, withdrawing from contact.'[10] When Watts quizzed her about the inspiration for *Carol* and her relationships with women, Highsmith responded, 'I don't want to say. People's emotional life . . . I think it's all accidental, and not planned. It is very hard to talk about.'[11]

It wasn't only journalists who had a problem getting close to her. Daniel Keel, her literary executor and president of Diogenes Verlag, the Zurich-based publishing company, says it took Highsmith twenty years before she trusted him enough to share her thoughts and feelings. 'Before that it was simply "yes" or "no",' he says. 'There were great holes in the conversation.'[12] Another friend, the writer and art collector, Carl Laszlo says, 'She was a writer, not a speaker – one always had the idea she concentrated so as *not* to say anything, *not* to give anything away.'[13]

Barbara Roett, the partner of the late Barbara Ker-Seymer, remembers how Highsmith would tense up when touched. 'She wasn't a sensual person at all – when you embraced her, it was like holding a board. I always remember that she was quite shocked when I once said, "I must go and lie in the bath". She'd never actually laid down in a bath – rather, she would sit bolt upright in it. I said, "Pat, how can you? How could you sit upright in a bath?" She replied, "I would never lie down." I just had the feeling somehow she was not comfortable in her own body.'[14]

Vivien De Bernardi, a friend who lived near Highsmith in Switzerland, and one of her executors, believes the writer had a problem with intimacy. 'She may have had numerous sexual partners but she did not have that many people with whom she was genuinely intimate. Her relationships never lasted very long.

'She was sincere and direct – those are two key words that describe Pat – and she did not have a drop of dishonesty in her. Yet, I didn't like the ranting and raving, the nastiness, the hatred which would overflow. She would get on a subject and she would not give it up. She was like a dog gnawing on a bone. There were some subjects that, when she talked about them, I considered her to be a raving maniac. Her really true friends loved her in spite of some of her behaviour.

'It was obvious that this tremendous emotional reaction had nothing to do with reality. It was something internal and it was agonising for her. The nastiness had much more to do with her – with her inner state, her depression, her anger, and her self-hatred – than anything external.

'She did not understand her immediate reality because she had such a strange interior world. I felt strongly she needed to look into her own shadow.'[15]

Critics have wrestled with Highsmith's place in modern literature since the 1960s, when book reviewers and editors first began to notice that her novels were rather different to the mass of pulp fiction being churned out by crime writers. Even today, trying to 'locate' her in a literary context or tradition is almost impossible, as she herself admitted. 'I never think about my "place" in literature, and perhaps I have none. I consider myself an entertainer. I like to tell a fascinating story.

But every book is an argument with myself, and I would write it whether it is ever published or not.'[16]

Her gothicism – her insatiable appetite for the grotesque, the cruel, and the macabre, particularly evident in her short stories – owes a great deal to Edgar Allan Poe, with whom she shared a birthday, 19 January, while the tone of her books was also influenced by the 'noir' novels of the thirties and forties. Yet the themes and philosophical arguments that lie at the heart of her fiction reflect the bleak existentialist writings of Dostoevsky, Kierkegaard, Nietzsche, Kafka, Sartre and Camus, all of whom she read. Behaviour or destiny, Highsmith felt, could not be predicted and deterministic readings of life leached man of the very thing that differentiated him from lower forms of life. 'Admit that human life can be guided by reason and all possibility of life is annihilated,' she wrote, quoting Tolstoy, in one of her journals.[17] She celebrated irrationality, chaos and emotional anarchy, and regarded the criminal as the perfect example of the twentieth-century existentialist hero, a man she believed was 'active, free in spirit'.[18]

The year before she wrote her first published novel, *Strangers on a Train*, she read Albert Camus' existentialist classic, *L'Étranger* or *The Stranger*, whose narrator, Meursault, embodies the dislocated hero so favoured by Highsmith. The hero, she surmised in a 1947 journal, represented, 'willness, like the believer in Existentialism, perhaps?'[19] before going on to link the novel with Dostoevsky's *Notes from Underground*, another account of a man's disassociation from society. She observed how man would snuff out his existence rather than endure a life which was rational, determined, planned and predicted.

She loved the paintings of Francis Bacon and, towards the end of her life, she kept a postcard of his *Study Number 6* on her desk. 'To me Francis Bacon paints the ultimate picture of what's going on in the world,' she said, 'mankind throwing up in a toilet with his naked derrière showing.'[20] Highsmith's fiction, like Bacon's painting, allows us to glimpse the dark, terrible forces that shape our lives, while at the same time, documenting the banality of evil. The mundane and the trivial are described at the same pitch as the horrific and the sinister and it is this unsettling juxtaposition that gives her work such power. As Terrence Rafferty, writing in *The New Yorker*, said, 'Patricia Highsmith's novels are peerlessly disturbing – not great cathartic nightmares but banal bad dreams that keep us restless and thrashing for the rest of the night . . . Our minds have registered everything, the ordinary and the horrible, with absolute neutrality; we seem to have been marooned in a flat, undifferentiated territory, like a desert – a place without values, without the emotional landmarks of our fictions or our waking lives.'[21] Highsmith, although working within the suspense genre, not only transcended its confines, but created a whole new form. 'Popular fiction isn't supposed to work on us this way,' added Rafferty.[22]

The writer Will Self, in a BBC2 television programme discussing Highsmith's legacy, said, 'I think she's only a crime writer in the sense that you would say Polanski made thriller movies; that's not what they're about. To me the experience of reading my first Highsmith book was a physical experience of being confronted with evil . . . I put it [the book] away because I felt tangible evil coming off the page . . . I think she'll be remembered as one of the great mappers of this topography of criminal psychopathology, and an anticipator, in a way, of the collective obsession with serial killers and evil that has come to pass, a precursor if you like.'[23]

According to Daniel Keel, 'She was better than other American writers such as Philip Roth and Norman Mailer. In the future she'll be remembered long after more "fashionable" novelists have faded into obscurity. Her voice is unique in fiction.'[24]

Highsmith's most famous creation is Tom Ripley, the charming psychopath who features in five of her twenty-two novels. He is a cold-blooded killer with a taste for the finer things in life. He paints and sketches, plays Bach's Goldberg variations and Scarlatti on the harpsichord, reads Schiller and Molière and is rather proud of his art collection (van Goghs and Magrittes, together with drawings by Cocteau and Picasso). The thud of a corpse falling into a freshly dug grave gives him a positively delicious pleasure and he laughs at the sight of two of his victims burning in a car – yet this is the same man who is moved to tears at the sight of Keats' grave.

Highsmith used Ripley as a device with which she could dismantle the cosiness of conventional crime writing. According to W.H. Auden, the basic formula of detective fiction could be plotted out as follows: 'A murder occurs; many are suspected; all but one suspect, who is the murderer, are eliminated; the murderer is arrested or dies.'[25] Not so in a Highsmith novel. 'I think it is a silly way of teasing people, "who-done-it",' she said of the detective novel. 'It doesn't interest me in the least . . . It is like a puzzle, and puzzles do not interest me.'[26]

She cleverly seduces the reader into identifying with Ripley until by the end our moral responses have been so invaginated, we are actively on the side of the killer, hoping he will escape punishment, as indeed he does, with increasing bravura, in each book. Without a doubt, High-

smith admired her rather superior breed of murderer and often regarded their victims as second-rate citizens. 'In some of my books the
victims are evil or boring individuals, so the murderer is more important than they,' she said. 'This is a writer's remark, not a legal
judge's.'[27] Graham Greene, one of her greatest fans, called her 'the poet
of apprehension',[28] a writer who has created a 'world without moral
endings . . . Nothing is certain when we have crossed *this* frontier.'[29]

From the second novel in the series, Ripley lives in a house near
Fontainebleau named 'Belle Ombre' and the metaphor of the 'beautiful
shadow' is an appropriate one for Highsmith. Not only does she
legitimise entry into a world where we can savour, as Graham Greene
said, a range of 'cruel pleasures',[30] but her work explores the motif of
the double or splintered self. The changeable nature of identity fascinated her both philosophically and personally. 'I had a strong feeling
tonight . . . that I was many faceted like a ball of glass, or like the eye of
a fly,' she wrote in a 1942 journal.[31] Highsmith's friend Julia Diethelm
testifies to the truth of the notebook entry. 'With every person she
knew, she was always a different Pat,' she says.[32] Diethelm's husband,
Bert, adds, 'That's why it is so difficult to define her character. She had
many facets, many different projections.'[33]

If such a thing is possible, her private notebooks can be seen to
represent, if not an authentic self, at least an identity that is somehow
more substantial than the one she chose to show to the outside world. In
addition to keeping incredibly detailed diaries, she recorded her creative
ideas, observations and experiences in what she called her 'cahiers' or
working journals. She was also a prolific letter writer, dashing off
several hundred each year, an activity which earned her the epithet
'post-addicted'. It is these private documents – the diaries, notebooks
and letters held at the Swiss Literary Archives in Berne – together with
interviews with Highsmith's friends, colleagues and lovers, which form
the core of this book.

Many writers' diaries are works of self-mythology, often more
fantastical than their own fiction, but after checking Highsmith's
documents with other archival sources and information gleaned from
my interviews, it is clear that her private journals were written without
artifice. Her voice was tormented, self-critical but, significantly, brutally honest. She kept a diary, she said, because she was interested in
analysing the motivation of her behaviour. 'I cannot do this without
dropping dried peas behind me to help me retrace my course, to point a
straight line in the darkness.'[34] Throughout her life she toyed with the
idea of burning these most personal of journals, and although she was

given the opportunity to incinerate any incriminating material before her death, she only chose to destroy a few letters from one of her younger lovers.

Writing was Highsmith's way of exploring the darker aspects of her personality. 'She wrote from her unconscious,' says Daniel Keel. 'It just came out of her. She used herself, her life as a source.'[35] If she didn't write, Highsmith felt she merely existed. 'She was an obsessive writer, these stories just boiled up from her,' says Larry Ashmead, her editor at Doubleday in the sixties.[36] Highsmith herself admitted that she was never short of ideas; in fact she had them, she said, as frequently as rats had orgasms. Writing was a compulsion for her. 'I'm miserable when I can't write,' she said.[37]

I never met Patricia Highsmith, but like most biographers I have dreamt about my subject many times. The first time she 'appeared' to me was about four years ago. She was sitting at a large wooden table and the first thing I noticed about her were her extraordinarily large hands. Her complexion was tinged with green and she looked rather forbidding. She stared at me with her dark, haunted eyes and with a slight nod of the head, gave me permission to embark on her life. It may well have been wish fulfilment on my part, but I like to think the dream was a good omen. Highsmith, with her guarded eyes and the mane of black hair that she would occasionally wear like a curtain to shield her face, was so secretive that by the end of her life she had been dubbed, quite wrongly, a 'recluse' by journalists.

Like her fiction, Highsmith, who was appropriately ambidextrous, was dyadic – both self and spectre, her identity constantly in flux. 'Dostoevsky is criticised for ambivalence, for illogic, contradictions – worst of all, ambivalences in his philosophy,' she wrote in 1947. 'But there are always two. Perhaps this wonderful, magical, creative, public & private number is the mystic secret of the universe. One can love two people, the sexes are within all of us, emotions directly contrary do exist side by side. This is the way I see the world too.'[38]

For this reason, writing about Highsmith is a dangerous undertaking, one which she would, with her streak of black, sometimes cruel, humour, have no doubt appreciated. Confronted with her diaries, I paused for a moment before leafing through their delicate, leaf-thin, pages. Of course, I was curious to know her secrets, keen to hear her distinctive voice talk to me from the past. But I also felt guilty, like a character in one of her books, especially when I opened the pages of her 1942 diary, and found this:

> Look before and look behind,
> There's still time to change your mind;
> Perfidy no time assuages;
> Curst be he that moves these pages.[39]

A chilling note. Yet, on other occasions, I have felt quite blessed. Doors seemed to open, letters from long-lost friends arrived through my letter box and her inner circle, keen to protect her memory, began to reveal itself. Highsmith was adamant a biography should not be written while she was alive – indeed, she blocked several attempts – but secretly quite proud that one might be written when she was no longer around to witness the result. Biographers who swooped around her like vultures disgusted her, but she realised, as she wrote to her friend, Charles Latimer, 'I do NOT mean to sound as important as Winston Churchill, but am absolutely sure someone will wish to "write something" when I'm dead.'[40] She also stated that an examination of her relationships was a legitimate subject for investigation. 'In case of biog how much of my personal liaisons should be mentioned, and I replied if they picked me up or let me down, they should be mentioned . . . I said it would be hypocritical to try to avoid the subject, and that everyone must know I am queer, or gay.'[41]

Writing a life of anyone, let alone someone as perplexing as High-smith, is a highly subjective task. No one, even with access to the fullest and most intimate of diaries, can document a life in all its richness. Highsmith, too, was aware of this, as she wrote in her 1940 journal. There were, she said, certain emotions or incidents which she had failed to record. Those memories, as she said in a poem, were, 'Fixed in my head/And there they'll remain/Even after I'm dead.'[42] Even so, the novelist realised that it was still possible to trace the complex matrix of connections that link the present to the past. She was so obsessed with recording and analysing her life that the journals, diaries and letters which survive provide a rich source of material so alive with detail that the current biographical trend to turn to more fictional methods was unnecessary.

Highsmith herself said, in a journal entry discussing a biography of Dostoevsky, that the most intimate way of knowing any writer was to make a chronological history of their 'moods, fits and daily activities',[43] together with details about what they wrote when. That, surely, was the best way of understanding them and that is what I have attempted to do here. This is a biography first and foremost and although I have attempted to set Highsmith within her historical and cultural context, expansive literary criticism is outside the scope of this book. I have, however, for those readers unfamiliar with her work, tried to explain why her novels and short stories are superior to the mass of popular crime fiction, citing the sources from which she drew her ideas to help explain the power of her writing. As Highsmith writes in *The Blunderer*, 'if you knew the kind of books a man wanted, you knew the man.'[44]

After reading her private, unpublished papers, I felt like her confessor, like the imaginary empathetic friend she wrote about in one of her notebooks, whom she describes lying before a fire, with their hands behind their head, listening to the author talk about 'the little dark pockets of the past'.[45] As the wood smoke twists and curls its way towards me, Highsmith starts speaking. 'I could tell you many stories, some of them bitter, many of them strange, but all of them true.'[46]

I

The forever seeking

1921 and before

In one of Highsmith's early notebooks there is a short vignette about a boy who wonders why he is happy at one moment and sad the next. As the boy grows older, he becomes increasingly fascinated by the nature of consciousness and people come from afar to ask him the question: 'What and why am I?'[1] Like the boy in her story, Highsmith was a writer in search of identity. On every page of her cahiers and diaries the same self-searching questions are asked over and over again. Was she the sum of her consciousness? Or was her self merely made up of the perceptions of other people? 'There is an ever more acute difference . . . between my inner self which I know is the real me, and various faces of the outside world,' she wrote in 1947.[2] And could a writer, forever assuming the personalities of his or her characters, even have such a thing as a stable identity?

Towards the end of her life, Highsmith became fascinated by genealogy, building up a mass of papers which purport to trace her lineage, through the Stewarts, her maternal grandmother's line, back to James I. She wrote to distant relatives, genealogists, the College of Arms in London and local historians so as to piece together the fragments of her family history. Running parallel to this desperate urge to find roots in the past, was the instinct to escape the present and a desire to chase the unobtainable. This manifested itself by her nomadic journeying around the world, from her birth place in Fort Worth, Texas, to New York, Mexico, Germany, Austria, Italy, England, France and Switzerland. In a poem she wrote when she was only twenty she imagined what her state of mind would be like in the future – after travelling around the world, she surmised, she would know hundreds of people in a clutch of different cities and yet she would still be lonely. 'I am the forever-seeking,' she said.[3]

When Highsmith was thirteen years old she bought a pair of Confederate swords for $13. Later in life, each time she moved house, she would make sure these weapons from the American Civil War were displayed in a suitably prominent position. For all her European veneer – she had a working knowledge of French, German, Spanish and Italian – she was undeniably Texan. Her favourite food was the traditional cooking of the South – cornbread, collard greens, spare ribs, black-eyed peas and peanut butter – and towards the end of her life she felt most comfortable dressed in the basic uniform of the off-duty cowboy: 34-inch-waist Levis, sneakers and neckerchiefs.

'The fact that Pat was from Texas is incredibly important for an accurate appreciation of her character,' says her friend, the American playwright Phyllis Nagy, who knew Highsmith when she was in her sixties. 'When you say things like this to people who aren't American they think it's terribly facile but Southern conservatism was deeply ingrained in her. People forget that she was a very conservative person – she wasn't bohemian like Jane Bowles and she did hold some very weird and contradictory views.'[4]

Highsmith was born on 19 January 1921 in Fort Worth, thirty miles west of Dallas. In addition to Poe, she shared her birthday with Robert E. Lee, the US Confederate commander in the Civil War, whom she later named as her favourite historical figure. She would leave Texas for New York at the age of six, returning intermittently for short periods throughout her childhood, including an unhappy year when she was twelve, but the spirit of the Lone Star state, with its molten-hot, colourless sun, 'like something grown white with its own heat',[5] ran deep in her veins. Later in life, when asked by a journalist whether she was aware of any typically Texan characteristics in her personality, the writer replied, 'Maybe a kind of independence.'[6] As a young woman she also enjoyed horseriding – the one sport she indulged in – which she said was 'perhaps the only respect in which I resemble a Texan'.[7]

At school, Highsmith would have learned about the history of her home state before that of America: 'We chose this land; we took it; we made it bear fruit,' was a common mantra heard in many a Texan classroom. The phrase accurately articulated the 'territoriality of Texans – the feeling for place and tribe'[8] and the passion its people felt for the land no matter whose flag – Spanish, French, Mexican, Texan,

Confederate, American – could be seen blowing in the wind. 'The Texans in the 19th century did not create a "usable past", or one that buttressed 20th-century American mainstream thought,' writes historian T.R. Fehrenbach. 'The Texans emerged with a "blood memory," in the Texan writer Katherine Anne Porter's memorable phrase.'[9]

The Lone Star flag flew over Texas, proclaiming its independence, for ten years, before it was annexed by the United States. Yet the struggle for the frontier continued, a savage confrontation between the so-called 'civilising' elements of America and the untamed world of the Indian; a war of identity which, when retold through the generations, transformed itself into a near-mythical story of epic proportions, a tale the young Highsmith found fascinating. The constant battle for land on what was called the 'raw scar of the frontier'[10] – as late as 1870, the Kiowas, Comanches, Cheyennes, Kiowa-Apaches and Arapahoes prevented white men from stepping foot in nearly half of Texas – contributed to the Texan's belief in the rightness of his own law-making. In a land where opposing groups were battling for dominance, each man had to make his own rules, a structure of self-regulating morality which must have also interested the writer in later life. Texans were typically atomistic, empiricist of mind and independent, and, like Highsmith and many of her characters, they tended to shy away from groups in order to pursue their own physical and psychological journeys.

Running parallel to this rather creative approach to morality was the rich tradition of fire and brimstone inherited by detailed reading of the Bible. The Old Testament, with its graphic descriptions of good and evil, appealed to the Texan frame of mind. 'The young Texan read of evil that was ancient and ever-present, requiring eternal discipline of man . . .' writes Fehrenbach. 'And although few could articulate or explain it, Texans gained a timeless portrait of man's world, of the rise and fall of peoples, of bondage and deliverance, of God's patience and wrath, and man's enduring inhumanity to man.'[11]

Fort Worth – Highsmith's birthplace – was the site of many a brutal confrontation. Founded in 1849 by Major Ripley Arnold, the frontier town served as a military outpost to guard against Comanche Indian raids, protecting the white population to the east. The army left the town in 1853 but three years later, Fort Worth superseded neighbouring Birdville as the Tarrant county seat. From the 1870s onwards, Fort Worth became a place associated with movement, transition and the free flow of people, products and livestock, acting as a stopover point for the longhorn cattle drives on the Chisholm Trail, the route which ran from south of San Antonio, Texas, across Oklahoma, towards

Abilene, Kansas. Its position as a cattle-shipping boomtown was
secured with the arrival of the Texas and Pacific Railway in 1876,
by which time Fort Worth could boast thirteen saloons, with such
names as 'Red Light', 'The Waco Tap', 'Cattle Exchange' and 'Our
Comrades'. 'Fort Worth was less conscious of her morals than some of
her neighbors,' one old timer is recorded as saying.[12]

With the opening of the Fort Worth Stock Yards Company in 1893
and the development of the railway, Fort Worth transformed itself from
a dusty cow town into a major trading centre. The railroads had
revolutionised both its geography and its status and the city now
proudly declared itself to be the 'Queen of the Prairies', attracting
an influx of immigrants that only served to increase its prosperity. The
population grew from 3,000 in 1876, to 23,076 in 1890, and 27,000 by
the turn of the century. By 1910, 75,000 people lived within the city's
limits[13] and the discovery of oil in northwest Texas in 1917 fuelled the
economic boom even further. By 1924 – three years after Highsmith's
birth – the nine refineries in the area produced petroleum products
valued at $52 million a year, making Fort Worth the 'oil capital of
North Texas'.

From where Highsmith was born, two streets south of the Texas and
Pacific tracks that slice the city in two along an east-west axis, she
would have heard, as she describes in her first published novel,
Strangers on a Train, the roar and 'angry, irregular rhythm' of the
trains that tore through the 'vast, pink-tan blankets' of the prairies.[14] In
that novel, Guy on a visit back to his home, the fictional Texan town of
Metcalf, hears a locomotive wailing in the distance, a sound which
reminds him of his childhood, a noise which is 'beautiful, pure, lonely.
Like a wild horse shaking a white mane.'[15] And it was the railroad, with
its distinctive tarantula-like network, and the ensuing employment
boom, that attracted Highsmith's family to Fort Worth.

In 1904, Highsmith's maternal grandparents Daniel and Willie Mae
Coates travelled from Alabama to Texas in a bid to capitalise on Fort
Worth's economic buoyancy. Both husband and wife had come from
solid, respectable, upwardly mobile backgrounds. Daniel was the son of
plantation-owner Gideon Coats (the 'e' was added at some point at the
end of the nineteenth century), while Willie Mae was the daughter of Dr
Oscar Wilkinson Stewart, a surgeon. Highsmith was particularly proud
of these two great-grandfathers, men who symbolised the spirit of
American adventure and pioneering. She could not understand how her
family could have fallen, as she saw it, so far down the social scale and

she constantly turned to the past as a way of reassuring herself of her origins.

Gideon Coats, born in 1812, came from South Carolina and travelled to Alabama to resettle. After exploring the state, looking for a suitable place to build a plantation, the bearded, dark-eyed man found Coats Bend, then nothing more than a mass of dense forests and windswept sagebrush fields. In true pioneer style, he bought 5,000 acres from the Cherokee Indians for an undisclosed sum and in 1842 constructed what became known as the Coats mansion, a ten-room house with twenty-foot rooms and fourteen-foot-high ceilings. The whole house was built without the use of nails; instead it was fixed together using nothing but wooden pegs, an architectural detail that delighted Highsmith. In fact, she was so taken with the plantation house she kept a photograph of it in one of her albums. Later in life she would confess that one of her favourite books was Margaret Mitchell's Civil War classic, *Gone with the Wind*, 'because it is a true novel about the South', before adding, perhaps somewhat naively, that, 'My great-grandfather in Alabama had something like 110 slaves and they were not unhappy.'[16]

Gideon Coats married Sarah Deckered in 1842 and together they had eight children, including Highsmith's grandfather, Daniel, born on 13 October 1859. The Coats were famous for having large feet and hands, physical characteristics inherited by Highsmith. 'I think most of us were "bent too soon" in that we have large feet, also large hands,' wrote one relative to the author, unable to resist making a pun on the name of the family's birthplace.[17]

Willie Mae's father, Dr Oscar Wilkinson Stewart, was born in 1829, one of the sixteen children of Elizabeth Dechard and William Stewart, a Scot so pious he wore holes in the carpet of his bedroom by his 'frequent and protracted kneeling in the act of prayer'.[18] Oscar grew up to be a physician who served as a Confederate States surgeon in the Civil War, and with his wife, Mary Ann Pope, he raised eight children, including Willie Mae, who was born on 7 September 1866 in Auburn, Alabama. The girl was only seven when her 44-year-old father died of yellow fever, in Memphis, Tennessee, in September 1873.

The two families were united when, on 25 December 1883, Daniel Coates and Willie Mae Stewart married in Coats Bend, Alabama. Although Daniel was given a grist mill, store and sawmill by his father, during the early years of the new century the couple, with their five children – Edward, Dan, John, Claude, and Mary, all of whom were born between 1884 and 1895 – decided to travel 600 miles west in search of a better life. 'They packed up everything they had, their china, crystal and silver, and drove west,' says Don Coates, Willie Mae's great-grandson. 'One of the reasons they decided to move was, I suppose, quite a selfish motive: they only wanted to look after their own family, not the extended family back in Alabama.

'My great-grandmother did not go to college but she was self-educated and was a voracious reader. Willie Mae was also amazingly strong-willed, like Pat. I recall once going over there for Sunday dinner and I was slightly taken aback because she was sitting very upright in her rocking chair, not at all in her usual relaxed state. When Daddy asked what was wrong, she finally admitted that she had fallen off the ladder while painting the ceilings. Even though she was that old she was painting the twelve-foot-high ceilings, but that was Grandma, she was going to do what she wanted to do and you weren't going to tell her otherwise. She was her own woman.'[19]

Don's brother, Dan, also remembers the matriarchal Willie Mae, who died in 1955 at the age of eighty-eight. 'She was a very small woman – I guess she was five foot one – and kind of wiry, with little metal-framed glasses,' he says. 'She used to work hard, had a head of stone and was rather outspoken and opinionated. She was extremely independent and was not afraid of the Devil himself. And she made the best milkshake in America. Pat really identified with her and respected her for her work ethic.'[20] Highsmith remembered Willie Mae as an extremely moral woman who taught her the difference between right and wrong: 'She was a Scot, very practical, though with a great sense of humor, and very lenient with me.'[21]

The Southside of Fort Worth, the part of the city in which High-smith's family made their home, was already a residential area by the end of the nineteenth century, but during the first decade of the twentieth century the neighbourhood witnessed a massive influx of new residents. Transport links were improved and the area boasted a street railway system, running in a square south down Main Street to Magnolia Avenue, west to Henderson Street, north to Daggett Avenue and east to Jennings.

Willie Mae and Daniel first settled in Fort Worth at 523 West Daggett Avenue but by 1910 they had moved further along the street, to 603, into a traditional wooden-frame structure that looked like a miniature version of the Coats mansion, where they opened a boarding house. They did this, according to Highsmith, 'with practically no capital . . . catering at first to young gentlemen of talent and sensibility.'[22] Enterprising to the last, the couple also rented out a number of small, wooden, red-painted shacks to black families at the back of their house, an area which came to be known as Red or Negro Alley.

'Behind the house was an alley, a large alley, in which there were little red-painted cottages that Willie Mae would lease out to black families,' remembers Dan, 'and that was part of her income. She was a pretty good business-woman and did a good job. One day the people back in the alley had a big party, and they all got drunk. There were about twenty-five blacks back there raising hell and cursing. She grabbed a white robe – I'll never forget it – and went out to confront the blacks who were all boozed up. She walked straight out and told those who did not live there to get home where they belonged and she meant right this minute. And you know what? They did as they were told – oh gosh, the way they behaved, you'd have thought she was carrying a shot-gun.'[23]

Sometimes, black children who lived in 'Red Alley' would knock on the back door of the Coates' house and ask if she had any leftovers. 'She would fix them a dish of what was left from the noon meal and the children would take the food out to the alley,' remembered Willie Mae's grandson, Dan – the father of Dan and Don – who came to live with his grandparents in 1913 after the death of his parents.[24] 'The house, though plain and ramshackle, showing a hint of poverty even here and there, could always make room for one more, could always provide food for one more mouth, and generously, and love for one more heart,' Highsmith wrote in her journal.[25]

Across the street from the boarding house was a two-storey factory built from brick and occupied by Exline-Reimers Printing Company, whose employers also enjoyed Willie Mae's hospitality. 'She had quite a few mail carriers [men who sorted the mail for different towns as they travelled on the railroads] that ate there,' wrote Dan to Highsmith, his cousin, 'as well as the folks at X-REIMERS [sic] printing across the street.'[26]

Willie Mae and Daniel's only daughter, Mary Coates, was born in Coats Bend, Alabama, on 13 September 1895, the youngest of five children. She was striking-looking, 'a double for Greta Garbo'.[27]

A photograph taken of Mary a couple of years after giving birth to her daughter shows that she was a slim, elegant woman, with a fashionable flapper haircut framing a perfectly made-up face, while her knowing pose – hand placed seductively on the knee, ankles neatly crossed, eyes looking mischievously to one side – betrays a self-confident sexuality. It is obvious from the portrait that Mary took a keen interest in her appearance, not unusual in an age when, according to contemporary advertisements, a woman's beauty really did make the difference between romantic success and failure. 'The first duty of woman is to attract . . .' ran one advertisement. 'Your masterpiece – yourself,' another promised its readers.[28] In the same photograph, sitting next to Mary on the grass in front of the Coates house, is her daughter, Patricia, but Mary seems uninterested in the boyish-looking girl with her anxious expression, basin haircut and pudgy face.

Mary confessed that there was a certain distance and frostiness between herself and her own mother. She was doted upon by her father, but Willie Mae never told Mary that she loved her and as a result Mary said that she grew up feeling rejected by the one person she wanted to please, an emotional pattern which Highsmith, too, would inherit.

'You spoke of what your grandmother [Willie Mae] wouldn't do,' Mary wrote to her daughter, in an undated letter. 'She treated you differently than she did me. It was as if she was not the same person. She went to her grave never letting me know that I ever made the grade. But my father wasn't like that – he told her I was better than all the boys put together.'[29]

Mary showed an early talent for drawing and painting and hoped to become a fashion illustrator. 'She was incredibly creative and a very visual person, skills which Pat inherited from her and there's no doubt that Willie Mae, Mary and Pat were all extremely strong-willed women,' says Don. 'Pat as a child had certain needs and wants which she felt Mary didn't provide. But because of her success and her hard work, Mary was able to provide her daughter with an education. In many ways she did a lot more for Pat and her future than if she had been right there playing mom and baking cookies.'[30] 'Mary was, bless her soul, a very eccentric woman,' adds his brother, Dan. 'Oh my God, she was more fun than a barrel of monkeys, just a wonderful lady. She was very outgoing but probably not the best mother in the world. She was a very career-minded person, not a little homemaker at all.'[31]

One day, when Mary Coates was in her early twenties, she was walking past a photographer's window in Fort Worth when she saw the image of a black-haired, dark-eyed man with rather simian features and a slight, wiry body; apparently she was so struck by the picture that she sought him out. That man was Highsmith's real father – Jay Bernard Plangman.

Jay Bernard Plangman, or Jay B as he would later be called, was born one street south of the Coates family home in Fort Worth, at 508 West

Broadway, on 9 December 1887. His parents, Minna Hartman and Herman Plangman, were both from German stock, and, perhaps unusually, it is from this side of the family that Highsmith inherited her dark hair and eyes and her somewhat sallow complexion.

Highsmith's physical characteristics intrigued her, but when anyone tried to suggest that she might have had black ancestors she acted swiftly to squash the idea. Five years before she died the writer received a letter from a man in Bradford, England. He enclosed a picture of his paternal grandfather, Henry Highsmith, a black man born in South Carolina, and asked whether she belonged to an offshoot of the same family. Highsmith – who thought herself a liberal but at this point in her life also believed blacks were responsible for the welfare crisis in America – gave the inquiry short shrift. She wrote back a sniffy letter, stressing that Highsmith was not the name of her biological father – Stanley Highsmith was her stepfather – nor did he have any black or Red Indian blood.

Yet her colouring was so swarthy that she felt compelled to make some discreet inquiries into her background. 'Some time ago you inquired whether my mother (and Jay B's) had any Indian blood, because of her dark complexion and dark hair and eyes,' replied Walter Plangman, Highsmith's uncle 'She definitely had no Indian blood.'[32]

The dark features could be traced back to Jay B's grandmother, Liena, who, together with her two sisters, arrived in Galveston, Texas, from Germany, in the late 1850s. 'They were servants in well-to-do homes in Galveston, which at the time was the largest city in Texas,' said Jay B.[33]

During the 1850s, nearly one million Germans settled in America, making it one of the peak periods of German immigration. The failure of the revolutions of 1848 to establish democracy, plus the subsequent crop failures and potato famines, caused hundreds of thousands of Germans to leave their homeland and sail to America. So substantial was the community that by the 1860s, around 200 German-language magazines and newspapers were published in America. Guidebooks were published in Germany to outline the range of opportunities offered in America, while a number of societies were formed to make the immigration process easier.

Soon after stepping foot in Texas, age sixteen, Liena married Henry Hartman, another German immigrant, and on 6 September 1865, she gave birth to a daughter, Minna, in Indianola. When Minna, whom Highsmith only met on a couple of occasions, describing her as 'very jolly, not tall and very dark-haired',[34] was twenty-one she married

Herman Plangman, who, together with his parents Gesina and Herman, left their home in Emden, Germany, for a new life in Texas. 'They were all Lutherans, I think,' Highsmith later said, 'hardworking, respectable, mildly prospering'.[35]

Liena had another child, a son, Oscar, but after the death of her husband, from tuberculosis, Highsmith's great-grandmother married again, this time a merchant, Ernest August Kruse, who had been born in Germany in 1839 and who owned property on Houston Street and Main Street, Fort Worth. By the 1880s, Liena and Ernest August Kruse were living in Fort Worth in a house across the street from her daughter, Minna, and grandchildren, Bernard, Herman and Walter. The latter remembered that Liena 'taught me to speak German before I learned to speak English.'[36] Although many first-generation German immigrants reconstructed much of their Old World culture, by 1917, as a consequence of the First World War, the majority of German Americans in Fort Worth had taken out citizenship in order to advertise their loyalty to their new country.

Jay B, like his future wife Mary Coates, was artistic from an early age and as a pupil at the Sixth Ward School, the same school Highsmith would attend, he remembered that he 'always liked to draw'.[37] After a spell working for the Texas and Pacific railroad – he was a railroad buff all his life – he enrolled at the Chicago Academy of Fine Arts, graduating in 1912. The following year he started work at the *Fort Worth Star-Telegram* as a staff artist and at the time of his daughter's birth he was a draftsman at Pearce Oil Company. During the Depression, Jay B taught art in the Fort Worth Public School system and one fellow teacher later recalled his kindness. 'He [Jay B] got $3 a day for teaching and gave me a dollar of it,' said commercial artist Marvin Van Orden. 'That shows you what kind of a man he is, what kind of character Mr Plangman's really got – giving away a third of his salary when money was really short.'[38]

It would be simplistic to link Highsmith's fictional fixation with identity too closely with her own unhappy circumstances, but her familial history was so dysphoric that it's hard to see how it could fail to play some part. After all, Highsmith wasn't even her real name – she was born Mary Patricia Plangman – and she didn't meet her biological father until she was twelve years old.

The marriage between Mary Coates and Jay Bernard Plangman took place on 16 July 1919, but a year later, the couple experienced a crisis that eventually resulted in divorce. In the summer of 1920, Mary discovered she was four months pregnant; she wanted to keep the child, but Bernard suggested she have an abortion. Five months before the birth, Mary tried to rid herself of her unborn child by drinking turpentine. 'It's funny you adore the smell of turpentine, Pat,' her mother would tell her later.[39] Fifty years after her birth, Highsmith asked her parents to explain the exact circumstances surrounding the attempted termination.

'(I believe in abortion, and the decrease of the population, so you must not think for a moment I am annoyed by this idea),' Highsmith wrote to her father in 1971, 'and according to my mother, she wanted a child, and she divorced you to have it in peace.'[40]

Jay B confessed that the abortion was his idea. 'I did suggest an abortion as we were just getting started in the art field in New York and thought it best to postpone a family until some time later,' wrote Jay B to his daughter. 'The turpentine was suggested by a friend of Mary's and tried with no results.'[41] Jay B planned to travel with Mary to Manhattan, where she could work as a commercial artist, and he could act as her manager. 'He thought that with her ability and his selling they could make good money,' wrote Dan Coates to his cousin. 'And when she became pregnant he thought she should abort because a baby didn't fit into his plans at the time.'[42]

After a short period of separation, when Mary was in Anniston, Alabama, on a three-week vacation, she returned to her husband and told him she wanted a divorce, not such an unusual request as one might think. Between the years 1870 and 1920, the number of divorces in America shot up by a factor of fifteen, and statistics show that in 1924 one marriage in seven ended in divorce. 'More wives than ever before had done paid work during marriage,' says Sarah Jane Deutsch, outlining women's history between 1920 and 1940, 'and they knew they had options other than staying in an unsatisfactory marriage.'[43] Women felt newly emancipated – in 1920 women could vote in national elections on the same basis as men everywhere in the United States, the result of a seventy-year battle by American suffragettes. 'Above all, in the 1920s, there was a pervasive sense of newness,' Deutsch adds.[44] It was, of course, the age of the flapper, when, according to Frederick Lewis Allen, whose classic book *Only Yesterday* defined the era, 'women were bent on freedom – freedom to work and play without the trammels that had bound them heretofore to lives of comparative inactivity.'[45] Women, with their bob hairdos and hiked skirts, mutated themselves into what Allen called unripened youths, 'hard-boiled adolescents' who no longer thought in terms of love, but sex.

Jay B offered to 'do anything to keep the marriage intact',[46] but it was no use. The union lasted only eighteen months in all. 'I remember them [the Coates family] getting a lawyer and filing for a divorce and telling him [Jay B] they didn't want anything he had,' said Dan.[47]

The minutes of the District Court 67th Judicial District of Texas, lodged at Tarrant County Court in Fort Worth, show that a divorce between Mary Coates Plangman and Jay Bernard Plangman was granted on 10 January 1921. Nine days later, at 603 West Daggett Avenue, Fort Worth, at 3.30 on the morning of 19 January 1921, Mary gave birth to a baby daughter, an only child.

The man who would assume the role of her father was yet another commercial artist, Stanley Highsmith, who was five years younger than Mary and lived at 2424 College Avenue, Fort Worth. 'Stanley was an extremely quiet man, very low-key, but he had a great, but rather dry, sense of humour and was a fabulous photographer,' says Dan Coates.[48] Photographs show him to be quite a dapper man, with a neatly clipped moustache and small, round spectacles. Born illegitimately in 1900, his mother was left to raise him single-handedly, until she married again. Pat did not know about the circumstances surrounding her stepfather's birth until much later, when she was in her forties.

'His character is not weak, but he has no push . . .' she wrote to her mother about Stanley. 'It's plain now, from what you tell me, that he had "obstacles", things that would make him feel shy and inferior since his early days.'[49]

Mary Coates Plangman married Stanley Highsmith on 14 June 1924, when Patricia was three years old. Her family, which Highsmith would later look back upon as a little hell, was formed.

2

Born under a sickly star

1921–1927

Highsmith was born into an America on the cusp of change, a country caught between nostalgia for the past and the exciting promise of the future. For the first time in its history, the United States, according to the census of 1920, was officially recognised as an urban nation, with over 50 per cent of its population living in towns or cities. (Ten years later the corresponding figure had increased to 69 per cent.)

In the autumn of 1920, 16 million Americans – just over 60 per cent of those who voted – opted for the well-dressed, silver-haired Republican senator from Ohio, Warren Harding. Harding promised a return to 'normalcy' – 'not revolution but restoration; not surgery but serenity'. Harding was quick to realise that what ordinary Americans wanted was not further involvement in world politics – the country's backing of the Allied cause in the First World War had left it in a state of crisis, with increased inflation, unemployment and social unrest – but an increased investment and improvement in their own affairs. When Harding made his inaugural speech in 1921, an address broadcast on radio, the Republican promised to lower taxes and reduce legislation, measures which he hoped would boost the economy by helping to promote the rapid rise of the individual. Under President Harding – and subsequently, John Calvin Coolidge, Republican vice-president and presidential successor from 1923 – America recovered from its post-war depression and entered a feverish boom, which saw the economy flourish and consumer spending increase. By 1929, the gross national product increased by 40 per cent with corresponding low inflation.

The twenties was the first mass-media age. Advertisers were labelled the new 'captains of consciousness'[1] and by the end of the decade three

out of four Americans owned a radio and said they went to the movies
at least once a week. Henry Ford's ideas of mass production of low-cost
luxury goods – and the payment of higher wages to workers so as to
boost their power as consumers – were seized upon by America's
corporations. Yet the country could not sustain such high-energy
intensity for long, and, like a person suffering from particularly serious
case of bipolar disorder, in 1929, the mania that had gripped America
was replaced by another crushing depression.

Ironically, for all of Harding's pledges to return America to a state of
'normalcy', the era was defined by fragmentation, social unease, and
cultural crisis. From the beginning of the decade the United States was
gripped by a fear of social revolution and paranoia surrounding
anarchic uprisings; there was, according to one commentator, a strange
poison in the air. In 1921, the year of Highsmith's birth, Nicola Sacco
and Bartolomeo Vanzetti, two Italian immigrants and self-confessed
anarchists, were sentenced to death for the payroll murders in Brain-
tree, Massachusetts, on the basis of what many believed to be flimsy
evidence. 'I am suffering because I am a radical . . . an Italian,' said
Vanzetti, while the judge in the case concluded that although the men
may not have committed the murders they were nevertheless 'the enemy
of our existing institutions . . . The defendant's ideals are cognate with
crime.' Despite a vigorous freedom campaign led by some of America's
leading intellectuals, including Albert Einstein, John Dos Passos and
Dorothy Parker, the two men were executed in August 1927. The case
split the country. 'All right, we are two nations,' wrote John Dos Passos
in his novel *USA* – a book which Highsmith read – referring to the
public's reaction to the prosecution.

At the same time, European and American art and literature was
experiencing something of a cultural schism. 'The world broke in two in
1922 or thereabouts,' said Willa Cather, referring to the year which she
thought served as a barrier between the traditionalism of the past and
the new modernism. That same year, Harold Stearns edited a book of
essays, *Civilization in the United States*, which concluded that America
did not have a civilisation, echoing the voices of disillusioned writers
such as Ernest Hemingway, Ezra Pound, Katherine Anne Porter,
William Carlos Williams and F. Scott Fitzgerald, all of whom left
America for Europe. 'We have no heritage or tradition to which we
cling,' said Stearns, 'except those that have already withered in our
hands and turned to dust.'[2]

The concept of a culture in crisis was reflected in 'The Waste Land',
T.S. Eliot's epic exploring the fragmentary nature of modern life –

which Highsmith would study in 1941 while at Barnard – a work published in 1922, the same year as Joyce's *Ulysses*, Katherine Mansfield's *The Garden Party* and F. Scott Fitzgerald's *The Beautiful and the Damned* and *Tales of the Jazz Age*. A year before, the year of Highsmith's birth, Einstein delivered a lecture on relativity at Columbia University in New York; Wittgenstein's *Tractatus Logico-Philosophicus* was published; Freud's *Dream Psychology* was printed in America and Rorschach's 'ink-blot' test was introduced into the country. It was during the twenties that terms such as 'libido', 'id' and 'superego' first entered popular discourse and, in the 1924 trial of the so-called 'thrill killers' Leopold and Loeb, two wealthy University of Chicago students who murdered a fourteen-year-old boy and who modelled themselves on Nietzsche's concept of the 'superman', Freud was cited in their defence. The popularity of Freud tapped into a desire for novelty and rebellion, and many young Americans, according to one historian, looked upon his theories as a 'justification against all accepted conventions, especially sexual ones'.[3]

At the same time the country developed an insatiable appetite for tabloid sensation stories and gruesome murder cases, such as the Snyder-Gray trial, in which a married woman, Ruth Brown Snyder and her lover Henry Judd Gray were each accused of murdering her husband; the case received wider coverage than more 'serious' subjects such as politics or international affairs. When Nan Britton, the secret mistress of the late Warren Harding and mother of his illegitimate child, published her autobiography, *The President's Daughter* in 1927, America's decade of 'normalcy' was finally exposed as a sham. The mood of the modern age – its superficial gloss and corresponding dark underside – was articulated by Amory Blaine, the hero of F. Scott Fitzgerald's novel, *This Side of Paradise*: 'Here was a new generation . . . grown up to find all Gods dead . . . all faiths in man shaken.'[4] Such a world would find a perfect chronicler in Patricia Highsmith.

It is all too easy for a biographer to trawl retrospectively through their subject's childhood searching for clues that might solve the mystery of creativity. The temptation is to hunt for an incident that occurred when the individual was an infant, an unarticulated psychological trauma that caused a dislocation of identity which then predisposed them to think of themselves as an outsider. Unhappy childhood plus repression equals a writer, runs the equation. As theories go, it is an attractive one – indeed, one that Highsmith herself occasionally subscribed to – but this neat explanation never quite captures the mysterious quality that defines the literary imagination. Highsmith's childhood was, in many ways, a desperately unhappy one, but of course, this does not explain why she became a writer.

That is not to say, however, that a detailed investigation of her early years cannot provide insights into the familial and cultural influences that shaped her character. Each of us, she wrote in her 1941 journal, is forced to confront the fact that our personalities are largely formed by our childhood and adolescence and although one might try and change certain aspects or qualities, any substantial transformation of our character is impossible. These early formative experiences, she said, 'now control what one is and what one is to be henceforth'.[5] She believed that heredity was more important than environment, yet also felt that the experiences of the first five years of life also shaped the personality.[6] In an interview with Diana Cooper-Clark, in 1981, Highsmith said that she believed in the concept of the 'bad seed' – that individuals were born evil – but yet also put some faith on the transformative potential of the individual personality. 'The phrase "poor schools" makes me laugh,' she said. 'I went to several. What counts is individual motivation. Ambition and drive count.'[7] And although some people maintained that they were not able to trace back the source of their problems to their childhood, Highsmith believed that if one looked hard enough, such a connection was always possible, 'some little thing will be the cause . . . a multitude of tiny things contribute like sand grains to a dune,'[8] she wrote in her journal in 1942.

A portrait taken of one-year-old Patsy, as she was then called by her family, shows her sitting in a little chair clutching a ball; her dark hair is cut in a rather severe style and her almond-shaped, intelligent eyes give her the look of an oriental baby. In fact, several neighbours who lived near the house in Fort Worth took her to be of Chinese origin. Her mother spent a great deal of time outside the home trying to establish her career – Mary travelled to Chicago to work just three weeks after the birth[9] – and as a result Patsy was largely brought up by her grandmother, Willie Mae, who taught her to read. 'My family says that I read nursery rhymes fluently aged two, but probably I knew them by heart,' she said.[10]

The bond between the women in the house was a strong one, until Stanley Highsmith arrived on the scene. From their first meeting, Highsmith disliked her stepfather, she said. She remembered Stanley appearing, when she was three years old, like an intruder and she was acutely aware that he was not her father. Interestingly, later in life

Highsmith would associate her stepfather's entrance into her life with the loss of a private, imaginary language. Patsy was reading a book when the tall figure walked into the room and asked if she could pronounce a particular word on the page. 'Open see-same!' shouted the little girl, proud she knew this magical phrase. Stanley corrected her pronunciation to 'Sess-a-mi!' but when Patsy repeated the word, her spirit was crushed. Stanley smiled indulgently down at her, 'his red heavy lips tight together and spread wide below his black moustache,' and although logically she knew his teaching was in her best interests, she loathed him at once.[11]

'And I knew he was right, and I hated him because he was right like grown-up people always were, and because he had forever destroyed my enchanting, "Open See-same," and because now the new word would have no meaning to me, had destroyed my picture, had become strange, unfriendly and unknown.'[12]

After the wedding, Stanley moved from his home on College Avenue, Fort Worth, into one of the apartments at Willie Mae and Daniel Coates' house, which he shared with his new wife. While he worked in the copy department of the Wimberly-Hubbard Agency, Mary tried to make a name for herself as a commercial artist and illustrator. 'She was also (is) definitely a feminine type,' said Highsmith about her mother. 'She simply considered it quite normal for a woman to be interested in her work, to act upon this, but my mother never preached one word about this that I recall; she simply did it.'[13]

Growing up in the Coates' house, ruled over by the kind-hearted, but terrier-like Willie Mae, Patsy realised that the women in her family were the dynamic ones; the men, she thought, were slightly insipid. Her grandfather, Daniel, worked as a district manager for the local Fort Worth newspaper, the *Star-Telegram*, but it was his wife who was the real force in the family. 'There weren't any strong men in my family,' she said later.[14] This view of men as the weaker of the two sexes is at odds with her later belief that they were, in fact, far superior creatures to women – an opinion which was reflected in her writing, particularly the sharp, acidic collection of short stories, *Little Tales of Misogyny*. This reassessment was, no doubt, connected to Highsmith's complex and, at times, contradictory emotional responses relating to her own sexual identity.

Talking to the writer and academic Bettina Berch, in 1984, she said that she saw women only in relation to men. They were, she thought, mere appendages – either married or totally dependent. 'Which is very curious because my mother was very . . . she was definitely rather brave. She had a career since she was twenty . . . So I had in my childhood the image of a rather strong independent woman – and yet I don't see them that way. I see them as a bunch of pushovers, for the most part. I see them as whining, to tell you the truth . . .'[15]

Six months after Stanley's arrival in the household, Patsy was still not comfortable with him. In the Christmas of 1924, when she was nearly four, her mother recalled that her daughter was 'silent, looking serious and apprehensive, as well I might, as my stepfather had in the last months come on the scene.'[16] That Christmas morning, as Patsy peeked through the sliding doors which separated the living room from the parlour – the room which housed the tree with its red and silver torch-shaped decorations and tinfoil icicles – she felt wary and unsure of herself. 'As I child, I was never ebullient, unless outdoors playing,' she said.[17]

That day the family breakfasted on coffee and oatmeal, followed by eggnog served from a large silver bowl and as they sat down to open their presents, they nibbled on home-baked cookies made by Willie Mae. Although they didn't go to church, Daniel said a short grace before sitting down to eat. Lunch consisted of roast turkey, cornbread, mashed sweet potatoes mixed with walnuts and topped with marsh-mallows, onions and celery, followed by home-made vanilla ice cream and a slice of Willie Mae's brandy-dosed fruit cake.

Just over one month later, in February 1925, four-year-old Patsy had her first taste of the exhilarating qualities of literary suspense as she read the newspaper coverage of the Floyd Collins saga, a compulsive, real-life drama that gripped the nation. On 30 January, Collins, a cave explorer hoping to find a new entrance to the Mammoth Cave System, in Kentucky, was trapped when a twenty-seven-pound rock fell on his foot. For more than two weeks, Floyd was imprisoned in the cold, wet passage, waiting to be rescued, while above ground something of a media frenzy developed.

The public's appetite for news was insatiable and the case was reported around America. However, after fifteen days under ground, Collins died. The authorities thought it was too dangerous to remove the body and left it there for eighty days. The drama – the struggle to rescue the trapped man before he perished, together with the story's gruesome climax – appealed to the young girl's imagination.

'I remember racing barefoot in my dropseat overalls,' recalled High-smith, 'down the hall to pick up the Fort Worth *Star Telegram* from the front porch and racing back to the kitchen to read aloud to my Scots grandmother, who at 7 a.m. would be standing at the stove, stirring a pot of oatmeal. This was my first adventure story, strung out with all the suspense of instalments.'[18]

Highsmith was four when she was involved in a life-and-death drama of her own. In 1925 she fell victim to a one of the most lethal epidemics in modern history – Spanish flu. From 1918 to 1919, the illness killed between 20 and 40 million around the world. In America, an estimated 25 million people, a quarter of the population, contracted the disease, between 375,000 and 550,000 fatally. The doctor, according to Highsmith, wrote her off as a certain death and stopped coming to the house because he didn't want another fatality on his hands. 'My grandmother, who was the daughter of a doctor, gave me calomel, which is a kind of laxative with mercury in it. I made it through on that.'[19]

'Where does guilt come from?' Highsmith asked. She rejected the concept that a child was born feeling guilty, but located its source in early infantile experiences. Later in life she would talk about how all her novels reflected her interest in the subject and how she created characters who were driven by the absence or presence of guilt. 'I am interested in whether certain people have or have not a sense of guilt under certain circumstances,' she said,[20] while critics have, quite rightly, highlighted the fact that culpability or the lack of it is one of her most powerful themes.

'It is the terrain of guilt and the effect of guilt, of fear and fear's destructive potency, the territory of pretence and desperation and unease,' says William Trevor of Highsmith's world. 'Hatred interested her more than love, the skewed more than the normal, the defeated more than the successful.'[21] In a Highsmith novel, says Susannah Clapp, 'guilt can seem to leak from one cracked vessel to another.'[22]

Prompted by Willie Mae's descriptions, Highsmith remembered herself as 'a small, dark figure,' 'an alert, anxious-faced child over whom hangs already the grey-black spirit of doom, of foreordained unhappiness, the knowledge of which made this child weep often.'[23] As authenticity is often inimical to recollection, it's questionable whether she actually felt this at the time or whether these were memories she subsequently projected onto her past. But by the time she had reached her late teenage years, she looked back at her childhood with a mixture of poetic longing and terrifying alienation, as she wrote in a 1942 verse, which begins, 'I was born under a sickly star.'[24]

Towards the end of her life, when she was engaged in a certain amount of soul-searching and self-analysis, she confessed to her friend

Vivien De Bernardi, that she thought she had been sexually abused between the ages of four and five.

'She told me once that she thought she might have been sexually abused at her grandmother's house,' says Vivien. 'She didn't have a clear memory of it, but she was a small child, around four or five, and remembered two men, whom she thought could have been salesmen, coming into the house. One of the men lifted her up and sat her on a counter or the kitchen sink. What exactly the abuse consisted of, I don't know but I certainly didn't get the impression that she was referring to anything like a rape. She had a sense of having been violated by these two men in the way she didn't really understand. She didn't understand what was going on and her memory of the occasion was not clear.'[25]

Of course, although this incident doesn't explain her sexuality, Highsmith could have been referring to the experience when she wrote to the American right-wing, anti-gay rights campaigner Anita Bryant. 'I did not say people are born homosexual,' she said, 'but they are quite often made homosexual by certain family conditions, as early as six or eight.'[26] If indeed Highsmith had been sexually abused it would have most likely have contributed to the feelings of alienation and disloca- tion which haunted her throughout her life. It could also go some way to understanding the roots of the overwhelming sense of guilt from which she suffered as a young child.

As a little girl, Highsmith had a terrifying recurring dream about being born, a nightmare which clearly symbolised the guilt which overshadowed her young life. Seven nurses and doctors stood around her small body in an atmosphere of 'murk and gloom'. She lay on a table but all she could see, from this strange, out-of-body perspective, was herself surrounded by the medics, who stared at her with a mixture of curiosity, pity and horror. 'They nod in solemn agreement over some unspeakable defect in me,' she wrote. 'It is an irrevocable pronounce- ment, worse than death because I am fated to live. I had this dream, or vision, before the age of six and frequently afterward.'[27]

From around this time, too, she was plagued by an hallucinatory spot, a grey blob that would dance and dart diagonally across the upper left-hand corner of her vision and which took the form of a mouse. The 'mouse' would appear whenever she was reading or staring at anything intently. The phantom creature did not, in itself, disturb her so much as the reaction of those around her when they witnessed her surprise at its sudden appearance. 'I was ashamed to tell them, of course, about my "mouse". But the imagined figure was so lifelike, I was never able to control my shock . . .'[28] The vision continued to appear between four and five times a week from the age of about five until she was seven. Then she was given a brindled cat for her birthday and shortly after this the mouse disappeared.

Whatever the truth about the suggestions of childhood sexual abuse, Highsmith did have some fond memories of growing up at her grandmother's house. She would sit in a pair of overalls, before the gas stove in the living room, reading the serials in the Fort Worth local press. From an early age she had an almost physical love for the written word and while she was reading she would often bring the newspaper close to her nose so she could breathe in the fragrant aroma from the ink, which was sometimes still warm from printing. She was also fascinated by a book about the history of the First World War which contained gruesome black and white photographs of injured and dead soldiers. Not all her reading matter was so bleak, however, as she also took to browsing through a book about Hollywood, which was packed full of photographs of matinee idols and starlets. 'On the nose of one of the blonde, cupid's-bow-lipped beauties, a little girl chum and I succeeded in smashing a large housefly by slamming the book shut. Gales of mirth!' she remembered.[29]

Nevertheless, she pinpointed this time in her life, when she was six years old, as the moment she first became aware that her emotional and sexual identity was somehow different from the norm. 'My character was essentially made before I was six,' she wrote to her stepfather.[30] Six years old may seem like a precocious age at which to become aware of one's sexuality, but she was conscious of feeling strangely different, an awareness she connected with her desire for other girls and its subsequent repression. Of course, she did not articulate it in these terms when she was a child, but later she would write, in an autobiographical, untitled, poem:

> It was no doubt a tragedy that I saw
> 'Forbidden' written like a word in red paint,
> 'Stop,' and could read it, when I was six.[31]

It is also clear that she resented Stanley's presence in the household and she blamed him for coming between her and her mother. By the time she was eight she had repeated fantasies about killing Stanley, confessing in her journal the 'evil thoughts, of murder of my stepfather, for example, when I was eight or less'.[32] When Highsmith was twenty-one, during a row with her mother in which she was accused of being odd, she told Mary that the reason why she was different from other people was because of 'sex primarily and my maladjustment to it almost from babyhood as a result of suppressed relations in the family – which is all a child's world for many years.'[33] Highsmith repressed and internalised these poisonous emotions. 'I learned to live with a grievous and murderous hatred very early on. And learned to stifle also my more positive emotions,' she wrote.[34] The dark fantasies nourished her gothic imagination. 'All this probably caused my propensity to write blood-thirsty stories of murder and violence,' she said.[35]

3

A house divided

1927–1933

When Patsy was six years old, she moved with her mother and stepfather from Fort Worth to New York. The Manhattan of 1927 was a city of contradictions, both beautiful and sordid, situated somewhere between the old certainties of the past and the exciting prospects of the Machine Age. '1927 may be regarded,' writes New York architectural historian Robert Stern, 'as the fulcrum on which the balance between the old and the new tipped with finality in favor of the latter'.[1]

Regarded as the nation's cultural and economic capital, New York epitomised the 'nothing is impossible' attitude which was sweeping America in the late twenties. Developments in technology were speeding forwards at an astonishing rate – the same year that the Highsmiths moved to Manhattan, the first national radio networks were established; television was given its first public demonstration at Bell Telephone's laboratories on West Street; a radio-telephone service was established between New York and London; movies began to 'talk'; and Charles Lindbergh was welcomed back to the city with 'the Great Blizzard', an extravagant 1,800-ton ticker-tape parade after completing the world's first solo transatlantic flight between New York and Paris. Skyscrapers – those totems of American capitalist mythology – rose from the city's streets, climbing ever higher in a seemingly never-ending quest to reach the heavens.

Arriving in New York – described by one contemporary visitor as 'like a young girl, eager, healthy, vivacious and still full of illusions'[2] – would have been an exciting experience for the young Highsmith. The sense of dynamism, self-confidence and optimism was unmistakable –

New York was the first conurbation to become, in Oswald Spengler's phrase, a 'world city' – and yet it would have been almost impossible for the small girl not to have felt dwarfed by the enormity of the buildings and the sheer size of the crowds. In 1925, central London had a density of sixty people per acre, whereas in New York the corresponding figure stood at 162.[3] Its people were unmistakably heterogeneous: figures for 1927, as listed by the Works Progress Administration's *New York City Guide*, show that there were 465,000 Jewish residents in Manhattan, making up just over a quarter of the population, while in 1930 there were 224,670 'Negroes'; 117,740 Italians; 86,548 'Free State Irish'; 69,685 Russians; 69,111 Germans and 59,120 Poles.[4] In addition, the number of cars in the city increased from 125,101 in 1918 to 790,123 in the late 1920s, meaning that there were more vehicles in Manhattan than in the whole of Europe.[5]

Twenty years later Highsmith would express the sense of alienation she and her family felt on arriving in New York in the short story, 'The World's Champion Ball-Bouncer', published in *Woman's Home Companion* in April 1947. The Leverings – mother, Leila, father, A.J. (a letterer like Stanley) and daughter, Elspeth – have recently arrived in New York from the south. Although Elspeth had had dreams of the wonders of the Empire State building, as she breakfasts on oatmeal and cream the little girl feels an overwhelming sense of isolation and strangeness and realises that, after all, she does not want to make the trip up to the tallest skyscraper in the world. She notices the soiled walls of the apartment – a sign that the flat has been occupied by countless families before hers – and feels distinctly ill at ease in her new environment. After spotting a girl playing with a ball on the sidewalk, her mother suggests to her daughter to go and make friends, but when Elspeth introduces herself, she is met with an unfriendly stare and the comment, 'You sure talk funny.'[6] Elspeth's face crumbles, she rushes inside but lies to her mother and father about speaking to the girl. Tears roll down her cheeks as her parents comfort her, who 'were both as quiet as she during that long minute while she held her breath.'[7]

Counterpointing the constant trill of the newest, the best, and the latest which echoed throughout Manhattan at this time was a darker undertone which threatened to destroy the city, a mood which was described by Walter Lippmann in 1929 as 'a dissonance comprised of a thousand noises',[8] and articulated by F. Scott Fitzgerald. 'By 1927 a wide-spread neurosis began to be evident . . . contemporaries of mine had begun to disappear into the dark shadow of violence,' he wrote in an essay entitled, 'My Lost City'.[9] One of his classmates killed his wife and himself on Long Island, another tumbled accidentally from a skyscraper in New York, while one of his friends was brutally beaten in a speak-easy club in Manhattan and crawled into the Princeton Club to die. 'These are not catastrophes that I went out of my way to look for – these were my friends; moreover, these things happened not during the depression but during the boom.'[10] Figures show that in 1929 there were 401 reported murders in New York, while Chicago had none.[11]

One of the unfortunate by-products of the new Machine Age – the title of a 1927 exhibition held in a gallery on West 57th Street – with its drive towards progress and its obsession with convenience and commerce, was its corresponding dehumanisation, a leaching of the soul which Highsmith would later explore in her writing. 'It is the city of the Good Time,' wrote Ford Madox Ford of New York in 1927, 'and the Good Time is there so sacred that you may be excused anything you do in searching for it.'[12] The city was so multifaceted and ambiguous that commentators found it beyond definition: 'of no other city can we say with equal truth,' wrote one observer, 'that it defies the effort to summarise briefly its typical characteristics.'[13]

It was against this backdrop that Mary and Stanley Highsmith settled in New York. The couple had left Fort Worth for Manhattan with the ambition of furthering their careers in the commercial art world and soon after moving to the city, Mary started working freelance as an illustrator. 'My stepfather, Highsmith, was working for the telephone – what do you call it? – the Yellow Pages, layout and lettering,' Highsmith told one interviewer, 'and my mother did fashion work for newspapers and *Women's Wear Daily* for a while.'[14]

The family lived in a flat on 103rd Street and Broadway and enrolled their six-year-old daughter under the name of Mary Patricia Highsmith – not her birth name of Plangman – at a school near their home.[15] On her first day, her mother walked her to the large building made from red brick and grey cement, where a few hundred small children were playing games of tag or tossing balls. Holding her daughter's hand, Mary led her through the playground into a large, gloomy gymnasium hall. The oppressive room was painted dirty grey and dark green and the few lights that existed were covered by wire cages. The windows seemed to tower above the little girl and were set far too high in the walls to see anything of the outside world.

She was assigned to class 1A, but after her reading was tested, and found to be superior for her age, she was transferred to 2B, where the children were two years older than her. Unfortunately, Patsy's skills in mathematics did not match her reading ability; she thought a multiplication sign was a plus sign that had fallen on its side. In each of her classes she sat near the back of the room and felt that her Southern accent marked her as an outsider. At the end of her first day, when her mother came to collect her at three o'clock, Patsy walked out of the building and down the steps of the school hand in hand with a black boy. She made friends with him, she assumed, because he was one of the few people who could understand what she was saying and vice versa.

'I had romped and played in my grandmother's "alley" ever since I could walk, with the black kids of the families to whom my grandmother rented houses,' she wrote. 'It was no surprise to me, it was indeed a pleasure, to find black children in the New York schools. I had not been to school before, not in the South, so I knew nothing of segregation.'[16]

Mary, who held liberal views, did not worry about her daughter mixing with black children, but Willie Mae was horrified. Playing with the kids in 'Negro Alley' was one thing, she thought; making friends with them at school in New York something rather different. She persuaded Mary and Stanley to take their daughter out of her school and transfer her to a 'private' one on nearby 103rd Street and Riverside Drive, overlooking the Hudson river. The girl, however, found her new school boring, as there were only around thirty pupils in the whole building compared to the hundreds of children in the previous one.

Highsmith remembered walking down to Riverside Park, just one street away from the school, in waist-high snow and returning blue with cold. She also recalled that on Fridays she would have kidneys for lunch, which she hated, and after being forced to clean her plate, she would often sneak off to the bathrooms to be sick.

In February 1929, the family moved back to Texas and eight-year-old Patsy was enrolled at the old Sixth Ward school, which from 1904 was called the Stephen F. Austin Elementary School, at 319 Lipscomb Street, Fort Worth. The school was located just a few blocks south of the Texas and Pacific Railway tracks and from the playground she would have been able to hear the roar of the trains. Her school records show consistently high marks in almost every subject: 92 in reading, 94 in spelling, 83 in language, 90 in arithmetic, 81 in geography, 85 in drawing and 88 in music. Her lowest mark was 70 for handwriting.

It was while she was at this school that Patsy became fascinated by American Indians. She looked forward to the hour each week when teachers allowed the class to browse in the library. In each session she would read about the 'Indians in their teepees, Indians making bows and arrows . . . I carried it in my head for a week and could hardly wait to plop down on my backless stool – a dark, docile lump – to reopen the book where I had left and go on, finding out about the people who had lived on the land where I was born, long before I was born.'[17]

She also read a book on Greek myths, given to her by her parents, and was spellbound by Arthur Conan Doyle's Sherlock Holmes stories. 'I was carried along by the atmosphere and action,' she said, 'I thought Sherlock Holmes was a genius.'[18] Between the ages of eleven and twelve she would also listen to them on the radio.

Her first experience of the magic of storytelling came after a summer trip with her mother and stepfather to the Endless Caverns near New Market, Virginia. On returning to school she had to complete an assignment in her English class, entitled, 'How I Spent My Summer Vacation', which she had to recite, without notes, standing at the front of the room. Shy and self-conscious as she was, Patsy made a nervous start, but as she started to describe the caves, with their natural limestone formations that took the shapes of flowers, she became aware that her classmates had become hooked by her story.

'The caverns had been discovered by two small boys who were chasing a rabbit,' she said. 'The rabbit dashed down a crevice in the earth, the boys followed it; and found themselves in an underground world – huge, cool, beautiful and full of color. When I came to this part, there was a different atmosphere in the classroom. Everyone had begun to listen, because they were interested. I had suddenly become entertaining, and I was also sharing a personal emotion. I forgot my self-consciousness, and my little speech went much better. This was my first experience at giving enjoyment through a story. It was like a kind of magic, and yet it could be done and had been done by me.'[19]

The Fort Worth of Highsmith's childhood was very different from the city as it is today. The Coates' house on West Daggett no longer stands, demolished to make way for a car park, and a large area of its south section seems to be nothing but a mass of industrial wasteland. A stroll through the centre, with its gleaming skyscrapers and soulless office blocks, is a slightly dispiriting activity. Yet for all of Fort Worth's modern blandness there are a few buildings still standing which Highsmith would have seen as she walked around her home town.

Around the corner from the site of the Coates' home on Daggett Avenue, sits the Rosenberg-Coomer House at 426 Lipscomb Street. Built in 1908, this one-storey, wood-frame house, with its flat-topped hip roof and small gables on the front and sides, is typical of the style of residence popular in the Southside at the beginning of the new century.

On Wednesday afternoons she would go into town with her grandmother. Walking across the viaduct she could look down at the Mexican settlement below, see the stray dogs and half-clothed children, the men lounging in their shanties or bringing home parcels of groceries for their families. When they reached the centre of town, Willie Mae and her granddaughter often went to see a film, as movies were cheaper on Wednesdays. During the film Patsy used to eat a Hershey bar, making one last the entire show and peeling down the tinfoil as the chocolate melted in her hands. Later, whenever she smelt cloves, she recalled the strong smell of the spice that her grandmother laid on her tongue to sweeten her breath during the film. After the movie, Willie Mae took her to Kresses, a dime store, from where she remembered buying a jumping frog. 'This was America – Texas – in 1929,' she wrote in her journal.[20] At school she also developed a crush on a fellow pupil. 'I remember sticking my folded notes in the crack of the stones in the old Sixth Ward building, notes to be found by a certain red-haired little girl in a lower class than mine.'[21] Twenty years later, during six months of analysis with a New York psychotherapist, Highsmith would remember the love she had felt for this unnamed flame-haired girl.

In January 1930, Highsmith and her family moved once again to New York – the yo-yoing between the two states was a common feature of her childhood – this time to Astoria, Queens. A picture of her taken when she was living in Astoria shows her standing outside what was presumably her house with her stepfather, Stanley. The young girl, dressed in a smart winter outfit, complete with fur coat, hat and woolly gloves, is holding a bicycle (her first), but she gazes into the camera not with pride or joy, but with a look of uncertainty. She is sporting a rather severe fringe, her little black eyes squint into the light and from the shape of her mouth it looks as though she could have been biting the inside of her cheek.

When the family arrived in Astoria – they first settled at 1919 21st Road, near Astoria Park, and then, most likely in 1931, moved to an address on 28th Street[22] – the borough was experiencing something of a boom. The arrival of the rapid transit system in the 1920s and the five-cent fare triggered an enormous increase in the demand for houses and suddenly the area, situated in the north-west corner of Queens, came under siege from the white-collar worker. For $34 a month, two families could live in a new brick-built house only two minutes walk from Ditmars Avenue and a mere fifteen-minute subway ride from Grand Central Station or Times Square.[23] Although the new apartment houses would have been quite different to the elegant, aristocratic structures which lined the exclusive 12th and 14th streets north of

27th Avenue, an area known as 'The Hill', the homes, with their large windows, steps up to the porch and high ceilings were generally considered 'Greater value for less money'.[24]

The commanding prospect of Manhattan, as seen from Queens, across 'a foreground of verdure and water' was, according to the influential architectural critic, Lewis Mumford, 'one of the most dazzling urban views in the world'.[25] Manhattan was undergoing a dramatic transformation – between 1929 and 1930 five major skyscrapers, including the Chrysler and the Empire State buildings, were either completed or in the process of construction, while a whole series of new bridges and freeways sprung up around the island. According to *The New Yorker* of November 1929, the city had never before been so 'torn up'[26] as it proceeded to transform itself with increasing protean energy.

The young Highsmith would have also been intrigued by some of the sights closer to home: the wide boulevard of 30th Avenue, with its busy food and clothing shops; 'The Big House', the glamorous Astoria Studio, built in 1920, at 35th Avenue and 35th Street, by Players-Lasky Corporation (Paramount Pictures after 1927) as a rival to the Hollywood studios and the location for the Marx Brothers' first feature, *The Cocoanuts*; the newly built Church of the Most Precious Blood on 37th Street, with its thrilling references to the Jazz Age, Lutyens' Castle Drogo, Celtic Architecture and fin de siècle Vienna; and the ferry terminal lying at the foot of Astoria Boulevard and 92nd Street, which, until 1936, carried residents across the East River. She was fascinated by the 'strange power'[27] of Hell Gate Bridge, an imposing structure which served as a rail link between Canada, New England and the Southwest. In fact, when she was twenty-five she toyed with the idea of writing a novel about a young girl, Letitia, growing up in Astoria, using the bridge – with its distinctive parabolic steel arch – as one of the book's central images.

While at her new school – PS 122, 2101 Ditmars Boulevard – Highsmith earned high marks each term. She entered the school on 10 February 1930, in the fourth grade, and her records show that she was a conscientious and hardworking pupil, usually winning mostly As for both her conduct and work. Throughout her stay in Astoria, Highsmith – who in September 1932 weighed just over eighty pounds, with a height of fifty-seven and a half inches – never once turned up late for school.[28] As a child she was, by her own admission, 'lugubrious, and very grown up'[29] and it is therefore not so surprising, perhaps, that she felt drawn to more adult reading material. Fascinated by human behaviour and its motivation, she joined the Astoria branch of the Queens Borough Public Library – a brick structure built with money donated by Andrew Carnegie – from which she borrowed psychology books. 'I plunged at once into the psychology section, took books out, and often sat reading books which were not meant to be borrowed,' she said.[30]

It was while living in Astoria that Patsy developed a fascination with the psychologically 'abnormal' which would last the rest of her life. Other girls of her age were reading fairy stories, but Highsmith was gripped by Dr Karl Menninger's *The Human Mind*, a detailed account of so-called 'deviant' behaviour such as kleptomania, schizophrenia and pyromania. (Interestingly, a handful of Menninger's studies were culled from the research done by Robert Ripley, the flamboyant creator of 'Ripley's Believe It or Not!', who travelled the world in the early twentieth century in search of the bizarre for his world-wide syndicated newspaper column.) Published in 1930, *The Human Mind* was one of the first psychiatric books written for a mass audience, tapping into a wider cultural need to understand the darker aspects of human behaviour. It was selected by the Literary Guild, attracted over 1,000 reviews and became an instant bestseller, selling 70,000 copies on publication. 'It is a straightforward, non-argumentative presentation of the principles of dynamic psychiatry,' according to Sydney Smith, editor of *The Human Mind Revisited*, 'but it flashed a light on the shadows of the human mind.'[31]

Menninger, who founded a psychiatric clinic in Topeka, Kansas and later went on to be president of the American Psychoanalytic Association, became something of a celebrity and there was a national demand for interviews, speeches, advice and newspaper and magazine articles. His book was so successful, in part, because he explained complex psychological symptoms in a clear, concise style and illustrated his points with details from real case histories. Highsmith would have been intrigued when she read the book's opening lines.

When a trout rising to a fly gets hooked on a line and finds himself unable to swim about freely, he begins a fight which results in struggles and splashes and sometimes an escape. Often, of course, the situation is too tough for him.

In the same way the human being struggles with his environment and with the hooks that catch him. Sometimes he masters his difficulties; sometimes they are too much for him. His struggles are all that the world sees and it usually misunderstands them. It is hard for a free fish to understand what is happening to a hooked one.[32]

After school finished at 3.30 p.m., Patsy would come home to an empty house – both Mary and Stanley were at work – where she would sit in the green armchair in the living room and read Menninger's catalogue of case histories about the mentally disturbed: the happily married woman and mother of two who shot her children and yet could remember nothing about the incident; the well-off merchant who couldn't stop himself from robbing banks and the college girl who was sexually attracted to her female room-mate. 'To me they were real, of course, consequently more stimulating to my imagination than fairy tales or fiction would have been,' she wrote to Karl Menninger in 1989, one year before his death.[33]

No doubt what attracted the young girl, already feeling somewhat at odds with her immediate reality, was Menninger's rejection of the concept of normality. As Menninger wrote in the preface to *The Human Mind*, 'The adjuration to be "normal" seems shockingly repellent to me; I see neither hope nor comfort in sinking to that low level. I think it is ignorance that makes people think of abnormality only with horror and allows them to remain undismayed at the proximity of "normal" to average and mediocre. For surely anyone who achieves anything is, *a priori*, abnormal . . .'[34]

The book appealed to her already instinctive belief that behind an individual's respectable facade lay a mass of contradictions and perverse desires; a psychological dynamic that was ripe for creative exploration. 'I can't think of anything more apt to set the imagination stirring, drifting, creating, than the idea – the fact – that anyone you walk past on the pavement anywhere may be a sadist, a compulsive thief, or even a murderer,' she said.[35]

The drive to 'get under the skin' of her fellow man also manifested itself in her interest in human anatomy. Another influential textbook which was, perhaps again, unusual reading for a nine-year-old, was George Bridgman's *The Human Machine: the Anatomical Structure and Mechanism of the Human Body*, a guide to the underlying structures of the body written as a textbook for art students. 'It was an important book in the household as my mother and stepfather, as commercial artists, had to have some ability to draw the human figure,' she wrote to her publisher, Diogenes Verlag.[36] She also read Jack London, Louisa May Alcott's *Little Women*, Robert Louis Stevenson, Ruskin's *Sesame and Lilies* and Bram Stoker's *Dracula*, which she would prop up in front of her while she ate lunch alone in her parents' apartment. The book both transfixed and terrified her – as she turned its pages she would imagine that a ghost might appear in the hall doorway even though it was broad daylight.

In biology lessons at school she learnt about Mendel's research into pea plants and the laws of genetics. Her mother told her the truth of her parentage when she was ten, but she knew the details long before then, she claimed. She had long suspected that Stanley was not her real father – after all, she only had to look in the mirror to see how her dark eyes and hair bore no resemblance to either her mother nor her stepfather. And now Mendel's laws confirmed her suspicion. 'My mother is a blondish type with grey eyes and my stepfather has grey eyes too,' she said.[37] In addition, her mother had drawings in her grandmother's house signed Mary Plangman, not Mary Highsmith. 'I remember asking – why this name? Not to mention the fact that my stepfather came on the scene when I was three,' she told Craig Brown.[38]

The news came as no great shock to her, but the knowledge that Stanley was not her real father must have forced her, albeit unconsciously, to question the nature of her identity. Whatever the effect of this revelation, she was left feeling extremely disturbed.

'When I was nine or ten I had a feeling I would die when I fell asleep and I was afraid of that. It took me ages to fall asleep, I remember many a time I was awake until two. I had a feeling I would stop breathing, so I used to take water and snuff it up my nose a bit as if it would keep me awake somehow. It must have gone on several weeks, months even.'[39]

It also seems that as a child she suffered from some sort of health problem. In an undated letter to her grandmother – Highsmith's earliest surviving piece of writing – she refers to what she calls her 'poison'.

Dear Grandma,
    I have been bathing so much this summer at the beach that I did not have time to write to you like I did in the winter. I am saving up money to spend on you when you get up here . . . We are all anxious for you to come up here. Mother and Stanley are going to try to show you a good time.
    My poison is all cured up now. Mother cured it up. I am going to send an old letter I wrote long ago . . . Stanley says hello to all of you and looks forward to your visit . . .
    How is grandma – and I wish I was home so I could play in the back yard. love to all Patsy.[40]

*   *   *

One day in 1931, Highsmith was at school, trying to open one of the windows with a twelve-foot-long wooden pole, when she looked out and saw a man walking quickly down the street. He was wearing a dark suit, but no hat, and carried a briefcase under his arm, but the ordinary-looking man invested the young girl with a desperate longing for a time when she too would be able to walk down the sidewalk, free from the control of her elders and betters. To the intelligent ten-year-old girl, eager to experience the world, the man represented liberty, the power to do anything and go anywhere. 'The image made an indelible impression on me,' she wrote later, 'because from that moment, I felt that that was what I wanted too.'[41] Fascinated by the man and what he represented, she climbed halfway up the wooden pole and, so as to disrupt the class, pretended the window would not open.

'Patsy, will you come down!' said her teacher, as the pupils fell about with laughter.

'So I came down,' Highsmith remembered, 'but with my vision still in my eyes.'[42]

The incident is important because it indicates Highsmith's ambivalent attitude towards belonging to a group, a tension which would later shape both her career and her personal life. At one level she wanted to escape the confines of the classroom and be like the solitary man she saw walking down the street, but on another she clearly felt a strong impulse to amuse her fellow pupils. She said that her schooldays made her 'feel like a worker ant, without identity, importance, individuality or dignity'[43] and as a result from then on she battled against uniformity. At the age of eleven, she refused to be taught French before she started Latin classes – an idea she picked up from the 'Jeremy' books of Sir Hugh Walpole – and instead used her free time to read Hazlitt's essays and Boswell's *The Life of Samuel Johnson* in the school library. She may have loathed the thought of losing her identity in a crowd, but she confided to Vivien De Bernardi, that 'the happiest year of her life was when she was ten years old and she belonged to a gang.'[44]

At the onset of puberty, Highsmith was ignorant of the basic facts of life. When she started to menstruate at the age of eleven, she turned to her mother for emotional support. 'When I was eleven, my mother of necessity had to tell me about menstruation,' she wrote in a letter to her stepfather. 'She added, in regard to the facts of life, "Don't you think that a man has something to do with it?" I replied, "No – I don't know." That was the end of the talk on the facts of life.'[45]

At the same time, Mary and Stanley's relationship was becoming increasingly volatile. Highsmith later wrote to her mother, reminding her of the constant arguments which echoed around the house. 'I remember quarrels constantly, he was not my father, you threatened separation, packed (and sometimes unpacked) your suitcases, threatening departure and so forth.'[46]

In the summer of 1933, twelve-year-old Patsy escaped her hellish home environment to spend a month at a girls' camp near West Point and Walker Valley, New York. Each day she wrote home to her parents, letters which were published two years later in *Woman's World* magazine and which show her early aptitude for writing. She describes now she breakfasted on prunes and cereal, learnt how to swim and make fires, played tennis, toasted marshmallows and slept in dormitories. She was elected bunk leader, with duties to inspect the dorms, and on certain evenings she joined a group of girls who swam naked in the lake, an activity popularly known as 'swimming Diana'. 'Diana means without any clothes on at all,' she wrote. 'Do you think it's all right to go in Diana? It's very dark.'[47] From the letters, it's obvious she thoroughly enjoyed the experience. 'Some of the girls are saps but some are pretty nice,' she said, and she particularly admired her tennis coach, Miss Edna, who had 'a swell serve. She swings her racket around twice before she hits the ball.'[48] One of the highlights for her was the 'Campers-Councillors Day', when the staff swapped clothes and duties with the girls. 'The Councillors had to wear the Campers' clothes and vice-virtue. (I learned to say vice-virtue for vice versa out of a funny magazine.),' she wrote, illustrating an early love for the vibrancy and humour of language.[49]

During her stay at summer camp, Patsy missed her mother and wrote asking if she would come up and see her, while towards the end of her vacation, she expressed her eagerness and excitement at seeing Mary again. 'I'm packing tonight for going home. O joy, O joy,' she said.[50] In her absence, Mary and Stanley had obviously tried to sort out their differences, but when Patsy returned back home, her mother told her the marriage was over. She would divorce Stanley, take her daughter back to Fort Worth, where they would live with Willie Mae. The three women would be together again, just like the old days. 'The Highsmith house was a house divided if I ever saw one, on the brink of collapse,' Highsmith wrote to her mother, 'and indeed it was a collapse when I was aged 12–13.'[51]

At the end of the summer of 1933, Mary did leave her husband, travelling to Forth Worth with her daughter. But after only a few weeks in Texas, Stanley arrived and took his wife back to New York, leaving their daughter with Willie Mae. Highsmith's sense of loss was overwhelming.

'She had just found a social group in New York in which she felt really comfortable,' says Vivien De Bernardi. 'She was part of this group of kids and then she got shipped off to Texas when she was twelve. Taking a hypersensitive child – and this was a really bright child, for whom New York was like water for someone dying of thirst – and sticking them in cow country must have been incredibly traumatic for her.'[52]

Highsmith never forgave her mother for deceiving her at this crucial time in her life. Of course, she loved her grandparents dearly, but she felt bitter and betrayed that her mother could lie to her in this way. In a letter to her stepfather, she confessed how her mother's actions affected her.

'She never said in regard to the (to me) appalling year 12–13 which I spent in Texas, "We parked you with Grandma because we were broke." Or "I decided to go back to Stanley. I am sorry because I told you we were going to be divorced, but it is not so." Either of these statements would have made the situation easier to bear.'[53]

Her mother, she related to her father, Jay B, 'never realized what a devastating betrayal of faith this was to me, at that time'[54] and Highsmith later referred to this period as the saddest year of her life.[55]

4

Suppressions

1933–1938

Records kept by the Fort Worth Independent School District show that on 14 September 1933, Willie Mae, acting as guardian, made an application for her twelve-year-old granddaughter's admission to the junior high school on South Jennings Avenue. The continuous transfer between schools in New York and Fort Worth meant that Patsy found it difficult to make friends and the fact that her new fellow pupils were two years older than her only served to increase her sense of isolation. Her classmates invited her to a Hallowe'en party on 31 October, but she was considered too young to go and so, feeling alienated and alone, she went for a walk late at night and, in a rebellious moment, removed a tyre cap from a parked car. In her journal, exactly fifty years later, Highsmith wrote of the incident; of how she had toyed with the idea of letting the air out of the tyre, but decided against it and how, through-out the experience, she remembered feeling 'furtive'.[1]

At school she took a year's course in carpentry – a hobby she would later use to sculpt figures and animals out of pieces of wood – but she was the only girl in the class. It was at this point in her young life that she formulated an idea which helped her make sense of her confused sexual identity, viewing herself as having an unmistakable masculine essence secreted away within a female shell. 'I am a walking perpetual example of my contention: as I said brilliantly at the age of twelve, a boy in a girl's body.'[2] Later in life, in 1948, a New Orleans fortune teller would say to her mother, 'You have one child – a son. No, a daughter. It should have been a boy, but it's a girl.'[3] Highsmith confessed in her diary that she felt haunted by the remark.

For most of that year in Texas she felt bereft and utterly miserable and she turned to her twenty-three-year-old cousin, Dan Coates, who still lived with Willie Mae and Daniel, to raise her spirits. During this time the two became so close that they regarded each other not so much as cousins, but as brother and sister; later Dan would address letters to her 'Dear Sis Pat'. In a letter she wrote to Dan in 1968, she reminded him of the happy times they spent together, playing football on the front lawn, drying dishes in the kitchen and fooling about, 'snapping moist dishtowels at each other'.[4] On Sunday evenings, the local preacher would sometimes drop by for dinner at Willie Mae's house. Highsmith could remember that the dining room was often plagued by sex-mad flies, insects which seemed to be attracted not so much by the food on the dining table but by the embarrassment they knew they would cause the family. 'Those flies in the dining room were different from any flies I've seen before or since . . .' she said. 'Then one would catch the other and perform the sex act in the air.'[5]

Soon after moving back to Fort Worth, she met her real father, Jay Bernard Plangman, for the first time. Their meeting, at her grandmother's house, was a low-key, rather understated affair. She recalled feeling shy but curious about this shadowy figure, yet neither of them showed much emotion. Jay B merely took hold of her hand as if to say yes, you are my daughter, 'but he was almost a stranger, rather brusque and formal'.[6] After that first encounter, he walked her to school and back a couple of times, but their relationship was not a deep one and it was for her mother that she still yearned.

She was, by her own admission, in a 'very depressed state'[7] and, in an effort to brighten her spirits, she cut her grandparents' lawn at 50 cents a time so as to save the $12 she needed to buy a man's pocket watch she admired. In a letter she wrote to a family friend in 1972, Highsmith told how she looked upon the watch almost as a talisman, a rare object of beauty which she could use as a substitute for real happiness. Although she missed her mother terribly, working for – and then possessing – the watch helped her block out the misery of her life; it was, she said, 'something to work for, something to achieve, something to have to look at once I had earned it'.[8] Later she gave the watch to her stepfather, 'curious, as at that time I had reason to dislike him.'[9]

She would occasionally talk to her friends about her unhappy childhood, particularly this wretched year in Texas. 'From what she told me she suffered a lot as a child,' says Bert Diethelm. 'She was a person whom I could not imagine as a little girl with a doll, hopping around singing her songs. In all the photographs you see, she looks a sombre, introverted little kid, which no doubt must have had an influence on her work. As a child I think she did feel rejected and was rejected subsequently at a later time. I think she had very many unhappinesses.'[10]

She would look back on this time – and what she saw as her mother's betrayal of her – as being especially influential on her future relationships. 'If I have the steady thing, I reject it,' she wrote to her friend Alex Szogyi, 'this has happened over and over – rather, I made it happen. I repeat the pattern, of course, of my mother's semi-rejection of me. Her "abandonment" of me to my grandmother, when I was aged 12, when my mother took me to Texas, with a promise she would divorce my stepfather . . . I never got over it. Thus I seek out women who will hurt me in a similar manner, and avoid the women who are – good eggs.'[11] The separation from her mother only lasted a year, but as she saw it, the damage had been done. She was reunited with Mary, and, to her disappointment, her stepfather, again in 1934 when they called for her and told her that it would be best if she came to live with them in New York. The day she left Fort Worth, she remembered how her grandmother kissed her on the lips while standing on the steps of the house. As she drove away she felt 'Her kiss was wet on my upper lip, and I let it stay, dreading the inevitable time when the wind would dry it, and the coolness would be gone.'[12]

The stockmarket crash of October 1929 had a devastating, but far from immediate, effect on New York and on her return to Manhattan, Highsmith would have noticed a marked difference in the mood of the city. By 1932, 1.6 million Manhattanites received some sort of benefit and a third of the city's manufacturing plants had closed.[13] Nationally, the picture was even bleaker, with millions of people travelling around the country in a fruitless search for work. The unemployed – between 1929 and 1933 they increased from 500,000 to 12 million – constructed shanty slums, known as 'Hoovervilles', named after the Republican President Herbert Hoover who was elected in 1929, while beggars, bread-lines and apple-sellers appeared in every city in America. Hoover was voted out of office in 1932 and replaced by Democrat Franklin D. Roosevelt. The actress Lilian Gish witnessed his inaugural address in March 1933, in which he famously said, 'the only thing we have to fear is fear itself'; FDR, the father of the New Deal, seemed, she said, 'to have been dipped in phosphorus'.[14]

To offset the economic gloom casting a shadow over Manhattan, a massive building programme – a restructuring scheme which included the construction of new expressways, bridges and a mass transit system

– was initiated by the city's new mayor, Fiorello La Guardia, who held office between 1933 and 1945. Later, Highsmith, in *Strangers on a Train*, would describe New York, with its 'dirty jumble' of disorderly roofs and streets, as looking like 'a floor model of how a city should not be built.'[15]

The Highsmiths' new apartment at 1 Bank Street – so named after the temporary move of the Wall Street counting houses to the street following the yellow fever epidemic of 1822 – was in the heart of Greenwich Village, a district which had already established something of a reputation for non-conformity and a tolerance of artistic eccentricity. At the turn of the century the area had been inhabited by working-class Italians, followed by a new influx of writers and artists attracted by its winding streets, Old World charm, cheap rents and the ubiquitous 'ailanthus' or 'backyard tree' which thrived on poor soil, little water and the minimum amount of light. The Works Progress Administration *New York City Guide*, in a potted history of the area, concluded that the 'Village' 'was the center of the American Renaissance or of artiness, of political progress or of long-haired radical men and short-haired radical women, of sex freedom or of sex license – dependent upon the point of view.'[16] The Museum of Living Art at 100 Washington Square East was founded in 1927, housing works by Man Ray, Brancusi, Matisse, Picasso, Mondrian, Léger and Juan Gris, while three years later, the Whitney Museum opened its doors on Eighth Street, a pioneering space designed 'to help create rather than conserve a tradition'. Tom Paine spent the last years of his life at a house in Grove Street – to which the Highsmiths would move in 1940 – while Edgar Allan Poe, Walt Whitman and Henry James all lived in the area at some point in their lives. In fact, the artistic atmosphere of the Village soon became something of a cliché, and in 1935 the sociologist Caroline Ware described the area as being packed full of 'pseudo-Bohemians'.[17] Despite this, the neighbourhood west of Washington Square Park still held the power to shock – in 1936 one writer observed how the Village was a mecca for 'exhibitionists and perverts of all kinds'.[18]

On her return to New York in 1934, Highsmith enrolled in yet another school – Julia Richman High School, 317 East 67th Street, where she would stay until 1938. The single-sex school, named after the first woman district superintendent of schools in the City of New York, housed a total of 8,000 pupils – 60 percent of the girls were Italian, 30 per cent Jewish, the rest made up of Irish, German and Polish children, a mix which reflected the city at large – in four buildings. Pupils at

Highsmith's school had to share not only desks, but seats as well, as the influx of immigrants, particularly Jews fleeing Hitler, increased. Figures show that between 1930 and 1939, Jews comprised more than a third of those entering the school system,[19] an increase caused by Hitler's pre-World War Two policy of *Judenfrei*, together with the implementation of the 1921 and 1924 National Origins Acts, which calculated the number seeking immigration to the United States on the basis of a percentage of those already living in America. In fact, the demand for school places in New York was so enormous that the Board of Education was forced to erect portable wooden buildings, some structures which were used until after the Second World War.[20]

'I always had to share my seat, though some girls plumper than me had their seats to themselves . . .' Highsmith said. 'These were the Hitler years, and the school became so crowded, it had three shifts, one starting at 8:15 AM, the second at 9 AM, the third at 9:45 AM. The classrooms were packed, and there was no possibility of getting special help, in case one needed it.'[21]

Yet for all the school's cultural pluralism, Highsmith felt isolated. As a Protestant, she felt excluded from the Jewish or Catholic majorities, a social segregation she clearly resented. 'Non-Catholics and non-Jews were not invited from fourteen onward to parties given by Catholics or Jews, from which Catholics or Jews excluded the other. There were never enough Protestants to throw a party.'[22]

Twenty-six years before Highsmith entered the school, Julia Richman published a book which no doubt reflected the dominant ethos of the establishment which proudly bore her name. The 1908 title, *Good Citizenship*, co-authored with Isabel Richman Wallach, was written as a practical guide for children and outlines the basics of modern living, with chapters focusing on the fire service, the department of health, street cleaning and the police. The words that Richman wrote on the subject of crime would no doubt have caused the writer, later in life, to emit one of her distinctively throaty laughs. 'Crime is an ugly word, and it stands for ugly deeds. Disorder is bad enough to contend with, but crime is far worse . . . Men commit crime because of anger, envy, or greed; but they are generally very careful not to do it when the policeman is in sight.'[23] In Highsmith's world, crime may be ugly, but it is also something born of psychological necessity and described in such a logical, detached manner that the reader is tricked into believing it is simply part of the continuum of normal behaviour. Not only that: any policeman featured in one of her novels is just as likely to be as corrupt as his criminal quarry. Morality is shifted, unsettling one's vision, skewing perspective and undermining accepted notions of truth and justice.

Highsmith's move to a single-sex environment resulted in boredom. 'It was much more fun when I was going to school with boys before the age of fourteen,' she said later, 'because they have a sense of humor, much better than that of the girls, I must say, and it was amusing. And suddenly from fourteen to seventeen there was a bunch of girls . . . learning things by rote. Pretty boring.'[24]

Highsmith's school records from Julia Richman detail not only her academic record – from the beginning she earned high marks in most subjects – but offer an insight into her personality too. Observations noted on the card entry include comments such as 'Shy?', 'Always so very nice to me!', and 'worth watching'. Yet Highsmith's abiding memory of school is one of crushing boredom, and so, whenever she had a free moment, she escaped into a parallel universe: the endlessly thrilling world of fiction. So bored was she by her immediate reality that she would take a book with her to gym classes, which she would then read while hanging from the top of a rope. 'It never seemed to occur to the teacher or anyone to look up,' she said.[25]

Edgar Allan Poe was a particular favourite, especially his *Tales of Mystery and the Imagination*, 'with their ingenious fantasies about death, resurrection, and the possibility of life continuing after burial'.[26] 'His was a wild imagination in full flight. He chanced anything,' she said.[27] She visited his cottage in Fordham, thirteen miles from New York, where she delighted in seeing a sample of his writing in a notebook and one of his sketches of his wife, Virginia, together with his cat. She was also rather impressed to learn that one day Poe walked from the house over the Bronx River bridge, and down to Manhattan in order to deliver a manuscript. Another literary hero, Joseph Conrad, whose *Typhoon* was one of her favourite books, prompted a fantasy of running away by hiding in the bowels of one of the ships stationed by the piers of the Hudson River, just a few blocks away from the family's apartment: 'I . . . used to gaze at the rusty prows of freighters docked at the end of Christopher Street and Morton Street, and wished that I could climb on one of them and escape from school and family. The ships' names attracted me, many strange and unpronounceable.'[28] This desire was shared by one of her characters, Guy, in her first published novel, *Strangers on a Train*, who remembers he had been 'wild to go to sea at fourteen'.[29] In addition to its ocean setting, it's not difficult to understand why Conrad's novella attracted her; its structure is deter- mined by the dualistic, slightly homoerotic, relationship between Captain MacWhirr, driven by instinct, and his chief-mate Jukes, a symbol of intelligence, a male-male dialectic she would explore in greater detail in her own work.

Patsy also experienced escapism – and a certain amount of vicarious pleasure – in January 1935, as she followed the high-profile prosecution of German immigrant Bruno Richard Hauptmann for the kidnapping and murder of Charles A. Lindbergh Jr, the baby son of the aviator. The fourteen-year-old was so transfixed by what became known as 'the trial of the century' that she took to summarising the findings in her diary. 'Hauptman [*sic*] trial. Yells: "Stop lying . . .",' she wrote, before noting the guilty verdict, in February, 'Hauptman [*sic*] guilty, sentenced to chair'.[30] Twelve years later, in 1947, when Highsmith was writing *Strangers on a Train*, she would unite the names of murderer and victim in this, the most sensational crime of the early twentieth century, to create the first of her psychopathic killers – Charles A. Bruno.

When Patsy was fourteen, her mother asked her, 'Are you a les?' before adding cruelly, 'You are beginning to make noises like one.' Later Highsmith would recall how this 'rather vulgar and frightening remark'[31] made her feel even more alienated and introverted. 'It reminds one of "Look at that hunchback isn't he funny" on the street. I was not a cripple on the street, but a member of my mother's family.'[32]

At school, she was already forming crushes on fellow pupils and in her diary she noted that after a 'fingerclasp' with one girl she was too nervous to sit in the same German class with her. Her relationships, at this time, were most likely to have been romantic, non-erotic affairs, but, to a certain extent she still felt she had to suppress her sexual identity. 'A most important fact in my character is that I did not begin, as a child and an adolescent, open, free, naive, gullible and so forth. Naive I was, no doubt of that, but I was closed up and reserved.'[33]

Mary became concerned about her daughter's odd behaviour, but didn't make an effort to understand what she was going through, simply saying, 'Why don't you straighten up and fly right?'[34] before walking out of the room. Mary Highsmith wanted her daughter to 'be like other people'[35] but Patsy was left feeling confused by her stinging remarks. How could she, the girl asked herself, 'be like other people' when her own background was so strange? Did her mother not realise the effect she had had on her own daughter when she continually rejected her? Looking back on the incident as an adult, Highsmith remembered how belittled she felt by her mother's comments. Had Mary really cared about her, she said, surely she would have attempted to help her or at least tried to seek the opinions of a child psychiatrist?

Patsy, like one of the snails which would obsess her later in life, turned in on herself and erected a psychological shell which she thought would protect her from the outside world. 'Until around thirty, I was essentially, like a glacier or like stone,' she wrote in her journal. 'I suppose I was "protecting" myself. It was certainly tied up with the fact I had to conceal the most important emotional drives of myself completely.

'This is the tragedy of the conscience-stricken young homosexual, that he not only conceals his sex objectives, but conceals his humanity and natural warmth of heart as well.'[36]

Muriel Mandelbaum, née Wiesenthal, a fellow pupil at Julia Richman High School, remembers Highsmith as being amazingly bright but terribly reserved, someone who kept a certain distance from the other girls. 'She, like me, lived on the west side and we went to school together on the bus,' she remembers. 'We would compete with each other to see who could do the *Herald Tribune* cryptogram first, in the shortest amount of time. She was very good at crosswords.

'She was extraordinarily pretty – beautiful and tall and slender – with, quite appropriately, patrician features. I was shocked to see the pictures that were taken towards the end of her life. When I knew her she wore lipstick and had long hair. She was feminine and there was nothing butch about her at all. Of course I was an innocent, but there was no suggestion that she might be lesbian.'[37]

Highsmith not only repressed her emotions at home and at school, but felt she had to censor herself even when she was writing her diary. 'I cannot write what I want. Suppressions,' she wrote in 1935. 'M. [her mother] says I am very x and I think so myself for the first time,' runs another entry.[38]

It's not surprising that Patsy felt the need to stifle the expression of her burgeoning sexuality. She may have been living in Greenwich Village, but the onset of the Depression in 1929 put a damper on the expression of female independence. During the three years following the Wall Street Crash, society became increasingly antipathetic towards working women. If a job existed it should, general opinion insisted, go to a man rather than his female counterpart. In 1931, the dean of Barnard College – the women-only college Highsmith would attend between the ages of seventeen and twenty-one – suggested each graduate should ask herself whether it was strictly necessary for her to work. If not then perhaps 'the greatest service that you can render to the community . . . is to have the courage to refuse to work for gain,' she said.[39]

The prevailing attitude towards lesbianism was even more negative. Menninger's *The Human Mind* classified lesbianism under 'Perversions of Affection and Interest' – along with fetishism, paedophilia and even satanism – and discussed the case of a college girl enamoured of her room-mate. 'They attend each other like lovers,' said Menninger. 'They have violent quarrels, demonstrations of jealousy, and rapturous reunions.'[40] A front-page feature in the *New York Times*, in 1935, headlined, 'Women's Personalities Changed by Adrenal Gland Operations', revealed that women who suffered from 'masculine psychological states' – obviously a euphemism for same-sex relations – could now be treated, indeed 'cured', of their unnatural desires by the removal of an adrenal gland. The surgery would, it was claimed, help such women battle against their 'aversion to marriage' and make them less mannish.[41]

In fiction, too, lesbians were regarded as somewhat freakish characters. The publication, in 1928, of Radclyffe Hall's *The Well of Loneliness* helped increase lesbian visibility, but it portrayed them as 'inverts', men trapped in women's bodies, rather than as simply women who happened to love other women. It whetted the public's appetite for the subject matter, and a spate of novels were published which served to increase hatred of lesbians, classifying them as 'crooked, twisted freaks of nature who stagnate in dark and muddy waters'[42] while journalists took to lampooning them in the popular press. 'Greenwich Village Sin Dives Lay Traps for Innocent Girls,' ran the headline in a 1931 edition of the *New York Evening Graphic*. The piece described the clientele of the Bungalow, a bar full of 'lisping boys and deep-voiced girls . . . They display their jealousies and occasionally claw at each other with their nails. They talk loudly, scream, jibe at each other and order gin continually. Always gin.'[43]

Lesbians were 'considered monstrosities in the 1930s'[44] and many young women, like Highsmith, felt compelled to repress their desires. Perhaps it was this mood of self-censorship which contributed to Highsmith's fascination with the idea of the fantasy lover, the ghost-like woman who existed purely in her mind. If she couldn't have the reality, she would have to make do with a figure conjured from her imagination. When she was fourteen, she fell in love with someone, most probably another girl, with whom she had only the briefest of contacts. 'I was in love aged 14 to 17 and more with someone I saw only for a few weeks in school aged 14 . . . we went to different high schools in New York, never saw each other again, and indeed we'd never been friends or even shaken hands.'[45]

It would be a pattern she would repeat over and over again, forever investing her lovers with qualities they blatantly did not possess. In an unpublished interview with Bettina Berch, Highsmith was asked about the nature and essence of love. 'Imagination,' she replied. 'Because it's all in the eyes of the beholder. Nothing to do with reality. When you're in love it's a state of madness.'[46]

After school she would stop by at Caso's, a drugstore on 68th Street and Third Avenue, for a soda. She revisited the shop fourteen years later; as she walked past, age twenty-nine, the bittersweet memories of youth flooded back to her. 'And the crises I have known here, the faces I looked for, and saw, or missed, the afternoons metamorphosed by some overwhelming event that had happened in school that day, days that twisted one's life around completely and permanently, I remember them.'[47]

Life was, at times, as she confessed in her diary, 'an endless hell on earth'.[48] Stanley and Mary argued constantly and, although she dreamed about the possibility of a divorce between the two, she realised that it was unlikely. 'M. will never leave S. and never never know real happiness,' she wrote.[49] At nights, she would often cry herself to sleep.

In April 1935, however, she received news from Ray Wallace, the editor of *Woman's World* that his magazine would not only publish the series of letters she had written to her parents from summer camp two years previously, but he would pay her $25 when the piece ran in the July issue. Writing – the ordering of experience – appealed to her, she surmised, because her own home life was so chaotic. She remembered feeling immensely satisfied after writing her first fictional sentence, age fourteen – 'He prepared to go to sleep, removed his shoes and set them parallel, toes outward, beside his bed.'[50] Whatever happened next, she did not remember, but 'it gave me a sense of order, seeing the shoes neatly beside the bed in my imagination . . . I longed for order and security.'[51] When she was fourteen or fifteen, she also started work on an epic poem in the style of Tennyson's 'Idylls of the King' that, in blank verse, told a romantic story set in a world of castles and battles, but which does not survive today. Her IQ she recorded as 121 and she read works as diverse as Wilkie Collins' *The Moonstone*, Melville's *Moby-Dick*, Erich Maria Remarque's *All Quiet on the Western Front*, and books on heredity, palmistry and Christian Science.

Her mother was a keen disciple of the Church of Christ, Scientist, created by Mary Baker Eddy in Massachusetts in the 1870s, a movement which can be seen as a by-product of the unrest which gripped

America after the end of the Civil War. Eddy's aim was to restore what she saw as primitive Christianity and its lost element of spiritual healing through a number of alternative remedies, including homeopathy. The roots of disease, she believed, could be traced back to the mind and the only true cure was brought about by spiritual healing. By 1930, Christian Science churches in America numbered around 2,400, while the 1936 US Bureau of the Census recorded membership of the church in the United States as totalling 269,000. 'The public wants . . . to obtain . . . cloying sweetness . . . optimism . . . and peppermint sayings . . .' wrote one early twentieth-century commentator. '[It] pays a high price to Mrs Eddy for the privilege of being deluded into believing that all is sweetness and light in a era of stress and materialism.'[52] However, it's not hard to see why Eddy's book, *Science and Health with Key to the Scriptures*, originally published in 1875, but continually revised over the next thirty-five years, influenced Highsmith throughout her teens. Central to Eddy's thesis was her belief that the human mind and spirit determined reality. 'There is nothing either good or bad, but thinking makes it so,' runs the quotation, from Shakespeare's *Hamlet* at the beginning of Eddy's text, a principle which appealed to Highsmith and one she would reassert at low points throughout her life. 'Sometimes one has the mental habit, well, really tricks, to continue to be cheerful and to continue to imagine that one's making progress when one really isn't,' she said.[53]

By the time Highsmith reached her early twenties, she found the whole premise of Christian Science a ludicrous one and she distanced herself from the movement. At twenty-seven, Highsmith assessed the methods advocated by Eddy to lift one's spirits and their influence on her mother, concluding them to be 'hysterical'.[54] However, as a young girl, shy and insecure, anxious that her sexual instincts would mark her out as a freak, she turned to Christian Science as if towards a beacon of hope. After resolving to apply the teachings of Mary Baker Eddy to her life, she believed that she did indeed feel more 'hopeful'.[55] 'The physical healing of Christian Science results now, as in Jesus' time,' Eddy promised her, 'from the operation of divine Principle, before which sin and desire lose their reality in human consciousness and disappear as naturally and as necessarily as darkness gives place to light and sin to redemption.'[56]

At fifteen, Highsmith started to keep what she called her 'cahiers', journals measuring seven by eight and a quarter inches which she would use to jot down germs of inspiration, which she referred to as 'Keime', and began to mix with a group of 'intellectual' girls who liked to be seen carrying volumes of Hemingway, Katherine Mansfield, Proust and T.S. Eliot. Each day she made sure she read the *Herald Tribune* newspaper on the way to school.

'Ever since I was sixteen or seventeen I got what is [*sic*] sometimes called creepy ideas, I suppose,' she recalled, 'but I don't consider it gruesome.'[57] In June 1937, she wrote a story called 'Crime Begins', which was described by one of her teachers as being the best in the school that term. Its theme was one she would return to in various guises for the rest of her life – the interplay of morality and guilt – and its inspiration came from personal experience.

'The first story I really remember was when I was sixteen years old. In the high school where I was going there were three copies of a certain history book, there were so many girls – it was an all-girls high school – trying to get at the book at the same time . . . It occurred to me to steal it, so I wrote a story about a girl who did. *I* never stole the book.' In the story the girl cut out a section of a very thick notebook and hid the book inside. 'It was not bad – the same style I am using now, very simple, a very simple style.'[58]

Another story, 'Primroses Are Pink', published in the fall 1937 issue of the school literary and art magazine, *The Bluebird*, deals with a psychological crisis brought on by something as trivial as the colour of primroses. Two versions of the story survive – the one that was printed in the *The Bluebird* and a slightly longer, more confident, study which exists in manuscript and which reads like a later rewrite.

The opening of the story printed in the school magazine reads as follows: 'Mr. Fleming was a man of very exacting nature. For a long time he had wanted a sporting print for his study, but he had never found any suiting both his pocketbook and his taste.'[59] The opening paragraph of the manuscript story is much more unsettling, terrifying as it is in its banality: 'The beaming Mr. Theodore Fleming strode into the lobby of his apartment building, greeted the elevator boy, and stepped into the elevator. At the twelfth floor he got out and walked gaily into his apartment. His wife was in the living room.'[60]

Fleming buys a monotone picture of a jockey on a Derby-winning racehorse and after learning of the authentic colours of his silks – primrose and white – he sends it away for painting. However, on seeing the transformed print, Fleming's wife, Catherine, thinks the primrose sported by the jockey should be pink – not the greenish-yellow colour in the painting. After all, her mother always had pink primroses in her garden. Doubt and an overwhelming sense of anxiety cloud Fleming's vision and he becomes obsessive about the correct colour of the primrose, prompting conflict between him and his wife. Although he decides to hang the painting in the apartment, he feels compelled to tell guests, 'That's primrose. English primroses are yellow, you know.'[61] Obviously the experience has left him somewhat disturbed.

Writing, it seems, was Highsmith's only outlet. 'I know why I began writing – to get an emotion out of myself, to see it on paper, organized as best as I could organize it,' she said later.[62] But at the same time as she purged herself through the experience of writing, she deliberately starved herself as a form of punishment. The sixteen-year-old girl weighed only 106 pounds and until she was nineteen she suffered from a range of health problems which would, later in the century, be classified as anorexia: failure to eat, low body weight, lack of menstruation, constipation, overactivity, blue extremities, slow heart rate and a downy skin. 'I had all these symptoms aged 15–19,'[63] she scribbled next to a newspaper feature on the subject in 1969.

In Highsmith's case, anorexia – a manifestation of extremely low self-esteem – can be read as a sign of an almost pathological desire to rid herself of her identity, a drive towards self-erasure which would later find expression in many of her novels, particularly *The Talented Mr Ripley*. This compulsion to fade away out of existence can be traced back to a mass of complex emotional factors: her unhappy childhood, her rejection by her mother in early puberty, her sense of dissociation from reality and confusion about her sexuality. She described her behaviour in her journal: 'Saving part of anything, living like a rat. Self-depreciation. Lack of food intake in adolescence, to get attention of parents, also to punish myself, for sex reasons etc.'[64]

The theories surrounding writing and sex are manifold but Highsmith herself believed that her creativity was an expression of frustrated and repressed desires. In a fictional sketch written in 1942, she drew heavily on her own experiences of her sixteenth year to paint a portrait of a girl called Henrietta. On Sundays the Henrietta/Highsmith figure would be possessed by the spirit of creativity – expressed as an urge to write and paint – but at the end of the day would only feel unsatisfied, desperately unhappy and on the verge of tears. Refusing the coffee and ice cream offered by her parents, she would stay in her unlit room, hunger tearing at her stomach, tears smarting in her eyes. Writing, Henrietta felt, was a cathartic process, a way of eliminating the toxic emotional mass that had built up inside her. But when she experienced a block, she was left feeling wretched. 'Then she associated the frustration and the desire with unfulfilled sex impulses, which was a . . . reasonable one at that age.'[65] These impulses would not remain unfulfilled for long.

Mary Highsmith, observing how little Pat was interested in the opposite sex, took it upon herself to find her daughter a boyfriend. Pat and her date would go out for a meal followed by dancing, but when it came to kissing goodnight, the sixteen-year-old girl found the practice disgusting. 'It's like falling into a bucket of oysters, isn't it?' she told her mother.[66] She hoped Mary would give her some maternal advice, but her mother was not forthcoming on the subject.

'I thought, if that's what I have to pay, at the end of the evening, for a young man's having paid my dinner check, I would rather pay my own dinner check. It never came to that, because I ceased seeing this young chap – a waste of time on both our parts, it was.'[67]

However, at some point when she was sixteen she did, according to Vivien De Bernardi, sleep with a man. 'She told me once that her first sexual experience was when she was sixteen. It was with a man. She hated it. It wasn't at all pleasurable. She had no relationship with this person at all – she was just curious. Like a medical experiment.'[68]

She found women more emotionally engaging and the 'accidental touch of the hand of a girl was a whole heaven!' she remembered later.[69] In November of 1937 she went on a date with another girl in her year at Julia Richman High School, Judy Tuvim, the actress who would later take the name Judy Holliday and win an Oscar for the 1950 film *Born Yesterday*. The two young women had a great deal in common, as both had suffered unhappy childhoods; Judy's parents' marriage had disintegrated a year after her birth and when she was a child her mother had tried to kill herself by putting her head in the oven and switching on the gas, only to be saved by her daughter. Highsmith and Tuvim were teenage misfits and yet they both had visions of forging better lives for themselves. 'I guess I was a natural snob. I got a kick out of being different and improving myself and everyone around me,' said Judy later.[70]

But any teenage relationships Highsmith entered into had to be put on hold: after graduation from high school, in January 1938, she intended to go back to stay for a few months with her grandparents in Fort Worth. In her last year at Julia Richman she had decided to work hard and aim for good grades and in her Regents, the standardised examinations for the state of New York, she received a distinction, a mark of 88 out of 100. Her final report stated that she was awarded 90 for English, French and Oral English, 85 in German, 93 in

American History, 91 in Hygiene, and 85 in Physical Training. She was let down by Social Training, which netted her only 75 marks. Her average mark totalled 79.6 per cent, ranking her 116 out of a group of 502 graduating girls.

Before she left New York she visited New York University on Washington Square, one of her choices of college. Although she had once relished the company of boys, she decided she couldn't face the reality of a mixed-sex environment. 'At any rate, in 1938, the student body of NYU looked twenty-five years old to me, though I am sure it wasn't,' she said, 'everyone seemed to weigh two hundred pounds and to be covered with hair, and I knew what it was to be bumped by one of them while walking in a hall or climbing a stairway.'[71]

In late January, she took a boat from New York to Houston and while sailing off the coast of Miami she was thrilled to see the city's lights shimmering in the dawn, a rainbow curving its way across the sea. She arrived at Willie Mae's home in Fort Worth in February, observing that the house had become rather neglected since her last visit. She also met up again with her real father, Jay B.

Father and daughter went out to dinner and spent an increasing amount of time together, culminating in what appeared to be a clumsy attempt by Jay B to seduce her. 'And now to my father,' she wrote to her stepfather over thirty years later. 'There were some lingering kisses when I was seventeen in Texas, not exactly paternal. This is all I meant. I do not want to make a big thing out of it. The word incestuous is a strong one. That my father is a gentleman has nothing to do with it. It makes as much sense as saying gentlemen have no sex drives, a patent absurdity . . .'[72] There is also a suggestion that he could even have shown her pornographic material. 'B shows me pornographic pictures (to my mingled disgust & fascination, & shame for him),' she noted in her journal.[73] Obviously their father-daughter relationship was an unusual one; he didn't look upon her as his child, while Pat didn't regard him as a fully-fledged parent. In contrast to the messy emotional spillage Highsmith had witnessed at home – the constant arguments between Mary and Stanley, rows which drove the girl further within herself – it's inevitable Pat would have seen her real father, absent as he was for such a long time, as something of an idealised figure. Like many of the silhouettes which would obsess her later in life, shadow figures she glimpsed from a distance which inspired her to write her fiction, Jay B served as a *tabula rasa*, a vessel on to which she could project her own fantasies. Not only that, but Jay B was, without a doubt, the closest living person she had encountered who bore a striking physical resemblance to herself. As she stared at him, she would have seen a glimpse of what she might have looked like had she been born a boy, a narcissistic fascination which must have drawn her closer. Undoubtedly, both father and daughter would have been confused by their feelings, an empathy and recognition that somehow mutated into sexual attraction. However, whereas Highsmith was happy to record a number of traumatic incidents in her cahiers and diaries, she chose not to document this subject in detail; perhaps it was just too raw and painful to write down.

While she was in Fort Worth, Pat made the decision to go to Barnard College, a single-sex college and part of Columbia University, New York. She spent her days reading – her favourite authors at this time included Proust, and the eighteenth-century English essayists Addison and Steele – and riding with her Fort Worth friend Florence Brillhart. One day, she remembered, she took a taxi with her grandmother, nearly blind from cataracts, from Fort Worth to a movie house out of town to see the 1935 film, *A Midsummer Night's Dream*, directed by Max Reinhardt, starring James Cagney, Dick Powell, Mickey Rooney and Olivia de Havilland, with music by Mendelssohn. 'I thought that evening, "Mendelssohn was no older than I when he wrote that overture. What a genius!"'[74]

In the evenings, she loved to walk the streets of her birthplace and imagine the psychological torment being suffered by the occupiers of the respectable houses. Clearly influenced by her early reading of Menninger, she passed the affluent homes on the west side of the city and dreamt that in one lived a madman, the son of a rich cattleowner, while another building housed an unhappy, grey-haired woman whose sons had disgraced her. 'The walks I made at seventeen out to the west, late at night,' she wrote in her journal, 'were full of surprises that were yet not quite surprises.'[75]

During this trip she also met a boy who would later be re-born as Bruno, the psychopathic killer of her first novel, *Strangers on a Train*. 'When I was 17, in Texas, I met briefly, a very spoilt boy who was very much like Bruno, completely dissolute,' she said. 'He was an adopted boy in a wealthy family and completely worthless, and he was the sort of the genesis of Bruno, who was really quite a psychopath.'[76]

In June, she sailed back to New York. She would start at Barnard College in September, and so had three months in which to enjoy the city. She went to the Metropolitan Museum of Art for a series of lectures on Egypt, bought a set of Dickens novels and resumed her relationship with Judy Tuvim. 'I see much of Judy. Though I don't like her family.'[77]

She began to feel open to the possibilities of pleasure. 'In the last month I have changed so much,' she wrote in her diary on 8 September 1938. The future presented itself as a terrifically thrilling prospect. 'I dream of the good days that lie before me, I hope.'[78]

5

The taste of freedom

1938–1940

On 28 September 1938, Highsmith walked up Broadway, through the tall iron gates of Barnard College, and registered for her four-year Bachelor of Arts course in English Literature. 'Here was the taste of freedom I craved,' she wrote of her undergraduate years.[1]

Barnard, a women-only college, and part of Columbia University, was noted for its high standards and, as part of the Ivy League, had a reputation for being somewhat exclusive. When it opened its doors, in the autumn of 1889, the institution was the first independent college in the city of New York to offer a four-year bachelor's degree to women. Former graduates who attended Barnard before Highsmith included the astronomer Henrietta Swope, authors Margaret Mead, Zora Neale Hurston, Phoebe Atwood Taylor and Elizabeth Janeway, and the poet and critic Babette Deutsch. Officially, its motto is the same as that of Columbia University – '*In Lumine Tuo Videbimus Lumen*' – 'In thy light shall we see light' – but for years the female students have adopted the Greek phrase, translated as 'Pursuing the way of reason' which appears on either side of a figure of the goddess Athena. In Highsmith's case a more fitting motto might be, 'In thy light shall we see darkness' or, 'Pursuing the way of unreason'.

At this time, Barnard's selection methods were strict: requirements included proficiency in fifteen units of secondary school subjects, including English, mathematics and a foreign language; good grades in the Regents exams, with a honour at high-school level; a glowing reference from the principal; and a suitably high grade in the Barnard entrance exam, a paper which tested the applicant's knowledge of a wide range of subjects. 'In the 1930s, only girls of exceptional accom-

plishment attended four-year colleges like Barnard,' says Donald Glassman, the Barnard College archivist.[2]

In addition to studying English Literature, Highsmith also took classes
in the short story and playwriting – interestingly, never the novel –
together with Greek, Latin, and zoology. The atmosphere at Barnard
was intensely academic, and the courses were designed to give the 950
young women admitted each year a thorough, deep and wide education.
It was, she recalled later, 'Ivory tower in those days, one long book list.'[3]
During her four-year course, Highsmith studied a wide range of English
texts ranging from *Piers Plowman, The Pearl, Sir Gawain and the Green
Knight* and Chaucer's *The Canterbury Tales* to Conrad, James, Lawrence and Eliot, as well as a number of classics from other cultures, such as
Homer's *Odyssey*, Ovid's *Metamorphoses*, Dante's *Divine Comedy*,
Goethe's *Faust*, plus works by Proust, Schiller and Pushkin. It was while
she was at Barnard that Highsmith experienced what she later described
as her 'Eureka' moment, when she realised that all of the arts were one.
'All art is based on a desire to communicate, a love of beauty, a need to
create order out of disorder,' she wrote.[4]

During Highsmith's time at Barnard, the college was presided over by
Dean Virginia Crocheron Gildersleeve, an ex-Barnard pupil and former
teacher of English. Fellow Barnard pupil Kate Kingsley Skattebol, then
Gloria Kathleen Kingsley, and one of Highsmith's closest friends,
remembers the Dean as the epitome of the bluestocking. 'We found
her formidably austere and remote, primarily because we had almost no
personal contact with her,' she says. 'I recall a speech in which she said
she wanted Barnard to turn us out as "trained brains" in order to put
our education into useful service to society.'[5] Dean Gildersleeve maintained that the function of the college was to produce young women
who not only had a deep knowledge of their chosen academic subject,
but girls who were well-rounded individuals. Barnard, she said in one of
her reports, 'is concerned with every side of the student's life, and tries
to provide an all-around civilizing environment. Public opinion expects
it to furnish residence, social development, health instruction and
supervision, vocational advice, and a position after graduation.'[6] Some
people, she added, jokingly, 'even suggest we should provide hus-
bands'.[7]

One of Highsmith's favourite teachers was Ethel Sturtevant, Assistant Professor of English, who taught her the art of short-story writing,
and to whom she would later dedicate the novel, *A Game for the
Living*. Sturtevant, an elegant woman with a passion for Jane Austen,
the Brontës, Henry James, and George Meredith, had taught at Barnard

since 1911, and she remained there until her retirement in 1948. 'I always like my students to do things for themselves,' she said. 'What one works for, one remembers.'[8]

She was, according to those who knew her, 'charming, humorous, wilful, with a magical voice and the airs of a beauty. Wearing her large garden-party hat she would toss her head like a Gibson beauty. Her students of course adored her.'[9] Her two favourite words of praise were 'significant' and 'exciting', qualities she would have recognised in the young Highsmith's writings. Like Highsmith, she never married; she shared her apartment on West 116th Street with her mother, and on her retirement, moved permanently into the old family home in East Lyme, Connecticut. It was there, in 1950, two years after Sturtevant had left Barnard, that Highsmith showed her extracts of her lesbian novel, *The Price of Salt* (later republished as *Carol*), prompting her to respond, 'Now *this* packs a wallop! This is an excellent piece of writing, Pat.'[10]

In the latter part of 1938, Highsmith had a vision of a young, ghost-like girl dancing by herself to the music of a Tchaikovsky waltz. As the girl moved around the room, she had a sense that the music was emanating from within her. It had, she thought, taken years for the melodies to form themselves, but now the rhythm was born effortlessly and with a life of its own. There was no difference between herself and the music that played, no break between the inner and outer worlds. Not only was her self the source of the art, but it was, in a way, also its subject.

This fantasy, recorded in the opening pages of her first cahier, can be interpreted as a symbol of her burgeoning creativity, an imaginative quality that expressed itself as a terrifically powerful force, ready to 'burst forth in the selfless spontaneity'.[11] At college Highsmith's creative instinct found expression in the pages of the college magazine. In December 1938, she was elected as one of the literary staff on *Barnard Quarterly*, the college journal which she would go on to edit in her senior year and which in the fall 1939 issue, published her short story 'Quiet Night'. The unsettling tale, about two old women, Hattie and Alice, who share a room in a New York hotel, articulates the twinned motives of tender affection and violent loathing that would characterise so much of her work. In the middle of the night, when Alice is asleep, Hattie takes a pair of scissors and purposefully makes a number of slashes in Alice's new sweater, a gift from her niece. 'In the moonlight her face gleamed, toothless and demoniacal,' she wrote. 'She examined the sweater in the manner of a person who plays with a piece of steak with a fork before deciding where to put his knife.'[12] When Alice discovers what her friend has done, she is utterly bereft and, in revenge, one night takes the scissors, determined to slice off Hattie's only vanity – a two-foot long braid of hair – but stops herself as she is about to make the first cut.

Highsmith would, in 1966, rewrite the story – under the title 'The Cries of Love' – so that Alice does cut off her friend's hair, leaving her with nothing but an ugly stump. And although the two women apologise to one another, there's no doubting that their repressed feelings will continue to interrupt their lives, further suggesting that neither of them can survive outside this strange sado-masochistic relationship.

The germ for this story had its origins in a walk Highsmith made through Gramercy Park, where she observed a number of old ladies sitting on benches. Increasingly she looked to real life to provide the base for her fiction. 'I can never make a character unless I take him from actual life – with as little changes as possible. Sturtevant says the ability to create abstractly comes with experience. But even Proust had a germ of reality for each of his characters. And why not?'[13] Later in *Plotting and Writing Suspense Fiction*, Highsmith would write about how she would sometimes milk friends and acquaintances for inspiration, occasionally taking the physical characteristics of someone she knew, or using their personality as a base for further development. However, she said she never transported anyone in their totality from real life into her fiction, preferring a mix-and-match approach.

The supernatural, which she had once adored, now bored her – ghost stories were simply childish and idiotic. Yet her stories did at this stage still bear the traces of her gothic perspective. One of the reasons why her work is so powerful and so disturbing is precisely because, while her subject matter may be the fantastical, the perverse and the bizarre, her style is pared-down, documentary and almost super-realist in tone. In 1940 she said she admired Maupassant because of his 'economy in writing'.

'What immense satisfaction it must be to fashion a story like his! One must say "fashion" because it is not merely writing, but massing and cutting away like a sculptor, chiseling lean and clear. And to put one's work confidently in the crucible of Time; to know that in six perfect pages is the finest form of one's idea: This satisfaction is the only true reward of the artist, and this his highest possible joy on Earth.'[14]

She had always been a voracious reader, but now she turned down invitations to dinner in favour of staying at home and immersing herself in the dark imaginative landscapes of Thomas Mann, Strindberg,

Goethe, Joyce, T.S. Eliot and Baudelaire. The mere thought that she was alone and surrounded by books gave her a near-sensuous thrill. As she looked around her room, dark except for the slash of light near her lamp, and saw the vague outlines of her books, she asked herself, 'Have I not the whole world?'[15]

During her time at Barnard, Highsmith embraced a number of different ideologies with the hope of finding an interpretative tool which would help her understand the world. When she was seventeen she became fascinated by Eastern philosophy, a system of thought which she would later describe as having a 'powerful'[16] influence on her and something she would study for two years. In her first cahier, in an entry dated August 1939, she made a list of the major character traits of Hinduism, detailing the Yogic explanation for how the universe came into being. She also outlined a number of rules and codes of behaviour designed to promote a deeper level of consciousness: non-violence, truthfulness, non-stealing, moderation, non-possessiveness, purity, contentment, austerity, study and surrender. However, for all her reading and thinking, Pat abandoned the East as a source of possible philosophical illumination because she felt that ultimately she could not relate to it, 'never getting anywhere with a real connection with my life of the Western World'.[17]

Perhaps communism would give her the answers she was looking for? During her teenage years she had positioned herself as an intellectual and as such aligned herself with other writers who, like Thomas Mann, believed that 'politics is everybody's business'.[18] When, in July 1936, she heard the news of the outbreak of the Spanish Civil War – which began as a civil conflict but which soon translated into an ideological battle – it seemed natural for the fifteen-year-old's sympathies to lie with the Republicans, fighters for democracy and freedom, rather than the fascist military regime imposed by Franco. Within the space of a few months, Spain had become a symbol of hope for anti-fascists everywhere; the conflict set the intellectual world aflame, foregrounding the power struggles that would dominate world politics throughout the twentieth century. According to W.H. Auden, the struggle 'X-rayed the lies upon which our civilization is built'[19], while C.S. Lewis articulated the conflict as 'a battle between light and darkness'.[20]

During the Spanish Civil War, the written word was used as a shield to protect the country from the sting of fascist bullets and the stirring language employed by authors such as John Dos Passos in his 1938 work *Adventures of a Young Man*, appealed to the young Highsmith, passionate as she was in the fight for liberty, compassion, tolerance and free speech. Many American intellectuals like Highsmith turned to communism because they realised that, in Spain, democracy had failed to stop the rise of fascism – in 1939 the Nationalist forces squashed the Republican uprising and Franco ruled over the country as dictator – and they felt frustrated by their own country's hypocritical attitudes to the conflict. Highsmith became a communist, she said later, simply 'for the good reason USA was financing Franco, who was being supported by Hitler and Mussolini.'[21] Franco's victory also forced people to question accepted notions of morality and many young writers like Highsmith were left feeling increasingly depressed and alienated by the modern world. Their state of mind, described by Frederick R. Benson, in *Writers in Arms: The Literary Impact of the Spanish Civil War*, has particular resonance with Highsmith's work.

> The war revealed, in the case of fascism, a capacity for evil in human beings that negated certain optimistic psychological assumptions and destroyed the basic political arguments advanced in the democracies by right-wing defenders of 'national socialism' . . . Often the individual conscience was numbed, and acquiescence to nihilism as a result of the loss of human identity was the immediate consequence.[22]

The Spanish Civil War 'made a great impact on me, on all my generation',[23] Highsmith said, and in 1939 she joined the Young Communist League, an organisation created in 1922 that by 1935 boasted a membership list of 8,000. Later, she would confess to Patricia Losey – whose husband, the film director, Joseph Losey was blacklisted – that she had been placed on the S-list because of her one-time communist sympathies. Highsmith read her way through Karl Marx's *The Class Struggles in France 1848–1850*, Marx and Engels' *The Communist Manifesto*, and a number of other key Marxist texts such as *The Civil War in France*, *The 18th Brumaire of Louis Bonaparte* and Stalin's *Foundations of Leninism*. 'How Socialism works,' she noted passionately. 'One hates the rich!'[24] Despite European unrest, Barnard was an extremely conservative college. 'There were only two girls in my dorm who were Democrats, the rest were Republicans,' says fellow pupil Rita Semel.[25] Undoubtedly, Highsmith's decision to sign up as a party member would have shocked, had she chosen to tell them, many of her contemporaries.

Throughout the thirties, the communist party took advantage of

America's failing economic and spiritual health. During the first three years of the Depression, in a seismic societal shift appropriately dubbed the great 'American earthquake', the communist party doubled its membership, then doubled it once more in the first two years of Roosevelt's New Deal, and once more again in the following two years. By October 1936, the majority of its members were native-born, rather than immigrants.

'Second generation Americans found the communist movement a channel for their rebellion,' writes Joseph Starobin, a historian of American communism, 'a cure for their anomie, a vehicle for ambitions.'[26] Similarly, the Young Communist League appealed to the nation's increasingly dissatisfied youth, men and women who felt at odds with mainstream society. The first ambition of the League, as expressed by its leader, Gil Green, was the destruction of the capitalist state and its replacement by the dictatorship of the proletariat.

During her two years as a member of the YCL, Highsmith would have been told that the organisation could be compared to a machine operating on a belt system connecting it both directly and indirectly to various sections of society, including student networks and young workers. 'In turn, as a result of our mass work,' according to Lewis Miller, compiler of the YCL's handbook, 'we recruit new members for the Young Communist League.'[27]

In January 1941, Highsmith heard Earl Browder, the general secretary of the communist party of the United States, speak at the Lenin Memorial meeting in Madison Square Gardens. 'Lenin died seventeen years ago,' said Browder. 'But his spirit lives as the beloved teacher and guide of tens of millions in all lands, because he and his party alone showed the way out of the last imperialist war, the way to peace and socialism.'[28] Browder went on to attack Roosevelt's politics, arguing that American democracy was in fact a whitewash, merely imperialism in disguise. Instead, the people of America should look to the USSR, which Browder claimed somewhat naively, was the 'embodiment of the rule of the people', a 'realisation of the teachings of Lenin, and of his great and wise successor and continuator, Stalin.'[29]

However, by late 1941 Highsmith started to feel uneasy in the company of her fellow young communists. 'A meeting this evening of the League,' she recorded in her diary in September 1941, 'I feel uncomfortable with them & useless, because now we are all supposed to be collecting money. I wonder if I should tell them I am a degenerate & be expelled.'[30] In November, she dashed off what she thought was a well-worded epistle outlining her reasons for leaving the party and by the end of December, after mixing with a more sophisticated – and wealthy – crowd, Highsmith wrote in her diary about her new appreciation for money. Whereas previously she thought that having money dulled one's artistic instincts, lately she had come around to the view that it actually helped one appreciate aesthetics.

Many of her contemporaries experienced a similar disillusionment with the movement. Arthur Koestler, whom Highsmith would meet in October 1950 and who would become a close friend, was so depressed by the state of the world – by the failure of Marxist ideals to prevent the rise of fascism and the Stalin-Hitler pact – that he wrote how he had, like Picasso, rushed into communism as one goes to a spring of fresh water and yet turned away from the movement like a man desperate to climb from the murky waters of a poisoned river, 'strewn with the wreckage of flooded cities and the corpses of the drowned.'[31]

Even before Highsmith resigned from the YCL she was having serious doubts about its effect on her creativity. She rejected the concept that novels should be structured according to a philosophy which is then, through the development of the plot, proven to have some kind of universal application. If she tried this approach, she said, the end result would be forced and dry; not so much a story but merely a vehicle for ideas. Rather, she believed a more fruitful approach would be to think up a narrative and then, after she had sketched out the shape of the story, she could ask herself whether it contained a 'universal idea'. 'If it could not be contained,' she wrote in her journal, 'the story could then be rejected.'[32]

From October 1939, paralleling her interest in Marx, Highsmith started to study the other great pioneer of twentieth-century thought: Freud. Later in life, Highsmith said she mistrusted psychoanalysis, but from reading her diaries and journals it is clear that the movement shaped both her character and her writing. 'Conscious thinking is the weakest (How I believe this!),' she wrote in 1940,[33] while three years later, she said, 'The highest good is the use of the subconscious mind entirely, almost to the exclusion of the conscious mind, which is patterned after those around us. Within the subconscious lies all one's oil, one's fire, one's flavor, and the measure of divinity allotted to all of us.'[34]

Her best ideas, she believed, came when her rational mind was switched off – when she was doing activities such as the ironing or gardening – and she allowed herself to daydream. The ideas that rose to the surface of her consciousness and articulated themselves in her early, experimental fiction were, from the beginning, dark, sinister and expressive of a haunting sense of isolation. The nine stories published in *Barnard Quarterly*, between 1939 and 1942, illustrate her already expert ability at conveying unease and building up suspense even in the most mundane of situations. 'Pat the distinctive . . . Pat the ultra,' reads her entry in the college magazine, *Mortarboard*, of 1942, 'Pat the gal who reads standing up . . . all Barnard shivers to the tune of her smoothly-written *Quarterly* masterpieces . . .'[35]

'A Mighty Nice Man', published in *Barnard Quarterly* in spring 1940, is about a kerbcrawler whose efforts to try and entice a girl into a car with some sweets are frustrated by an onlooker. Later when the girl's mother asks her to explain her eagerness to get into the stranger's car, she replies, 'But he was a mighty nice man'.[36] 'A suspense story, you see,' said Highsmith later.[37] 'Eel in the Bathtub', published in the autumn of 1940, is so called because its central character, bachelor Nicholas Carr, is just as difficult to catch as the slippery, snake-like fish. He is obsessed with the objects that surround him – his watch, his clothes, his Abercrombie Fitch horsehide picnic kit – and turns down a weekend trip with friends, and a date with a prospective girlfriend, so he can be alone. 'Movie Date', in the winter 1940 issue, is a cruel, but poignant, story about Danny – dull, boring and spotty – and Helen, the girl he loves. She can't stand his company and she tells him that she is going to marry an older man, knowing that the revelation will crush him. Indeed, the news does shock him and the tale ends with Danny's announcement that he will quit not only his job, but may even give up on life itself. Instead of resorting to melodrama, Highsmith skilfully underplays the emotional intensity of the situation, articulating the torment through its banality.

'The Legend of The Convent of Saint Fotheringay', published in spring of 1941, tells in a comic style the story of a baby boy brought up as a girl, Mary. One day the child is found by a nun from the convent of Saint Fotheringay, an institution that prides itself on its all-female environment. Not only are all the pupils girls, but they are are denied the knowledge that there is another sex. Mary is raised as a girl, but all the time the child knows that she is different from the others and eventually blackmails the nuns into letting her leave the convent by threatening to blow it up with firecrackers. She eventually does escape, but the building is mysteriously destroyed, along with all its inhabitants. Too much shouldn't be read into this story, but it's intriguing to note that Highsmith's middle name was Mary, and she felt from an early age that she had an unmistakably masculine identity. 'It is

forbidden me to mention his name in connection with the Legend of
Saint Fotheringay,' she says at the end of the story, 'but each of you, I'm
sure, dear readers, would know him if I did.'[38]

Her favoured style was crisp and concise, employing the same
economic technique she would use until the end of her career, but
there was one exception, 'Silver Horn of Plenty', published in *Barnard
Quarterly* in the winter of 1941. She said later that she could never have
written the story, a stream of consciousness prose-poem, focusing on a
woman's preparation for a New Year's Eve party, 'on my own
observation of parties, but only if I had attended them with my
parents.'[39] Clearly influenced by the modernist movement, the impressionistic story lacks a strong central narrative and is composed of a
series of fragmented images. Yet it is still typically Highsmithian, as its
central themes are splintered identity and simmering sexuality.

Just as Menninger exposed the psychological torment that lurked
inside the most respectable, seemingly well-balanced men and women,
so Highsmith, with her instinctive feel for the subject, stripped back the
mask of normality to reveal the horrors underneath.

'Almost every man in the world prides himself on his delicate
understanding, his magnanimity, his kindness, his wisdom, in the
unreal sanctity of his study room,' she wrote in 1940. 'But each
man when he goes into the world puts on his armor, even armor for
his heart, and firms his mouth . . . In each man's heart sits loneliness
and shame and pride.'[40]

Above this notebook entry, Highsmith later scrawled the word,
'Important'.

When Highsmith stepped out from the safe confines of her study room,
her armour appeared to be intact, quite invincible. The face she chose to
show the world was one which bore no trace of her inner, private
torments. Her fellow students at Barnard thought her a reserved,
reticent, and rather shadowy figure. 'She was a loner, rather superior
but very efficient, and I don't remember her associating much with
anyone very closely,' says Deborah Karp (then Burstein), who succeeded her as editor of *Quarterly*.[41]

Rita Semel, editor of *Barnard Quarterly* in 1941, with Highsmith as
her deputy, thought Pat mature for her age. 'She was very different from
all the other girls,' she says. 'She knew what she was going to do with
her life and what she wanted to be – a writer. Words were her life then
and it was clear she would succeed in her ambition. I liked her but I
couldn't say I *knew* her. I could tell she was a very complex person, but

she was hard to get to know. We had as good a friendship as any we were likely to have because she was private and gave nothing away. I worked for hours on *Quarterly* with her and yet I can say I knew nothing about her.'[42]

The writer Mary Cable (then Mary Pratt), who was in the same writing class at Barnard, and who met her in 1940, also remembers Pat as quite a distant figure, a handsome girl who made no effort to integrate with her peers.

'I recall distinctly that she was not very communicative,' she says. 'She simply did not make an effort. For instance if both of us were early to class she would go and sit at the back. We never really had a conversation and that was, in a way, quite off-putting.

'Yet she was very good looking and always well dressed and nicely made-up. Both of us were taught by Ethel Sturtevant, and from the beginning it was obvious that Pat was very good at writing. But she did not express much emotion when she was praised – maybe she always knew that she was good.'[43]

Rather, Highsmith was racked by self-doubt. In 1938, she wrote a poem about the process of creation, how when she sat down to write she felt inspired by a 'white heat', a fury which possessed her, but a force which ultimately manifested itself by nothing but a wastebasket full of scribbles, nicotine-stained fingers and an unpleasant taste in the mouth.[44] She spent hours recording her thoughts, observations and creative ideas in her cahiers, but after looking through them she was left feeling disappointed, convinced that her writing betrayed nothing but signs of immaturity and unoriginality. She was also terribly insecure and still felt at odds with the world around her, as she recorded in a poem in one of her notebooks.

> I have been sadder than any man could be:
> For nothing in the world was made for me.[45]

At times she wanted simply to disappear, to erase her identity, and imagined herself to be nothing more than an abstract fragment of a thought drifting across a desert. In her journal she wrote a poignant account of how the joyous anticipation of going on a date with a woman turned into embarrassment after she became tongue-tied and self-conscious: the more she failed to communicate, the more she thought her date assumed she was stupid and had nothing to say, which then resulted in further verbal constipation. As she walked home, ashamed of her behaviour, she castigated herself for not being able to express her thoughts and feelings. This crippling sense of shyness would stay with her until middle age, as she wrote in a later letter to Arthur Koestler, describing the 'dreadful shyness, of teens and twenties, that was like a physical pain. I think some psychiatrists call such shyness an inverted arrogance and conceit. This explanation doesn't help the pain of it.'[46]

Her home life, too, made her feel ill at ease and uncomfortable. In the latter part of 1939 the family moved to a flat at 35 Morton Street, also in Greenwich Village, but the relationship between Mary and Stanley deteriorated to such an extent that he moved out for a few months and took an apartment on Charles Street, a few blocks north. At the same time, too, Pat had begun to see her mother in a new light. Although Mary had abandoned her with her grandmother in Texas, emotionally she still felt close to her mother. However, from the age of seventeen she started to realise that it was Mary – not Stanley – who was to blame for the harsh-sounding arguments that echoed around her throughout her early years. As she wrote to her friend Alex Szogyi in 1967, she believed her mother to be not only irrational but of questionable intelligence too. The slow realisation that Mary was the source of the problem caused her to reassess her 'childhood hell', she said. 'It is dreadful when love turns to hate,' she wrote. 'There is nothing worse.'[47] She articulated these ambiguous feelings for her mother in a telling poem written in July 1940, a two-line fragment which could be compared to one of Sylvia Plath's poems about her relationship with her father.

> I am married to my mother
> I shall never wed another.[48]

There was a lasting bond between mother and daughter, but, as in the worst of marriages, it comprised of a combination of love and loathing that she found impossible to escape. In the future, her relationships with women would always be shaped by her paradoxical emotional attachment to Mary Highsmith, a compulsion which clearly tormented her.

Her peers misread this sense of alienation and inner despair, confusing it with superiority and haughtiness. Most of them also failed to appreciate her black – and often ribald sense of humour. It was this quality which initially attracted Kate Kingsley Skattebol, then Gloria Kathleen Kingsley – Pat would always call by her maiden name – who enjoyed a close friendship with her until Highsmith's death in 1995. The two young Barnard students met in the offices of *Quarterly* when Kingsley gingerly handed Highsmith a short story for her appraisal.

When the two students next saw one another, they exchanged limericks over the reading desk. Highsmith loved limericks, the bawdier the better, as this one, written in 1940 shows:

> A clever old maid of Hampstead
> Kept a burglar for year half-dead
> By threat of betrayal
> Should he ever fail
> To bugger her nightly in bed.[49]

'She was fun to be with,' says Kingsley, 'and her sense of humour was great. She loved to shock people. She was like a shot in the arm for me. I remember seeing her in the library – she always stood up to read – and I have this picture of her standing there surrounded by books. She had a beautiful figure, very slender, well dressed, and had exotic looks. There was a certain mystique about her and she was very alluring. After swapping limericks, we started talking and it was clear that she read an awful lot.

'However, the only reason, I'm sure, that I lasted so long as a friend of hers is that we never had an erotic relationship. And so we were never subject to these emotional frailties. I had a great crush on her, but it was nothing sexual. She did not fancy me and I certainly did not fancy her in a sexual way. But aesthetically – I thought she was an object of adoration, an idol to me. I think I knew that Pat was gay from the beginning. I grew up in a fringe theatrical world, and I knew about gay people. But I think the fact that Pat was gay had extraordinarily little to do with her writing.'[50]

Highsmith was far from sexually innocent – from November 1938 she started to see a twenty-year-old woman called Virginia, whom she described as looking like Virginia Woolf – but during her early days at Barnard there was something almost schoolgirlish about her appreciation of the feminine form. On 13 April 1940, Pat competed in the hurdles of the Greek Games – Barnard's 'attempt to reproduce, as nearly as modern conditions permit, a classic festival'[51] – complete with contests in athletics, costume, dance, music and lyrics and dedicated to the God Prometheus. The occasion also gave her an opportunity to ogle the other girls in their short skirts. In her programme for the event, she scribbled next to one fellow contestant the word 'legs!'

'Barnard was very prim and proper in those days,' says Rita Semel. 'It may sound dumb now but back then I didn't even know what a lesbian was – I had never heard the word.'[52] Deborah Karp remembers that Pat often wore riding breeches into college. 'She was extremely dashing-looking and it never occurred to any of us that she might like women,' she says.[53]

Highsmith idealised her relationship with Virginia, describing their union as 'the first glimpse of a piece of heaven brought down to earth'.[54] Pat credited the slightly older woman with investing her with sharper powers of observation and a new sense of self-worth. The 'real love'[55] which they shared, she believed, had truly metamorphic qualities. As she walked down a sidewalk, through the dappled shadows cast by a group of low arching trees, Highsmith had the sense that she could walk for ever and that the whole world was singing. She compared the sun to Beethoven; the whisper of the grass was like Chopin; the sharp, atonal screeches of the birds sounded like Stravinsky, while the wind in the trees she likened to Debussy, phrases she would work into her 1952 novel, *The Price of Salt*, to describe Therese's love for Carol. 'But the tempo? The tempo was mine . . .' she wrote in her notebook. 'I was the beat, and the whole world marched to my pace that afternoon.'[56]

Falling in love, she thought at the time, allowed her to feel and act like other people, 'seeing what should be seen . . . having the correct reaction'.[57] Later she would add, tellingly, that 'The real return to normality is after falling out of love. Not while being in love.'[58] Significantly, the eighteen-year-old Highsmith already connected the misery brought on by personal relationships with the need to write. Whenever she felt unhappy about Virginia's cruel treatment of her, Highsmith translated this into a compulsive desire to expunge her feelings through her fiction. 'I miss Va., can't end it,' she wrote in March 1939. 'Must write something good to calm & satisfy myself.'[59] Writing became a cathartic process for her, a way of expressing the contradictory responses of love and hate that seethed inside her. 'I read, write and create,' she wrote in December. 'I must lose myself in work, so that there is no space for the other/anything else.'[60]

6

A trail of unmade beds

1940–1942

'The undergraduate of 1940 . . .' wrote Barnard's official historian, 'seemed even younger than her age in her loafers and ankle sox, her casual sweaters and skirts, and with her hair often in little pigtails. If she wore make-up at all it was only lipstick, and she acted like the most carefree and comfortable of girls.'[1] This saccharine description is one entirely at odds with the image of Highsmith as a young woman, a figure who felt dislocated from the world around her. What, she asked herself, could she do to force herself to experience life more acutely? Her adolescence had been a sheltered one, as she believed she had lived for the most part within the prescribed confines of a fictionalised reality defined by the books she had read. As she left her teenage years behind she realised it was time to move away from an imaginative landscape composed of only make-believe characters into a world inhabited by 'real people'. The ideal, she would soon learn, was a union of the two – the knowledge gleaned from reading grafted on to the fruits of direct experience.

She turned for inspiration to the American novelist Thomas Wolfe, whose posthumous novel, *You Can't Go Home Again*, Highsmith read in June 1941. He believed one's personal experiences lay at the foundation of all great fiction. 'Nowhere can you escape autobiography whenever you come to anything that has any real or lasting value in letters,' he wrote.[2] The notion of writing about one's immediate life and experience appealed to Highsmith and she later compared the self to a patch of fertile soil from which she could draw creative nourishment. 'Mother says that he [Wolfe] was a colossal egotist and that I resemble him in that respect,' she wrote in her diary. 'Egotist, yes, and genius too.'[3] Highsmith regarded him as a poet, a writer who used his self as the central theme of his work, as opposed to novelists such as Somerset Maugham, passive bystanders, who merely observed the world. Although she was not interested in imitating Wolfe's 'overwritten', somewhat retrogressive style, peppered as it was with commas and semi-colons, Highsmith nonetheless admired him for his dedication to his craft and for being 'true to himself'. Yet she also knew that if she wanted to succeed as a writer, she would have to find more interesting material than Barnard's daily tittle-tattle.

Highsmith connected her progression from literary junkie – using books as drugs to shield herself from reality – to active participant in life with her burgeoning sexual identity. At nineteen, she went along, initially quite reluctantly, with a group of other Barnard girls to a bar in Greenwich Village. There she met Mary Sullivan, a butch, five-foot-tall, middle-aged lesbian who ran the bookshop at the Waldorf Astoria Hotel. Mary invited Pat to a party – her friends declined the offer – and within the space of a week her 'monastic adolescence was ended'.[4] She described every detail of the resulting sexual awakening in her diaries, drawing a brutally frank and viscerally powerful account of her relationships with a large number of men and women, including Mary Sullivan. This intimate account of what went on behind the closed doors of the near-incestuous, web-like network of forties gay New York makes for powerful reading. While the writer's cahiers, or notebooks, functioned as the storehouse for her creative and philosophical thoughts, split into sections such as quotations from other writers, places and people, and 'Keime' or germs of ideas, Highsmith used her diaries as a collecting bowl into which she could spill the residue of her frequently chaotic personal life. This compulsive mapping of her emotional and sexual experiences raises the question of motivation: why did she feel the urge to document so fully such an intimate part of her life?

Pat's promiscuity and her obsessive need to record it can be traced back to the same source – an overwhelming quest towards greater self-knowledge. She was conscious that she needed to become better 'acquainted with myself'[5] and throughout the diaries she connected this search for self-revelation with two interlinked activities: intimacy with women and the act of writing. She believed in the spiritualising effect of the women she loved, viewing them as muses who would inspire her to create work of which she was proud.

'Our works are the mirror wherein the spirit sees its natural lineaments,' she wrote in the opening pages of her 1941 diary, quoting a

passage from Carlyle's *Sartor Resartus*.[6] Taking the metaphor one step
further, the portrait which emerges from the diaries is one composed of
the many glistening shards of a broken mirror, reflective splinters
through which she attempted to reconstruct and review her ever-
changing identity. Gushing, naive, contradictory, touching, banal
and romantic, the diaries may not be interesting for their inherent
literary merit, yet they bear the details which Highsmith would subsequently refashion into fiction. By writing about her various liaisons,
Highsmith hoped to stir up her creativity by bringing about a sort of
catalytic chain reaction. She believed that the act of recording would
help recapture the emotional essence of each experience, feelings which
could then be channelled into a short story or novel. 'All these bits of
information and observation in this notebook should, some day, make
a novel,' she said. 'The question is what should be the glue to hold them
together? My work now is the quest for the glue.'[7]

Throughout Highsmith's confessional journals there exists a tension
between the two sides of the writer's nature, a confrontation between
puritanism and promiscuity, mind and body, conscious and unconscious, the philosophical and the mundane. Pleasure is pursued only for
it to be sullied by guilt; statements are made which are then contra-
dicted; and lovers lauded and worshipped only to be cast aside with the
sudden discovery of a new source of wonder. As such, the diaries can be
read as discourses of desire, documents which detail the protean,
chimeric nature of love.

While Highsmith was at Barnard, she immersed herself in Proust's *A
la recherche du temps perdu*, finding the work 'a delight and an
inspiration'.[8] Her work would stand at the opposite pole of the stylistic
spectrum – Proust's opaque prose is discursive and digressive, while
Highsmith's near-transparent writing is crisp and compact – but
thematically she was drawn to explore the same subject: the illusory
nature of love. When the young Highsmith opened her copy of *Swann's
Way*, the first volume of the French *roman-fleuve*, she would have seen
herself reflected in its pages and there is no doubt that, subsequently,
Proust's vision of the nature of desire informed both her writing and her
personal life. When we love, said Proust, we focus not on the real
qualities of a particular person nor the relative merits of their appearance or character; instead, we create a fantasy of our own making
which we then project on to the unsuspecting individual. Far from being
empirical, love is eidetic, a mental image made visible. At the first
suggestion of falling in love, says Proust, 'we falsify it by memory and
by suggestion; recognising one of its symptoms, we recall and recreate

the rest.'[9] Each object of one's love is a mere silhouette, a blank canvas which acts as a base for the construction of an imaginative fantasy. As such there could never be merely one Albertine, the women enamoured by Proust's narrator; like the appearance of the ever-changing sea, his loved one's identities were legion. Just as the narrator feels the need to give a different name to each of the Albertines he conjures in his mind, so he is compelled to regard his own self as composed of many different personae. 'To be quite accurate, I ought to give a different name to each of the selves who subsequently thought about Albertine; I ought still more to give a different name to each of the Albertines who appeared before me, never the same'.[10] Happiness is impossible, he says, as 'the advantage one has secured is never anything but a fresh starting-point for further desires'.[11]

Highsmith continued her relationships with Mary Sullivan – who sent Pat a bunch of gardenias every afternoon under the name of 'Mike Thomas', before the couple eventually separated in July 1941 – and her old girlfriend Virginia, but neither woman was enough for her. She recognised her insatiable appetite for a constant supply of new conquests and the inherent destructiveness of her habit, yet she felt unable to resist its power, classifying herself as something of a 'degenerate'.

Fellow Barnard student Rita Semel remembers how on one occasion Pat invited her to dinner at her apartment. 'I went around for dinner, her mother wasn't there, and she came on to me,' she says. 'I was very confused I didn't know what was happening. She tried to seduce me both with words and actions but I think I just pushed her away and left soon after. Only years later did I realise what she was up to. I didn't say anything afterwards and neither did she.'[12] A friend once said of Highsmith that she left a trail of unmade beds behind her. 'How Pat ever got to class – she was hungover so many times – I'll never know, with all this coming and going,' says Kingsley. 'It's a mystery to me how she managed to get anything done or read anything at all.'[13]

Paradoxically, Highsmith's seemingly unstoppable sexual drive was fired by a sense of incompleteness, the frustrating sense that, during lovemaking, she was forever the observer rather than the active participant. Sex, for her, she said, was very much a hoax, an overrated con-act as false as a Coney Island sideshow. 'Yet why must I always stand aside and watch myself and others as though we were on stage!' she wrote.[14]

One of her associates at this time was the 'charmingly naive'[15] painter Buffie Johnson, whom Pat met at the beginning of July 1941. 'She stood out from the crowd, she was very handsome,' says

Buffie of that first meeting.[16] Pat asked for Buffie's telephone number and astounded the painter by telling her she didn't need to write it down as she had memorised it. 'To my surprise she did,' says Buffie, 'and I was impressed with this trick of memory especially since my own is poor.'[17] On the 19th of the month, Buffie, who was friends with New York's literary set, including Tennessee Williams, Truman Capote and Paul and Jane Bowles, took her new friend to a party, which she knew would be a good opportunity for Pat to meet people in the publishing world. 'Although they were much older, she immediately busied herself among them,' says Buffie. 'Emerging from a deep conversation, I suddenly realised that all the other guests had left the party. Without even saying goodnight, Patricia had left with the group of editors.'[18] One of those women was Rosalind Constable.

Rosalind was an elegant thirty-four-year-old British-born woman and a researcher on *Fortune* magazine, but to Highsmith, the New York magazine journalist with her 'blond Dutch boy hair and frosty light eyes'[19] could have walked straight out of the pages of Proust. To Highsmith, Rosalind was not so much an individual as a symbol, embodying an idealised love of her own making. 'I don't think anything ever did happen between them, but Pat absolutely adored her,' says Kingsley. 'She was a true role model for her.'[20]

The day after they met, Pat telephoned Rosalind, who invited her over to her apartment on Madison Avenue, where the women drank and played records. At 2 a.m., the younger woman made moves to go, but Rosalind invited her to stay in her roommate's bedroom, where, 'We were both kidding around and laughing a lot.'[21] Pat was particularly touched that Rosalind – who went on to forge a formidable reputation as the avant-garde specialist and cultural trend-spotter across a number of titles at Time Inc. – kept a piece of string from her dress as a memento of their time together.

From this briefest of encounters, Highsmith immediately concluded that she was in love with the older, Scandinavian-looking woman, feelings which were strengthened by a period of separation. During a four-week driving tour of America in late July and August, which Highsmith made with her uncle, John, and his wife, Grace, the writer composed an evocative word-picture of Rosalind in her diary. At each of the stops on the cross-country trip – Chicago, Sioux Falls, across the Badlands and the Rockies, to Reno, Sacramento, San Francisco and Los Angeles – Highsmith checked the post office for letters forwarded from Rosalind. Together with her relatives, she drove west on roads that ran straight for forty miles, riding through the night, under a half moon, thinking of 'happiness and love to come'.[22]

The language she chose to describe Rosalind indicated the special status she afforded her new figure of worship, casting her as a perfect statue, a Titan, an angel. She was Beatrice to Highsmith's Dante, her one source of inspiration, her 'bit of heaven'.[23] Rather than view Rosalind as a sexual object, Highsmith saw the cultured sophisticate – of whom it was later said, 'Everyone knew that Rosalind Constable was The person to ask about anything ranging from the latest slang to the first stirrings of a literary style or new art movement'[24] – in Platonic terms. She would, she confessed, rather worship her from afar and bask in the unsullied purity of their relationship than take pleasure in the sordid madness of the moment. From the beginning of their friendship, Highsmith knew that Rosalind was attached – her partner was the artist and gallery owner Betty Parsons – and it seems her very unobtainability was one of her most attractive qualities. 'When we love unrequited we are very much conscious that we are in love. That is all we have to think about,' she wrote. 'When our love is returned there is, in me, at least, a holding back, almost a fear of perfection.'[25]

On her return to New York at the end of August, Highsmith resumed her relationships with a number of individuals of both sexes. One prospective lover wryly observed that Highsmith was rather like the Allied army in that she was '"too thinly deployed on too many fronts"'.[26] But Pat justified her promiscuity by telling herself that it was better to have sex than 'stagnating'; otherwise she wouldn't be in any condition for her true love: Rosalind. 'I shall take the rest holding my nose,' she wrote, 'like a dose of castor oil.'[27]

Rosalind, for her part, certainly flirted with Pat. She walked through the streets of Greenwich Village holding her hand, called Pat 'Baby', before her friends and invited the younger woman to sit on her lap in taxis. But the relationship did not progress as quickly as Pat wished and she turned to fantasy as a way of channelling her desires. Highsmith realised that her obsession with Rosalind could unbalance her: she forced herself to think of her only at certain times of the day, when she was in a room full of people, for example, or in bed. As a result her mental image of Rosalind became a stand-in for the real thing. 'Unfortunately it has had to do for seeing you many times, and one gets rather good at pretending after a while,' she wrote.[28]

Mary and Stanley saw their daughter's fixation on Rosalind as the cause of her odd behaviour at home. 'Pat's mother thought that

Rosalind led Pat astray,' said Kingsley.[29] Mary Highsmith wrote to her daughter later, 'Stanley and I were with you 100% on everything you wanted. That was our pleasure. Then you met Rosalind – you changed. We were no longer your friends . . . Stanley says now that you wanted to make us out ignorant, crude and unthinking so you could show people how far you had sprung from your poor and slimy background.'[30]

Highsmith thought that her mother was jealous of her new sophisticated friends such as Rosalind, while Mary just could not understand why her daughter behaved so strangely. In an effort to pull her into line, Mary went so far as to threaten to take Pat out of Barnard. Fundamentally, however, Rosalind was not responsible for what Mary and Stanley thought was Pat's increasingly peculiar behaviour. 'Rosalind is supposed to have changed my character,' she wrote to her stepfather.[31] But she didn't meet the older woman until she was twenty and her personality, Highsmith said, was formed much earlier in life. The real source of her problems was her relationship with her mother.

Although Highsmith missed her mother when Mary went back to Fort Worth on the death of her father, Daniel Coates, on 28 December 1941 – she symbolised, Pat said, 'the stability, the femininity, the comfort and warmth of my life'[32] – after her return the two women were at each other's throats again within a matter of days. Pat knew that she had a problem with Mary and that it was a deep-seated one; in her diary she even went so far as to posit the theory that she was in love with her own mother. She still resented Stanley's presence – she told her mother that they would never be content as long as he was around – and she felt at ease only if she, not her stepfather, was in control. 'I'm happy if I can be boss,' she said, 'lighting her cigarettes and dominating as I did yesterday.'[33] Mary thought that her daughter was 'an intellectual snob',[34] while Pat said her mother was boring and obsessed with celebrity tittle-tattle such as Fred Astaire's status as a romantic hero and Carole Lombard's death in a plane crash. 'Mother of course says I'm inhuman, I treat her like a dog, I don't do a thing around the house – every whit of which is a) jealousy b) inferiority c) retribution for her not getting work and consequent worry.'[35]

Highsmith's mother became anxious about what she saw as her daughter's difference from other young women and gave her lectures on how she would never succeed or get a job after graduating from Barnard. A husband and babies were the secret of female happiness, Mary added, a comment which disgusted her daughter. Stanley, too, joined in the character attack, informing Pat that she only liked people who complimented her. Highsmith was desperate to leave home – in 1940 the family had moved to a flat at 48 Grove Street, Greenwich Village, before switching to an apartment at 345 East 57th Street in March 1942 – but she felt powerless and trapped. While Mary relied on Christian Science and Dale Carnegie, one of the world's first self-help gurus with his bestseller, *How to Win Friends and Influence People*, her daughter, aware there was the possibility that there was something not quite right about herself, wanted to explore the possibility of serious psychiatric help. 'I talked of a psychiatrist, & she talked of MB Eddy!' she wrote in her diary.[36]

In June 1942, Mary slapped her daughter across the face after Pat, then aged twenty-one, accused her mother of only being able to have 'trite conversation'.[37] Nine days later Highsmith wrote an outline for a story about a young girl putting her mother to bed. The seemingly dutiful daughter agrees to all the older woman's demands – including her mother's wish never to see the daughter's boyfriend again – and, like the kind soul she appears to be, gets the frail figure ready for the night, pouring out her toilet water and fetching her a nice cup of hot milk. Then the girl takes out a pair of scissors from her pocket and, with a smile, plunges them into her mother's breast, turning and twisting them with all her might. 'What do they know,' she wrote of her mother and Stanley, 'of my fury, impatience, frustration, ambition, energy, desperation, loves & hates, and of my ecstasies!? Nothing! & they never can.'[38]

The substitution of fantasy for reality was the central motif of many of the novels Highsmith would write later in her career, but the appearance of the theme can be traced back to her earliest work. In September 1941, she wrote the short story 'The Heroine', a chilling tale about a governess, Lucille, who deliberately sets fire to her employers' house in order to satisfy her perverse desire to save their children, Nicky and Heloise. The girl dreams about guarding the children from an intruder, rescuing her charges from a flood or saving Nicky and Heloise from an earthquake. In such a scenario, she imagines, she would be able to show her bravery and devotion by dashing back into the wreckage to rescue not only the children but their toys too. As the story progresses, Lucille becomes more and more divorced from reality until she eventually surmises that if she were to start a fire herself, then she would really be able to prove how much she cared. 'She would let the flames leap tall, even to the nursery window, before she rushed in, so that the danger might be at its highest.'[39] Smiling, she takes a tank of petrol from the garage, empties its contents around the house, sets it alight and then stands back to watch the flames. The story ends with the tank exploding, as she walks towards her employers' home to do her duty. Throughout 'The Heroine', Lucille battles with the memory of her late mother's insanity, conscious that she has inherited her madness. As she stands in front of a mirror, her eyes stretching ever wider, she desperately tries to control the mania which is erupting inside her, until it eventually possesses her.

Highsmith sent the story off to a number of magazines, but received nothing but rejections. Even *Barnard Quarterly* turned down the chance of publishing 'The Heroine'; the tale, it seemed, was judged to be too horrific and might even encourage vulnerable young women to copy Lucille's bizarre behaviour. However, she eventually sold it to *Harper's Bazaar*, which published it in its August 1945 issue, and a year later the story was anthologised in the prestigious *O. Henry Memorial Award Prize Stories of 1946*.

Increasingly, Highsmith had become fascinated by what psychiatrists at the time called 'deviancy'. 'Each person carries around in himself a terrible other world of hell and the unknown,' Highsmith wrote in her notebook in 1942. 'It is an enormous pit reaching below the deepest crater of the earth, or it is the thinnest air far beyond the moon. But it is frightening and essentially "unlike" man as he knows himself familiarly, so we spend all our days living at the other antipodes of ourself.'[40] Her own behaviour, she recognised, was far from conventional but her bohemianism was tempered by other, more stabilising qualities such as her strong work ethic and her tendency to suppress her feelings. Her heart she likened to a dammed-up river, which one day would flood its banks, the water washing away all traces of ugliness. She felt compelled to drive herself forward, setting herself new challenges, ones she knew were impossible to meet. At times she felt in need of punishment and these masochistic impulses expressed themselves through tortured poetry; one poem she wrote at this time begins, 'I am too much master of my self.'[41]

Towards the end of 1941, the stark difference between the targets she set for herself and her actual achievements left her feeling on the verge of suicide. Why wasn't she better? More successful and creative? 'Passed my first suicide moment this evening,' she wrote in her notebook. 'It comes when one stands confronted with work, empty sheets of paper all about, and inside one's head, shame and confusion.'[42]

One of the problems, as she saw it, was the fact that creative people like her were born without protective barriers. Depression – or, in her terms, melancholy – was a result of letting oneself be blown about like grass in the wind, sometimes beaten and broken and trampled underfoot and this blackness, this overwhelming sense of despair, was reflected in her work. She would never be able, she said, to write about apple-blossom faces, Valentine cards, roaring kitchen fires and old-fashioned bedsteads, and there was little point creating work which affirmed man's status quo. She was not interested in these well-worn clichés; rather her approach was to dismantle and subvert normality until the comfortable and the conventional took on a more dangerous, sinister edge. After all, there was too much wrong with both the individual and the world.

On 7 December 1941, the Japanese made their surprise attack on Pearl Harbor, precipitating America's entry into the Second World War. Highsmith had often analysed the causes of the war in Europe – in June of that year she had had an argument with her stepfather about its origins, he blaming 'inherent wickedness', she citing the machinations of profiteers. Since the mid-thirties, America had been committed to the principles of isolationism set down in the Neutrality Acts of 1935–1937, but after the Nazi invasion of Czechoslovakia in 1939, Roosevelt attempted and failed to repeal the legislation so the country could offer financial assistance. Although the laws were finally relaxed after the German invasion of Poland, and Congress rubber-stamped FDR's appeal for a $7 billion 'lend-lease' in 1941, the bombing of Pearl Harbor forced America to abandon to its position of neutrality in favour of a full-scale aggression on the enemies of democracy. Historians have singled out the attack – articulated by FDR as 'a date which will live in infamy' – as the moment that America lost its innocence. There is no doubt that the mood of the nation was deeply affected by Pearl Harbor, but the bombing brought about not so much a transition from innocence to experience as a realisation that American arrogance – an unshakeable belief in its own strength and impenetrability – had been well and truly punctured. The age of anxiety – the era of paranoia which could be traced back to the late thirties and Orson Welles' 1938 *The War of the Worlds* radio broadcast – had been crystallised by a defining historical event.

To help the war effort, Barnard arranged courses for students to learn the basics of first aid, map reading and aerial photographic interpretation, while from March 1942, Highsmith regularly joined Kingsley at training sessions where the young women learnt how to identify enemy planes. Dean Gildersleeve was adamant, however, that her students should not be used as mere pen-pushers. 'The brains of its young people are among the most precious assets of our country . . .' she wrote at the time. 'We must not, therefore, waste on the lower, simpler types of work minds which might become chemists, economists, mathematicians, social workers, educated secretaries . . . Many more of them are needed to help win the war.'[43]

However, it is obvious that Highsmith was, at this time, much more interested in affairs of the heart than the implications of international conflict. Her diary tells of a short, but intense relationship with another Barnard student, Helen, who was, by all accounts, heterosexual and engaged to a young man. In fact, the unavailable straight woman was a type which would attract Highsmith throughout her life. In her diary she confessed her desire for Helen, comparing her attraction to how she felt towards 'all the straights I was so violently in love with when I was younger'.[44] On the first day in college after news of the bombing of Pearl Harbor broke, the two women took a walk down to the Hudson River and then, over a glass of beer, the writer confessed her love to Helen. Since the beginning of their relationship in October of 1941, Highsmith had treated her new dalliance badly – flirting with other women in front of Helen and at times regarding her with indifference. Yet, fearing that Helen finally might pledge herself to her sweetheart about to be called up to fight, Highsmith felt unable to keep her feelings to herself any longer. The scene was a poignant one with Highsmith crying and Helen asking, 'What do you want me to do, Pat?' Helen felt that she could not send her boyfriend off to war in such circumstances and she wrote a letter to Pat, telling her that she would have to end their friendship, while relations between the two women deteriorated even further when Helen discovered that Highsmith had been telling fellow students that she would soon make her lover forget 'her little boyfriend'.[45] In her cahier, at this time, Highsmith wrote, 'Love is a monster between us, each of us caught in a fist,'[46] a line she would rework into her 1952 novel, *The Price of Salt*, to describe the souring of the relationship between Therese and Carol. Highsmith obviously had high hopes for her friendship with Helen and although they carried on seeing one another throughout the first half of 1942, the relationship with the woman she once described, in typically romantic language, as 'a slice of heaven walking around on earth',[47] failed to develop.

A true understanding of the problems of the twentieth century, Highsmith believed, could only be achieved by a person who rejected the concept of the normal, someone who was able to approach societal and individualistic complexities from a marginalised position. In order to present the truth of the situation, it was necessary, she said, to strip away the protective patch of normality to reveal the festering wound underneath. Highsmith said that writers interested in representing the truth of the times had a duty to scrape away at the red raw skin and journey down to the rotten core of the problem, and, switching metaphors, she likened the artist who successfully represented this reality to a spider spinning a web from within itself. She decided she would use her sense of strangeness, her own psychological quirks as a basis for her peculiar fictional fantasies. In order to create it was necessary to exploit the self and as such she looked to what she thought was the most important force in her life: sex. 'Yes, maybe sex is my theme in literature – being the most profound influence on me – manifesting itself in repressions and negatives.'[48]

In January 1942, she plotted out a short story about a woman alone in a room who hears scratching in a chest. Terrified of mice, she opens one of the drawers and sees nothing unusual, only the bodice of her wedding dress, but a few days later, when the noise has ceased, she finds a little mouse, dead and stiff, lying on the lace. Two months later, Highsmith had a moment of inspiration when she realised that the time was right 'for a good, classic, beautiful prose thriller like Collins' *Moonstone* . . . which might even contain the metaphysical'.[49] She looked back at the story she wrote as a teenager, 'Crime Begins', and realised that suspense was her forte. 'The morbid, the cruel, the abnormal fascinates me,' she said.[50]

An effective method of writing such a book, Highsmith decided, would be to cloak the fantastical subject matter with a realist style, 'The tone of verisimilitude made by realism'.[51] The archetypal twentieth-century man, its true Everyman, would be the psychopath. 'The abnormal point of view is always the best for depicting twentieth-century life, not only because so many of us are abnormal, realizing it or not, but because twentieth-century life is established and maintained through abnormality. I should love to do a novel with all the literary virtues of *Red Badge of Courage* about one abnormal character seeing present day life, very ordinary life, yet arresting through it, abnormality, until at the end, the reader sees, and with little reluctance, that he is not abnormal at all, and that the main character might well be himself.'[52]

This notebook entry, written six years before *Strangers on a Train* and twelve years before *The Talented Mr Ripley*, is a neat summary of her basic literary method and a clue to why her novels and short stories are so haunting. Highsmith's world is seen through the distorted perspective of an 'abnormal' man, but the style of writing is so transparent and flat that by the end the reader aligns himself with a point of view that is clearly unbalanced and disturbed. In Highsmith's work the tension between the forces of the conscious and unconscious mind is articulated in such a seamless manner that the reader is gradually drawn into empathising with the illogical, the irrational and the chaotic, but this skewed perspective is normalised by virtue of her monotonal style.

Highsmith challenged herself to dream up a plot every night while under the shower, and she already felt drawn to the theme which would distinguish her novels: the ambiguous feelings of attraction and repulsion experienced by two very different men. 'A strong character – appears weak when pulled equally in an opposite direction,' she noted.[53] At this stage she considered the possibility of writing a novel with a lesbian theme, but quickly rejected it and, in a way, there was no need, as, she said, 'it comes out well enough in other themes as well. One can't help it.'[54]

Imagining what she would be like in the future, she realised that, essentially, her character would not change. She could see herself becoming more disciplined, but still only able to create by means of her unconscious. She would have a tendency to be even more addicted to alcohol and cigarettes; would still be shy when it came to expressing her emotions and disturbed when feeling was displayed. And she would be forever prone to falling in love but always happiest when alone.

Like one of Dante's wandering souls she said she would be destined to live neither for God nor the Devil, but for herself. 'Mercy & Justice scorn them both,' she wrote in her notebook, quoting from Canto III of *The Inferno*. 'Without praise or blame, with that ill band of angels mixed, who nor rebellious prov'd, Nor yet were true to God, but for themselves were only.' It would be the motivation for many of the characters she created. And, as the note she added next to the quotation testified, this was a 'terrifying thought'.[55]

7

The dungeon of thy self

1942–1943

Highsmith resisted literary categorisation, but if one was to search for a school which encapsulated her fictional obsessions at this stage in her life one could do no better than to call her a Greenian. Highsmith immersed herself in the work of the American-French writer Julian Green throughout the early 1940s. In September 1941, as she was working on 'The Heroine', she read his 1934 novel, *Le Visionnaire*, translated as *The Dreamer*, while sixteen months later she wrote in her diary of her admiration for his 1941 novel, *Varouna*, describing the book as one that gave her more than any other. In 1944, she wrote about how she turned to Green for 'life, courage, quietness'.[1]

Born in Paris in 1900, Green was Irish-American by heritage and French by education and culture. As a child he felt like an outsider and, like Highsmith, would draw on these feelings of isolation and disloca-tion throughout his life, describing his childhood as 'the subterranean stream that runs obscurely through adult life'.[2] At fourteen, he lost his mother and, at sixteen, he converted from puritanical Protestantism to Catholicism, but also took a keen interest in Buddhism and Eastern philosophies. From an early age he realised that, again like Highsmith, he was attracted to members of his own sex and subsequently acknowl-edged that one of his fictional obsessions was the battle between the aspirations of the spirit and the urges of the body. At twenty-eight, he decided to document the tensions within himself in a personal journal, diaries which were published, first in French and then English, from the late 1930s onwards. 'This diary, which I intend to keep as regularly as I can,' he writes, 'will help me, I think, to see more clearly into myself.'[3]

These confessional documents bear a striking similarity, both in tone and subject matter, to Highsmith's notebooks and help illuminate the myriad connections between the two authors' works. When Highsmith read Green's *Personal Record* in 1943, she wrote in her diary, part of which she kept in French, 'Je sens une amitié rare avec J. Green . . . je reconnais comme mes propres pensées.' ('I feel an exceptional friendship with J. Green . . . I almost recognize my own thoughts.')[4] Like Highsmith, Green felt wretched when he did not work, almost as if he did not exist; he admired the work of Edgar Allan Poe; sourced his creativity in his early formative experiences – 'Everything I write proceeds in a straight line from my childhood'[5] – and believed in the fragmented nature of human identity. 'I think there is in each of us, not only the two men spoken of by St Paul,' he wrote in 1938, 'but a good dozen persons who rarely agree among themselves and are almost always in contradiction . . . one of these persons is a lunatic . . .'[6] Similarly, he regarded reality as simply the projection of an individual's thoughts – a man, he said, could travel between paradise and hell simply by the nature of his consciousness – and, again like Highsmith, was fascinated by the nature of the self. 'Tired of always being my same old self. Has anyone ever said a word about this particular form of sadness?'[7] he wrote in 1940, in what could be interpreted almost as a literary *cri de coeur* from Green to Highsmith. Whether Highsmith read these words is unknown. What we do know is that she was already obsessed with exploring similar ideas in her own work.

Green was convinced that his work stemmed from his life – from his dreams and his repressions – and claimed, rather like Highsmith, that happiness and contentment negated the writing process. 'Writing books comforts the author for everything life has refused him,' he wrote in 1948. 'It might even be that an overgratified, successful life could have produced a sterile one for him. A surfeited man does not write.'[8]

Green's novel, *Si j'étais vous*, or *If I Were You*, bears a remarkable similarity to Highsmith's *The Talented Mr Ripley*. The book, published in 1947 in France and 1949 in America, investigates, according to Green, the sadness expressed by Milton in *Samson Agonistes*: 'Thou art become, (O worst imprisonment!) the Dungeon of thy self.'[9] Like Highsmith's Tom Ripley, a young man with a near-pathological sense of self-hatred, the central character of Green's novel, Fabian Especel, is motivated by a desire to shed his own skin and take on the personality of another. Fabian could not bear the fact that, 'all his days, his soul would inevitably stay firmly encased in the same body'[10] and so, when a stranger offers him the opportunity to change bodies with the person of his choice by the pronouncement of a magic phrase, he readily accepts.

In the foreword to the book, Green addressed the subject that Highsmith would take as her own. 'Which of us, after all, has never said to himself, "If I were he," or "If I were you?"' writes Green. Discontent, he says, 'arises from the perpetual sameness in which were are enveloped',[11] the realisation that each of us is eternally trapped within the barriers of our solipsistic prisons. Quoting Donne, a poet who influenced both Green and Highsmith, the French writer concludes that man was a 'sick god' – 'Nothing could better describe present humanity.'[12]

Writing with 'a simplicity and directness of language, a sparseness that can hardly be called "style" at all'[13] Green's novels and short stories, like Highsmith's, force the reader to suspend their critical faculties. Although it resists interpretation and analysis, his work is distinctive for its curious hybridity, its mix of two very different literary traditions: realism, passed down from Balzac and Flaubert (with whom Highsmith said she felt 'a strong kinship'[14]) and fantasy, as embodied in the work of Hoffman and Poe. Highsmith too could be analysed in this way, a writer of unobtrusive prose who seamlessly combines the surface authenticity of detailed literary mimesis with the subversive under-current of the abnormal and the delusional. This would prove to be an intoxicating mix.

Highsmith graduated from Barnard College with a Bachelor of Arts degree on the 2 June 1942. Her grandmother gave her $20, which, rather than spend on herself (apart from the small sum she set aside for a piece of wood for a sculpture), she decided to use to take her friends and family out for dinner and drinks. Money had always been in short supply, but now, desperate to leave home and find a room of her own, it was a matter of real urgency.

Yet she set herself some standards. 'I wanted to avoid learning anything useful,' she told an interviewer. 'I never learned to type properly because I didn't want to be stuck with a secretarial job.'[15] Working in the world of magazines appealed to her and, encouraged by Rosalind Constable, she applied to *Mademoiselle*, *Good Housekeeping*, *Time*, *Fortune*, and *Vogue*. But the capacity to look as if she had just stepped out of one of the magazines' fashion spreads was, un-fortunately, quite beyond her. In early June she had an interview at *Vogue*, but two weeks later received a telegram to say that she had not been successful. Apparently, she had an image problem. 'They said you looked like you'd just got out of bed,' Rosalind told her.[16] Her jacket was suitable, but the white blouse she had worn to the interview was not clean and they were appalled that she had not even bothered with a hat. She was disappointed, but she reasoned 'there'll come a time when I shall be bigger than *Vogue* and I can thank my stars I escaped their corrupting influences.'[17]

Like many writers, both aspiring and established, Highsmith's dream was to work for *The New Yorker*. On 16 June, she met William Shawn, then the magazine's managing editor, and the next day followed up the visit by sending him four issues of *Barnard Quarterly*. Although later in the year she was asked to write a couple of sample *Talk of the Town* pieces, nothing came of the association and she was forced to settle for a position which she described, in a letter to Shawn, as 'not a job to be excited about'.[18] The job was as editorial assistant to Ben Zion Goldberg, the Russian born, ex-managing editor of the *Jewish Morning Journal*, author of the book *The Sacred Fire*, and a prolific newspaper columnist. She had applied for the position at the publishing house, FFF Publishers, which supplied copy to various Jewish outlets, and in late June, after an interview, Goldberg offered her the job on a salary of $20 a week. 'I didn't haggle,' she said, 'being poor at haggling.'[19]

Her duties involved writing and editing the household section of *The Jewish Family Almanac* and compiling pieces on Jewish art and culture, cooking and interior decorating. This was, perhaps, a surprising choice considering the fact that she had held anti-Semitic prejudices since she was at school. Indeed, when, in 1993, she was asked to describe her first job in a piece for *The Oldie* magazine, she omitted the fact that she had ever worked for the Jewish firm. 'She did not care to acknowledge her association with FFF then or later,' says Kingsley, although Highsmith stayed in touch with Goldberg.[20]

In November, after she had contributed to a book about the Jews' historical and cultural influence on the United States, the publishing house was forced to lay her off because of lack of work. But Highsmith made sure that she put her time with FFF to good use, mining the company for characters which she could then work into fiction. She found one employee, a dumpy, pudgy little man with a limp, so fascinating that she felt inspired to write a tale based on him, 'Mountain Treasure', a story which, after a few drafts and rejections, was published in the August 1943 issue of *Home & Food*, under the title, 'Uncertain Treasure'.

The story centres on two men – Archie, the cripple, and an unnamed bookkeeper – who both spot an unclaimed bag on a station platform. What follows is a bizarre cat and mouse game around the streets of New York as Archie pursues the man for the bag. Eventually, motivated by a mixture of fear and shame, the unnamed man drops the bag. Archie takes it home to his shabby flat, where, with almost unbearable excitement, he unzips it – to find, not money as he thought, but row upon row of sweets and chocolates.

The story is interesting not only for its own merits, but because this is one of Highsmith's first fictional attempts to explore the theme of two men in pursuit of one another, a motif she would later develop further in novels such as *The Two Faces of January* and *Those Who Walk Away*. It is also fascinating to see how the two characters fetishise the objects that surround them, believing that the mere possession of a bag and its contents will make them happy. 'The gold colored zipper sent a chill of pleasure through his fingers,' Highsmith writes. 'Its purr was a song of richness, or mechanical beauty.'[21]

Writing stories was all very well, but she knew that, at this stage in her career, it would not win her financial independence. In order to earn money she typed letters for magazines and, in December 1942, went so far as to take a temporary job which involved standing outside a number of department stores and asking customers a series of questions about deodorants and liver pills. 'It was a long way from Homer's *Iliad*, asking total strangers to concentrate for a moment on the state of their underarms,' she said.[22] But on 23 December she was thrilled to hear that she had been successful in securing another full-time job, salary at least $30 a week, with the producers of comic books, Michel Publishers. 'I walked into a comic book outfit with posters of "Black Terror" on the walls and various characters who could fly in the air and rockets and all that,' she told an interviewer. 'It was like learning a trade . . . Four fellows were sitting there and drawing and three fellows writing the stuff, besides me.'[23]

The job enabled her, in early 1943, to move out of her parents' into an apartment of her own – at 353 East 56th Street at the intersection with First Avenue – which she would rent for thirteen years. Later in life, Highsmith compared her little apartment to the one Carson McCullers described in 'Court in the West Eighties'. 'Mine happened to be in the East Fifties,' she said, 'but the second floor apartment looked onto a small court, and the neighbours' window opposite or at right angles were not so far away – perhaps six metres.'[24] In a letter to her god-daughter, Winifer Skattebol, Highsmith spoke of the place fondly, describing its 'one-room which doubled as living-room and bedroom, with three-quarter bed that served as "couch", plus a real kitchen, plus a bath with tub and shower.'[25]

Wandering around Sutton Place the writer would have been aware of the striking economic differences of the district's residents. Indeed, the area down by the dock of East 53rd Street is said to have inspired Sidney Kingsley's 1935 play *Dead End* about the extreme contrasts between rich and poor. 'Here drying winter flannels are within fishpole reach of a Wall Street tycoon's windows,' reads one entry in the *New York City Guide*, 'and the society woman in her boudoir may be separated only by a wall from the family on relief in a cold-water flat.'[26] If Highsmith walked out of her apartment and down to the East River she would have seen both the splendour of Vincent Astor's yacht *Nourmahal*, which would often drop anchor off the dock at the end of East 52nd Street, and the squalor of the sewage outlets which spilled into the water.

Highsmith's first assignment at Michel was to write, in comic book form, the story of Barney Ross, the boxer and World War Two hero, which she then followed with an account of the life of Edward Rickenbacker, the World War One ace who shot down twenty-six enemy planes. Both men were enormously popular subjects during the current conflict and these stories no doubt helped raise morale. Highsmith's position on the war was an ambiguous one; she no longer subscribed to the simplistic anti-capitalist theories of communism but neither did she feel completely at ease with straightforward patriotism. 'We talked vaguely of the war,' she said of a meeting with Rosalind Constable. 'I am always vague, because I am neither communist nor reactionary.'[27]

Other subjects she worked on for Michel included Einstein, Oliver Cromwell, Sir Isaac Newton, Galileo and Dr David Livingstone. 'My work had nothing to do with literature,' she said later of her time writing comic books, 'but it did stimulate my imagination.'[28]

The writer and critic Susannah Clapp believes that comic books were the perfect medium for the young writer. 'Her language is not self-consciously elegant,' she says. 'The syntax isn't supple. She isn't discursive or elaborate; she worked for a time writing plots for comic strips; and their pungency must have suited her.'[29] The following year, after a few months working for Michel, she switched to another publishers, Fawcett, where she produced scripts with titles such as 'Golden Arrow', 'Spy Smasher', 'Pyroman', 'Black Terror' and 'Captain Midnight'. 'These insane stories had to have a beginning, middle and end,' she said later, 'but otherwise it was a ridiculous formula, like a brush with the enemy on page two . . . It was like grinding out two grade B movies per day. I had to come up with two ideas a day.'[30]

In the evenings and at weekends, however, she wrote stories of a very different kind; ones set in a world bereft of superheroes, often without happy endings. In order to help place her in a more creative state of mind, after working on what she described as 'hack' work during the day, Highsmith would often take a nap at six in the evening, have a bath and change her clothes. 'This gave me an illusion of two days in one and made me as fresh for the evening, under the circumstances, as I could possibly be.'[31]

She had an intuitive insight into the unseemly impulses that lurked behind the sweetest of smiles and an insatiable appetite for the horrific. She sketched out one story about two murderers, each plotting the other's death – father and son both in love with the same woman, one's wife, the other's mother. The father stabs his son in his back as he bends over to kiss his mother goodnight. Another idea was to write about a homosexual man, Jack, who lives with his mother. When his diary goes missing he assumes his mother, who doesn't know about his sexuality, must have read it and, unable to bear the shame, he kills himself. In fact, she has never read the diary and when his mother finds it she decides, out of respect for her dead son, not to open it.

Highsmith also played with the possibility of writing about the frustrations and hatred felt by an ordinary woman, who, as she is cleaning up after her husband, fantasies about killing him by taking hold of a rock and crushing his skull. 'I might see the dark red blood gush out like a great river, watch him bleed and bleed and bleed,'[32] imagines the woman. For many, Highsmith's horrific snapshots of contemporary life were just too sickening to stomach – one reader at *The New Yorker* described one of Highsmith's unsolicited stories, 'These Sad Pillars', about a man and woman who try to make dates by scribbling on the pillars of a subway platform, as 'sordid'[33] – but the young writer was determined not to let rejection get her down. After all, she reminded herself, America's greatest writers, men such as Melville, Poe and Whitman, went unrecognised during their lifetimes. 'They wrote in a vacuum – of themselves,' she said.[34]

In December 1942, she started to experiment with satire, a style she would later use to great effect in collections of short stories such as *Little Tales of Misogyny* and *Tales of Natural and Unnatural Catastrophes*. She dreamt up the plot for a modern-day morality story about a man, Roderick, who is obsessed with saving. He adores and fetishises money to such an extent that he takes to hoarding it in his rafters, but eventually the roof collapses, kills him and his body has to be dug out of half dollar pieces. The moral? 'If you hate money, then stay away from it and if you like it, spend it. And if you save it, at least don't keep it hanging over your head.'[35] This is advice Highsmith herself could have benefited from later in life; friends testify that as she aged, she became increasingly obsessed with not spending money. 'She was pathologically stingy,' says her friend Peter Huber. 'I could go on for hours about how stingy she was.'[36]

Highsmith wasn't interested in writing about healthy, happy, well-balanced people; as she saw it, contentment equalled stupidity. Madness, rather than being seen by psychiatrists as something that should be curbed and normalised, should, she believed, be celebrated. 'I believe people should be allowed to go the whole hog with their perversions, abnormalities, unhappinesses,' she wrote in her journal in 1942. 'Mad people are the only active people, they have built the world.'[37]

The difference between the inner self and the facade which one chose to show to the outside world intrigued her. The people who could successfully paper over the cracks between the two selves were, in her opinion, dishonest, while those who were not even aware of this fundamental philosophical problem were unperceptive. She admired only the men and women who were unable or unwilling to hide these psychological fissures. 'I like people in whom the wrestlings are visible,' she said.[38]

She read William Blake avidly, noting down his words, 'Active evil is better than passive good',[39] and in September 1942 she stated, somewhat chillingly, 'Perversion interests me most and is really my guiding darkness . . . I love to write of cruel deeds. Murder fascinates me . . . Physical cruelty appeals to me mostly. It is visual & dramatic. Mental cruelty is a torture, even for me, to think of. I have known too much of it myself.'[40] Two weeks after recording this in her journal, she acknowledged that her own prose was 'psychopathic'.[41]

It was in this state of mind that she started to plot out the story that would eventually form the basis of her first, albeit unpublished and unfinished, novel, The Click of the Shutting.

She looked back through her old notebooks and diaries for source material, hoping that by reading them she could encourage her unconscious to create a suitable story, 'merely trying to distil the murk of emotions inside me'.[42] She felt her creativity growing and stirring within her: 'My time is coming like a pregnant woman's,' she said.[43] She would look to her own life to provide the emotional core of the book and even, in an early version of the manuscript, went so far as to base the characters on herself and the young women she had loved. Alex would be Judy Tuvim – the schoolfriend at Julia Richman High School who went on to become the actress, Judy Holliday; Christina was modelled on Virginia, and Gregory, a writer and the novel's hero, would be an extension of herself.

Yet she knew the matter of transforming homosexual women into sexually ambiguous men – a technique of transposition of the sexes she had gleaned from Proust – was not as straightforward as simply providing her real life characters with fictional male names. The expression of homosexuality was, of course, a taboo subject and if she stripped her characters of this fundamental quality she would be left with odd, etiolated creatures, personalities robbed of the very quality which defined them – their sexual difference. If she was to write of characters who were 'abnormally inhibited . . . this makes, generally, a sexual weakling, a schizophrenic, an inhibited suppressed person of a vigorous one.'[44]

Whatever decision she made regarding her fictional dilemma over the gender and sexuality of her characters it was clear that, to a certain extent, the central figure, Gregory, whom she would follow from adolescence to maturity, would be based on herself. Gregory 'often amused himself before falling asleep by finding . . . sensations of being another person – someone of course he did not know'.[45] Highsmith was likewise obsessed with 'the insolvable problem of what am I?'[46]; not only did she practise losing herself so she could inhabit the world of her imaginary characters, but, at times, she genuinely felt that her identity was slipping away from her.

Another preliminary sketch for the novel introduces a character called Michael, Gregory's friend and idol; the psychological and sexual tension between them is something she would go on to explore in greater depth in novels such as *Strangers on a Train* and *The Talented Mr Ripley*. In one scene, Gregory, who feels a strange sexual attraction to Michael, mentions to his friend that many of history's greatest men were, in fact, homosexual; a segment which bears strong resemblance to the homo-erotic relationship between Tom Ripley and Dickie Greenleaf in *The Talented Mr Ripley*.

'It is at all times essential to Gregory to have a hero,' Highsmith recorded in her journal. 'He is nothing in himself . . . He knows all about the study of homosexuality and once to Michael when they were walking . . . told to Michael all the list of names, Alexander the Great, Julius Caesar . . . who were homosexual.'

Michael rejects him with the words:

'Crap! . . . How do you know they were homos?'
    (The word sent a thrill of shame down Gregory's spine . . .)[47]

*   *   *

Homosexuality, its theory as well as practice, informed all of High-smith's writing. In each of her cahiers she would introduce her ob-servations on the subject under the heading, N.O.E.P.S. – Notes On Ever Present Subject. When she was nineteen she stated that relations between people of the same sex would always be transitory and never ultimately satisfying because each person always thought they would be happier with another. The problem with homosexuals, she declared a year later, was that they unconsciously associated expressions of emotion with secrecy, thereby censoring in themselves even the most warm and positive feelings. Most gay women disgusted her. Not only were the majority of them, she believed, stupid and dirty but socially they were beneath her. Expanding on the negative aspects of her own sexuality, she went onto say that while homosexual males sought out intellectual equals, lesbians were merely would-be men who never expected to meet their match.

'The Lesbian, the classic Lesbian, never seeks her equal. She is . . . the soi-disant male, who does not expect his match in his mate, who would rather use her as the base-on-the-earth which he can never be.'[48]

Her admiration for gay men was not purely conceptual. In the summer of 1942, she met the German-born photographer Rolf Tiet-gens. They were introduced by a mutual friend – another photographer, Ruth Bernhard – and by August, Rolf, a gay man, and Pat, a gay woman, found themselves strangely attracted to one another. Bernhard – Highsmith always called her by her surname – informed Rolf, with whom she shared a studio in New York, that he did not have a snowflake's chance in hell of sleeping with Pat.

'Pat Highsmith was a very interesting and handsome woman,' remembers Ruth. 'She looked wild, her facial expression was extremely intense and I liked her an awful lot. She was very direct, she said what she believed – she was unforgettable. I took some nude photographs of her – her figure was very slim, boyish. She was reserved, I did not know much about her, but she was a person with whom it was always very interesting to spend time. Our relationship was platonic, but intense. I did not have a romance with her.'[49]

In August the two women, together with Rolf, enjoyed a few days at the house of the artist Jack Augustin, in Valley Stream, Long Island. While out walking in the swampy forest, Pat was bitten on the 'rear end' by a police dog. But the incident seemed to affect Bernhard more than the real victim. 'The funniest thing,' wrote Highsmith, 'is that Bernhard was trembling and crying as soon as it happened, embraced me all the way home & practically had to be treated for shock.'[50]

It seems Bernhard had a crush on Highsmith, but the writer judged her to be 'unfortunately feminine inside'.[51] On their return to the city, Pat felt herself increasingly drawn to Rolf, a man she knew was gay. 'I shall someday marry just such a man as he,' she said.[52] He was tall, dark and good-looking, but primarily Rolf appealed to her intellect; he spoke 'like Christ and John Donne.'[53] She would later dedicate *The Two Faces of January* to him. He was, in a way, 'her alter ego', says Dorothy Edson, who was associate editor of *Harper's Bazaar* and a good friend of both Tietgens and Highsmith. 'I recall Rolf asking Patricia what lesbians did when they made love and she said, "They just lie together and embrace". Rolf said, "How dull." '[54]

Rolf, too, took seductive photographs of Pat, some of them nudes, and felt attracted to her rather gamine figure. Showing her one of his portraits, he said to her, 'I knew you'd like that one. Because you look very boyish. You are a boy, you know.'[55] He liked her, she knew, because of her lean and hard body and because she was not afraid to speak her mind. 'Yes, he fancies me a boy,' she said.[56]

The couple walked down 57th Street to the Hudson River, where they watched the boats and embraced. 'He kissed me a few times – rather a mutual thing for a change,' she said. 'It was quite wonderful and perfect, and for several moments I could see happiness and read it in the sky like a strange new word written . . . He broke off several times to laugh at himself for liking a girl, because the girls have pursued him, and he has dodged . . . So tonight – I am new . . . I should like very much to sleep with him. And I know he wants it.'[57]

Both of them talked openly about their sexuality, but, rather than mark them out as being off-limits to one another, this only increased their mutual attraction. In the middle of September, the couple attempted to sleep together. They took their clothes off, lay down on the bed, but 'neither of us feel any physical excitement and neither want nor cause anything to happen'.[58] She told Rolf about her past, particularly her ongoing emotional attachment to Rosalind Constable and realised that, 'I have a definite psychosis in being with people,' she wrote. 'I cannot bear it very long. Perhaps in all the world there is only Rosalind with whom I can feel calm for hours on end.'[59]

Two days later, however, after an afternoon at a Toulouse-Lautrec exhibition and a chicken dinner with her mother, they tried it again, this time at his apartment. She found herself aroused but Rolf failed to get an erection. Their failure to make love wasn't that bad, she reasoned; after all, she only ever wanted Rosalind anyway. 'I love Rosalind &

want nothing else in the physical sense – really I don't want her, because I love her in such a beautiful way. The fact is, I worship her.'[60]

Pat's almost holy adoration of what she saw as this golden-haired goddess would continue for the next eight years – until their friendship eventually cooled – but throughout her life, Highsmith looked for women whom she could worship. Sex was far from the most important factor in any relationship; rather, it was this near-divine quality for which she yearned.

As 1943 progressed, Highsmith sought out a number of women whom she imagined might be able to share space with Rosalind in her affections. From the beginning of her relationship with the painter Allela Cornell – a short, but intense liaison which lasted from May until September – Highsmith regarded her new lover as a spiritual soulmate. Allela was an odd-looking woman, thin and boyish, with a mop of dark hair and small, round glasses which magnified her eyes. In a sketch Highsmith did of her, in which Allela is reading a book, she drew her eyes as two large spirals made up of a seemingly infinite number of smaller vortexes, giving her the look of a woman who was clearly disturbed.

'Allela was rather unattractive, borderline ugly,' says her friend, the composer David Diamond, who shared a loft-studio with her in Greenwich Village. 'So it surprised me that Pat, who I met through Allela, and she became intimate. Pat was absolutely stunning – she had a wonderful complexion, her skin was peach-like, her face beautiful and I'll always remember her large hands and her terribly expressive fingers. Pat walked with this Garbo-like slouch, dressed in open-necked boy's shirts and well-tailored jackets; she was more silent than talkative and there was something enigmatic and quite mysterious about her. But for all the difference in their physical appearances, Pat and Allela were enormously fond of one another.'[61]

Allela had had some success as a painter – in 1934 she exhibited a picture in the New York Watercolor Club and five years later won a prize at the Golden Gate Exhibition, in San Francisco. Yet commercially she went unrecognised and was forced to do pen and ink portraits on the sidewalks of New York for a dollar a time. Allela and Pat attended art classes together, and Highsmith often sat for her new lover. Allela's large oil portrait of Highsmith, dressed in a red jacket and white blouse, with large, haunted owl-like eyes and a complexion tinged with green, later took pride of place in the writer's various houses around the world. 'Pat loved that portrait,' says Kingsley. 'But I think there's something almost evil in that face, as if it's just come out of the grave'.[62]

Highsmith never found Allela physically attractive – she regarded her not so much as a real woman, but as 'an idea, born by an X-ray'[63] – and the relationship imploded. She proceeded to find another instant replacement in the form of a thirty-year-old married woman and model, Chloe, whom she described as 'slim', 'dark' and 'neurotic'.[64] In the early days of the friendship, Chloe made it known that she only wanted a limited physical relationship: Pat was allowed to share her bed and kiss her, but nothing more. This 'beautiful – terrible'[65] torture appealed to Highsmith's fetishistic nature and she admired Chloe's beauty as if she were an alabaster statue or a mannequin in a shop window. Yet when, in October, the two finally consummated their relationship, Highsmith felt strangely disappointed, confessing to Rosalind, 'there is something perverted within me, that I don't love a girl any more, if she loves me more than I love her.'[66] Rosalind leafed through one of Highsmith's journals, and, after reading a couple of entries about Chloe, asked Pat whether the book was a diary. No, replied the young writer, it was merely a literary notebook, one of her cahiers in which she recorded ideas for novels and short stories. 'Well, then your diary must be a feasting,' she responded.[67]

Bored with her job, which she found increasingly dull, Highsmith dreamed of escaping the frenetic pace of Manhattan for Mexico, where she hoped to write her novel. She was initially thrilled by the news that Chloe agreed to accompany her, but realised that, in fact, her new lover now held little power over her. After negotiating with her employers – who told her that she would be sacked if she left, before finally agreeing that she could send stories into their New York office from Mexico – she started to make preparations for her adventure south of the border. She sublet her East 56th Street apartment for $65 a month, sold her radio and record player to her mother and stepfather for $75, busied herself learning Spanish, ordered her train ticket and endured a painful typhoid vaccination, but was annoyed that Chloe did not seem to share her sense of enthusiasm for the trip. 'Chloe changes [her plans] faster than the Russian front line,' she said.[68]

In December, with the $350 which Highsmith had managed to save, the two women left New York for Mexico.

8

A carefully nurtured bohemianism

1943–1945

'Things were not always logical in Mexico,' wrote Highsmith in her 1958 novel *A Game for the Living*.[1] It was this very quality of irrationality which attracted the writer to the country. She thought she did her best writing at night, when her intellect was at its weakest; dreaming she believed was 'the highest function of the mind'[2] and later she would write to Kingsley of her ambition to write a novel which had more in common with Carroll's *Alice's Adventures in Wonderland* than Dostoevsky's *Crime and Punishment*.[3]

Highsmith was well aware of the allure the country held for writers – D.H. Lawrence, Hart Crane, Aldous Huxley, Katherine Anne Porter, John Dos Passos, Tennessee Williams, Malcolm Lowry and Paul and Jane Bowles had all journeyed south of the border. During the Depression years, post-revolutionary Mexico was seen by writers and artists as a land of promise, a place where one could discover a spirit of primitivism, an invigorating earthiness which was absent from the 'Machine Age' culture of more 'sophisticated' countries. 'Here I feel that life is real, people really live and die here,' Hart Crane told Katherine Anne Porter. 'In Paris . . . they were just cutting paper dollies.'[4] A travel guide, written in 1935 for the American market, enthused about the country, despite its somewhat violent reputation. 'Mexico shows a wealth of contrast: the hot country and the mountains; the quiet noble-looking Indians, and the (sometimes pleasantly, sometimes savagely) drunken ones; the constant sight of machetes, carbines, .45 automatics, and yet very little shooting . . .' wrote its authors. 'All life and death are vividly present: a little closer than we are used to seeing them.'[5]

Paralleling its reputation for vibrancy and emotional rawness, Mexico was also known for its capacity to corrupt the artistic sensibility. 'Mexico . . . is the most Christ-awful place in the world in which to be in any form of distress,' wrote Malcolm Lowry in his novel, *La Mordida*,[6] while Highsmith herself acknowledged 'the subtle and pernicious effects of this Latin atmosphere'.[7]

From New York, Highsmith travelled first to San Antonio, Texas, arriving with Chloe on 14 December, and then on to Mexico City, where she spent Christmas. During that fortnight the relationship between the two women degenerated – Chloe accused the writer of being neurotic and even questioned why she had brought her to Mexico. On Christmas Day, Highsmith walked through the quiet streets of Mexico City up the hill towards Chapultepec Castle, where she stopped to chat to a group of Mexican soldiers. 'Because of my limited Spanish, there was more laughter than conversation,' she wrote. 'I still recall their short figures, their small feet in thick army shoes, their smiles and their friendliness.'[8] Yet the following Christmas Day, she looked back on her time in Mexico City with sadness. 'A year ago I was miserable,' she wrote in her diary.[9]

That Christmas Day night, after a disastrous evening out drinking with Teddy Stauffer, the Swiss-born jazz musician and club owner who went on to marry the actress Hedy Lamarr and who helped establish Acapulco as an international resort, Pat came to the conclusion that Chloe was bad for her. As long as they kept seeing one another, she would not be able to write. It was obvious, Highsmith observed in her diary, that Chloe was still in love with her husband and that she preferred going out drinking with Teddy Stauffer to spending an evening with her. For all Pat's bravado it's obvious from her diary that the collapse of the relationship saddened her. In the first few days of the new year, she wrote in her notebook of a future which, like a powerful geyser, stretched high into the air only for it to disappear back into the earth as it reached its zenith. 'How rich your flesh,' she said of her beloved, 'but how poor your spirit.'[10]

From Mexico City, Highsmith travelled south alone, arriving in Taxco, the charming town spread out 6,000 feet above sea level, along the south-eastern slope of the Atachi hills, on 7 January. She liked Taxco so much – it was, she noted in her diary, one of the few Mexican towns where women could wear trousers – that she made plans to settle there. The origins of the town are not certain. Legend has it that in 1717 a French prospector Joseph de la Borde, later known as Jose de la Borda, was travelling on the way back from an unsuccessful trip to

Acapulco when his burro stumbled upon a rock. On closer inspection the stone appeared to be glistening and snaked through with silver. Subsequently Borda's silver mines netted him a fortune and in 1748, in order to thank God for his good fortune, the entrepreneur financed the building of the cathedral of Santa Prisca. The twin-towered Baroque fantasy still dominates the landscape; Aldous Huxley, after a visit to Taxco, described it as 'one of the most sumptuous and one of the most ugly' cathedrals he had ever seen, calling it 'an inverted work of genius',[11] while Malcolm Lowry referred to it as 'Borda's horrible beautiful cathedral'.[12]

Just as silver boosted Taxco's economy in the eighteenth century, so the precious metal helped rejuvenate the town in the twentieth. In 1931, architect William Spratling – who had bought a house in the town in 1929 and who later became one of Highsmith's acquaintances when she lived in Taxco – turned his hand to silversmithing and opened his shop Las Delicias. Spratling, a friend of William Faulkner and Diego Rivera, acted as something of a cultural beacon, enticing a wide range of artists and writers to Taxco. Hart Crane – who was in Mexico trying to write his epic poem about the Conquest – was a regular visitor and for years after the event residents talked of the time the poet climbed to the turret of Santa Prisca cathedral and rang the bell so loud it could be heard all around the town. This was, as Paul Bowles said, 'something he had no right to do, but for which apparently he was not punished, drunkenness not being considered a serious evil in that tolerant place.'[13]

Bowles, together with his wife, Jane, moved to Taxco in 1940, returning for another summer in 1941, and although she preferred it to Acapulco, he could not bear the town's artistic pretensions and loathed its 'carefully nurtured bohemian atmosphere'.[14] Aldous Huxley, who had visited in the early 1930s, had taken a similar view, noting how it was populated by 'artists and those camp-followers of the arts whose main contribution to the cause of Intellectual Beauty consists in being partially or completely drunk for several hours each day.'[15]

After living in Taxco for some months, Paul wrote to Virgil Thomson of the creative lethargy which hung over the town like a stifling, suffocating pocket of heat. 'The old, accustomed paralysis takes hold of one's consciousness here,' he said. 'The place is nonexistent . . . one is tempted to look down at one's toes and think of life and death.'[16] In fact, Bowles very nearly died there, when in the summer of 1941, he contracted a severe case of jaundice, an illness which forced him and Jane to leave Taxco for good.

When Highsmith arrived in Taxco in early January 1944, she would have been well aware of the town's literary and artistic associations. She may even have read William Spratling's 1932 book, *Little Mexico*, with its foreword by Diego Rivera and illustrations by the author. The slim volume is an evocative, impressionistic sketch of Taxco life in the early 1930s, details which Highsmith herself would have recognised as she strolled around the town just over ten years later. 'Seen from above, the highway through town, the *camino real*, is a twisted vine with tendrils . . .' wrote Spratling. 'Signs of the zodiac, heroic bulls, stars and other favourite insignia are wrought in a mosaic of black basalt in the cobbles of the *camino real*.'[17]

On a typical late afternoon, one could see a line of old women sitting on the cobblestones, baskets in their laps, hawking their tamales or steaming hot tortillas; the daily ritual of parading around the square at six o'clock when mothers would coo over newborn babies; and the menfolk sitting under the majestic trees discussing finance or news from the mines nearby. Above their chatter one could hear the soporific sound of guitar-playing and gentle singing drifting out of the unplastered adobe or palm-thatched 'jacal' houses.

Highsmith's own house, which she rented, was called Los Castillo Casa Chiquita; a sketch she made of it shows her new home to be a single-storey, traditional Mexican structure, with decorative tiles framing the wooden doorway and tall, fleshly cacti growing in her garden. Small lizards scampered in and out of the house and over its pitched roof, while through one of her windows she could hear the noisy slavering of a pig chomping on leftovers. She paid $54 a month for her rent, food and part-time maid and in her diary she said she thought the house was the most beautiful in Taxco. She had space in which to write, enough money (theoretically) for a few months in Mexico and a typewriter which she had brought with her from New York. She wrote letters home to her friends, mother and grandmother describing her life in her new environment, complaining about the trouble she had with her maid and being bitten to death by the dreaded *pulgas* or fleas.

She spent her mornings painting or drawing, her afternoons walking, while in the evenings she would write until late into the night. In her free time she would jot down poems about cats – in April she acquired a kitten, which she named Fragonard after the French rococo painter – read about the history of Mexico and Eastern philosophy, which she described as a 'balm to the soul'.[18] She enjoyed the juicy tomatoes which she compared to the shape of handbags with drawstrings, but after a few weeks she found herself becoming bored by the monotony of Mexican cuisine and the toughness of its meat. Some evenings she would walk down to the Hotel Victoria where she would drink with fellow Americans, noting that in Taxco people did not 'drink to fill social intervals . . . but for total oblivion'.[19] Alcohol, for Highsmith, was another way of accessing her subconscious mind and throughout her notebooks and diaries she repeatedly refers to drink as essential for the true artist, as it 'lets him see the truth, the simplicity, and the primitive emotions once more'.[20] Yet she was also conscious of its potentially destructive effects – especially when combined with the distracting influences of her Taxco acquaintances. She wrote in her diary of her decision to leave Taxco in May and how distancing herself from the town's drinkers and its 'corrupt atmosphere'[21] would enable her to get down to work. For all the village's seemingly idyllic setting, she found life there hard, especially as her money was running out. At times, it was all too much. 'Fleas, ants, cats, dogs, the Mexicans – all prey on me,' she wrote. 'Some want money, some food, some flesh, but all want something, and as this is their country they get it.'[22]

Despite her involvement in Taxco's lively social scene, at times Highsmith felt terribly lonely and often thought about Allela Cornell and Rosalind Constable. In the evenings, she longed for the presence of a 'solid embrace', a desire she had to suppress. 'Sometimes the desire is a ghostly counterpart of me,' she wrote, 'and stands beside me sadly. In the nights I lie and watch the moon . . .'[23]

In March she was visited by Ben Zion Goldberg, her ex-employer, who would often come by late at night to talk through her work. 'He does many things in the same way as I do,' she wrote in her diary, originally in Spanish. 'He's pagan, so he says (and has had success with this philosophy).'[24]

In mid-March, the pair, together with some other Taxco friends, drove south to Acapulco, which Highsmith would describe in her novel, *A Game for the Living*. 'Acapulco presented its brilliant, smiling crescent at mid-morning, a tumbled ring of golden green hills, a fringe of hotels that seemed to sit right in the blue ocean. White flecks of sails looked perfectly still on the surface of the bay.'[25]

While in Acapulco, Highsmith witnessed a sea tempest whip up the ocean like a ferocious monster, a detail she would use in her unfinished, unpublished novel, *The Dove Descending*, written in 1946. The storm left the beach devastated and the water alive with phosphorescence; as she stomped her feet in the wet sand a host of green sparks shimmered on the shore.

Back in Taxco, Highsmith concentrated on her writing. She toyed with the idea of a book of short stories about the American expatriate community in Taxco, in which she would highlight the difficulties they experienced choosing whether to keep their distance or assimilate themselves into the new environment. 'They try to do both, and lose their souls, their mores, their minds . . .' she wrote. 'It is this split personality that makes the American a total failure, and tears him apart.'[26] She never completed the project, but the Jamesian idea of an American at odds with a foreign milieu is one she would go on to explore in many of her novels, particularly *The Talented Mr Ripley*. As she worked, her mood fluctuated between all-consuming joy and utter desperation according to the quantity and quality of her writing. On one particularly depressing day, she wrote in Spanish in her diary, 'I think about my life, of my work, and think I will never accomplish anything.'[27]

During those five months in Mexico, Highsmith worked on her novel *The Click of the Shutting*, which she had started to plan the year before. By now the work had developed into a gothic novel set in contemporary New York featuring two boys, Gregory Bulick – who lives in Greenwich Village with his boorish alcoholic father and whom Highsmith had initially modelled on herself – and George Willson, a privileged youngster whose family enjoys a lavish and opulent lifestyle. 'In these two boys,' Highsmith said, 'I now see the pattern I was later to follow in so many novels, the meeting, the close friendship of two people who are unlike one another.'[28] As she was writing the novel, she mused on the dangers facing the first-time novelist – that 'every character is one's self.'[29]

The manuscript which survives is only 272 typewritten pages Although it remains unfinished, the novel is fascinating as it features what can be seen as quintessential Highsmithian themes – homo-eroticism, the allure of the double and the erasure of identity. The story opens with the sentence, '"I'll pretend that I live there," Gregory whispered as he came into the block,'[30] – a line she wrote while living at Los Castillo Casa Chiquita and one of which she was proud. The first few pages describe how the insecure adolescent follows the rich and glamorous George back to his home, imagining what it would be like to cast off his own identity and cloak himself in another, infinitely more intriguing, self. 'He thought often, and sometimes with an eerie sense of possibility, that he could have been born George Willson instead of himself . . . Was it his body that made him what he was or something inside him?'[31]

Highsmith would explore this concept in her later novels, particularly in *The Talented Mr Ripley*. The character of Gregory also shares with Ripley an indeterminate, ambiguous sexuality. Twenty pages of *The Click of the Shutting* are taken up with a description of a sexually charged dream, in which George visualises his school friends, Charles and Bernard, waking up in a life-saving station by the river. Bernard, whose eyelashes and voice are described as girlish, watches as Charles parades around the room, displaying his body, 'holding his arms a little behind him so Bernard could admire his chest that was grooved down the center and segmented with muscle like a giant insect's thorax or like some kind of armor.'[32]

Another of Gregory's dreams can be seen as a metaphor for Highsmith's thematic obsession with the concept of the double. New York has had to be evacuated, but Gregory misses the last boat and he is the only soul left in the city. Then, as he walks down Fifth Avenue, he sees the shadow of a man in the distance and starts to run in pursuit of it, 'fear and curiosity warring in his spine, and the shadow had ducked in and out of streets trying to avoid him'.[33] The spectre, when he eventually confronts it, transforms itself into another friend and idol, Paul. 'Paul, displeased with him, scowling, displeased at something he had done.'[34]

Eventually Gregory successfully infiltrates the eccentric Willson household – he becomes particularly close to Margaret, the mother – and the book ends with his request to stay with the family in their attic. Highsmith planned to continue the novel and a possible climactic flourish she sketched out included a fight between Gregory and George over Margaret, during which the woman would hit her head and die.

Although Highsmith was often besieged by uncertainties and doubts – she asked herself, how was she going to complete the story, did she even have anything worthwhile to say? – she also realised that the novel was essential to her development. 'It is a heightening and romanticising of my own aspirations, found-delights, and material disillusionments coupled with, I believe sincerely, a spiritual awakening,' she wrote in her diary.[35] After reading through her first chapter, she compared the style to that of Carson McCullers, but friends who read the early draft of the manuscript told her that it lacked a certain intensity.

Highsmith herself was clearly dissatisfied with the material she had composed in Mexico. In a letter to Kingsley, dated 12 May 1944, she considered scrapping everything she had written except for the first six pages. Yet *The Click of the Shutting*, for all its clunky sentences and melodramatic plotting, takes on a fresh, new perspective when compared to the book which so clearly inspired it – André Gide's 1925 novel *The Counterfeiters*. Highsmith first read the novel in 1941 and the following year she noted how, 'Adolescents have enormous possibilities in a novel. Witness what André Gide did with them in *The Counterfeiters*. They are good because they are extremes . . . What keeps returning to me as a fundamental of the novel is the individual out of place in this century.'[36]

Like *The Click of the Shutting*, Gide's novel focuses on the fragmented world of the adolescent; it contains characters called Bernard, George and Margaret (Marguerite in French); explores similar themes such as homo-eroticism and the fabricated personality, while its climax, in which Boris takes a gun into the classroom and kills himself, is similar to the one in Gregory's dream in which Charles and Bernard take a dead dog to school. Like Proust, Gide, via the character of Edouard, a writer whose journal forms a large part of the book, posits the theory that love is essentially illusory. 'Involuntarily – unconsciously – each one of a pair of lovers fashions himself to meet the other's requirements – endeavours by a continual effort to resemble that idol of himself which he beholds in the other's heart . . .' runs a passage from Edouard's journal. 'Whoever really loves abandons all sincerity.'[37]

Highsmith, too, believed that love was based on a fantasy, as is evident from the title of *The Click of the Shutting* which she borrowed from one of Elizabeth Barrett Browning's *Sonnets from the Portuguese*. Sonnet XXIV in the sequence describes a self-enclosed, self-created world which enshrouds and protects the loving couple from outsiders, a solipsistic imaginative space which the poet likens to a warm hand clasping hold of a folding knife. 'After the click of the shutting. Life to life – I lean upon thee, Dear, without alarm.'

For Gide and for Highsmith, feelings, like love, were prone to the fantastical fluctuations. Highsmith's protagonists bore witness to Gide's theory, outlined at the end of *The Counterfeiters*, that emotions taken on as pretence, those which are feigned, can be felt as keenly as so-called 'real' feelings. Just as Gide uses the counterfeited gold coins to symbolise the notion of the fabricated personality, so Highsmith would work out elaborate plots featuring fakes and con-men in order to explore the mercurial fluidity of human identity.

It seems as if Highsmith used Gide's novel as a blueprint for her writing; she reread it in late 1947, together with his journals and *Corydon* and looked to the character of Edouard as a kind of fiction-alised mentor figure. Like Edouard, Highsmith believed that reality did not exist unless she saw it reflected in her journal, while she also subscribed to his theory of depersonalisation, the ability of writers to negate their identities and take on the qualities of others. Such writerly empathy, Edouard states, 'enables me to feel other people's emotions as if they were my own'. Similarly, Highsmith, in her notebooks, often wrote about how her imagination provided her with inner experiences which were more 'real' than the actuality being played out around her. Although she was occasionally attacked for creating characters riddled with inconsistencies and illogicalities, Highsmith articulates the paradox of human nature: the irrationality of the civilised rational man. Gide, in *The Counterfeiters*, expressed another contradiction – the fact that in fiction one is often presented with men and women who behave in a logical fashion, while in real life it is common to meet people who behave irrationally.

'Inconsistency. Characters in a novel or a play who act all the way through exactly as one expects them to . . . This consistency of theirs, which is held up to our admiration, is on the contrary the very thing which makes us recognize that they are artificially composed.'[38]

The point was taken up by Graham Greene in his foreword to Highsmith's book of short stories, *Eleven*. 'Her characters are irrational; and they leap to life in their very lack of reason; suddenly we realize how unbelievably rational most fictional characters are as they lead their lives from A to Z, like commuters always taking the same train.'[39]

Ultimately, although Highsmith was thrilled by the philosophical arguments expounded in Gide's novel, she rejected meta-fictional literary self-consciousness in favour of stylistic simplicity. She admired the work of James M. Cain – author of *The Postman Always Rings Twice*, *Mildred Pierce* and *Double Indemnity* – describing him as 'a kind of genius',[40] and rating his *Serenade* as 'a great book – brilliant'.[41] Although she identified with Kafka, she decided not to try and emulate his style. 'Tales of horror, physical or mental, of bizarre, startling events, physical or mental,' she wrote in her notebook in October 1944, after reading his *Metamorphosis*, 'are more impressive when told in ordinary (but excellent) prose, when they are the more memorable for their uniqueness in the everyday world symbolized by the everyday prose.'[42]

After five months in Mexico, Highsmith ran out of money and at the beginning of May she started to make her way back home. On 8 May she stayed overnight at the Hotel Monte Carlo in Mexico City –

described in *Strangers on a Train* as 'a great shabby building that looked like the former residence of a military general'[43] – where she met with her 'alcoholic beauty',[44] Chloe, who had decided to stay on in the country. Four days later, in Monterrey, she gathered her energies ready for the officials at the border town of Laredo, men she knew would be especially suspicious of the number of books and papers she had in her possession. From Monterrey, she wrote a letter to Kingsley, telling her friend about her progress on her novel – she had written 160 type-written pages of *The Click of the Shutting*, but she described it as 'mediocre stuff'.[45] Of course, it didn't help that she was reading Joyce's *Portrait of the Artist as a Young Man* and she asked herself 'what need of more after this?'[46] She quizzed Kingsley about a handful of Barnard friends and wondered whether any of them were directly involved in helping with the war effort. Approximately six million American women went to work in the war plants, while around 100,000 joined the armed services, but Highsmith, like many educated young women, opted out. If she had wanted to take on one of the war jobs offered to women, she would, she said, rather flee to Russia, where at least they might have let her train as a fighter pilot.

Surely, such a role was better than mucking out kitchens? 'Pat was not one to be lost in a crowd of uniformed servicewomen or to be joining Rosie the Riveter in a gaggle of female factory workers,' says Kingsley, 'but it might have been a different story had there been an opportunity to distinguish herself as an individual. One must also take into account her abhorrence of war no matter who was waging it.'[47]

She arrived back at her grandmother's house in Fort Worth in June, where she spent her days writing, reading and drawing. Her visit, although initially pleasurable, was not particularly creatively stimulating and she found she couldn't bear to engage in typical topics of conversation such as the merits of the local golf courses, the selection of songs on the radio and the state of the weather. Fort Worth, she said, was a 'city of the truly dead',[48] and after one of her cousins refused to sit still long enough for her to paint their portrait, she left the house and, in frustration, walked out to the edge of town. Logically, she knew something so trivial should not, by rights, produce such powerful emotions in her, but nevertheless she felt on the verge of taking her own life. '(At such raging times, "suicide" flashes to my mind, as inevitably as lightning produces thunder.)' she wrote. 'I walked home, feeling such unnameable melancholic emotion I wondered what it was?'[49]

Yet her wicked sense of humour had obviously not deserted her, as is clear from another entry in her notebook about a family pet, a fox terrier called Trixie Queen. 'Should like to see her do her business in her initials – TQ – an exercise for the dog and a novelty for her owners.'[50]

Considering Highsmith's emotional attachment to painting, it's perhaps not surprising that the interrupted sitting should precipitate such an extreme reaction. In her late teenage years and early twenties, Highsmith flirted with the idea of dedicating her life to art, instead of writing. 'I was on the fence 'till I was 23 as to whether I wanted to do drawing or painting or writing,' she said,[51] but for her painting did not provide as much of an intellectual and creative challenge as writing. In 1947, she would come to acknowledge that she had made the right decision to concentrate on fiction. 'Painting could never have been sufficiently complex, sufficiently complicated and explicit to please me,' she said.[52] However, she did acknowledge that the lessons she had learnt from art had influenced her writing. 'Think of each story to be written, as a painted picture,' she noted. 'I think more clearly in a painter's terms. There is a choice of words, as there is a choice between gouache and watercolor.'[53] Even when she had dedicated herself to writing, she continued to paint and sketch; drawing, she said, opened her heart.[54]

The paintings, sketches and drawings gathered together by Diogenes Verlag after her death and published as the 1995 book, *Patricia Highsmith Zeichnungen* represent only a tiny fraction of her artistic output – landscapes; lovers; pets (particularly her cats); the view from her window in New York, New Orleans, Venice, Rome, Florence, Positano and Paris; together with the occasional surreal work such as *Marcel Proust Examining Own Bathwater*, showing the writer, eyes ringed by shadows, holding a test-tube full of water taken from a miniature bath which is sitting before him; and *Departure*, a 1948 piece showing a truncated female form, breasts mutated into square eyes, a navel fashioned into a nose, and a waistline drawn as a smile. 'I thought Pat was extremely gifted as an artist,' says Vivien De Bernardi. 'She had a real talent for drawing, an exceptional line and extraordinary eye. I suspect her talent came largely from the genetic inheritance from her parents – her mother had the same eye for line.'[55] When Janice Robertson, Pat's editor at Heinemann, visited Highsmith at her house in Moncourt in the early seventies, she noticed that some of the floors, 'were painted these jewel-like colours – bright red and brilliant blue – and the effect was almost magical; there was no doubt about it, these were the floors of an artist,' she says.[56]

Drawing gave free rein to Pat's *jeux d'esprit*, says Kingsley. 'Images under her hand breathed a kind of reality that made the ordinary seem better than it was. Atmosphere, intention and nuance, were present in a pen stroke. This is Pat unbound, expressively so artless as to be able to see past the visible shape of things to the "itness" of whatever it was she chose to portray. I do not claim for her art any esoteric singularity, only that it has humor, personality and visual resonance – I'd know that street scene, that bell tower, that person anywhere. It was Degas, I think, who said that art does not render what is visible, it renders visible. That's what I meant by saying that Pat could evoke the "itness" of things.

'We'll never know how much she might have refined and enlarged herself as a visual artist had she chosen to follow that particular calling. For while Pat's life was not without its pleasures, it was art, even more than love, that released her inborn creativity and showered her with torrents of joy. She gravitated to art in all its forms, primarily to drawing, painting, sculpture, all of which and more, including wood-carving and carpentry, she turned her hand to. And quite a remarkable hand it was – noticeably larger in size and stronger than one might consider "normal".'[57]

It is no coincidence that many of Highsmith's characters are artists of one kind or another. Guy in *Strangers on a Train* is an architect with a penchant for sketching the buildings and people of New York; Jack Sutherland in *Found in the Street* is an illustrator and graphic artist; Dickie in *The Talented Mr Ripley* is a painter, as are Theodore in *A Game for the Living*, Ed Coleman in *Those Who Walk Away* and Jensen in *The Tremor of Forgery*, while Therese in *The Price of Salt* is a stage designer. In that novel, Therese compares a square window open to the white sky beyond to a work by Mondrian, in Chicago she likens the 'fuzzy' horizon to a Pissarro painting, and at one point describes the elongated features of one of her friends as being similar to an El Greco. Sitting down and sketching gives Therese, as it gave Highsmith herself, an exhilarating sense of creating something anew. 'A world was born around her,' writes Highsmith of Therese the artist, 'like a bright forest with a million shimmering leaves.'[58]

Tom Ripley in the later Ripley novels is a keen amateur painter and art collector (he possesses a number of Van Gogh, Magritte, Picasso and Cocteau drawings), while the whole plot of *Ripley Under Ground* centres around the questionable authenticity of a group of paintings by an artist who we know to be dead. 'If one painted more forgeries than one's own paintings,' Highsmith asks at one point in the novel, 'wouldn't the forgeries become more natural, more real, more genuine to oneself, than one's own painting?'[59]

Highsmith saw the world with an artist's eye. Not only does she meticulously describe the objects which surround her characters with a poetic claustrophobia, but her language also teems with metaphors which are almost painterly in their visual flair. A dish of tinned peaches swim around a bowl 'like little orange fishes'[60] (*The Price of Salt*) and in the same novel a mountain range is described as looking 'like majestic red lions, staring down their noses'.[61] In *The Blunderer*, Kimmel's fat lips, are said to look like 'an obese, horizontally divided heart',[62] a vase full of philodendrons is compared to an abstract painting and a group of willow trees reminds one character of the spectral winged figures hovering over the tombstones of the dead in Blake engravings.

Although her strong visual imagination made it easy for her to plot out comic book storylines, when Highsmith returned to New York in July to resume her strip-writing, she felt like a failure. She had no money and had produced a novel she knew was unpublishable. Her only option, she felt, was to return to the kind of work she had first embarked upon after graduation, but this time on a freelance basis, which earned her about three times more than an equivalent full-time position. Writing for a pulp market worried her; she was anxious not to imitate the genre's lazy plotting and stereotypical characterisation and she questioned whether churning out comic strips might somehow corrupt her own work, comparing her talent to a building that was gradually being undermined by termites.

She would carry on writing comic strips for the next six years, but she soon got bored of thinking up new ideas and eventually regarded them as nothing more than an easy way of making money, cynically viewing each page as a visual representation of between four and seven dollars. The comic stories were written to a strict formula, one which required the minimal investment of inspiration, but at least the hack-work enabled her to set aside enough time in which she could write fiction.

As the summer of 1944 ebbed away, Highsmith's love life was as topsy-turvy as ever. In her diary she confessed to overlapping several love affairs, including one with twenty-three-year-old Natica Waterbury, a glamorous, New York-born blonde who went on to become a photographer, pilot, patron of abstract art and sculpture, and an editorial aide of Sylvia Beach at the bookstore and publishing firm Shakespeare and Company in Paris. Highsmith realised that her emotional well-being was in a precarious position, and even when she was momentarily happy, she never expected the bliss to last, continually waiting for the end of the affair. Cumulatively Pat's affairs had an anaesthetising effect on her emotions, 'until where one's heart is, is so thickly padded, nothing can any longer be felt'.[63] Yet, in contrast to most homosexuals, Highsmith said, her nature was fundamentally a romantic one. Seemingly insignificant gestures and tokens thrilled her, such as the strand of her lover's hair, a desperately longed-for letter, the scuff on her shoes she could not bear to clean off, and the telephone call that had the potential to transport her to heaven or to hell. 'Shadowed people are we,' she said, referring to her relationship with Natica, 'a melancholy soul have I, for this unknown parting hangs over me even when I am with you.'[64]

After the collapse of each of her brief, but intense, relationships, she felt so depressed that she sometimes felt incapable of writing. Her melancholy was so deep, her spirit so paralysed, she felt she could not even summon up enough energy to commit suicide. Ultimately, she was left wondering whether any kind of emotional attachment was worth the pain. 'Love should be reduced,' she said, 'to a simple, unbalanced equation: put the days of exquisite happiness in the beginning of love against the inevitable hell at the end.'[65]

9

The strange, subtle
pluckings of terror

1945–1948

New York immediately after the war found itself at the centre of a creative explosion precipitated by the intellectual dynamism of European émigrés who had fled Hitler to settle in America – a diverse group including Mann, Nabokov, Marcuse, Brecht, Stravinsky, and Mies van der Rohe. Some historians have gone so far as to categorise this westward move as the most important cultural event of the second quarter of the twentieth century, signalling as it did a major shift in the centre of intellectual power. America was exposed to many of the ideas that had disturbed European modern consciousness in the years between the wars, themes which were articulated by W.H. Auden's 1947 poem, 'The Age of Anxiety'. 'It seems to me now that Americans were confronting their loneliness for the first time,' wrote Anatole Broyard about the post-war years. 'Loneliness was like the morning after the war, like a great hangover. The war had broken the rhythm of American life, and when we tried to pick it up again, we couldn't find it – it wasn't there. It was as if a great bomb, an explosion of consciousness, had gone off in American life, shattering everything.'[1]

Much of the creative energy centred on the activities of the writers and artists who lived in Greenwich Village. It was, said Broyard, who then ran a bookshop on Cornelia Street, as if the writers and artists who lived and congregated around the Village were forging an identity for themselves which was unmistakably new, one dislocated from the comfortable platitudes of the American tradition. Broyard and his contemporaries, like Highsmith, 'didn't know where we ended and books began . . . We didn't simply read books; we became them . . . Books were to us what drugs were to young men in the sixties.'[2] The bleak, existential modern nightmare envisioned by Kafka particularly resonated; indeed during the post-war years, 'Kafka was the rage',[3] 'as popular in the Village at that time as Dickens had been in Victorian London.'[4]

Highsmith first read Kafka in late 1942 and early 1943. She worked her way through *The Castle*, published in America in 1930, but felt that she had failed to understand the complex novel. However, by August 1945, it was obvious she had grown more confident in her interpretative approach to the Czech-born author, and had developed a kind of empathy with him. In her notebook, she observed how an analysis of Kafka's work in the *New York Times* by Charles Neider isolated concerns that echoed her own: how the compromise between idealism and realism resulted in guilt, how the modern world was bereft of moral certainties and how 'everything is fluid and ambivalent, the "right" way far from certain.'[5] Neider went on to write: 'Greater knowledge, by its expansion of the conscience, involves the possibility of greater sin. Therefore a sense of sin and ambivalence is characteristic of our time. And Franz Kafka is unique because he perceived these facts so completely on the imaginative, emotional, poetic planes, giving us, through his conscious dreams, a more intense and complete and, above all, experiential awareness of these factors in ourselves.'[6]

In February 1948, she read Edwin Berry Burgum's *The Novel and the World's Dilemma*, an analysis of modern prose fiction, which included essays on Proust, Mann, Joyce, Woolf, Huxley, Wolfe, Faulkner and Kafka. In the book, she read how Kafka was a 'diseased personality', someone who 'verged on the psychopathic', a novelist who wrote about the bankruptcy of faith and the breakdown of mysticism. 'Fantasy and hallucination,' wrote Burgum, 'now are the last resort of a man who never had faith in humanity and could never secure a faith in God.'[7] After reading Burgum, she wrote in her cahier that, like Kafka, she felt she was a pessimist, unable to formulate a system in which an individual could believe in God, government or self. Again like Kafka, she looked into the great abyss which separated the spiritual and the material and saw the terrifying emptiness, the hollowness, at the heart of every man, a sense of alienation she felt compelled to explore in her fiction. As her next hero, she would take an architect, 'a young man whose authority is art and therefore himself,' who when he murders, 'feels no guilt or even fear when he thinks of legal retribution'.[8] The more she read of Kafka the more she felt afraid as she came to realise, 'I am so similar to him.'[9]

Like Lucille, the disturbed heroine of 'The Heroine', Highsmith acknowledged that she saw life through what she called 'a distorted lens'.[10] Instead of taking events and experiences at face value, she had a tendency to exaggerate their importance and feel their impact – whether it be joy or misery – too acutely. In her notebooks, she set down her thoughts on the subject, concluding that she would not try to refocus her skewed psychological vision, but would merely make a series of minor adjustments. At times, however, her mental instability frightened her. Often she would feel gripped by 'the strange, subtle pluckings of terror'[11] which overshadowed her, an anxiety which she felt unable to explain. She worried about her hormonal problems – months could go by between her periods – and even visited a doctor, who prescribed ergot to help regulate her menstrual cycle.

If she saw an acquaintance walking down the sidewalk she would deliberately cross over so as to avoid them. When she came in contact with people, she realised she split herself into many different, false, identities, but, because she loathed lying and deceit, she chose to absent herself completely rather than go through such a charade. Highsmith interpreted this characteristic as an example of 'the eternal hypocrisy in me'[12], rather her mental shape-shifting had its source in her quite extraordinary ability to empathise. Her imaginative capacity to subsume her own identity, while taking on the qualities of those around her – her negative capability, if you like – was so powerful that she said she often felt like her inner visions were far more real than the outside world. She aligned herself with the mad and the miserable, 'the insane man who feels himself one with all mankind, all life, because in losing his mind, he has lost his ego, his self-ness',[13] yet realised that such a state inspired her fiction. Her ambition, she said, was to write about the underlying sickness of this 'daedal planet'[14] and capture the essence of the human condition: eternal disappointment. Plotting, she said at this time, was not so important to her; she was much more interested in the exploration of consciousness, inhabiting the mind of her characters and representing this on the printed page.

When 'The Heroine' appeared in the August 1945 issue of *Harper's Bazaar* it attracted the attention of one of the editors at the publishing house, Knopf. 'Your characterization of Lucille is extraordinarily real and poignant,' wrote Emily Morison. She praised Highsmith for her skilful handling of the tragic ending and her clear, direct style. 'I am so impressed by this story, in fact,' she added, 'that I would like very much to see a book of yours, with of course a view to publication.'[15] After a meeting with the young writer, Morison wrote an internal memo, recording the fact that Highsmith was working on a forty page story, which she promised to show the editor when it was complete. Pat also told the publisher that she planned to start another novel that winter, and once she had written sample chapters and an outline these too would be sent to Knopf. However, after repeated requests for material – Morison wrote to Highsmith in 1946 and 1948 – the publisher failed to secure the author.

Despite Knopf's keen interest, during the late summer and autumn of 1945, it still seemed impossible that she would ever publish a novel. Her New York agents told her frankly that if she did not make the endings of her short stories more upbeat, they would remain, for the most part, unsaleable. 'Too bad you had to write like that,' they said. 'It's sad to write and not be published.' Such a prospect, however, did not seem to bother her. As she walked out of their office into the blinding August sunlight, she concluded that her way of perceiving the world was vastly different from the rather business-minded approach of the agent. 'We do not speak the same language,' she said.[16]

In October 1945, Jean-Paul Sartre delivered an influential lecture, 'L'Existentialisme est un humanisme', translated into English and published in America in 1947 as *Existentialism*, in which he said that for human beings 'existence precedes essence'. There was no such thing, he believed, as preordained human nature; rather individuals are free to make certain choices, with each one of us responsible for determining one's being, a concept articulated in Sartre's play *Huis Clos* – 'You *are* your life and nothing else.' In his 700-page epic, *L'Etre et le néant*, *Being and Nothingness*, published in 1943, Sartre stated, in a teasingly enigmatic line, that 'the nature of consciousness simultaneously is to be what it is not and not to be what it is'.

His ideas instantly appealed to Parisian intellectuals, encapsulating as they did the aspirations and anxieties of post-liberation France. 'Sartre is automatically fashionable now among those who once found surrealism automatically fashionable,' wrote Janet Flanner, later a friend of Highsmith's, in her *New Yorker* column in December 1945.[17] The philosophical revolution centring around individual freedom also set New York buzzing and thousands of column inches were devoted to trying to untangle Sartre's complex ideas. 'There is much talk in Paris, in Greenwich Village, even in the center of Manhattan,' wrote Jean

Wahl, in the October issue of the *New Republic*, 'about existence and existentialism',[18] while the mass market *Time* magazine, in January 1946, proclaimed that existentialism 'had called forth more words and more ink than any intellectual movement since Dadaism ushered in Europe's "lost generation" after World War I. Existentialism has its long-haired snobbish fringe . . . But the word has filtered down to everyman's and everywoman's level.'[19] The philosophy also appealed to the post-war sensibility of pessimism. After Hiroshima in August 1945, America woke up to the fact that, as one historian put it, 'the bomb became the possible instrument of universal extinction and Americans wondered how they would live with it, as though civilization had inherited an incurable disease.'[20]

The philosophical issues surrounding being and nothingness had always intrigued Highsmith and after reading his work, she felt stimulated by Sartre's audacious attack on conventional thinking. 'The riddle of the universe,' she wrote in her notebook, 'the relation of the individual to one other person, to the rest of humanity.'[21] What particularly intrigued her was Sartre's analysis of subject-object relations – the impact of other people on the nature of our consciousness – which he illustrated by the use of an anecdotal example. In *Being and Nothingness*, Sartre imagines being possessed by jealously and peering through a keyhole to find out what is happening on the other side of the door. At first he is completely immersed in the scene in front of him and in this state – the non-thetic or pre-reflective mode of consciousness – he is unaware of himself as a self, only of the images before his eyes. But then he hears footsteps behind him and realises, shamefully, that someone is looking at him. He is shocked into acknowledging that he himself is an object, something viewed by another consciousness. One's self is not, after all, an extension of the world but merely, and quite inevitably, another object contained within it. This stinging realisation is one Highsmith would explore throughout her fiction. Indeed, Ripley in *The Talented Mr Ripley*, murders Dickie partly because of the shock of discovering that he could not be one with him or anybody else.

The sense of strangeness – of alienation, separateness and despair – felt by Ripley articulates the existential nausea expressed by Sartre. One of the ways man could free himself was by writing and reading, as Sartre explained in his seminal book, *What Is Literature?*, which Highsmith read in January 1948. Literature, instead of serving as a mere exercise in escapism, could act as an agent of liberation, a catalyst of real change enabling man to move towards personal freedom. Such a book was Albert Camus' *L'Étranger*, first published in French in 1942 and read by Highsmith in the spring of 1946. 'People told each other that it was "the best book since the end of the war",' wrote Jean-Paul Sartre in February 1943. 'Amidst the literary productions of its time this novel was, itself, an outsider.'[22]

The book, narrated by Meursault, opens with, 'Mother died today. Or maybe yesterday. I can't be sure.'[23] Meursault, like one of Highsmith's heroes, is a man dislocated from reality. He kills an Arab in self-defence, but at his trial he is so indifferent to his fate that he refuses to play by society's unspoken rules and, as a result, is condemned to die for it. 'Gentleman of the jury,' the prosecutor says in his summing up of the case, 'I would have you note that, on the day after his mother's funeral, that man was visiting a swimming pool, starting a liaison with a girl and going to see a comic film. That is all I wish to say.'[24]

His greatest virtue – his honesty, his refusal to say what is expected of him – is also his downfall and as he waits in his prison cell he realises that life is unreal; only now, faced with death, can he contemplate freedom. Albert Camus, in a preface to an edition of the book published in 1955, describes Meursault, as a man driven by the passion for truth. 'He says what he is, he refuses to hide his feelings and society immediately threatens. For example, he is asked to say that he regrets his crime, in time-honoured fashion. He replies that he feels more annoyance about it than true regret. And it is this nuance that condemns him.'[25]

When Highsmith read the book she described it as an example of the 'twentieth century's annihilation of the individual . . . It is a tour de force. It is a piece of brilliant impressionism.'[26] Like Camus, she was interested in exploring what she thought was the saddest aspect of her generation, 'the absence of personality'.[27] Just as the French novelist's anti-hero meandered through the novel in an emotionally anaemic daze so Highsmith started to think about writing about 'a man to whom events become progressively less real'.[28]

One day, late in 1945, Highsmith was walking by the Hudson river with her mother and stepfather when she had the idea of writing a novel about two men who exchange murders. On 16 December, she opened her notebook, and wrote the outline of a plot which would eventually form itself into her first published novel, *Strangers on a Train*. The original plot centred around, two men, Alfred and Laurence, both of whom wanted to kill women they no longer loved.

'An exchange of victims would clear us both by eliminating all possible motivation,' thinks Alfred, whose name Highsmith later changed to Bruno. 'Yes, we shall each let ourselves be caught for the crime, but the police will find no motivation. We shall go free!'[29]

Alfred goes through with the murder, but initially Lawrence cannot reciprocate and begins to hate his doppelgänger. Finally, however, he kills Alfred's wife and is arrested. It is guilt that has destroyed him. The characters and their motivation would change many times over the next four years, but the central theme of the double murder would remain the same. Highsmith put the idea on hold until the spring of 1947 when the plot fired her imagination once again.

Her favourite technique to ease herself into the right frame of mind for work was to sit on her bed surrounded by cigarettes, ashtray, matches, a mug of coffee, a doughnut and an accompanying saucer of sugar. She had to avoid any sense of discipline and make the act of writing as pleasurable as possible. Her position, she noted, would be almost foetal and, indeed, her intention was to create, she said, 'a womb of her own'.[30] Later, in *Plotting and Writing Suspense Fiction*, Highsmith revealed that in order to write she often deliberately thought herself into a different frame of mind, by pretending she was not herself, moving herself 'into a state of innocence', free of the day-to-day worries and anxieties of life. 'I suppose it's a measure of how professional one is, how quickly one can do this,' she said. 'The ability does improve with practice.'[31]

She started writing *Strangers on a Train* on 23 June 1947 and in her diary outlined her vision for its beginning. 'I want a brief first part, in which the two young men and the possibility of the murders are presented,' she wrote.[32] She worked intensely and, less than a month later, she had produced eighty pages. Ben Zion Goldberg, her one-time boss, admired the first chapter, judging it to be an 'excellent story', while the black poet and writer Owen Dodson, whom she met in August, praised her for her economy of style. She found the experience of writing therapeutic and described the book as 'a too open description of my feelings, of the mystery of my self'.[33] Goldberg also pointed out to her that the theme of novel, 'the relationship between two men, usually quite different in make-up, sometimes an obvious contrast in good and evil, sometimes merely ill-matched friends'[34] was one she had also used as a basis for *The Click of the Shutting*. As she explored the relationship between the two male characters – psychopath Bruno and the target of his corruption, who at this point she called Tucker, later to be called Guy – she realised she was falling in love with the amoral killer. 'I am so happy when Bruno reappears in the novel,' she said. 'I love him!'[35]

She regarded the novel as a nine-month-old foetus in a womb of literary creation and, as she worked, she read 'cheap' or pulp novels, analysing their fictional techniques. She admired them for their clear-cut narratives and simple style, but at the same time she also revelled in a sense of superiority, a knowledge that she, in fact, could do better. At the end of November, she wrote herself a list of stylistic pointers. When working she should remember to set the scene quickly and get straight to the point; she should write quickly and with ease, as too much effort would result in a tired style; describe only the feelings and viewpoint of the main characters; make sure the end result was entertaining, as this was the prime reason people picked up a novel; and always try to leave the reader begging for more.[36]

In an old journal, which she later used as a scrapbook for recipes, she sketched out an experimental fragment of the book. Tucker, like Guy in the final version, is an architect, who has a loathing for his wife, Miriam, and a desire to marry his new girlfriend, while Bruno cannot bear his rich father. Although the basic premise is, roughly, the same as the published version, Highsmith's writing is not nearly so accomplished. In this scene, Tucker recalls the previous night on the train when he had met Bruno, whose idea it was plot kill Miriam.

'He saw her now, because of the talk last night with the fellow on the train. To murder her? . . . He saw Bruno's gleeful face. "If I killed your wife, say –" A person like Bruno would do it. How simple everything would be if Miriam were dead!'[37]

It is Tucker's ambition to build a spectacular city of glass – he admires the work of Mies van der Rohe and Frank Lloyd Wright – but his vision is clouded by a 'shadow': Bruno, who haunts his every moment. This fascination with duality expressed itself in early titles such as 'The Other Side of the Mirror', 'Back of the Mirror', and 'The Other', and an empathy with Dostoevsky's novels.

Highsmith's splintered point of view confused publishers, however. Her new agent, Margot Johnson of A & S Lyons, sent off Highsmith's incomplete manuscript to Marion Chamberlain at Dodd, Mead & Company for an early assessment, but while she obviously had great enthusiasm for the book, the editor felt it still needed a great deal of work.

'I think she has to make a choice and unless she does there will be a fatal flaw in the book,' she wrote in a letter to Johnson in January 1948. 'I think it either has to be Bruno's story, clearcut and undeviating, or it has to be an "entertainment" of the [Graham] Greene school where the two young men are actors but the real meaning of the story lies in the spectator sport – a character who is involved by them but who is in the end free of them both.'[38]

Marion Chamberlain advised her to 'heighten' Bruno and 'shade down' Tucker; if Highsmith did this the result would be a tragic novel, one which was 'grim but moving'. The young writer, she concluded, was not, however, ready for a contract; what was more important was the reshaping and rethinking of the novel. Highsmith was disappointed, but not destroyed, by the rejection and she discussed her characters with her new friend, Lil Picard, who told her that Tucker was a somewhat insubstantial character compared to Bruno. 'I think and think – of my uncle Herman, and also of Rolf,' she wrote in her diary, trying to visualise Tucker's appearance. 'Yes, he becomes a darker shorter version of Rolf T[ietgens].'[39] Highsmith started to rework the novel, but she realised the truth of the Dodd, Mead editor's observation, 'She has a bigger book on her hands than perhaps she conceived and it will take all she's got.'[40]

10

How I adore my Virginias

1945–1948

Highsmith's long intellectual love affair with Dostoevsky began at the age of thirteen. 'I was very impressed in my adolescence by *Crime and Punishment*,' she said, 'its theme, the justification that Raskolnikov tried to convince himself of, and his failure in this. I know morally this had a great effect on me.'[1] In the summer of 1945, she scribbled a quote from Dostoevsky on the inside cover of her thirteenth cahier, 'Oh, do not believe in the unity of men!'[2] She admired him for his rejection of conventional naturalism in favour of a more shocking psychological realism and there is no doubt that the nineteenth-century Russian author, particularly his novel *Crime and Punishment*, which she read once again in May 1947, had an enormous impact on her work. Indeed, after reading the novel, Highsmith wrote in her diary that Dostoevsky was her 'master'. She later said that *Crime and Punishment* could be read as a story of suspense, an opinion shared by Thomas Mann, who wrote in his introduction to the short novels of Dostoevsky, published in America at the beginning of 1946, that the book was 'the greatest detective novel of all time'.[3]

The parallels between *Crime and Punishment* – the story of how an impoverished student Raskolnikov comes to murder an old pawn-broker and her sister – and Highsmith's first published novel, *Strangers on a Train*, are striking. Like Dostoevsky's anti-hero, the two strangers on a train, Bruno and Guy, fantasise about the murders in their minds before carrying out the acts. Indeed, the psychological rehearsals for the killings are so fully imagined that they almost serve as substitutes for the actual murders. As Raskolnikov thinks himself into a state of near hysteria he asks himself, 'If I feel so timid now, what will it be when I come to put my plan into execution?'[4] Similarly Bruno, while shadow-ing Guy's wife, Miriam, through the surreally carnivalesque amusement park in Texas, runs through all the different ways he could kill her – taking hold of her head and pushing her under the water; stabbing her to death with his knife, his beloved 'clean instrument'; clapping his hands over her mouth and snuffing out her life – before eventually deciding to strangle her. Guy, unable to sleep and eaten away by guilt, visualises how he would murder Bruno's father, leaving a clue so as to incriminate his son: 'he enacted the murder, and it soothed him like a drug'.[5] Of course, in typically Highsmithian fashion, the fantasy mutates into reality and the world of reason is tipped on its side.

Whether conscious or not, Highsmith's description of Bruno echoes Dostoevsky's of Svidrigailov, the rich Russian degenerate. The wealthy psychopath from Long Island is a 'tall blond young man', with a 'pallid, undersized face', and skin as 'smooth as a girl's, even waxenly clear',[6] while Svidrigailov is described as having blond hair, a face which 'might almost have been taken for a mask; the complexion was too bright, the lips too ruddy, the beard too fair, the hair too thick, the eyes too blue, the gaze too rigid'.[7] Although Raskolnikov is disgusted by Svidrigailov, he is drawn towards him by a strange combination of love and hate. Hurrying to meet his alter-ego, Raskolnikov remarks that the figure concealed some hidden power that held sway over him, a feeling shared by Guy for Bruno, a symbol of his unconscious desires. 'Hadn't he known Bruno was like himself? Or why had he liked Bruno? He loved Bruno.'[8]

Like Raskolnikov, a law student, Guy, an architect, is a man representative of order, while Svidrigailov serves as an embodiment of disorder, as does Bruno. In fact, both novels can be read as fictionalised arguments which explore the battle between the conscious and the unconscious minds, the eternal conflict between Apollo and Dionysus.

'I have my own idea of art, and it is this: what most people regard as fantastic and lacking in universality, I hold to be the utmost essence of truth,' Highsmith wrote in her notebook, transcribing a passage from one of Dostoevsky's letters.[9] Rather than serving as a caricature or stereotype, a flat signal for one aspect of human behaviour, Raskolni-kov is an example of the contradictions in everyman – 'One might almost say that there exist in him two natures, which alternately get the upper hand.'[10] Highsmith, who was equally as fascinated by dualism, explores the issue further in *Strangers on a Train*. Guy, archetype of reason and order and a reader of Plato and Sir Thomas Browne's

Religio Medici, initially views evil as an external force, something distinctly apart and outside of him. He rejects Bruno's belief in the universality of criminal desires – that each of us harbours a potential murderer – but after killing Bruno's father he realises the truth, that 'love and hate . . . good and evil, lived side by side in the human heart'.[11] Just as Svidrigailov exists in relation to Raskolnikov, so Bruno serves as Guy's 'cast-off self, what he thought he hated but perhaps in reality he loved'.[12]

In *Crime and Punishment*, Dostoevsky's anti-rationalism is articulated by Razumikhin, who, while discussing his friend Raskolnikov's article about the relationship between criminals and society, concludes that the living soul does not obey the laws of logic. Motivation is far from transparent; actions are often precipitated by a number of conflicting impulses. Both writers, instead of presenting the reader with a clear-cut, fully defined portrait of a particular character, suggest that while consciousness can be glimpsed through fiction, it cannot be explained. In one of her notebooks, Highsmith transcribed an insightful quote from Dostoevsky's novel *The Idiot* on this very subject. 'Don't let us forget that the motives of human actions are usually infinitely more complex and varied than we are apt to explain them afterwards, and can rarely be defined with certainty. It is sometimes much better for a writer to content himself with a simple narrative of events.'[13] It is a neat summary of Highsmith's literary method and, in addition, a wise piece of advice for any biographer.

Taking her lead from the Russian novelist, Highsmith explored these ambiguities and contradictions, these paradoxes of human consciousness with skill and subtlety. For instance, in *Strangers on a Train*, when Bruno breaks into an apartment house in Astoria – just for the thrill of it – he takes a table model, a piece of coloured glass, a cigarette lighter. 'I especially took what I didn't want,' he says.[14] At the end of the novel, Guy, after his confession to Owen, turns to Gerard, the detective who has heard his every word, and starts to speak, 'saying something entirely different from what he had intended'.[15] The scene alludes to one in *Crime and Punishment* when Raskolnikov feels he has to unburden himself to Sonya. Like Guy, after his outburst, he realises 'the event upset all his calculations, for it certainly was not *thus* that he had intended to confess his crime.'[16]

Although Highsmith's fiction almost bristles at any attempt to slot it into a given category, if one was forced to impose an interpretative model on her work one could say that, like Dostoevsky, she was working within the tradition of fantastic realism. Many of Dostoevsky's writings on the subject echo Highsmith's own; indeed both writers were heavily influenced by the work of Edgar Allan Poe. In an essay Dostoevsky wrote in 1861, he sets out the relationship between fantasy and realism in Poe's fiction. 'But in the tales of Poe you see all the details of the image or event presented to you with such great plasticity that in the end you are convinced of its possibility, or its reality although the event in question is either almost entirely impossible or has never yet occurred in this world.'[17] He analysed this further in a letter he sent to an aspiring writer in June of 1880. 'The fantastic must be so close to the real that you *almost* have to believe in it . . . '[18] Highsmith anchors her novels and stories in reality by listing a cloying number of details – clothes, physical appearance, food and wine, description of houses – the minutiae of life which carries the reader seamlessly over into the world of the uncanny. Jean-Paul Sartre, in his essay on the fantastic, describes such a technique as one of semiotic excess – 'the innumerable signs that line the roads and that mean nothing'[19] – a method particularly suitable for describing, and critiquing, the modern world.

Tzvetan Todorov, in his influential book on the fantastic in literature, shows how modern detective stories have replaced the ghostly tales of the past. Indeed, many of Todorov's statements defining the fantastic could be seen to apply directly to Highsmith's fiction. All works of fantasy literature, he says, share a number of common elements: fractured identity; the breakdown of boundaries between an individual and their environment; and the blurring of external reality and internal consciousness. These features, he concludes, 'collect the essential elements of the basic network of fantastic themes.'[20] Highsmith's characters, like Dostoevsky's, occupy a paraxial realm, one described by Mikhail Bakhtin in the following terms. 'In Dostoevsky the participants in the performance stand on the threshold (the threshold of life and death, truth and falsehood, sanity and insanity) . . . "today's corpses", capable of neither dying, nor of being born anew.'[21] Highsmith compels the reader to align his point of view with the hero, whose task it is to sail us, like Charon, across the dark waters to the otherworld of Hades. 'We know that the reader begins his reading by identifying himself with the hero of the novel,' says Jean-Paul Sartre. 'Thus, the hero, by lending us his point of view, constitutes the sole access to the fantastic.'[22]

Highsmith also felt a personal empathy with Dostoevsky. Like him, she realised that she was to some degree in love with suffering and at times exposed herself to situations she knew would hurt her. While reading a biography of the author in 1959, she noted that she too often wanted to suffer humiliation, to be 'personally degraded, cursed, spat upon,' for her 'finest emotions'.[23] She traced her fascination with duality and ambiguity back to her own childhood, acknowledging that the strands of love and hate which were woven through her character had their roots in her early relationship with her parents. Yet she knew that such dark, murky territory was a fertile breeding ground for her fiction. 'Out of this, I shall create, discover, invent, prove and reveal,' she said.[24]

Those close to her, particularly her family, often commented on how Highsmith's vision of reality was a warped one, however. In April 1947, she transcribed into her notebook what was, presumably, a real dialogue between herself and her mother, in which Mary accused her of not facing the world. Highsmith replied that she did indeed view the world 'sideways, but since the world faces reality sideways, sideways is the only way the world can be looked at in true perspective.'[25] The problem, Highsmith said, was that her psychic optics were different to those around her, but if that was the case, her mother replied, then she should equip herself with a pair of new spectacles. Highsmith was not convinced. 'Then I need a new birth,' she concluded.[26]

Stanley Highsmith had finally adopted his stepdaughter in November 1946, at an official hearing of the surrogate's court in Westchester County, New York, which Pat said was done so as to secure a passport. There, Pat made a formal oath to the effect that she had lived with Stanley since her mother's marriage to him in 1924. During that period, she looked upon him 'with daughter-like love and respect and desire now to make him my foster father in the eyes of the law as well.'[27] She added that she had gone under the name of Mary Patricia Highsmith both professionally and socially since she was a child, and now wished to change her name legally from Plangman to Highsmith. The statement, 'That for the past 21 years we three, my mother, Mr Highsmith and I have lived together as one closely knit family,' was, perhaps, the most galling for her to utter.[28]

In the gap between the initial inspiration and the plotting and writing of *Strangers on a Train*, Highsmith started work on yet another book, one she called *The Dove Descending*. She began writing it in the summer of 1946 and named it after a line in T.S. Eliot's poem, 'Little Gidding' from *Four Quartets*, which is suggestive of spiritual redemption. The incomplete manuscript runs to only seventy-seven pages and eight chapters, but she worked out the whole story in her notebook. The novel was narrated in the first person – a style she was not at all comfortable with – by a young, repressed girl, brought up by her aunt after the death of her architect father from tuberculosis and her mother in a car accident. The girl, called Leonora in the synopsis, but referred to as Marcia in the surviving draft, bears a strong resemblance to Highsmith herself. 'Dark-eyed' and 'thin faced', she attends Briarley Academy, an all-girl college and, like Highsmith at Barnard, studies English.

In the synopsis, the girl's affections are divided between her childhood sweetheart, Martin, who is a kind, but conventional man, and the wild anarchy of alcoholic Carl, a sculptor in Mexico. She travels to Mexico with her aunt, where she elopes with Carl. But in Acapulco there is a terrible storm and Carl drowns. His death, however, is not in vain, as it forces the girl to undergo an emotional reawakening, and, rather than settle for the safety of Martin she opts for the more spirited qualities of another man, Cappie. The plot is somewhat contrived, and even though she thought the eight pages a day, which she tapped out on her typewriter, read well enough for a first draft, she still remained dissatisfied, comparing her feelings to those suffered by a lover who has failed to pleasure his mistress.

If Highsmith believed in the creative and transformative powers of love, as she suggests, surely one of her greatest muses was the woman she starting seeing in June 1946. Her name was Virginia Kent Catherwood.

Virginia, whom she had first met at a party of Rosalind Constable's in November 1944, could not have come from a more different background from Highsmith. Born in 1915, she was the daughter of wealthy Philadelphia inventor and radio manufacturer Atwater Kent. The young Virginia Tucker Kent attended finishing school and studied sculpture in Paris and, in 1933, was presented at court to King George V and Queen Mary. Her debutante ball, in late December 1933, was the most lavish party Philadelphia had seen since before the Depression. Atwater Kent hired a sixty-piece orchestra to play at the grand Bellevue-Stratford Hotel – the music alone cost between $5,000 and $10,000. 'Not in years has anyone had the temerity to engage such a colossal orchestra for a private party,' commented a Philadelphia reporter.[29]

Virginia was also a favourite of the gossip columns; in January 1935 her name was linked with Franklin Roosevelt Jr, but in April of the same year, she married the wealthy banker Cummins Catherwood. On her wedding day, at the Church of the Redeemer, Bryn Mawr, Virginia wore a 'shimmering white satin', high-waist dress, with a train of five and a half yards and close-fitting sleeves. 'Her veil of tulle,' gushed the extensive newspaper description, 'is arranged with a close fitting cap of tulle, and a satin bandeau over the forehead fastened at the sides with tiny clusters of orange blossoms. Of three widths of tulle, seven and a half yards long, the veil completely envelopes the satin train. White satin pumps complete her costume. She will carry a bouquet of white orchids and lilies of the valley.'[30]

On return from their honeymoon, the couple leased a country estate in Bryn Mawr, then valued at $200,000, with twenty rooms, a gardener's cottage, garaging for four cars, and a swimming pool. But the romantic idyll did not last long and on 4 April 1941 the couple were divorced in Blaine County, Idaho. The circumstances of the divorce remain unclear, but according to Ann Clark, who had a relationship with Highsmith in the late 1940s, the relationship broke down because of Cummins Catherwood's discovery of his wife's lesbianism.

'Pat only told me the story once, but apparently Virginia lost custody of her child after a recording made in a hotel room and exposing a lesbian affair was played in court. Of course there is something of this tale in The Price of Salt.'[31]

Highsmith herself acknowledged the similarity. 'I worry that Ginnie may feel Carol's case too similar to her own,' she wrote in her diary in 1950, 'though Ann knows another woman in the same predicament now.'[32] Later, Highsmith would write about how Virginia occupied a central position in her imaginative landscape and how she would repeatedly use her in her work. 'Where is Ginnie – without whom the Price of Salt would never have been written,' she wrote in her diary in 1968, two years after Virginia's death, age fifty-one. 'How I adore my Virginias. She is "Lotte" in The Tremor of Forgery – the woman whom my hero will always love, with his body, with his soul also.'[33]

Two weeks after embarking on her relationship with Virginia, Highsmith wrote in her notebook about the importance of a lover in her life, someone who was able to cast light on all the wonders of the world. Without their presence, she said, she was a mere shadow. Love, she observed, acted rather like lubricant on machinery, performing as a catalyst sparking off new reactions. Certainly, the rich, glamorous socialite gave her a 'oneness' and a 'timelessness' that allowed her to enter a creative state of mind.[34] She was the 'other half of the universe' and 'together we make a whole'.[35] She compared herself and Virginia to the negative and positive components of an atom, halves which could not exist singly, only in conjunction; this desire to search out a defining doppelgänger figure reveals itself as a prominent theme in her writing.

But just as she was beginning to sample the possibility of happiness with Virginia, she heard the news, in September 1946, that her former lover, the painter Allela Cornell, had attempted suicide by drinking nitric acid. The effects of the acid were not immediate and, although Allela was in a great deal of pain, she remained conscious in her hospital bed for two weeks. Tragically, during this time she realised she did not want to die. She talked about what she would do when she regained her health, telling one of the doctors, 'I want you to pose for me, and I'll never have to look for a model again.' She believed that she would be discharged from the hospital within a month – a hope that made the doctor put his face in his hands and cry – but then, on 4 October, she slipped into a coma and died.

It seems the reasons Allela took her own life were nothing to do with Highsmith. 'Allela was lonely,' says one of her friends, Maggie Eversol.[36] 'Pat played no part in her suicide.'[37] 'Allela was involved with another woman who treated her appallingly,' says David Diamond. 'She came back from a disastrous trip to Alabama with this woman – Allela was in love with her, while this woman clearly did not feel the same way – and a few weeks later drank an entire bottle of nitric acid.'[38]

Yet Highsmith did, to a certain extent, blame herself. She asked herself why Allela had ever loved her, as it was inevitable she would drive her mad. She called herself an 'evil thing',[39] read through Allela's love letters and as she looked back over their time together, felt guilty at the way she had treated her. She said that in comparison to the angelic Allela, she, together with the rest of the living, were mere weeds, feeding on the waste products of the earth.

In the midst of mourning for Allela Cornell, Highsmith also became aware that Virginia Kent Catherwood was in danger of being snatched away from her by her excessive drinking, just as the painter had been stolen from her by death. The attack of paralysis suffered by Bruno in *Strangers on a Train*, brought on by his alcoholism destroying his nerve tissue, was clearly inspired by the terrifying physical breakdown suffered by Virginia in May 1947 when she lost her voice and couldn't feel her fingers. The scene Highsmith describes in the novel runs as follows.

He gasped. He couldn't talk, couldn't move his tongue. It had gone to his vocal chords . . . He gestured towards his mouth with his crazy hands. He trotted to the closet window. His face was white, flat around the mouth as if someone had hit him with a board, his lips drawn horribly back from his teeth. And his hands! He wouldn't be able to hold a glass any more, or light a cigarette. He wouldn't be able to drive a car. He wouldn't even be able to go to the john by himself![40]

By the summer of 1947, after only a year together, their relationship had deteriorated to such an extent that when they quarrelled, Virginia attacked Pat with her fists. Virginia had thrown herself into a new relationship with a photographer, Sheila, a liaison which Highsmith found unbearable, and in July, the writer walked in to find the couple naked in bed together. Pat tried to turn Virginia against Sheila, but when this failed, she began to fantasise about killing her rival, and wrote a poem in her notebook, entitled 'Murder fills my heart tonight'.[41] She could not bear the thought of Virginia and Sheila together and the potent mixture of love, hate, envy, anger and frustration resulted in a long stretch of insomnia.

On 23 October, at four in the morning, Pat sat up in bed, took hold of her cahier and recorded her anguish. 'In the night, alone, awake after sleep, I am insane . . . I am without discretion, judgment, moral code. There is nothing I would not do, murder, destruction, vile sexual practises. I would also, however, read my Bible.'[42] For the next few months, she kept Virginia alive in her mind and, to a certain extent, she worshipped the fantasy image just as much as she had loved the reality. She knew she would never forget her, precisely because, 'I know her so little, my conception of her is absolute, unchangeable.'[43] Yet the breakdown of their relationship that autumn forced her to question the state of her mental health and, in November, she wrote in her notebook about her worries. 'I am troubled by a sense of being several people . . . Should not be at all surprised if I become a dangerous schizophrene in my middle years.'[44]

In January 1948, as she cast her eye over the manuscript of the yet to be titled *Strangers on a Train*, Highsmith realised that the writing she had produced after the split from Virginia – seventy pages of the book – was weak and needed a thorough overhaul. 'It is as if I'd had a broken leg, when I wrote them,' she said.[45]

Without women, she said, there would be 'no tranquillity, no repose, no beauty in living'.[46] She needed them in order to work, simply to exist. But the idea that a relationship should better one's life was, she said, a falsity, noting that the act of love in the insect world often resulted in serious injury, if not death.

When Highsmith was at Barnard she spent a year studying zoology and throughout her life she felt a strong tenderness for animals, particularly cats and snails, both of which she kept as pets. She became so fascinated by the gastropods that she described her attraction for them in an imaginary interview which she conducted with herself. 'How did you hit upon this strange pastime or hobby, Miss H?' she asked. Her empathy for the creatures first manifested itself in 1946, she said, when she was walking past a fish market in New York and saw two snails, which were dark cream with brown stripes, locked in a bizarre embrace. She took the pair home with her, put them in a fish bowl and observed them mating, an activity she chose to describe in minute, almost scientific, detail. Later, during a radio interview in which she was asked why she kept snails as pets, she replied, 'they give me a sort of tranquillity'.[47]

In February 1947, she decided to write a story about the creatures, a blend of science and fantasy, but the result was judged by her agent to be 'too repellent to show editors'.[48] Nearly a quarter of a century later, Graham Greene would write of his admiration for the tale, 'The Snail-Watcher', in which a breeder of gastropods, Peter Knoppert, comes to a disgustingly sticky end. 'Mr Knoppert has the same attitude to his snails,' wrote Greene, 'as Miss Highsmith to human beings.'[49]

While Highsmith explored dualism philosophically in her work, it is also true to say that on a more personal level she always felt torn between the aspirations of the mind and the irrational drives of the body. Her intellect expressed itself in her tendency towards monasticism, while her bodily instincts pushed her towards promiscuity and, during the summer and winter of 1947 at least, a desire to surround herself with a crowd of like-minded artists, writers and intellectuals – a little Bohemia. After working during the day – on her comic books, short stories and novel – she would launch herself into the vibrant social whirl of post-war Manhattan.

Highsmith had first met Jane Bowles in late 1944, on her return from living in Taxco, but during the summer when Pat was breaking up with Virginia Kent Catherwood, the two writers began to see quite a lot more of one another. In her diaries she talks of their brief flirtation – at one point they had even planned on travelling to Africa together – but the relationship came to nothing. Highsmith, when contacted by Bowles' biographer, Millicent Dillon, told nothing of this, mentioning only that she had once been to a party at the Bowles' home on West 10th Street, in Greenwich Village, attended by various luminaries including John Gielgud, Jerome Robbins, and Oliver Smith, 'everybody notable except me – I felt!'[50] Another party at Jane Bowles' apartment which she described in her diary, was held for Simone de Beauvoir and Dorothy Parker, but unfortunately the guests of honour failed to turn up. Highsmith did, however, receive a piece of writerly advice from Bowles, who told her not to plan too much; rather she should let her imagination carry her along and rework later.

During this time, Highsmith also met the actress Stella Adler, the composer Marc Blitzstein, the writer and editor Leo Lerman, Bowden Broadwater, the third husband of Mary McCarthy, who worked at *The New Yorker*, and the German-born avant-garde artist Lil Picard, later known as 'the Gertrude Stein of the New York art scene' or 'the grandmother of the hippies'. Lil supported her through the trauma of breaking up with Virginia, while the two women attended sketching classes and a wide range of exhibitions together, everything from the 'La Licorne de Cluny' tapestries at the Metropolitan Museum to work by Rafino Tamayo and Salvador Dali.

'Pat was an inveterate gallery- and museum-goer and she seldom left home without a little three-by-five inch spiral booklet of blank pages which she filled on the spur of the moment or while taking in some especially pleasing sight,' says Kingsley. 'She believed that drawing, painting and music were among the noblest works – if not *the* noblest – works of man.'[51]

Highsmith, five years out of Barnard, still had an insatiable hunger to learn more about both classical and contemporary culture. During late 1947 and early 1948, she attended Edith Piaf, Bach and Hindemith concerts, in addition to playing the piano at her parents' new house in Hastings-on-Hudson; discussed existentialist drama with friends; saw one of the first productions of Tennessee Williams' play, *A Streetcar Named Desire*; and enjoyed films of *Crime and Punishment* and Eugene O'Neill's *Mourning Becomes Electra*, which she said was 'the best movie I have seen in the USA. Three hours of unrelieved tragedy, one sees life, but through murders and suicides. That's the way I want my book.'[52]

At times, Highsmith felt exhausted by the seemingly endless round of gallery openings, film and theatrical productions and non-stop cocktail parties. However, at one such gathering, in February 1948, she met the writer Truman Capote who would play an important role in securing her place at Yaddo, the artists' and writers' colony in upstate New York. Highsmith had been sniffy about Capote's work for some time, thinking him good at driving 'brilliantly from one phrase to the other'[53] but fundamentally flawed because of his inability to convey depth of character. Yet when she met him she was smitten. 'I like to go out with little Truman,' Highsmith wrote in her diary. 'He is so attentive, and so famous!'[54] She also found his carefree lightheartedness about his own homosexuality refreshing, regaling her with the anecdote that when he was fourteen he told his parents, 'Everybody is interested in girls, only I, T.C., am interested in boys!'[55]

Highsmith's new friend was already something of a Manhattan celebrity and on 1 March she invited Capote to her apartment on East 56th Street. She knew that a recommendation from Truman – who had attended the institution in the summer of 1946, at the same time as Carson McCullers – would make an impression on the Yaddo selection committee. 'He was in good with the people at Yaddo,' recalled Highsmith, 'and he said, "I'll help you get in if you'll sublet to me." So the deal was struck.'[56] Capote went on to finish *A Tree of Night* while staying in the apartment. But Pat also recognised that Capote's influence was potentially corrupting. One Sunday, soon after meeting him, he phoned her and invited her to tea. 'Now at that tea party was probably Irving Berlin and Bernstein, loads of people,' she later told Craig Brown, 'but I said I work on Sundays. I preferred to work. You can't do both.'[57]

Highsmith sent off her application to Yaddo at the beginning of March. Her novel was only one third done and she felt she needed the 'concentrated period of quiet such as Yaddo would provide'.[58] She submitted part of the book, which she described as 'a psychological one essentially, about two young men who exchange the task of doing a murder',[59] and examples of her published short stories, including 'The Heroine'. References came courtesy of Ethel Sturtevant, Rosalind Constable, her agent Margot Johnson, who recommended her as 'a serious young writer, who we believe to have a great deal of talent',[60] Mary Louise Aswell, the fiction editor at *Harper's Bazaar*, and of course, Truman Capote.

Highsmith's submissions, although not considered especially literary, were recognised to have a certain power and, according to one reader on the Yaddo selection panel, were actually much better written than the fiction of authors working within a 'higher' tradition. 'She *writes* better than most of our writers – not in the highest sense, of course, but just in the sense of movement, expertness, ease, and freedom,' wrote the advisor, 'and there is surely a very respectable place for such a writer in a time when even the best books, or some of them, are awkwardly written . . . But in any case my own vote would be Yes – unless there is a great deal more pressure than there seems to be from really *very* extraordinary people.'[61]

Ten days after this report was written, Highsmith received the news that her application had been successful. She was thrilled. 'Such a relief,' she noted in her diary, 'like a soldier, to have one's life planned for the next 10–12 weeks!'[62] Her grandmother, Willie Mae, was particularly impressed and she took the trouble to read the pamphlets sent by Yaddo. 'How wide in range are her interests,' Highsmith wrote about her grandmother, 'how much *grander* a person is she than all her offspring.'[63]

Pat regarded Yaddo as an opportunity to start life afresh, and so, before she made the journey upstate, she took the time to analyse her past mistakes. Highsmith, realised that her choice of partners was detrimental to her mental health and, to help herself understand her own motives, she sketched out a table, listing the most significant lovers by their initials, age, physique, colouring, personality type, duration of relationship, reason for the breakdown and the length of time she thought of them after the affair was over. Against each name, she added symbols, which when checked against the key, stand for, 'End due to my lack of sympathy', 'End due to her lack of sympathy', 'Bad judgment on my part', and 'most advantageous'.

This table, written on a scrap of paper which survives sandwiched between the pages of one of her notebooks, makes for fascinating reading; not only for what it tells us about her lovers, but for what it signifies about Highsmith herself. The very act of fashioning such a schematised grid, dissecting her relationships with almost mathematical preciseness, could be considered to betray a certain coldness of heart, a ruthlessness that negated her romantic nature. Rather, it seems like a desperate attempt to try and understand why she could never find lasting happiness, a question that tortured her for the rest of her life. The resulting self-analysis was a brutally honest, if perhaps Freudian-biased, indictment of her character, and she concluded that, 'I lack sympathy, am impatient with that which attracted me, therefore unconscious masochism. Have resolved to do better, as well as change my type radically.'[64]

11

Yaddo, shadow –
shadow, Yaddo!

1948

In the front of a copy of *Strangers on a Train* that Highsmith donated to Yaddo, she inscribed the words, 'To Yaddo – with profoundest gratitude for the summer of peace that let me write this book.'[1] At the end of her life she would show her appreciation by making the artists' and writers' colony the sole beneficiary of her estate, granting them, in addition to a $3 million bequest, the promise of any future royalties. It was quite a gesture, considering that Highsmith had only ever spent two months there fifty years before.

She arrived at Yaddo on 10 May 1948. No doubt the dark, sombre quality of the place, its bleakness and monastic atmosphere, appealed to her gothic imagination. It was said that Edgar Allan Poe composed part of his poem, 'The Raven', on the land which later became Yaddo and its history reads like the plot of a nineteenth-century sensation novel. In 1881, the site on which Yaddo now stands was bought by Wall Street financier Spencer Trask and his wife, Katrina. Trask's father, Alanson, made a fortune manufacturing boots for the Union Army during the Civil War while Spencer invested in a number of projects, including the rebirth of the *New York Times* in the 1880s. He also put money into Thomas Edison's incandescent lightbulb and his distribution grid for electricity in New York City; later he was the first president of what became Consolidated Edison and the General Electric Company.

Spencer and Katrina lived in Brooklyn, but after the death of their five-year-old son, Alan, in 1880, they took a summer house in Saratoga Springs, upstate New York, a place they finally decided to make their

permanent home. Soon after settling into the dilapidated villa surrounded by pine trees, which was originally built in the 1850s, the
family held a meeting about what they should call their new home.
According to family history, Katrina asked her daughter, Christina,
what name she would like to give it. The family was still dressed in
mourning clothes and Christina often heard her relatives speak about
how their lives had been shadowed by the tragedy. So the little girl put
her hands over her eyes, concentrated for a moment, and then said,
'Now I know. Call it "Yaddo", Mamma, for it makes poetry! Yaddo,
shadow – shadow, Yaddo! It sounds like shadow, but it's not going to
be a shadow.'[2]

Christina had unwittingly chosen an Old English word meaning
'shimmer'. 'She felt that the word (shadow) belonged to us,' recalled
Katrina Trask, 'and yet, instinctively, she shrank from the association.
Unconsciously, she gave us a prophecy for the years to come, for it grew
less and less to mean shadow, until at last, in the radiance of the life
here, it came to mean light.'[3]

The Trasks' lives continued to be beset by tragedy. Christina and her
brother Spencer Jr died in 1888 after they contracted diphtheria from
their mother. Katrina had been told that although she was due to die,
her illness had passed beyond the point of contagion, and so she called
for her two children to be brought to her so she could say her goodbyes.
The doctors, however, had made a terrible mistake, and the children
died within a few days of each other, while their mother survived. A
year later, in 1889, their fourth child, Katrina, was born but she too
died, twelve days after the delivery, due to birth complications. Then, in
1891, the Trasks' house burnt down.

The couple, however, refused to let themselves be destroyed by grief.
They commissioned a new house, which was finished in 1893, complete
with a Tiffany mosaic above the fireplace, emblazoned with the words,
Flammis Invicta per Ignem Yaddo Resurgo ad Pacem' – 'the flame
unconquered by fire, Yaddo rises up again in peace' – and in 1899,
while walking in the pine forest, Katrina had a vision. Katrina's account
of the birth of the Yaddo dream makes for embarrassing reading, as it
mixes mawkish melodrama with sham spirituality, but nevertheless her
idea was a noble one. The corporation of Yaddo was formed in 1900
and the first residents arrived in 1926.

'The vision of the future is clear to me,' Katrina told her husband.
Their home would be a refuge for writers and artists. 'At Yaddo they
will find the Sacred Fire, and light their torches at its flame. Look,
Spencer! They are walking in the woods, wandering in the garden,

sitting under the pine trees – men and women – creating, creating, creating!'[4]

Today, walking around Yaddo is an unsettling experience. The mansion is a harsh, almost brutal building, packed with Victorian-style furniture and decorated with sentimental portraits of the Trasks in gilt frames. The pine trees that surround and guard the house cast long shadows, and the four lakes – each representing one of the Trask children who died – shimmer in the sunlight. The local rumour that the children drowned in the waters here is unfounded, but in this isolated 400-acre site it is easy to understand how such stories gained a foothold.

For the two months Highsmith was at Yaddo she lived in the West House, on the first floor of a turreted building resembling something from a fairy tale, a few hundred yards away from the main house. On her first day, she was met by Yaddo's executive director, Elizabeth Ames, who, according to Truman Capote, looked and behaved like something from a modern gothic novel. 'She was a strange, creepy sort of woman, silent and sinister like Mrs Danvers in *Rebecca*,' he said. 'She was always going around spying, seeing who was working and not working and what everybody was up to.'[5]

Elizabeth Ames kept a close eye on Highsmith and, quite rightly, classified her as a 'hard drinker'.[6] In the mornings, before she could start work, Highsmith felt the need to have a stiff drink, not to perk her up, but to reduce her energy levels, which veered towards the manic. 'Until the period of my visit expired,' wrote fellow resident Chester Himes, the black crime writer whose room was across the hall from Highsmith's, 'I was drunk every day.'[7] Other residents included the man who would later become her fiancé, the writer Marc Brandel, together with Irene Orgel, Flannery O'Connor, Paul Moor, Vivien Koch Macleod, Stanley Levine, Gail Kubik, W.S. Graham, Clifford Wright, Harold Shapero and his wife, Esther Geller Shapero; men and women Highsmith described as sociable and unpretentious. In a letter Highsmith wrote to Ronald Blythe in 1967, she described Flannery O'Connor as, 'very quiet, stayed alone – while others of us were shockingly gregarious and unwriterlike. At that time, I fell between those two stools.'[8]

The problem was, Highsmith said in a letter to Kingsley, that after being cooped up in their rooms during the day, many of the residents were driven to walk into Saratoga Springs, two miles away, 'with the energy of mating salmon', in order to buy beers; the drinking was so excessive, she said, that they often suffered from two-day hangovers.[9]

On her tenth day at Yaddo, the group went into town for cocktails at a local bar, where Highsmith had five or six Martinis, two Manhattans and nearly blacked out. 'Mixing was the order – for a thrill,' she said. 'Marc soon succumbed, with carrot hair in his carrot soup.'[10]

Her daily regime, however, was a strict one, consisting of breakfast at 8 a.m. (half an hour later on Sundays), a packed lunch which she picked up in the mornings, and a working day which lasted until late afternoon. She often read the Bible in the mornings. The disciplined routine suited her perfectly, 'people work 30 per cent better under those conditions,' she said later.[11] If the novel she was writing was a baby inside her then Yaddo was the 'supreme hospital',[12] the perfect place in which to give birth.

Eight days after arriving, Highsmith read a piece in a magazine about the German-Swiss physicist Albert Einstein and was excited to learn that his scientific research echoed her own musings on the concept of duality. The lines she wrote in her diary echo those in chapter twenty-eight of *Strangers on a Train*, when Guy, just after committing a murder, thinks about the nature of man and the universe: 'Perhaps God and the Devil danced hand in hand around every single electron!'[13] Although Highsmith was conscious of her novel's underlying philosophical themes, she didn't let them interrupt the quick flow of the narrative or deflect attention away from the suspense. At Yaddo, she asked the painter Clifford Wright if he knew how to hold a gun[14] – unfortunately he didn't – and followed the case of Robert Murl Daniels, the twenty-four-year-old baby-faced murderer whose newspaper picture she pasted into her diary, next to the headline, 'KILLER NABBED'. Under this she then wrote, 'Bruno', the name of her psychopathic killer. 'Before I wrote *Strangers on a Train*,' she said, 'there was a photograph of this jolly boy . . . and he'd killed God knows, two, three, four people, absolutely joking and laughing with the police and it made an impression on me.'[15]

By 17 June, Pat thought she was nearing completion of another draft of the book. She could no longer think about its structure in a logical manner, and felt as if she was writing 'like the blind'.[16] Fatigue left her feeling crushed and weak, and yet, at night, she was so full of energy she could not sleep. The novel, she knew, had been written so hectically and she still remained dissatisfied with her first chapter and its overall tone. 'My book needs much relaxation on my part,' she wrote, 'a verification of all through the lens of meditation and reexperiencing.'[17] The process of creation, of writing at top speed, had its consequences and often, after a day at her desk, she felt like a 'coiled spring',[18] without a proper outlet for her sexual and emotional longings. Deliberately flouting Yaddo's rules, she arranged to see a girlfriend who drove up to Saratoga Springs, from where they travelled on to Glen Falls and then Hastings. Their two nights together were, she said, blissful; the girl was like a leaf from India or the Pacific, and when she departed, Highsmith could still sense her presence. 'I can feel our lips together,' she wrote, 'It frightens, delights and maddens me, because J. is not with me.'[19]

She also found herself growing closer to Marc Brandel, the twenty-nine-year-old son of the British novelist John Davys Beresford and whose real name was Marcus Beresford. Born in London on 28 March 1919, he was educated at St Catharine's College, Cambridge, and Westminster College, and in 1945 won early success with his first novel, *Rain Before Seven* – published in Britain as *The Ides of Summer* – followed by *The Rod and the Staff*, in 1947. One American critic commented of the latter work, 'if they [readers] retain any sensitiveness to good writing, will know that here is a first-rate piece of fiction and a novelist with something to say'.[20]

On 26 June, Pat and Marc walked down to the lake together and discussed homosexuality. She found his attitude incredibly tolerant and positive – it helped her feel more self-confident – and although she was open about her own sexuality, this didn't stop him from proposing to her – four times. Marc left Yaddo on 28 June, but wrote to her the week after, declaring his love for her again and mooting the idea of a trip together. 'He considers me very feminine,' she wrote, 'and that he likes me better etwas schwul [translated as: somewhat gay] because it excuses his peculiarities of temperament.'[21]

She continued to see him on her return to New York in July. As he was a published novelist, Pat valued his opinion about her writing and so she was pleased when he told her, near the end of August, that the 235 pages she had written were 'very, very good'.[22] She had a strong desire to make her relationship with Brandel work, but she also realised that she was only sexually attracted to women. 'Marc always said that she was very beautiful, that was his first impression of her,' says Brandel's second wife Edith, who herself became a friend of Highsmith's in later years. 'He was very much in love with her at that time, but although they slept together, the next morning she would be very resentful, due to the fact she resented herself when she did it.'[23]

In September, Marc Brandel rented a house in Provincetown, the fishing village at the tip of Cape Cod; he hoped that, in the few weeks they would spend together there, Pat and he would not only finish their novels, but resolve their difficulties and move towards a greater level of intimacy. Provincetown should have been the perfect setting for the culmination of such professional and personal epiphanies, as the quaint village located on the knuckle of Cape Cod's clenched fist had long acted as a magnet for a wide range of artists and writers seeking inspiration and insight. In 1899, attracted by the near-Mediterranean quality of light, impressionist Charles Hawthorne opened the Cape Cod School of Art, and frequently held classes *en plein* on the beaches and wharves, capturing the essence of the Portuguese fishermen who had long made Provincetown their home. By 1916 – the year in which Eugene O'Neill had his first play, *Bound East For Cardiff*, produced by the Provincetown Players – there were five summer art schools in the village; from the 1920s onwards the area acted as a creative mecca for modernists such as Marsden Hartley, Charles Demuth and Stuart Davis and, later, teachers such as Hans Hofman, who was instrumental in the development of Abstract Expressionism; while during the forties and fifties it attracted Tennessee Williams, Marlon Brando, Jackson Pollock and Mark Rothko.

By the time Highsmith arrived in 1948, Provincetown flaunted its reputation as a Greenwich Village by the sea, a centre of bohemianism and avant-garde experimentalism. Although Brandel was aware of the village's easygoing ways, nothing could have prepared him for the consequences of Highsmith's visit. Rather than bringing them closer together, Provincetown only served to drive a further wedge between them. Nervous of Pat's arrival, Brandel enlisted a stranger, Ann Clark, then Ann Smith, who was vacationing in a nearby fisherman's shack, to help; little did he realise that the two women would become lovers within a few hours of meeting. Ann, a painter and designer, was twenty-five, slim, tall, gamine, an ex-fashion model for *Vogue*; drawings Highsmith made of her portray her as a girlish figure with impossibly long legs.

'I had met Marc the night before and had taken an instant dislike to him,' says Ann. 'He was unattractive because of being so sneering and [a] nasty drunk, but also he had white white skin, freckles and looked unhealthy. He launched into a recital of his great success in England with his first novel and how he'd gotten high praise from Elizabeth Bowen for whom he had no regard and then after more unpleasant conversation he leaned over the deck rail and threw up.

'The next morning he came over to my deck and he was a shattered wreck. He told me he'd been at Yaddo and had met a writer, Patricia Highsmith, who said she was gay, but he'd fallen in love with her and he

wanted to marry her. He'd talked her into joining him in Provincetown
to spend a few weeks finishing their novels, and she was arriving that
day on the five o'clock bus. He was terrified and asked would I please
come over at five for a drink? He begged and begged and I finally began
to feel sorry for him. So I told him that me and a friend, who I was
expecting for the weekend, would be over at five.

'It had started to turn cold, it was rainy, and I hoped Marc had heat.
Marc met us at the door and we went into the cavernous, dim living
room. There, near the only lamp, behind a desk, stood Pat. Typical Pat,
she took a step back, not forward, when she saw us, she was completely
silent, looking apprehensive but perfectly beautiful.

'After a great deal of drinking, the next thing I remember is
standing near the main wharf, next to Marc, who was challenging
me to dive in. Apparently the attraction between Pat and I was
obvious and this was the only time in my entire life that I got into
any sort of competition with a man over a woman. Marc dived in but
I was scared and, instead, I decided to slide down a piling covered
with mussels. But my legs got all cut up and I started to bleed
through my pants. But there was no pain at all. The next memory I
have is being in the women's room of a big dance hall, where a black
band was playing. Pat was on her knees sopping up blood and I was
saying, "Don't bother, it doesn't hurt." Then I remember it raining
and Pat and I were on a pile of ropes on a little wharf near my deck
and we were making love and I was going absolutely out of my mind.
I'd never felt anything like that in my life.

'The next morning of course my legs hurt and I felt thoroughly
ashamed, hungover, and at the same time terrified I'd never see Pat
again. As I started to pack to go back to the city, there was a knock on
the door and it was her.'[24]

The two women swapped addresses and as soon as Pat arrived back
in Manhattan, at the end of September, she took a cab over to Ann's
tiny, roach-infested apartment on West 12th Street, where they went
straight to bed.

'Considering I'd been in bed with more men than I could remember, I
couldn't believe what was happening. The next morning I said, "I just
lost my virginity." She couldn't believe I'd never been in bed with a
woman before. But that was the truth. I told her she was everything I'd
ever wanted in another – and I meant it. I also said I was floored
because I thought I knew something about sexuality and obviously I
didn't. She said, "I didn't invent it, you know." I said, "For me you
did." Her first gift to me was a little three-minute egg timer encased in

sterling silver on each end. With it came a note: "Dear Ann – the best things in life last at least three minutes – Love, Pat".'[25]

Ann has vivid memories of Pat's apartment on East 56th Street. One entered, she said, through an iron gate, next to another residential building that opened into a courtyard, then one turned right into a separate two-storey structure and walked up one flight of stairs. The entrance led directly into a small kitchen, there was a bathroom and a closet, and on the wall outside the living room hung a photograph by Ruth Bernhard, a picture of a wooden arm holding a doll's head. An archway led through to the living room, which had two windows and which overlooked the courtyard below, but, because there was no fenestration on the building opposite, the apartment was incredibly private. In the bedroom there was a three-quarter size bed, over which hung a painting by Allela Cornell. Near the window, Pat had placed a table on which stood a plant and her bowl of snails. Still in the bedroom, there was her desk, complete with typewriter, and the shelves above housed her notebooks and a dictionary which she would add to when she came across a new word. ('What a pleasure is reading the dictionary!' Highsmith wrote in her notebook. 'The only book I know that is true and honest.'[26]) There was a record player, and a stack of records, including their favourite, Lee Wiley singing 'A Ship Without A Sail'.

Ann worked only a few blocks away from Pat's apartment and so, at the end of the day, they would meet at a little park at the end of 57th Street, or back at the flat, where Pat would cook Ann garlicked lamb chops or steak and a green salad. 'We'd wander home to her apartment for coffee and at some hour or other we'd start to undress, to take showers and we'd start kissing and stand for hours, it seemed, not able to move,' she says. 'It was never that way with anyone else – if we touched it was like fire. We'd finally get to bed and make love until dawn. I'd wake up in time for work and I'd leave her sleeping and she seemed to sleep so deeply and serenely. There was something very quiet about her.'[27]

The two women had a fondness for word games and Ann found Pat to be extraordinarily witty and humorous; they would clown around the apartment, dancing to music and saying silly things. In fact, they behaved, says Ann, very much like children when they were together. In the aftermath of Pat's death in 1995, Ann was so grief-stricken she felt as though she was walking around with a gaping hole in her middle. 'She was the only person with whom I was truly deeply in love – she pleased my eyes, my mind, my body, my spirit. She was the first woman

I went to bed with and I would have been very happy if she'd been the last.

'My memories of Pat and me are of laughter and music and passion in bed. But it seemed to me that she was slamming a door on her best ability – that is, her humour, her tenderness, her capacity to love and laugh and have a marvellous time in the sunlight, not the shadows.

'I guess I always thought of Pat as essentially very feminine though she had distinctly boyish characteristics at times, and some boyish characteristics in structure. She always seemed so fragile in my arms – I was taller and though I have a small skeletal structure, I always felt stronger than Pat and had the wish to protect her. I never felt she was in good health. She was very careful of her eating habits and her weight never varied. She got me into the habit of keeping little bits of leftovers and never eating a big meal. Sometimes she seemed so exhausted and her colour seemed too pale. Well, writers often do have a haunted look.'[28]

At the end of November 1948, after a recommendation from the composer David Diamond, Highsmith embarked on a course of therapy with the New York psychoanalyst, Eva Klein Lipshutz. In post-war New York, psychoanalysis was almost de rigueur. 'There was an inevitability about psychoanalysis,' says Anatole Broyard. 'It was like having to take the subway to get anywhere. Psychoanalysis was in the air, like humidity, or smoke . . . The war had been a bad dream that we wanted to analyze now . . . There was a feeling that we had forgotten how to live.'[29] Highsmith had tried one session of therapy before – in March earlier that year, after an unsuccessful sexual experience with a man, she had visited Dr Rudolf Lowenstein, who told her she would need approximately two years of analysis – but now she was determined to try and change. Highsmith hoped that the therapy would help her be able to enjoy sex with Marc, whom she wanted to marry. Could she learn to become heterosexual?

Freud believed that it was pointless trying to 'cure' homosexuals of their same sex desires; rather, psychotherapy could be used to help patients come to terms with their sexuality. However, American psychotherapists of the late 1940s and early 1950s, spellbound by the cult of self-improvement and the promise of restoring 'normality', translated Freud's writings into a belief system which they thought could be used to erase 'unhealthy' erotic drives and banish all traces of homosexuality.

'According to some psychiatrists of the post-war years, same-sex love

was simply a symptom of a more general character disorder,' writes
Lillian Faderman, author of *Odd Girls and Twilight Lovers: A History
of Lesbian Life in Twentieth-Century America*. 'It would disappear if
the disorder were resolved, and the woman would then be content to
marry and stay home, raising babies and tending to hubby's needs.'[30]
The zeal to 'cure' gays of what psychotherapists perceived as their
'mental illness' continued throughout the 1950s. Indeed, one therapist,
Albert Ellis, went so far as to claim that after 'treatment', one-third of
his lesbian patients were 'distinctly improved', while two-thirds were
'considerably improved', in their quest towards conventional sexuality.
'The metropolitan lesbian who has not, at one time or another,
embarked on this voyage, is a rarity,' wrote therapist Dr Richard
Robertiello, in his 1950s book, *Voyage from Lesbos: The Psychoanalysis of a Female Homosexual*.[31] The book focused on a lesbian
woman happy with her sexuality who came to the therapist complaining of insomnia. Robertiello seized on her case and claimed to cure her
of her 'perversion' (though unfortunately, not of her insomnia).

Highsmith's therapist, Eva Klein Lipshutz, whom the writer only
ever referred to by her unmarried name, gained a degree in psychoanalysis from Columbia University in 1947 and went on to write
research papers on the treatment of alcoholics, the comparison of
dreams in group therapy and the psychodynamics of skin disease.
When Highsmith came to her for help, Klein was working at the New
York Medical College. The money Highsmith earned from her comic
books averaged $55 a week, and therapy took $30 of this, a situation
that clearly did not please her. But at the time she thought that if the
analysis helped her become heterosexual, then it was money well
spent. Klein told her that sex with a man was 'quite normal.
Everyone does it',[32] but Pat found it physically impossible. 'Sexual
intercourse', she wrote in a letter to her stepfather later, explaining
the situation with Marc Brandel, 'is steel wool in the face, a sensation
of being raped in the wrong place – leading to a sensation of having
to have, pretty soon, a boewl [*sic*] movement. If these words are
unpleasant to read, I can assure you it is a little more unpleasant in
bed. I tried . . .'[33]

Today the therapist's interpretation of Highsmith's case seems laugh-
ably simplistic and over-dependent on Freudian theory. At the time,
however, Highsmith took what Klein had to say seriously, describing
each visit to her in a separate section of her diary devoted to analysing
her analysis. After her first session, at the end of November, she
concluded that the therapy was 'a way to me',[34] and she soon looked

upon the analyst as a mother substitute – 'the feeling already, that Mrs Klein is my mother', she wrote.[35] Klein questioned her about her childhood, particularly what happened in 1926, the year in which Highsmith could, according to Vivien De Bernardi, have been sexually abused. 'Tried to remember the year '26,' wrote Highsmith. 'I have no memory of my parents' sexuality.'[36]

After sitting a Rorschach test and enduring a session of free association, Klein concluded that Highsmith's basic problem was that she resented her mother. She felt guilty about her hatred of her and, to overcompensate, entered into relationships with other women with whom she then acted out a pattern of loving and leaving. Her experience with Virginia Kent Catherwood typified all her affairs with women. 'Yes, what I loved in her was, that she was a mother to me,' wrote Highsmith in her diary. 'And didn't she always say that I were a child?'[37]

Klein informed Pat that she'd never been happy, that she actually hated women and loved men and, quite absurdly, interpreted a dream of flushing the lavatory and flooding the bathroom floor as a sign that her patient wanted to flush her mother down the drain like human faeces. Highsmith had, Klein concluded, a 'basic maladjustment to people and to sex from earliest anal-sadistic years'[38] and recommended she start group therapy with four married women who were, Klein, said, latent homosexuals. 'Perhaps I shall amuse myself by seducing a couple of them,' Highsmith noted in her diary.[39]

It's questionable whether the therapy actually helped Highsmith. It certainly forced her to examine the nature of her unconscious – she often dreamt about being a man threatened with castration – which was, after all, the source of her creativity. During the analysis, she also acknowledged that she could not, ultimately, have a so-called 'healthy' relationship, as she found it impossible to 'merge' with anyone, male or female. But there's no doubt that Klein's interpretation of homosexuality as a mental illness, together with Highsmith's reading of psychiatrist Edmund Bergler – who believed that lesbians were sick and could only be happy if they underwent intensive psychotherapy three times a week for one or two years – left her feeling even more confused.

It's ironic then that the therapy which was designed to cure Highsmith of her homosexuality inadvertently brought about the necessary conditions for the creation of a novel about lesbian love. In order to pay for the services of Eva Klein, Highsmith was forced to get a temporary job and in early December, she took a position in the toy department of

Bloomingdale's, the famous Manhattan department store. The experience was a profound one, personally and creatively, as it inspired a book that is both significant in terms of twentieth-century gay literary history and a powerful novel in its own right: *The Price of Salt*, or, as it was later titled, *Carol*.

12

Instantly, I love her

1948–1949

On 8 December 1948, a few days after starting at Bloomingdale's, Highsmith was working in the toy department when in walked an elegant, blonde woman. Pat had never seen her before, but she was immediately infatuated. Not only was she a beautiful and alluring figure, but, according to Highsmith's diaries, she reminded the writer of Virginia Kent Catherwood. The woman bought a doll for one of her daughters, left her name, address and delivery details and then walked out of the store. The two women never met again but her influence was ineffable and she was reborn, Highsmith later claimed, as the character Carol in *The Price of Salt*.

When the book was republished under her own name, Highsmith wrote in the afterword, 'Perhaps I noticed her because she was alone, or because a mink coat was a rarity, and because she was blondish and seemed to give off light.'[1]

But was there really such a woman? And if so, who was she? When the book was reissued as *Carol* in 1990, journalists questioned Highsmith about her inspiration, but the famously private author refused to divulge any further information. 'I don't answer personal questions about myself or other people that I know, anymore than I give out people's telephone numbers,' she told Sarah Dunant on BBC2's *The Late Show*.[2] However, in Highsmith's diaries she names the woman as a Mrs E.R. Senn, of North Murray Avenue, Ridgewood, New Jersey – in the novel she is Mrs H.F. Aird, also of New Jersey. When I checked the 1952 Ridgewood directory which sits in the reference section of the Ridgewood Public Library, there was an entry for a Mr E.R. Senn, first name Ernest, who worked as an executive in New York City. A scan of the local high school alumnae directory also revealed the names of two ex-pupils who had been born with the name Senn and who could, I thought, have been the children of this marriage. I wrote to both of them and a few weeks later received a letter from a man informing me that unfortunately his father was not the Mr E.R. Senn that I was looking for. Weeks passed and then, one day, I received a reply from one of the Senns' daughters.

'Can't tell you what a surprise it was to read your letter and realize the effort you have put into locating me on behalf of my mother!' it read. Eventually, after months of communication, I arranged a meeting with one of Mrs Senn's other daughters, Priscilla Kennedy, who was visiting London from America, and who was able to tell me about the woman who captured Highsmith's imagination back in 1948.

She was called Kathleen Senn and she lived with her husband, Ernest Richardson, and her family in North Murray Avenue, Ridgewood, then a wealthy suburb of New Jersey. Kathleen Senn was born in 1911, in Denver, Colorado, and her father was Elmer W. Wiggins, owner of Wiggins Airways, which operated out of Dedham, Massachusetts. This is already more than Highsmith knew about her blonde-haired inspiration – she never even knew her Christian name, let alone her background, but if she had, she might easily have fallen in love with her.

'She had been to Skidmore College and she looked like a socialite,' says Priscilla. 'She had a maid to do the menial tasks for her in the house and spent time at the country club. She was incredibly self-sufficient, not afraid of anything, but unfortunately she was alcoholic and was in and out of psychiatric hospitals in New York all the time.'[3]

After that briefest of brief encounters with Kathleen Senn in Bloomingdale's, Highsmith came home from work feeling unwell and the next day, on 9 December, she wrote down the plot of a lesbian love story about a young shop girl and an older, more sophisticated woman. 'I see her the same instant she sees me, and instantly, I love her,' she wrote in her journal. 'Instantly, I am terrified, because I know she knows I am terrified and that I love her.'[4]

Initially, in this sketch, narrated in the first person, Highsmith called the young shop girl, an eighteen-year-old orphan, Liselle Freyer, and the blonde-haired woman Mrs Sean, of Ridgefield, New Jersey. The older woman asks Liselle out to lunch, where after cocktails, she compliments Liselle on her prettiness. The orphaned girl, although shy, manages to confess that she thinks Mrs Sean is magnificent and they arrange to meet the following Saturday. Mrs Sean picks Liselle up

'There is an ever more acute difference . . . between my inner self which I know is the real me, and various faces of the outside world.' Highsmith on the Staten Island ferry, New York, in the early 1930s.

Highsmith's maternal great-grandfather, Gideon Coats.

Minna Hartman (left), Highsmith's paternal grandmother, taken in 1885.

Daniel and Willie Mae Coates, Highsmith's maternal grandparents, with whom she spent many years of her childhood.

Mary Coates,
Highsmith's mother.

When Mary discovered
she was pregnant, she
tried to rid herself of her
unborn child by drinking
turpentine. 'It's funny
you adore the smell of
turpentine,' she would
later tell her daughter.
The attempted
termination was
unsuccessful and the
couple were divorced
nine days before their
only child was born.

Jay B Plangman,
Highsmith's father.

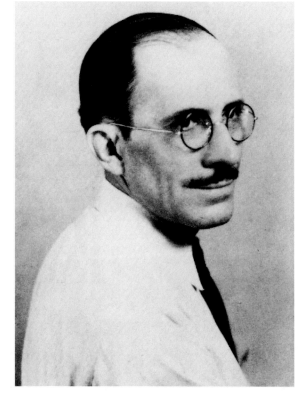

Mary with 'Patsy', as Highsmith was called by her family.

Mary with Stanley Highsmith, whom she married in 1924. Later, Highsmith would confess in her journal to 'evil thoughts, of murder of my stepfather . . . when I was eight or less'.

Patsy on the veranda of her grandmother's house in Fort Worth. She later described her childhood as a 'little hell'.

Highsmith as a young girl, probably taken in Texas.

Pat while at Barnard College, New York. 'Here was the taste of freedom I craved,' she said of her undergraduate years.

Highsmith, aged twenty-one, just after leaving Barnard, photographed by Rolf Tietgens.

Kate Kingsley Skattebol, Pat's friend from her Barnard years until her death.

The photographer Rolf Tietgens, who Highsmith met in the summer of 1942. He was one of the few men to whom she felt attracted.

One of the nude photographs of Pat taken by Rolf Tietgens in 1942.

The artist Allela Cornell, with whom Highsmith had an affair in 1943. Highsmith confessed she regarded her not so much as a real woman, but as 'an idea, born by an X-ray'. Cornell committed suicide in 1946 by drinking nitric acid.

Virginia Kent at her wedding to Cummins Catherwood in 1935.

Virginia Kent Catherwood, Highsmith's lover from 1946 until 1947, was one of the inspirations for Highsmith's character Carol in *The Price of Salt*. 'I worry that Ginnie may feel Carol's case too similar to her own,' wrote Pat in her diary.

Yaddo, the writers' and artists' colony in upstate New York which Highsmith later named as her sole beneficiary.

Pat's writing studio, the West House, Yaddo, as it is today. She thanked Yaddo for the 'summer of peace' of 1948 during which she wrote a large part of her first published novel, *Strangers on a Train*.

Novelist Marc Brandel, Highsmith's fiancé. It was for his benefit that Pat underwent six months of therapy in New York in an attempt to make herself heterosexual.

Farley Granger as Guy and Robert Walker as Bruno in Hitchcock's film of *Strangers on a Train*, released in 1951.

'My most persistent obsession – that America is fatally . . . off the mark of the true reality, that the Europeans have it precisely,' Highsmith wrote in her notebook before sailing from New York to Europe in May 1949.

Kathryn Cohen, a doctor, former Ziegfeld Follies girl and the wife of
Highsmith's British publisher. Highsmith and she had an intense relationship
in September 1949.

Kathleen Senn, the 'real-life Carol', who Highsmith encountered in Bloomingdale's, New York.

in her car in New York, and they drive back to her house in the suburbs. There, the two women kiss, before Mrs Sean puts her to bed like a child and gives her a cup of hot milk.

'I can envisage an entire book,' wrote Highsmith, 'with enough human play on the seventh-floor toy department . . . The toy world within the commercial prison. The captured dream . . . Only parts of it fool the child. The child knows. I saw no delighted child while I was there.'[5]

Three days after writing this, Highsmith left Bloomingdale's. Then on 22 December, she came down with a fever and fainted on the subway. Her therapist, Eva Klein, asked her what she was thinking about as she lost consciousness. 'About death,' Highsmith replied.[6] She was eventually diagnosed as having chickenpox and over Christmas, her face, body, scalp, upper arms, ears and throat were covered in spots, blood and weeping pus; it looked to her, she said, as if she had just been hit by a shower of flak.

At her parents' house in Hastings-on-Hudson, she was confined to bed, but instead of receiving appropriate treatment, she was subjected to her mother's experiments with Christian Science. 'Shall I read you some Mary Baker Eddy?' she asked. 'Just an aspirin, please,' Highsmith replied.[7] Finally, her case became so serious a doctor had to be called, who although he was aware of Mary Highsmith's unorthodox approach to treatment, decided to keep his comments to himself.

Highsmith continued with her psychotherapy in early 1949, recording her progress in a diary. Her motivation was to 'get myself into a condition to be married',[8] but the more she analysed herself, the more she realised that a life with Marc Brandel would be disastrous. Yet she failed to extract herself from the relationship and, over the next few months, she veered wildly between a desperate wish to be married and the sickening knowledge that if she did so, she would not only destroy him, but herself as well. At the end of March, she feared she was pregnant and took a urine sample into a laboratory for analysis. 'She was hysterical when she phoned to tell me,' says Ann Clark. 'I told her she could always have an abortion – I had had one – but thankfully it never came to that.'[9] The two women celebrated her pregnancy-free state with a toast of beer. 'Amazing how good the world can look in one moment!' wrote Highsmith in her diary.[10] She was fitted with diaphragm and although she carried on sleeping with Marc, she told him she would see him only a couple of nights a week, not every evening as he wished; yet the day after this decision she agreed to become officially engaged to him. ' "You'd better make up your mind whom you love," ' Ann told her, ' "because you're wasting a hell of a lot of valuable time." ' [11] This inability to chose between lovers would cause Highsmith a great deal of emotional disturbance over the next few years. One of the reasons why she found it so difficult to separate herself from Marc was her idealisation of his intellect; she respected the fact that he was a published writer and no doubt felt a little flattered by his interest in her. Highsmith thought of herself as something other than a woman and the psychological dynamic that attracted them was far more complicated than the male-female roles of a traditional relationship. As both of them were artists, Highsmith liked to think that they existed outside the rules, yet ultimately she would learn that a life lived only in the mind had devastating consequences on the emotions.

During her forty-seventh, and last, analysis session on 24 May 1949, the therapist advised Highsmith not to attach herself to anyone for the next few months; that way, she wouldn't feel too disappointed if they rejected her. Pat's last word on the subject, however, took a more pragmatic view: 'Bloody angry at having to pay this bill before I leave.' [12] Pat's dream of travelling through Europe had finally materialised and the delights of the Continent beckoned.

Europe, and particularly England, had long since captured Highsmith's imagination. When she was a teenager she had been moved to tears by George Cukor's 1935 film *David Copperfield*, and after reading *Tom Brown's Schooldays* by Thomas Hughes, she felt so inspired she wrote a short composition based on the book. In 1947, she noted, 'My most persistent obsession – that America is fatally . . . off the mark of the true reality, that the Europeans have it precisely.' [13] To her, Europe represented sophistication, reverence of the intellect, the source of mind-expanding philosophies, and, above all, freedom. 'Expatriates,' she wrote in 1953, 'are accused of escaping. They seek, on the contrary.' [14] Her initial impulse to travel to the Continent probably stemmed from her reading, 'as nearly all her literary interests were embedded in the works of what the politically correct today characterize as dead white European males,' says Kingsley. 'One also should not discount the change of scene, recharging her batteries and the appetite for adventure, the opportunity to experience something completely different.' [15]

She had first been invited to make the transatlantic crossing by Lil Picard in September 1948, and although she turned down the offer, she decided that travelling to the Continent was one of her most pressing ambitions. She saved money from comic-book writing and in May 1949, booked her ticket. She felt optimistic about the trip – after all, on 20 May, only a fortnight before she was due to sail on the *Queen Mary*, her agent told her that Harper & Brothers wanted to publish her novel, the as yet untitled *Strangers on a Train*. That same night, over a bottle of champagne, she and Marc Brandel decided to get married on Christmas Day. 'Three high points in my life – definitely!' she wrote in her diary.[16]

Before she left for Europe, she had lunch with her editor at Harper & Brothers, Joan Kahn, who would work closely with Highsmith for the next thirteen years. Pat was nervous before the lunch, but Joan told her that the book was a fine first novel. On 4 June, Marc, Rosalind and her mother came to see her off. Pat was disappointed that her cabin, which she had to share with three other women, was on the D deck and that she had to travel tourist, instead of first class – she blamed her therapist for her lack of funds. Noel Coward was on board, but as she was sailing 'below deck', she had no way of orchestrating a meeting. The meals, she said, were thrown at the passengers and then quickly snatched away. 'No one attractive in tourist class,' she sneered.[17]

Aboard the liner she slept, bashed out comic stories on her typewriter and imagined the life she would return to in America. But the more she thought about the prospect of marriage to Marc, the more she dreaded it. Domesticity, she said, repelled her and the idea of a life of babies, cooking, false smiles, vacations, movies and sex, particularly the latter, disgusted her. By the time she had docked at Southampton on 10 June, she had decided wedded bliss was not for her. She took a first-class carriage up to the capital and was met at Waterloo station by her London hosts – Dennis Cohen, the wealthy founder of the Cresset Press (which would publish *Strangers on a Train*, *The Blunderer* and *The Talented Mr Ripley* in Britain), and his wife, Kathryn. The couple drove her to their rather grand house in Old Church Street, Chelsea, in a Rolls-Royce and laid on a superb lunch, complete with Riesling wine. Highsmith had first met the Cohens at a party of Rosalind Constable's in New York, on 10 March, that was also attended by the writer Mary McCarthy and her husband.

Pat was captivated by the beautiful Kathryn Cohen who worked as a doctor at St George's Hospital in London. American by birth – her maiden name was Kathryn Hamill – she had spent the first part of her life working as an actress, appearing in Cochran's *Revue Sketches*,

Farjeon's *Nine O'Clock Revue*, and had met her husband, Dennis, while she was starring with the Ziegfeld Follies. After working for a brief period as Aneurin Bevan's secretary, Kathryn enrolled at Newnham College, Cambridge, to study medicine.

Kathryn played the part of the sophisticated – and well-connected – hostess to perfection. She invited Pat to lunch with the actress Peggy Ashcroft, took her to the Tate Gallery, and accompanied her on a trip to Stratford-upon-Avon, where they saw Diana Wynyard as Desdemona. Quickly the two women became close and, during her two-week stay at the Cohen's house, Pat felt able to talk in detail about her complicated emotional life. She also asked Kathryn's advice about the hormone deficiency that still worried her. 'If you were added up,' Kathryn told her, 'I think you'd have a little more on the male side – from your reactions to men I mean.'[18]

On 25 June, Highsmith took a train from Victoria, a boat across the Channel and then another train to Paris. The distractions of the city, which Highsmith described as 'bold, squawking, dirty, magnificent in a thousand places'[19] – she frequented the louche nightclubs of the Latin quarter, including the notorious Le Monocle – should have been enough to take her mind off Kathryn. But she still yearned for the kind of emotional intensity not provided by instant sexual gratification. 'No such dissolute three days in all my life before,' she wrote in her diary. 'I am lonely. I need Kathryn, or Ann!'[20] While in Paris, she visited the Louvre, where she saw the Winged Victory of Samothrace, the headless Grecian statue which she later described as the perfect embodiment of courage and female beauty and which she would use in *The Price of Salt* to describe Therese's attraction to Carol. 'Carol's beauty struck her like a glimpse of the Winged Victory of Samothrace,' she wrote.[21]

A few days later, after travelling south to Marseille, where she was staying with a family friend, Highsmith decided for her health that it would be better if she took Eva Klein's advice and shunned any emotional attachments for the foreseeable future, and she wrote to Marc temporarily breaking off relations. From Marseille, she travelled by bus to Genoa, where she discarded a pair of pyjamas, the 'horrors', given to her by her fiancé. The next day, in Milan, she visited the cathedral at dusk, where she was mistaken for a prostitute. She then journeyed on to Venice, Bologna, Florence and Rome. Two days after arriving in Rome, she felt ill and was confined to her hotel bed, thinking that nobody would care if she were to die alone. She wired Kathryn in London, who telephoned her the following day. Yes, she said, she would come out and meet her in Naples; immediately Highsmith's spirits rose.

Pat fell in love with Naples, the capital of the *mezzogiorno*, as soon as she arrived on 24 August. Standing in the filthy streets she could hear the ringing of church bells, the spit and hiss of the espresso machines, the constant barking of dogs, the honking of car horns, the clatter of dishes and the plaintive echo of American songs on street radios. Beggars loitered everywhere and the city smelt of stale sweat, rotten fruit, urine and faeces. It was here that she felt inspired to start writing the novel based on her experiences in Bloomingdale's.

Kathryn arrived in Naples on 3 September. Initially the two women were somewhat timid with one another; Pat wanted to kiss Kathryn good night, but did not dare, for fear of being rejected. Like the character of Tom Ripley she thought herself shabby next to her object of adoration and felt self-conscious about her bad teeth, unkempt hair and untidy shoes. On 7 September, the two women drove with a friend of Kathryn's to Positano, the magical village on the Amalfi coast, which would be recast in *The Talented Mr Ripley* as Mongibello. Highsmith found the place enchanting. 'I love the name,' she said, 'and down to the sea, an ideal rock bordered cove . . .'[22]

From Naples, Kathryn and Pat took a boat to Palermo, Sicily. Sitting out on deck, under the moonlight, the writer observed how, as the ship gained speed, white crested waves formed at the prow and the lights of the boat flashed like a strange silver forest fire. 'At night, sitting in the soft wind on the top deck . . . a happiness and promise suffuses one like an enthusiasm, a spell cast by the gods, and one falls in love with whomever one is near, one is filled with giving.'[23]

During the days that followed the two women became lovers, but as they travelled back on the night boat to Naples, they realised their time together was limited. Kathryn was due back in Britain and Highsmith's summer jaunt had come to an end. On 23 September – 'the horrible day' – Highsmith closed the door to their hotel room feeling utterly dejected. Kathryn, as a parting gift, gave her a pink and blue scarf which she had bought in Capri. Highsmith travelled to Genoa from where she would sail back to America.

Looking back at her trip, she realised that her three and a half months in England, France and Italy had stimulated both her senses and her literary imagination. 'It widens one's interests again,' she said of Europe, 'makes [one] more diverse as at seventeen.'[24] As her ship sailed through the wine-dark sea, Highsmith pondered her future. Her affair with Kathryn had been intense and passionate, but Pat realised that she had, essentially, a flighty nature and could not sustain a relationship for longer than two or three years. 'But at least the two years are worth it, worth anything,' she concluded. 'I can envisage England & Kathryn for two years . . .'[25]

While in London, Highsmith had purchased a Kierkegaard anthology, edited by Robert Bretall, into which she scribbled the words, 'Truth is subjectivity', a neat summary of the Danish writer's philosophy. After reading the anthology, Highsmith referred to Kierkegaard as her 'master', the same term she had applied to Dostoevsky; indeed the two writers explored similar themes – irrationality, loss of identity, and the fragmented nature of consciousness – motifs which worm their way throughout Highsmith's work. In Kierkegaard's *The Sickness Unto Death*, written in 1849, the philosopher wrote about a man desperate to lose his identity. 'Such a despairer, whose only wish is this most crazy of all transformations, loves to think that this change might be accomplished as easily as changing a coat . . . he recognizes that he has a self only by externals.'[26] The words sum up the underlying motivation that governs many of Highsmith's anti-heroes, particularly Tom Ripley in *The Talented Mr Ripley*.

Although Søren Kierkegaard died in 1855, readers of English had to wait until the 1930s and 1940s for the publication of his complete works in translation. This 'tardy recognition', in Bretall's words[27] was due not only to the fact that Kierkegaard wrote in a so-called 'minor language', but also to the sheer modernity of his ideas, concepts which seemed to have a greater resonance for the twentieth century than the nineteenth. Indeed, Kierkegaard has been seen as the father of existentialism – freedom, he believed, lies not in choice itself, but in the decision to choose whether to choose. 'It is, therefore, not so much a question of choosing between willing the good or the evil,' Kierkegaard wrote, 'as of choosing to *will*, but by this in turn the good and the evil are posited.'[28] The only truth, as Kierkegaard saw it, was 'subjectivity, inwardness',[29] the flux-like irrational state of mind Highsmith hoped to capture in her writing. If she knew she was going to die, what, she asked herself in her notebook in November 1950, would she like to have achieved in her work? 'Consciousness alone, consciousness in my particular era, 1950,'[30] she wrote.

Highsmith also found parallels between the work of Kierkegaard and Proust, especially in their writings on the nature of love. Only by believing that one had a duty to love, by seeing the object of one's affections as a fixed and static being, was it possible to make that love last. 'For in that love which only has continuance, however confident it is,' wrote Kierkegaard, 'there is still an anxiety, an anxiety about the possibility of change.'[31] It is not hard to see why Kierkegaard's notion of love appealed to the romantic in Highsmith.

13

Carol, in a thousand cities

1949–1951

If Highsmith thought her adventures in Europe would sort out her unresolved emotional life she was wrong. If anything, the trip only made the situation worse. After docking at Philadelphia, Highsmith took a train to New York, arriving in Manhattan on 15 October 1949. Four days later she had dinner at her apartment with Marc, who told her that he was still keen on marriage and that he was sure he wanted to spend the rest of his life with her. They started sleeping together again, but she only wanted Kathryn. 'I feel I am in love with her, really,' she wrote, 'as I have not been with anyone, anything *like* this, since Ginnie.'[1]

Each day she waited for a letter from Kathryn. Pat sent her lipstick, butter, figs and chocolate bars – still rationed in post-war Britain – but was too timid to dispatch the letter she had written confessing her love. Inspired by the agony of waiting for a word from Kathryn, at the end of October she had an idea for a story about a man suffering from the same inner torment. The story opens, 'Every morning, Don looked into his mailbox, but there was never a letter from her.'[2]

After a holiday romance, Don is overcome with a passion for Rosalind and he is so smitten he wants to marry her. He sends her a letter, but when she doesn't write back, he becomes convinced that her reply has been delivered to the wrong mailbox. In the first of a series of irrational acts, Don breaks into the box of his neighbour, Dusenberry, and reads a letter he has been sent by lovesick woman, Edith. Don then assumes his neighbour's identity and writes to her as Dusenberry, arranging a time to meet at Grand Central station. Eventually he receives a letter from Rosalind, refusing his offer of marriage. In a state of madness, he keeps his appointment with Edith, watching her from afar, before walking up to her and saying, 'I'm sorry'. The story ends with him striding up Lexington Avenue, thinking about the letter he must write to Rosalind, in tears.

She called the story, which she typed up in mid-November, 'Love is a Terrible Thing', which could almost be taken as the subtitle of Highsmith's own life. 'The story is so much K and myself,' she wrote in her diary.[3] It was published in 1968, in *Ellery Queen Mystery Magazine* as 'The Birds Poised To Fly', and anthologised in Highsmith's collection, *Eleven*. 'Neurotic' and 'degenerate' were the words her family used after she read the story to them; they asked her why she was obsessed with such dark subject matter. The comment was a measure of how little Stanley and Mary understood the source of their daughter's fiction and its overwhelming power.

During the autumn of 1949, Highsmith continued to write her lesbian novel. Inspired by the Bloomingdale's incident of December 1948, and her relationships with women such as Virginia Kent Catherwood and Kathryn Hamill Cohen, the book, she realised, took the form of an autobiographical confession. In October, when she showed a page of the novel to a friend, he 'remarked it was entirely myself,' she recorded. 'So it is. Perhaps that accounts for my confidence . . . Have never felt such outpouring of myself – in all forms of writing. A great gush.'[4]

The book is written in the same precise, yet unsettling, style as one of her suspense novels, yet it is, essentially, a love story and its plot is a simple one. Therese Belivet is an aspiring stage designer who takes a temporary job in the toy department of a New York department store, Frankenberg's. One day, close to Christmas, she finds herself attracted to a customer, Carol Aird, a woman who is buying a doll for her daughter. The two meet, fall in love, and then go on a driving trip together across America, a plotline which foreshadows Jack Kerouac's 1957 novel *On the Road*. But they are pursued by a private detective hired by Carol's husband, in order to amass evidence that can be used against her in divorce, so as to gain custody of their child.

Carol is clearly an amalgamation of all the qualities Highsmith admired in a woman. Like Kathleen Senn, the woman who walked into Bloomingdale's, she has blonde hair and grey eyes, while her characteristics – grace, elegance, femininity, and a certain goddess-like unattainability – reflect the personalities of Highsmith's most alluring muses. Highsmith wrote Therese as a slightly younger and more naive version of herself. Like the writer, Therese is unsure of her real identity, seems insubstantial and defines herself through others, particularly her lovers – 'all she saw, she seemed to see through Carol.'[5] Highsmith also placed her own words, ones that she had previously recorded in her notebooks, straight into the mouth of her fictionalised self. In 1942, she wrote in one of her cahiers, after drinking a glass of hot milk, 'It tastes organic, of blood and hair, meat and bone. It is alive as an embryo sucked from a womb.'[6] In the novel, after Carol gives Therese a glass of milk, Highsmith writes, 'The milk seemed to taste of bone and blood, of warm flesh, or hair, saltless as chalk yet alive as a growing embryo.'[7]

The character of Richard, Therese's boyfriend, whom she subsequently rejects in favour of Carol, also seems to have been inspired in part by Marc Brandel. Sex between the two writers had always been difficult – Highsmith simply loathed it – and, in the novel, lovemaking is described in the following terms.

> She remembered the first night she had let him stay, and she writhed again inwardly. It had been anything but pleasant, and she had asked right in the middle of it, 'Is this right?' How could it be right and so unpleasant, she had thought.[8]

When the character of Richard discovers his girlfriend's 'unnatural' predilections, he writes Therese a letter expressing his disgust, calling her relationship with Carol 'sordid and pathological', 'rootless and infantile'. In May 1950, Marc, too, wrote Highsmith such a letter, 'telling me I cling to my disgusting, infantile sicknesses as a little girl clings to a doll'.[9]

However, Marc, unlike Richard in *The Price of Salt*, ended the note with yet another request that they marry. His feelings for her were much more complex than those of Richard's for Therese; after a great deal of persuasion from Pat, he was eventually forced to admit that one of the reasons why he felt attracted to her was because she reminded him of one of his brothers. 'I shall leave it to his psychoanalyst to tell him that he is attracted to me for homosexual reasons, which I have always known,' she wrote in her diary.[10] In addition, he confessed he preferred women who had lesbian tendencies.

In its early stages, *The Price of Salt* had a working title of 'The Argument of Tantalus', a reference to Greek mythology. Tantalus, the son of Pelops and Niobe, was punished for his sins in a variety of ways, all of which Highsmith took to symbolise the agonising position occupied by homosexuals in society; today, the word 'tantalise' bears the etymological root of his name. In Hades, Tantalus, desperately hungry and thirsty, was placed near a group of fruit trees, and next to a pool of water. But every time he tried to pick the fruit, the wind would sweep the branches aside, and as he was about to wet his lips, the pool would recede and drain away. Another account has Tantalus sitting before a lavish banquet, knowing that if he were to touch even a morsel of food, a huge stone suspended above his head would crash down and kill him.

In the same way, homosexuals, as she saw it, were in a no win situation – they needed the love of a member of their own sex to survive, both physically and emotionally. But as soon as they sought this out, they were victimised by society and left fearful of their own desires, unable to conquer their repressed wishes. 'Those were the days,' Highsmith wrote in an afterword to the novel when it was reissued as *Carol* five years before her death, 'when gay bars were a dark door somewhere in Manhattan, where people wanting to go to a certain bar got off the subway a station before or after the convenient one, lest they be suspected of being homosexual.'[11]

Highsmith's initial idea was to end the novel on an unhappy, tragic note, with Therese and Carol going their separate ways; after all, this was true to her own experience, as none of her relationships had been, so far at least, particularly long-term. It was her agent, Margot Johnson, who in October 1950, after seeing an alternative, more positive ending that Highsmith had written, persuaded her client to choose the more optimistic version. 'Shall show MJ both versions,' Highsmith said, 'and am sure she will prefer the "lift" ending in which T & C go back together.'[12]

The choice of the more optimistic denouement – the final scene has Therese walking towards Carol – is, perhaps, even more surprising considering the climate of fear that existed in America at the time. The Republican senator Joseph McCarthy took advantage of the paranoia that was sweeping post-war America to conduct a 'witch-hunt' that initially targeted communists, the so-called 'enemy within'. Tapping into an envy of the intellectual classes, McCarthy, who attacked communists as young men 'who are born with silver spoons in their mouths', articulated these ideological societal tensions as a simple war between good and evil, with capitalism and moral certainty clearly on the right side. Political undesirables would have to be culled, he maintained; otherwise civilisation, as the American people knew it, would come to an end. He was so successful at whipping up mass hysteria that, after persecuting communists, he widened his field to include homosexuals. 'Perhaps as dangerous as the actual communists are the sexual perverts who have infiltrated our government in recent years,' Republican National Chairman George Gabrielson wrote in 1950 in an official report.[13]

Homosexuals, said McCarthy, posed a security risk and as such the Senate had every right to dismiss them from government. This was merely a cover for a wider suspicion of lesbians and gay men. Homosexuality, according to a Senate sub-committee report, was considered, 'so contrary to the normal accepted standards of social behavior that persons who engage in such activity are looked upon as outcasts by society in general'.[14] By April of 1950, ninety-one homosexuals had been sacked from the State Department alone, while gays who worked in any public sector position also felt at risk. McCarthy's virulent attack on nonconformity lasted until 1954, when he was eventually censured by the Senate. He died three years later, but his influence was widespread. The very existence of homosexuality caused mass moral panic, with magazines declaring it a threat to the nation's mental and physical health, linking it to murder, crime and drug addiction, while so-called respectable journals such as *Human Events*, whose target audience was made up of professional and business leaders, claimed that gay men and lesbians should be hunted down. 'By the very nature of their vice they belong to a sinister, mysterious and efficient International [conspiracy].'[15]

Highsmith was acutely conscious of the the apocalyptic visions that haunted early 1950s America. In *The Price of Salt*, there are references to bomb shelters, while at one point Therese asks an acquaintance, a physicist, whether he intends to work on the atom bomb. In fact the whole novel could be interpreted as as a critique of McCarthyism. Therese escapes the soul-destroying conformity of the prison-like department store and her stifling relationship with Richard to pursue her dreams of freedom, both personal and sexual, with Carol. But as the two women drive across America they are spied upon and pursued by a private detective, hired by Carol's husband, and clearly a symbol of the sinister Senator. To Therese, it seemed as though the detective gained a sadistic pleasure from the possibility of separating them.

> She had seen just now what she had only sensed before, that the whole world was ready to be their enemy, and suddenly what she and Carol had together seemed no longer love or anything happy but a monster between them, with each of them caught in a fist.[16]

Just as McCarthy and his aides resorted to underhand measures to trap their victims, so the detective bugs the women's hotel room in

Waterloo and the tape is then used to blackmail Carol into relinquishing Therese. 'Everything was very simple this morning – I simply surrendered,' Carol writes in a letter to her young lover before she finally decides to sacrifice her child for Therese[17]. Highsmith writes, 'It would be Carol, in a thousand cities, a thousand houses, in foreign lands where they would go together, in heaven and in hell.'[18]

It may seem tame by today's standards, but the idea that a novel could end with two women settling down together was in fact extraordinarily radical. 'Prior to this book,' Highsmith wrote in her 1990 afterword, 'homosexuals male and female in American novels had had to pay for their deviation by cutting their wrists, drowning themselves in a swimming pool, or by switching to heterosexuality (so it was stated), or by collapsing – alone and miserable and shunned – into a depression equal to hell.'[19]

Lesbian pulp novels, often written for heterosexual men as a form of soft-porn fantasy, were popular from the beginning of the 1950s. But the balance that existed between the expression of sexual freedom and establishment conformity was a fine one. For example, Tereska Torres' bestselling *Women's Barracks*, published by Fawcett under its Gold Medal imprint in 1950, and advertised on its cover as 'The Frank Autobiography of a French Girl Soldier' became the subject of a Senate investigation into pornography. So, in order to carry on releasing what was, plainly, a highly popular and profitable sub-genre, publishers imposed strict censorship rules on their authors. Lesbian pulp author Ann Bannon says 'There was some kind of retribution that was essential at the end so that you could let them have a little fun in the meantime and entertain the reader.'[20]

Marijane Meaker, who would later have a relationship with Highsmith, was a secretary at Fawcett at this time. After an editor asked her about homosexuality at boarding school and college, she wrote *Spring Fire* under the pseudonym Vin Packer, published in 1952. At the end of the novel, one lesbian converts back to heterosexuality while the other ends up in a mental institution. Meaker was told by her editor to make the ending an unhappy one, 'otherwise the post office might seize the books as obscene'.[21] 'In the end,' says Jaye Zimet, author of *Strange Sisters: The Art of Lesbian Pulp Fiction 1949–1969*, 'the lesbian gets her due . . . marriage, insanity or . . . suicide.'[22]

In August of 1950, Highsmith went to the cinema alone to see John Huston's *The Asphalt Jungle*, the adaptation of W.R. Burnett's novel about a gang of thieves who fall apart after robbing an upmarket jewellery shop. Not only did Highsmith enjoy it on a superficial level, but she was also impressed by the way it forced the viewer into identifying with a criminal perspective. As she walked up Third Avenue, her eyes looked into shadowy corners and dark alleyways seeking out the strange and the forbidden. The fictional exploration of criminal psychology, she mused, was a natural subject matter for the post-war sensibility. 'If I could but gather all the chaos of the world today and of my own soul and shape it to a story!' she said,[23] significantly locating the source of her work not only in the world around her, but also in her frighteningly anarchic emotional landscape. So tangled was High-smith's personal life that, in the winter of 1949 and throughout 1950, she noted that at times she felt like she was losing her grip on reality. She defined herself as basically 'polygamous'[24] and was con-scious of the fact that her free-form sexuality, together with her tendency to lose herself in those close to her, could easily result in a complete mental breakdown. The world that spun from the web of her imagination was manifestly more real to her than what she saw before her. It was as if, like her fiction, she inhabited a paraxial region, an area which, like one of the working titles for *Strangers on a Train*, could be said to lie at 'The Other Side of the Mirror'.

In January 1950, after a driving trip with a friend from New York to Fort Worth and back again, Pat wrote in her notebook of her fear of insanity. It wasn't as if she had a series of irrational thoughts; rather it was like 'the entire structure of one's information slipping',[25] as though the earth's fixed points, such as the North and South Pole, had suddenly swapped places. At the same time, she sketched out the plot of a story in which a woman living alone in New York hears scratches in her apartment at night. Eventually, she realises that her fear is not caused by an external monster, but something located within her, 'in some part of her life she knows not'.[26] Later, this horror would articulate itself in her disturbing tales such as 'The Empty Birdhouse' and 'The Terrors of Basket-Weaving'.

In April, just after she had written a letter to Marc, informing him that she finally wanted to break free of him – a decision which she failed to stand by – she received a note from Kathryn Cohen politely refusing any further emotional involvement. Although what the two women had experienced in Italy had been based on a deep mutual attraction, it was obvious from the tone of the letter that she thought they had no future together. The irony was almost too much to bear, as Marc must have received her letter the same day as she opened the one from Kathryn. 'Thus we both get it in the neck the same day.'[27]

Bruised by the latest rejection, Highsmith retreated into her imagination and lost herself in the fictional world of Therese and Carol. She compared the process of writing the novel to documenting her own birth and although she found the process agonising, she predicted that, once completed, it would be her finest book, an opinion shared by her mentor Ethel Sturtevant, to whom she showed one chapter. Sturtevant read the first half of a page, looked up at her former pupil and exclaimed, ' "But this is love!" ' Pat, still somewhat ashamed of admitting the true nature of Therese and Carol's relationship, tried to convince her it was nothing more than a misplaced yearning for the maternal, but Sturtevant was having none of it. ' "That's a sexual awakening," ' she countered. ' "It's fascinating." '[28]

Highsmith's identification was total and, like Therese, she found herself falling for Carol. 'I live so completely with them now,' she said, 'I do not even think I can contemplate an amour (I am in love with Carol, too).'[29] Reality and imagination were now dangerously close and, in June, the melancholy of the past few months was replaced by a state resembling mania. She felt deliriously happy, due in part to the feelings of ecstasy she experienced when she dreamt of Carol. 'I want to be faithful to her,' she said.[30] Sinus problems forced her to see a doctor who diagnosed her condition as nervous strain, she was prescribed sedatives and after a dramatic falling-out with Rosalind Constable – in which the older woman accused her of being eccentric, lazy and promiscuous, nothing but 'a bum' – she was left feeling vulnerable and shaken.

Having taken her own experiences and transferred them into art, Highsmith now found herself behaving like a character in one of her books. On 30 June, she took the train out to Ridgewood, New Jersey, to spy on Kathleen Senn. 'Today, feeling quite odd – like a murderer in a novel, I boarded the train for Ridgewood, New Jersey,' she wrote in her diary.[31] On returning to New York, Highsmith wrote a poem for the stranger, detailing the love she felt for her, love which she compared to a faint, but permanent stain on her heart.[32]

Although she fantasised about placing her hands on the woman's throat, and squeezing until she was as still and cold as a statue, she was motivated not by hate, but love. It was essential she found someone to give her love to; if there was no one near, she would seek out a woman who could play the role. It didn't matter that her feelings were not reciprocated, as 'The gesture is the thing! The thought, the privilege of that dedication!'[33]

*   *   *

'To all the Virginias', reads the dedication in *Strangers on a Train*, which was published on 15 March 1950. Although Marc Brandel had played a crucial role in fashioning the novel, prompting her to rewrite the final chapter and even providing her with its title, Highsmith chose not to grace the first page of the book with his name. Instead, she decided to dedicate it to the women she had loved, her first girlfriend, Virginia, and Virginia Kent Catherwood.

Two days after publication, Highsmith hosted a party, attended by friends such as Kingsley, Rosalind Constable, her editor, Joan Kahn, and a smattering of journalists. Djuna Barnes was due to attend, but called Highsmith to say that she couldn't make it as she had sprained her back. Later, Highsmith recalled her thoughts on seeing her first novel in print. 'I remember opening the carton [of books] on the floor in my apartment in New York, and my first thought was, "These are taking up a lot of space in the world." There it was – a sort of cube – and it was funny that that should have occurred to me. I didn't feel particularly proud . . . but I thought, "these take up space".'[34] She could still remember the sense of embarrassment she felt years later, as she told Ronald Blythe in 1971. 'I thought, "How have I got the nerve to stick my neck out like this, to assume I can entertain the public, to assume I'm a writer – like Dickens or – or Graham Greene?"'[35]

Yet the reviews of the book were positive. 'There is a warning on the jacket that this book will make you think twice before you speak to a stranger on a train,' wrote an unbylined writer in *The New Yorker*. 'This is unquestionably the understatement of the year . . . A horrifying picture of an oddly engaging young man, who has all the complexes you ever heard of. Highly recommended.'[36] The *New York Herald Tribune Book Review* said that the novel was, 'one of this year's most sinister items. It has its obvious faults. It is not always credible, and the characters are not entirely convincing. Nevertheless, it is a highly persuasive book . . . as one reads it page by page throughout a full-length novel, one is held by an evil kind of suspense. It becomes more believable than one would suppose – a rarely perceptible study in criminal psychology.'[37]

Within a few days of its publication, *Strangers on a Train* attracted interest from film-makers keen to turn the novel into a movie. On 22 March, her agent turned down an offer of $4,000, before finally accepting one of $6,000 (for rights in perpetuity) plus an additional fee of $1,500 for any work on the script. The successful bidder was Alfred Hitchcock, who only revealed his identity after Margot Johnson had finalised the deal – on 17 May he wrote to the publicity director at

Harper & Brothers, Ramona Herdman, thanking her for sending him the novel and telling her that he was using it as the basis for his next movie.[38] (In 1961, Hitchcock would buy the television rights to Highsmith's novel *This Sweet Sickness* for transmission in November of the following year – 'Of course Hitchcock has all the rights now, and until "perpetuity",' she wrote in a letter to her French publisher Robert Calmann-Lévy in 1967.[39]) Although Highsmith would later vent her anger at the amount of money Hitchcock had paid for *Strangers on a Train*, she also acknowledged, 'That wasn't a bad price for a first book. I was working like a fool to earn a living and pay for my apartment.'[40] In September, while Highsmith was holidaying with Ann Clark in Provincetown, Hitchcock telegraphed her, requesting her presence on the set, but the writer refused in spite of the fee he promised. 'I was surprised because I felt Pat had such a drive for money at that time,' says Ann.[41] Yet Highsmith obviously felt enormously proud of the fact that she had sold her first novel to the director as, according to the writer Brian Glanville, who met her in Florence in 1952, 'She carried with her the letter from Alfred Hitchcock telling her, in little more than a couple of lines, that he had decided to make her book *Strangers on a Train* his next film.'[42]

Adapting Highsmith's novel for the screen proved to be a troublesome experience for Hitchcock, who in July enlisted the services of Raymond Chandler at $2,500 a week. 'I'm still slaving away for Warner Brothers on this Hitchcock thing . . .' Chandler wrote to Bernice Baumgarten on 13 September. 'Some days I think it is fun and other days I think it is damn foolishness. The money looks good, but as a matter of fact it isn't.'[43] Chandler completed the script on 26 September, but after sending it off to Hitchcock, via his agent, the writer received a curt telegram telling him he had been sacked. The director subsequently appointed Czenzi Ormonde to rewrite it. 'The great difficulty of the story always was to make it credible to an audience that Guy should behave in the damn-fool way in which he did behave,' wrote Chandler in a letter to Hitchcock, which he never sent,[44] concluding that the film had, 'No guts. No characters. No dialogue.'[45] 'A Hitchcock picture has to be all Hitchcock,' he wrote to his literary agent. 'A script which shows any sign of a positive style must be obliterated or changed until it is quite innocuous.'[46]

In an introduction to a book about Chandler, Highsmith wrote of her admiration for the creator of Philip Marlowe and the difficulties he encountered while adapting her novel for the screen. 'A book of mine called *Strangers on a Train* gave Chandler fits during his Hollywood scriptwriting period, and from his grave Chandler has given me tit for tat,' Highsmith said in 1977. 'It is difficult to sum up Raymond Chandler . . . Chandler wrote in a letter, "I suppose all writers are crazy, but if they are any good, I believe they have a terrible honesty." That sounds indeed like a writer, not funking the job, honest according to his own lights, and willing to work his heart out – maybe in two senses of the phrase.'[47]

The movie opened in America in July 1951, but as Highsmith was in Europe, she didn't see it until October. She was initially quite pleased with it, especially Robert Walker's portrayal of Bruno, but later voiced her disapproval at the way Hitchcock drained the work of its power to shock – in the film, Guy, played by Farley Granger, now a professional tennis player instead of an architect, fails to carry out his murder – and the casting of Ruth Roman as Ann, Guy's love interest. 'I thought it was ludicrous,' said Highsmith. 'It's even more ludicrous that he's [Guy's] aspiring to be a politician, and that he's supposed to be in love with that stone angel.'[48]

After months of procrastination, Highsmith's relationship with Marc Brandel finally broke down in the fall of 1950. In November, she opened Brandel's new novel, *The Choice*, and read the standard abrogation at the beginning of the book. 'None of the characters portrayed in this book is intended as a reflection on any actual person.' From the briefest of perusals, it was obvious that this was not so, as Highsmith herself recognised. 'I am Jill Hillside & there down to the last detail . . .'[49]

Superficially Brandel's book is a thriller – it concerns the strange case of Nat Mason, a roach exterminator who steals women's underwear and sends poison pen letters – but really this is just an excuse for Brandel to explore his unhappy love affair with Highsmith. The book centres on the relationship between Ned Marlowe, a freelance comic book artist, his girlfriend, Jill, and her lesbian lover, Ann Dawson, and as such is a fictionalised account of the triangular situation that existed between Brandel, Highsmith and Ann Smith. Jill is a slender girl with dark hair, a woman with square and strong-looking hands, fragile thighs and small, childish breasts. Ned loves her but feels that she is distant towards him, especially during lovemaking. Sometimes in the middle of kissing her, she asks questions like, ' "What date's Wednesday?" ', or she reminds herself to pick up some toothpaste the next morning. 'Oh, God, if he could only just once *reach* her, he thought,' Brandel wrote.[50]

When Ned realises the truth about the Jill and Ann, he is shocked and disgusted, and likens the discovery to that of a having a bandage removed: 'You had known all along how bad it was, the doctors had told you, but you hadn't believed it until you saw the stump.'[51] The homosexual world sickens him, he thinks it seethes with jealousy, transitoriness and hysteria while he describes gay bars as 'freak-show places,'[52] and Ned does everything he can to fight for his lover. One day he meets Ann, who tells him Jill regards him as nothing more than an ugly brute. But after a rather ridiculous climax, in which the roach exterminator is exposed and subsequently kills himself, there is the vague suggestion that Ned and Jill may get back together, something that was by now an impossibility for Brandel and Highsmith.

In October 1950 Highsmith started to have doubts whether her novel about the love between Carol and Therese should be published at all. She had, after the publication of *Strangers on a Train*, been labelled as a mystery writer; the last thing in the world she wanted was to be known as a lesbian novelist. Agent and writer compromised, however, when, Margot Johnson suggested she publish it under a pseudonym. Highsmith also worried about what eighty-four-year-old Willie Mae would think. 'Pat said she wanted to use another name because she didn't want to upset her grandmother,' recalls Ann.[53]

The pseudonym, Claire Morgan, was decided upon in January 1951 and was Ann's idea – her mother's cousin was married to Rex Morgan, an architect, while Claire was a friend of her mother's.[54] This was, as Highsmith wrote in her diary, a 'temporary, partial relief from shame'.[55]

Although Highsmith had written an upbeat ending for her lesbian novel – which was accepted for publication by Harper & Brothers in January 1951 – the greatest irony of all, she said, was that in life she had only ever experienced frustration and rejection. 'Oh, I write a book with a happy ending, but what happens when I find the right person?' she asked.[56] Finding a woman who could act as lover and muse was essential for her survival. Without such a woman, 'I cannot even develop as a writer any farther, or sometimes, even exist'.[57] She planned another trip to Europe – *Strangers on a Train* was due to be published in Britain in February 1951 by Cresset Press and in France by Calmann-Lévy early the following year – but when she returned she wanted to live with a woman whom she loved. Surely this wasn't too much to ask?

Before she left, she decided to make one last trip to see Kathleen Senn.

On 21 January, she travelled out to Ridgewood, New Jersey, to spy on the woman who had inspired her lesbian novel for the last time. Closing her eyes, she forced herself to submit the image of the house, with its fairy-tale-style towers, to memory. As she did so, she thought back to their meeting in the toy department and how that moment had changed the course of her life.

When *The Price of Salt* was published in May 1952 it was described by the *New York Times Book Review* as being written 'with sincerity and good taste'. The same reviewer, however, also remarked how the book 'in spite of its high-voltage subject – is of decidedly low voltage . . . Therese herself remains a tenuous characterization, and the other personages are not much more than silhouettes.'[58] Yet the public disagreed with this glib dismissal and, when it was published as a Bantam 25-cent paperback in 1953 it is said to have sold over a million copies. 'The novel of a love society forbids,' ran the catchline on the front cover of the mass-market edition; below was printed the lurid image of a troubled, innocent-looking girl, her shoulder being caressed by an older, more sophisticated woman, while in the background lurked the figure of an alarmed young man. The response from gay men and women around America was nothing less than phenomenal. Highsmith received between ten and fifteen letters twice a week for months on end.

'The letters were very touching and revealed just how terribly repressed gay women were in small-town America, what with the Bible and the idea of Sin,' says Ann Clark. 'I remember particularly a letter from a woman in a small town, saying that until she read the book she thought she was the only woman in the entire world who had had such a strong feeling for another woman.'[59]

Kathleen Senn, however, never had the chance to read the book she had unknowingly inspired. On 30 October 1951, she walked into her garage, closed the doors and switched on the engine of her car. Highsmith never knew what became of her real-life Carol or that she had ended her life.

14

Two identities: the victim and the murderer

1951–1953

Slightly hungover, Highsmith boarded a plane from New York to Paris, arriving at Orly airport early on 5 February 1951. She would stay in Europe for the next two years, flitting between London, Paris, Venice, Florence, Rome, Salzburg and Munich. Like her character Tom Ripley, whom she would create three years later, she had no permanent address and was forced to pick up her mail from American Express offices. She was, she noted, always, ' "care of Mrs Somebody" . . . I have never a home.'[1] Europe, she told Kingsley, helped her in many ways: she found it easier to make friends than in America; she liked the people, whom she thought more serious and considered than the folk back home; the change in environment gave her a fresh perspective on life and stimulated her creative imagination and, on a practical note, the day-to-day expenses she incurred were less than in the States. Although individual items such as tissues were more expensive, 'to have an elegant good time, with beautiful surroundings, is cheap,' she wrote to her friend.[2]

After a few days in Paris, where she enjoyed cocktails with Janet Flanner – 'Genet', *The New Yorker*'s Paris correspondent – and her partner, the book publisher, Natalia Danesi Murray, Highsmith boarded a flight to London on 16 February. At Northolt the writer was met by reporters, who interviewed her in the rain about her new novel, *Strangers on a Train*. 'Miss Highsmith is a modest, serious person,' observed the *Evening News*, 'and today she was dressed in a black suit, grey sweater and flat-heeled shoes.'[3]

Highsmith took a taxi from the airport to 64 Old Church Street,

Chelsea. Kathryn Cohen, she thought, looked thinner and less radiant; although she gave her guest a warm welcome, Pat knew that they would never be able to resume their once passionate relationship. Highsmith went to bed, but couldn't sleep and during the night had an idea for her next book, which she would call, initially, 'The Sleepless Night'. Its plot would be 'wild . . . involving much sex and violent action would naturally evolve'[4] and would centre on a young man, who allowed his wife to become the mistress of his friend. The next day, she developed a 103-degree fever – just as she had when she contracted chickenpox and *The Price of Salt* was born – which turned into bronchitis and she had to spend three days in bed.

The idea for the novel, in itself, was not new; the central theme had haunted her thoughts for months. The previous November she had sketched the bare bones of a story about a husband who stands by while his wife sleeps with another man, noting that the cuckold could be used as a symbol for the pain of life itself. 'We are all waiting in passive anger, resignation, or bewilderment, while the dearest thing we possess goes a-whoring: that is, the meaning of life, whose face we have even long ago forgotten, and never ever knew.'[5]

Staying with Kathryn, and knowing that she was not going to leave Dennis for her, was a painful experience and as the days passed Pat began to imagine that their time together had been nothing more than a dream. She showed Kathryn her lesbian novel, but felt disappointed by what she interpreted as her indifference towards it. 'I don't think she likes it enough to recommend it to Dennis as she did the last,' Highsmith noted, feeling that she had failed her both as a person and as a writer.[6]

From London, she travelled first to Paris, then Marseille and arrived in Rome on 17 April, where the city had been taken over by crowds jostling to get a look at the visiting Princess Elizabeth and her husband, Philip. While in Rome, she received the news that *Strangers on a Train* had been nominated for the prestigious Edgar Allan Poe award in America. She acknowledged that most people in her situation would make the most of their 'tour of triumph',[7] but she felt crushed by an overwhelming sense of inadequacy. When she met Natalia Danesi Murray, who as the American representative of the Italian publishing house Mondadori kept an apartment in Rome, together with a villa in Capri, she felt shy and tongue-tied.

In the Italian capital, she visited the Keats-Shelley Memorial House, on the Piazza di Spagna, and wrote pieces about the city's 2,700th birthday, which she sent off to the Fort Worth *Star-Telegram*. With

Natalia, she travelled to Naples, from where they took a boat to Capri. Retracing the journey she had made with Kathryn was agonising; everything she did reminded her of the moments of happiness they had shared in the late summer of 1949. Back in Rome, exploring the catacombs of San Callisto, she remembered the time when she had kissed Kathryn in the shadows of the underground burial site in Siracusa. Highsmith wondered why Kathryn did not write to her, conjecturing that she must hate her, an emotion she preferred to blank indifference.

Continuing her own idiosyncratic version of the grand tour, Highsmith journeyed to Florence and Venice, which she once described as a miracle, both because of its beauty and because it still existed. In Venice, she met Peggy Guggenheim and Somerset Maugham for cocktails, but the two writers didn't talk about their work; she admired Maugham, who she said was 'short, stutters, extremely polite',[8] for his ability to make the perfect dry Martini.

While travelling she heard her first novel had failed to win the Edgar Allan Poe award – the honour went to *Nightmare in Manhattan* by Thomas Walsh – and when she arrived in Munich, she received the bad news that Harper & Brothers had, after all, rejected her lesbian novel. Apparently, the editorial board had decided that she was too close to her subject matter and that her approach was not mature enough. Yet the setbacks failed to depress her and three weeks later, on 6 July, Margot wrote to tell her that Coward-McCann had accepted the book and that they would give her $500 on delivery of the finished manuscript.

From Munich, where she was staying at the Pension Olive, on Ohmstrasse, she wrote to her mother about her recent sightseeing trips and informed her that her health had improved – she put this down to drinking more milk and eating simpler food. Privately Highsmith wondered how many times the heart could renew itself – 'I have been five or six people in thirty years,' she said[9] – and started to ponder her mortality. On 4 July – the day the Hitchcock film opened – she lay in bed, feeling old and, quite preposterously, fat. She listened to her heart beating in her chest and was forced to confront the fact that one day she would die. She recalled Natalia Murray's words in Capri that one didn't start to live until one was at least thirty years old, but nevertheless the thought of death unsettled her.

She had problems with abscesses in her mouth, which necessitated the removal of two teeth, but by August as she worked on her lesbian novel, now retitled *The Price of Salt*, and plotted 'The Sleepless Night', she felt creatively invigorated. 'I have never felt so (dangerously) alive at all pores as in these last days,' she noted.[10] 'The Sleepless Night', later called *The Traffic of Jacob's Ladder*, ran to nearly 400 pages, and was, she said, 'a very long straight novel . . . it concerned eight people instead of just one'.[11] The book was rejected by Coward-McCann in October 1952 and then subsequently by Harper & Brothers because of its 'disjointedness and mostly, I think, for the lack of conclusion to all of it,' she wrote to Kingsley. 'Some have said the triteness of the ideas.'[12] Although the manuscript was mysteriously misplaced in 1958, hidden away in one of the boxes at the Swiss Literary Archives in Berne lie the last ten pages of Highsmith's lost novel, a book described by Kingsley, who read it, as having 'nothing to do with suspense . . . It was a serious book and I thought if she went on like this she would have something'.[13]

The fragment – typewritten, on paper discoloured by age – reveals that the climax of the novel, set in Paris, focuses on the close relationship between two men, Gerald and Oscar. In typical Highsmithian fashion, the bond between the two male characters has homoerotic undertones.

> [Gerald] would recreate him forever with love and as a brother with no doubt of why, of wherefore and without judgement. And the urgency in his fingers spread up his arms, becoming a desire to embrace the stranger behind him with a love beyond brother's love, beyond friend's.[14]

In the final pages, Gerald discovers that Oscar has taken an overdose of nembutol and learns that he is the sole beneficiary of his friend's estate (an interesting parallel with the climax of *The Talented Mr Ripley*). The book ends with Gerald taking hold of his suitcase and turning away into the darkness, a solitary figure facing an uncertain future.

Despite all her physical and emotional problems, however, in August 1951 Highsmith believed her own future could not be brighter. Walking through a Munich park in the moonlight, under the weeping willows, she felt alive to every possibility and was conscious that her imagination was soaring to new heights. 'I am alive! (O this trip! Just enough sex experiences to keep my appetite whetted, never half satisfied. Perhaps it is creating better . . .'[15]

Two weeks after writing this in her notebook, Highsmith met the sociologist Ellen Hill, a woman who would shape her life for the next four years and to whom she would remain bonded, by a combination of love and loathing, until just a few years before her death. Ellen, like the lovers that came before her, would inspire some of Highsmith's most powerful novels, but in her case, the resulting fictional portraits were far from flattering.

Their relationship was a tortured one from the very beginning. 'Ellen was like a governess,' says Kingsley. 'They had a love-hate relationship.'[16] 'She was quite brilliant, very intelligent, but a little bit snobbish,' says Peggy Lewis, who knew both women.[17] 'She was one of the most unpleasant women I have ever met,' says Peter Huber, Highsmith's friend and neighbour in Tegna. 'But for some reason, even though they tormented one another, there was some sort of bond between them. I remember that Pat made her an ashtray and, enjoying the word play, inscribed it with the word "Forellen", which means "trout" in German, and decorated it with three fish. Ellen didn't like it, so Pat kept it.'[18]

Pat and Ellen met in Munich in early September 1951, via a mutual friend. Ellen, when arranging what to do on their first date together, asked Pat whether she preferred rococo to baroque castles. The couple drove to Tegernsee, the lake outside the city, where they had coffee and wine before lunch. Highsmith noted that the slight, well-groomed forty-two-year-old was 'sharp, rather humourless, very polite',[19] and she found her mildly attractive. Two days later, Ellen invited her back to her apartment on Karl Theodorstrasse where the two women listened to poetry and a music programme on the radio. Then Pat asked Ellen to come and sit by her on the sofa. Ellen's hands and body reminded her of Virginia Kent Catherwood's and it was this similarity that she responded to when they slept together. 'Ah, she is much like Ginnie,' Highsmith wrote in her diary. 'Tonight was the only wonderful sensation – blotting out everyone who's been between Ginnie and her.'[20]

Ellen told Pat that not only was she the best lover she had ever had, but better than any she had ever heard or read about. 'Ellen Hill told me that Pat was a marvellous lover,' says Kingsley.[21] But Ellen, who was fiercely intelligent, also realised Highsmith had an impulse to invest lovers with imaginary characteristics; she knew that this tendency was not concomitant to a happy relationship. The older woman provided the writer with an accurate summary of exactly what was wrong with her. 'She says, I fit the person to my wishes, find they don't fit, and proceed to break it off,' Highsmith noted. 'So she analyses my past pattern.'[22]

Unfortunately this pattern was about to repeat itself. Both women knew the risks, but neither of them was prepared to end the relationship. Pat felt herself to be passionately in love – she couldn't sleep or eat, and her waist was shrinking to almost doll-like proportions – even though, or precisely because, Ellen was so obviously bad for her. She found Ellen's lack of warmth astonishing and the snobbish attitude she showed towards her friends mortifyingly embarrassing. '"I hate the common man,"' Ellen told her,[23] a view which obviously did not alter over time. 'I often talk with a sociologist friend,' Highsmith told an interviewer in 1981, 'and her opinion is that most people are quite ordinary, that universal education hasn't brought the happiness and beauty that people had hoped.'[24]

Ellen complained that since they had met a month ago, she had never had a decent night's sleep; that Pat drank too much; she was sloppy, careless and absent-minded. If Highsmith so much as spilt a little milk, this was enough to send Ellen into paroxysms of rage. Six weeks after meeting, Pat noted that living with Ellen, whom she described as a harpy, upset her digestion. 'She loves to dominate me, I feel,' Highsmith said, 'by ordering my life to give me a sense of helplessness and dependence upon her.'[25]

At the beginning of February 1952, Ellen and Pat drove from Munich to Paris, and then to Nice, Cannes, Le Perthus, Barcelona, before sailing to Mallorca. As the trip progressed, their relations steadily worsened. Highsmith became increasingly resentful of Ellen's dog, to whom she had to give half her steak one night at dinner. This hatred of the animal caused her to analyse the source of her animosity and, perhaps pushing the psychoanalytic parallels too far, she found similarities between her feelings for the dog and her stepfather's attitude towards her and her mother when she was a little girl. In addition, Ellen, she felt, did not respect her as a writer and treated her as if she were of low intelligence. In Mallorca, they slept in separate beds and didn't even kiss one another goodnight. In March, back in Cannes-sur-Mer, where they rented a three-storey house together for a month, costing $35, Pat wrote a poem which articulated the mutual sense of loathing that, in a way, held them together. She contemplated leaving Ellen, but her feelings veered wildly between utter hatred and a sense that she would go insane without her. In April the couple took a house in Florence for a couple of months, and while Ellen looked for a suitable job, Highsmith tried to finish her novel, *The Traffic of Jacob's Ladder*. But she found work almost impossible with Ellen around, as she was constantly interrupted by her incessant nagging about domestic details. 'She could not be sabotaging it more effectively – unless she burnt the manuscript,' noted Pat.[26] They argued during the day, and made love at night – 'Ellen's last effort (always) to hang onto me.'[27] The atmosphere between them was, she said, so putrid that it threatened to poison the spring blossom on the trees.

A warm Florentine night, June 1952. Highsmith is dreaming. She is in a room with Kathryn Cohen and a naked girl who resembles herself. Highsmith is overcome by a desire to set fire to the girl and orders her to stand in the bath. She gives her a small effigy, a doll of her grandmother, and sets the girl alight. As the flames begin to dance and lick around her, Kathryn starts to cry, resting her head on her shoulder. She tells Kathryn not to forget that the girl asked them to set her on fire, it was she who wanted it. At that moment, the victim's lips begin to move and she turns her head in misery, avoiding the cruel flick of the flames. As Highsmith watches her burn, she is horrified by her own actions, but then as the girl stands up and steps out of the bath, she realises she is unharmed except for a few singes that darken and brown her skin. She feels guilty, worries that the girl will report her for this terrible crime, but then she wakes up. Musing over the dream, Highsmith has the feeling that the girl in the bathtub somehow represented herself. 'In that case,' she wrote in her journal, of this disturbingly vivid dream, 'I had two identities: the victim and the murderer.'[28]

From Florence, Pat and Ellen travelled to Positano, the fishing village on the Amalfi coast, vertiginously spread up a hillside, set by the glistening azure blue of the Mediterranean. It was here, while staying at the Albergo Miramari Hotel, that one morning, at about six o'clock, Highsmith walked out onto her balcony and saw a young man strolling along the beach – the man who would be later be born in her imagination as Tom Ripley.

'All was cool and quiet, the cliffs rose high behind me and were out of sight then, but visible to right and left . . . then I noticed a solitary young man in shorts and sandals with a towel flung over his shoulder, making his way along the beach from right to left . . . I could just see that his hair was straight and darkish. There was an air of pensiveness about him, maybe unease. And why was he alone? . . . Had he quarrelled with someone? What was on his mind? I never saw him again. I did not even write anything in my cahier about him.'[29]

She would return to this image two years later when she started to write *The Talented Mr Ripley*. During that summer of 1952, however, she started to channel her creative energies into another novel, a book based on her love-hate relationship with Ellen Hill. The basic idea was about a man who murdered by imitation. 'A model of brevity, with good humor, and tragedy in the hopelessness of his unhappy marriage,' she wrote in her diary on 4 July, 'which I shall create from the worst aspects of mine.'[30] Reading that novel – which had working titles of 'A Man Provoked' and 'A Deadly Innocence', but which was eventually published in 1954 as *The Blunderer* – at the same time as Highsmith's diaries is a chilling experience as she based Clara, the highly strung, manipulative, domineering wife of Walter Stackhouse, on Ellen Hill. Like Ellen, Clara seems more in love with her dog, Jeff, than with her partner, an affection that fosters resentment. ' "If you have fish again," ' Clara tells her husband one night in a restaurant, ' "Jeff gets *nothing* today!" '[31] Not only is she anti-drink, and anti-sex, like Ellen, but Clara hates Walter's friends. 'He was married to a neurotic, a woman who was actually insane in some directions, and moreover a neurotic that he was in love with.'[32] When Walter reads in a newspaper the case of a woman's body found in Tarrytown, New York – the wife of Melchior Kimmel, who really did commit murder – he begins to fantasise about killing Clara.

There's no doubt that the venomous emotions expressed in *The Blunderer* had their roots in real life. In the idyllic setting of the Amalfi coast, with its sparkling blue waters, paradisal views, and citrus-blossom scented breezes, the two women waged a psychological war. Again, Ellen accused Pat of interrupting her sleep and whenever the writer wanted to read, she was forced to retire to the bathroom, where she would sit on the lavatory, the door shut, sweltering in the heat. A simple purchase of a couple of bottles of gin and vermouth was enough to send Ellen crazy and she accused Pat of drinking when her back was turned. Sex between them was non-existent and Ellen behaved towards her like a sour governess might towards a rather slow-minded charge.

Like Walter, Highsmith felt a prisoner in an unhealthy relationship. Suffering from toothache and low blood pressure, she felt drained of energy and depressed. Logically she knew she should leave Ellen, but emotionally she still felt bound to her and 'a persistent fear of violent consequences prevent me from breaking off.'[33]

At the end of July, Highsmith paid a visit to W.H. Auden at his home in Forio, where she found him barefoot and tended by what she described as a young Italian pansy. 'I was prepared to talk of poetry,'

Pat wrote later to Kingsley, 'and all he spoke of was the cheaper prices of things there.'[34]

In September, after trips to Ascona and Munich, the two women moved to Paris, where Ellen was due to start her job with the Tolstoy Foundation. The change of scene, however, did not improve the relationship and on 10 September, in the middle of the night, Ellen woke Pat, and in a fury, launched herself at her younger lover with her fists. The argument raged on for an hour, centring around Ellen's determination to extract from Pat how many evenings she wanted to spend out socialising; if Pat did meet friends, she wanted to know how many times a week this would be. Ellen, now hysterical and playing the martyr, said she would be prepared to kill her dog to please her. 'How can I stand it,' Highsmith noted. 'It is worse than being married.'[35]

They moved into an apartment together at 83 Rue de l'Université, but the arguments continued and Highsmith started to think about the possibility of fleeing to Florence and living alone. 'The horrible flaw in my make-up is that I never have cared for the artistic type like myself,' she told Kingsley, 'so that sooner or later, one comes upon that shoal (to mix my metaphors) and there is a shipwreck. A fundamental incompatibility.'[36]

The situation reached crisis point when, in early November, Ellen reached across the bed in a bid to be affectionate. 'I struck at her,' Highsmith noted in her diary, 'had to, to ward her off. By Christ, I do believe she is insane.'[37] Pat refused to accompany her on a short trip to Geneva and the next morning, she awoke to find that Ellen had gone. Highsmith made up her mind to leave. She bought a plane ticket back to Florence, went out to the Le Monocle, where she danced with several girls, none of whom she found attractive, and wrote Ellen a farewell poem.

On Ellen's return from her trip to Switzerland, the two women tried to talk logically about their relationship. But, once again, Ellen broke down, threatened to commit suicide if Pat left and pleaded with her to make a date – for Christmas Eve in Venice – when they could sleep together once again. 'She said I was the first and last person she'd want to sleep with,' Pat wrote in her diary.[38] Highsmith refused. The next morning, looking worn out and miserable, Pat and Ellen parted at the Gare les Invalides. As she looked out of the aeroplane's window and saw the snow-capped Alps below, Highsmith felt suddenly liberated.

That late November, in bitterly cold Florence, Highsmith booked herself into the Pensione Bartolini. With its maze of dark corridors, bleak rooms and rather primitive plumbing system, the cheap pensione seemed a strange place for such a sophisticated young woman, according to fellow guest, the British writer and sports journalist Brian Glanville, then twenty-one. 'The Bartolini was hardly right for her, *Studentesco*, the Italians would have called it, and indeed it was full of students and painters,' he said.[39] She was, remembers Glanville, 'much fuller in the face than in the grim photographs of her declining years, high cheekboned, with a touch of what one then would have called Red Indian.'[40] The two became friends almost immediately. In the evenings they would meet at the bar of the Excelsior Hotel, where John Horne Burns, author of *The Gallery*, was slowly drinking himself to death.

'I found her very charming and she had a wonderful sense of humour,' says Glanville. 'But she never talked about her sexuality and there were no indications that she was a lesbian. But I could tell she was unhappy and quite lonely. She had little, or no confidence, and would often show me extracts of the novel which would eventually become *The Blunderer*. I thought it was clumsy and naive, quite poor, but of course I did not say so, and she subsequently scrapped this version.'[41]

After a few days alone in Florence, Pat began to yearn for Ellen. One night, at 2 a.m., unable to sleep, she phoned and told her how she felt. Highsmith could not bear to stay away from her tormentor any longer and in December, after receiving a letter from Ellen, she took a train from Florence to Geneva, where they met in a hotel. From there they travelled back to Paris, before setting out again to Basel, St Moritz, Venice and eventually Trieste, settling at 22 Via Stupavich, in January. For Highsmith, Trieste should have held a special resonance, conscious as she was of its literary history – Freud and Joyce had both lived there, the latter writing *Dubliners*, *A Portrait of an Artist as a Young Man*, *Exiles* and draft sections of *Ulysses* while in the city. 'And Trieste, ah Trieste ate I my liver!' Joyce wrote in *Finnegan's Wake*. The port city on the Adriatic, spread out on terraces, rising from the gulf up towards the Carso Hills also bristled with symbolic associations representative of fractured identity. Immediately after the Second World War, Trieste looked set to be a source of conflict between East and West – it was liberated by both Yugoslav and Anglo-American troops – until a settlement was finally reached in 1954, partitioning the land between Italy and Yugoslavia. Yet Highsmith did not warm to Trieste, finding it gloomy and depressing. Via Stupavich was, she wrote to her French agent, Jenny Bradley, of the Paris-based William A. Bradley literary agency, who had taken her on in early 1951, not a particularly pleasant-sounding street name, but the house she and Ellen shared was quite pretty and she looked forward to the summer when the bone-chilling 'bora' would cease blowing in from the east. Although she assumed she would stay in Trieste for at least a year, her time in the city was limited to a mere four months, a miserable interlude during which she came down with a bout of flu and was plagued by toothache; she often dreamed about her bad teeth and in fact thought she would be quite a different person if she had a perfect set.

No doubt her perception of the city was shaped by her life with Ellen. Their arguments were just as heated and intense as before and Ellen continued to criticise the younger woman: the drawers in the bedroom were not straight; she did not tip adequately; she left a stain on the kitchen table. The constant bullying left Pat feeling depressed and shaken. The inequality in their incomes also caused a problem and Highsmith realised that she would not win Ellen's respect unless she made some money. She tried her hand at writing a lesbian pulp novel, which she called 'Breakup', and applied for a job teaching English, which would net her $45 a week, but nothing came of either plan. By March, Highsmith was in such a low state that she declared herself a nervous wreck. She told Ellen the relationship was over. Predictably, Ellen took the news badly, breaking down in tears and, as always when Pat attempted to finish it, she tried to win her back with the promise of sex. Their life together had become impossible. Nevertheless, in April 1953, instead of splitting up, they travelled from Trieste to Genoa, then sailed to Gibraltar and toured southern Spain, before journeying by boat together to New York, arriving on 13 May. As the ship sailed by Long Island and towards Manhattan, the early morning fog cleared and the sun came out, wrapping the city in a warm glow.

Back in New York, Highsmith arranged to rent an apartment from a friend for two months for $150 a month. She was initially optimistic about her future with Ellen and wrote in her diary of how she dreamed about sharing a house with her. But the day after recording these thoughts in her diary, she saw the photographer Rolf Tietgens, the homosexual man to whom she felt strangely attracted, and after a steak supper, went to bed with him. The liaison wasn't wholly successful but the best yet, and she, at least, enjoyed it. 'In my system of morals,' she added, 'I do not feel this in the least unfaithful to Ellen.'[42]

Writing her new suspense novel left Pat feeling physically and emotionally exhausted and in June she felt gripped by a depression just as deep and as black as the one she suffered during the winter of

1948–49. In New York Ellen's jealousy reached monstrous proportions – she could not understand why Pat didn't want to spend every evening with her. During one argument about a party – Highsmith wanted to go along, Ellen, as usual, forbade her – Ellen became so angry she ripped her lover's shirt from her back. On 1 July, Highsmith decided she had finally had enough. She decided they would have to separate, once and for all. Ellen became hysterical and, after downing a couple of Martinis, knocking them back like water, she threatened to take an overdose of veronal. 'I love you very much,' said Ellen, sitting naked on the bed as she swallowed eight pills. Highsmith, sickened by the sight of her, left the apartment, called on Kingsley and her husband, Lars, before going to have a supper of hamburgers with a friend. She arrived back at home at two in the morning to find Ellen in a coma. On the typewriter, Ellen's suicide note read, 'I should have done this 20 years ago. This is no reflection on you . . .' Coffee and cold towels were no good so Pat had to call a doctor, who tried to pump Ellen's stomach. Still Ellen was unconscious, so she was forced to call the police and then Bellevue, the psychiatric hospital.

The next day, however, Ellen showed no sign of coming out of the coma. The doctor at Bellevue gave Ellen a fifty-fifty chance of survival, but rather than hang around her bedside, Pat took her lover's car and drove up to Fire Island with a friend for the Independence Day holiday weekend. 'I am escaping from hell,' she wrote.[43] She sunbathed on the beach at Cherry Grove, posed for some pictures, and forced herself to work, 'believing Ellen is dead at this point'.[44] In the evening, after drinking heavily, she picked a fight with a bunch of girls who turned on her and beat her up.

Ellen had half-heartedly tried to commit suicide before – in June 1952, after reading Highsmith's diary – but it was this second, more serious, attempt that Highsmith used as a basis for the incident she describes in *The Blunderer*. Clara, the neurotic wife, threatens to take an overdose of veronal, but Walter, her husband, ignores her and, like Highsmith, deliberately leaves the house so as to let her kill herself. 'Walter could not escape the fact,' Highsmith wrote in the novel, 'that he had known she was going to take the pills.'[45] Walter wonders whether his actions could be considered to be a kind of murder, and, in a way, Highsmith's ruthless decision to leave Ellen, knowing she was going to swallow those pills, could be seen in the same light. 'The suicide & Ellen's character in the book,' Highsmith wrote in her diary, 'I find very disturbing & too personal.'[46]

After the weekend in Fire Island, she returned to Manhattan and found that Ellen had survived. At the hospital, Pat held the older woman in her arms for nearly an hour; Ellen wanted her back, it was obvious, but Highsmith was undecided. 'I am very unhappy – because of sheer indecision . . .' she wrote. 'So I drink.'[47]

15

Pat H, alias Ripley

1953–1955

'My personal maladies and malaises are only those of my own generation and of my time, heightened,' Highsmith wrote in her notebook in September 1950.[1] Highsmith's absence from America had sharpened her powers of perception and on her return in 1953, she viewed the country from an outsider's perspective, shocked at the mood of paranoia which was sweeping the USA. The Korean War, which rumbled on between 1950 and 1953, a battle between the communist North, backed by China, and the non-communist South, supported by America, symbolised the ideological battle which was raging in the United States. By the time a settlement had been reached – in July 1953 – over five million people had died, but to the vast majority of Americans who were convinced that sending troops to a far-flung land actually helped guard their security and protected themselves from communist aggression, it was a worthwhile sacrifice. President Eisenhower, inaugurated in 1953, even discussed the use of atomic weapons in order to try and settle the conflict.

Highsmith was dismayed by the news of the imminent execution of Julius and Ethel Rosenberg, the Jewish couple accused of stealing the secrets of the atomic bomb, and she worried about America's global reputation, one which was looking increasingly soiled. McCarthy's continuing communist witchhunt was reaching near-hysteric levels – a phenomenon exposed in Arthur Miller's 1953 play *The Crucible* – and in the same year librarians were ordered to remove books by 'Communists, fellow travelers, and the like'. 'The whole nation is protesting, some for humanitarian reasons, some because it would endanger our international prestige,' Highsmith noted in her diary about the Rosenberg electrocution at Sing-Sing prison, New York. 'Though how it could sink much lower with the present book burning of the Amerika Hauser I don't see. D Hammett's *Thin Man*, Howard Fast, Langston Hughes, were among those which were removed from libraries.'[2]

The Eisenhower years, post-Korean War, have been mythologised as an era of peace and prosperity, the 'bountiful new world'[3] of *I Love Lucy*, bobby sox, cashmere-cardiganed preppies, drive-in movies, barbecues and convenience living. Between 1950 and 1958 the economy expanded with an annual growth rate of 4.7 per cent and living standards increased. It was the age of the baby boom – in 1940 the population of America was 130 million, by the mid-1950s the figure had risen to 165 million. The suburbs, which to many crystallised the essence of the fifties, expanded and consumers embarked on a frenzied spending spree. Yet the new uniformity of living was also symptomatic of the hollowness of the American dream. Columnist William Shannon observed that, 'The Eisenhower years have been years of flabbiness and self-satisfaction and gross materialism', while Norman Mailer dismissed the fifties as 'one of the worst decades in the history of man.'[4]

In 1950, the social scientist and lawyer David Riesman published *The Lonely Crowd*, a controversial book that triggered a national debate into the changing nature of the American psyche, and a work which Highsmith read. Riesman, whose books analysed the place of the individual in a modern, increasingly media-driven society, believed that there were three types of man: the 'tradition-directed', those in pre-industrial communities, who inherited their values from their predecessors; the 'inner-directed', formed in the nineteenth-century capitalist boom, who relied on their consciences to shape their behaviour; and the 'other-directed', people living in a mass society like modern America, men and women whose beliefs were shaped by their peers or from the media. As Riesman saw it, man had moved from the inner to the other-directed and, as a result, had made a transition from industry and achievement to conformity and adjustment. What is common to all other-directed people, wrote Riesman, is that 'their contemporaries are the source of direction for the individual – either those known to him or those with whom he is indirectly acquainted, through friends and through the mass media.'[5]

The problem was Americans were suffering from oversocialisation. 'For centuries moralists had warned that people become unhappy when they get what they want – or think they want,' writes historian John Patrick Diggins of the fifties. 'Suburbia offered Americans the cleanliness and safety of a planned community, but nothing is more hopeless than planned happiness.'⁶

Highsmith's novel *The Blunderer* explores just such an identity crisis, a hollowness situated at the heart of the American everyman. The novel takes as its central character Walter Stackhouse, a typical other-directed man. To the outside world, thirty-year-old Walter seems to have it all – a successful and highly paid wife, Clara, who is an estate agent, a house in Long Island given to his wife by her mother, a good job as a lawyer in Manhattan and an enviable lifestyle. Yet Walter feels alienated. 'There were times, standing with a second highball in his hand on somebody's lawn in Benedict,' Highsmith wrote, 'when Walter asked himself what he was doing there among those pleasant, smugly well-to-do and essentially boring people, what he was doing with his whole life.'⁷ His marriage was unhappy, married as he was to a pleasure-denying woman with 'acid in her voice',⁸ and his job at the large law firm in New York left him unstimulated. Walter dreams of setting up a law practice of his own in the West Forties, dealing with minor cases rejected by other offices, and he is highly conscious of the fact that he feels frustrated with the banality of his life. 'At thirty, Walter had concluded that dissatisfaction was normal. He supposed life for most people was a falling slightly short of one ideal after another.'⁹ In his spare time, Walter compiles a list of 'unworthy friendships', an analysis of the unequal relationships that existed between various pairs of men, a dynamic which Highsmith returned to again and again in her work. Most people, Walter believed, struck up a friendship with at least one person who was inferior to them, 'because of certain needs and deficiencies that were either mirrored or complemented by the inferior friend.'¹⁰

Ironically, Walter himself is drawn into just such a relationship with Melchior Kimmel, whom he reads about in a newspaper under the headline, 'WOMAN FOUND NEAR TARRYTOWN, N.Y.' The story relates how Kimmel's wife, Helen, has been found stabbed and beaten at the bottom of a cliff, a case which Walter cannot get out of his mind. As his own relationship with Clara degenerates, he starts to imagine the details of the case, visualising the body in a clump of trees, with a long bloody gash running down its face. Like many of Highsmith's heroes, Walter's fantasy, his fictional recreation of the murder, his psychological rehearsal of the killing, is responsible for trapping him. Although he doesn't murder Clara – she throws herself off a cliff, in circumstances which echo the Kimmel case – Walter's obsession with Melchior brings about his downfall. By the end of the book, Walter, like one of

Riesman's lonely crowd, has been stripped of his individuality. ' "You became a living cipher," Walter thought . . . Did a cipher have the capacity to love?'[11] At the climax – as Kimmel stalks Stackhouse through Central Park – Walter is conscious of thinking of nothing, his identity reduced to a vacuum. There is, ultimately, only one logical conclusion – death. Kimmel jumps on him, brandishing a knife, and stabs him in the face – Walter hears the blade scrape across his teeth – and then in the throat. As the blood flows out of him, Walter loses the will to live. The scene, in which external events are juxtaposed against fragments of an imploding consciousness, is a masterly denouement to an utterly compelling novel.

By 26 August, Highsmith had written 100 pages of the novel which would become *The Blunderer*. However, she wrote the bulk of the book – which at this time she called 'The Man on the Queue' or 'A Deadly Innocence' – in Fort Worth, where she lived from the end of September 1953 until early January 1954. During this time she stayed first at the Coates Hotel, the apartment hotel owned by her uncle, Claude, and then at the house of her cousin, Millie Alford, on Ash Park Drive. The novel, she thought, was much more complex and sophisticated than *Strangers on a Train*, and consequently, a lot more difficult to write. However, her main motive was to make it a good read. 'I only hope it is entertaining,' she wrote to Kingsley, 'as that is the prime purpose.'[12]

In an interview she gave to the local paper in Fort Worth, Highsmith said that the secret of her success was 'plenty of quiet and afternoon beer'[13] and named her favourite American writers as Robert Penn Warren and William Faulkner. She wrote in a white heat – 'writing,' she said, 'is no good for the health'[14] – purging herself of the emotions she associated with her unhappy relationship with Ellen, which had finally broken down in September. She was afraid that Ellen, who left New York for Europe, might try and commit suicide once again and the parallels between real life and the events she described in her novel continued to disturb her. 'Perhaps life will outrace me yet. Just as it did about the sleeping pill episode, which is also in the book. Rather uncanny,' she wrote to Kingsley.[15]

She felt deeply depressed – trivial incidents were enough to leave her feeling crushed and on the verge of tears – although she realised that, on the surface, she had little to feel melancholy about. This was, she surmised, because of 'an obvious form of masochism'[16] and, in order to get through the day, she needed constant bolstering from friends and lovers. She found the people down in Texas too 'surface-dwelling' and, in order to concentrate on her book, often pretended to go to bed early so she could be alone.

She finished the first draft of the novel in early November and on 9 November, decided on the title, *The Blunderer*. 'C'est plus qu'un crime,' she noted, describing Walter's actions in the novel, 'c'est une faute. (It's more than just a crime, it's a mistake (in the moral sense). Walter really is a Blunderer.'[17] She reworked and retyped the novel until she had written what she thought was a satisfactory ending, and she enclosed the final page in a letter she wrote to Kingsley on Christmas Eve.

When not writing, she spent time with her family, went riding with her old friend Florence Brillhart, sketched, watched television (which she did not particularly care for), travelled into Dallas for lunch, played golf and frequently got drunk with her cousin, Millie, with whom she became particularly close. She had, since her Barnard days, been a heavy drinker, but by now her alcohol consumption – Martinis, gin, rye, Bourbon, wine – was becoming dangerously high and she continued to overdo it when she arrived back in New York, in early January 1954. On her first day back in the city she went to bed at four in the afternoon, with a bottle of gin, and then, while out at dinner with Ann Smith, went on to drink seven Martinis and two glasses of wine.

'Last year nothing made sense,' she said of 1953, 'My attitude was, "Have another drink" . . . I spent my money like a drunken sailor.'[18] One of the most galling aspects of all this was the fact that she was aware of her actions and as such, she concluded, if she ran up huge debts she had nobody else to blame but herself. Highsmith's tendency towards degeneracy – her excessive drinking, her sexual buccaneering – was tempered by her instinct to punish herself for her pleasures. 'It does not matter that I have worked pretty hard, harder than many people, even,' she wrote. 'I have been imprudent, irreverent, false to myself, in fact'.[19]

When *The Blunderer* was published in September 1954 – its dedication simply read, 'For L.', a reference to Highsmith's latest muse. After Ellen – or rather during the dying days of their relationship – Highsmith embarked on another relationship with the aspiring actress, Lynn Roth, an ex-girlfriend of Ann Smith's. Lynn was twenty-eight, slim, blonde, almost pixie-like. Such was the power that Lynn held over her that, twenty-five years later, Highsmith made a list of her characteristics and qualities, a description prompted by her love for another woman who reminded her of Lynn – the twenty-five-year-old actress and costume designer Tabea Blumenschein. She went on to compare the two women, noting down that she admired the girls' artistic temperaments, their free spirits. Paraphrasing Proust, she said that fundamentally, when it came down to it, one's 'type' did not change. 'This is why one can say one is "always" in love with such a person, that the emotions do not change,' she wrote.[20]

Highsmith started dating Lynn in July 1953 – two weeks after Ellen's suicide bid – and although the two women lived together, briefly, at Lynn's apartment in Greenwich Village, by the spring of 1954 their affair had collapsed. Once again, Highsmith was forced to question why she had chosen yet another woman who was bad for her. The loss of Lynn Roth left her feeling disturbed to such an extent that she questioned her sanity. 'I am becoming a little odd, personally,' she said.[21] She also recorded in her notebook the fact that she had been told manic depression was one of the few types of mental illness which was 'innate' and as a result 'nearly impossible to cure'.[22] In order to prove that her mental state was, after all, still intact, she set herself a test: she sat in front of the radio and listened to the news, noting whether she could follow the broadcast. Of course, such an experiment was no real marker of sanity, but Highsmith needed something to boost her low spirits and she was pleased when she decided that she had 'passed'.

She had an infected tooth, her possessions were scattered across the country and her lover had just left her, but nevertheless there was something inside her – which she described as a strength – which kept her going. The breakdown of her relationship with Lynn Roth did give her a spiritual setback and she looked at the collapse of that affair as being symbolic of all past liaisons, 'which have and always will be beset with disappointment'.[23] Instead of wallowing in self-pity, however, Highsmith started to flesh out the plot of a book which would become one of her most powerful and celebrated novels. Early titles included, 'Pursuit of Evil,' 'The Thrill Boys', and 'Business is my Pleasure,' before she eventually settled on *The Talented Mr Ripley*.

The Talented Mr Ripley, the first of Highsmith's five Ripley novels, was written at speed in 1954, taking only six months. 'It felt like Ripley was writing it,' she said later, 'it just came out.'[24] Highsmith's novel centres on Thomas Ripley, an insecure young American enlisted by the rich father of an acquaintance to travel to Italy and bring back his estranged son, Dickie Greenleaf. Tom falls in love with Dickie's lifestyle (and a little with Dickie himself), but when he realises that he will never, ultimately, be able to be one with him, Ripley kills him and assumes his identity.

The story is a dark reworking of Henry James' *The Ambassadors*, which she read in 1940, and which she thought was rather overwritten and overlong. In case the reader is left in any doubt about the parallels between the two novels, Highsmith alludes to *The Ambassadors* – in which Lambert Strether is sent by Mrs Newsome to find her son, Chad, in Paris and return him back to his home in America – twice. The first mention is when an amused Herbert Greenleaf asks Tom whether he has read a particular work by James. The second is when Ripley requests a copy of the book in the library on board the liner taking him from America to Europe.

The central theme of *The Talented Mr Ripley* – the flux-like nature of identity and the difference between appearance and reality – was one which had, as we know, concerned Highsmith from an early age. 'Pretences when begun early enough become true character . . .' she wrote in 1949. 'And the curious truth in human nature, that falsity becomes truth finally.'[25] She also suffered the agonies of desiring the unattainable and realised that such a subject was perfect for fictional exploration. 'Frustration as a theme. One person, in love with another whom he cannot attain or be with,' she noted, again in 1949.[26]

She started plotting the novel at the end of March 1954, just before the split with Lynn Roth, when she jotted down some initial thoughts about the central character, a young American man living in Europe. The portrait she sketched out, although significantly different from the Ripley of the finished book, bears traces of both the amoral but charming psychopath and his victim, and love object, Dickie Greenleaf. At this point she imagined her hero to be an amateur painter, half homosexual, with an adequate private income, who found himself caught up in a smuggling plot. As the story progressed, she envisioned him discovering that he had a talent for – and took a pleasure in – killing, and, as a result, he is used by a gang to carry out their dirty work. 'Like Bruno, he must never be quite queer – merely capable of playing the part if need be to get information to help himself out of an emergency . . .' she wrote. 'His name should be Clifford, or David, or Matthew.'[27]

Highsmith thought back to the young man she had seen in Positano in 1952, the isolated figure strolling down the beach at six in the morning. She focused on this image, split it in two in her imagination like a scientist dividing a cell under a microscope, and came up with another of her powerful male–male dynamics to create the characters of Richard – or Dickie – Greenleaf and Thomas Ripley.

'Or Richard Greenleaf – the boy on the beach at Positano,' she mused. 'Tom . . . is the other, a perpetually frightened looking, vaguely handsome young man who has at the same time the most ordinary, forgettable face in the world.'[28]

One of Highsmith's early plot scenarios for the book had Dickie's father travelling to Positano, where the two young men murder him by pushing him off a cliff. Then Ripley lures Dickie to the same spot and watches him fall, believing him to be dead. But Dickie survives, returns to the house, and talks Ripley into taking part in a smuggling operation. Another possibility was to have Tom involved in smuggling from the start. Mr Greenleaf turns up at the house in Positano, orders Tom to leave, and Tom in revenge kills the father, whose body is then, quite ludicrously, used to transport opium.

The idea, like so much of Highsmith's fiction, had a root in her own life. She started writing the novel while living in a rented cottage near Lenox, Massachusetts, which she had rented for the summer of 1954. Her landlord was an undertaker and she became fascinated by the minute details of his job, particularly the tree-shaped incisions he made in corpses before he opened them up and the material he used to stuff the bodies (sawdust was his secret).

'I was toying with the idea of having Ripley engaged in a smuggling operation . . . during which Ripley would escort a corpse that was actually filled with opium,' she said later. 'This was certainly a wrong tack, and I never wrote it that way.'[29]

Thankfully Highsmith relegated this *grand guignol* plot to a comic episode in the final version, transforming it into Tom's suggestion that he and Dickie travel in coffins, accompanying a real corpse stuffed with drugs from Trieste to Paris and used the incident to symbolise the souring of the relationship between the two men. Ripley takes Dickie's dismissal of this idea as a personal rejection, an indicator of their essential difference, and as such it becomes a motivating factor which leads directly to the murder.

> They didn't know each other. It struck Tom like a horrible truth, true for all time, true for the people he had known in the past and for those he would know in the future: each had stood and would stand before him, and he would know time and time again that he would never know them . . .[30]

The central premise of the book – one man losing his identity as easily as a snake sheds its skin – also had a real-life inspiration. On 16 April 1954, Highsmith picked up a copy of the *Herald Tribune* and read the headline: MAN 'BURIED' AS FIRE VICTIM SEIZED AS MURDER SUSPECT. The story concerned Albert Paglino, of St Louis, who was presumed dead after the discovery of a charred body, which police took to be his. The man, however, was spotted drinking after his 'funeral' and he was arrested. Highsmith cut the piece from the newspaper and pasted it into her notebook, where it helped feed her imagination.

'I did not turn loose of my main idea,' she said, 'which was of two young men with a certain resemblance – not much – one of whom kills the other and assumes his identity. This was the crux of the story.'[31]

She started the book in what she described as a 'bucolic' mood. Certainly her life was more relaxed after the emotional turmoil of the last few years. In Lenox, she went to the local library, read de Tocqueville's *Democracy in America* and flicked through an Italian grammar, but she found this somewhat serene attitude out of kilter with her frantic subject matter. After writing seventy-five pages she decided her prose was too flaccid. She scrapped the lot, made a mental and physical effort to sit on the edge of her chair, and started again.

'It became a popular book because of its frenetic prose,' she said, 'and the insolence and audacity of Ripley himself. By thinking myself inside the skin of such a character, my own prose became more self-assured than it logically should have been. It became entertaining.'[32]

It was, however, not difficult for her to think like Tom Ripley. Not only had the character had a long gestation, but the timbre and tone of his voice were remarkably similar to Highsmith's own, as she later recognised. After the publication, in Britain, of her second Ripley novel, *Ripley Under Ground*, in 1971, she gave a copy of the book to her friend, Charles Latimer, with the dedication, 'For Charles with love – April 2 – '71 from Tom (Pat).'[33]

'After Pat's death, John Mortimer wrote a tribute, saying he thought she was in love with Mr Ripley,' says Charles Latimer, 'but actually she *was* Ripley, or, I should say, she would have liked to have been him.'[34]

When she spoke of Ripley in her later years, 'she would talk about him like he was a person who was very close to her,' says Bettina Berch. 'She'd defend him and think about what he would say about a certain situation. He was very real to her.'[35] At the end of a letter to her friend, the photographer Barbara Ker-Seymer, Highsmith signed herself 'Pat H., alias Ripley.'[36]

The painter Peter Thomson, now living in New York, remembers how in Positano, in 1963, he was coming off the beach after an all-night party when Highsmith, at the time a resident of the fishing village, walked up to him and said, 'You remind me of Tom Ripley.' 'It was,' recalls Thomson, 'as if she was talking about somebody she knew.'[37]

Knew him she did, for Ripley was an embodiment of her creative imagination at work, a representation of her unconscious and a shadowy symbol of her repressed, forbidden, and occasionally quite violent, desires. 'EVIL' she wrote, in capital letters, next to the heading 'Subject', at the beginning of her twenty-third cahier, the one she used as a notebook for *The Talented Mr Ripley*. She had been fascinated by the allure of evil as a subject matter for fiction ever since she started to keep her notebooks and in 1942, she observed that she felt herself strongly drawn it. While plotting the novel, in October 1954, she noted, 'What I predicted I would once do, I am doing already in this very book (Tom Ripley), that is, showing the unequivocal triumph of evil over good, and rejoicing in it. I shall make my readers rejoice in it, too. Thus the subconscious always proceeds the consciousness, or reality, as in dreams.'[38]

Ripley is not an author by profession, but there is a suggestion – in the first novel of the series at least – that, with his uncanny mimetic skills and his dynamic creative imagination, writing could be the greatest of his talents. After all, what else is fiction but an elaborate confidence trick? 'His stories were good,' Highsmith writes about Ripley, 'because he imagined them so intensely, so intensely that he came to believe them.'[39]

Early in the novel, while Ripley is sailing to Europe – first class courtesy of the Greenleafs – he sits down to write what is, at first, a polite thank-you note for providing him with such comfortable accommodation. But his imagination takes over and the letter turns into a fantastical account of life with Dickie, whom in fact he has not yet met, in the village of Mongibello (the name is a knowing reference to Mount Etna, as described by Dante in Canto XIV of *The Inferno*). After detailing the fishing, the swimming, and the cafés, Ripley writes about how Dickie is not really romantically interested in Marge, together with a complete character analysis of her character, 'until the table was covered with sheets of paper'.[40]

Ripley's chameleon-like personality – his ability to take over the identity of those around him, so essential in a writer – also expresses itself after he sees Dickie kissing Marge. In disgust, he pretends to be Dickie – he even goes so far as to step into a complete outfit of his clothes – and acts out a grotesque *tableau vivant* where he, still as Dickie, takes hold of Marge and strangles her. ' "Marge, you must understand that I don't *love* you," Tom said into the mirror in Dickie's voice . . .'[41]

His decision to kill the man he loves comes when he realises that he cannot take over Dickie's identity. And after the murder – he bludgeons Dickie about the head with an oar in a boat off the coast of San Remo – Ripley's talent for fictionality, for constant self-reinvention, comes into its own, with a series of elaborate twists and turns, disguises and fantasies. Like an author immersed in the world of his own creation, Tom loses whatever identity he ever had. 'It was a good idea,' Highsmith writes of Ripley, 'to practice jumping into his own character again, because the time might come when he would need to in a matter of seconds, and it was strangely easy to forget the exact timbre of Tom Ripley's voice.'[42]

With an ear attuned to the rhythms and codas of his main character's speech patterns, Ripley retypes a letter, written as Dickie, to Mr and Mrs Greenleaf, because there are too many commas in it, while after a few weeks living under the assumed identity of his dead friend, he finds it easier to write as if he were Dickie rather than himself. 'The dull yards of Dickie's prose came out more fluently now than Tom's own letters ever had.'[43]

When Ripley is forced to step back into his own self in the final chapter, he is, like a novelist who has fallen in love with his protagonist, utterly miserable. After all, being oneself again was so boring after the excitement and drama of pretending to be another. 'He hated becoming Thomas Ripley again, hated being nobody . . . He hated going back to himself as he would have hated putting on a shabby suit of clothes, a grease-spotted, unpressed suit of clothes that had not been very good even when it was new.'[44]

Ripley, with the reader's active encouragement, gets away with two murders and, at the end of the book, instead of being caught or punished, he is let off scot-free, his last words being, '*Il meglio albergo. Il meglio, il meglio!*' ('The best hotel! The best, the best!') Not only is the novel a radical celebration of amorality, but Ripley can also be seen as a metaphor for Highsmith's creative, and quite transgressive, imagination at work.

She herself realised the parallels between psychopaths and writers. 'In regard to future writing about the so-called psychopath,' she noted in 1949, 'writing is only living pared away somewhat, and made more definite. The psychopath of a book is an average man living more clearly than the world permits him.'[45]

She had experienced at first hand many of Ripley's characteristics – splintered identity, insecurity, inferiority, obsession with an object of adoration, and the violence that springs from repression. Like her young anti-hero, she knew that in order to survive, it was necessary to prop oneself up with a psychological fantasy of one's own making. 'Happiness, for me, is a matter of imagination,' she wrote in her notebook while writing *The Talented Mr Ripley*. 'Existence is a matter of unconscious elimination of negative and pessimistic thinking. I mean, to survive at all. And this applies to everyone. We are all suicides under the skin, and under the surface of our lives.'[46]

In September 1954, Highsmith moved from the rented house in Massachusetts to New Mexico, settling in Santa Fe, 'and I began writing the very next day,' she said later. 'It was one of those things. I didn't care whether my suitcase was quite unpacked.'[47]

Her companion was Ellen Hill, who had recently returned to America. From 1954 until 1962, Highsmith stopped keeping a diary because Ellen Hill had started to read it, so it is difficult to know exactly when and why she resumed her friendship with the older woman, but in a letter to a friend, Alex Szogyi, Pat revealed that her relationship with Ellen lasted four years in all. They spent two years in Europe together, 1951 and 1952, and two years in America, 1954 and 1955. 'I spent about four years of my life with her (Ellen) and her lugubrious influence carried over much longer,' she wrote.[48]

For all the problems of the past, Pat still admired Ellen for her intellect and the two women often had the most stimulating conversations. 'It was her challenging mind, often irritating, her point not always justified, that inspired the conversations generally,' she wrote in her journal.[49]

At the end of December, the couple, with Ellen's French poodle, drove from Santa Fe to the border town of El Paso and down through Mexico, stopping in Hidalgo del Parral, awaking to see the mountains covered in snow. If Highsmith thought that her relationship with Ellen would improve second time around, she was mistaken. Their mutual friend Peggy Lewis remembers a fraught three weeks when she went to stay with the couple in Mexico.

'They had arguments that were incredibly boring to listen to,' she says. 'They rowed about whether this person should come to dinner or that one. They took different sides about the people they liked and whether they were worth cultivating. I got the impression that Ellen went into a relationship for all the wrong reasons, because she thought it might benefit her one way or another. She would, I suppose, use people.'[50]

*   *   *

When Highsmith had finished *The Talented Mr Ripley* she sent a copy of the manuscript to her beloved grandmother, Willie Mae, in Fort Worth, because she was afraid the old woman might die before its publication late in 1955. On 5 February 1955, the eighty-eight-year-old woman collapsed, just outside the house in which Highsmith had been born.

'She was outside working in her flower garden – she had flowers everywhere, it was a real pretty garden, complete with a fish pond – and she had an aneurysm,' says Dan Coates. 'She dropped dead right there, which was perfect because she didn't linger or suffer and she was active until the very end. We'd kid her and say, "Grandma you've only got two more years to go and you'll be ninety," and she said, "Oh no, I've only got twelve to go and I'll be a hundred."'[51]

Pat would have been particularly upset by her grandmother's death. 'I remember – she adored her grandmother,' says Kingsley. 'She said her heart turned over when she saw a pair of her grandmother's slippers because they had taken the shape of her foot.'[52]

The copy of the manuscript of the novel was lost in the weeks following Willie Mae's death, an accident Highsmith blamed on her mother. 'Unfortunately, my mother lost the manuscript,' she said later. 'Inexcusable. Inexcusable. I said to my mother, "How could this happen?" and she said, "Well, the negroes were sorting it out," and I said, "The negroes were sorting out the . . . What are you *talking* about?"'[53]

Good reviews greeted *The Talented Mr Ripley* when it was published in December 1955. *The New Yorker* found the novel's hero was 'one of the most repellent and fascinating characters' of modern times, adding, tellingly, that Ripley 'kills one young man, for whom he feels a strong homosexual attachment, to get his money, and then murders another with whom he is hardly acquainted at all, on the ground that he may know too much'.[54] Highsmith, the anonymous reviewer concluded, told 'this remarkably immoral story very engagingly indeed'.[55] Connoisseur of detective fiction, Anthony Boucher, praised Highsmith for her 'unusual insight into a particular type of criminal'. He described Ripley as a 'three-dimensional portrait of what a criminal psychologist would call a "congenital psychopathic inferior"', and thought that the novel was a 'more solid essay in the creation and analysis of character' than *Strangers on a Train* and *The Blunderer*. It was 'skilful', he added, but perhaps 'somewhat overlong'.[56]

The novel went on to win numerous awards, including the Edgar

Allan Poe Scroll presented in April 1956 by the Mystery Writers of America. A few years later, when the certificate became mildewed, Highsmith removed the glass to clean it, but before she hung it back on her bathroom wall, she scribbed in the words, 'Mr Ripley and' before her own name. She thought that he deserved the honour as much as her. And, in a way, he did. 'I often had the feeling Ripley was writing it and I was merely typing,' she said.[57]

16

Each Man is in His Spectres power

1955–1958

Whenever Highsmith became weary of herself and her environment, she escaped into a rich, if slightly perverse, imaginative world. There she would create an alternative landscape inhabited by strange, irrational characters that represented various aspects of herself. Such was her state of mind in early 1955 when she started to think about her next novel. She found the process of fashioning a narrative satisfying. 'My story can move fast, as I can't, it can have a reasonable and perhaps perfect solution, as mine can't,' she said. 'A solution that is somehow satisfying, as my personal solution never can be.'[1]

She initially called her new novel, 'The Dog in the Manger' and although the book was eventually published, in 1957, as *Deep Water*, a title she originally recorded in her journal in 1950, the central theme – the vicious animosity between a husband, Vic, and his wife, Melinda – remained the same from the outset. Conveying an atmosphere of hatred was essential, she said, as she would focus on the 'sniping, griping, ambushing,' that can exist between people who are supposed to love one another, locked together in a 'ballet of the wearing of the nerves'.[2]

Highsmith herself had experienced such a dance and, travelling with Ellen Hill to Acapulco at the end of April, she found herself repeating the same excruciatingly painful, but familiar, steps. She stayed in Acapulco for about a month, before moving on, still with Ellen, to Ajijic and Taxco in June, and then to Oaxaca and east Mexico a month later. She did not keep a diary of hate, like the one she penned as she crossed Europe and America with Ellen – she knew the older woman would, no doubt, be tempted to read it – but it's clear from the entries in her notebooks that the experience was a sour one. Ellen continually complained about the noise of Pat's typewriter[3] and it was plain that whatever kept them together could no longer be classified as love. Pat likened living with someone she did not love to wearing a pair of spectacles fitted with lenses which skewed one's vision of the world. 'An unbearable fate for an artist!', she said.[4]

Just as she had drawn on their poisonous relationship to paint a picture of marital conflict in *The Blunderer*, so she looked to her own stifled emotional responses to create the character of Vic, a man driven mad by repression. 'The moral of the story,' she said of *Deep Water*, is how 'repressed emotions can become schizophrenic.'[5] She stole Vic's physical appearance directly from Ellen; like her he had 'thick, crisp brown eyebrows that stood out over innocent blue eyes,' with a middle-sized 'mouth . . . firm, and usually drawn down at the right corner with a lopsided determination or with humour, depending on how one cared to take it'[6] and his blue eyes, 'wide, intelligent, and unsurprisable', gave no clue 'as to what he was thinking or feeling'.[7]

Vic has not had sex since his wife, Melinda, started having affairs with other men three years before. However, he refuses to feel jealous of her extra-marital activities and sublimates his feelings in his work, as head of a small, and exclusive, publishing company, and in his hobbies – snail-breeding (one of Highsmith's favourite pastimes). To his friends in the affluent suburb of Little Wesley, outside of New York, Vic appears to embody success and sophistication. But beneath his mask of respectability lurk very different emotions which represent the darker side of the American dream.

'I want to explore the diseases produced by sexual repression,' wrote Highsmith in her notebook, as she plotted out the novel. 'From this unnatural abstinence evil things arise, like peculiar vermin in a stagnant well: fantasies and hatreds, and the accursed tendency to attribute evil motivations to charitable and friendly acts.'[8]

Like so many of her heroes, Vic is trapped by a fantasy. He deliberately starts a false rumour saying he has killed one of Melinda's lovers, McRae, but the idea of murder soon becomes a reality, a reality which appears like a dream – 'like something he had imagined rather than done'.[9] He is incapable of perceiving the magnitude of his violent acts and, as a result, feels no guilt. He waits for the terror to creep across him, darkening his conscience, but instead all he experiences is a bland memory from childhood of when he won a prize in geography for making a model Eskimo village out of eggshells and spun glass. The act of murder frees him from his repression and after drowning a man in a swimming pool at a party, Vic feels remarkably liberated. The char-

acterisation certainly impressed Anthony Boucher who, writing in the
New York Times Book Review, called the book 'a full-fleshed novel of
pity and irony'.[10]

Ironically, the crimes also make Vic feel vastly superior to the
common man and in the last paragraph of the novel, he believes himself
to be an 'überman', a Nietzschean superhero whose intellectual skills
single him out from the crowd. Unlike Ripley, with whom he shares
quite a few characteristics, Vic is caught at the end of the novel.
Significantly the man who brings about his downfall, Don Wilson,
is a writer of detective novels, and the final paragraph of *Deep Water*
can be read as a self-referential statement about Highsmith's transgressive methods, a measure of just how disruptive her anti-heroes were to
the genre of crime fiction.

Vic has been brought to justice by a crime writer – a man working in
a fictional form which was famous, pre-Highsmith, for restoring order
and bolstering up morality – but he is resistant to the neat narrative
closure imposed upon him. He cocks a knowing snook to the well-worn
ending of the traditional suspense story and curses the mediocrity of
conventional morality. Murder, he believes, has made him a great man.
Like an eagle, he is capable of flying over the mass of little birds without
wings.

The novel does make a moral point of sorts. Surely, Highsmith
believes, modern society must share some of the blame for the dead-
ening of an individual's soul, together with the topsy-turvy morality
promulgated by the media that persuades us to regard murderers as
heroes. Vic's six-year-old daughter, Beatrice, or Trixie, is the typical
product of post-war society: 'in that little blonde head was no moral
standard whatsoever, at least not about a matter as big as murder,'
Highsmith writes.[11] Although she wouldn't dream of stealing so much
as a piece of chalk from school, murder was something else. 'She saw it
or heard of it in the comic books every day, saw it on television at
Janey's house, and it was something exciting and even heroic when the
good cowboys did it in Westerns.'[12]

Highsmith is so skilful at immersing the reader in the abnormal
psychology of her anti-heroes, it's easy to forget that she was also a
political writer. *Deep Water* contains references, albeit subtle ones, to
the Cold War, H-bomb shelters and the paranoia surrounding communism. As Vic says, ' "If the Americans go over to the Reds, they call
them 'turncoats'. If the Reds come over to us, they're 'freedom-loving'.
Just depends from what side you're talking." '[13]

Academic Russell Harrison believes that Highsmith's use of these oblique references reflects the suppressive politics of Fifties' America. 'Because this displacement mimics the displacement the Cold War effected in American life . . . it is more profound and harder to see,' he writes. 'As sex is everywhere in Highsmith's novels, though not necessarily treated directly, so the political is similarly pervasive, if even more invisible. Although her novels from the late 1960s on dealt more directly with social and political change in the United States, the earlier novels were products of (the suppression of) politics that constituted Cold-War America.'[14]

Towards the end of 1955 Highsmith and Ellen Hill parted, this time for good. Although they would remain friends, of sorts, until a few years before Highsmith's death, their intimate relationship was now over. Pat moved back to New York, to her small apartment on East 56th Street, where she finished the first draft of *Deep Water*. In mid-December she analysed, yet again, why her relationship with Ellen was doomed to fail. It was, she concluded, because they were both fundamentally pessimistic. From now on she would, she added, only ever ally herself with women with more sunny dispositions.

As the new year began, she felt completely paralysed, incapable of reading or picking up the phone. 'I can feel my grip loosening on my self,' she wrote. 'It is like strength failing in the hand that holds me above an abyss.'[15] She wished there were a more awful-sounding word for what she was feeling than simply 'depression'. She wanted to die, she said, but then realised that the best course of action would be to endure the wretchedness until it passed. Her wish was, 'Not to die, but not to exist, simply, until this is over'.[16]

In the midst of her depression, she had an idea about the gaseous after-effects of a bomb, which had the power to wipe out the memories of an entire population – the resulting story, 'Blackout', was apparently thrown away in December 1974. The hellishness of the city was a theme which obviously concerned her at this time, and in February 1956, she thought of another story which expressed the malaise. The story was inspired, she said, by an incident several months previously when Highsmith had walked into her first floor apartment to find a group of five or six boys hunched over her desk. She had left one of the windows open and the boys had, it seemed, entered via the fire escape. When they saw her they rushed out, but they had daubed a suitcase with paint which then had to be removed with turpentine. Months later she was reminded of the experience when, sitting at her desk, she heard the sound of shouting coming from the fire escape, and, automatically, retreated into the corner of her room like a frightened rat.

'I do not understand people who like to make noise; consequently I fear them, and since I fear them, I hate them,' she said. 'It is a vicious emotional cycle.'[17] The experience inspired 'The Barbarians', a story anthologised in her collection, *Eleven*, about a man, Stanley Hubbell, who enjoys painting on Sundays, but whose hobby is interrupted by the noise of a group of baseball players below his flat. Highsmith purged herself of the hatred she felt for the boys outside her own apartment by having Stanley take hold of a large stone and drop it on to one of the rowdy men's heads.[18] But the reader is left with the unsettling question: who is the greater barbarian?

As spring warmed the city, Highsmith's spirits received a well-needed boost by the start of a new relationship with a thirty-four-year-old female copywriter who cannot be named. By May of 1956, Highsmith had started dedicating poems to her and then in June, after a trial period of living together in New York, they moved to the countryside. With them came a new chrome and black Ford convertible, a boxer dog and a pair of Siamese cats. Highsmith kept her East 56th Street apartment for the summer, but vacated it at the beginning of September.

Their house, a converted barn in four acres of land, was situated in Sneden's Landing, Palisades, an hour's drive from Manhattan. Domestic life, it seems, was idyllic; each night Highsmith set her alarm for seven in the morning, her girlfriend drove into the city to work, while she spent the summer finishing off the still untitled *Deep Water*. 'The trust in the eyes of a girl who loves you,' she said. 'It is the most beautiful thing in the world.'[19]

Yet only four months after the start of their relationship, Highsmith was already feeling uncomfortable with the situation. It was, she said, too easy, too comfortable, too safe for her. 'The danger of living with somebody, for me, is the danger of living without one's normal diet of passion,' she noted at the end of July.[20] Life with Ellen Hill had been full of passion, she recalled, precisely because the older woman's behaviour made her so angry and resentful she could not fail to feel stimulated. Her new lover, however, was simply too nice. A new piece of furniture, an extra pet, or an amazingly sophisticated labour-saving device could not satisfy Pat's spiritual and emotional cravings. Perhaps the fault lay with her subject matter; writing about hatred, sexual repression, murder and violence left little room for the expression of love, 'and it is necessary for me to express love,' she said. 'I can do this only in dreaming, it seems.'[21]

A friend suggested therapy, but after her experience with Eva Klein, she felt reluctant to rush back on to the psychotherapists' couch. The best solution, she reasoned, was to express herself through her writing and drawing. 'And when all's said and done, the final comment will be (from me at least) so what? I'll live with my neuroses. I'll try to develop patience, with my handicapped personality. But I prefer to live with my neuroses and try to make the best of them.'[22]

In June 1956, Highsmith started to make notes for what would become her sixth novel, *A Game for the Living*. It would, she said, focus on two men, dark-haired Ramon and the more Germanic-looking Theodore, both in love with the same woman. In addition to the genre-driven quality of suspense appropriate to such a book, Highsmith wanted the novel to explore deeper, philosophical issues, particularly existentialism. While working on the book, she read Kierkegaard, transcribing into her notebook one of her favourite quotations; which she would use at the beginning of the published novel. 'Faith has taken all chances into account . . . if you are willing to understand that you *must* love, then is your love eternally secure.' Next to this, Highsmith wrote in her notebook, 'This illustrates the appeal of Kierkegaard for the neurotic of our time.'[23]

But Highsmith's attempts to fuse the whodunnit form with philosophical inquiry were not wholly successful. Whereas in her previous novels, she had skillfully managed to convey her ideas through character dynamics and subtle narrative patterns, in *A Game for the Living* the themes are signposted in such a self-conscious way that the result seems forced. 'He believed the world had no meaning,' Highsmith writes of Theodore in the novel, 'no end but nothingness, and that man's achievements were all finally perishable – cosmic jokes, like man himself.'[24]

The setting for the book was inspired by a two-month-long trip she made to Mexico with her copywriter girlfriend at the beginning of 1957, stopping in Mexico City, Veracruz, and Acapulco. Sitting on the terrace of her hotel in Acapulco, Highsmith opened her artist's pad and sketched the breathtaking view that stretched itself out around her. Clearly, the process of transforming what she saw into art gave her a sense of order – it helped her to assimilate what she perceived and to make sense of her emotional life.

'Order in my life,' she wrote in her notebook on 20 February. 'It has to be an internal order, of course. To make a sketch of a view from my Acapulco terrace conquers the muddled scene in front of me . . . The veil comes between me and the person I am supposed to love, also. This

I do not like but cannot help. It will be so with any individual with whom I am in love or with whom I live.'[25]

While in Acapulco she analysed herself using Riesmanian terminology; since 1951 she had, she said, moved from a state of being what she called 'inner-directed' – defined by the fact that she was ambitious, idealistic and self-driven – to a person who was more 'other-directed'. This had manifested itself by a certain carelessness with money, the abandonment of her daily exercise regime, laziness, an over-tolerance of mediocrity and 'a general lowering of sights in my themes'.[26]

Arriving back in Sneden's Landing in March – the same month 'A Perfect Alibi', the first of her many stories for *Ellery Queen's Mystery Magazine*, was published – Highsmith started work on *A Game for the Living*. But two months later, after writing fifty-eight pages, she remained dissatisfied with what she had produced. She did not see the character of Theodore fully and thought she had made him too comic a figure, while Ramon's emotional history was still unclear. 'Don't know where I'm going,' she said, 'resulting in static effect.'[27] Reading Kierkegaard, however, helped crystallise Ramon's motivation and by 27 July, as she told her editor Joan Kahn, she had written 285 pages and was within twelve pages of finishing.

'To me it is a "different" book, I mean for me, but may be considered the same old stuff by reviewers . . .' she wrote. 'I am prepared for a rejection, having imagined all this in the weeks past. I do think I can pull it off, which I wasn't sure of at first.'[28]

Her agent, however, thought otherwise, labelling the book a 'crashing bore . . . without suspense and with too much talk'.[29] After reading through the novel again, Highsmith agreed with her assessment and immediately started the arduous task of rewriting. As she did so, perhaps she followed the tips she set down in her notebook at the end of September for an article which would eventually be published in *The Writer* magazine and then reworked for her 1966 non-fiction book, *Plotting and Writing Suspense Fiction*.

Privacy. An expensive thing in the modern world . . . Take yourself seriously. Set a routine. Once you are alone, relax and behave as you will . . . While you are writing a book, you must carry around your own stage full of characters with their emotional changes – you have no room for another stage.[30]

The same month she read Colin Wilson's influential study of literary and artistic alienation, *The Outsider*. The subject matter of the book –

an examination of the works of writers and artists including Blake, Kafka, Dostoevsky, Kierkegaard, Nietzsche – had always intrigued her both on a personal and intellectual level. 'The enigma of consciousness, of self, of destiny,' she wrote, 'which has fascinated me, specifically since I was seventeen, when I asked myself no longer why but how I was different from other people. The book stirs my mind to the murky depths (emotional depths) in which I lived my adolescence like van Gogh and T.E. Lawrence trying to "gain control" by fasting, exercise, routines for doing everything.'[31]

The book, published in 1956, analysed the links between the outsider figure and creativity, drawing on an enormous range of literary and artistic references to flesh out the characteristics of the twentieth-century everyman, a figure who has all the attributes of a Highsmithian anti-hero. The outsider, concludes Wilson, sees 'too deep and too much'[32] (quoting from Henri Barbusse's novel *L'Enfer*); feels as if he 'had died already and am now living a posthumous existence'[33] (Keats, in a letter to Browne just before his death); finds his identity fracturing into splinters, observing how he is 'dividing into parts'[34] (T.E. Lawrence, *The Seven Pillars of Wisdom*); and is plagued by a deep sense of nausea – 'The nausea is not inside me; I feel it *out there*, in the wall, in the suspenders; everywhere around me. It makes itself one with the café; I am the one who is within it.'[35] (Jean-Paul Sartre, *The Diary of Antoine Roquentin*.) The emotional anaemia, indifference to life and the horror that one might be controlled by a hidden aspect of the self, complete the outsider's profile. It could be argued that each of High-smith's novels explores the theme, articulated by Blake and quoted by Wilson in *The Outsider*, that 'Each Man is in His Spectres power'.[36] The phrase captures the Jungian archetype of the shadow. 'The shadow,' wrote Jung, 'personifies everything that the subject refuses to acknowledge about himself and yet is always thrusting itself upon him directly or indirectly – for instance, inferior traits of character and other incompatible tendencies.'[37]

Now that Highsmith was, to some degree, in control of her life – she was in a settled, and seemingly happy, relationship – it is ironic that the writer produced work which could be said to rank as the weakest of her oeuvre. In November she started writing what she envisaged as a 'political satire, in the manner of Voltaire',[38] entitled 'The Straightfor-ward Lie'. The completed, but wisely unpublished novel, focuses on the experiences of George Stephanost, a twenty-one-year-old engineering student who is chosen by his country as an informal representative on a trip around the world. While the theme of this picaresque novel is the cultural specificity of morality – and in particular a critique of American values – Highsmith's satirical touch is so heavy that she leaches the tale of humour. Halfway through the novel, a four-foot-tall figure appears to George and tells him that he can read his mind and that the student has evil, selfish thoughts. Prompted by his encounter with this dwarf-like creature, on his return home George informs the government officials of the shocking sights he has witnessed around the world. 'Truth is evil, evil is truth,' he concludes, inverting the Keatsian phrase. 'There is some good, but it is hard to find. If anybody doubts this, he should make a trip around the world . . . Now repeat after me our creed. Truth is evil –'[39] The government, however, doesn't take kindly to their fledgling diplomat's discoveries and the novel ends with George being confined to an asylum.

Although 'The Straightforward Lie' never found a publisher, she did, at least, manage to put the title to good use, selecting it as the name of the book Theodore is due to illustrate for his writer friend, Kurt Zwingli, in *A Game for the Living*. In that novel, Theodore describes the book in his journal as, 'A satire of modern life. A young man who never existed – like those in the exercises of old-fashioned grammar books who stay at *pensions* in London in order to learn the language . . . travels around the world today and finds everybody dubious about the good and value of everything, cynical and pessimistic.'[40]

Highsmith herself realised that her powers were not at their peak. Perhaps, she asked herself, this was because of her comfortable relationship with her new girlfriend? The situation was only compounded when, in November, she was reminded of what she was capable of when the news arrived that she had won the Grand Prix de Littérature Policière for *The Talented Mr Ripley*. Three days into the new year of 1958, Highsmith opened her notebook and tried to analyse just what had gone wrong. She looked back upon her old self – what she called her 'adolescent-adult status quo' – when she spent a greater proportion of time alone, and acknowledged that the swing between elation and depression produced some of her best writing.

> If my new book, *A Game for the Living* is well received, my mind will
> be set at rest insofar as worldly opinion goes, but not so far as my
> own mind goes . . .
>   My present house is not big enough for two people, especially if
> one is a writer . . . The interesting thing is why I endure it. Is it not a
> further and more serious dissipation under the guise of the bourgeois,

the healthy, conventional, comfortable and orderly? It is no guise to me. I have always consciously hated it.

Perhaps what it comes down to is that I have had about enough, perhaps spoilt my last book effort. I am trying to save myself! Like Gide, I can exist, and of course grow, only by change, a challenge to which I have to make an adjustment, an upsetting, of course, which in the end is beneficial, though in the course of it I may lose an eye or a leg. What proffiteth it a man, however, tranquility and orderliness, if thereby he lose his soul?[41]

On 14 February, Highsmith received the news she had been half expecting – Joan Kahn's five-page analysis of exactly why *A Game for the Living* was so flawed. Having Salvador, a boy from the streets, as the murderer of Leila, was just not convincing, she said. 'The boy gets two lines on page seventy-one – and is not mentioned again until page 202 . . .' Kahn wrote. 'The strength of the suspense novel, and the strength of any novel, is that the author does not introduce personalities and incidents, however interesting, that have no particular bearing on the particular book the author is writing . . . as is obvious from all the above, I hope you will consider changing the ending.'[42]

After suffering what she described to Joan as a 'brief attack of nervous indigestion'[43] prompted by the letter, Highsmith replotted the novel, finishing another draft by the middle of March. Kahn agreed that Pat had improved the ending, but, as the stern taskmaster she so clearly was, she requested further work on the book, including the addition of more detailed character descriptions within the first few pages. In September 1958, in an attempt to garner some publicity for the novel, Joan Kahn sent off the galleys to a number of influential figures, including Alfred Hitchcock, Katherine Anne Porter and the celebrated mystery novelist Dorothy B. Hughes, author of *In a Lonely Place*. On 9 November, Hughes wrote back apologising for her late response and her inability to supply Kahn with a pithy quote, confessing her dislike for Highsmith's novels, 'and I particularly did not like what (to me) was her lack of empathy to the Mexican nationals in this, although her scene was a good one'.[44] Kahn admitted that Highsmith wasn't 'everyone's meat'.[45]

Later, Highsmith came to regard *A Game for the Living*, published in November 1958, as one of her worst novels. 'The murderer is off-scene, mostly,' she said, 'so the book became a "mystery who-dunnit," in a way – definitely not my forte.'[46] She concluded that the book, which she said was 'the only really dull book I have written',[47] lacked the elements which she thought were vital in her novels – 'surprise, speed of action, the stretching of the reader's credulity, and above all that intimacy with the murderer himself . . . The result was mediocrity.'[48]

As a form of light relief from the intensity of novel-writing, Pat turned to her sketchpad, first knocking off a couple of drawings which she thought might suit *The New Yorker* – unfortunately she found the literary journal so intimidating she failed to do anything with them. Then she concentrated her artistic efforts on a children's book, *Miranda the Panda is on the Veranda*, written with her friend Doris Sanders. Highsmith would do the illustrations, while Doris would provide the captions such as, 'A tinkling bell on a gazelle'. 'Some myrtle on a turtle', 'A monk and a skunk and some junk on an elephant's trunk', and 'A veil on a snail'. The book was accepted for publication by Coward-McCann and published later in the year.

As Highsmith worked on the children's book, her relationship with her girlfriend started to deteriorate. Highsmith found the atmosphere of the house in Sneden's Landing claustrophobic and in June she wrote in her notebook of how much she dreaded not so much the rows but the resulting reconciliations. 'Give me fantasies any day! Fantasies of making love to an attractive friend who is unavailable . . .'[49]

This last telling statement was soon to manifest itself not only in her work, with the creation of her next novel, *This Sweet Sickness*, but also in her life. As we know, the two were so intertwined it was often difficult to tell them apart.

17

This sweet sickness

1958–1959

Highsmith's *This Sweet Sickness* – published in 1960 – tells the story of David Kelsey, a chemist and chief engineer at a fabric company in the fictional New York town of Froudsburg, who is unable to forget his former girlfriend, Annabelle Stanton. After Annabelle rejects him she marries another man, Gerald, but Kelsey refuses to accept what he refers to as 'the Situation', reasoning, 'I am incomplete without you.'[1] Kelsey is so obsessed with his ex-lover that he creates another identity – that of William Neumeister – through whom he feels able to satisfy his repressed desires and live out his dreams of domestic bliss with his fantasy image of Annabelle.

The name of the protagonist's alter-ego – translated literally from the German it means 'new master' – was an apt one for a writer interested in exploring Nietzschean themes of power, guilt, repression and the concept of the superman. Highsmith had first read Nietzsche's *Ecce Homo* in 1939, while she was a student at Barnard. It was, she found, a book which articulated many of her most pressing concerns. 'Studies should come to answer a personal need, and for no other purpose,' she noted at the time.[2] Nietzsche's autobiography, written in 1888 and published posthumously in 1908, with its radical reassessment of morality, daring dismantling of traditional power structures and play-ful spirit of subversion, sparked Highsmith's imagination.

The famous nihilist, who spent the last eleven years of his life in a state of complete mental collapse – Nietzsche's last letter to Cosima Wagner read, 'Ariadne, I love thee. Dionysus' – influenced Highsmith throughout her career. Indeed, Bruno in *Strangers on a Train*, Ripley in *The Talented Mr Ripley* and subsequent Ripley novels, and Vic in *Deep*

Water could each be classified as a Nietzschean *Ubermensch*. Yet David Kelsey who literally transforms himself into a 'new master' must surely be the most fully realised embodiment of the superman in Highsmith's fiction. 'Active, successful natures act, not according to the dictum "know thyself",' wrote Nietzsche in *Assorted Opinions and Maxims*, 'but as if there hovered before them the commandment: *will* a self and thou shalt *become* a self.'[3]

Kelsey's will to create another self is initially staggeringly successful. Reluctant to face up to the uncomfortable truth of rejection, he escapes into not so much a fantasy life as another parallel reality. Although Kelsey pretends to his friends and fellow residents at his run-down boarding house that his weekends are taken up by visits to his invalid mother in a nursing home, in fact each Friday evening he discards his monotonal existence in favour of the rather more colourful life of William Neumeister, who believes he does indeed live with his paramour in a large, luxurious house in the New York countryside.

'With the new name came to some extent a new character,' Highsmith writes, 'William Neumeister, who had never failed at anything, at least nothing important, who therefore had won Annabelle.'[4] The split between the two selves – between the lonely, sordid, Hopperesque urban existence of Kelsey, and the glamorous, sophisticated, but ultimately fantastical, rural dream of Neumeister – can be read as a fictional reworking of Nietzsche's exploration of the 'will to power'. 'Not necessity, not desire – no, the love of power is the demon of men,' he said.[5] So strong is this urge, Nietzsche argues, that some men actually seek out a way of punishing themselves so as to regain a sense of self-control, as Kelsey does by immuring himself during the week at his drab boarding house.

Nietzsche outlined the concept in *Human, All Too Human*. 'For certain men feel so great a need to exercise their strength and lust for power that, in default of other objects or because their efforts in other directions have always miscarried, they at last hit upon the idea of tyrannizing over certain parts of their own nature, over, as it were, certain segments or stages of themselves . . . Thus a man climbs on dangerous paths in the highest mountains so as to mock at his fears and trembling knees . . . This division of oneself, this mockery of one's own nature, this *spernere se sperni* of which the religions have made so much, is actually a very high degree of vanity . . . In every ascetic morality man worships a part of himself as God and for that he needs to diabolize the other part.'[6]

The two sides of Highsmith's Nietzschean hero fall into such a dialectical pattern. So pure is Kelsey that fellow residents at his boarding house nickname him 'The Saint'; he seems to show no interest whatsoever in women and all his weekends, so it is generally believed, are taken up by visiting his sick mother. His more diabolical self, however, in the assumed identity of William Neumeister, is dedicated to pleasure, indulging in bottles of Pouilly-Fuisse and Frascati, endless Martinis and imported mustards, and is rather partial to a good steak. His taste in interior design, in stark contrast to the ugly yellow walls of the rented room in Froudsburg, with its worn carpet and shabby, brown-coloured double bed, is impeccable. The house near Ballard – his temple to Annabelle – is fitted out with brown and white cowhide rugs, comfortable sofas and all the aspirational trappings of the post-war American suburban dream.

Surrounding himself with possessions, he is able to slip into his new identity and forget the truth of the Situation. 'In this house, his house, he liked to imagine himself William Neumeister – a man who had everything he wanted, a man who knew how to live, to laugh and to be happy.'[7] As the reificator he so obviously is, Neumeister casts Annabelle as one of the many beautiful objects in his country home and, like a modern-day Pygmalion dreaming about his Galatea, comes to believe in the fantasy rather than the reality, in her presence, rather than her absence. 'He behaved as if he were with her, even when he meditatively ate his meals,'[8] Highsmith writes. The frisson he gets when thinking of Annabelle is unmistakably erotic and when he goes to bed he fills the empty space next to him with a vision of the object of his adoration. 'Her head lay on his arm, and when he turned to her and held her close, the surge of his desire had more than once reached the summit and gone over with the imagined pressure of her body . . .'[9]

As Kelsey retreats further into fantasy, so Neumeister the superman comes to dominate his character. 'Overcome, you higher men,' wrote Nietzsche, 'the petty virtues, the petty prudences, the sand-grain discretion, the ant-swarm inanity, miserable ease, the "happiness of the greatest number".'[10] As if obeying Nietzsche's command, Kelsey rejects the ordinary world of the boarding house and posits himself as a man superior to the mass of mediocrity which surrounds him. He compares Gerald's underlip to a 'monkey's behind',[11] regards Annabelle's life without him as unbearably 'dreary',[12] her new partner as 'another nobody . . . another second rater',[13] and snobbishly dismisses her wedding ring as 'one of those plain bands of gold, solid and convex, that had become too common in the world for David's taste'.[14]

His final gesture as an *Übermensch* occurs after he nihilistically articulates the bleakness of the universe, commenting that, 'Nothing was true but the fatigue of life and the eternal disappointment.'[15] On the run from the police after he has accidentally killed Gerald in a fight, Kelsey becomes trapped on a window ledge of an apartment block eight storeys above Manhattan. Unable to accept the thought of being punished by laws not made by himself, he chooses to step into nothingness. As he lifts his foot away from the solidness of the stone, all he sees is 'a memory of a curve of her shoulder, naked, as he had never seen it'.[16] The denouement is a perfect Nietzschean moment.

'Is a state of affairs unthinkable in which the malefactor calls himself to account and publicly dictates his own punishment . . . that by punishing himself he is exercising his power, the power of the lawgiver? . . .' Nietzsche wrote. 'Such would be the criminal of a possible future, who, to be sure, also presupposes a future lawgiving – one founded on the idea "I submit only to the law which I myself have given, in great things and in small." '[17]

The general idea of a love affair conducted purely within the confines of the imagination had intrigued Highsmith for years – she had written the sketch for such a story as early as January 1947 – but her thoughts on fashioning the subject into a book started to take shape in the summer of 1958. The novel was born after her copywriter girlfriend, with whom she still lived, suggested she write about a man who 'creates a second character, another man whose life he leads at certain times'.[18] After metaphorically 'killing off' his invented persona, the man, Barry, is suspected of murder after his fingerprints are found at the scene of the crime. The first draft, which at this stage she called 'I Thee Endow', could have turned into a rehash of *The Talented Mr Ripley* had it not been for the entrance into her life of the woman whose shadow haunts every page.

In Highsmith's journals for 1958, the inspiration for the book is only mentioned by a coded capital letter – M. But from the clues scattered throughout her unpublished notebooks, together with fragments gleaned from other sources, it is possible to piece together a picture of the woman – the artist and illustrator, Mary Ronin – who, like those who came both before and after her, served as a muse for Highsmith's fiction. On 12 August 1958, Highsmith wrote in her cahier of the parallels between her feelings for her new 'lover' and the emotions she was experiencing while plotting her latest book, which she had now entitled *This Sweet Sickness*. What appealed to her was the fact that, in each case, her love affair and her book existed only within the perimeters of her imagination; she could preserve the purity of her relationship by circumscribing its limits and, at the same time, relish the thrill of anticipation she knew she would experience as she retreated from everyday reality and stepped into the world of fiction. Just as David Kelsey fantasised about his non-existent relationship with Annabelle Stanton, so Highsmith conducted an imaginary love affair with Mary Ronin, whom it seems she met in July. Without her, as Highsmith admitted in a cahier entry dated 5 November, 'it would have been quite a different book'.[19]

Mary Jane Ronin was born on 18 December 1912 in Sycamore, Illinois, to Jas Ronin, a horsetrainer and his wife Blanch Darling, and spent her childhood in Nebraska. After studying art at Omaha University, she arrived in New York, age twenty-five, and in June 1938 started work in the advertising art department of Bloomingdale's – the same Manhattan department store Highsmith would work in ten years later. 'I drew everything they sold,' she said. 'Pots, pans, shoes, furniture – everything.'[20] From Bloomingdale's, she moved to Young and Rubicam, where she took a position as an art director, one of the first female art directors in New York. After seven years with the advertising agency, she took a sabbatical year in France, returning to Manhattan in 1953 to freelance. Photographs show her, glasses in hand, sitting at her drawing board; a slim, elegant woman with delicate features and a stylish dress sense. She described her home in Westport, Connecticut, situated on a wooded hillside, as 'a Hansel and Gretel house',[21] while her studio appeared almost alive with colour, packed as it was with sketches, watercolours and art books.

By the autumn of 1958, Highsmith's affair with Mary Ronin had moved out of the realms of the imagination into reality. On 5 November, Pat recorded in her notebook that her new lover had called her 'darling' for the first time, after three months. She also wrote a poem to the woman whom she credited with sweetening her summer. Letters from Mary – signed with a lower-case 'm.' – which Highsmith preserved in the pages of her notebook and which the author later dated as October or November 1958, reveal the romantic passion which underlined their affair. In one letter Mary talks about her love of Schoenberg's 'Transfigured Night' – 'Somehow it now reminds me of us!'[22] – and describes Highsmith's physical characteristics according to the range of colours set down by Abraham Werner in his 1821 book, Werner's Nomenclature of Colour. According to Mary's trained eye, Highsmith's hair was not simply black, rather it could be compared to Werner's Scotch Blue, Throat of Blue Titmouse and Blue Copper Ore.

Continuing with the allusions, she went on to describe Highsmith's lips
– minus lipstick – as a mixture of Aurora Red, Vent Converts of Pied
Wood-Pecker, Red on the Naked Apple and Red Orpiment, while her
skin was a blend of Celandine Green, Phaloena Margaritaria, Back of
Tussilage Leaves and the mineral Beryl. Towards the end of the letter,
after making an error in spacing, she comments, 'The above skipped
line should prove to you that people in love do not make ggood [sic]
typists.'[23] From the letters it can also be gathered that Highsmith sent
her lover a flower in the midst of a snow flurry and that Mary
rapturously described Pat as having 'a beautiful figure and legs like
a thorobred'.[24] Highsmith thought her lover possessed an intriguing
combination of innocence and wisdom – not only was she as impulsive
as a teenager, but she seemed to be generous and open-hearted. How,
Highsmith asked herself, could she have remained so fresh and seemingly uncorrupted by the disappointments of life? 'Or has she had so
few?' Highsmith asked. 'Perhaps she did not repeat mistakes over and
over, as I did.'[25]

Pat started writing *This Sweet Sickness* at the end of September. Five
and half weeks later she had written nearly half of it, but as she took a
break from work she became acutely conscious of the creative process.
She compared it to watching a performance at a theatre during which
the stage machinery was exposed revealing the clumsy mechanics
behind the magic. The realisation – the glimpse into the dark heart
of creation – left her frightened, scared of 'this abyss in the middle of
myself'.[26] Intriguingly, Highsmith went on to draw parallels between
the black hole inside herself – clearly a symbol of her creativity – and the
concomitant need for that space to be filled by an 'innocent victim'.[27]
There was, she said, surely no sensation like falling in love – the blend of
mental and physical feelings could transport one completely, give one a
brief flash of heaven. Even if she was seventy-five and knew she did not
have much longer to live, she would still believe in the metamorphic
power of love; if she could no longer feel its influence, she said, she
would surely remember its effects.

Despite the affair with Mary Ronin, Highsmith continued to live with
her copywriter girlfriend. The couple moved into a larger house
together in nearby Sparkill in late September, but by the end of
1958, their relationship had broken down. In early December, Pat
returned to New York City, into an apartment at 76 Irving Place, where
she lived alone. After living with her girlfriend for two years, she
enjoyed the sense of isolation, happy that there was nobody around to
interrupt her flow of consciousness, yet she was also more aware of her

irrationality – her fear of insanity – than before. During January, she worked on a second draft of the novel, and on 12 February she wrote to Kingsley that she had 'just quickly written a book I am quite pleased with, appropriately entitled *This Sweet Sickness*'.[28] After submitting the novel to Joan Kahn, her editor wrote back to her, on 8 May, with a critique of the book. Her main worry was the accepting behaviour of the characters who surrounded David Kelsey, the feeling that, 'people's reactions to him and his dual role, etc. are too often not real enough so that the reader feels, Oh, it's all so easy on him.'[29] She followed this up with a list of minor editing queries, but concluded, 'I think the book is so good that I want everyone to share my enthusiasm for it.'[30]

Yet during early 1959, Highsmith realised that her affair with Mary Ronin, once suffused with romance, now seemed slightly soiled. It had became obvious that the illustrator was involved with another all along, whom Highsmith only identified by the initials R.B. On 18 February she wrote in her notebook that she had had her 'faith shaken in the girl who inspired the book'.[31] However, this was not Mary's fault; it was Pat's own fickleness which was to blame. As her mania flared up once again, her libido peaked and she said she felt like making love ten times a day. 'And it is surprising how the girls come!'[32] In March, Pat and Mary quarrelled when the artist misunderstood her lover, assuming that Highsmith had presented her with an ultimatum: if she did not choose her, the writer would end their relationship and take another. During the encounter, Mary's composure crumpled – she sat staring silently at the floor and Highsmith said that she looked like she had suddenly aged by fifteen years.

Pat was constantly anxious. She worried that her pet cats might be hit by a passing car or one day fall out of the window of her Manhattan apartment – a feeling which was, she said, a projection of the guilty feelings which festered inside her, emotions brought about as a by-product of involving herself with another woman's lover. 'I worry, subconsciously, about the responsibility of M. and myself, and my guilt feelings in regard to R.,' she wrote in her notebook. But why should she care about hurting another person? 'Because I doubt my reliability . . . It is an endless chain, going back into the unconscious, the little shames best left buried.'[33]

Although Highsmith did not document how her relationship with Mary Ronin ended, by June she noted that, after eight months together, the 'fire of love dies down'.[34] The writer hoped that Mary would accompany her on a trip to Greece, but in October, while she was in Paris, she learnt the disappointing news that her lover would not meet her after all. Her future, she saw, would comprise of yet another foreign city experienced alone; a tiny room in a hotel, the glinting lights of a nearby restaurant where she would dine by herself. 'Out of these things come my stories, books, and my sense of life,' she wrote.[35]

'Things were not so good in the late fifties when I was broke,' Highsmith said, referring to the state of her finances,[36] and it was time, she thought, to do something about it. At the end of 1958, soon after moving into her new apartment in Irving Place, Highsmith severed contact with her agent Margot Johnson. From 1953, Highsmith had expressed doubts about Johnson's ability – she believed she just wasn't working hard enough to sell her books and raise her advances. In late 1958, she also felt confident enough to start asking her French agent Jenny Bradley, of the William A. Bradley Literary Agency, to push for more money. She had been disappointed when, in October 1957, an offer of $10,000 for the film rights to *The Talented Mr Ripley* had been withdrawn after the producers failed to find a *metteur en scène*. But one year on she thought it only appropriate to ask for more. On 29 December 1958, she wrote to Jenny Bradley, telling her, in a friendly manner, that she would like $12,000, perhaps even $15,000, for the film rights of *The Talented Mr Ripley* – 'one can always come down in price, if necessary,' she said.[37] (The producers Robert and Raymond Hakim bought the book in early 1959, using it as a basis for the sumptuous *Plein Soleil* starring Alain Delon and directed by Réné Clément.)

In early 1959, after sacking Johnson, she appointed Patricia Schartle, a partner of the of New York-based agency Constance Smith Associates as her American agent. 'At the time when I asked Highsmith direct [why she had left Margot Johnson], she said that she was disappointed in sales,' says Patricia, who subsequently married the novelist Anton Myrer, and who represented Highsmith for twenty years.[38] Schartle – who was head of the book department and who would take Highsmith with her when Constance Smith retired and the business was merged with McIntosh & Otis, where Schartle was appointed president – remembers how difficult it was selling Highsmith's, and many other suspense writers', work. 'In the early fifties, the lending library market in America totally disappeared almost overnight, where suspense and mysteries had received their support,' she says. 'Publishers panicked and declined mysteries despite [the] efforts of agents and booksellers, who always believed the market . . . would again flourish. But only [Agatha] Christie and Mickey Spillane were selling and it was not until

P.D. James that the broad market recovered. Highsmith suffered at that time, in the late fifties, and sixties.'[39]

Schartle believes that Highsmith experienced 'two almost perfect flashes of brilliance'[40] in her career: the idea behind *Strangers on a Train* and the characterisation of Ripley. 'There had been rascals before in suspense writing, of course, but her sense of amorality or evil was particular in Ripley – not always as consciously as some critics thought perhaps; she often showed contempt for human beings.

'My first impression of her was a loneliness, a sadness in one so young (we were both in our early thirties) with absolutely no sense of joy or balance. Gauche to an extreme, really physically clumsy as well as boyish, it was almost impossible to put her at ease. It was as if she felt a deep distrust of everything. She was totally secretive about her past – I asked a few questions about Texas, which she refused to answer. She really didn't want anyone to know about her American origins and always avoided it. She tried to assume a superior European view even in that first meeting, which was rather pathetic. Highsmith had absolutely no grace – poor woman, she thought having an espresso machine made her sophisticated.

'What I did like about her was her openness about her lesbianism, although we never once discussed it. I had the feeling that she had gone abroad so often . . . because she was more at ease in France, Germany – boring Munich seemed great to her . . . But she had the courage, after the success of *Strangers on a Train* to come out of the closet in days when it was not easy to do. One felt she had consciously decided to make a career virtue of it and to live abroad and be appreciated. She thought it made her more interesting as a writer. But she had never read Colette or Stendhal or George Sand at that point. I did respect her work ethic – she kept to a good regular working schedule daily in an almost Germanic sense.

'What did I dislike? Slyness, a certain meanness. She showed no interest really in other serious artists in any field, unless they were hugely famous, and she was curiously bourgeois – a mixture of contrasts that must have cost her emotionally. The very things I personally disliked, I also recognized probably helped her to achieve a certain individuality as a writer: misanthropy, malice, which I think ran deep in her nature.'[41] The only time she can remember Highsmith laughing was when the writer saw 'a poster-ad in the New York subway where some creep had gouged out the eyes of the child'.[42]

18

A lurking liking for those that flout the law

1959–1960

Towards the end of 1959, Highsmith wrote in her notebook that there was one thing that interested her more than morality *per se* – the collapse of moral structures and the sense of despair which was clouding the post-war era. 'We have to doubt the "reward of virtue", certainly in the next world, and also its power to bring happiness here,' she said.[1] She was echoing the views of a number of social commentators who had been quick to articulate the new sense of moral relativity which had wormed its way through Eisenhower's America.

Although the Republican President linked the quintessence of America with religion – 'Recognition of the Supreme Being is the first, most basic, expression of Americanism. Without God, there could be no American form of government, nor American way of life,' he said in 1955 – the truth was very different. Perhaps a more insightful – and honest – assessment of the moral landscape came from Eisenhower's opponent in the 1952 election, Democratic candidate Adlai Stevenson: 'Some of us worship in churches, some in synagogues, some on golf courses,' he said. It was true that, in 1955, the weekly church attendance totalled 49 million adults – half the total adult population – yet a deep unease threatened to undermine the collective health of the nation. It was also true that America seemed to have been blessed with an unprecedented affluence, but could, as some observers suggested, this new celebration of materialism actually be the root cause of the nation's malaise? A 1957 magazine survey, investigating the morals of the modern American, concluded that the average man or woman thought it acceptable they should carry on just as they liked so long as their behaviour was accepted by their neighbours.

The notion that America's increasing obsession with personal wealth had played its part in the disintegration of contemporary morality was explored by David M. Potter in his 1954 book, *People of Plenty: Economic Abundance and the American Character*. Borrowing from the work of Karen Horney, Potter stated that affluence was one of the central contributing factors of modern neurosis, and, in an observation that could act as a summary of Highsmith's fictional obsessions, stated how, 'aggressiveness [had] grown so pronounced that it cannot be reconciled with Christian brotherhood; desire for material goods so vigorously stimulated that it cannot be satisfied; and expectations of untrammelled freedom soaring so high that they cannot be squared with the multitude of responsibilities and restrictions that confine us all.'[2]

It was no wonder that, although America was one of the richest nations on the planet, its inhabitants were amongst the most anxious, alienated from both the workplace and themselves. According to the sociologist C. Wright Mills, writing in 1951, it was necessary to analyse the American character in more psychological terms. 'The problems that concern us most border on the psychiatric,'[3] he wrote. 'Internally, they [the American middle classes] are split, fragmented.'[4] As we have seen, Highsmith – together with a number of other writers, artists and film-makers – had already taken on the task, documenting the heart of darkness in modern America. 'Crime, in many ways,' said Daniel Bell, whose work Highsmith read, 'is a Coney Island mirror, caricaturing the morals and manners of a society,'[5] and by extension crime novels serve a similar purpose. In a piece for the *Radio Times*, to tie in with the BBC1 programme, *Omnibus File – Thrillers and Crime Fiction* in 1972, the author defined herself as a novelist who found crime 'very good for illustrating moral points'.[6] This preoccupation – her view of herself as a documenter of degeneracy – lasted throughout her life and in an interview she did with Neil Gordon in 1992, to coincide with the American publication of *Ripley Under Water*, she 'spoke at great length about the decline of American culture, the horror of TV. She hated Reagan and Bush, but seemed rather to feel that we were getting what we deserved in them, given how irresponsible had been our own safeguarding of our culture.'[7]

As her early novels reveal, Highsmith's position on morality was far from straightforward. In *Strangers on a Train*, it is clear that an essentially 'good' man, Guy, has been corrupted by the evil influences of Bruno. At the climax of the novel, Guy confesses all to Owen Markman – the former lover of his dead wife, Miriam – and tries to engage him in a debate on individual moral responsibility only to be met by blank, drunken indifference and an apathetic response of 'Live and let live.' Although Guy has committed a murder, he chooses not to align himself with the hollow, unfeeling emptiness of Markman and when faced with news that his confession has been overheard by the detective, Gerard, says simply, 'Take me.' The ending, in a sense, is a conventional one – the law is finally imposed and the guilty are punished – in *The Blunderer, Deep Water, A Game for the Living*, and *This Sweet Sickness*, the transgressors are similarly brought to justice. Yet one gets the sense that order is imposed not because these characters inhabit a rational, God-governed universe, but because of the intervention of chance or circumstance. Indeed, the innocent are just as likely to be punished as the guilty – Walter is killed by Kimmel in *The Blunderer* before Kimmel is, in turn, trapped by the police – while the enforcers of the law often seem more morally corrupt than the criminals they are trying to entrap. At one point, Walter in *The Blunderer* views Kimmel – a wife-killer – to be angelic when compared to a 'diabolic' Corby, the detective.[8] Not only that, but a certain amoral leakage occurs, spilling over from the personalities of Highsmith's hollow men and infecting the reader with a skewed vision. 'The effect is chilling,' wrote one critic, 'partly because it seems to Patricia Highsmith that eating breakfast, walking the dog, and committing murder have come to occupy the same moral space.'[9]

By privileging the perspective of the abnormal and amoral, she both subverts the expectations of the genre and questions one of the central conventions of the Western tradition – the idea that art is supposed to be morally edifying. Highsmith describes murder with a certain *joie de vivre*, while it is clear that many of her killers – Bruno, Kimmel, Vic, and of course Ripley – relish the act of snuffing out another life. The intensity with which she wrote about the abnormal, amoral personality and, in *The Talented Mr Ripley, Deep Water* and *This Sweet Sickness*, the sheer totality of her vision – achieved by confining her point of view to the warped perspective of the central character in each of these books – naturally begs the question: What was Highsmith's own relationship towards morality? Just where did she stand?

Craig Brown remembers once discussing *Deep Water* with High-smith and her astonishing reaction when he suggested that perhaps Vic was rather a weak and pathetic man before he embarked on his mission to murder his wife's lovers. 'She leapt to his defence,' Brown remembers. ' "He's mentally a bit odd, but at least he finally has a go. To impress on his wife that he's not taking any more, he eliminates those boring lovers. At least he *has a go*. At least he *tries*." Her vehemence quite took me aback. Her lack of enthusiasm for the victim set her at odds with her times.'[10]

Otto Penzler of the Mysterious Press – who published five of her books in America between 1985 and 1988 – believes that one of the reasons Highsmith never became a big seller in the States during her lifetime was because of the amorality of her fiction. She was too dark for mass consumption. 'There's a certain repellent quality about them all in a way,' he says of her novels. 'Certainly the Ripley books are so amoral that a lot of people are simply uncomfortable, because they don't have a guide post, they don't have the author leading them along, saying, "Look here's somebody you should really despise." . . . You're sort of at sea in her books, you don't know who are the good guys and the bad guys because there are no nice people. Nobody's nice, nobody's good. There's no one you can relate to and I think that's disquieting for a lot of people.'[11] H.R.F. Keating, the veteran crime author and president of the Detection Club, remembers that, 'When Highsmith was invited to join the Detection Club one member was so outraged by the amorality of her books that they said, "If she's in, I leave".'[12]

The late Julian Symons, the crime novelist, biographer, and former president of the Detection Club, remarked that although reader identification with a criminal perspective was far from new – E.W. Hornung's portrayal of the nineteenth-century gentleman-burglar, Raffles, had prompted his brother-in-law, Conan Doyle to say, 'You must not make the criminal a hero'[13] – Highsmith's novels went one step further. 'Tom Ripley is the gentleman as occasional murderer, a difference expressive of the ethical gap between the late nineteenth century and late twentieth,' he said.[14] Symons believed that Highsmith's novels were remarkable as they suggested 'that a different and wholly personal code of morality should be substituted for the code of what society generally regards as important.'[15] Indeed, Highsmith more or less stated as much in her 1966 book, *Plotting and Writing Suspense Fiction*. 'I find the public passion for justice quite boring and artificial, for neither life nor nature cares if justice is ever done or not.'[16] In 1981, she elaborated on this when she told Diana Cooper-Clark of her fascination for amorality. 'I suppose I find it an interesting contrast to stereotyped morality which is frequently hypocritical and phony. I also think that to mock lip-service morality and to have a character amoral, such as Ripley, is entertaining.'[17] After all, if people found her work morally objectionable, they should realise that she was merely reflecting the reality of the modern world. 'This is the way life is,' she said, 'and I read somewhere years ago that only 11 per cent of murders are solved. That is unfortunate, but lots of victims are not so important as the President of the United States. The police make a certain effort, and it may be a good effort, but frequently the case is dropped. And so I think, why shouldn't I write about a few characters who go free?'[18] She also told one interviewer that she aligned herself with the criminal perspective because of her own innate sense of strangeness, which she traced back to her family background. 'It's true, I understand nuts, kinky, kooky people,' she said. 'I don't understand ordinary people. Housewives. Maybe it's because I am not entirely normal! I myself have a criminal bent . . . I have a lurking liking for those who flout the law which I realise is despicable of me.'[19] Although she found Clément's *Plein Soleil*, which she saw in September 1961, while she was living in New Hope, 'very beautiful to the eye and interesting for the intellect',[20] she was rather dismayed by the moralistic ending tacked on to the end of her story. The producers of the film – Robert and Raymond Hakim – told her that they would have preferred to highlight the homosexual subtext of the novel, but as they would have been refused permission by the authorities, there was little use attempting to tackle the issue. Later she would also voice her dismay that Ripley was captured, telling one interviewer that 'it was a terrible concession to so-called public morality that the criminal had to be caught'.[21]

It can't be denied that Highsmith experienced a thrilling *frisson* when she encountered – at a safe distance, of course – amorality or violence. She loved reading about the psychology of killers, pasted newspaper reports about murderers into her notebooks, admitted that she found writing about psychopaths 'easy',[22] and, in later life, enjoyed flicking through *A Colour Atlas of Forensic Pathology*, a veritable gore-fest of images containing, as she told one journalist, colour photographs of 'car accidents, murders and rape cases: the really shocking images that don't reach the public'.[23] The writer and journalist Roger Clarke, who met Highsmith in 1982, believes that 'the amorality [in Highsmith's work] is genuine. Some writers, like Martin Amis, do a very good job of amorality, but the bottom line is Amis is probably not an amoral person. But I think Pat really was amoral. There was this strange blankness about her.'[24]

Other friends point out that, later in life, she could be ridiculously repressive – and terribly moralistic – in her view of how other people should lead their lives. 'There was one woman [who lived nearby] who had been living with a man for five years and Pat would go on and on about this relationship, about "her latest lay",' says Vivien De Bernardi. 'I said once, "Pat, how many years do they have to be together before this gentleman goes on to a higher level than 'her latest lay'?" But Pat did not approve. She was very judgmental about people's sexual inclinations, which is kind of funny when you think of her own. I think it represented the flip side of her idealisation of the intellect – up there she had created an altar to logic, but accompanying this was a tremendous disgust for copulation. I said to her, "Jesus, could we not find something in the middle? After all, there are limits to what you can do with a very logical mind. People sleep together, Pat – human beings do that." '[25] 'Highsmith was amoral, but only vicariously,' adds Kingsley. 'As a person she could be quite conventional, but she bought into the prevailing idea at the time that as an artist one was outside the norm.'[26]

Her notebook entries reveal similar contradictions. As early as 1942 she wrote of how she found it difficult, if not impossible, to reconcile conventional morality with the quirks of her personality. She frequently located herself outside the confines of generally accepted, popular notions of right and wrong, noting that she occupied a marginalised position on the fringes of society. In 1954, she wrote:

There is no moral to my life – I have none – except:
'Stand up and take it'.
The rest is sentiment.[27]

Yet, she clearly knew when she fell short of her own expectations. In October 1950, she was so ashamed of her own behaviour – her drunkenness, her promiscuity, her lack of control – that she wrote in her diary of her self-disgust. 'And I feel I sink as low morally as any of the Village, wastrels of whom I have heard, have known, all my life, without suspecting I could ever be like them.'[28] Writing a diary, she said in June 1955 – a year after abandoning the exercise to avoid Ellen Hill's snooping – had helped keep her on the right moral pathway. It's certain that she did not believe in moral platitudes – her sharp intelligence could easily see through the pretensions of bogus emotion – yet Highsmith, for all her aspirations towards amorality, had some standards that grounded her. One's moral foundations, she told one interviewer, were laid down in the first five years of life: if a child was raised in a 'decent' home then the likelihood was he or she would grow up to be a good person, but if a youngster was the product of a broken home or similarly unstable environment then they were more likely to face the temptations that could lead them into crime.

Like the fifties themselves, Highsmith had a paradoxical attitude towards morality and it is these contradictions, revealed by the very real wrestlings of conscience she documents in her notebooks, that are reflected in her work. As she said, each of her books, far from being a clear moral statement, was an argument with herself. It is this indefinability – an ambiguity that she claims, in *A Game for the Living*, as 'the secret of life, the very key to the universe'[29] – which invests her work with such power.

'It is very, very difficult for me to know what to forgive among people's vices (mine, too),' she wrote in her notebook in 1959.[30] How was it possible to make a value judgement about the morals of others or even oneself? At what point, she asked herself, did one no longer believe in the innate goodness secreted within each individual? She was certain that Europeans were brought up with a clearer idea of right and wrong than Americans and, as a result, they could at least find a position for themselves on the sliding scale of modern morality. Not only was she an American, but she also believed that, 'only out of personal chaos and failure and humiliation can truth and real character come,' and consequently it was, she said, 'twice as hard for me'.[31] Ultimately, she realised, it was impossible to lay down any fixed laws regarding morality because of the difficulties inherent in discerning motivation and the fact that interpretation of behaviour was not a science, but an art. 'It is because of its flexibility that it torments me,' she said.[32]

Highsmith boarded a plane in New York, bound for Paris, arriving in the French capital on 28 September 1959. Accompanying her on her trip – a publicity tour – was her mother. The two women checked into their hotel, the Hotel du Quai Voltaire, where, a few days later, Highsmith was due to be interviewed by a couple of journalists. On the agreed day, the writer was waiting in her room, wondering why the reporters were late, when the telephone rang. 'The journalists told me that my mother was downstairs and for five minutes or more had tried to convince them that she was me,' Highsmith wrote in a letter to her cousin, Dan Coates. 'They took a snap of her to please her.'[33] She went on to say that if she or Dan were to mention the incident, Mary would deny it ever happened or dismiss it as a silly joke. 'I think a psychiatrist would put another meaning to it,' she said.[34]

Highsmith had worried about the state of her mother's mental health since the mid-1940s, when her parents had moved to Hastings-on-

Hudson. When Marc Brandel met Mary in 1949 he told Pat that he thought her mother 'weird',[35] while the following year she wrote in her diary of the older woman's anxieties and neuroses, psychological problems which she thought might drive her to commit suicide. By 1959, it was obvious that there was something seriously wrong with Mary and while in Paris, Highsmith noticed the terrifying resemblance between her sixty-four-year-old mother and her late grandmother, Willie Mae, at a much older age. It seemed, she said, as though Mary was suffering from a form of dementia – not only was she absent-minded, but she repeated herself incessantly and would often puncture the conversation with remarks Highsmith regarded as ridiculous and self-aggrandising. 'My mother seems already to have entered anility,' she wrote in her notebook, before adding, 'It's inevitable, too, to think that there go I in another twenty-five years.'[36]

Mother and daughter spent just under a month together in Paris, before Pat waved her off, with an overwhelming sense of relief, on a flight to Rome. It had been a long time since she had been so repulsed by anything as her mother's behaviour in Europe, she said. Detailing these feelings in her notebook, she expanded from the personal to the general and mused on how she might be able to explore such a personality – seemingly passive and feminine but in reality scheming and selfish – in her fiction. 'Her unconscious is more intelligent than her conscious,' she noted.[37]

From Paris, Highsmith took a week's break in Marseille, before returning to the French capital in November. In early December she travelled to Salzburg with a friend and then on to Greece, arriving in Athens at the end of the month. 'Christmas will find me drinking ouzo, probably, instead of egg nog,' she wrote to Joan Kahn before the trip.[38] She was not overly impressed by Athens, finding the city a dusty mass of yellowing, flimsy buildings and its people primitive and ill-mannered. She spent the first day of the new year in Napflio, the elegant fortified town on the Peloponnese which was the fledging capital of modern Greece. From Heraklion, she wrote a cheery postcard to Jenny Bradley telling her French agent how much she was enjoying the holiday, although she was finding daily existence rather primitive, yet her note-book entries for the same period reveal a despondency she chose to keep to herself. As she gazed at the cold, turquoise waters of the Mediterra-nean it's likely she would have looked back to the blissful holiday she had spent with Kathryn Cohen in the summer of 1949. Indeed, Kathryn had haunted her thoughts before she had left for Greece and in late September 1959, while in Paris, Highsmith had a dream that she was a man, coughing up blood the colour of pale lavender into a pristine white napkin. A doctor examined the evidence and diagnosed a fatal condition. Analysing the dream, Highsmith believed that she associated lavender with Kathryn, and her stay with her in London ten years before. The dream proved to be bad omen; over the New Year weekend of 1960, just as Highsmith was travelling through Greece, fifty-four-year-old Kathryn Cohen committed suicide by taking an overdose of barbiturates at her house in Chelsea. 'DEATH OF A ZIEGFELD GIRL' screamed the *Daily Mail* headline on 5 January 1960. Highsmith never recorded how or when she heard the news – she did, however, keep the newspaper reports of the death – but on 3 February she wrote about how wretched she felt in her journal. 'One interesting thing is that a stage is reached when nothing hurts any more . . .' she said of her depression. 'Things cannot become any worse, finally, for the one who is really depressed . . .'[39] The same month she also noted how easy it was to hate the whole human race. 'I cannot figure out how I must live,' she added.[40]

19

The ultra neurotic

1960–1962

On her return from Europe – she arrived at her New York apartment in February 1960 – Highsmith was greeted by the favourable reviews of *This Sweet Sickness*, published the same month. 'The singular Patricia Highsmith has a cool affinity for aberration,' wrote James Sandoe in the *New York Herald Tribune Book Review*. 'Her treatment is internal, not clinical, and this makes for a sharp immediacy rather than a case history . . . It's not so much that Miss Highsmith makes these proceedings plausible as that she makes them unquestionable. I think the world of Miss Highsmith because while she has me in her firm grasp, she is quite simply the world.'[1]

Back at her desk, Highsmith started to muse on how she could transform the sights and sounds of Europe, particularly her out-of-season trip to Greece, into fiction. 'I remembered a musty old hotel I had stopped at in Athens, where the service was not very good, where the carpets were worn out, in whose corridors one heard a dozen different languages a day, and I wanted to use this hotel in my book,' she said. 'I wanted also to use the labyrinthian Palace of Knossos, which I had visited.'[2] She also recalled, from the same trip, feeling 'slightly rooked by a middle-aged man, a graduate of one of America's most esteemed universities'; she thought she could use him as a basis for a character, a con-man. At the beginning of May she wrote in her notebook the idea for a 'comic-tragic novel'[3] focusing on the experiences of Chester MacFarland, who has embezzled $35,000 by selling shares in non-existent properties, and his arrival in Athens. This plot would eventually, after a great deal of heartache, form itself into her 1964 novel, *The Two Faces of January*.

She worked on the book throughout 1960 and by mid-July she wrote to Jenny Bradley to tell her she was halfway through the as yet untitled novel. At the beginning of September she moved from New York to Pennsylvania, into a light, two-storey house set in the middle of a large field, on Old Ferry Road, ten miles from New Hope, where she lived for six months with the writer Marijane Meaker (aka M.E. Kerr, Vin Packer, Ann Aldrich) and where she continued work on the novel. 'I began a book in the heat of this summer . . .' she wrote to Joan Kahn on 6 September, 'one of those books which midway necessitated some re-thinking, which I did during this rather colossal moving from city to country. I am going to plunge in again in this quieter atmosphere, and I expect to have it done before Christmas.'[4] In October, she wrote to Jenny Bradley of the difficulties she faced reconciling the necessary, but time-consuming, chores of country living with the fact that she would have to expend most of her energy writing her novel. She confessed she had not yet resolved the matter.[5]

As she wrote, she noted how the writer, by the very nature of his or her profession, was without a fixed personality, as 'he is always part of his characters'.[6] By November, after toying with 'The Power of Negative Thinking' – a title she would later use as the name of one of Howard Ingham's novels in *The Tremor of Forgery* – and 'Rydal's Folly' she settled on calling her new novel *The Two Faces of January*, appropriate for the Janus-faced, flux-like nature of her protagonists. On 7 December she wrote to Jenny Bradley to inform her that she had finished the novel. Her editor, Joan Kahn, however, thought otherwise and later Highsmith had to admit that it was 'quite a mess in its first version'.[7]

She submitted the novel to Harper & Brothers early in 1961, but in February, Joan Kahn wrote to Highsmith's agent, Patricia Schartle, telling her that although she thought the author's writing was still 'fine, the book escapes us'.[8] The main structural flaw, as she saw it, was Highsmith's trio of characters – Rydal, Chester, and his wife, who at this stage was named Olga, but whom she would later call Colette. 'The book makes sense only if there is a homosexual relationship between Rydal and Chester . . .' wrote Joan. 'We cannot like any of the characters, but more difficult, we cannot believe in them . . . it's all so far in a dream now it makes no sense. If our worries make any sense I would like to see the novel salvaged – but I feel we cannot publish as it stands . . .'[9]

Highsmith set about reworking the book almost immediately. She told her editor that she was 'revising with a will',[10] but privately she felt furious that she was being forced to rethink her characters. By mid-April, Highsmith resubmitted the novel, but still it failed to capture Joan Kahn's imagination. In her assessment, the characters did not jump off the page. 'It would need a major character revision to make the novel make sense,' wrote Joan. 'Perhaps you'd never want to do that . . .'[11]

Instead of trashing the novel, Highsmith said she would completely rethink the motivation of her characters and, at the same time, eliminate any suspicion of a homosexual relationship between the two men. Although she agreed to rework the book – *A Game for the Living*, she reasoned, had also 'presented ghastly problems, too, but [they] were at last overcome'[12] – she confided to her French agent, Jenny Bradley, that such revisions were in her view 'unreasonable'.[13]

Highsmith's revisions on the book stretched into 1962, but still Joan Kahn wasn't happy. A reader's report submitted to Kahn, written on 28 May 1962, found that for all of Highsmith's reworking, the writer had failed to improve the novel. In fact, they concluded, damningly, 'There is a frightening sense of the neurotic about the author's approach to and conception of character. There is no reason or motivation for their actions . . . A very unhealthy air hangs over it all and I finished it all with a strong feeling of revulsion.'[14]

As a result Kahn felt obliged to send the manuscript back to Patricia Schartle. 'I'm very sorry, but I still don't like *The Two Faces of January*,' Kahn wrote to Highsmith on 6 June. 'I don't believe in any of the people – oh, dear. I couldn't be sadder.'[15]

The book, after being rejected by Harper & Brothers, was eventually published by Doubleday in America and Heinemann in Britain in 1964. Ironically, it was the book's 'unhealthy air' and Highsmith's 'frightening sense of the neurotic', which actually attracted the attention of the critics. The writer Brigid Brophy, one of Highsmith's greatest fans, claimed that, 'Highsmith has superbly carried out Dickens's task of making the crime story literature'.[16] She praised the novel for the 'cold-crumpet clamminess' of the characters and summed up the book as 'a thriller chiefly in the sense that every good novel is . . . It is the story not so much of a chase as of moving, uneasily, on. Shifts of ground stand metaphor for shifts in relationship; psychology is beautifully interleaved with a gritty *genius loci*.'[17] Julian Symons, writing in the *Sunday Times*, lauded Highsmith for her subtle characterisation and her unremittingly bleak vision of modern life. 'The book confirms the fact that Miss Highsmith has no rival in writing crime stories that show us a doom-laden world where human beings, all of them emotionally lame, deficient or perverse, are destroyed not by events but by each other.'[18] In 1965 the novel won the Crime Writers Association of England Silver Dagger Award for the best foreign crime novel of the previous year; she used the dagger she received to open her mail from then on.

Rejection was something all aspiring writers must face as a reality of the profession, she said.

> These little setbacks, amounting sometimes to thousands of dollars' worth of time wasted, writers must learn to take like Spartans. A brief curse, perhaps, then tighten the belt a notch and on to something new – of course with enthusiasm, courage and optimism, because without these three elements, you cannot produce anything good.[19]

While plotting *The Two Faces of January* Highsmith noted how she thought about basing the characters of the novel on certain aspects of herself. She particularly wanted to articulate the paradoxical, nihilistic elements of her personality, which she found best expressed in Dostoevsky's *Notes from Underground*. 'The ultra neurotic, which is myself. The Underground Man,' she wrote in her cahier. 'To hell with reader identification in the usual sense, or a sympathetic character.'[20] The parallels between Highsmith's novel and the nihilistic Russian text, written in 1864, are striking.

Although the majority of Highsmith's fiction addresses the transitoriness and unknowability of identity, *The Two Faces of January* takes the concept to its extreme, as each of its three main characters – Chester, Colette and Rydal – assume and disrobe new selves with alarming regularity. Chester MacFarland is at once 'himself', a rich American con-man on the run from the authorities, but also in the course of the novel adopts the personae of a range of men with different names, ages and backgrounds: Howard Cheever, Richard Donlevy, Louis Ferguson, William Chamberlain, Philip Jeffries Wedekind and Oliver Donaldson; his wife, Colette, was born Elizabeth, but changed her name on a whim at the age of fourteen, while Rydal Keener, the son of a sophisticated, but controlling Harvard professor, takes on a number of names, including Joey, French-born Pierre Winckel and the Italian Enrico Perassi. As the three characters flit between Athens and Crete, with later scenes between Chester and Rydal being acted out in France, they each undergo a quest for self-knowledge only to be met by a brain-numbing sense of anticlimax. Chester's future self would be 'something yet unknown',[21] while Rydal, who at one point escapes from the police and finds himself without an assumed identity, declares that 'he was free, as only a nameless person of his time could be free.'[22]

The tone of the novel echoes the shrill, taunting voice of Dostoevsky's Underground Man, who warns that, no matter how hard one tries to ape the behaviour of others, 'there is no way out for you, that you will never change into a different person'.[23] Highsmith seems to have initially read the book, described by Colin Wilson as 'the first major treatment of the Outsider theme in modern literature'[24] in 1947, when she wrote in her notebook that she agreed with Dostoevsky's narrator's belief, 'strip the personality and will will be found, not intellect'.[25] Dostoevsky's text self-consciously celebrates its own perverseness and 'paradoxalist' ambiguities, continually suggesting uncertainties only for them to be subsequently subverted. Yet, for all its slippery, enigmatic qualities it seems to posit a theory that reason, self-interest and logical thinking will always be undermined by chaos, desire and the unstoppable rush towards self-destruction.

What else explains Rydal's curiously perverse, self-destructive behaviour outlined in the opening pages of Highsmith's novel, when he chooses to help Chester dispose of the Greek agent's body in the cleaning cupboard of an Athenian hotel? 'Rydal didn't know why. It had been such a fast decision,' Highsmith writes.[26] Rydal is motivated by the irrational, by a desire to live out a fantasy both with Chester, who reminds him of his dead father, and Colette, who resembles a cousin he was accused of raping at the age of fifteen. But he recognises that what spurs him on is beyond explanation, as he writes to his brother. ' "I am using this man for my own inner purposes . . . A psychological purge by some sort of re-enactment that I don't even understand yet is going on in me." '[27] Highsmith, of course, was herself prone to similar elaborate psychodramas, in which she used friends, lovers, even strangers to play out certain patterns from her past; an urge articulated by Rydal in the novel. 'He remembered Proust's remark, that people do not grow emotionally. It was rather a frightening thought.'[28]

The love-hate bond between the two male protagonists, a relationship which clearly worried Highsmith's editors and which the writer described as a 'game of shadowing',[29] also has a precedent in Dostoevsky's text.

Reality, consciousness and self-awareness, as expressed in *The Two Faces of January*, equal alienation, nausea and hellishness. When Chester, who spends most of the book staggering about in an alcohol-induced daze, contemplates his own real identity he feels distinctly uncomfortable. 'It was he. It was awful.'[30] Similarly, the narrator of *Notes from Underground* comments, 'to be overly conscious is a sickness, a real, thorough sickness . . . any consciousness at all is a sickness'.[31] Writing the book, Dostoevsky's narrator concludes, was a form of 'corrective punishment'.[32] At times, such a motive could also be said to drive Highsmith herself.

New Hope, situated on the banks of the Delaware River in Bucks County, was an idyllic place in the late fifties, early sixties. 'New Hope was a beautiful little town, with a very European look and almost a fairy-tale feel,' says Peggy Lewis, who worked as the book review editor of the *Bucks County Life* and who was a friend of Highsmith's from New York. 'It was a very pleasant place to live, people felt very warm towards each other and we had street fairs once a year.'[33] The area was also well known for its artistic connections. In the nineteenth century Bucks County, named after the English county of Buckinghamshire following William Penn's settlement of the territory in 1680, acted as a haven for painters seduced by the sylvan charms of the countryside and during the 1930s and 1940s a wide range of literary figures, many from New York, bought properties in the region. Nathanael West, together with his brother-in-law S.J. Perelman, owned a converted farm in Erwinna; Dorothy Parker lived in Pipersville as did James A. Michener; Nobel Prize winner Pearl Buck resided in nearby Perkasie; in the early fifties Arthur Koestler bought an island in the Delaware River, near New Hope, and the town itself was home to the famous Bucks County Playhouse, opened in 1939. 'In the glittering thirties and forties, so many nationally famous literary figures owned country homes in Bucks County,' says biographer Dorothy Herrmann, 'that the New York press dubbed the area 'the Genius Belt'.[34]

Running parallel to the writing – and rewriting – of *The Two Faces of January*, Highsmith busied herself by working on a clutch of short stories such as 'Camera Finish', published in *Cosmopolitan* in 1960 and 'The Terrapin', which a year after its publication in *Ellery Queen's Mystery Magazine* in 1962 won a 'Raven' award from the Mystery Writers of America. She also dashed off regular book reviews for *Bucks County Life* – writing about subjects as diverse as America in the thirties, prehistoric Crete, and the anatomy of prisons – and thought about how she could develop an idea she had had for a second lesbian novel. In May 1960, she thought about writing a sequel to *The Price of Salt*, but as she couldn't figure out how to introduce Therese into the narrative, she concluded that it would be better to think up a batch of new characters. Later in the year, in December, she jotted down her thoughts on a possible book written under her pseudonym of Claire Morgan. Each of the seven scenarios would outline one of her past relationships. 'Possibly each story told from older and younger point of view,' she said. 'Complete new beginning & end of each.'[35] Then in January 1961, she sketched the basis for an incomplete, unpublished novel to which she originally gave the working title, 'Girls' Book,' before settling on *First Person Novel*.

The book comprises of the letters and diary of Juliette Tallifer Dorn, a forty-one-year-old Philadelphia-born teacher, living in Geneva with her husband, Eric, an electrical engineer and their seventeen-year-old son, Philip John. Juliette is staying in the fictional town of Gemelsbach for the summer, where for two hours a day she sits down and writes the history of her homosexual affairs for the benefit of her husband. 'Should I do my life first or tell about the First Girl?' she asks herself. 'My life being not the facts that you know, but the trail, the chain of crushes and loves, amounting to nothing but memories – but such memories!'[36]

Her first love dated back to childhood, when she was six and the other girl, Marjorie, was ten. 'The important fact is that she was a girl, a female,' Highsmith writes.[37] Then, aged ten, she had a crush on another girl, Helen, although neither of them touched one another. 'I knew so well the pleasure, through imagination, knew through its intensity and through some sense I cannot give a name to that it was tabu, unnatural, that I would be punished for it if caught, and possibly scorned by the object of my affection, if I made any advances to her. This was enough to keep me in check.'[38]

Juliette recounts how at eleven, she was browsing in the psychology section of the local library when she came across the word 'lesbian'; the term sent a chill of fear through her body. Three years later, age fourteen, she caught a glimpse of a girl and immediately fell in love with her, an infatuation which lasted for three years. Then, when she was sixteen, she attempted to make love with a nineteen-year-old man, an indifferent experience she didn't particularly want to repeat. By the time she was seventeen, and her parents had moved to Switzerland, she knew that she was odd. Like Highsmith, Juliette refused to eat, a condition which eventually resulted in low blood pressure and anaemia. At boarding school, she met another girl, Veronica Miniger, who had a long history of sleeping with other women. But although their affair lasted three years, the relationship came to an end when Veronica's mother discovered the truth about her daughter. The short novel ends with a return to the present and a series of letters from Juliette's latest love interest, Penelope Quinn, a twenty-three-year-old ballet dancer.

The book, although fictional, obviously had its base in Highsmith's own life. In fact, throughout the first quarter of 1961, she looked back on her past affairs for inspiration, noting down the initials of her various lovers and how her life had been affected by them. The heroine herself would be based on none other than Ellen Hill, 'with many of her attractive qualities and few of her faults'.[39] The novel, she said, would draw on her friendships with a range of women including her first girlfriend, Virginia; Helen (the girl at Barnard); Allela Cornell; Virginia Kent Catherwood, 'the inevitable Lilith. Physical pure and simple';[40] and possibly Chloe, with whom she had travelled to Mexico, 'although she gave me no roots, and I could not write of her as a love with any feeling'.[41] The objective of the book would be, she said, 'to depict the mature woman (in every sense) who cannot keep herself from practising homosexuality, even if for social reasons she would wish to'.[42]

Highsmith, however, only wrote fifty-nine pages of this lesbian novel. In April 1961, just as she was splitting up from Marijane Meaker, she felt compelled to write a story which had even greater resonances for her own life – *The Cry of the Owl*, part of which is set in Lambertville, just across the Delaware River from New Hope. The novel takes as its subject matter the warped relationship between a stalker, Robert Forester and his victim, Jenny Thierolf. The opening scene, in which Highsmith describes the thrill Robert experiences as he gazes at Jenny in her fairy-tale style house – it bears a remarkable similarity to the Ridgewood home of Kathleen Senn, the woman Pat had served in Bloomingdale's – one gets the impression that Highsmith was writing about her own voyeuristic pleasures eleven years previously.

> Whenever Robert looked at her of an evening, for the first time in two or three weeks, he felt struck or smitten in a way that made his heart jump, then beat faster for a few seconds . . . What he felt, what he had was like a terrible thirst that had to be quenched. He had to see her, had to watch her.[43]

Indeed, at the end of May, while Highsmith was working on the outline of the novel, she wrote to Kingsley, 'I am writing something out of my system, which is not so therapeutic as it sounds; all my books come out of my system, but this one more so. I only hope I have the real distance, which makes for art not therapy. I only know that I must do it before I do anything else. It is really only a character which is from "my system", the story is of course totally invented, and not from real life.'[44]

In the middle of June, Pat found that she couldn't abide light and noticed that she was feeling unusually nervous. Then, spots began to pepper her stomach, back and upper arms – she had developed a case of German measles. The symptoms were physically painful – in addition to the spots, she developed tender, swollen glands in her neck and her face flushed roseate – but, as when she developed chickenpox and conceived the plot of *The Price of Salt*, she found the measles beneficial to her imagination. During the illness she settled on an ending to her novel. By 7 July she had written 263 pages of her first draft. 'Good books,' she said, 'write themselves',[45] and, sure enough, by the beginning of February 1962 she had finished it.

Yet after the book was published – by Harper's in 1962, and by Heinemann in Britain the following year – Highsmith considered *The Cry of the Owl* one of her weakest books, describing the hero as 'rather square . . . a polite sitting duck for more evil characters, and a passive bore'.[46] Critics, however, thought it one of her most powerful novels. 'As Sophocles hit on the incest, so Miss Highsmith hits on the murder which is in the unconscious and will out,' commented Brigid Brophy. '*The Cry of the Owl* builds up Websterian tragedy.' She went on to praise the novelist for tackling 'what Dickens more than once approached but veered away from, the psychology of the self-elected victim'.[47] In 1967, Brophy would tell an interviewer from *The New York Times Book Review* 'I think, in the last twenty years, there have been five or six novels that have been very good, and that is all one is entitled to expect. Two that I think of are Patricia Highsmith's *The Cry of the Owl* and Nabokov's *Lolita*.'[48]

Underpinning the novel is an unsettling nexus of voyeuristic compulsions and delusional fantasies. Robert is driven to spy on Jenny because the sight of her cooking in the kitchen or pottering about her home, makes him, on one level, feel undeniably happier and calmer. Jenny represents idealised domesticity and, like Annabelle in *This Sweet Sickness*, an unreal image of femininity – 'To Robert, she was all of a piece, like a properly made statue.'[49] Watching her also seems to satisfy an unconscious need in him as Jenny reminds him of 'a picture or a person he already knew from somewhere'.[50]

The discovery of a strange man lurking in the bushes could, in a lesser novelist's hands, have been reduced to a melodramatic scene full of horror and disbelief. But when Jenny sees Robert watching her she does not behave hysterically or call the police, perhaps the 'logical' reaction in such a situation. Rather, she invites the prowler into her house and offers him a cup of coffee. ' "I suppose you think I'm insane, asking you to come in," ' she says.[51] Her irrationality, like Robert's, stems from a feeling that the stranger is representative of a larger symbol, one she does not yet fully understand. It is the recognition of this emotional blueprint, rather than the personality, intellect or physique of Robert Forester, that Jenny falls in love with. As Robert gradually loses interest in her – the reality of her is just too much for him to bear – so Jenny becomes increasingly obsessed with her one-time stalker.

Jenny's fiancé, Greg Wyncoop, also develops an unhealthy desire to spy on both his girlfriend and love rival, Forester, thereby completing the voyeuristic matrix. ' "I have the definite feeling if everybody in the world didn't keep watching to see what everybody else did, we'd all go beserk." ' Robert tells his therapist. ' "Left on their own, people wouldn't know how to live." '[52]

Written in Highsmith's distinctive, cool, detached style, *The Cry of the Owl*, juxtaposes the everyday and the extraordinary, the pathetically banal and the genuinely tragic. For instance, Robert's friend from his days in army service, Kermit, was killed not in the Korean War, but by a freak accident involving a catapult while training in Alaska. Throughout the book, incidents which run the risk of tipping over into excessive melodrama are undermined by being grounded in the mundane and the ordinary. When Robert and Jenny are in the middle of a heated argument about whether he should admit to the police about his fight with Greg, Highsmith introduces a line about cooking frozen chicken pies for supper. 'These chicken pies won't be done in half an hour,' says Jenny, before worrying about whether they are cooked all the way through and when they should be eaten – before or after the visit from the police.[53] Conversely, everyday objects are posited as strange and otherworldly – a bank of used cars is described as looking like 'a vast army of dead soldiers in armor',[54] while the cry of an owl in the wood becomes symbolic of death.

When Greg disappears and an unidentified corpse is found downriver. Jenny jumps to the conclusion that Robert is responsible for her fiancé's death and, in a disturbed state of mind, realises the symbolic meaning of the man who used to watch her from the woods. Robert is, like the cry of the owl, representative of death. The chapter in which Highsmith describes Jenny's unsettled mind as she prepares to kill herself must rank as one of the most compelling and convincing suicide scenes in fiction as it documents the sordid reality of the act, while at the same time capturing the stream-of-consciousness images which flit through a despairing and dying mind. Jenny walks outside, into the garden where she first met Robert, drowsy from sleeping pills, carrying a sweater she was knitting for him. There she lies down and cuts her wrists. 'It was too dark to see, or her eyelids were closing, but she could feel warm blood flowing down her raised forearm . . .'[55]

The final climax of the book is, as Brigid Brophy suggested, reminiscent of the last act of a Jacobean tragedy set in suburban America. The scene – a confrontation between Robert, his ex-wife Nickie and Greg – is awash with blood and gore; a wound is described as 'like a little mouth with bright blood jetting from it',[56] while the red stain on one of the characters' shirts is likened to a strange flower 'blossom'.[57]

Reading the book can be likened to taking a hallucinogenic drug, one that alters one's perceptions and uncomfortably shifts the basis of reality. It's hardly surprising then that Joan Kahn, after reading the manuscript, described the novel, in a letter dated 8 February 1962, as, 'a strong drink, and may not be everyone's curl-up-with choice . . .'[58] A few days later a contract was drawn up promising an advance of $1,500. Kahn, the fierce task-mistress, was, as Highsmith knew only too well, not easily pleased, but she was astounded by the novel's intensity. 'You've done an amazing job,' she added.[59]

After a spate of disastrous affairs, Highsmith was understandably anxious about entering into another relationship. Flicking through old diaries, she came to the conclusion that her personal life had been, so far, 'a chronicle of unbelievable mistakes'.[60] Why did she keep repeating the same patterns? What lessons could she learn? Would she ever be happy? Although in the future she resolved to try and avoid women who were fundamentally sadistic in temperament, the problems were, she realised, so deeply ingrained in her personality that it was unlikely anything would change. 'I avoid nothing,' she wrote in her notebook. 'I show everything I feel, even without speaking. I play nothing cautiously, and last of all will I ever save myself in an emotional situation.'[61]

In March 1961, she moved from her house in Old Ferry Road to another rented property in New Hope, at 113 South Sugan Drive, a three-bedroom, two-storey building with views overlooking a brook. In the summer she embarked on a relationship with thirty-nine-year-old Daisy Winston, who at the time worked as a waitress in New Hope. 'Daisy had black hair and was of small build,' says Peggy Lewis. 'I remember her as being very bright and lively.'[62] Daisy's best friend was New Hope woodworker and craftsman Phillip Powell, who settled in the town in 1947. 'Pat was quite a character, very dour but my first impression of her was her shyness and it was clear that she needed booze to keep her going,' he says. 'Daisy never admitted that her relationship with Pat was an intimate one. New Hope was very free but she was a very private person. There was no question about the nature of their short – but intense – relationship, yet it remained unspoken.'[63]

In August 1961, Highsmith, ever the romantic, composed a love poem for Daisy, in which she said that she pledged herself to her new lover, her 'Little jewel of black and gold.'[64] Daisy, in letters she wrote later to Highsmith, recalls how, in 1991 she found a batch of Pat's notes, 'some very dear, some humerous [sic] but all brought back very fond memories',[65] written to her thirty years before. 'But you never brought me flowers – oh well – I won't hold that against you,' she added. 'But fear not – it all went up in smoke.'[66] Highsmith's intimacy with Daisy lasted less than a year, yet their emotional attachment was deep and long-lasting and she dedicated *The Cry of the Owl* to her. When Highsmith was living in Europe, Daisy, who called herself Pat's 'adopted daughter', would send her packages containing chillies, Campbell's split pea soup and shoes – US size nine – from America, while Highsmith, who later developed a reputation as something of a miser, would think nothing of lending her friend money to cover her bills. In fact, in 1967, Highsmith made a will, one which she would subsequently rewrite, bequeathing half her 'wordly' goods to Daisy. 'What a charming Freudian mistake,' Pat wrote to Kingsley, correcting herself. 'I mean, of course, wordly . . . and I have done it again. I mean, of course, worldly.'[67]

A cold winter night, December 1961. Highsmith is dreaming of murder again. She takes hold of an axe and slowly raises it above her head before bringing it down on a defenceless old woman, splitting her face open. Blow after blow reduces the woman to a bloody mass. The murder is without motive, but nevertheless the police have no doubt who committed the crime and arrest her soon after. The dream, she said, 'was representative of guilt and of a deep fear that I might someday do this. In a fit of drunkenness or anger. But the victim in my dream was unknown to me, and ergo the murder had no objective. So much the more a crime of sheer brutality, wantonness, insanity, even.'[68]

In March 1962, Highsmith drew up an advertisement to sublet her house in New Hope. Her relationship with Daisy was over, she planned a three-month European trip and needed someone to pay her $150 monthly rent and feed her two cats. Before she left, she said her goodbyes to her friend Alex Szogyi whom she had met in the spring of 1960, when he was a French professor at Wesleyan University, Middletown, Connecticut; later she would dedicate her short-story collection, *Eleven*, to him.

'I thought she was just wonderful,' says Alex. 'She was quite beautiful then, but her face became quite tortured and unfortunately most people remember that and not the beauty of her earlier years. At the party when I first met her we talked for hours and we became close immediately – she told me she wanted me to be a friend of hers for the rest of her life. I was just so honoured that she liked me. I could have been the brother she never had. She was an only child as I was and we both had difficulties with our parents. I know that had she remained here I probably would have had her with me, because I was bisexual. It probably would have happened, but it never did because she went away, she was no longer part of my life and I was very shy. Before she left, she gave me her writing desk, which I still have.

'She was never happy, not that I know of, but she was curious and interested in people and very loyal to her friends. Yet some of my friends were afraid of her – she wanted to really find out their essence, I guess; she had a mind of an inquiring novelist. She was a wonderful prober. Pat was always going to the very depths of experiences. There was never a dull moment with her and I do believe that she is a major American writer. Later in life, however, she became very possessive, controlling and jealous and eventually our friendship soured.'[69]

Highsmith arrived in Paris in mid-May, where she stayed for ten days, after which she took a flight to Rome, travelling on to Cagliari, Sardinia. Her companion for the summer would be Ellen Hill. From Sardinia, the two women took a boat to Naples, and they arrived at the house they had rented in Positano at the beginning of June.

Within moments of settling in at the house at 15 Via Monte, the psychological battle between the two ex-lovers resumed. Ellen started to hark back over what she thought was Pat's ill-treatment and neglect of her and, in response, Highsmith reminded the older woman of her own hellish behaviour and suicide attempts. Highsmith decided that she would never share a house with another person again (a vow she would subsequently break); she could not bear the thought of being told what to do or the idea that someone was dominating her. 'I have a real knack for finding people who do this,' she wrote, 'apart from this, my past associations have left me either emotionally or financially bankrupt,

and the prospect of another such abyss and of hauling myself out of it
utterly dismays me. I am to [*sic*] old to have that kind of courage any
more.'[70]

From Positano, the two women travelled to Rome, and at the end of
June, Highsmith journeyed on to Venice, where she stayed at the
Pensione Seguso, an establishment which would feature in her 1967
novel *Those Who Walk Away*, and then Paris. On 12 July she paid a
visit to Oscar Wilde's grave in Père Lachaise cemetery – with its
tombstone designed by Jacob Epstein – and where she read the lines
inscribed on his grave, from his 'Ballad of Reading Gaol', 'And alien
tears shall fill for him/Pity's long broken urn,/For his mourners shall be
outcast men,/And outcasts always mourn.' Highsmith had long felt an
empathy for Wilde and earlier in the year had transcribed a passage
from his letters into her notebook, a sentence which she would use at
the beginning of *Ripley Under Ground*; it could have been an epigraph
to her own life: 'I think I would more readily die for what I do not
believe in than for what I hold to be true . . . Sometimes I think that the
artistic life is a long and lovely suicide, and I am not sorry that it is
so . . .'[71]

20

A freedom from responsibility

1962–1964

Highsmith had no qualms about using the emotional core of her experience as a basis for her work; what was more unsettling was when her novels then started to play themselves out in her life. In the summer of 1962, she met the wife of a London businessman, a woman with whom she would conduct a four-year affair. The scenario echoed the one described in her incomplete, unpublished *First Person Novel*, which was narrated by an older, married woman and took the form of an extended analysis of her lesbian relationships.

When Highsmith met the woman, whom I shall call X, she was immediately infatuated. She wrote a poem in which she compared her new object of idolisation – who was middle-aged, middle-class and a mother – to an orchid of white crystal in a mountain cave and, as she flew back to America that summer, she pledged her undying love for her. For once, however, it seems that the woman's infatuation matched Highsmith's for intensity; in her letters X described how after Pat left England she felt as though her oxygen supply had been cut off.

Back in New Hope, Highsmith tried to concentrate on work, but all she could think about was the woman who had recently captured her heart. In a piece Highsmith wrote for the *Sunday Times Magazine* in 1974, she recalled how, at forty-one, she sat on the edge of the sink in her house in New Hope in the early hours of the morning thinking how wonderful it was to be in love. ' "What a pleasure just to exist!" ' she thought. ' "Why haven't I ever realised this before?" It really seemed to me then that I hadn't thought of it or felt it before.'[1] Highsmith felt frustrated because she knew her letters might be read by X's husband. Was there, she asked, a place where she could send her notes so that she

could tell her exactly how she felt? Unfortunately not, the other woman
replied. But the quantity – eight in five weeks – and the depth of feeling
expressed in the letters she sent over from England helped ease Highsmith's anxiety.

Highsmith felt desperately in need of her. 'I am nearly sick,' she wrote
in her diary, 'and must get hold of myself or crack up.'[2] Her friends
counselled her to find a love within fifty miles of New Hope, rather than a
woman on the other side of the Atlantic, and although Highsmith knew
she should follow such logical advice, she was, like one of her characters,
motivated by a totally irrational and irresistible desire. 'I am so much in
love – obviously,' wrote Highsmith, 'that I cannot see anything else.'[3]

When X suggested that, as she was staying in Paris for a week that
autumn, Pat should fly over and join her, Highsmith did not hesitate.
The writer flew from Idlewild airport to Paris, meeting her lover off the
London train at the Gare du Nord the next day. According to Highsmith, their initial awkwardness at seeing one another was soon
replaced by passion and, after dinner, while walking along St Germain,
the two women kissed, Pat losing an earring in the process. 'She is quite
aware of her charms,' wrote Highsmith in her diary, 'and melts into my
arms as if she were smelted by Vulcan expressly for that purpose.'[4]

The two women travelled separately to England – Pat by plane, her
lover by train – but in London they met at Highsmith's hotel and at X's
house. They talked about whether they should tell X's husband about
their relationship, but Highsmith cautioned against it. As it was, the
woman said, her husband was behaving extremely oddly, telling his
wife of a strange dream he had had seemingly based on Ibsen's play,
The Master Builder, remarking that 'the women with strange names
enter people's lives and destroy them'; apparently he thought that
Highsmith's name had an odd ring to it.

Highsmith flew back to America in November, and on arrival in New
Hope she once again found it hard to focus on work. In her diary she
wrote of how her lover made her sick with desire and the same month,
in a bid to be nearer X, she decided that she would leave America and
base herself at the house she rented in Positano. When interviewers
asked Highsmith why she left the United States for Europe – she made
the permanent move in early 1963 – the writer replied that she was
'bored with going backwards and forwards and I thought that Europe
was more interesting'.[5] The statement no doubt contains a grain of
truth, but it does not reflect the driving force behind the transition – her
love for the woman who would soon push her to the edge of reason.

*   *   *

In September 1962, Highsmith started to plot the book which would eventually – after heavy rewriting and a final rejection from Harper's – be published, by Doubleday in America and Heinemann in Britain, as *The Glass Cell*. She had first had the idea of setting a book in a prison in 1961 when she received a letter from a thirty-six-year-old inmate of a Chicago penitentiary convicted for forgery, breaking and entering and parole busting, telling her how much he had enjoyed *Deep Water*. 'I don't think my books should be in prison libraries,' Highsmith said later.[6] Prisoner and author stuck up a correspondence and Highsmith asked him to describe a typical day for her. The resulting three type-written pages – details of his meals, his work in a prison shoe factory, his relationship with his cell mate and the sounds that echoed around the building after lights out – was, she said, 'the kind of information one cannot get from any book',[7] and, inspired by her epistolary communication with her new pen-pal, she became increasingly fascinated by the subject. 'A few months later . . . I read a book about convicts, a non-fiction book, which told the story of an engineer imprisoned unjustly, a man who was strung up by the thumbs by sadistic guards, and afterward became a morphine addict because of his constant pain . . .' she wrote. 'Here was part of a story ready-made.'[8] Indeed, *The Glass Cell* centres around the experiences of such a man – Philip Carter, an engineer serving a six-year sentence for a fraud he didn't commit and who is strung up by the thumbs for two days and becomes addicted to morphine while in the prison hospital.

While researching the novel, Highsmith also read John Bartlow Martin's *Break Down the Walls*, a non-fiction analysis of the 1952 riots at the State Prison of Southern Michigan in Jackson, described by the author as 'the most dangerous prison riot in American history'.[9] The influence of the book on Highsmith is clear, both in terms of its subject matter and its documentary style. Martin writes of 'The Hole' – a name Highsmith borrowed for her book to convey the hell of the solitary confinement quarters – describing in detail the solid steel doors, the bare wooden bench for sleeping, the absence of wash bowl, bed, and light bulbs. Martin goes on to trace the roots of the Jackson riots – and explores the history of the prison system, debating the reasons for its failure and suggesting solutions to the problem of crime and punishment. In *The Glass Cell*, Highsmith is quite clear in her condemnation of the prison system, serving as it does only to corrupt an innocent man, Philip Carter, and opinion which reflects Martin's bold statement at the end of his book: 'The American prison system makes no sense. Prisons have failed as deterrents to crime. They have failed as rehabilitative institutions . . . Prisons should be abolished . . . Prison is not just the enemy of the prisoner. It is the enemy of society.'[10]

Highsmith was keen to see inside a prison for herself and on 19 December 1962, together with an American criminal lawyer, she visited one in Doylestown, near her New Hope home. 'He [the lawyer] could not get me past the bars, but at least I could wait in the lobby just outside and see the prisoners walking freely in and out of cells whose doors stood open . . . and I watched them for perhaps forty minutes.'[11] Although she had researched the novel carefully and admitted that it would be a 'challenge to my imagination, a difficult job to do well',[12] she could not have foreseen the trouble she would have with the book.

Originally she conceived the story in allegorical terms, envisioning the prison as representative of the world, but soon realised that such a heavy-handed approach would be unfeasible. She thought she was ready to start writing the novel in mid-December, just before her visit to the prison in Doylestown, but she missed X in London, a feeling of wretchedness which threatened to unbalance her. She wrote in her diary, 'Such unhappiness and loneliness as I felt today must be counter-acted by work, or I shall go mad.'[13] By 11 January 1963, she had written forty pages, but the book was interrupted by ill-health – in early February a doctor diagnosed exhaustion and prescribed Vitamin B12 shots together with the advice that she should eat more liver – and the move from New Hope to Positano. She sailed across the Atlantic in February, stopping in Lisbon and arrived at the house at 15 Via Monte at the end of the month, just as Positano was in the grip of a cold spell. As she tried to settle down to work she received a telegram from London asking her to call X – she was upset and could no longer hide the truth about her affair with Highsmith from her husband. According to Highsmith, although her lover's husband had guessed the truth of the situation, he did not bear the couple any ill-will and even thought that Pat's presence in London might help lift his wife's spirits. 'It seems I'll never have the tranquillity or the time to work again,' wrote Highsmith in her diary. 'The prison book is in my head, but however to get it on paper?'[14] The next day, the writer took a taxi to Naples, a train to Rome and then a flight to London. Over the next few days, X's mood gradually improved until she felt well enough to accompany her husband out socially. Meanwhile, Highsmith stayed home alone. Later, in 1968, after the relationship between the two women had failed, Highsmith wrote in her diary of her stupidity for being fooled by her lover's sudden recovery. 'I should put her in a book one day,' she concluded.[15]

While in London, Highsmith did a couple of interviews to help publicise *The Cry of the Owl*, due for its British publication in May, including a radio broadcast with literary journalist Francis Wyndham. 'I remember both of us were so nervous we needed a drink,' says Wyndham, 'but her hands were shaking so much that the sound of ice in the glass blocked out her voice. I liked her immediately. She was very unpretentious and did not behave like she was a great writer – she talked about how much her books sold and things like that. I could tell that she was shy and reticent, a woman with deep feelings, someone who was affectionate, but also difficult. I don't think she was a very happy person. She wasn't a pretty woman, but she was attractive. She was like a certain sort of American woman who wears slacks; there was nothing feminine about her at all. Some of her books are terrifying and I soon realised that she couldn't *not* have a dark side.'[16] Wyndham followed up the interview with a piece in the *New Statesman*, the first article in a British newspaper or magazine to analyse Highsmith as a serious novelist rather than as an author of genre fiction. Highsmith liked the critique so much that she wrote to Wyndham from Positano to thank him. 'Guilt is her theme,' wrote Wyndham, 'and she approaches it through two contrasting heroes. These may be simplified as the guilty man who has justified his guilt and the innocent man who feels himself to be guilty.'[17] Her 1955 novel, *The Talented Mr Ripley*, he believed 'sheds more light on "the problem of identity" than many solemn approaches to a fashionable subject.'[18] Although the reviewer thought Highsmith in *The Cry of the Owl* was 'writing well below top form,' nevertheless 'she still maintains an exciting pitch of narrative tension . . . Miss Highsmith's plots are often praised for being ingenious, but they are never tidy; chance, coincidence, silly misunderstandings play their part, as they do in life. She knows that people do not always act in their own best interests, and that their motives are more obscure than psychological novelists often care to admit.'[19] Wyndham's acute observations on Highsmith's work also offer a prescient insight into the writer's life: for all the self-analysis contained in her cahiers and diaries, her motivation was often just as self-destructive, irrational and opaque as that which drove many of her characters.

That spring, the writer travelled back to Italy with X, but soon after arriving in Positano, Highsmith was struck down by acidosis and vomiting, an attack which lasted twenty hours. 'It was the most painful night of my life,' she wrote.[20] Yet she was touched by her lover's kindness and although their relationship was far from easy – X believed homosexual relations were flawed and she was constantly torn between conventional and bohemian instincts – Highsmith was upset when she had to return back to London after less than a month away. Indeed, over Easter, after receiving no letter from X, Highsmith confessed in her diary that she could imagine ending it all. 'I have imagined killing myself, strangely more strongly now than with anyone else I have ever known . . . I set this down because for the first time suicide has crossed my mind – I think only in a romantic way . . . It is generally selfish, which is my main objection to it.'[21] If her lover did leave her, she was certain she would do it. However, after a letter in which X told Pat of her continuing love for her, she felt so happy she changed her will, leaving half her estate to her mother, half to X in London, while her literary manuscripts she bequeathed to Kingsley.

Alone in Positano, Highsmith worked on *The Glass Cell*. 'The book still uncertain,' she wrote on 3 May, noting that she had completed 104 pages, 'am not in the depths yet, but reasonably confident & happier than I've been in many a month.'[22] But, by the time she had finished another 150 pages, a month later, she realised that 'at p 245 it is only now breaking into the story!'[23] Most evenings she spent by herself, writing letters to X about their forthcoming summer holiday in Aldeburgh, Suffolk; reading T.E. Lawrence's *The Mint*, Golding's *The Lord of the Flies* and Balzac's *Père Goriot*; and subsisting on spaghetti with meat sauce. Occasionally she met fellow resident Peter Thomson for drinks. 'Pat was an enormously attractive person and she did not suffer fools at all,' recalls Peter, whom Highsmith thought the most talented painter in Positano. 'She was basically very honest and said what she felt. She was also a jolly good painter – I remember this one work she did of a gigantic cat's head, which I thought was quite magical. Both of us were heavy drinkers in those days and her capacity for alcohol was certainly very impressive.'[24]

That summer, just as she was putting what she thought were the finishing touches to *The Glass Cell*, she received a telegram from London requesting her presence; according to Highsmith, once again X was unsettled by the situation. Dutifully, Highsmith packed her bags for London, from where the two women travelled to Aldeburgh for a month's holiday. She described the Suffolk seaside town as 'full of the atmosphere and domestic decor which I call 1910 or Edwardian', and recorded in her notebook that a haircut cost 2/6 and a small lobster, 5/6.[25]

Highsmith returned to Positano – alone – in early August, where she conceded that her prison novel was 'messy in spots, long in others'[26] and plotted a new ending. She flirted with the possibility of wintering in

Rome and although, in early October, she did rent an apartment in the Italian capital, at 38 Via Vecchiarelli, her stay was a short one. On 5 October, she wrote to Jenny Bradley telling her that she had just finished *The Glass Cell* and had sent off the manuscript to America. Ten days later, Joan Kahn wrote to Patricia Schartle, thanking her for sending her the first 188 pages of the novel. Although she thought Highsmith described the terrors of prison life in graphic detail, some of the details were rather repetitious. In addition, the pace of the book was too slow. 'But more important – the people don't come through . . .' she wrote, 'one can't identify with the characters . . . On the basis of what's here, I'd have to say "no contract".'[27] Patricia Schartle sent Harper's the remaining pages of the novel, but on 13 November, Joan Kahn wrote to Highsmith, still in Rome, outlining the problem with the book. As she saw it, the character of Carter was unclear: 'Carter before prison we know too little. Carter after prison is certainly a man in a mess – but the mess seems to us one that, though prison may have enlarged it, probably existed before . . . there isn't enough surprise, or depth, to keep us interested – and not enough to make us care.'[28]

Highsmith's spirits were already low before she received the letter. She regretted leaving Positano for Rome and she worried about her finances – at the end of October she had estimated that her total income for the year came to $4,400, and she was sure she was spending more than she earned. On 26 October she wrote in her diary of her increasingly anxious state of mind. 'I was quite frantic & exhausted Mon–Wed & thought I might have to go to a hospital, a psychiatrist – or whatnot – for some manner of sedation. Everything has gone wrong this year, financially, with the sole exception of Heinemann buying [*The Two Faces of*] *January* & I have not sold anything I have done in the last 15 months. Is there any wonder I am discouraged?'[29]

She left Rome at the beginning of November and, after a brief spell in London, she moved into a house in Aldeburgh – at 27 King Street – which she rented for five guineas a week. It was in the Suffolk seaside town that, on 22 November, while in Jay's Hotel, packed with Americans, she heard of the assassination of John F. Kennedy. 'I only saw her in despair once, and that was after the murder of John Kennedy,' says Richard Ingham, who lived in Aldeburgh at the time. 'She came bursting into our flat . . . just a few yards along from her own house, and absolutely bellowed, "Oh, Richard, what the hell's wrong with America?"[30] In her diary, Highsmith noted how the whole world was just as shocked as America.

Alone in Aldeburgh – X tended to treat the house more as a holiday home than a permanent base, visiting only at weekends – Highsmith was at a loss about how to rework *The Glass Cell*. Her confidence was lifted, however, with the news from Patricia Schartle just before Christmas that her seventeen-month 'jinx' as she called it, had finally come to an end. Doubleday would publish *The Two Faces of January* in America if she cut thirty-two pages, while *Ellery Queen's Mystery Magazine* had bought her short story 'Who is Crazy', which she had written in October. On 13 January of the new year she came up with a strategy – she would rework the prison novel from page 120 – and at the end of the month she conceived a new ending for the book.

She finished the heavy rewrite by 22 March, and in June she heard that Heinemann planned to publish it early in 1965. She also submitted the manuscript to Doubleday, which accepted it on condition that she cut forty pages, and which published the book in December 1964. 'After all my cuts,' she said, 'first in black and then in red for the second round, some of the pages had only three lines left.'[31]

On the novel's publication, some reviewers admitted they were baffled by it. 'I don't know quite what to make of Miss Highsmith's book,' said the critic from the *New York Times Book Review*.[32] Others attacked Highsmith for her stark portrayal of a world in which good men can be corrupted by the so-called civilised justice system, go on to kill and remain unpunished at the end of it all. 'There are not many nastier fictional worlds than Patricia Highsmith's, and soon they sicken, worlds for sadistic voyeurs who get their kicks from seeing the poor worms hooked and squirming,' wrote a reviewer in the *Times Literary Supplement*. 'There is not much else to do with her new anti-hero, Philip Carter, but pity him or enjoy his pain, and the first without any kind of catharsis soon comes to feel very like the other.'[33] He concluded, however, that the book was well-structured and well-written and, ultimately, any objections 'must be moral, not technical'.[34]

Highsmith often drew inspiration from her surroundings, jotting down details about cities and countries in her cahiers under the special heading of 'Places'; journeying to foreign countries, she said when still a teenager, was surely the 'most desirable thing on earth'.[35] In 1947, she wrote how travelling was one of the activities – along with ironing, sewing and receiving dental treatment – which helped her in the act of creation. She later recalled how, as a young woman, she adored prowling around strange foreign cities, seeking out new places with an 'indiscriminate curiosity'.[36] In a piece she contributed to the *World Authors* series, she wrote of how since leaving New York she had had a 'rocky time geographically', but confessed, 'the fact is, I do like travelling and making acquaintance with new scenes. I always use them.'[37] After a trip to Mexico she wrote *A Game for the Living*; on returning from Greece and Crete she plotted *The Two Faces of January*; a holiday in Venice resulted in *Those Who Walk Away*, and a journey to Hammamet, Tunisia, was used as backdrop for *The Tremor of Forgery*. Most of her novels set outside the USA feature Americans cast adrift in foreign settings. Such locations, noted Julian Symons, 'often give the Highsmith characters a freedom of action, springing from what they feel is a freedom from responsibility, which makes them do strange – but, in the context of place and person, convincing – things'.[38]

On 26 April 1964, Highsmith bought Bridge Cottage, Earl Soham, Suffolk, a seventeenth-century, three-bedroom, pale pink cottage. The house, she told Arthur Koestler, was 'very good for working, due to extreme English quietude' and the fact that for 90 per cent of the time her lover was in London.[39] In a letter Highsmith wrote to Kingsley, just before moving into the property, she described the house, formed by knocking together two workers' cottages, and boasting a black weathervane, as 'so picturesque it is rather unbelievable'.[40] Outside there was a reasonably sized garden, stocked with old-fashioned roses and camelias, at the bottom of which ran a stream. The writer Ronald Blythe, whom Highsmith met in January 1964 and who lived nearby in the village of Debach, was a frequent visitor to Bridge Cottage. 'It was very clean and comfortable, orderly and warm, but there was, as they say, nothing "good" in it,' he says. 'It was as if she had just gone out and got the basics. She wasn't at all a good hostess – she was rather bad at it really – but she liked to invite me over for supper. After a while, however, it was obvious that she wanted her life back to herself again, to go back to her typewriter and work. That was her reality more than anything else – the act of writing made her happy, gave her something that nothing else could.'[41]

Ten days after moving into her new home, she wrote in her cahier the plot outline for a book set in Suffolk. The result was *A Suspension of Mercy* (published as *The Story-Teller* in America), and its opening description of the Suffolk countryside was obviously inspired by the land near Highsmith's new home. 'Since I had been living in Suffolk . . . I wanted to use this new ground and atmosphere and set the book there,' she said.[42] Yet there is nothing high-blown or purplish about the prose; if anything the portrait of the place veers towards the quotidian.

The land around Sydney and Alicia Bartleby's two-story cottage was
flat, like most Suffolk country. A road, two-laned and paved, went by
the house at a distance of twenty yards. To one side of the front walk,
which was of slightly askew flagstones, five young elms gave some
privacy, and on the other side a tall, bushy hedge provided a better
screen for thirty feet. For this reason, Sydney had never trimmed
it . . .[43]

The book also grew out of the working relationship between Highsmith and aspiring writer Richard Ingham, then teaching mathematics
at Woodbridge School. In the spring of 1964, she set time aside from
her schedule to work on an idea for a television 'cliffhanger', *It's a Deal*,
with Ingham. Like Sydney and his writing partner Alex in the finished
novel, she would plot the synopsis, while he would bash out the words.
In the script Lucy Lucas is having an affair with Robbie Vanderhof.[44]
Each Friday afternoon the couple meet for regular lovemaking sessions,
an arrangement Lucy finds increasingly sordid. As she tries to convince
her lover of her need for a greater level of commitment, Robbie lashes
out and hits her, leaving her sobbing. When Lucy's husband, Joel,
returns home and finds his wife surrounded by evidence of the fight, he
kills her, planning to frame Robbie for the murder. Dressed in the kind
of gardening clothes favoured by Robbie, Joel buries the body under
one of the newly planted trees in the nearby forest. In the middle of
digging up the earth, Joel is caught in the act by a young girl, Elinor, and
as she cannot see his face, he confesses to the crime. Joel reports his wife
missing and, after Elinor reports the crime to the police, investigators
subsequently find the corpse under one of the trees. Robbie is found
guilty and, in the last scene, just as Joel is about to celebrate his wife-free
status, his sluttish neighbour, Betty, turns up at the house and makes an
announcement. She knows that it was Joel, not Robbie, who killed Lucy
and unless he agrees to marry her she will inform the police. 'It's a deal,'
says the horrified Joel.[45]

'*It's a Deal* is rather slight and unconvincing,' admits Ingham, 'but I
think it reflects Pat's view that, be as clever and resourceful as you may,
life will screw you in the end.'[46] Later, in a letter to Ronald Blythe,
Highsmith confessed how she had transplanted the character of
Richard Ingham from life into fiction. 'I "used" Ingham as the . . .
writing partner in *A Suspension of Mercy*,' she wrote in 1969.[47]

The gestation of the book – which had a working title of 'A Lark at
Dawn' – also had its roots in an idea she had once had to rework the
clichéd body-in-a-carpet trope. What would happen, she thought, if

there was nobody inside? What if the person carrying the carpet was seen acting in a suspicious manner and was suspected of carrying out a murder? She combined this idea with another one about a writer who becomes increasingly confused about the difference between the plots inside his head and his external reality. 'This kind of writer-hero, I thought, could be not only amusing – and I mean in a comic sense – but could explore the rather harmless, everyday schizophrenia which every-where abounds – yea, even in thee and me,' she wrote in *Plotting and Writing Suspense Fiction*.[48] In a letter to Kingsley, on 27 July, in the middle of writing the novel, she expanded on the point, drawing even closer parallels between the hero of her latest book, Sydney Bartleby, an American living in Suffolk, and herself. 'He is a writer, who gets life a little mixed up with his plots. Something that may happen to me. I think I have some schizoid tendencies, which must Be Watched.'[49]

Originally, she said, she wanted the writer in her story to commit no murder at all, only to be suspected of the crime. But it didn't quite turn out that way. 'Sydney does at last commit an odd murder, which he thinks of as a temporary "suspension of mercy" on his part,' Highsmith said. 'He kills his wife's lover by forcing him to take an overdose of sleeping pills. But Sydney is only slightly suspected of this, and nothing can be proven.'[50]

The correlation between writing and criminality is one of the most striking aspects of Highsmith's work. Many of her criminal-heroes – particularly Ripley – have imaginations that enable them to forget their immediate reality and live out the fiction inside their heads. But in Sydney Bartleby, Highsmith created the first of her writer protagonists, later joined by Howard Ingham (a novelist) in *The Tremor of Forgery*; Edith (a freelance journalist) in *Edith's Diary*; E. Taylor Cheever (a sub-editor turned aspiring, but failed, author) featured in the short story, 'The Man who Wrote Books in his Head'; Stanley and Ginnie Brixton (husband and wife novelists and critics) in 'Something You Have to Live With'; and Elinor Sievert (a freelance journalist) in 'The Pond' (the three stories can be found in the 1979 collection *Slowly, Slowly in the Wind*). In an interview with Diana Cooper-Clark, published in 1981, the author was asked about the connection between the artist and the criminal. Did she agree with George Bernard Shaw's idea that the two occupations bore some striking similarities? 'I can think of only one slight closeness,' Highsmith replied, 'and that is that an imaginative writer is very free-wheeling; he has to forget about his own personal morals, especially if he is writing about criminals. He has to feel anything is possible.'[51] In the same interview she explored the point further, adding that the criminal, 'at least for a short period of time is free, free to do anything he wishes'.[52] The issue was taken up by the writer Bettina Berch, who interviewed Highsmith in 1984. Did her writer protagonists function as alter egos? 'Yes, in the case of Sydney, definitely,' Highsmith replied, referring to A Suspension of Mercy. 'Because I was interested in the fact that I don't understand murder, or the very instant of one person, for instance, taking away the consciousness of another person – taking away the life – this very phenomenon or event I really don't understand . . .'[53]

Writers, like criminals, live outside the confines of the conventional, creating a environment which frequently transgresses so-called 'normal' moral perspectives. As she was working on A Suspension of Mercy, Highsmith scribbled in her notebook, 'It seems natural that a writer will tend to write about the "same kind" of hero – with the intellectual associations that he has himself.'[54] Charles Latimer, who met Highsmith in the early sixties when he was the advertising manager at William Heinemann and who later became one of her closest friends, remembers how the writer prepared herself for work. 'Pat liked to act out things to see what they felt like,' he says. 'I remember she buried some snails in the woods behind her cottage to give her some ideas or emotions for A Suspension of Mercy. Similarly, when I stayed with Pat at her house in Tegna, Switzerland, I remember seeing her prowl around the house late at night on several occasions. She was a night owl. The house would be in pitch darkness and Pat, wearing blue- and white-striped flannel pyjamas and a khaki, terry-cloth dressing gown, would walk cautiously through the rooms, shining her torch in all directions, sometimes stepping outside for a moment or two. I imagined her wondering what it would be like to find an intruder in the house, or perhaps she was thinking what it would feel like to be an intruder.'[55] According to Charles, Pat hated to be thought of as an intellectual. 'She loathed the term, and she told me she did things by instinct,' he says. 'As she wrote, she became the characters in her books.'[56]

Ronald Blythe recalls how, on occasions, he would cycle back from Bridge Cottage to his house in Debach, feeling upset and uneasy. 'Sometimes when I was with her, we strayed without words into this world where you did what you liked, so you were free as if you were a criminal,' he says. 'Although I didn't understand the psychopathic side that shows itself in her novels, now and again this despair and distress would overcome me; all we were doing was sitting together in a room. I don't think she was connected to what most people see as the "real world". She was cut off from what we think of as ordinary life, cut off by her genius.

'I remember one day I went over to her house for supper. We were just beginning to eat when a plop of water fell on to the table. I looked up and saw that the lightshade, one of those glass bowls, was full of water, which was pouring in from the ceiling. Although she said she had asked someone to come and fix it, I knew nobody would venture out on a Saturday night and told her I would do it. "Leave it," she said, but I ignored her. I left the table and went upstairs to the bathroom. The ball cock in the lavatory was bent and so I fixed it, pulled the chain and stopped the overflow. I came downstairs, cleaned everything up, but she didn't talk to me for hours after that. She was annoyed, I suppose, because I had disobeyed her.

'Yet there was a warmth about our friendship, which was affectionate and very caring, and she struck me as an intensely truthful person. She would stay over at my house if I thought she had had too much to drink and I would stay over with her because sometimes she was rather unhappy, but she wouldn't say why. I thought she was rather attractive in a strange way, so unlike anyone I'd ever met before. She had beautiful manners and a low voice and she smoked incessantly. She didn't walk or behave in a butch way at all, she was well-bred and had a kind of elegance. Yet her loneliness showed in her face – a cloudiness, an ugliness really – which would go when she laughed, a strange, low chuckle.

'We would sleep in the same room and talk; she needed some kind of closeness. We weren't lovers, but we did sleep together once or twice. We talked about gay love and the unsatisfactory nature of some of our romantic friendships – she knew all about my sex life – but we never analysed our relationship, whatever it was. Sex with her was like being made love to by a boy. Her hands were very masculine and big and she was hipless like an adolescent boy. She wasn't at all repelled by the male body, she was intrigued by it.'[57]

Perhaps Blythe reminded her of Rolf Tietgens, the homosexual photographer whom she had felt drawn to in 1942? In November 1966, Highsmith wrote a letter to Blythe outlining her thoughts on men and women in which she mentions her relationship with Rolf. The photographer had a Freudian complex about the opposite sex, a real fear of them, said Highsmith, and she was the first woman – 'if I can call myself that'[58] – of whom he was not afraid.

'It was unsettling finding myself being intimate with her, but she just wanted some warmth and it was never referred to again,' says Blythe. 'I was associated with things like the village church and although I'm far from a puritan – quite the reverse – I felt like she didn't have the same discipline or rules in her life that I had been brought up with. She had a psychological freedom.'[59]

Highsmith was aware of the anarchy of her inner world, of the sense that her writerly imagination was raw and unfettered, but at least the act of fashioning a novel or short story imposed a semblance of order upon it. She was all too aware of the games she played. 'No use asking if a crime writer has anything of the criminal in him,' she wrote in her notebook in December 1958. 'He perpetuates little hoaxes, lies and crimes every time he writes a book. It is all a grand masquerade, a shameful deception in the guise of entertainment.'[60]

A Suspension of Mercy reads like an exposé of the crime writer at work, a literary hall of mirrors in which reality and fiction are constantly reflected and, ultimately, confused. Although Highsmith would never have analysed it in these terms, it could be said to rank as the author's most postmodern novel, a book which constantly toys with the genre of crime fiction to tease out some of its most ridiculous stereotypes and tropes. This playfulness of spirit, however, results in an atypical lack of intensity, a lightness of touch which Highsmith later admitted lent the book a 'rather flippant tone',[61] and which was picked up by the critics. Julian Symons, usually a fan, declared that this was not one of Highsmith's best books, finding it unconvincing and contrived and the ending implausible.

Sydney is a man seduced by fantasy – the imaginative game of killing his wife, Alicia, carrying her body out in a rolled-up carpet and burying her in a field. Running parallel to this, Sydney dreams up the idea for a television series called 'The Whip' – a rather dashing character who bears a striking similarity to Highsmith's own Ripley. 'The Whip would be a criminal character who did something ghastly in every episode . . .' she writes in the novel. 'The audience saw everything through The Whip's eyes, did everything with him, finally plugged for him through thick and thin and hoped the police would fail, which they always did. He wouldn't carry a whip or anything like that, but the nickname would be suggestive of depraved and secret habits.'[62] After months of repressed resentment towards his wife, Sydney imagines killing her, visualising the murder in detail, positioning her as a character in one of his stories.

Sydney then acts out the murder, buries the carpet, and records the fantasy in his notebook, written from the perspective of a guilty man.

As he muses on the fictional possibilities of the situation, he notes, ' "*The Schizophrenic We* would make a rather a good title" ';[63] this was one of the working titles Highsmith had had in mind for *A Suspension of Mercy*. Sydney, like Highsmith, is driven by the desire to understand why some people commit murder, but when – after learning of Alicia's suicide – he forces his wife's lover, Tilbury, to take an overdose of sleeping pills, his novelistic imagination fails him. Ironically, the self-conscious, omnipotent author, so in control of his characters, becomes a mere character himself: 'it dawned on him that he hadn't remembered to think what it felt like to commit a murder while he was committing it. He had not thought at all about himself.'[64]

At the end of the book, not only does Sydney escape punishment, but he also receives the news that a publisher has accepted his novel, *The Planners*, a work in which the characters seek to live out self-determined destinies. Highsmith's book ends on a triumphal note of meta-fictionality. On the last page, Sydney toys with the possibility of writing about the murder of Tilbury in his notebook – read by the police and viewed as merely an imaginative vehicle rather than a representation of reality – 'the notebook was now, after all, the safest place in which to write it'.[65]

Highsmith wrote the novel quickly, in under six months, completing a rough draft before a trip to New Hope at the end of September. She stayed with Daisy Winston while sorting out her belongings and packing up anything that needed to be shipped over to England. While there, she suffered from more dental problems – an extracted tooth failed to drain properly – and complained of feeling exhausted. In New York, she showed a rough manuscript of the yet untitled novel to Larry Ashmead, her editor at Doubleday, who remarked that it looked 'very promising'.[66] She arrived back home at Bridge Cottage on 7 October, where she struggled with the cold – the house did not have central heating – and tidied up the novel, which she finished typing in mid-November. The usual 'post-natal' depression she experienced when finishing a book descended on her once more, and, as the Suffolk winter set in, she felt plagued by insecurity, anxiety and money worries. (She noted that she would have to earn around $1,600 extra a year to keep her in cigarettes and alcohol alone.)

'Fantasy, an unflagging optimism is necessary for a writer at all stages of this rough game,' she wrote in her notebook on 15 December. 'A kind of madness is therefore necessary, when there is every logical reason for a state of depression and discouragement . . . Perhaps the fact that I can react with utter gloom to this is what keeps me from being psychotic and keeps me merely neurotic . . . I am doing quite a good day's work today. But I am also aware of the madness that actually sustains me, and I am not made more comfortable or happy by it.'[67]

21

Love was an outgoing thing

1964–1967

Writing was always a near-mystical process for Highsmith. When journalists asked her where her inspiration came from, she tended to answer, 'out of thin air'. Ideas came to her, she said, like birds that she saw in the corner of her eye; the challenge was to try and get a closer fix on these elusive creatures. During the bitterly cold winter of 1964–1965, Highsmith tried, once and for all, to pin down those creatures so she could work out exactly what inspired her and how she turned an initial germ of an idea into a finished book. The impetus came from The Writer Inc., the Boston-based publishing company which produced a number of how-to guides for aspiring authors. In December 1964, as she prepared a short essay on suspense, she listed in her cahier a number of writers, including Dostoevsky, Wilkie Collins, Henry James and Edgar Allan Poe, whom she believed could be said to belong to the tradition; 're-member you are in good company,' she added.[1] Highsmith expanded the essay into the book *Plotting and Writing Suspense Fiction*. When the slim title was published, in January 1966, she sent Arthur Koestler a copy, with the note, 'It could be better. It's the product of a month's work; my agent didn't want me to take it on.'[2]

As she worked on the guide in January and February of 1965, Highsmith dreamt of the ripe avocados, juicy oranges and warm sunlight of California, where Koestler was then living. 'This British Isles climate,' she wrote to him, 'plus all-pervading gloom, is finally bothering me.'[3] She kept warm by taking hold of her largest carpenter's saw and working on a piece of wood until she started to sweat. 'I become,' she told Kingsley, 'more Scrooge like with age.'[4]

She began the non-fiction book with a chapter about inspiration, the germs of an idea, outlining how she had first thought of the plots of *Strangers on a Train*, *The Blunderer*, *This Sweet Sickness*, *The Two Faces of January*, *A Suspension of Mercy*, and the origin of the short story, 'The Terrapin'. Intriguingly, Highsmith speaks of some ideas, such as the one behind *Strangers on a Train*, as forming in her mind by a process of parthenogenesis – springing to life without any external influence – while others, she admitted, needed a certain amount of cross-fertilisation to form themselves clearly in her imagination. But how did one recognise ideas when they came? She said she knew of their significance because of a 'certain excitement which they instantly bring, akin to the pleasure and excitement of a good poem or line in a poem.'[5]

She went on to recommend that aspiring writers keep a notebook in which to jot down thoughts or ideas, that they should trust in the power of the unconscious and that they shouldn't force inspiration. In addition, it was important to avoid those who negated the creative process, sometimes people *per se*. 'The plane of social intercourse,' she said, 'is not the plane of creation, not the plane on which creative ideas fly . . . This is a curious thing, because sometimes the very people we are attracted to or in love with act as effectively as rubber insulators to the spark of inspiration.'[6] She devoted subsequent chapters to the suspense short story, the use of personal experience, the development of the story, plotting, the first and second draft and a detailed analysis of the problems she had encountered while trying to write *The Glass Cell*. She was, she said, constantly aware of the possibility of failure; it was, simply, an occupational hazard. 'I have dwelt as much on my failures as successes here,' she wrote, 'because one can learn a lot from failures. By revealing my sometimes formidable losses of time and effort and the reasons, perhaps I can save other writers from suffering the same things.'[7]

Although she never particularly liked to discuss her work in interviews, she did expand on the points she had covered in *Plotting and Writing Suspense Fiction* in a short piece she wrote for another book, *Whodunit? A Guide to Crime, Suspense and Spy Fiction*, edited by H.R.F. Keating. She had no hard and fast rules when writing a novel, she said; neither did she set out with a definite kind of reader in mind. Her ideas began 'with a situation of surprise or coincidence, some unusual circumstances, and around this, and forward and backward, I create a narrative with a beginning and an end.'[8] She liked to write three or four hours a day and she often found it helpful to take regular breaks and do something manual and non-creative, such as washing the dishes.

It was while she was in this state, she said, that her mind was able to make a creative leap. 'Hard thought never did me very much good,' she wrote. 'I believe in letting one's mind alone.'[9] In ideal conditions, she said, she could write 2,000 words a day, but in reality such circumstances only presented themselves every other day. She wished she could use the method adopted by one famous author who said that he bashed out the action parts of the story first, only going back to fill in details later. She, however, had to write everything down as she went along. 'Maybe this is inevitable because of the subjective attitude I generally take: I describe what is in the head of the protagonist, psychopath or not, because what is in his or her head must explain as well as advance the story.'[10]

Ronald Blythe remembers how seriously Highsmith took her work. 'She didn't think of herself as a writer of detective fiction at all,' he says, 'but she liked the idea of suspense and she was fascinated by amorality. We used to talk about books and our work – how she had done seven pages or whatever that day and how I had done 700 words or so. Although her novels didn't really appeal to me at first, they intrigued me and eventually I saw how they reflected her. She had a great memory for details and often she would write out bits of conversation we had had in her books. One did feel sometimes as if one was subject matter. It's difficult to describe her in a way, except as an artist. She saw herself as a very serious writer.'[11]

In March 1965, Highsmith felt so piqued that she wasn't getting the respect she deserved from her French publishers, Calmann-Lévy, that she wrote to Robert Calmann-Lévy to tell him that she had signed a contract with a rival publishing house, Laffont. Money wasn't so much an issue – as she said, 'It is Laffont with prestige and Gallimard with money, & I prefer prestige.'[12] What annoyed Highsmith was the fact that Calmann-Lévy had released her books so slowly in France that she had 'four novels, written in the last years, that are unpublished'.[13] The staff at Calmann-Lévy were so shocked by what they saw as her rather impulsive behaviour that editor Manès Sperber wrote a letter expressing his astonishment. Surely, he said, it would have been better to raise this matter with Calmann-Lévy first before she rushed into a contract with another publishing house? As it was, Calmann-Lévy had not even been given the opportunity to see the manuscripts of the two novels Highsmith thought they had rejected – *The Two Faces of January* and *The Glass Cell*. The problem, he outlined, was one of sales – the company could not publish all her novels in quick succession because, 'the commercial reasons to do it were rather weak; on the other hand, it was extremely difficult to arouse the public attention your great talent deserves.'[14]

Highsmith wrote back, explaining how she did not make the decision lightly, but after the rejection, in America, of *The Two Faces of January* and *The Glass Cell* by Harper's – books subsequently published by Doubleday – she felt compelled to take action. 'As for Calmann-Lévy, I have felt for three years that I might as well have been dead as far as they are concerned,' she wrote to Sperber.[15] Why had she not heard about the publication of *This Sweet Sickness*, which was, she said, 'so well received in the United States and in England, chosen by Hitchcock for his hour TV programme, and now in the Perennial Library (pocket-book) of Harper & Row'?[16] After the heated exchange of letters, Calmann-Lévy offered to publish *This Sweet Sickness* as *Ce mal étrange* in 1966, agreeing to an increase in her advance from the usual $200 to $500, and continued to act as her French publisher after the expiry of Highsmith's contract with Laffont – who would publish three of her books, *The Two Faces of January*, *The Glass Cell*, and *The Suspension of Mercy*. 'I have always considered your novels not as crime-stories,' wrote Sperber in a letter to Highsmith, 'but as a peculiar kind of psychological fiction.'[17]

Like the character of Sydney Bartleby in *A Suspension of Mercy*, Highsmith expressed a desire to write for television. 'Would love to learn to write for TV,' she told Peggy Lewis. 'I now have a set, on the rental plan, which is what all the English do – and never buy one, as the models change too quickly,'[18] a line she used, in a slightly different form, in the first chapter of *A Suspension of Mercy*.

One Sunday, in early May 1965, Highsmith was at home in Bridge Cottage, when she received a call from the BBC. Would she be able to give them a 250-word synopsis of a play by the next day? They had seen an old script of the story, which had originally started life as a synopsis for an eighty-page novella for American *Cosmopolitan*. The magazine turned it down, but Highsmith subsequently sold it to television in the USA and the BBC wanted to know whether it could be brought up to date. Mary Highsmith was staying with her daughter at the time, and so Highsmith locked herself in the study and in under two hours wrote an outline of the story she initially called 'The Prowler'. 'I got the assignment – L600 it was,' she wrote to her stepfather later.[19] The deadline for submitting the play was 25 June, and although she admitted that it was 'quite full of old-fashionedness and corn',[20] it was accepted. It was broadcast on BBC1 on 22 September as 'The Cellar', as part of *The*

Wednesday Thriller series. From reading the script, however, it's obvious that dialogue was not Highsmith's forte. In fact, the play is populated by characters who are nothing more than murder mystery stereotypes, including an hysterical wife, Hilda, a duplicitous husband, George, and Peggy, an over-zealous mistress.

Although Highsmith's later experiments in screenwriting were equally unsuccessful, her aspirations did not go to waste, as her second Ripley novel, *Ripley Under Ground*, published in 1970, grew out of a play she had planned to write for television. She started work on the plotting of the screenplay, which she entitled 'Derwatt Resurrected', in July 1965, drawing inspiration from the death of her ex-lover, the painter Allela Cornell. 'Ripley was not in it at all,' she told Julian Jebb, who would later become a close friend, 'but it had to do with a painter who had died. Actually something of the same thing happened in my own life, a great friend of mine died, age twenty-nine, a woman . . . I for one showed a portfolio of her work on 57th Street and they said, "It's very good, but we're really not interested in dead painters, there's no use in having a show." So that was the end of that. I never thought about it for fifteen years and then it occurred to me that with rather crooked fraud someone could continue painting in the same style.'[21] The problem with writing a play, she told an interviewer from *The Times*, was the fact that 'It doesn't form itself in my mind in the same way as a novel because there you can show what a person's thinking without other people knowing.'[22] In a novel she would not hesitate in shaping her characters according to her will, but, as she wrote in her notebook in March 1977 (after four months of trying, and once again failing, to write a television drama), when she was working on a script she always tended to see the characters as 'living people whom I can't touch, rearrange, change'.[23]

On finishing the synopsis of 'The Prowler' or 'The Cellar', Highsmith unlocked her study to be met by her enraged mother whom she could hear 'yacking' outside the door. The relationship between the two women was already strained but the visit culminated in an attempt by Mary to attack her daughter with a coat hanger – 'fortunately I looked over my shoulder on that occasion'.[24] Highsmith called a local doctor, who prescribed sedatives for both women and after the six-day trip was over, she was left feeling emotionally exhausted. She was convinced her mother was suffering from manic-depression, while friends were less kind, simply labelling her as 'mental – their word for insane'.[25]

In March 1964, Mary had written her daughter a twenty-nine-page diatribe which Highsmith called an 'insane blast . . . dredging up all the sludge of ancient time',[26] adding that her mother was 'a bitter old woman with nothing else to do'.[27] In the letter Mary articulated a whole range of issues which clearly bothered her, some dating back to the time when Highsmith was at Yaddo. 'Then I learned to my horror you flatly lied about me to Mamma to the effect that I was jealous of you being at Yaddo,' she said. 'God how that information shook me . . . Ever since I ever looked at you I lived to serve you & give you all the things I never had & do everything I could for you & I've not changed one iota . . . Yes, I know why you burst in tears at the drop of a hat. It's because you have to live with you and it's your conscience. I've seen you drop a friend without a qualm – I hate to witness it but I hate lying more.'[28] The letter, the first of many vituperative attacks on her daughter, left Highsmith feeling upset for several days after reading it. 'I had to puncture this festering abscess,' was Mary's parting shot, 'I've lost nothing because we cannot face the future without confronting the past. It was constantly between us. If it separates us completely – let it. I've lost nothing – because I had nothing.'[29] In her diary, Highsmith tried to analyse her mother's motives, believing them to spring from jealousy of her relationship with X. 'She wants my attention, devotion, etc. hence is so jealous of the women in my life.'[30]

Just as Mary's attitude towards her daughter was sullied by the resentment she felt towards the women in Pat's life, so the writer's relationships with her lovers were constantly undermined by the damaged foundations that lay beneath her emotional attachment to her mother. At the end of 1964, Highsmith wrote a number of poems expressing her tortured inner life. She wrote of her complex feelings of love and hatred, expressing both the tenderness and the sadistic impulses that welled inside her. 'Small wonder I would both kiss your feet/ And imagine beating you cruelly.'[31] Two days later, she wrote another autobiographical poem charting the roots of her ambiguous feelings back to her childhood, when she had to stifle and repress the love she had felt for girls – 'resentment was my second emotion', she said.[32] X had accused her of both loving and hating women, a contradictory response Highsmith accepted. In the new year, Highsmith wrote to Alex Szogyi about the problems in her new relationship, of her jealousy of X's family and the fact that they had more contact with her than she did. Whenever the two women did manage to spend time together, she felt as though there was an atmosphere of 'something snatched',[33] and, instead of being spontaneous and enjoyable, sex had become vulgar and embarrassing. 'I have never been a sex fiend, it's always been fun, the greatest pleasure, something one doesn't think about for days, and then one does – but this is when things are calm, and one sleeps every night with the person one loves . . .' she wrote to Alex. 'I have accused her of teasing me and other things not pleasant . . . She accused me of inner violence (not physical).'[34]

When Highsmith made a short trip to Paris in March 1965, X seemed to resent the fact that she had travelled with Daisy Winston, even though the writer explained that she had no longer felt any 'emotional involvement' for her old friend whatsoever.[35] According to Highsmith, her lover threatened to cancel a holiday to Venice the two women had planned for May, a trip Pat had been looking forward to throughout the long, dreary winter. She was baffled as to how to progress. Eventually, however, the two women sorted out their problems, temporarily at least, and in mid-May they arrived in Venice. They stayed in a hotel close to the house where John Ruskin once lived and worked, and it was while in the watery city that Highsmith conceived the idea for the Venice-set novel, *Those Who Walk Away*. After ten days in Venice, she travelled alone to Rome, where she stayed with Ellen Hill for a week, and then to Positano to see her cat, Spider. In Positano, she met by accident the novelists Edna O'Brien and Brigid Brophy, but Highsmith, who loathed the 'literary scene', tried to keep her distance – she was, as she admitted to Kingsley, 'not very sociable'.[36]

Sir Michael Levey, former director of the National Gallery and Brophy's widower, recalls the meeting and tells how, over time, he and his wife became friends of the writer. 'I, in particular, was eager to convey my admiration to her. But I had no preconceived idea of the writer and barely realised it was she when our party was joined by a rather severe-seeming woman, looking neither young nor old, with a shock of untidy, straight, dark hair, and casually dressed in buff safari jacket, open shirt, khaki chinos and moccasins. Perhaps it was the moccasins that raised Red Indian associations. I came to think that there was something of the Red Indian about Pat's appearance and even her manner, while the clothes she wore that evening became familiar, in my experience, as her unvarying uniform.

'Although notably silent that evening, she appeared less shy than reserved, and by no means ill at ease sitting among strangers. Enthusiasm of the kind I wanted to convey seemed to cause her mild amusement, and she responded with a grunted yet not unfriendly, 'Ugh, huh', which I would later recognise as a typical Pat conversational response. She was far from intimidating, however, nor at all aloof. Rather, I had the impression of a personality quietly idiosyncratic and distinctly intriguing, whom one would like to know better.

'I doubt whether she and Brigid talked much on that occasion. Each of them had, in her own way, the capacity – indeed, a preference – for silence in lieu of uttering social banalities . . . Nevertheless, I think that some sort of rapport must have been established between them . . . What Brigid enjoyed in Pat's company – and, I would guess, vice versa – was especially the sharpness of mind and the sardonic, frequently deadpan humour . . . Although it would be rash to try to sum up a person one did not know well, I retain a very clear sense of Pat's personality. Never getting close to it actually was, I would say, part of its spell. It embodied "cool", though coolness might have been achieved only after considerable turmoil, emotional and otherwise. That is pure hypothesis, yet hints seemed to lurk, indicating if not earlier unhappiness then earlier vulnerability. By the time we met her, Pat appeared solitary but not lonely, profoundly self-contained but not at all self-assertive – always friendly, kind and notably courteous in behaviour, despite her inner reserve . . . She seldom, if ever, referred to her books, and it was hard to make much correlation between her and the writer of them, except that their protagonists are so often loners of some sort.'[37]

Back in Suffolk, Highsmith spent the summer plotting *Those Who Walk Away*, writing it between October 1965 and March 1966. During this time she barely saw her married lover and the couple did not sleep together, sending Highsmith into another dark depression. 'Some of my blackest days – I passed then,' she later recalled, adding that she turned to her doctor for a prescription of barbiturates.[38] In September, she travelled to Mallorca, where in Deya she met the poet Robert Graves, whom she described as having 'an air of self-esteem and smugness'.[39] She caught a boat from Palma to Barcelona, journeying on to Paris, and stopping briefly at Koestler's house in Alpbach, Austria.

In December, she had another dream about Lynn Roth – she had last dreamt about her 'girl of magic'[40] in August – in which her former lover was five-months pregnant. On seeing her waters break, Highsmith said that she was sorry as she wished the child could have been hers. 'I wanted us to have one,' she said.[41] In the same entry, she said that it was obvious she longed to have someone to love and feel the same way about her. 'I have reached (again),' she said, 'a point of preferring to forget that the person I am supposed to love exists.'[42]

Highsmith's passion for snail-breeding paid off when in January 1966 *Nova* magazine bought her short story, 'The Snail-Watcher', for £70. The grotesque tale focuses on Peter Knoppert, whose passion for breeding the creatures results in his death. Trapped in his study, which has been colonised by snails, Knoppert uses a hose pipe to try and clear some space from the ceiling. A clutch of gastropods hits him on the head, he trips on the slimy floor, a sea of snails begin to crawl across and into him. As he cries for help, a creature slips into his mouth and then more slime their way across his eyes. Eventually he swallows one; he cannot breathe. The last thing he sees before losing consciousness is two snails making love on the rubber plant. 'And right beside them, tiny snails as pure as dewdrops were emerging from a pit like an infinite army into their widening world.'[43] In his introduction to the collection, *Eleven*, Graham Greene commented, 'for pure physical horror, which is an emotion rarely evoked by Miss Highsmith, "The Snail-Watcher" would be hard to beat.'[44]

Pat was still fascinated by the creatures she had first encountered in 1946 and she housed 300 snails in her back garden in Suffolk. According to those who knew her she became so fond of them she couldn't travel without them.

'After staying with her at her house in Suffolk, I met her the following week at a cocktail party in London,' says Peter Thomson. 'She walked in with this gigantic handbag, which she then opened with pride and which contained a hundred snails and an enormous head of lettuce. She absolutely adored the snails, they were her companions for the evening.'[45]

Her editor at Doubleday, Larry Ashmead, recalls that when Highsmith moved to France in 1967, she told him that she smuggled her pet snails into the country under her breasts. 'You couldn't take live snails into France so she was sneaking them in under her breasts,' he says. 'And that wasn't just on one trip – no, she kept going back and forth. She said that she would take six to ten of the creatures under each breast every time she went. And she wasn't joking – she was very serious.'[46]

On return from a trip to Paris, in March, where she was due to help publicise the French edition of *The Glass Cell*, she completed another horror story about snails, 'The Quest for Blank Claveringi' about a professor of zoology, Avery Clavering, who, searching for a giant snail on an uninhabited island, is overwhelmed by the creatures. 'Our hero kills the male,' she wrote in her notebook, 'but is overcome by the female, who leaves his corpse disdainfully for her little ones to devour – this he realizes as he is being eaten alive . . .'[47] The tale ends on a wonderfully macabre note, as Professor Clavering, running into the sea, fleeing a fast approaching giant snail, muses over his fate. 'He was waist-deep when he stumbled, waist-deep but head under when the snail crashed down upon him, and he realized as the thousands of pairs of teeth began to gnaw at his back, that his fate was both to drown and to be chewed to death.'[48]

In October 1969, Highsmith thought about the possibility of writing a third story about snails, this one focusing on an apocalyptic, post-nuclear world in which all life on the planet has been destroyed except for snails. A spaceship carrying the last 150 members of the human race arrives on the planet and they set out to destroy the gastropods, many of which have mutated – some creatures sport two heads or have grown to giant proportions, some possess remarkable intelligence, while others have developed cannibalistic habits. The battle between the snails and the humans is a fierce one – the creatures proceed to attack the men and eat them – but a few people manage to flee back into the spaceship and escape. Unknown to them, however, there is a small batch of snail eggs on board.

In April 1966, just as Pat's relationship with X had started to improve, her familial situation began to worsen to such an extent that she took the extreme step of writing a harsh letter to her mother. Highsmith tried to make her mother believe that she harboured no resentment towards her even though Mary deserted her and left her with her grandmother in Texas when she was twelve; nor did she feel any bitterness about the sniping remark her mother had made when she was fourteen, to the effect that 'Why don't you straighten up and fly right?' Yet the fact that Highsmith chose to highlight these incidents suggests the opposite, that she could not forgive her mother for what she had done. She told her mother that she was quite happy. She enjoyed her life and the rewards her writing brought her. 'If you would get rid of your guilt, it would make things better . . .' she wrote. 'If there is anything in the above you would like me to elaborate on, or clarify, I'll be glad to. With much love.'[49] Highsmith left the letter unsigned.

Later in the year, Mary and Stanley Highsmith, who had moved back to Fort Worth, were referred to a psychiatrist by their doctor. At issue, as their psychiatrist correctly diagnosed in a letter to Highsmith, was their 'conflicted' relationship with their daughter. It was a conflict which had still to reach its inevitable and ugly conclusion.

In June, Highsmith joined a friend, Elizabeth, in Paris, from where they drove down to Marseille and took a boat to Tunis, settling in Hammamet, which she described as a 'real Arab village',[50] and which would form the setting for her next novel, *The Tremor of Forgery*. 'We walked in the native quarter,' she wrote in her notebook, 'white arches, dirt street, but all more reasonably clean.'[51] The extent to which an individual exists without the framing presence of his or her normal society had intrigued Highsmith back in 1954 when she wrote *The Talented Mr Ripley*, but as she travelled through Tunisia, she became increasingly interested in the contrast between the so-called 'civilised' culture of Europe and the anarchy and unknowability of Africa. She likened the continent to an obese woman, stripped of her clothes, lying fast asleep in a comfortable bed, indifferent to any approach. Tunisia certainly inspired her senses – she wrote a travel piece about it for the *New Statesman* – but on her return from the six-week trip she told a journalist that she would never go back. 'I got fed up with it – the petty thieving and things. It's said to be the most progressive part of Africa – which is a terrifying thought.'[52]

The country, for all its exoticism, failed to make her forget her difficulties back in England; rather, she found her new environment gave her the opportunity in which to think freely. Standing next to the white walls of the Arabic houses she felt, she said, naked, as if her problems had been stripped of all their complexities; she reworked this observation, first recorded in her notebook, into the third chapter of *The Tremor of Forgery*. From Tunisia, Highsmith wrote X a letter outlining how she could not endure any more of her 'nonsense'. The week before their fourth anniversary, Highsmith wrote a vicious poem which articulated the psychological battle that was raging between them, a four-line stanza peppered with military metaphors. The passion and affection of their early days had now been replaced by indifference and hatred. Highsmith acknowledged that although she did admit to a strong masochistic streak, she did not believe X's accusation that she was destructive to all human relationships. Instead she blamed her lover, citing her request that Highsmith encourage her husband's presence at the cottage as one of the main contributory factors in the breakdown of their affair. 'It is a curious request from a lover,' she wrote to Alex Szogyi, 'to insist upon the presence of a person who inevitably separates us.'[53]

From Tunisia, Pat and Elizabeth sailed to Naples, from where they travelled to Alpnach, Austria, arriving home in August. The next month she was on the move yet again, this time to Nice, where the director Raoul Lévy wanted her to help work on the script of her novel, *Deep Water*. The trip was not a successful one, as she suffered from a range of what she described as neurotic symptoms, including exhaustion, inability to sleep, lack of appetite and fear of failure. Even though Highsmith wrote a ninety-three-page script, the film never got made, as Lévy shot himself in St Tropez later that year. 'Alas, I never liked him,' wrote Highsmith in her notebook of Lévy, 'and obviously he did not like himself.'[54]

While in the south of France, Highsmith met the photographer and artist Barbara Ker-Seymer, and her partner Barbara Roett, women she came to regard as two of her closest friends.

'Pat was best at friendship at a distance,' says Barbara Roett. 'I got that feeling from her that she could not sustain relationships, she didn't even try. She was strange with me, she used to talk to me as though I were another man, and she had no idea about what other women were feeling and thinking. In fact, there could have been something hormonally strange about Pat. She had the most beautiful hands, but they were really not a woman's hands – they were strong, large and square, but absolutely did not belong to a woman. She made half-hearted concessions to womanhood – for instance, she'd put on a necklace almost apologetically – but she was happiest when she had on her blue jeans and checked shirt. I remember Pat had thick black hair and she would stare at the ground with her hair falling forward and then suddenly a black eye would peek out and pin you to the wall. She did, however, have a very good brain – considering, that is, how imbalanced she was in other ways.

'When I first met her, I suppose it was her vulnerability that I found appealing. She really did seem to be drinking herself to death, I felt sort of protective towards her and thought, "If only she could meet a nice person." Eventually I saw what a monster she could be in any relationship so I quickly changed that view. Having said that, I still liked her a great deal, much better than I liked a lot of more balanced people. She was a natural eccentric and she had a tremendous talent.'[55]

Back at Bridge Cottage, Highsmith's relationship with X reached crisis point one night in mid-October. Highsmith came up to bed five or ten minutes after her lover and then, in what Pat thought was a 'silent huff', the other woman walked out of the bedroom. Highsmith couldn't bear it any longer. She took hold of X's overnight bag and threw it into the next room. The next morning Pat saw that she had spent the night in the guest room, with one pink blanket for warmth. 'I told her in the morning I had had enough huffs and was finished, and she left at 4PM,' noted Highsmith.[56]

And with that their four-year relationship came to its end. It was, she said, 'the very worst time of my entire life'.[57] Mozart, her composer of choice in moments of utter hopelessness, came to Highsmith's aid in the immediate aftermath of the split. She had chosen to listen to his music rather than take a sedative at other times of crisis and she hoped he wouldn't let her down. 'With Mozart's courage, I could face lions,' she said.[58]

What Highsmith tried, but failed, to achieve with *A Suspension of Mercy* – the creation of a suspense novel that did not feature a murder – she succeeded in doing with her next book, *Those Who Walk Away*, which she dedicated to one of her 'more inspiring friends' Lil Picard. The book opens in Rome, with the attempted murder of Ray Garrett, the twenty-seven-year-old son-in-law of painter Ed Coleman, whom the older man blames for the recent suicide of his only child, Peggy. As the novel progresses, it becomes clear that the two men – as with Rydal and Chester in *The Two Faces of January* – are locked in an intense symbiotic relationship, each of them drawing out of the other previously repressed internal feelings. Rather than flee, Ray follows Ed to Venice, where his father-in-law is wintering with his girlfriend, Inez, and the setting for the unsettling game of cat and mouse that follows. 'There are no more genuine agonies in modern literature than those endured by the couples in her books,' wrote Julian Symons of Highsmith, 'who are locked together in a dislike and even hatred that often strangely contains love.'[59]

Ray is haunted by a sense of guilt – an after-effect of the suicide of his young wife – and, well aware of Coleman's violent intentions, repeatedly places himself in positions of danger and self-abnegation. His death wish is echoed by the eerie setting of Venice in winter, the breathy whisper of San Marco, which seems to emit a strange noise like 'an unending exhalation of a spirit'.[60] It is Ray's masochism which leads him, in the early hours of the morning, to accept a lift from Coleman in a motor-boat, to take him from the Lido to a point near his hotel, the Pensione Seguso. Sailing across the lagoon, Coleman lunges towards his son-in-law and pushes him overboard, and as Ray feels the icy, black water beginning to numb his body, he says to himself, '*It's what you deserve, you ass!*'[61] Ray then pretends Coleman has actually killed him, a process which involves in true Highsmith fashion, the assumption of a number of false names and accompanying feelings of both exhilarating freedom and overwhelming emptiness. By playing dead, Ray begins to feel like he is invisible – like a ghost wandering through the streets of Venice. When he sees his jacket, peppered with the gunshots fired by Coleman, he views the item of clothing with a distant, and clearly disturbed, perspective, as if it was 'a bridge between two existences'.[62]

On its publication in America in April 1967, Anthony Boucher noted how the book was 'as absorbing as it is inconclusive . . . This is a book to some extent exasperating . . . But it is often illuminating – and always compelling.'[63] J.M. Edelstein, writing in *New Republic*, was correct in pointing out Highsmith's radical decision not to include a murder in a book which seemed to bear all the hallmarks of a suspense novel. 'The movement of hunter and hunted, and their occasional contact is seen as less the attraction of opposites, of evil and good, or evil and weakness, than it is as the attraction of like to like. The psychological truth thus implied may be a greater horror than any climatic act of violence.'[64] After the novel's publication in Britain, the *Times Literary Supplement* observed, in its 1 June issue, how Highsmith's books continued to vex literary editors, uncertain whether to send out her work with the likes of Agatha Christie or the more highbrow Iris Murdoch. 'The carpet she skilfully weaves is of popular material and in strong colours, but the pattern in it is subtle, elusive and unfinished . . . [Though] it may seem ungrateful to crab about the entertainment she offers, one wants her now to develop forms that would extend what after all the "crime novel" cannot properly comprise, the truly serious side of the novelist's art.'[65] The critic from the *Times Literary Supplement* failed to notice the fact that *Those Who Walk Away* was already an example of the new form which he or she was advocating. As Julian Symons noted, 'The deadly games of pursuit played in her best novels are as subtle and interesting as anything being done in the novel today.'[66]

Those Who Walk Away can be read as a novel of ideas – an exploration of the means by which individuals construct reality, a philosophical examination of the nature of identity and an analysis of the complex relationship between consciousness and art. Although Ray's wife, Peggy, kills herself ten days before the opening of the novel by slitting her wrists in the bath, her ghost-like image haunts every page, her absence proving the driving force behind the two protagonists. Peggy thought 'ideals were real, even indestructible, maybe the realest things on earth'[67] and committed suicide because of her dissatisfaction with the external world. She wanted more than life itself could give, constantly believing that sex was something divine and repeatedly striving for a mystical experience. It is clear Peggy lived in a parallel world, a universe of dreams, full of fruit orchards and brightly coloured birds, and expected her transition to married life to be something of an epiphany, 'like paradise or poetry – instead of a continuation of this world'.[68] Peggy, a painter, ultimately felt let down by her reality; her artistic vision no longer fulfilled her; sex did not offer her an insight into the mystical universe she so craved and so she chose to kill herself. The world was not enough, she had said. 'It might have been her death cry, Ray thought, if she had had one. *The world is not enough, therefore I leave it to find something bigger.*'[69]

Just how do we construct reality? the novel asks. Is it merely the perception of one's external surroundings or is it shaped by memory, association and expectation? How does art change our view of the world? Highsmith plays games with the notion of the Platonic ideal, the concept that art is merely an image twice-removed from true reality. In the Platonic universe, there exists perfect forms, abstracts which are then made concrete by man – for instance, God created the form of the bed, which is then copied by a carpenter into what we think of as a 'real' bed. If an artist were then to paint it then all he would be doing would be holding up a mirror to what was, in effect, an imperfect image of the original as conceived by God. In this way, Plato argued in *The Republic*, artists interfere with rather than encourage our perception of reality and have no place in the idealised community.

In *Those Who Walk Away*, the characters constantly try to grasp reality through the appreciation of artistic form, a process which seems constantly elusive. Ray, like his wife, aspired to be a painter, but abandoned it at the age of twenty-four, believing he would never be good enough, settling on a career as a gallery owner, while his father-in-law, Coleman, a former civil engineer, is an artist who considers himself belonging in a 'European' tradition. Throughout the novel there are a proliferation of images which suggest that both characters construct reality through the medium of artistic association. Ray sees Inez standing in the dim interior of a bar, drinking a cup of coffee, a composition which suggested a work by Cézanne. As Ray lowers himself into a bath, he looks at the red, green and cream patterned linoleum on the floor, worn down in spots and revealing a dark red weaving. 'Not beautiful, but in a Bonnard it might have been,' thinks Ray,[70] referring to the French painter whose work Highsmith saw at the Royal Academy in London in February 1966. After Coleman's fall in a fishing boat his knee swells, something which looks like a drawing by Hieronymus Bosch.

In Highsmith's world – an environment like the cave of shadows portrayed by Plato – reality is insubstantial and constantly in flux. In *Those Who Walk Away* this is best illustrated by something as mundane as the protagonists' attitude towards a scarf. On arriving in Venice, Ray passes a shop window displaying a floral-patterned, green, black and yellow scarf, which reminds him of his dead wife. Although she never possessed an item of clothing like it, he was sure she would have adored the scarf and so, on impulse, buys it. To Ray, the scarf acts as a talisman, as an associative aid to help conjure the memory of Peggy. But when his father-in-law sees it, he projects on to it his own feelings of loss and guilt – by taking hold of the scarf, which he believes Peggy once owned, he thinks he will hang on to a part of his dead daughter. The revelation, during his interrogation at the end of the novel, that Peggy never once held or wore it is all too much for Coleman. His vision of the truth, his interpretation of reality, crumbles.

Similarly, Ray's attitude towards love is revealed to be based on nothing more than fantasy, but at least it is an illusion of which he is aware. Towards the end of the novel, he realises that his affection for Elisabetta, a waitress in a coffee bar, is founded on a delicate, and fundamentally insubstantial, matrix of projected feelings. 'Suddenly it seemed to him that love – erotic and romantic love – was nothing but a form or various forms of ego. Therefore the right thing to do was to direct one's ego to recipients other than people, or to people from whom one expected nothing. Love could be pure, but pure only if it was unselfish . . . It was important that the objects of love be nothing but recipients, he thought again. Love was an outgoing thing, a gift that one should not expect to be returned. Stendhal must have said that, Proust certainly, using other words: a piece of wisdom his eyes had passed over in reading . . .'[71]

Clearly autobiographical, the words could have been lifted straight out of one of Highsmith's notebooks.

22

This shimmery void

1967–1968

After the collapse of her latest relationship, Highsmith chose to leave England and move to the Île-de-France, the lush, forested countryside encircling Paris, defined by the eighteenth-century landscape painter Corot as the area bordered by the rivers Seine, Marne, Oise and Aisne, and a 'royal fief *par excellence*'.[1] Traditionally renowned as the birthplace of Gothic architecture – its cathedrals include Saint-Denis, Noyon, Laon, Senlis, Mantes, Soissons and Chartres – and the seat of the ancient French kingdom, it served as a pastoral paradise in which royalty and aristocracy built some of the most opulent palaces in the world: Versailles, Fontainebleau, Saint-Cloud, Meudon, Chantilly, Vincennes, Sceaux, Marly, Sevres and Malmaison. The Île-de-France was also famous for the quality of its light, described by one writer in 1929 as lending the 'limpidity and delicacy of crystal to the song of the poet and the picture of the painter'.[2] Highsmith would move house four times over the course of the next thirteen years, yet she always chose to stay within a twenty-five-kilometre radius of Fontainebleau, at the southern edge of the Île-de-France, near to Nemours, with its medieval castle, and the fortified town of Moret-sur-Loing, where the impressionist painter Alfred Sisley had lived and worked, producing 'glittering landscapes bathed in light'.[3]

Highsmith first had the idea of living in Fontainebleau in January 1967 during a driving tour with her friend Elizabeth. Together the two women drove from the French capital to Tours, from where Highsmith travelled by train to Montbazon en Touraine, where she was due to sit on a panel to judge the best short films at the Festival International du Court-Metrage. The jury comprised of seven people, including Victor

Vasarely, the Hungarian-born Op art painter; Slawomir Mrozek, the Polish playwright; the Japanese film star Keiko Kishi; Andrei Petrov, the Russian composer; the actor Guy Coté and the French novelist José Cabanis. The atmosphere of the occasion reminded her of Yaddo, she said, except for one important difference – a certain initial frostiness, which she put down to the fact that the other panellists were, like her, somewhat guarded, 'more suspicious, more jealous of our (already gained) reputations'.[4] One lunch time, sandwiched between a table of yacking Tours' women, a glass cage full of parakeets, and Vasarely and Cabanis talking, in French, about incomprehensible art theory, Highsmith felt like she wanted to scream. After being interviewed for television, Highsmith questioned, in her notebook, the validity of verbal expression, observing, 'What a lot of nonsense, all this communicating! Foreign to most artists.'[5] From the film festival, Highsmith sent a card to Kate Levey, the daughter of Michael Levey and Brigid Brophy, on the back of which she had drawn a quick pen sketch of the jury members pretending to kill each other by firing bread pellets.

In March, Elizabeth informed her friend that she had spotted a house she thought would be perfect for her – a two-bedroom, furnished property within a walled estate in Bois Fontaine – and, after going to see the house, Highsmith decided to take it. The rent would be the equivalent of $170 per month. 'I look forward to a new life,' she wrote to Alex Szogyi, 'even though I am 46.'[6] The writer moved into 57 Rue Saint Merry in June, but on receipt of $26,000 from Columbia Pictures for the sale of the film rights of *Those Who Walk Away* (a movie which failed to materialise), Highsmith decided it would be better if she bought a house, costing $20,900, with Elizabeth in nearby Samois-sur-Seine, a charming village built of pale stone nestling next to the Seine.

Highsmith moved to her new address at 20 Rue de Courbuisson in September. Her new home was a stone farmhouse with two doors, two bathrooms, and one kitchen. It was four minutes walk from the river, where one could swim. Elizabeth, who kept on her flat in Paris, and Pat were never anything more than just good friends but Highsmith was flattered that the fifty-nine-year-old woman she had known for nineteen years wanted to live with her. She should, however, have trusted her instincts when she wrote in a letter to Alex Szogyi, 'I can never imagine that anyone can tolerate me.'[7] It was not an auspicious beginning. After lugging the furniture from eight rooms into one so as to paint and clean the house, Pat felt exhausted, 'older than Methuselah',[8] but instead of being praised by her friend for her efforts she was attacked. 'You have a disorderly mind,' Elizabeth barked at her. 'The state of your room indicates a disorderly mind!' Why, she wondered, had she chosen to align herself with yet another overly dominant woman? She admitted, as she wrote to Alex Szogyi, that she was 'juvenile, self-centred, selfish, not mindful enough of work other people do for me, and in the last five years I can have a temper on occasion, especially when "Baited".'[9] But surely she wasn't to blame this time, was she? 'I have a pattern of choosing people with whom I don't feel comfortable,' she continued in the same letter. 'Maybe this is because I am attracted to perfectionists, people who boss me . . . (For goodness sake, don't show this letter to a psychiatrist, for he would say, Highsmith is the nut!)'[10]

Pat and Elizabeth shared only the kitchen and living room – but even so, from the first day, they obviously found living together impossible. Rosalind Constable, who got back in touch with Pat in 1967 and to whom Highsmith dedicated *The Tremor of Forgery* 'as a small souvenir of a rather long friendship'[11], pleaded with her to wrestle herself free of the situation, even if she had to lose out financially. Did she, asked Rosalind, who visited Highsmith in October 1967 when Elizabeth was in New York, like to be bullied by small, fierce women? Weeks could pass by between Elizabeth's visits, but nevertheless Pat found living in Samois physically and mentally depressing. Not only was she cold – the oil furnace which heated the house was on Elizabeth's side of the house – but she felt like a shabby visitor messing up a stranger's beautiful home. Her so-called friend had made her feel that the house 'was not half mine, that my possessions were sordid, that I was hopelessly disorganized – by nature',[12] and she hated the expense of living in France. She felt particularly outraged that a bottle of Johnny Walker Scotch cost her 35 francs.

As she endured yet more domestic difficulties, Highsmith tried to concentrate on writing her Tunisian novel, *The Tremor of Forgery*, which she started to plot in detail in January 1967 and which she completed and sent off to her publishers in February 1968. Graham Greene named the book as Highsmith's finest, 'and if I were to be asked what it is about I would reply, "Apprehension".'[13] The unsettling nature of the prose is achieved not through sensational or violent action, but rather an uneasy sense that nothing is certain, that character, language and beliefs are equally fluid and subject to change. Like Camus' *L'Étranger*, Highsmith's *The Tremor of Forgery* is an unnerving study in alienation, a work which should not be read as a work of

crime fiction but as a serious, non-genre novel. The novel tells the story
of thirty-four-year-old Howard Ingham, a divorced American writer
who travels to Tunisia to wait for a film director, John Castlewood,
with whom he is to work on a movie, only to hear that he has
committed suicide. One night he awakens to see the door of his hotel
bungalow open. Without thinking, he takes hold of his typewriter and
throws it at a receding turbaned figure, who collapses on the terrace.
Any evidence of the attack is cleared by hotel workers and although it is
suspected that Ingham killed the Arab, nothing is certain; in fact we
learn nothing more of the incident.

Wrenched away from a familiar environment, Ingham feels he is
gradually losing his bearings, and in the noisy surroundings of Melik's,
the local restaurant, he likens himself to a small, empty, silent room
boxed in by the larger one of the outside world. To pass the time, he
starts working on a novel, a book which he originally entitles *The
Tremor of Forgery*, about a man, Dennison, who leads a double life and
who, like the imaginative creations of Highsmith's other writer-pro-
tagonists, such as Sydney Bartleby's character of 'The Whip,' can be
likened to Ripley. 'His book was about a man with a double life, a man
unaware of the amorality of the way he lived'.[14]

Like Highsmith herself, Ingham occupies a world confused by the
constant intertwining of reality and fantasy, an environment in which it
is difficult to decide what is fake and what is authentic. While in Sousse,
Ingham notices the counterfeit Levi's on sale in shop windows, complete with the tell-tale label, ' "This Is A Genuine Pair of Louise" . . .
The forgers had given up.'[15] (Highsmith would explore the issue of
forgery further in her next novel, *Ripley Under Ground*.) Just as
Ingham's loss of identity echoes Dennison's, so his life begins to parallel
the triangular scenario he had imagined in his synopsis for *Trio*, the film
he intended to make with John Castlewood. The boundaries between
the real and the created become even more uncertain in the days after
the typewriter incident. The Arab boys employed by the hotel deny all
knowledge of the attack and it becomes relegated to the realms of
illusion. Living in an alien environment has washed all traces of his self
away.

The sojourn in Tunisia strips Ingham of his morals, breeds doubt and
anxiety, even forces him to question the nature of his sexuality. North
Africa was notorious for its blurring of masculine sexual identity, and
in Tunisia, as Highsmith writes in the book, boys could be bought for
sex for half a packet of cigarettes. In the early stages of plotting the
novel, in January 1967, Highsmith visualised the central character as a

recently divorced man who has an affair with an Arab boy, 'because he reverts to childhood – consequent shame',[16] but in the final version she toned this down to a mere frisson of temptation due to his nervousness about exactly what to do with a boy in bed, which was, as she writes in the book, ('. . . Hardly a moral reason for chastity.) He [Ingham] was surrounded by a sea of Arabs who were still mysteries to him . . .'[17]

The book stands as a complex exploration of the intersections between life and its ever-reflecting imitations and an autobiographical expression of the writer at work. The novel functions, as Tunisia affects Ingham's consciousness, like a 'wavy mirror or a lens that inverted the image,'[18] constantly undermining the accepted and the fixed, subjecting everything to an unsettling 'fuzziness, or inversion of things'.[19]

The Tremor of Forgery is also one of Highsmith's most political novels, set as it is during the Arab-Israeli Six-Day War of June 1967. In chapter two, news of the start of the hostilities is relayed by an unnamed Western man who had just heard on television that the Israelis had started to blast several Arab airports. By chapter three, the war is over – the Israelis had secured a victory – but the conflict continues to resonate throughout the novel. Highsmith was decidedly anti-Israeli later in life – she boycotted the country from 1977 and despised Ariel Sharon. 'I think the Jewish lobby, on the Middle East, is pulling Congress around by the nose,' she told Ian Hamilton in 1977. 'These little Congressmen are afraid of losing their jobs, frankly, if they don't send money and arms to Israel . . . I don't know why America should support a country that is behaving like that.'[20]

Yet the portrait of the conflict which emerges from the novel is an uncertain one. Several of the characters, living in an Arab country, express strong anti-Arab feelings, including the Danish-born homosexual Jensen, who is not averse to a spot of sexual exploitation and whom a reader might expect to hold more liberal opinions. After the disappearance of his dog, Hasso, which he presumes to have been killed, he says to Ingham, 'But I'll tell you one thing, I hate the thought of Hasso's *bones* being in this goddamn sand! Am I glad the Jews beat the shit out of them!'[21] Similarly, Francis Adams – also known as OWL, an acronym for 'Our Way of Life' – whom one might think would proffer more pro-Israeli sentiments, criticises the Jewish state for its arrogant nationalism, ' "which was the hallmark of Nazi Germany, and for which Nazi Germany at last went to her doom"'.[22] Ingham's reaction is interesting because, against all expectations, he agrees, at least in part, with Adams' beliefs, but he chooses to keep his opinions to himself. It just wasn't worth it, he reasons, as the problem was not his –

a lethargy suggestive of Ingham's gradual collapse of his self. His lack of action after attacking the Arab with his typewriter could, in the same way, be seen as a symbol of the moral apathy at work in the world at large.

After finishing the novel, in February 1968, Highsmith mused on the nature of evil, believing that fundamentally it was rooted in jealousy, adding that she was living through what she described as the 'Age of Hypocrisy'. 'This is the age of knowing – thanks to first hand witnesses, reports, television, photographs – how everyone else everywhere is living and just what kind of corruption is being practised by various parties.'[23] Highsmith reflected the growing dissatisfaction with politics, a realisation that Robert Frost's hope of a 'golden age' – words written at the same time as John F. Kennedy's presidential inauguration – had come to naught.

While writing *The Tremor of Forgery* she commented that she wanted the novel to reflect the 'general sadness and futility of much of the world', particularly Vietnam.[24] Although the Vietnam War started in 1954, it wasn't until America's backing of the South against the communist North, in 1961, that the world began to take notice. By 1969, 550,000 American troops had been dispatched to the area, and by the end of the conflict, in 1975, with the communist North emerging victorious, 50,000 Americans had lost their lives, in addition to 900,000 Viet Cong and North Vietnamese and 400,000 South Vietnamese. High-profile names such as Martin Luther King, Norman Mailer, Noam Chomsky, Robert Lowell and Benjamin Spock all voiced their protest against America's actions. Highsmith was vehemently anti-war and in July 1968 she wrote to her friend Barbara Ker-Seymer telling her how she had penned a letter to the Barnard magazine attacking another alumna for what she saw as her whitewashing of Vietnam. She later told Ian Hamilton of the shame Americans felt over the Vietnam debacle. 'Vietnam was exporting rice before we set foot there,' she said. 'Now they have to import it.'[25]

The Tremor of Forgery explores the contradictory responses towards Vietnam by the use of two opposing characters, Francis Adams, who is pro-war and Ingham, very much against it. For Adams, 'OWL', the action in Vietnam is simply an extension of the American way, a conflict which he hopes will result in the Vietnamese believing in God and democracy. To Ingham, as to Highsmith, the war represents something more sinister, 'introducing the Vietnamese to the capitalist system in the form of a brothel industry, and to the American class system by making the Negroes pay higher for their lays'.[26] Adams may preach the message of universal democracy and global Christianity as the twin virtues which lie at the foundation of modern morality, but Ingham asks how a country can call itself Christian when it arms itself with nuclear weapons. In one of the tapes he plays to Ingham, Adams – who broadcasts behind the Iron Curtain under the name Robin Good-fellow, 'an ordinary American citizen' – addresses the issue of propaganda and asserts the moral superiority of capitalist society. Ironically, as Ingham realises, the clumsiness of his approach could actually have the opposite effect and culminate in an increase in anti-American feeling. Ultimately the real danger lay in American foreign policy. 'The harm OWL did (and he might, by his absurdity, and by making nonsense of the Vietnamese War, be doing some good) was infinitesimal compared to the harm done by America's foreign policy makers who actually sent people off to kill people.'[27]

In November 1967, as Highsmith was near to completing the novel, she wrote to Barbara Ker-Seymer of her ambivalent feelings for the book, telling her friend that she was at once 'pleased and doubtful about it',[28] while in January of 1968, she voiced her concerns in her notebook. She was worried, she said, that 'its themes are not great enough, that it is not as "great" a book as I had wished',[29] and afraid that it wouldn't be anything more than a popular success. Yet she was heartened by the opinions of Daisy Winston, who visited Highsmith over Christmas, who regarded it as a serious novel, and her agent, Patricia Schartle Myer, who asked Doubleday for a $3,000 advance, rather than Highsmith's usual $1,500. Larry Ashmead, her editor at Doubleday, believed it to be one of her best books. 'When I received *The Tremor of Forgery* I started to note down certain things from the book so I would know who was doing what and when and although it was so very complex, it all fell together beautifully,' he says. 'She was what I call a real caviar writer.'[30] Highsmith was delighted by the news that Doubleday would publish it not in their Crime Club series but as a straightforward, non-genre novel, yet dismayed by the fact that her American publishers had problems with the title. According to Highsmith, Doubleday complained that 'it sounds too much like a suspense book – so this is a slight pain to me, and I think I will argue about it and keep the title,' she wrote to Alain Oulman. 'It is *not* a suspense, etc. book, and you know how categorized the Americans are.'[31] Although Highsmith was keen for the book to be taken seriously she was also conscious that it should appeal to as wide a readership as possible. While working on the novel she read Iris Murdoch's *The Sandcastle* and *The Severed Head*, Golding's *Lord of the Flies* and Joyce's

Finnegan's Wake. She dismissed Joyce's epic as too stylistically experimental for its own good – 'A writer cannot write for his own pleasure alone and expect to be admired, loved, respected,' she said[32] – and later, in a letter to Alain Oulman, she described Pynchon's *Gravity's Rainbow* as 'lively and funny in spots . . . a bit insane and too full of whimsical humor . . . without form'.[33]

When *The Tremor of Forgery* was published by Heinemann, complete with a dustjacket Pat thought 'boring . . . all black, a drawing of Arab houses in white penline, and a sun which resembles a frying egg with orange yolk,'[34] some of the reviews were, in Julian Symons' words, 'obtuse'.[35] However, Symons, for one, was sure the novel was Highsmith's most accomplished yet, precisely because 'nothing much happens'.[36] Janice Elliott, writing in the *New Statesman*, commented on the ambiguous nature of the prose, observing that Highsmith was in the process of almost creating a whole new novelistic form. 'Thriller addicts can seize on it to prove that Crime has grown up to become Art,' she wrote. 'In fact, I doubt if there was ever this distinction in Miss Highsmith's mind; so closely are the two elements fused, enriching each other, that a third genre is created . . . Miss Highsmith's dry simplicity conceals a labyrinthian complexity it is a challenge and a pleasure to entangle.'[37] Nearly twenty years later the novel was still attracting attention; in 1988 the Spanish film director Pedro Almodóvar expressed interested in filming it, while Terrence Rafferty, writing in *The New Yorker*, explained that he regarded the novel as Highsmith's best. The author, he said, conjured her narrative as a series of mirages which disappear on closer inspection. 'In this shimmery void, the only real movement is internal,' he wrote.[38]

Early in 1967 Highsmith's agent told her why her books did not sell in paperback in America. It was, said Patricia Schartle Myrer, because they were 'too subtle', combined with the fact that none of her characters were likeable. 'Perhaps it is because I don't like anyone,' Highsmith replied. 'My last books may be about animals,'[39] an observation which presaged her 1975 book of short stories, *The Animal-Lover's Book of Beastly Murders*.

The resentment that had simmered inside her ever since she was a child, combined with the bitterness she felt at having suffered nothing but broken relationships, was now resulting in an increasing intolerance towards the outside world, a misanthropy which was made only slightly more palatable by its accompanying black humour. In her notebook, she wondered whether a use could be put to the growing number of what she described as 'morons'. 'How about training them as casual servants, people who empty ashtrays, polish brass, made beds, wash dishes and generally go about picking up? . . .' she wrote. 'This idea would give the morons a home, not an institution, and a form of family life. (Best not to get a moron fond of fires.)'[40] She directed her hatred towards other targets including babies, whom she thought could be 'killed early, like puppies or kittens'[41] so as to solve the problem of overpopulation, and the Vatican, which she hoped would be destroyed by American bombs. 'I propose a toast to the Pope,' whom she hated for his resistance to birth control. ' "I wish you, eternal pregnancy!" . . . "May your vagina be torn to pieces!" '[42] Her loathing of particular institutions and hypocrisies would later from the basis of her short-story collection, *Tales of Natural and Unnatural Catastrophes*, published in Britain by Bloomsbury in 1987 and in America by Atlantic Monthly Press two years later.

Counterpointing this splenetical streak was her tendency to romanticise the past, forever fantasising about the return of lost lovers. Throughout the writing of *The Tremor of Forgery* she had been sustained by the memory of her relationship with Virginia Kent Catherwood – whom she recast as Lotte, Ingham's ex-wife, in the novel – who had captured her heart twenty-two years before. During this time, she also had recurring dreams of Lynn Roth, her girlfriend from 1953. She dreamt that she was lying on a grassy sward reading a newspaper and next to her lay Lynn. Then a honeysuckle started to grow out of the top of the paper, from which the two women proceeded to suck honey. Lynn, she said, was the joy of her life and in December she noted in her diary, after another dream, that, 'I am still in love with Lynn Roth and always will be.'[43]

Then in January 1968, Highsmith wrote a letter to Ann Clark, telling her that *she* was the love of her life and how much she regretted what had passed. 'I wonder if anything will ever come of it?' she asked.[44] Of course nothing did, because Highsmith, as she herself realised, was in love with the idea of woman, not the reality. 'It is quite obvious that my falling in love is not love,' she wrote in her notebook, 'but a necessity of attaching myself to someone. In the past, I have been able to do this without any physical relationship – just to prove my point here. Perhaps a great source of shipwreck in the past has been to expect a physical relationship.'[45]

Feeling alone and unhappy, musing on what might have been, Pat once again worried about her sanity. Her nervous system, she said, resembled that of her mother and she was all too aware of how Mary's mind had degenerated into madness. Highsmith told a friend, the writer and critic Maurice Richardson, that she couldn't bear his presence in her house as he acted as a catalyst to her anxiety. 'As I said to him (quite honestly),' she wrote to Barbara Ker-Seymer in February, 'I fear the madness in me, quite near the surface.'[46]

On Saturday 2 March, Madeleine Harmsworth, a twenty-six-year-old journalist from London, arrived in Samois-sur-Seine to interview Highsmith about her work for *Queen* magazine. Highsmith found the Oxford graduate, with her long black hair and subtle oriental features, to be 'most charming'[47] and, emboldened by a few glasses of Scotch, proceeded to try her luck. Finding herself being seduced, Madeleine, who admired Highsmith so much she refused to call her Pat – she said it would be like calling Shakespeare, 'Willie' or Dickens, 'Charlie' – acquiesced and they spent that night together.

'She was an idol of mine and it was flattering,' says Madeleine. 'I wasn't averse to trying a bit of bisexuality. I was very young and impressionable, keen as a journalist and it seemed quite exciting. I was intrigued to know what sort of person could produce those books. I expected a fairly tortured soul because of the nature of the writing and I suppose that's what I found.'[48]

Madeleine stayed for the weekend and then went back to London, from where she wrote Highsmith a number of 'increasingly warm letters'.[49] Highsmith, in typical romantic fashion, asked the girl to 'marry me for a year'.[50] The couple planned when they would next see one another again and in April, Highsmith asked her housemate, Elizabeth, whether she was going away over Easter as she would like the house to be free so she could invite a friend – Madeleine. Although the request, in itself, seems reasonable enough, Highsmith may have phrased it in an insensitive way. Whatever the case, Elizabeth was incandescent for two days and demanded Pat find herself another house.

'I have had to engage a lawyer myself, to protect myself from whatever "charges" are in store for me . . .' Highsmith wrote to Barbara Ker-Seymer. 'My stomach is in a state of upset. I do hope to get out of here within a week.'[51]

From the 25 April until 6 May, Highsmith stayed with Barbara Ker-Seymer and Barbara Roett in London, where she attended the Crime Writers dinner at the Park Lane Hotel with Madeleine as her guest. When she was in Britain she always took advantage of what she saw were the cheaper prices, stocking up on shirts and typewriter ribbons. 'I dislike paying $2.10 for a typewriter ribbon here, e.g., so I stock up on such things in London,' she wrote to Alex Szogyi.[52]

Before she had left for her London trip, Highsmith had found a new house – in Montmachoux, six miles south-east of Samois-sur-Seine – and she signed a contract for its purchase for the equivalent of $18,000. 'I shall be living alone, thank God,' she said.[53] When she returned to France, shocked by the student uprising, strikes and riots – in addition to the recent assassinations of Martin Luther King, in April and then Robert Kennedy, in June – she declared that the world had gone mad. France seemed on the verge of a revolution. The Paris Metro was daubed with graffiti: '*Metro-boulot-dodo*' or 'Metro-work-sleep', an attempt by radicals to rouse what they saw as the non-questioning, robotic mind-set of the French workers. President Charles de Gaulle responded by labelling the protesters, '*Cette chienlit*' – 'This shit-in-the-bed' – a charge which was then scrawled over posters of the French leader, with the accompanying insult, '*La chienlit c'est lui!*'[54]

Highsmith's own immediate circumstances did not help the situation. Elizabeth, via her lawyer, refused to pay Highsmith for half the house. 'One's friends are not even one's friends,' she wrote in her notebook. 'I hate the dog-eat-dog of the atmosphere here.'[55] She loathed the fog of 'corruption & dishonesty'[56] which she thought permeated the whole country. 'Hoarding Gauloises, filling bathtubs with petrol,' she wrote to Koestler about the effects of the general strike. 'It is no wonder this country lost the last war.'[57]

On 20 June she moved into her new house in Montmachoux, a quiet rural village which had a population of only 160, mostly agricultural workers, labourers and their wives. From the church perched on a hillside Highsmith would have seen expanses of farmland and forest surrounding the village and the sweeping grandeur of the nearby Aqueduc de la Vanne. Above all she valued its isolated setting, almost revelling in its unsophisticated, non-bourgeois authenticity. 'I have to dump my own garbage, take it in a big plastic bag in the back seat of the car about one kilometre to a sort of First World War battlefield,' Highsmith said. 'You have to collect the milk at 6.30 or else. There's no bakery and no butcher in the village. I have to drive four to five kilometres to get meat for my cat.'[58] She enjoyed the peace, especially the lack of people, and any inconveniences, she said, were 'worth it to me to have a sense of elbow room'.[59]

Ten days after moving in, Madeleine arrived to help her unpack and weed the garden, while Highsmith worked on a play, *When the Sleep Ends*, for the London theatrical producer Martin Tickner. It was during this visit that Madeleine came to realise that Highsmith's image of herself was vastly different from the reality.

'I'm afraid that Pat was given to delusions and thankfully, for my sake, I quickly discovered that,' she says. 'To begin with these comprised of very simple fantasies. For example, she gave the impression that she was a great gardener, that she loved cats and adored good food. My first impression was of her garden – a barren piece of dried-up grass, which I thought was a little odd. I'm very keen on animals but all I can say is that I would not like to have been her cat; the way she handled it or didn't handle it was not that of an animal lover. And as for food – it didn't enter into her mind at all.'[60]

Throughout the summer Highsmith journeyed back and forth between her house in Montmachoux and London. In October, she and Madeleine were invited by Martin Tickner to a villa near Albufeira, Portugal, where she could work on *When the Sleep Ends*, which was set in a London drawing room and which she described as 'slightly misogynistic'.[61] Highsmith wrote the female part for her actress friend Heather Chasen. 'Pat was such a wonderful writer, but she couldn't write dialogue,' says Heather. 'When I read the play, a thriller, I hated the role – this woman was a terrible bitch. I thought if that's what she thinks of me, well that's charming. She never wrote well of women, she didn't seem to have any inside knowledge about them, they were all like cardboard figures. It didn't come to anything; it wasn't a very good play.'[62]

'I do remember Pat trying to write a play which wasn't at all successful,' says Madeleine. 'At that point I really was trying to distance myself from her, but she was persuasive and I went. It was as bad as I expected it to be. I was rather fond of Portugal until then. She was an extremely unbalanced person, extremely hostile and misanthropic and totally incapable of any kind of relationship, not just intimate ones. I felt sorry for her, because it wasn't her fault. There was something in her early days or whatever that made her incapable. She drove everybody away and people who really wanted to be friends ended up putting the phone down on her.

'It seemed to me as if she had to ape feelings and behaviour, like Ripley. Of course sometimes having no sense of social behaviour can be charming, but in her case it was alarming. I remember once, when she was trying to have a dinner party with people she barely knew, she deliberately leaned towards the candle on the table and set fire to her hair. People didn't know what to do as it was a very hostile act and the smell of singeing and burning filled the room.

'Of course she was an alcoholic and maybe that had something to do with her odd behaviour. Alcoholics are extremely boring people and the combination meant that one was associating with somebody who, I thought, was quite deranged. Young I may have been, but I wasn't interested in being associated with someone like that. Had she been living in England our relationship would have stopped early on, but because of the distance it took a long time. And she was quite clever at hiding things, including her alcoholism. It took me a while to spot the nine-o'clock-in-the-morning drink. She didn't fall about, like most alcoholics don't, but the drinking would start the moment she got up. Once the initial excitement of being with a famous person wore off and I realised she had all these problems, I started to back away.'[63]

Before Christmas, Madeleine had tried to split from Highsmith, but the affair lingered on into the new year. Then, while Pat was on a visit to London in January, Madeleine decided the time was right for her to tell Pat the truth, that she didn't think their relationship had a future. '"Maybe we shouldn't sleep together,"' said the younger woman, '"but maybe we can be friends."'[64] In a letter to Alex Szogyi, Highsmith attempted to analyse what exactly had gone wrong.

'I think it was decidedly my fault for making a play for Madeleine, succeeding, leading her on, with my letters. We had an acquaintance of 24 hours, in Samois, the rest progressed by letters . . . I must write to her again . . . and apologize for my own behaviour. I feel I have led on someone younger than I, unfairly. At the same time, I think she is thicker-skinned than I, so I hope there will be not a single tear shed. Madeleine is a political conservative. I find these people land on their feet. Or other people's.'[65]

Although Madeleine, when making the break, asked whether she could remain friends with Pat, she had no real intention of doing so. 'I would have liked to have stayed a friend – she had precious few of them – but I couldn't because she would make other assumptions and I didn't want her to think there was any possibility that we might get back together,' she says. 'I always continued to admire her as a writer. And, in fact, her writing saved her. She knew that. She knew that it stood between her and, I would say, insanity. If she hadn't had her work she would have been sent to an insane asylum or an alcoholics' home. If you look at the characters she writes about, they are her. It took a little while for me to figure this out, but all those strange characters haunting other people, and thinking and fantasising about them – they were her. She *was* her writing.

'To me, her novel *This Sweet Sickness* is the one which most closely represents her. Like the book's hero, she had a perception of her lovers which was different from reality. Without that, we wouldn't have had the books, but unfortunately, it was a harsh price to pay.'[66]

23

The false, the fake
and the counterfeit

1968–1969

Highsmith's sequel to *The Talented Mr Ripley* had a long gestation. In 1958, three years after publication of the first Ripley book in America, she toyed with the possibility of a follow-up, which she thought she might call 'The Alarming Return of Mr Ripley', and although nothing came of it, her amoral hero refused to die. At first he found expression in her novels under an assumed identity, particularly the fictional creation of Bartleby's 'The Whip' in *The Suspension of Mercy* and Ingham's character of Dennison in *The Tremor of Forgery*. In July 1965, while planning the unfinished television play, 'Derwatt Resurrected', she made the first notes for what would shape itself into the plot of the second Ripley novel, *Ripley Under Ground*, published in 1970. At this early stage, the story centred on an artist, Derwatt, who committed suicide, and whose friends claim to have witnessed him rising, like Jesus, from the dead. Another plot line, one which she would expand to form the basic narrative of the Ripley sequel, focused on the attempts of the dead man's friends to exploit his reputation for their own financial benefit. 'Bernard thinks of forging some paintings,' Highsmith wrote in her notebook, 'and the others, with one eye closed at first, fall in with it.'[1]

In February of the following year she thought about how she could meld together a daring narrative with philosophical inquiry, noting how such an approach would be perfect for the second Ripley novel, in which she imagined her favourite character at the age of twenty-eight and having secured an education. The result, she said, would be a 'more intellectual and funnier' novel than *The Talented Mr Ripley*.[2] By October of 1968, she felt she was ready to start work on plotting the book in detail. In her thirtieth cahier, she outlined her initial thoughts regarding an art forgery plot centring on the manufacture of paintings supposedly done by Derwatt, whose death Ripley and his associates have kept secret from the world. As she imagined it, Ripley would be living near a French town with a 'nice old lady' housekeeper and a wife, 'who is frequently away from home, pursuing her own affairs, since Tom is not very ardent in bed'.[3] Indeed, Ripley 'cares nothing sexually about his wife'.[4] By 5 November she had broken down the story into a series of key points, which she detailed in her notebook. Ripley's comfortable world would be shattered by the news that his art fraud is about to be exposed by the grumblings of an American collector convinced his Derwatt is a forgery and the arrival of Chris Greenleaf, Dickie Greenleaf's cousin. Point nine in the list expressed the theme of the book: 'Tom persuades Chris that a falsification can be as aesthetically satisfying as an original. In fact the falsifier has in his own way developed his talents, starting on Derwatt's principles, so that one cannot tell where the one begins, the other ends.'[5] Ripley, as Highsmith saw it, would be characterised by 'constant schizophrenia. He is happiest playing the role of someone else.'[6]

By Boxing Day, Highsmith had written 160 pages of the novel in four weeks, which she described as her 'normal speed' of work,[7] but which seems remarkable even for a writer of her prolificacy and in fact she confessed to Barbara Ker-Seymer that she was working in a 'manic' state.[8] Her imagination was stimulated by the newspaper coverage of the Mary Bell case – from 6 December issue of the *Daily Mail* she cut out the story headlined 'MURDER FOR PLEASURE', pasting it into her notebook – and towards the end of year she dreamt up a number of ideas for increasingly violent and horrific short stories.

'A man asks a father for his daughter's hand, and receives it in a box – the left hand,' she scribbled in her notebook on 15 November.[9] The first sentence of the final version of the tale, 'The Hand,' which would appear as the first story in her 1975 collection, *Little Tales of Misogyny*, differs remarkably little from the cahier entry: 'A young man asked a father for his daughter's hand, and received it in a box – her left hand.'[10] On 17 December she had the idea about a young boy who slaughters the staff of a house-of-horrors wax museum and arranges the bodies like a gory tableaux, a story published as 'Woodrow Wilson's Neck-tie', in *Ellery Queen's Mystery Magazine* in 1972 and anthologised in Highsmith's 1979 collection, *Slowly, Slowly in the Wind*.

After the mania of the previous month, at the end of December Highsmith fell into a depressingly debilitating fatigue. She had experienced a setback in plotting the second Ripley book, 'it won't move', she said,[11] and she remained so dissatisfied with her play *When the Sleep Ends* that, in December, she suffered what she believed to be a nervous breakdown. 'I continued, barely, to get out of bed in the morning, exceedingly late,' she wrote to Barbara Ker-Seymer in January 1969. 'At least now I can say I've had a breakdown, and I used to be a bit in awe of people who had had one, not really knowing what it is. It's a particularly hellish mental and physical discomfort – at the bottom of which is frustration.'[12] During a visit to London in January 1969, to publicise the launch of *The Tremor of Forgery*, journalists noted that Highsmith's beauty had started to fade. A writer for the *Guardian* described her as sitting 'hunched back in an armchair, the light falling sharply on dilapidated, almost Mexican features. She smokes untipped Gauloise down to the last quarter inch. She runs her hand through her straight, now greying hair, making her fringe stand on end . . .'[13] Highsmith thought the piece was 'pretty stinking all round'[14], yet even her close friends had to acknowledge the accuracy of its physical description. 'Pat's face barely reveals the beauty she once was,' wrote Cynthia Koestler in her diary,[15] after seeing Highsmith in the flesh at the house in Montpelier Square, and then on television, as one of the guests on *Late Night Line-up*. 'A. [Arthur] thought her v. good,' she added, 'inarticulate & because of that the honesty coming through.'[16]

Retreating from reality once more, Highsmith took refuge in another, hopeless romantic fantasy, by pretending to herself that she was in love with a Parisian friend, Jacqueline. In a poem she wrote about her feelings towards Jacqueline, entitled 'Togetherness', which she composed in early January 1969, Highsmith refers to the 'completely false love,/Made of imagination'.[17] Love, as she had said many times before, was nothing more than illusion, so why not use it to one's advantage?

Preoccupied by health problems, driven to distraction by the protracted rewrites of *When the Sleep Ends* and slowed down by domestic difficulties, the Ripley sequel had to be put on hold until May. When finally she settled down to look at the 190 pages of the manuscript, she said that she had been 'interrupted badly', but she thought that when finished it would be a 'nice book, a good one'.[18] By 28 June she had completed 210 pages of the novel and, after a trip to Salzburg, in July, she decided to set the climactic scene in the Austrian city. From Salzburg, Highsmith travelled to Koestler's chalet in Alpbach, where the two writers watched the moon landing on television. 'On the telly was a picture of ghostly figures moving around a ghostly American flag, throwing an elongated, narrow shadow,'[19] wrote Cynthia Koestler in her diary. At lunch Highsmith and Arthur Koestler discussed ideas for his new novel. 'He found the clue he was searching for for a novel on the madness of man . . .' Cynthia added.[20]

Highsmith finished the second Ripley novel, which she decided to call *Ripley Under Ground*, on her return to Montmachoux in August, and was so pleased with it she wrote in her diary, 'I am afraid to say how much I like it.'[21] She continued polishing and cutting the manuscript in October, when she decided she would dedicate it to her Polish neighbours, Agnes and Georges Barylski, 'my friends of France, 77', a reference to the region of Seine-et-Marne.[22] When Hester Green, who worked for the London literary agency A.M. Heath which represented Highsmith's American agent in Britain, visited Pat with a friend during the summer of 1972, the writer took her guests to meet the Barylskis. For most of her stay, Hester recalls, Highsmith had seemed to be in a state of inner torment, hardly relaxing for a moment. It was only when the author was with Agnes and Georges Barylski that she calmed down. 'It was extraordinary how when Pat took us to meet these friends of hers – who seemed to us to be simple farming people – she was like a different person,' says Hester. 'She was totally at ease with them as she could never be with anyone in the literary world.'[23]

Six years have passed since the last time we saw Tom Ripley, stepping off a ferry to discover that he had not only escaped punishment for his crimes, but had inherited a considerable sum of money from Dickie Greenleaf as well. Now age thirty-one, he has reinvented himself as a wealthy man of leisure living in the French countryside. Married to Heloise Plisson, the twenty-five-year-old daughter of a French pharmaceutical millionaire, Ripley lives in the magnificent surroundings of 'Belle Ombre', a large two-storey building made from grey stone, sporting four turrets over four round upstairs rooms, 'making the house look like a little castle',[24] located in the fictional village of Villeperce-sur-Seine, which Highsmith said was inspired by the countryside of the Île-de-France. 'Ripley now lives in a village about 15 miles from here,' said the writer in 1972, when she was living in Moncourt.[25] Although Ripley has no need to earn a living – his allowance from Heloise's father keeps the couple in style – he supplements his income with regular 'fence' jobs for Reeves Minot, an American living in Hamburg, and the profits which flow in from Derwatt Ltd, an art forgery business.

The plot centres on Ripley's increasingly desperate measures to maintain his reputation. The public believe the painter Derwatt to be living as a recluse in a remote Mexican village, but in fact he has committed suicide by drowning and his body has never been found. When an American art collector Thomas Murchison questions the authenticity of a forged Derwatt, Ripley disguises himself as the artist in order to convince him that he is still alive. When this scheme fails, he invites Murchison over to France where he kills him in his well-stocked wine cellar. Whereas in the first novel, Ripley seemed to be motivated by repressed sexual desire, a yearning to lose his identity and take on the personality of another and a vision of fashioning a better life for himself, it is clear that in this book his various machinations have had a corrupting influence on his personality. He is no longer a gauche, insecure young man, but of 'mystic origin, a font of evil',[26] a quality highlighted by the review in the *Times Literary Supplement*, which described Tom's murders as those of a 'contented psychopath, as if Ripley's real inheritance from Dickie Greenleaf was not normality but the confidence to nourish and exercise abnormality'.[27]

In *The Talented Mr Ripley*, it was quite clear that Tom's motivation was shaped by his own, albeit unacknowledged homosexuality, yet in the sequel his sexual identity is almost opaque. He may have married at twenty-eight, but the union is far from romantic. Highsmith tells us that, during the wedding service in the south of France, Ripley's face turned an unsightly shade of green, while on his honeymoon in Spain, Tom felt like he couldn't make love because of the noise of a parrot singing *Carmen*. Whenever he and Heloise do have sex it was a strangely disconnected experience, one in which Ripley viewed himself from a detached perspective, 'as if he derived pleasure from something inanimate, unreal, from a body without an identity'.[28] Indeed, he regards his wife not so much as person, but as an object, comparing her to one of his pictures which line the walls of 'Belle Ombre', and likening her skin to polished marble. Although critics have attacked Highsmith's Ripley novels for their one-dimensional portrait of Heloise – one writer in the *New York Times* described the character as 'zombielike'[29] – it should be remembered that the books, while written in the third person, present the world through the perspective of the criminal-hero's warped vision. Reading the books could be compared to viewing a Derwatt painting, as if one was 'looking at the picture through someone else's distorting eyeglasses'.[30]

Ripley behaves like the author of his own narrative, inventing characters and scenarios, manipulating the plot-line of his life like a piece of fiction. Tom creates the back-story of the novel – the impersonation of Derwatt's work by Bernard Tufts after the artist's suicide – and constantly reorders events, fictionalising them and presenting them as truth, so as to escape punishment. After killing Murchison and disposing of his body into the Loing, he follows Bernard to Salzburg, where he forces the forger, depressed and spiritless, to commit suicide, an act which Ripley regards as a 'curious murder'.[31] Tom's refiguring of Bernard's suicide, and his subsequent story that Bernard's remains are those of Derwatt, read like an author's attempt to smooth out the narrative blips in a particularly tricky plot. Interestingly, throughout his imaginings Ripley sees himself in the third person, as one of the characters in the dramatis personae, and at the end of the fictional rewriting of reality, he concludes, 'The story, so far as it went, began to fall into place.'[32] After burning Bernard's body and smashing up his skull and teeth, Ripley returns to his hotel room at the Goldener Hirsch – the same hotel Highsmith stayed in while she was in Salzburg researching the novel – and prepares himself for the inevitable questions from the police. 'He was imagining conversations with Bernard and Derwatt in various Salzburg Bier and Weinstubl.'[33] He tells the inspector that Derwatt killed himself by first taking an overdose and then throwing himself off a cliff; Bernard and he then burnt his body and Bernard disappeared, presumably having committed suicide by throwing himself in the river.

The audacity of the narrative – its sheer pace and drive – is, at times, almost too bewildering, yet Highsmith maintains the level of suspense until the very last sentence. Would Ripley be caught for his actions – for dreaming up the Derwatt forgery plot, for killing Murchison, for driving Bernard to suicide, for pretending Bernard's remains were those of Derwatt? On the last page, the telephone rings in 'Belle Ombre'. The caller is the inspector, Ripley thinks.

> Tom's hand stopped in the act of reaching for the telephone – only for a second, but in that second he anticipated defeat and seemed to suffer it. Exposure. Shame. Carry it off as before, he thought. The show wasn't over as yet. Courage! He picked up the telephone.[34]

Although it is a compulsive read, the novel can also be seen as an exploration into the nature of aesthetics. In a more self-consciously literary novelist, the critic from *The Times* argued, an examination of such a subject would no doubt be bogged down with ponderous, overly written speculation. Highsmith, however, examines the subject with verve, weaving it naturally into the narrative. 'This is Miss Highsmith's secret,' said the reviewer. 'By her hypnotic art she puts the suspense story into a toweringly high place in the hierarchy of fiction.'[35]

When Highsmith was working on the book she told an interviewer from *The Times* that it was 'more intellectual, curiously enough'[36] and indicated that her inspiration for the novel came from the notorious Dutch painter, Hans van Meegeren, who for years duped the art world into thinking that his forgeries, such as *Christ at Emmaus*, were the work of Vermeer. 'I like the way he stood up for himself,' commented Highsmith on van Meegeren, 'saying his paintings were damn good anyway so why not like them?'[37] In the novel, Ripley brings up the subject of forgery in his conversation with Murchison, observing how it is possible to enjoy and appreciate a fake just as much as the 'real' work of art. 'Van Meegeren's forgeries of Vermeer had finally achieved some value of their own . . .' writes Highsmith, 'aesthetically there was no doubt that van Meegeren's inventions of "new" Vermeers had given pleasure to the people who had bought them.'[38] In Tom's world the false, the fake and the counterfeit always triumph over the true, the real and the authentic. In Ripley's living room, it is one of Bernard's forgeries, rather than his real Derwatt, that takes precedence, situated in the prime spot over the fireplace and, whatever form Tom assumes – whether it be disguising himself as the bearded, D.H. Lawrence-like Derwatt, or taking on false identities such as Daniel Stevens, William Tenyck or Robert Fiedler Mackay – the fictional always seems more truthful than his 'authentic' self, whatever that may be. Indeed, Ripley's sense of self now seems so dislocated and fragmented, he can hardly be said to have any essence whatsoever. It is clear that Ripley is just one of many personalities which jostle beneath the surface of the man, as is illustrated by Highsmith's use of language in the following sentence, indicating a split between his self and his name: 'On impulse on Thursday afternoon, Tom bought a green raincoat in Athens, a raincoat of a style he would never have chosen himself – that was to say, Tom Ripley would never have touched it.'[39]

Although Ripley's loss of self enables him to commit the most heinous acts without disturbing his conscience, the impersonation has devastating consequences for Bernard, the forger. After years of painting as Derwatt he no longer has a style that he can call his own. In fact, whenever Bernard does try to work as himself, ironically it feels as though he is faking it as opposed to the working on his 'authentic' paintings as Derwatt. Bernard is so denuded of his true identity that he fashions a dummy of his self, complete with trousers, and hangs the effigy from a noose in Ripley's house – ' "It is Bernard Tufts that I hang, not Derwatt," ' reads his 'suicide' note.[40] After believing he has killed Ripley, he travels to Salzburg, where Tom haunts him, finally driving him to commit suicide for real. When Tom tells his wife of Bernard's death, relating the events so Heloise knows what to say to the police if she is questioned, he tells her that the events should be easy to remember because they are true. 'Heloise looked at him askance, a little mischievously. "What is true, what is not true?" ' she replies.[41] The question articulates the underlying theme of the book: the slippery nature of reality and its representation in art.

It's no coincidence that Highsmith chose a quote from Wilde as an epigraph for the book. Throughout her career, she found herself attracted both by his work and his extraordinary life; according to Kingsley, Highsmith read all his plays, poems, letters, essays, as well as *The Picture of Dorian Gray*. While at Barnard she copied Lord Alfred Douglas' sonnet, 'The Dead Poet', into her notebook, and five years before her death she felt moved by Richard Ellmann's 1987 biography, describing reading about Wilde's life as a truly cathartic experience. Highsmith took particular notice of Wilde's epigrammatic remark, that the Americans, as great hero-worshippers, always took their heroes from the criminal classes, transcribing it into her notebook in September 1962, two months after visiting Wilde's grave. Like Highsmith, Wilde believed, that 'to be a criminal takes imagination and courage'.[42]

Perhaps it is not too surprising then to discover that Ripley, Highsmith's most famous criminal-hero, has more than a touch of the Wildean decadent about him. According to Wilde's Dorian Gray – the beautiful, aristocrat who stays forever young while his portrait grows old – 'man was a being with myriad lives and myriad sensations, a complex multiform creature that bore within itself strange legacies of thought and passion'.[43] Dorian constantly desires to lose himself and take on another's identity; like Ripley he believes, 'Perhaps one never seems so much at ease as when one has to play a part.'[44] Dorian proceeds to murder Basil Hallward, 'the man who captured his bewitching image, stabbing the artist in the neck and blackmailing a friend to dispose of the body, but he eventually suffers from an attack of conscience, a psychological crisis which results in his own death. Unlike Dorian, Highsmith's gentleman-killer is immune to the effects of guilt. Just before murdering Murchison, Highsmith writes of the split in Ripley's reasoning. 'He saw the right and the wrong. Yet both sides of himself were equally sincere.'[45] But Ripley, like Dorian, can be seen as one of the protégés of Wilde's Lord Henry Wotton, who believes in the notion of individualism – a concept which, in the twentieth century, transformed itself into the cult of existentialism – precisely because of its rejection of mainstream morality. As Lord Henry says, ' "I consider that for any man of culture to accept the standard of his age is a form of the grossest immorality." '[46] Books which are called immoral, says Lord Henry later in the novel, are simply works which show the world its own shameful image.

The mask of respectability and seemingly ever-youthful beauty is one worn by both Dorian and Ripley, creatures who surround themselves with aesthetically pleasing *objets* in the belief that surface and style are more important than substance. 'He has a sense of aesthetics,' High-smith said of Ripley, 'and he likes handsome boys and good looking men . . . he likes good clothes.'[47] The sickly style of *The Picture of Dorian Gray* – its endless lists of perfumes, embroideries, art works, elaborate decorations, jewels and fabrics – was influenced by Huys-mans' *À Rebours* or *Against Nature*, a book which Highsmith also read. A distant echo of both works can be discerned in the semiotic overloading that occasionally weighs down the usually bare and transparent sentences of Highsmith's prose, particularly her descrip-tions of food and wine, the layout of rooms and the details of personal appearance and dress. After all, in Dorian's, as in Ripley's world, 'manners are of more importance than morals'.[48]

Wilde, too, was fascinated by the idea of forgery, particularly the work of Thomas Wainewright and Thomas Chatterton, men who symbolised the triumph of artifice. Wainewright, according to Wilde, writing in his essay, 'Pen, Pencil and Poison', was a 'young dandy', an art critic, poet, painter and poisoner, who, rather like Ripley, 'sought to be somebody, rather than to do something', a man who 'recognized that Life itself is an Art'.[49] Chatterton, the eighteenth-century poet who used his genius to forge Jacobean plays and who even staged his own death by penning a pretend suicide note, was the subject of one of Wilde's lectures in 1888. Wilde believed him to be a great artist because of his 'yearning to represent and if perfect representation seemed to him to demand forgery he needs must forge. Still this forgery came from the desire of artistic self-effacement.'[50]

Men like Wainewright and Chatterton were, Wilde believed, works of art in themselves and, similarly, Ripley can be read in this way. Emptied of his essence, he is the perfect embodiment of modern man – self-created, self-determined, a constantly changing, protean personality existing in a world where, as Wilde said, 'lying, the telling of beautiful untrue things, is the proper aim of Art'.[51] The artistic life is a long and lovely suicide precisely because it involves the negation of self; as Highsmith imagined herself as her characters, so Ripley takes on the personae of others and in doing so metamorphoses himself into a 'living' work of art. A return to the 'real life' after a period of creativity resulted in a fall in spirits, an agony Highsmith felt acutely. She voiced this pain in the novel via Bernard's quotation of an excerpt from Derwatt's notebook: ' "There is no depression for the artist except that caused by a return to the Self." '[52]

24

An equal opportunity offender

1969–1970

Highsmith was often accused of having a negative attitude to women in her work. The charge was levelled at her by critics after the publication of her book of short stories, *Little Tales of Misogyny*, firstly in German in 1975 and then its English language edition two years later. (The book did not appear in America until 1986.) After reading the collection, the critic and poet Tom Paulin attacked Highsmith for what he saw as her 'thin collection of failed fables in which various hairy, possessive or over-fecund women are murdered by their mates'.[1] Paulin felt that Highsmith took a perverse delight in describing the brutality with which the women in her stories were killed, adding that it would be 'wrong to read these stories as indirectly feminist satires on dependency'.[2]

Highsmith wrote most of these satirical, acid-drop stories during the first few months of 1969. 'All the women,' she said in a letter to Kingsley, 'come to terrible, well-merited ends, need I say.'[3] Written as transgressive fairy stories, the tales include Oona, the 'jolly' cavewoman used as the local easy lay by a tribe of men and killed by a jealous wife; the coquette bludgeoned to death by her lovers, who subsequently get away with her murder; and the middle-class housewife who attends a women's lib protest to put forward her conservative views and who is killed by a blow to her temple by a tin of baked beans. By 10 March, she had written seven such stories.

The issue of Highsmith's misogyny still divides critics. In 1985, Kathleen Gregory Klein argued that 'almost unconsciously Highsmith validates the concept of women as appropriate victims of murder or violence',[4] an idea questioned by Philippa Burton, whose statistical survey of her work suggests that the writer cast more men than women as victims.[5] But what did those closest to the author think? Did Highsmith really hate women? 'If she were a man I would have no doubt in saying that she was a misogynist,' says her friend Barbara Roett. 'The only aspect of sex she talked about to me was the feeling that she wasn't a woman, and she didn't quite understand what women were about.'[6] This view is reinforced by the actress Heather Chasen, who first met Highsmith in the sixties. 'Pat didn't like women,' she says. 'I always thought she had a mind like a man and she really got on much better with men. Of course, she fancied women but I don't think she really *liked* them.'[7] In a letter Highsmith wrote to Ronald Blythe, she expressed the opinion that, in many ways, men were superior to women, in that they generally possessed, 'a straight-forwardness, a sense of humor about sex, and a happy-go-lucky attitude sometimes toward sexual intercourse, for which I greatly admire them. Women can be so lugubrious and tedious about sex, always saving it – and for what and for whom?'[8]

When Highsmith was questioned about her attitude towards women by the writer Bettina Berch in 1984, she confessed that she loathed the feminist movement, which she believed to be headed by harridans who were always 'whining, always complaining about something'.[9] A woman who married, became pregnant and then moaned about the drudgery of her life only had herself to blame, she said. 'And she didn't foresee that [if] she got married and had the two kids, she'd be stuck in this particular trap[?]' Highsmith added. 'So this is why women mainly bore me . . .'[10] When feminists asked her whether she was discriminated against she would reply, 'Not one bit . . . I had a job, age twenty-one, twenty-two, had a job in New York . . . never did I feel myself discriminated against. And I'm not going to have it poked down my throat. Because I never had it from men.'[11]

The idea of women in a library appalled her, the thought that they could be menstruating at the same time as reading was disgusting, she said. The writer Michael Kerr – a friend of Charles Latimer's – remembers Highsmith telling him, 'that she preferred men in lots of ways. Women, she said, were dirty, physically dirty.'[12] In the early 1940s, Highsmith wrote that she found her own sex to be 'pitifully passive',[13] stating that, in their intellectual capacities, she admired and respected men over women. 'A woman's stupidity, absence of imagination, her childlike, retarded cruelty, cannot be equalled in the animal kingdom,' she noted in 1942. 'Men's energies are naturally more constructive and therefore more healthy . . .'[14]

Her position on the issue was complicated by the feelings she had forced herself to repress as a young girl. In late 1964, in a poem she wrote to X, her married lover, she spoke of how she realised that the emotions she felt for her own sex had had to be stifled and, as a result, she grew up feeling bitter and resentful. In the poem she writes of the time when, age sixteen, she had seen a heterosexual couple walking hand in hand down the street and how envious she had felt. 'Now you say I hate as well as love/Women, and you are quite right./They have the power to hurt me.'[15]

Yet her ambivalent responses to her own sex – her idolatry of women and its concomitant enmity – were, Vivien De Bernardi believes, symptomatic of a larger misanthropy. 'Kingsley told me – which I think is a perfect phrase – that Pat was an equal opportunity offender,' says Vivien. 'You name the group, she hated them. She said awful things about everything and everybody, but it wasn't personal. It was just hot air coming out – she opened her mouth and out it came. It sounds bizarre, but although she said terrible things, she wasn't really a nasty person.'[16]

For all her contradictory feelings towards women, she did not intend her *Little Tales of Misogyny* to be taken as serious attacks on her sex; rather, she conceived them as satires whose purpose it was to entertain. While writing the stories – which won the Grand Prix de l'Humour Noir in 1977, a prize shared with the illustrator Roland Topor – she told Alex Szogyi, 'frankly, I laugh myself – onto the floor, or such, the kind of laughter that makes tears at the same time . . . Thus I approach the real joy of a writer – or any other artist – amusing other people . . .'[17] A few years later she confessed to Barbara Ker-Seymer that two of the stories, 'The Breeder' and 'The Middle-class Housewife,' were actually inspired by anecdotes told to her by her married lover, X. When Highsmith sent X the tales, her ex-lover was far from amused. 'My misogyny she had always found one of my less endearing qualities,' she wrote.[18] Although Highsmith maintained that she found these stories absolutely hilarious, X hated them to such an extent that she told Pat it would be better if the collection was never published. 'I consider it satire, not misogyny,' was Highsmith's response.[19]

Highsmith had pondered the nature of her sexual self since she was a young girl, often describing herself as having a male identity. But in the spring of 1969, Highsmith's not altogether serious view of herself as a man in a woman's body was confirmed by the outside world when strangers started to mistake her for a member of the opposite sex. Even though she had long hair and wore a touch of lipstick and a necklace, waiters would stop Highsmith, in her white Levis, as she was entering the ladies' and say, looking aghast, 'Monsieur, not THAT door'. She blamed this on the fact that she had enormous feet and skinny thighs, but the experience was, quite clearly, an unnerving one. 'This of course contributes to my current schizophrenia,' she wrote to Barbara Ker-Seymer.[20]

Plagued by another bout of insomnia – she had not been to sleep before 3 a.m. since November of the previous year – accompanied by loneliness and mania, she felt that she was going slightly mad. The bureaucracy of the French and what she saw as the unreliability of its people made her feel as if she was trapped within a Kafkaesque nightmare. During one interview with a French journalist she commented, 'I feel like Alice in Wonderland here, it is a country where people break dates, lie . . . but I continue in this battle which I shall lose.'[21] Her uncertain liaison with her Parisian friend, Jacqueline, was another destabilising influence and although she tried to remain detached, Highsmith let herself be drawn into another unfulfilling, one-sided relationship. 'I am quite in love with her,' she wrote to Alex Szogyi, 'but as I think I said, I try to "keep my distance" for self-protection.'[22] While visiting Jacqueline at her apartment in Paris, where Pat had gone for a round of interviews, the constant ringing of the telephone made Highsmith so tense that she stomped into the kitchen, ripped down a twelve-foot-long curtain and proceeded to throw it into the bath on the grounds that she thought it was filthy and needed cleaning. Jacqueline could not bear her friend's eccentricities any longer. 'Jacky was so furious,' Highsmith wrote to Alex, 'she pulled my hair and slapped my face . . . Yet she loves me very much, oddly. She made a speech that she does not want me to stay at the house again.'[23]

In April, Pat channelled her feelings of disjointedness and fractured self-identity into the creation of a story about schizophrenia, which she would name 'One is a Number You Can't Divide'. The story centres on the experiences of a young woman, Evelyn, who sees no meaning in life. After breaking off her engagement with her boyfriend, she goes to see a psychiatrist without success, but on the way back from her appointment she meets a mysterious woman, who gives her a reason to carry on. Although 'One is a Number You Can't Divide' was not published during her lifetime, the tale can be seen as an articulation of Highsmith's deep anxieties and psychological conflicts, as well as her undying belief that she might find salvation through the love of another woman. Despite all the evidence to the contrary – her string of unhappy affairs and her inability to live intimately with another person – Highsmith forced herself to believe that one day she would find happiness. But, like many of her relationships, the source of her solace was illusory, its existence fragile and transitory. 'My self-esteem has a duration of not more than twenty-four hours,' she said.[24]

As soon as Highsmith cured her crushing fatigue – eating raw beef upped her energy levels overnight, she said – she started to suffer from a cyst in her throat, a swelling which felt as hard as a misplaced bone. In April, she travelled to London where the problem was diagnosed as a fibroid on her thyroid, necessitating a stay in hospital. She also thought she was beginning to show the first signs of the menopause, alongside what she assumed were symptoms of an ulcer, telling Barbara Ker-Seymer that she had 'been living under ulcerous mental conditions since June 1967'.[25]

While in London, bored and frustrated with her play, *When the Sleep Ends*, Highsmith informed Martin Tickner of her dissatisfaction and told him he could appoint another writer if he so wished, a move which effectively erased her from the project. She was also introduced to Shelagh Delaney, a meeting organised by Charles Latimer. Although Highsmith thought it had gone swimmingly, describing the author of *A Taste of Honey* as friendly, Charles remembers the occasion rather differently. 'I thought it would be an interesting meeting but it was just a nightmare,' he says. 'They just didn't get on, mainly because of Pat's crippling shyness. It was excruciating.'[26]

Keen to get rid of her house in Earl Soham, Highsmith had arranged for Daisy Winston to fly over from America to help her clean the cottage and get it into a saleable condition. Their four days' work paid off and in May, Highsmith received an offer of £3,000, a price which she eventually reduced by £500. The same month she also put the house which she had shared with Elizabeth in Samois-sur-Seine up for auction.

Back in Montmachoux – which she jokingly called Mount My Shoes – Highsmith received a letter from Daisy confessing her love. Unfortunately, Pat no longer found Daisy attractive; she also acknowledged that she was forever cursed to fall in love with women who were fundamentally bad for her. 'My gambling, my vice, my lure, my evil, is a woman who is not exactly honest . . .' she wrote in her notebook. 'It is the same things with my writing, an attraction for the evil. Not by any means, that I can consider myself the "good" side of this picture.'[27]

She confessed that her character was becoming 'increasingly misan-thropic . . . an old tendency, now becoming stronger with age',[28] and, at forty-eight, worried by recent health problems, she started to think about her own mortality. As she sorted through her desk, she realised that she had three boxes of carbon paper – enough, she said, to last her the rest of her life. The thought so utterly depressed her that she was tempted to throw one box away.

After finishing *Ripley Under Ground* and hearing the news that a short-story collection, *The Snail-Watcher and Other Stories*, was due to be published by Doubleday in the summer of 1970 and in Britain by Heinemann under the title *Eleven*, she felt optimistic about her work. In June, she received a commission to write a feature on Billy Wilder's film, *The Private Life of Sherlock Holmes* (which was published in *Queen* magazine in November) and news that she would be paid $10,800 for a film option on *A Suspension of Mercy*. She also received a $2,000 advance for the collection of stories, which went on to sell 4,000 copies in its first week on sale in America. She felt confident that Graham Greene would write an introduction to the short story book – she thought of Arthur Koestler as a replacement – yet in November she heard that Greene's agent was demanding a fee of $500; Doubleday, her American publishers, were only prepared to pay $100, and so she decided to make up the difference.

The rest of the year she felt dogged by health and domestic problems – firstly with toothache, which resulted in the extraction of more or less all her lower teeth, carried out by dentists in London, and then an attack of flu. In November, her Volkswagen was stolen from Montereau railway station and then, in December, on returning from a trip to London, where she had had yet another tooth out, she discovered that her beloved seven-year-old Siamese cat, Sammy, had died, finding her 'not yet stiff with death'.[29] Highsmith was 'paralysed' by shock and gripped by a 'grief that cannot be shared by well-meaning friends'.[30] She had no idea what had killed her, but she suspected that neighbours had poisoned the animal. As she had no proof of this, her brain, she said, whirled around in a turmoil of unhappiness.

Faced with the prospect of a black depression, Highsmith once again retreated into fantasy, dreaming about an affair with the actress Anne Meacham, whose picture she had seen in a magazine publicising her role in the Tennessee Williams' play, *In the Bar of a Tokyo Hotel*. After the disasters of recent years, she reckoned that the safest option was to escape into romantic imagination. She reviewed her failures over the past five years and concluded that 'the moral is: stay alone. Any idea of any close relationship should be imaginary, like any story I am writing. This way no harm is done to me or to any other person.'[31]

As she gazed at the actress's face in the magazine, Highsmith surmised that her new object of adoration was intense, neurotic and expressed a great deal of sexual energy, a combination she found irresistible. 'I have not seen such a bewitching face since I fell in love with Lynn Roth . . .' she wrote to Alex at one o'clock in the morning on 14 November. 'She probably is married with two children. That's my fate.'[32] The same night, unable to sleep, she wrote a poem to the actress, in which she said, 'It's funny to pledge all my energy/To you. It's laughter and anguish. Take me. Because I will completely take you.'[33]

Barbara Roett remembers how Highsmith kept a newspaper clipping about Anne Meacham in her wallet for years. 'Then, one day, she was dining with friends and they mentioned this particular actress in conversation,' she says. 'Pat immediately said, "Oh, but she is the love of my life!" Her friends told her that she lived upstairs, they knew her very well, and at this point Pat became pale with horror because she would rather flee than meet her.'[34]

As the year drew to a close, Highsmith found herself disenchanted with the country she had initially thought of as a new-found land teeming with possibilities. Now she thought the people were rude, dishonest and untrustworthy; she loathed the noisy behaviour of her Portuguese neighbours – a sound which she likened to the squeal made by pigs after having boiling water thrown over them – and the death of Sammy was, she said, the final blow. She needed, she decided, a break. 'I have learned a lot in France,' she wrote to Alex, 'and I shall never be quite the same again.'[35]

Prompted by an invitation to stay with Rosalind Constable in Santa Fe and flirting with the idea of moving back to America to live, Highsmith flew to New York in the first few days of February 1970. In Manhattan, she stayed at the $14-a-night Chelsea Hotel, on West 23rd Street, and after three weeks in New York, she travelled down to Fort Worth, where she saw her family at their house on Martha Lane. The ten-day visit was a disaster, as all the tensions that had been repressed over the last few decades boiled to the surface. Mary blamed her daughter for what she saw as her particularly cruel 'technique of torture',[36] while Highsmith believed the problem was caused by her seventy-four-year-old mother's manic depression. Pat, busy trying to finish off the corrections to *Ripley Under Ground*, was already feeling anxious that she wouldn't be able to meet her deadline of 31 March. The noise of the television interrupted her thoughts and she felt uncomfortable working in what she saw as such a disordered environment. Then her parents organised an informal buffet to celebrate their daughter's visit. During the party, the local preacher asked her whether it was true she had written a book under another name. 'Who told you that?' Highsmith asked, appalled that anyone could know about *The Price of Salt*. 'Your mother,' replied the preacher.

Highsmith was furious. When *The Price of Salt* was published in 1952, she had decided not to give her mother a copy of the novel, but Mary discovered her daughter's secret when she stayed in Highsmith's East 56th Street flat in 1956. 'Would it not occur to any idiot that if a person writes a book under another name, that person (the writer) wishes to keep the fact secret from the public?' Highsmith wrote to her stepfather, Stanley, who was suffering from Parkinson's disease.[37]

Mary Highsmith, upset by her daughter's 'inhuman treatment'[38] of her, asked her friends what they thought what was wrong with her, receiving a range of replies including one which accused the writer of being jealous of her mother. 'My doctors say if you had stayed 3 more days I would be dead . . .' Mary wrote to her daughter. 'All your schooling, college, Europe and the group of intelligensia [*sic*] friends, rubbed off no culture on you . . . You once wrote, "To visit your family is hell". Well, if it isn't you are going to see it gets that way . . . Don't feel bad if I don't write – I wish you well. I've tried with all I have and failed.'[39]

Reeling from the emotional violence of Fort Worth, Highsmith was relieved to join Rosalind Constable in Santa Fe at the beginning of March. The two friends had initially planned to stay in Santa Fe for two months and drive to Los Angeles and then back to New York in Rosalind's Karmann Ghia, but the older woman decided to sell the car. They stayed at the La Posada Inn – 'Santa Fe's Motor Hotel' – each taking a large suite, complete with kitchen, for $9 a day, and Highsmith went to dinner with Mary Louise Aswell and Agnes Sims. The peacefulness of Santa Fe came as a blessing and she soon finished her revisions of the second Ripley book.

Santa Fe was one of the towns in which Highsmith thought she might settle, but obviously during her time there she changed her mind. 'My idea of coming back to America is to push myself (professionally, ugh) for the next few years,' she wrote to Ronald Blythe from Santa Fe. 'Maybe it is not a bad idea, as I have been entirely too much of a recluse for the past nine years.'[40]

In mid-March, she flew back to New York, from where she travelled on to New Hope, to see Daisy, and Rockland County, another possible venue for her new home. At the end of the month she visited Sneden's Landing, Palisades – yet another potential relocation venue – and saw that the barn she had once rented had burnt down two years before.

Her fantasies about moving to America came to nothing, however, and once back in France, where she arrived in April, she decided to move to Moncourt, eighteen kilometres from Montmachoux, into a house next door to her journalist friends, Mary and Desmond Ryan.

Before she left New York, while staying at a hotel in Washington Square North, Highsmith had the idea for a story told from the perspective of a cockroach, a tale which was eventually published as 'Notes from a Respectable Cockroach', in the 1975 collection *The Animal-Lover's Book of Beastly Murder*. 'The roaches were, in their fashion, a good deal more decent than the clientele,' Highsmith wrote of her brief stay in the rundown hotel.[41] Manhattan, she observed, was depressingly illuminating – 'an eye-opener – on the future, perhaps'[42] – and the High School system a shambles. 'A knowledge of midwifery is now compulsory for all New York high school teachers,' she wrote to Koestler.[43]

The rest of 1970 was overshadowed by increasingly vicious letters from her mother, who not only criticised her daughter but attacked her real father, Jay B, to whom Highsmith would dedicate *A Dog's Ransom*. In June, Highsmith became so sick of her mother's epistolary assaults that she wrote to Stanley to tell Mary not to write any more. If she did, Highsmith would not even bother to open them; instead she would re-direct them, slowmail. Her stepfather, in a letter sent to Highsmith in August, rigorously defended his wife, but Pat could not understand why he failed to recognise Mary's real character, 'her buck-passing, evasions, arrogance, stupidity'.[44] Not only this, but Mary also refused to acknowledge that she had played any part in determining her daughter's sexuality. 'She refuses any bit of blame or responsibility for my character, or to put it bluntly queerness,' she wrote to Alex. 'Not that I blame her. We all become reconciled to being queer and prefer life that way. But she refuses to see that her very muddled married life had anything to do with it. Need I say, she thinks herself an angel, and me a destructive old bitch.'[45]

The subsequent series of letters written between Pat and Stanley in August and September can be read as key documents which articulate, in an autobiographical framework, themes Highsmith explored in her fiction. Highsmith herself realised the importance of these letters; in fact, later she would tell Kingsley that the fifteen-page potted psychological self-portrait was, 'good for biographer, I assure you',[46] while in 1974, one of the author's friends, Mary Sullivan, told her that she should use the testimony as raw material for her try at the great American novel.

On 23 August, Stanley wrote to his stepdaughter with a heavy heart, 'How I've hoped it would not come that I was to be faced with answering your last written pages,' he said.[47] First of all, he felt he had to address the question of his stepdaughter's assumption that she would inherit her grandmother's house at 603 West Daggett Avenue, Fort Worth. The house, he explained, was left to Mary and her brother, Claude; there was never any suggestion that she would share in the $30,000 resulting from its sale. It was, said Stanley, difficult for him to believe how Pat had behaved on her trip to Fort Worth earlier in the year. He was amazed at her cruelty. 'When you had gone and I saw what you had done to her [Mary] I regretted so very much that I didn't step in and stop it,' he wrote. 'You would have had more respect for me and maybe for yourself. Mary was always ready to meet you with love and friendliness and so was I. You talked to her in the most disrespectful manner and constantly and most of it with untruthful accusations. She made the mistake of fighting back and denying them when what she should have done was to turn and leave the room. Once she did just that then you started wrecking the kitchen. Throwing a big container of milk all over the place and breaking the louvered door, like a mad woman.'[48]

After a few days in her daughter's presence, Mary became so nervous that after each meal she would vomit, 'not from illness but from your treatment'.[49] Stanley believed what lay behind his stepdaughter's behaviour was 'liquor', since he knew that, at other times, she was capable of showing love and affection. However, he also recalled the time when Mary visited her daughter at her apartment on East 56th Street in New York, picking up French pastries from the bakery, thinking that they could have a nice chat, only to be met by Pat's iciness. 'There would be no satisfactory contact and she'd spend the time in the kitchen,' he wrote, 'cleaning and scrubbing the bath, or ironing until time to go.'[50]

Mary had recently finished reading a copy of Marc Brandel's autobiographical novel, *The Choice*, in which his relationship with Highsmith was described, and she concluded that it was her daughter's intention to destroy him. 'She [Mary] thinks he really loved you with a tenderness that you do not possess or feel for him,' wrote Stanley. He concluded that his stepdaughter's letters to his wife were peppered with lies. 'There's no end to your injustice and wasted years and you won't have her always,' he said.[51]

As soon as she received his letter, Highsmith sat down to respond, touching upon her rejection by her mother when she was twelve; the confusion over her surname; her mother's disgust at what she saw as her daughter's lesbianism; her relationship with Marc Brandel and the analysis she underwent so she could transform herself into a hetero-sexual. At the end of this extended *cri de coeur* to Stanley, written on 29 August and 1 September, she concluded, 'I am not playing the martyr. In fact, I often wonder what my mother thinks is so wrong with me. I have not been in prison, I do not take drugs, I have had no car accidents, no broken marriages, no illegitimate children, I earn a good living – I am even in Who's Who.'[52]

In November, Highsmith wrote once more to Stanley, stressing how she did not want to receive any more barbed epistles from her mother, whom she said would kill her in less than a year if they were to live together. In addition, she sent her parents an insurance policy originally taken out by her grandmother, Willie Mae, when Pat was in college. 'I have nothing to do with this money,' she said, 'and if you send me the proper papers, I shall be glad to sign them and pass over this money ($600 or what-not) to you and to my mother.'[53]

Two weeks after receiving this last letter, sixty-nine-year-old Stanley Highsmith was dead as a result of the side-effects of treatment for Parkinson's disease. He had been in hospital for three days when an artery in his abdomen ruptured. 'I am concerned, of course, with how my mother will make out,' she wrote to Kingsley, after Stanley's death, 'not so much financially as emotionally.'[54] Although Mary wrote her daughter an affectionate letter in December, in which she asked about her new cat, Tinkerbell, and wished her 'Good Night and My Love – Mother', Highsmith recognised that their relationship had deteriorated to such an extent that caring for her would be an impossibility. 'My mother is the type who fires a shotgun and then wonders why some of the birds are killed,' she wrote, 'others wounded and the rest scared. "Why don't the birds come back?" I came back several times to suffer always the same shots.'[55]

Spiteful, recriminatory letters from her mother continued to drop through Highsmith's letter box in early 1971, accusing the writer of treating her badly. 'I paid all Stanley's funeral $800 plus $65 blanket of yellow roses for the closed casket,' wrote Mary. 'You did not offer a cent. So I paid all of it. You did not even wire a flower. Yet you acted like you adored him.'[56] It is clear that, at times, Mary was so incensed by the contents of her daughter's letters that she sent them back to Pat, complete with annotations and deranged scribbles. Highsmith then used the letters like scraps of paper, noting down telephone numbers over and around the handwriting. The feud between mother and daughter obviously upset both women, yet for all their protestations to the contrary, Mary and Pat prolonged their relationship by the vicious epistolary exchange. 'As Stanley used to say –' wrote Mary to her daughter in February, 'you can be wrong so fluently . . .'[57]

25

Name: Ishmael

1970–1971

Highsmith thought 1968 'shocking' and 1969 was, she said, 'cata-strophic'.[1] Although she was referring to her personal life, she might well have selected such words to describe the cataclysmic sequence of events being being played out in the international political arena, especially in relation to America's increasing world dominance. The optimism of the early sixties – a promise of a new idealism – had been tainted by the continuing war in Vietnam and a sense that society, particularly in urban centres, was so divided that traditional structures might be on the point of collapse. Richard M. Nixon, the Republican who had served as Eisenhower's vice-President and who had been elected as President in 1968 – his 43.4 per cent victory was the lowest presidential margin since 1912 – stood as a representative of an old, traditional America in frighteningly anarchic times. The counterculture – drugs, political rebellion, new sexual freedoms – threatened to topple established hierarchies as an increasing number of groups and coalitions continued to express their anger. In April 1968, a group of students occupied the office of the president of Columbia University, Highsmith's alma mater. The following year, 448 universities across America were forced to close or declared they were on strike as students articulated their dissatisfaction with academic life by demanding sweeping changes to admissions policies and the way they were taught; in June, rioting broke out after New York police tried to raid the Stonewall gay bar in Greenwich Village. In an effort to restore order, Nixon declared that the radicals were a minority; it was the unprotesting silent majority which mattered. He maintained that drugs, crime, student revolutions, racial discord and draft resistance all threatened the old standards, even civilisation itself.

Nixon's public image, however, took a battering – nothing, of course, compared to the Watergate scandal which forced him to resign in August 1974 – after his decision, in May 1970, to invade Cambodia. In an address justifying the bombing of Vietnam's neighbour, Nixon told the world that America was a strong nation; that the country had never been defeated in its 199-year history and that it would succeed in both Cambodia and Vietnam. America would not be humiliated, he said, nor would it act like a pitiful, helpless giant. Not surprisingly, Highsmith did not believe such empty rhetoric. 'The American picture is so appalling, it defies comment,' she wrote to Ronald Blythe on 24 May.[2] Although a Gallup survey concluded that half of all Americans backed the invasion, with 35 per cent against, the student population and radical elements in the US were furious. National Guardsmen, employed to contain a demonstration at Kent State University, accidentally killed four students, including two women as they were walking to class. The news only served to inflame the already volatile mood of the nation: 400 campuses shut down and two million students announced they were on strike. 'Really, at last they are holding up IMPEACH NIXON placards,' wrote Highsmith to Ronald. 'He's the most unpopular president we've had since Hoover – who had the misfortune to lead USA into depression in 1929.'[3]

It was in this climate of unrest and rebellion that Highsmith started work on one of her most overtly political novels, A Dog's Ransom, set in New York. The plot focuses on the repercussions of the kidnapping of a black poodle, Tina, owned by a well-to-do Manhattan couple, Ed and Greta Reynolds, whose student daughter, Margaret, was killed in a shooting accident in a Greenwich Village bar. The kidnapper, Kenneth Rowajinski, an unemployed ex-construction worker with a limp, and a writer of poison pen letters, demands a $1,000 ransom for the safe return of the dog, money which the Reynolds' agree to give him. But, unknown to them, the poodle is dead; Kenneth hits its head with a rock and then dumps its body in a refuse bin. The case attracts the attention of a twenty-four-year-old New York patrolman, Clarence Duhamell, a graduate of Cornell, who tracks down the sociopath to a squalid basement flat on West End Avenue and 103rd Street. Rowajinski dupes Clarence into believing that if Ed and Greta give him another $1,000 he will, after failing to do so the first time, finally return the poodle to them. Highsmith confessed she had modelled Greta after her friend, Lil Picard.

Highsmith started to plot the book in May 1970, writing in her notebook of the 'saddest, meanest thing in the world – "poison pen" letters'.[4] She toyed with having the dog owner think about the possibility of having sex with the poodle, an idea which both repelled and disgusted him, but she rejected the idea. By 11 June, she had started to type out the first few paragraphs of the novel and by the middle of August she had completed 258 pages. There were, however, problems. She had not been clear about the book's theme when she started writing, but after working on it for two months she realised she would have to rework the front section of the novel. 'Usually my books romp along – as to plot,' she wrote to Alex Szogyi. 'Maybe a bad sign that this one doesn't. My plot idea is all right, but it doesn't romp in the writing.'[5] She also admitted that she was creating a book which featured a New York cop without having met one and confessed that she knew nothing about technicalities such as gun calibres and the workings of police precincts. She wished she could find a friendly cop, so she could ask him questions by letter and send 'a handsome present later for the information'.[6] By February 1971, she had written the bulk of the novel but felt anxious about shaping the conclusion. 'I wish some explosion would happen in my head so that I could come to a decision about the rest of the action,' she told Ronald Blythe.[7]

In addition to being an entertaining novel of suspense, the book can be read as an exploration of class relationships, the immigrant experience, and the instability of the law. In August, she wrote to Ronald Blythe of her vision of Clarence as someone 'caught between being square and far-out or anti-Establishment'.[8] She visualised him as being anti-Vietnam, but far from supportive of all civil rights, 'not really pro the blacks who raise hell in USA courts'[9] – a position more or less analogous with her own. Of course, she added, one could not lecture about these points in a novel – didacticism was anathema to Highsmith – but nevertheless she intended the book to serve as an analysis of contemporary American society. Highsmith, like Clarence, thought that New York was a 'disgusting city',[10] and believed, as Ed did, that it was nothing more than 'a conglomeration to make money'.[11]

Clarence Duhamell's downfall stems from his contradictory attitude towards power. Whereas his girlfriend, Marylyn, a freelance typist, believes in anarchy and disorder – she loathes the police – Clarence positions himself as a moderate, somebody who, although against the Vietnam War, subscribes to the view of the necessity of the law. While studying psychology at Cornell, he spoke at anti-war rallies, yet refused to accompany a group of protesting students who planned on wrecking the faculty's offices and library. Motivated by a sense of idealism, he entered the police force with a hope of bettering the world and, equipped with the knowledge gleaned from reading Freud, Dostoevsky, Proust and Krafft-Ebing, embarked on what he assumed would be a rewarding and satisfying career. 'A policeman today was in a unique position to make contact with his fellow men,' he believes, 'and to steer wavering individuals and families back into a happier path.'[12] When Rowajinski accuses him of pocketing $500 of the second lot of ransom money, Clarence, who is resented by the rest of the police officers for being a college boy and immune to the common practice of kickbacks, begins to disintegrate. Thrown out by Marylyn, who has been pestered by Rowajinski, and, infuriated by the fact that his fellow officers, particularly Manzoni, seem to believe his guilt, he vents his anger on a passing drunk by knocking him out. 'The act exhilarated Clarence, as if it were some kind of triumph',[13] an attack which prefigures his frenzied murder of Kenneth. Initially Clarence feels little guilt for the killing of 'the Pole' – when he hears the news of his death on television all he thinks about is how he has no appetite for his mother's lemon pie – but he soon realises that he has failed in every sense and contemplates suicide. As Highsmith was working out the climax of the novel, she wrote to Ronald Blythe about the implosion of Clarence's character – although he does not confess to the murder, 'he is in a sense ruined and weakened by inevitable guilt feelings. It is this that is so hard (now) for me to illustrate.'[14]

The book ends with the shooting of Clarence by Manzoni, another attack motivated by frustrated power relations. As he begins to lose consciousness, Clarence thinks of what might have been – his relationship with Marylyn, his love of Ed and Greta: '*I had wished for so much better.*'[15] As a representative of the law, Clarence not only commits murder, but is killed by one of his own, suggesting chaos and anarchy at the heart of the justice system. The novel highlights the suppressed tensions and contradictions which bristle under the surface of a modern 'civilised' society and implies how difficult it is to simply exist as an individual in a capitalist system, an opinion articulated by Marylyn in her view of the police: 'they were *all* tough, corrupt, fascist, and not above persecuting individuals if they could gain anything from it.'[16] Although some try and change the world through political intervention – both Marylyn and Greta attend regular protest meetings, at which Greta plays the piano and sings Vietcong lyrics and 'The Battle Hymn of the Republic' – Highsmith questions whether such actions actually make any

difference. How is it possible to subvert the world order when so many –
like the Reynolds' friend, Eric, who observes the unfolding dog-kidnap-
ping drama 'as if he were watching a TV show instead of being present at
something real'[17] – are disconnected from it? What is the use of political
statements if the general populace is apathetic? Although Highsmith still
took a keen interest in world affairs – in France she read the *International
Herald Tribune*, the *Sunday Times*, the *Observer* and a number of
weekly news magazines – she was aware that she was far from a political
idealist as she had been in her youth. 'At twenty and thirty, boycotting
stinking countries (like Spain then, like Greece now) had a point,' she
wrote in her notebook, referring to the military coup of 1967 and the rule
of Papadopoulos.[18] Yet in early January 1970 she contemplated travelling with Rosalind Constable on a cruise around Greece the following
summer, a holiday which never materialised.

Although the novel has its faults – its conclusion is unrealistic, the use
of coincidences is too clumsy and occasionally the dialogue is far from
believable – *A Dog's Ransom*, with its atypical use of multiple perspectives, offers a wide sweep of contemporary American society, a
portrait of bleakness which serves as a prologue for Highsmith's later
dystopias. It's hardly surprising that Gore Vidal, who later corresponded with Highsmith, called her one of the most interesting writers
of this dismal century. 'My bad temper about our times quite fitted
hers,' he says.[19]

In an essay she wrote on the subject of her favourite authors, Highsmith
selected Saul Bellow as her chosen 'all round good and probably great
writer'[20] and his 1970 novel *Mr Sammler's Planet* as his best work.
Highsmith praised the novel for its portrayal of 'a man and his family
who come from Europe to settle themselves in America – a sophisticated, extended Jewish family who experience cultural shock, tragedy
and think a thousand thoughts on the subject of life . . . For depiction of
the contrast between European and American values, *Mr Sammler's
Planet* can scarcely be topped.'[21]

Both Bellow and Highsmith represent a world proliferating with a
surfeit of signs and symbols, but the excess of messages is ultimately
without meaning. Individuals try to escape their spatial-temporal
prisons, but constantly meet with failure. People quest for the acquisition of the material and in doing so lose whatever spiritual life they once
had. Man is at once a killer and yet possesses a moral nature, a
contradiction that can only be resolved by insanity. Highsmith admired
Bellow, as she did Conrad too, for his 'moral attitude', for the fact that

he cared about the degeneration of society and the individual. Ultimately this was her intention: 'sometimes a novelist can combine his own genius with a comment, as did Dickens frequently,' she said. 'So maybe this is what I hope for.'[22]

As Highsmith read *Mr Sammler's Planet*, she identified a number of intellectual obsessions that she shared with Bellow. How was it possible to retain a sense of individuality in an increasingly consumerist world? What did it mean to connect to reality? Could one ever understand how the unconscious shaped our behaviour? And how could one survive as a European in an environment dominated by America, where, as one of the characters in the novel says, '"the whole world is now U.S."'[23]? Highsmith empathised with Artur Sammler, the central character of Bellow's novel, as she too felt distinctly at odds with an increasingly vulgar world, 'separated from the rest of his species, if not in some fashion severed – severed not so much by age as by preoccupations too different and remote'.[24]

Highsmith's awareness of herself as a marginal figure found expression in the beginning of her thirty-first cahier – which covers the two years between 1969 and 1971 – where she wrote the words, 'Name: Ishmael',[25] a reference to the Biblical figure described in Genesis as 'a wild man; his hand will be against every man, and every man's hand against him', and the narrator of Melville's *Moby-Dick*. Highsmith first read the novel when she was fourteen and, like Bellow's *Mr Sammler's Planet*, she counted it as one of her favourite books. She particularly relished the ending in which Ishmael survives the whale's destruction of the Pequod by clinging on to a coffin. 'Maybe Melville's perverse turn of mind (saved from drowning by a wooden coffin) influenced me in my plotting for my books,' she said.[26]

In addition to the thematic similarity of *Moby-Dick* to her own work – the constant allusions to male-male shadowing, the power of obsession, the elusive search for meaning and the mysteries surrounding the nature of consciousness – Highsmith felt a bond with Ishmael. She had adored books about the sea since she was a young girl and, like the disaffected sailor, she viewed the ocean as symbolic of escape and self-renewal. In a letter she wrote to Janice Robertson, her editor at Heinemann in London, she said, 'I am feeling unusually depressed this evening, without knowing why and I wish I were on the high seas . . .'[27]

She admired Melville, as she did Poe and Hawthorne, because he was, as she explained in a 1942 undergraduate essay, 'synonymous with literary rebellion and independence'.[28] The phrase could almost describe her own position: like Ishmael, Highsmith was both a teller of tales and an exile. In 1954, nine years before her permanent move from America to Europe, Highsmith described the United States as 'a second Roman Empire', and noted that as it was not in her nature to align herself with the 'top dog', she would one day have to leave.[29] According to Frank Rich, she 'made a life's work of her ostracization from the American mainstream and her own subsequent self-reinvention'.[30] She was an American citizen who had absented herself from the US and who adopted a European sensibility; a writer who employed many of the tropes and devices of suspense fiction only to then subvert its conventional form; a woman whose sexuality was neither easily codified nor well-defined.

Highsmith may have learnt her trade by writing for comic books, but as a novelist she refused to write to order or tailor her inspiration to meet the demands of genre publishing. 'I cannot continue in a certain vein unless a real idea comes to me,' she told Lucretia Stewart. 'It will not come to me just because someone says it's a good idea to carry on in a particular vein. That's what troubled me with *Strangers* [*on a Train*], or rather it didn't trouble me: my agent said, "Write another now, follow it up," like a one-two in a boxing match, and I didn't have the inspiration. I felt like writing *Carol* so I did. And then after that I had no more ideas in that vein.'[31]

Although Highsmith strove for stylistic simplicity and easy readability, she refused to allow her work to be corrupted by the brash forces of commercialism and she was frequently broke, she claimed, at the ages of twenty-nine, thirty, thirty-three and thirty-seven. Highsmith loathed the suggestion that she should make her novels less psychological and put more sex into her books to boost their sales: 'I think a novel *is* psychological . . . and I'm not going to throw in sex just to sell a book.'[32] She hated the aggressive marketing of popular fiction, rejecting bestselling novels such as *Jaws* and *Roots* as 'temporary fads' and 'rubbish'.[33] She was not above writing stories which, in her opinion, were a little 'gimmicky' ('You Can't Depend On Anybody') or 'a bit flippant, and by no means literature' ('Home Bodies'),[34] but it would be wrong to say, as some critics have suggested, that Highsmith wrote 'unashamedly for the marketplace'[35] just because her stories appeared frequently in *Ellery Queen's Mystery Magazine*. As she told Alain Oulman, her pieces of short fiction would often make the 'rounds of well-paying magazines in USA'[36] before they were finally accepted by *Ellery Queen*, 'the last resort',[37] for around $300 each. Stories such as 'Not One of Us' and 'The Terrors of Basket-Weaving' were, she believed, perfect for *The New Yorker*, but publication by the literary magazine eluded her during her lifetime. 'Irony of ironies!' says Kingsley. 'Try as she might, Pat was never able to get a story published in *The New Yorker*. It was only after she'd gone that the magazine ran one of her unpublished stories.'[38]

The narrow-mindedness of the publishing industry was also to blame for her relative lack of success in America, according to Gore Vidal. 'Our American book-chat deals only with categories so she was never really reviewed until European critics instructed Americans that Highsmith – or [Georges] Simenon – could be taken as literature,' he says.[39] When *Edith's Diary* was due to be published in America, Highsmith wrote to her agent asking whether she should bother to fly over for a publicity tour. 'It's only worth it in the United States if you get yourself on TV,' Highsmith said. 'And my agent wrote back, it's only junk books that get on TV, quirky books such as *Jaws*, the bizarre, sex books, how to feel good . . . Truman Capote has always been excellent at that [publicity]. But I've never bothered to be in America when a book was coming out in order to try and push myself. I didn't bother enough.'[40] As Craig Brown commented, whereas Capote spent his life cultivating the image of a writer, Highsmith spent hers writing. 'The recognition awarded by the world is probably unfairly distributed,' he said.[41]

Despite this, none of her editors remember her complaining; in fact, they testify to Highsmith's meticulousness, professionalism and dedication to her craft. 'She was a brilliant storyteller, a splendid stylist and she left no loose ends untied' says Larry Ashmead.[42] 'There was never any problem about putting a small error right,' adds Janice Robertson. 'But it was not a creative partnership – Pat knew what she wanted to say and wrote it meticulously. So the script came to Heinemann very much as she wanted it to be. It's interesting that when she wrote to me in March 1972 that she had no idea where the new Ripley would go, I had no sense, then or now, that this was a request for help.'[43] Robertson remembers how Pat would type her own manuscripts on her old Olympia, a workmanlike process which was integral to her writing. 'I should like to be the kind of writer (Simenon!) who could have [*sic*] a MS to a typist, but I'm just not,' Highsmith wrote to Janice in February 1973.[44]

'She was extremely good company, quirky and very generous,' adds Robertson. 'I remember when I left Heinemann she gave me a Gucci purse. Lots of authors said that they would really miss me, but nobody else gave me anything. She was not in the least ostentatious, but she gave me this lovely gift, which I still have. She wrote in a genre of her own; she was an individual in every respect.'[45]

When Roger Smith took over from Janice Robertson as Highsmith's editor at Heinemann in 1972, he recalls feeling proud that he was connected to her as she was regarded as one of the company's most respected authors. 'I felt that if it was necessary to make radical suggestions, I wouldn't have got very far,' he says. 'She was grateful for careful editorial reading – I would suggest a little rephrasing or the correction of minor inconsistencies – but I remember once, when she submitted a manuscript, she said to me, "I hope there won't be too many twiddly things." That made me laugh, as I had spent my life doing these "twiddly things". She did not have a great love of America, she was a difficult person to promote there and, to be honest, we found her the same in Britain.'[46]

Sales figures from Heinemann show that *The Tremor of Forgery* sold 6,760 copies in 1970 and *Ripley Under Ground* 6,345 between the book's publication in January 1971 and October.[47] The Heinemann memo also reveals that for *A Dog's Ransom*, Highsmith received an advance of £1,500 and that the board decided to print 8,000 copies of the book.

Gary Fisketjon, Highsmith's editor first at the Atlantic Monthly Press and then at Knopf in the US, recalls how, for many years, she was almost invisible as a writer in America. 'She defied categorisation, but was temptingly close to fitting into the category of mystery and she had a cynicism about human transactions that wasn't particularly user-friendly,' he says.[48] The fact that she kept flitting from country to country also didn't help, he says, 'as she presented a moving target both in her life and her work – nobody could quite fix on her'.[49] Larry Ashmead believes there was a division between her high critical opinion and her poor US sales figures, which he estimates never peaked above 8,000 for each novel. 'Her books were invariably well-received in the US and often in important journals and by important critics,' he says. 'She certainly had her fans but the core audience was consistently small . . . She didn't appeal to the mass market because her books were dark, often terrifying and the reader had to pay careful attention . . . Finally she wasn't agreeable to promoting her books and she was hardly mediagenic . . . It all added up to wide and serious review attention but minimal sales. All very frustrating at least to me because I considered her a singularly fine writer, and original voice and one of the best authors I'd ever published.'[50]

One publisher who recognised Highsmith's worth – and perhaps did more than any other to push her as a serious literary writer – was Daniel Keel, founder of the Swiss company Diogenes Verlag. Keel first became aware of Highsmith while watching Hitchcock's *Strangers on a Train* in a small Zurich cinema in the early sixties. He was so intrigued by the film that he stayed in his seat to watch the credits to find out whether it was an original screenplay or whether it had been adapted from a novel. 'It said, "Based on the novel by Patricia Highsmith", and that's how I found her,' says Keel.[51] Although Rowohlt had published several of her novels in German – starting with *The Talented Mr Ripley* in 1961 – Keel persuaded Highsmith to switch to the Swiss firm for the publication of *Those Who Walk Away* in 1967. 'I was willing to do a hardback at once, so I acquired Highsmith's rights and eventually the world rights,' he says.[52]

It may seem odd that Highsmith – writing in English – should want to appoint a Swiss publisher as her representative, but there's no doubt that she respected and admired Keel, described by Fellini as a man who 'knows how to surround himself with creative forces. He loves his work and allows his artists to flourish and develop'.[53] Pat thought him 'very friendly',[54] 'a darling'[55] and, according to Kingsley, she 'owed him a lot, he made her so to speak'.[56] Keel acted as Highsmith's champion, promoting her name not only in German-speaking countries – the publisher included her in his distinctive black and yellow paperback series, launched in 1974, a list which also featured novels by H.G. Wells, Joseph Conrad, Eric Ambler, Dashiell Hammett and Raymond Chandler and which became known as the '*crème de la crème* of crime literature' – but also around the world. 'Highsmith is an American classic who could be up there with Edgar Allan Poe one day,' he says.[57]

As she approached the age of fifty, Highsmith's misanthropic vision burned with an almost Swiftian intensity. On 5 January 1970 she wrote in her cahier of how she felt eaten up by resentment, acknowledging that if she did not check herself she would find herself slipping into paranoia and insanity. 'I dislike the adrenalin in my veins,' she added.[58] One of the targets of her irrational hatred was black people, a prejudicial attitude totally at odds with her view of herself as a liberal – she professed to loathing fascists and would later define herself politically as a 'Social Democrat or something'.[59] She was vehemently opposed to the introduction of Black Studies into American colleges – she felt it ignored, as she wrote in a letter to Alex Szogyi in June 1969, what she saw as the harsh reality, 'a few unpleasant facts such as the absence of a written language (save for a bit among the Zulus) and the fact that their own Black chieftains were very helpful in herding the slaves on the boats.'[60] She also blamed the entry of black people and Puerto Ricans into universities for the collapse of the US educational system. 'They enter college without high school diplomas now, and when they take one look at those books . . . they say to themselves cripes, I'll never make it!' she wrote to Ronald Blythe in August 1970. 'So they attack the professors and so on and so on. It's a hell of a way to cover up lack of brains.'[61] Her views are echoed in *A Dog's Ransom*, as Clarence muses on the chaos of Manhattan and its crime rate. 'A pity that New York had been overrun by blacks and Puerto Ricans instead of by some more advanced race that might have improved things.'[62] Before the novel was edited, Highsmith used the word 'superior' instead of 'advanced' in this sentence – it was Alain Oulman, her editor at Calmann-Lévy, who requested she tone it down as he thought it sounded 'dangerously like a racist's opinion which I know you are not'.[63] In her defence, Highsmith wrote back to Oulman, stressing that these were Clarence's thoughts, not necessarily her own. However, she did add: 'But not by any stretch of the imagination could the blacks and Puerto Ricans be deemed assets to the community in New York at the moment.'[64]

Her vision of the New York of the future is an apocalyptic one, a view shaped by what can only be interpreted as racial prejudice. She imagined life in New York in fifty years time when she would see, 'coons hanging from 50th story windows, plugging their neighbours (other coons) before taking the lift down to fleece their pockets,' she wrote to Barbara Ker-Seymer. 'It has already happened to Newark, New Jersey – which is now almost cleared of whites; they have a black mayor, even, and the highest crime and dope and welfare rate in all the USA.'[65] Highsmith had long nurtured an irrational hatred of Jews and now this too started to find expression in her notebooks. She observed how Jewish men said a prayer every morning thanking God that they were born male and not female. 'The rest of us give thanks that we were not born Jews,' she said. 'If the Jews are God's chosen people – that is all one needs to know about God.'[66]

During the oppressively hot summer of 1971, Highsmith's already black humour began to take on an even darker hue. Since dogs and cats now ate horsemeat, why, she wondered, shouldn't the foetuses of aborted babies be used to feed animals? In fact, as humans already consumed tripe, sweetbreads and bulls' testicles – the 'little maids' of Mexico – why couldn't waste foetal matter be served up to people as a delicacy? 'After all it is protein, which is becoming increasingly scarce as the world population increases,'[67] she wrote in her notebook in an entry anticipating her 1987 collection of stories, *Tales of Natural and Unnatural Catastrophes*. Later in the year she would also play with the idea of writing a novel about a character obsessed with the detritus of modern living – waste material including abortions, the contents of toilets, bedpans, diapers, hysterectomies. 'I need a character obsessed with all this,' she said. 'I've got one, myself.'[68]

As some people turned to religion for comfort, so, Highsmith wrote in her notebook in September 1970, she took refuge in her belief that she was making progress as a writer. But she realised that both systems of survival were, however, fundamentally illusory. She wrote, she said, quoting Oscar Wilde because, 'Work never seems to me a reality, but a way of getting rid of reality.'

In October she travelled into Paris for a book signing of *Ripley et les Ombres*, the French translation of *Ripley Under Ground*, published by Calmann-Lévy. While in the French capital, she attended a dinner party hosted by Alain Oulman. Her dining companions were Colette de Jouvenal – the daughter of Colette, whom she had met the previous year and who was accompanied by her Siamese cat – and the writer James Baldwin, whom she described as a 'rather hysterical revolutionary character . . . Jimmy assures all us whiteys we shall soon be murdered.'[69] A few days after the dinner party, she was invited to Zurich for a ball organised by Diogenes, which was attended by 800 people; although she tried to enjoy herself, she found it insufferable. Daniel Keel remembers how much Highsmith hated noise.

'Once we were in a restaurant and at the next table was a group of young girls, who were very pleasant, but who were laughing. I didn't think they were making a lot of noise, but Pat looked at them with hatred, then picked up her copy of the *International Herald Tribune* and brandished it at them, before using the newspaper as a screen, a barrier, between the two tables.'[70] If more than two people were talking in a room, Highsmith often found it difficult to hear, even if they were speaking English. In early 1971, she wondered whether she could have been going slightly deaf, or whether these symptoms were psychological. 'I remember Pat once going to La Scala in Milan and hating it,' says Vivien De Bernardi. 'She came back and told me that she could not bear the sound levels, she thought she would die. She had been invited by her editor in Milan, who thought that it would please her and although she loved classical music, Pat loathed the experience as she was particularly sensitive to noise.'[71]

Yet for all her spleen, one of the reasons why Highsmith moved from Montmachoux to Moncourt was to be nearer the people she liked. She eventually settled into her new house on 14 November 1970: Colette de

Jouvenal lived in Beamont, fifteen miles away, her translator friends Jeannine Herisson and Henri Robillot were only five miles from Moncourt, while Mary and Desmond Ryan lived next door. 'Thus I hope to pull myself out of this eremitic existence,' she wrote to Ronald Blythe.[72] Her new home, situated at 21 Rue de la Boissiere and which cost her 340,000 new francs, was one of a semi-circle of seven former farm cottages, situated by the Canal du Loing. When journalists asked her why she moved here, she had to admit that she didn't know, except that the house and her immediate neighbourhood was quiet, yet it was only one hour from Paris by car or train. The front of the house faced on to an unpaved courtyard, complete with a clutch of trees, and an old, redundant water pump. From the back windows she overlooked a garden, with an eight-foot-high stone wall covered with a mass of white grape vines, at the end of which was a wooden door which opened on to the banks of the canal, a waterway used by barges, carrying coal, oil, wood and sometimes cars and even the occasional yacht. When the writer Joan Juliet Buck visited Highsmith in 1977, she described the house as 'a low two-storey cottage of the type the French call *pavillon*, it is an austere place: lived in, but empty at the same time.'[73]

In March 1971, Highsmith's twelve-year-old godchild – Kingsley's daughter, Winifer Skattebol, to whom Highsmith would sign letters, 'Your loving witch God-mum' or 'Your evil godmother' – came from America to stay at her house in Moncourt, after which the writer accompanied her charge to London. Yet the trip was not a happy one. 'I was not a fan,' says Winifer. 'She was a weird, unkind and dissolute person. She was my mother's friend, but I did not care for her at all.'[74]

Barbara Roett, who visited Highsmith in Moncourt with Barbara Ker-Seymer in June, recalls being surprised at the writer's attempts at playing the perfect hostess, a role she had never associated with her before. When the two women arrived from London, Highsmith told them that she would take them to a wonderful market nearby, overflowing with delicious vegetables, meats and cheeses. That evening she would make, she said, a ratatouille. 'We'd never seen this side of Pat before and Barbara, who was a very good cook, well, her eyes lit up,' she says. 'Anyway, when we got to the market, we saw Pat make a beeline for this dark doorway which led to a very dingy bar. She said, "I'm just going to have a quick beer," but she never reappeared until Barbara and I had bought all the shopping. I know she didn't really care about eating – she only ever ate American bacon, fried eggs and cereal, all at odd times of the day – but it was obvious that she had this fantasy about cooking.

'I also remember one day, when Barbara and I were in the bedroom and Pat was in the garden, we were in the middle of chatting when suddenly we heard this thump. A dead rat had been tossed into the bedroom. Pat had swung it from its tail and thrown it from the garden through the window into the bedroom. She probably liked Barbara the best out of all her friends, and I thought if this is how she treats her, God knows how she behaves with other people.

'Pat did really love animals, but I must admit I used to worry about her cat as she would put the creature in this kind of hammock in a towel and swing her around the room. I said, "You're going to make that poor thing giddy," and indeed when the cat got out of the towel it would stagger dizzily around the room. She didn't know how to be gentle with it and that was towards something that she really cared about. It was hard to gauge her normal behaviour, because she was never normal around people.'[75]

During the hot summer of 1971, she typed up the final draft of *A Dog's Ransom*, wearing a pyjama top soaked in cold water, and sent the manuscript off to Heinemann on 5 August. Yet as soon as she had stopped work, she felt purposeless and quite at a loss about what to do with herself. 'There is no real life except in working,' she wrote in her notebook, 'that is to say in the imagination.'[76] It was in this state that she observed that only one situation would drive her to commit murder – being part of a family unit. Most likely, she thought, she would strike out in anger at a small child, felling them in one blow. But children over the age of eight, she surmised, would probably take two blows to kill. The reality of socialising with *anyone*, no matter how close, she said, left her feeling fatigued. After a visit from Daisy Winston at the end of September and then, in October, following a week-long trip to Vienna – where she stayed with her friend Trudi Gill, wife of Irwin Gill, the American ambassador to Panama – Highsmith felt tense and on edge. 'Is it because of the phoneyness?' she asked herself. 'I wasn't particularly phoney. It's my own inward tension.'[77]

As she was putting the finishing touches to *A Dog's Ransom*, Highsmith started to think about a number of film projects. In April 1971, while in London, she met the film producer Elliott Kastner, who asked her to think up an original storyline for a thriller; her 'flicker' of an idea centred around a man who assumed a woman's identity, killed his victim and then disappeared. During the same visit she also had a meeting with the film-maker Tristram Powell, son of the novelist Anthony Powell, about scripting a documentary for the BBC based on the French chateaux- and church-robbing gang headed by Xavier Richier. 'She was so keen on the project that she wrote a very lengthy treatment for the film,' says Tristram Powell. 'She was so generous because she never seemed to bother about payment, her only interest was the work.'[78] Yet for all Highsmith's efforts, neither film came to fruition.

That autumn, Highsmith worried about how *A Dog's Ransom* would be received by her publishers. Earlier in the year she had decided to switch to a new US publisher, Knopf, instead of Doubleday, as the latter, she told Koestler, had 'done not a thing for my reputation in the past – five books'.[79] Finally, she heard that Knopf had accepted her, and in December her new editor Bob Gottlieb requested a few minor revisions, as he considered her style, she said, 'pebbly'.[80] Although she agreed with most of the changes, which were, she said, done to try and smooth out her sentences, she later resented making some of them. Janice Robertson at Heinemann also asked her cut down the novel as a large part of it seemed to drag, while Alain Oulman thought it 'good', but one which 'might gain by a certain tightening here and there'.[81]

When the book was published the following year, it was met with mixed reviews. Mary Borg, writing in the *New Statesman*, thought it lacked invention, that its characters were unconvincing and that she could not believe in the 'glaring unlikeliness' of its plot.[82] The reviewer in the *Times Literary Supplement* expressed similar disappointment, adding that the novel 'belongs in what is becoming a depressingly substantial sector of her total output – it is a mechanical exercise in self-pastiche, employing all her familiar devices and rehearsing most of her familiar obsessions, but with none of the vigour, inventiveness or intensity which in her best work makes those devices and obsessions seem so rivetting'.[83] Such reviews compelled Graham Greene to write to Highsmith expressing his disgust at the stupidity of the critics and admiration for the book itself, noting that it was 'one of the best and most complex of all your novels'.[84] His opinion was shared by Diane LeClercq, writing in *Books and Bookmen*, who observed how the various elements of the plot neatly dovetailed together,[85] while the critic from *The Times* celebrated her subtle analysis of irrationality in the novel: 'Out at the edge Miss Highsmith flings back for us the new mirrors she finds there.'[86] In the *London Magazine*, Reg Gadney praised Highsmith for her understated narrative style and commended her for the way the novel dealt with contemporary issues. 'Technically, *A Dog's Ransom* is a considerable achievement; as a comment on the morality of American respectability, law and order, and the blurred edges of decency – in the best sense of the word – it is brilliant.'[87] Brigid Brophy, writing in the *Listener*, believed that the book was not only a virtuoso piece of suspense writing, but a serious analysis of the complex relationship between an individual, violence and society. 'Sociology and reporting, with their wide scatter, can set out contradictions in moral attitudes: *A Dog's Ransom* performs the indispensable function of fiction by taking the reader deep into the ironies of his own ambivalence.'[88]

26

What are the odds
of cat versus person?

1971–1973

At the end of October 1971, Highsmith started to have ghostly ideas for her third Ripley novel. In her notebook, she jotted down a series of possible plot outlines – some of which she would reshape and use in the finished book, *Ripley's Game*, some of which she would reject out of hand – sketches which functioned as an extended 'what if?' Ripley hears of a rumour that he has only six months to live; he receives a request from right-wing elements in the USSR for him to assassinate a liberal Russian leader, which he refuses because of his desire to protect political freedom; Tom carries out a number of revenge killings on behalf of a sixty-year-old poet, a scenario that Highsmith envisaged as, 'A dialogue with myself. Wishful thinking become a reality.'[1] By 24 November, she had settled on the main narrative line: that Ripley would spread a rumour that an acquaintance – who at this early stage she called Teddie Barnes, but who would finally be named Jonathan Trevanny – had only six months to live so he could be persuaded to commit murder on behalf of Reeves, Tom's 'fence'. She toyed with the idea that the victim should at first be one of Reeves' rivals, but then wondered whether a better target might not be the Mafia. After all, such a death would present 'no moral problem'.[2] The story, she said, would have to be presented from two points of view – Tom's and Teddie's – a major break from the claustrophobically privileged perspective of previous Ripley novels. Although such an approach would certainly be interesting, she felt anxious as it would inevitably result in, as she wrote to Barbara Ker-Seymer, 'a diminution of intensity, or Ripley's kind of madness, amorality'.[3]

Initially the book, like previous Ripley novels, seemed to write itself. By 12 January, she had thought of her first sentence, finally published as. ' "There's no such thing as a perfect murder." Tom said to Reeves. "That's just a parlour game, trying to dream one up." '[4] She started writing the novel on 27 February, dashing off 140 pages in two weeks. Yet in June she experienced a setback and wrote to Ronald Blythe of how she felt she had to rack her brain to work out the last half of the novel. She finished it in 1972, typing up a clean manuscript in January and sending off the final corrections to her publishers in June.

The book begins six months after the Derwatt affair described in *Ripley Under Ground* and centres on the relationship between Tom Ripley and Jonathan Trevanny, an English picture framer who is suffering from myeloid leukaemia and who knows he has only six to twelve years to live; a surreal foreshadowing of the blood disorder, aplastic anaemia, diagnosed in Highsmith twenty-two years later, in 1994.

When the two men are introduced at a party, Ripley senses Trevanny's dislike of him – Jonathan says, ' "Oh yes, I've heard of you" ', in a sneering manner – and, prompted by Reeves' request for a man to assassinate a member of the Mafia, Tom dreams up the rumour of the picture framer's imminent demise. Perhaps if Trevanny, who lives in Rue St Merry, Fontainebleau – Highsmith's home for a couple of months in the summer of 1967 – believes he has only six months to live he will be more likely to take on the gruesome task, especially since he would be rewarded with a $96,000 fee, money which would help his French wife, Simone, who works in a shoe shop, and young son, Georges. The premise had grown out of an idea Highsmith had had in August 1970 about a central character who, soon after meeting a stranger, falls ill. 'The stranger is not death,' said Highsmith, 'but the hero believes he is.'[5]

As in the previous novels in the series, Ripley spins the story out of his imagination, viewing those around him as nothing more than characters in the book of his own creation. Acting like a malevolent off-stage Prospero, Ripley manipulates the action, crafting the scenes of his amoral drama and shaping the lives of his characters as if they were mere puppets in a toy theatre.

Highsmith's cruel humour runs through the book like a rancid underwater stream, disturbing one's expectations of the genre by a series of violent, but hilarious, images. She seems to take delight in telling us that when Gauthier, the local art supplier, was knocked down by a hit-and-run driver, his glass eye flew out of its socket. 'Jonathan could see clearly Gauthier's glass eye on the black tar road, maybe crushed by a car wheel by now, maybe found in the gutter by some curious children.'[6] The murder scenes in *Ripley's Game* are described with such relish that it is, perhaps, surprising to learn that Highsmith would do almost anything – chores in the kitchen, daydreaming, pottering around the house or garden – rather than write them. On a train Ripley attacks Marcangelo, one of the Mafiosi, in a toilet, killing him by strangling him with a garrotte. Highsmith describes the victim's death in detail – the gurgling in his throat, the tongue protruding from his mouth – and then, with a deft touch, she adds that, during the murder, Marcangelo's bottom set of false teeth clattered on to the floor. The scene is almost Jacobean in its comedic horror. 'Tom picked up the teeth, and dropped them into the toilet, and managed to step on the pedal which dumped the pan,' Highsmith writes. 'He wiped his fingers with disgust on Marcangelo's padded shoulder.'[7] After assaulting another bodyguard and then proceeding to throw Marcangelo's body from the moving train, Ripley then sits down to a comforting bowl of hot goulash and a refreshing Carlsbad. Ripley kills Angy Lippari, another Mafia man, by bashing him over the head, first with a piece of firewood and then the steel butt of a rifle, yet seems more worried about the state of his carpet in 'Belle Ombre' than any moral concerns. ' "Mind the rug with that blood!" ' he tells Jonathan,[8] and a few seconds later he doubles up with laughter at the thought of attacking another intruder. He watches the car burn, containing the bodies of the two Mafia men, while whistling a jaunty Neapolitan tune, and as he hits another Mafiosi, trying to storm Jonathan's house, he slams a hammer into his forehead, 'straightforward and true, as if he had been an ox in a slaughter-house'.[9]

While in the early stages of plotting the novel, Highsmith wrote in her notebook that 'the chief reason for this book is to come to terms with the fear of death which we all have'.[10] In May 1970 she composed a poem about the mystery of death and then the following year she observed how, 'Every problem in life can be somehow solved – except the problem of death.'[11] Jonathan's illness serves as a constant reminder of his transient existence; during a fainting spell he imagines what it would be like to move from being to nothingness, comparing death to a 'wave sweeping out from a shore, sucking hard at the legs of a swimmer who'd already ventured too far, and who mysteriously had lost his will to struggle'.[12] Highsmith extends the watery metaphor to describe Jonathan's experience of death, his implosion of consciousness, following a shooting incident. Looking back on his thirty-four years. Jonathan realises that his life has been meaningless, nothing but an absurdity. 'He had a grey vision of a sea running out – somewhere on an English coast – sinking, collapsing.'[13] As Jonathan feels the energy ebb out of his body, he sees Tom, who is convinced Trevanny shielded him from the onslaught of Mafia bullets, at the wheel of the car taking him to hospital: 'Tom was driving the car, Jonathan thought, like God himself.'[14] With the corruption and death of an innocent, the transgressive deification – the transition of Ripley from self-invented man to amoral omniscient – is complete. Like one of the superheroes Highsmith created as young writer of comic books, Ripley's existence is seemingly eternal.

Not surprisingly, Highsmith's latest celebration of amorality divided the critics. The *Spectator* lauded her for the 'creation of an ambience – perhaps superior to that of the early Eric Ambler novels',[15] but Tony Henderson in *Books and Bookmen* condemned Highsmith's creation of Ripley for the very reasons why so many readers liked him – the fact that he is a 'monstrous paranoiac'.[16] Henderson believed that while Highsmith should rightly be applauded for the ingenious plotting and the surprising psychological insight of her first novel *Strangers on a Train*, her latest offering was too much to stomach. 'Something very sad is happening to the talented Miss Highsmith,' he said, 'and unless she hardens her heart and puts an end to her horrible brain-child, for whom she appears to have conceived an inexplicable affection, the fate of Baron Frankenstein will be hers also.'[17]

Two days after she started writing *Ripley's Game*, Highsmith made a note in her thirty-second cahier of an idea for a short story about a Siamese cat, Ming, which is jealous of his owner's new lover and which proceeds to kill him by pushing him off a yacht. In the final version, 'Ming's Biggest Prey', the lover, Teddie, tries to edge the cat overboard while sailing off the coast of Acapulco, but Ming avenges him later in the day when the couple return to their villa. As Teddie, who has been drinking, tries to capture him and throw him over the terrace, Ming jumps on to his shoulder and Teddie falls to his death. 'Ming was pleased, as he was pleased when he killed a bird and created this smell of blood under his teeth,' Highsmith writes. 'This was big prey.'[18]

After sketching the bare bones of the entertaining tale, Highsmith had an idea for a book of short stories, perhaps called 'The Beastly Book of Animal Murderers', 'Beastly Murders for Animal Lovers', or, the title she finally settled on, *The Animal-Lover's Book of Beastly*

Murder. Each story, she said, could show a creature or pet – horse, monkey, goat, elephant, dog, even hamster – taking their revenge on the human world, an environment which Highsmith believed was often more bestial than the animal kingdom. 'Victims will be hateworthy,' she wrote to Barbara Ker-Seymer, 'and the animals acting out of righteous instinct.'[19] Just as she had sublimated her contradictory responses towards women in her collection of stories, *Little Tales of Misogyny*, so she redirected her feelings of anger towards the human race in these revenge sketches about animals. Every time she re-read one of her stories, she had to admit that the experience left her doubled up, with tears of laughter rolling down her face. Some critics, however, took a decidedly po-faced stance. Marghanita Laski, for example, wrote in the *Listener* in November 1975, 'I used to be the only person I knew who loathed Patricia Highsmith's work for its inhumanity to man, but our numbers are growing and will be increased by [*The Animal-Lover's Book of Beastly Murder*], short stories about animals killing or mutilating people, with a strong flavour of being motivated less by pity for animals than by distaste for men.'[20]

Ever since she was a young girl, Pat had felt an extraordinary empathy for animals, particularly cats. The creatures, she said, 'provide something for writers that humans cannot: companionship that makes no demands or intrusions, that is as restful and ever-changing as a tranquil sea that barely moves'.[21] Her affection for cats was 'a constant as was feline companionship wherever her domestic situation permitted,' says Kingsley. 'As for animals in general, she saw them as individual personalities often better behaved, and endowed with more dignity and honesty than humans. Cruelty to or neglect of any helpless living creature could turn her incandescent with rage.'[22] Janice Robertson remembers how, after a particularly long lunch and a visit to Muriel's with Heinemann's Roland Gant, Highsmith was walking through the streets of Soho when she saw a wounded pigeon lying in the gutter. 'Pat decided there and then that this pigeon should be rescued,' says Janice. 'Although I think Roland persuaded her that it was past saving, she really was distraught. She couldn't bear to see animals hurt.'[23] Bruno Sager, Highsmith's carer at the end of her life, recalls the delicacy with which the writer would take hold of a spider which had crawled into the house, making sure to deposit it safely in her garden. 'For her human beings were strange – she thought she would never understand them – and perhaps that is why she liked cats and snails so much,' he says.[24]

Highsmith had first had the idea of writing about animals in 1946; in a notebook entry in June of that year she wondered why writers felt obliged to always focus their attention on people. 'What about animals?' she asked.[25] Yet the real genesis of the stories had its root in the troubled atmosphere of Rue de Courbuisson, Samois-sur-Seine, where she lived with her painter friend, Elizabeth. In a letter to Alex Szogyi in September 1967 she wrote of how her cat protected her against Elizabeth's temper. 'There are perhaps more brains in those Siamese tiny heads than we think,' she said,[26] while in another letter, to Koestler, she outlined a hypothetical battle situation between Elizabeth and her cat, positing the question, 'What are the odds, I wonder, of cat versus a person?'[27]

In December 1967, she told Ronald Blythe how his account of the barbarities of battery chicken farming had lingered in her mind, horrific details which, she said, might inspire her to write a story about it. After a couple of false starts, in October 1968, she finished the gruesome tale, 'The Day of Reckoning', one of the stories to feature in *The Animal-Lover's Book of Beastly Murder*, in which a profit-hungry farmer is pecked to death by the battery chickens he has driven insane, leaving him looking like 'a fallen column of blood and bone to which a few tatters of pyjama cloth still clung'.[28]

The premature death of her cat, Sammy, in December 1969, left Pat grief-stricken for months and the following summer she confessed that if she had a gun and she discovered which villager was responsible for docking the tail of a local black cat, Little Eddy, she would not hesitate in shooting them – 'and to kill,' she added.[29] She wrote moving poems about the creatures, adored sketching them and later told Vivien De Bernardi how her favoured form of exercise was late-night ping pong games with her cats. In 1991, perhaps not entirely capriciously, she said that if she came across a kitten and a baby both of which were obviously starving, she would, without a doubt, feed the cat first if nobody was looking. The painter Gudrun Mueller remembers the sad occasion when she accompanied the writer to the vet's to have one of her cats put down. 'She had this very old, crossed-eyed cat which she liked very much, but which was ill,' she says. 'The vet gave the cat an injection and Pat stood beside it sobbing – it was the only time I saw her cry. I was really touched as it was the first time she had shown her feelings.'[30] Highsmith told the writer Neil Gordon of the emotional impact of the experience. 'This affected me very much because it was much more important than a member of my family who might die of old age or God knows what, because I had the power to do it, but I didn't want the power . . .' she said. 'It's terrifying to have that power. I don't go to jail for it, [but] the cat is dead . . . They have a great right, these animals.'[31]

Soon after penning stories about the revenge of the battery chickens and Ming, the Siamese cat, in the summer of 1972 she wrote tales about a boy's pet ferret who kills the family's bully of a chauffeur ('Harry: A Ferret'); 'Eddie and the Monkey Robberies', about a nimble-fingered capuchin, used by a gang of burglars to open doors, who murders his owner, a female ex-convict, with a conch shell; 'Goat Ride', which focuses on the violent retaliation of a goat at an amusement park, and 'There I was, Stuck with Bubsy', about Baron, an aged poodle, who gets his own back on the brutal treatment meted out by his former owner's gay boyfriend, the slothful Bubsy. The two stories in the collection, 'Chorus Girl's Absolutely Final Performance' and 'Notes from a Respectable Cockroach', written in the first person – a style Highsmith rarely employed – stand as powerfully imagined interior monologues, fantastic glimpses into the consciousness of creatures that the human world, for the most part, regards as mere objects. By positioning the animals as subjects, by giving voice to their thoughts, Highsmith disrupts the Western philosophical tradition which celebrates the rationalism of man. 'When I see some of the people here, I count myself lucky to be a cockroach,' Highsmith writes in 'Notes from a Respectable Cockroach', a transgressive reworking of Kafka's *The Metamorphosis*.[32] The cockroach, who lives at the Hotel Duke in Washington Square, muses on how he would answer the questions on the US census, a document delivered to the residents. 'It was interesting to think of myself filling it out – and why not? I was more of a resident by hereditary seat than any of the human beasts in the hotel.'[33] If a cockroach – that most base and disgusting of creatures – can actually feel superior to a man then what, Highsmith asks, does it mean to be human?

Early in 1972 – after suffering from a six-week spell of lethargy, flu, toothache and depression during the winter – Highsmith wrote to Barbara Ker-Seymer about Daisy Winston's recent mid-life crisis. She related how the other woman, who was approaching her fiftieth birthday, seemed to be striving after answers as to the meaning of existence, before concluding, 'She cannot realize life is about nothing.'[34]

This bleak attitude was reflected in the stories she wrote over the next few months, tales which would be anthologised in her 1979 collection, *Slowly, Slowly in the Wind*. In January she had the idea for 'The Man who Wrote Books in his Head', featuring an aspiring novelist, Cheever, who never commits his thoughts to paper and who dies, age sixty-two, thinking he has written fourteen books and created 127 characters. On his death-bed, Cheever, another of Highsmith's characters imprisoned by a fantasy, believes that he will be buried next to Tennyson in Poet's Corner, Westminster Abbey, and remembered as a writer whose gravestone marked a 'monument to human imagination'.[35] The following month, in an attempt to explore the hypocrisies of the Catholic Church – what she saw as its leaching of the individual conscience – she wrote 'Those Awful Dawns', about an unwanted baby battered by its Catholic parents. In May she plotted 'The Pond', about a four-year-old boy, Chris, and his mother, Elinor Sievert, newly settled in Connecticut after the death of Elinor's husband, Cliff, in an aeroplane accident, who are both sucked to their deaths by malevolent vines in the garden pond of their house, a tale reminiscent of one of Poe's uncanny masterpieces. Highsmith neatly dismantles the American suburban idyll, subverting the clichés of domestic bliss – nice neighbours, a child's comforting glass of milk and the dream of growing radishes – with a macabre cruelty. 'She went face down into the water, but the water seemed soft,' Highsmith writes. 'She struggled a little, turned to breathe, and a vine tickled her neck . . . She breathed in, and much of what she took in was water.'[36] Elinor is punished for trying to poison the pond with weed-killer – the more chemicals she empties into the water, the more voracious the vines seem to grow – and as she battles against the vicious tendrils, she realises that her attempt to alter the course of nature will bring about her death. Highsmith would further explore the ecological nightmare she described in 'The Pond' – the apocalyptic imbalance between man and nature – in her 1987 collection, *Tales of Natural and Unnatural Catastrophes*. It is clear from all these stories that Highsmith had a real passion for the natural world. Detailing twenty of her favourite and least favourite things, she spoke of her joy at learning that the import of baby seal pelts had been banned from Europe, as well as her love of simple, 'authentic' pleasures – the sprouting of an avocado seed; carpentry; waking up without an alarm clock; the smell of old books; silence, and being alone.

'Work is the only thing of importance or joy in life,' Highsmith wrote in her notebook on 4 April 1972. 'Trouble begins when one pauses to consider what one has done.'[37] She told Ronald Blythe that the previous month she was happy, as her writing – *Ripley's Game* and the short stories – seemed to be going well and, for the most part, she spent the majority of her time alone, accepting only one date for drinks in the last thirty-five days. Then, however, on 2 May she attended a cocktail party at W.H. Smith's, in Paris, hosted by Penguin, the British company which republished her novels in paperback. She described the event as being full of 'French notables of the book world, also English', including Edna O'Brien, 'looking quite radiant', but, disappointingly, no Graham Greene.[38] Soon after the party, Highsmith had to steady herself for the arrival of her friends Daisy Winston from America and Lil Picard from Hamburg. The strain was too much for Highsmith and Daisy told her that she found her 'more tense, anxious about things that are not worth being anxious about'.[39] Highsmith was astonished at Lil's aggressive behaviour, especially when she attacked Pat for being pro-Nixon, a description totally at odds with her views. By the time the two women left, Highsmith admitted she was left feeling frazzled, confessing to Barbara Ker-Seymer that it took her a fortnight to get over the interruption, as 'half-insane people jangle me terribly, in a very inner way'.[40]

During the summer, she entered what she described as a manic phase – a state which she said was actually beneficial to her creative imagination – which was soon followed by its inevitable, and cruel, counterpart, a crushing depression. Hester Green, who worked for the London literary agency A.M. Heath, visited Pat with a friend that summer. She remembers how even the most trivial of incidents seemed to push Highsmith over the edge.

'Everything seemed to be a terrible psychological effort for her,' says Hester. 'I remember that we went around for lunch with her neighbours, Mary and Desmond Ryan, and all of a sudden, as we were sitting around the table, she put her head down on the table in a sort of terrible psychological state. I can't remember what precipitated it. Similarly, there was one occasion when she planned to have a barbecue, but it went wrong, I think because of the weather. She got into a terrible state about it, flung her arms around my neck – it really was a gesture of despair – and said that she was so sorry. It was only a little thing that had gone wrong, most people would have laughed it off, but to her it was a major drama.'[41]

Yet more barbed letters from her mother did not help Highsmith's state of mind, missives which stand as evidence of Mary's mental disintegration. Throughout the year, Mary took pleasure in denying her daughter the only two objects she knew Pat wanted from her – the watch she had given her stepfather when she was twelve or thirteen, together with an accompanying chain she had given him nine years later. Although the watch was a thing of beauty, she did not crave it purely for its aesthetic value; rather it represented, she said, a time in her life when she was utterly depressed, the year she spent with her grandparents in Fort Worth after being abandoned by her mother. As such, the watch, which she had bought after saving up the money given to her by her grandfather for cutting the lawn, became a symbol for her strong work ethic and a sign of just how much she had achieved.

Highsmith was so horrified by her mother's latest machinations that she wrote to her father, Jay B, asking him if he knew of a lawyer in Texas who could draw up a document legally separating her from Mary. Highsmith also wrote to one of Mary's friends asking her to inform Mary that she did not want to inherit anything from her when she died. Jay B, after being released from hospital following a kidney ailment, wrote his daughter a letter outlining the legal situation regarding parents and children. 'Regarding the request for a lawyer to draw up a legal separation paper,' he said. 'This is not necessary as under the law you are an adult of twenty-one years of age and a parent has no legal ties or control of your business or financial affairs or activities.'[42]

Emotionally, however, Highsmith would always be tied to her mother, even though she repeatedly tried to erase her from her memory. Each letter she received from Mary upset her for several days, during which she found it difficult to work and if this one, written in June 1972, is anything to go by, it is hardly surprising. 'You've treated me like a dog for 30 years,' Mary wrote to her daughter. 'That's why you look like you do.'[43] In the same letter, the issue of Highsmith's name once again came under discussion. Why, the writer had asked previously, did Mary enter her at school under 'Highsmith' when the name on her birth certificate clearly said 'Plangman'? There was a simple reason, Mary responded. 'The teacher did & the principal – they approved of the Highsmith name,' she wrote. 'Everything I did was in consideration of you . . . We wanted you to choose your name when you were old enough.'[44]

In October, Highsmith wrote to her friends to tell them how, the previous month, she had felt she was on the edge of another nervous breakdown and how she had been so depleted of energy that she couldn't work for six weeks. Once again, she fantasised about a move away from France, where she had now lived for just over five years, possibly to Switzerland. She wrote to Barbara Ker-Seymer, cursing France for what Koestler described as its 'bloody mindedness',[45] and in a letter to Ronald Blythe, she outlined her hatred of its bureaucracy and red-tape. She did not need to lead a blissful existence, she said, neither did she need a lover in order to be happy. 'It's impossible to justify my hopping about geographically, I know,' she wrote. 'I have been sustaining myself for the past two years by telling myself, "It isn't any better anywhere else, so why not stay?" I am not sure this is true.'[46]

After finishing *Ripley's Game* in the early part of 1973, Pat considered taking a four-month break travelling around Japan or Sri Lanka. She felt the need to 'get away from this solitary existence',[47] and, as money wasn't a problem, there was no reason why she shouldn't jet off on an extended holiday. Yet, fatigued by another bout of flu, toothache, and a swollen left cheek, Highsmith felt at a loss. Although she was initially heartened by the possibility that Marlon Brando might play Vic in a Hollywood film of *Deep Water* – Universal Pictures bought the film rights in 1972, but the movie did not progress beyond its planning stages – for the most part, Highsmith felt lonely and wretched during the first few months of the year. A horoscope plotted by Alex Szogyi suggested that she was passing through a period of great confusion, a point Highsmith expanded on in a letter to her friend. 'I feel disorganized,' she wrote to him at this time, 'as if I am no longer the captain of my usually tight-run ship.'[48]

Despite this, she was buoyed up by her black humour and her relish for the childish and the perverse. On 28 March, while waiting for a plane to take her back to France, after a trip to London to film the television book programme *Cover to Cover*, she was enjoying half a pint of bitter at Heathrow airport when she heard an announcement requesting that Messieurs Shit, Marchand and Shittal proceed to the information desk. Later in the year she would also be amused to see a typographic error in a French newspaper which read, instead of 'Travels with My Aunt', referring to the book by Graham Greene, the rather more ribald, 'Travels with My Cunt'. 'This sent her into gales of laughter,' says Charles Latimer. 'She clipped it from the paper and showed it to her friends. Pat had a raucous, earthy and quite unsophisticated sense of humour . . . She did not react to wit and any attempts at repartee with her were always deflated because she would usually admit that she didn't get the point of it. For example, it would have been futile to have taken her to a Noel Coward play. Yet her laugh was unexpected because as a rule she was very soft-spoken and had a fairly low, quietly modulated voice which was beautifully articulated. So when the laugh came out it was loud and uncontrolled, a bit what you might call thigh-slapping.'[49] 'Pat's laugh was a hoot, a guffaw, a snort,' recalls Vivien De Bernardi. 'Not at all ladylike. She'd kind of lose control and let it come up from the bottom of her belly in a deep throaty escape.'[50] Sir Michael Levey recalls one occasion when he and his wife Brigid Brophy met Pat for lunch in Paris. As they walked down a street, past a shoe shop, the couple observed Highsmith laughing to herself. ' "Did you see that notice?" she said, pointing out its wording: "Pour pieds sensibles". Tiny and trivial as the incident is, it somehow conveys a flavour of Pat's wry humour.'[51] She also delighted in telling Brigid that, as her initials were PH, she had the Greek letter φ ('phi') tattooed on the inside of her left wrist, a spot normally concealed by her watch strap. Although it was small, Highsmith joked that at least one day it might serve to identify her if she died in a plane accident and her severed arm was found at the crash site.

In the doldrums that always settled over her after finishing a book, Highsmith looked for ways in which she could fill her time, sorting through her accordion files and busying herself with projects around the house, none of which she found as satisfying as writing. Although she thought of some more story ideas for *Little Tales of Misogyny* and *The Animal-Lover's Book of Beastly Murder*, she admitted she felt uncomfortable with her excess leisure time. On 12 July she travelled to Hamburg, where she stayed for five days with her German translator Anne Uhde, before journeying on to Berlin alone. 'I must say I could not like or even understand Berlin,' she wrote on a postcard to Koestler.[52] Although she would learn to love the city, she initially felt distinctly uneasy as she thought Berlin had no discernible centre, an experience she likened to 'looking at a painting whose frame should have right angles, but has not'.[53]

On 19 July she took a trip to East Berlin, costing 15DM, which involved a close examination of her passport and a series of questions, including how many Deutschmarks she was carrying. 'At Checkpoint Charlie, a delay of at least 25 minutes,' she wrote in her notebook, 'while the grey-green polizei do God knows what . . . The Wall is in sight, looking like grey cement about 11 feet high. Dreary little cement huts about, all containing officials . . .'[54] While in Berlin she also visited the Schloss Charlottenburg and the zoo; the latter inspired an idea for a story about the animals taking over and placing their captors in cages, where the zoo-keepers would be 'forced to defecate and make love in the presence of spectators who laugh, point and stare . . .'[55]

On Highsmith's return to France, in late July, Heather Chasen and a friend visited the writer in Moncourt. Chasen recalls Highsmith as a figure of contradictions: a lesbian who didn't particularly like women; a writer of the most insightful psychological novels who, at times, appeared bored by people; a misanthrope with a gentle, sweet nature. 'I remember she always dressed very butch in jeans, but would wear beads around her neck as well, which gave her a slight feminine air,' she says. 'I think she was fond of me, and I was fond of her, but I felt desperately sorry for her. She wasn't a happy soul and needed friends. When I read her books later, I was astounded by her insight into human psychology – when I was with her she seemed so uninterested in people and what was going on around her. I think all her material came out of her head. As well as the aggression and vitriol that seeped from her – there weren't that many people whom she spoke well of – there was also an element of vulnerability and a sweetness about her.'[56]

The following month, Francis Wyndham wrote to Highsmith to ask whether she would be willing to write a piece for the *Sunday Times Magazine* entitled 'First Love'. Her first reaction was to turn down the commission – for which she would be paid £350 – but then, after a little thought, she realised that she could write about the experience she had had as a six-year-old girl. Highsmith's article, published in January 1974, is a masterpiece of equivocation, cleverly avoiding the names and gender of those she had loved. When Daisy Winston read the piece, she wrote Highsmith a letter telling her the feature had rather a stilted tone. 'I certainly have one helluva nerve being critical of an accomplished writer,' said Daisy, 'but it doesn't change the fact that I felt it lacking in a feeling I associate with love.'[57] Clearly, Highsmith had to censor herself; as she told Barbara Ker-Seymer, referring to the feature, 'Of course I could write a lot. But.'[58] Nevertheless it's obvious from reading the piece that Highsmith did not associate romance with happiness or contentment. 'If I don't speak of happy or successful first love, it is because I can't imagine it easily,' she wrote.[59]

People who fell in love at first sight, rushed home to their parents to tell them the good news and subsequently married were, she thought, retarded. Rather, a more honest appraisal of the nature of love positions it nearer to the horrors of mental illness. How else could you explain the fact that so many people were prepared to sacrifice the safety and cosiness of their lives for the thrill of a new romance? ' "I am sorry. I must have been mad," ' Highsmith writes, imagining the words of one such man afflicted by the 'condition', before she concludes, ' "Yes, that's it." '[60]

27

The summer soldier
and the sunshine patriot

1973–1976

During the autumn of 1973, Highsmith worried about the state of her health. Not only was she experiencing strange tingling sensations in her arms, which she put down to heavy gardening, but she was also plagued by digestive problems. She knew that she smoked too much – around twenty-three cigarettes, usually Gauloises, a day – and ate too little; the only food she could stomach were eggs, milk, mince and macaroni cheese. Rather than drink wine, she preferred beer and whisky, polishing off a bottle of Scotch every four days. In November, after a four-day publicity visit to Zurich, where she stayed at the Hotel Europe in a room complete with a trouser press that she imagined could double as a torture device, she returned home from the trip feeling wretched. Before she went to bed she felt nauseous and in the morning she was doubled-up with abdominal cramps and diarrhoea. The nervous strain of appearing on television, public readings and interrogation by journalists had taken its toll and it would, she said, take three or four days before she calmed down.

She was also apprehensive about a forthcoming medical examination in London. But after being checked over by a Wimpole Street heart specialist, in early December, she was told that she had nothing serious to worry about. Of course, if she wanted to prevent herself from suffering symptoms such as muscular pain in her calves after a brisk walk, she would have to give up smoking. Highsmith tried to cut her consumption down by half, but it was only a matter of time before she started smoking heavily again.

Highsmith spent Christmas and the first few weeks of the new year with Charles Latimer and his partner, the concert pianist Michel Block, in the Vallée du Lot region of France. 'I found her to be a tender soul hiding sometimes behind a gruff manner,' says Michel. 'She was quite shy and this translated often into an almost unfriendly attitude towards strangers. There was an almost "joyless" approach to life, or maybe "puritanical" is a better word, which was evident not only in the choice, for instance, of Moncourt, a dismal but expensive little hamlet . . . as her place of domicile in France, but the way her house looked inside – bare, severe, not overly comfortable. The same could be said of her large but sad (walled) garden. She loved to tinker in it and I remember how happy she looked burning leaves and sharing a beer and a cigarette with us afterwards – very much, "one of the boys".

'Her taste in women was unfortunate. I think she was both attracted and repelled by emotions and maybe because of this she never had a very happy love life: her women, at least the two lovers I met, were vivacious, temperamental, but ultimately unloving persons. Pat was a 100 per cent reliable, thoughtful and dependable friend. She was not your typical American expatriate. She was, in my opinion, an "exile", or maybe she was "in exile". Yet it was quite obvious to me she didn't particularly like France or the French. I was interested to hear her speak French, which up to that moment I didn't think she did; it was rather fluent, indifferent and most of the time, pleasantly incorrect. The reason she lived there I think is the same reason she had lived previously in Italy and the UK: she was admired and respected as a writer in Europe.'[1]

Once back in Moncourt, she started work on a number of short stories, including 'Hamsters vs Websters', one of the tales gathered together in *The Animal-Lover's Book of Beastly Murder*. At the beginning of March she travelled to London for a number of engagements to help publicise *Ripley's Game*. On 6 March, she attended a party at Bill Holden's bookshop in Regent's Park and then the next day, she gave a reading from *Little Tales of Misogyny* at a public house on the Fulham Road to raise money for the Writers' Action Group, the organisation created in 1972 by Brigid Brophy, Michael Levey, Maureen Duffy, Lettice Cooper and Francis King to campaign for the Public Lending Right. While in London, she met the Conservative MP and *Spectator* writer, Patrick Cosgrave – the two lunched together at the House of Commons – who described his meeting with her in a piece for the magazine. 'I found chatting to her last week, that Patricia Highsmith is still vaguely annoyed when her books are reviewed along with the crime fiction . . .' said Cosgrave. 'But there is something else about her work, which came over even more strongly in conversation than it does on the printed page. Miss Highsmith is an excellent hater.'[2]

Her novels, he added, were 'probably the most consistently excellent body of work of its kind produced since the war'.[3] An interviewer from the *Guardian*, whom she also met in London, described Highsmith as being cool, 'not in the nasty chilly sense but in the slow movements, the slightly separate air, the intensely dark yet not intense eyes, the easy politeness.'[4] Yet he failed, or chose not to describe, the novelist's demeanour, one which signified an overwhelming sadness; in the photograph, Highsmith's sloe-black eyes seem haunted and desperately sad, and her face, for all its deep lines, looks like that of a confused and lost child.

In early 1974, the blurring of fantasy and reality again left her feeling disoriented. In February, she dreamt that Ellen Hill wrote to her, declaring her love, and that Rolf Tietgens had died, visions she assumed were true for a couple of days afterwards. If Highsmith believed that each of her books was a fictional representation of her own internal wrestlings then her next novel, *Edith's Diary*, was one of her most personal dialogues yet, a work which explores the seductive, pain-relieving power of the imagination. 'Today I have the alarming feeling that fantasy alone keeps me going . . .' she wrote in her notebook just before starting to plot the book, an opinion she acknowledged she had voiced many times before.[5]

Before Highsmith could embark on what many regard as one of her greatest novels, the writer received a letter from her cousin, Dan Coates, requesting her presence in Texas; it was obvious Mary could not cope alone. At the end of September, Highsmith flew to Fort Worth, where she saw at first hand the sordid condition of her mother's house. There was so much rubbish in the Martha Lane property that Highsmith was forced to squeeze herself through the window in order to open the door. She was met by a shocking sight – a fridge full of rotting food, a sink breeding green slime, countless unwashed dishes, carpets covered in nearly a foot of newspapers and letters, cigarette butts, ashtrays and wigs lying in chaotic heaps throughout the rooms. Her mother resisted every move to clean up the house and when Highsmith picked up an old envelope and dropped it into a bin, Mary screamed at her to put it back where she found it.

Although they managed to acquire a power of attorney form from a lawyer, Highsmith and Dan Coates realised it was hardly worth trying to present it to Mary, since she would no doubt have refused to sign it.

During her time in Texas, Highsmith thought it best if she slept at her cousin's ranch, twenty-five miles away. 'Pat could not handle the fact that her mother was developing Alzheimer's,' says Don Coates. 'I think she could not accept that this might happen to her too.'[6] 'I didn't think Pat was very fair with Mary,' says his brother, Dan. 'What the hell difference does it make if something had pissed you off back when you were younger? I think Pat should have forgiven her mother and even if she did have to take some crap off Mary she should have come to visit. That was one aspect of her personality I didn't agree with. But you can like the person without having to like everything they do.'[7]

After Fort Worth, Highsmith spent some time in New York, where she met up with her editor Bob Gottlieb, friends Rosalind Constable, Lil Picard, Alex Szogyi and Rose Martini – who with her addiction to the telephone and constant mantra of 'Communication is everything', inspired the short story 'The Network' – and cousin Millie Alford, who gave her a letter from her mother. This last surviving letter from Mary Highsmith, dated 31 September, served to sever communication between the two women for ever.

> Well, you've done it – broken my heart – yet gave me a freedom I've not felt in many years. How sorry for you I am. That you could use the word to me that you used in describing the man you asked to adopt you. Many describe him as the finest man they have ever met – a gentle man. Better to you than your own blood father – wanted no man's money. Only wanted the best for you. Stanley and I made a great mistake – giving you everything we could . . . It's good you never had children – they'd be forever criticized and then never come up to your demands. You can think of no one but yourself . . . Don't write – I shan't.[8]

She signed the letter, not 'Mother', but a frosty and formal 'Mary Highsmith'.

On 6 August 1975, Mary Highsmith went out to lunch to a nearby diner, forgetting to extinguish a cigarette she had left burning. While she was out, a fire started which soon engulfed the house, destroying all her clothes, the piano, the paintings on the walls, her daughter's college diploma and her pet dog. Mary spent the remaining seventeen years of her life in a Fort Worth nursing home, where she slowly lost control of both her mind and body. Highsmith neither saw nor spoke to her mother again, but nevertheless her influence continued to shape her life and her work. 'Pat's mother was clearly the inspiration for some of her characters,' says Phyllis Nagy. 'Just because Pat didn't generally write about women doesn't mean her mother's not there. I don't think Pat was conscious of it, but her mother is there, in everything she wrote.'[9]

Highsmith expressed the essence of *Edith's Diary* – a book which she later described as 'more like a novel than a thriller'[10] – in a one paragraph summary she jotted in her notebook on 12 August 1974. The novel would focus, she said, on a middle-aged woman, Edith, 'a modern intellectual of considerable mental scope'.[11] Depressed by the trivialities of the modern media age, particularly its pernicious effect on her good-for-nothing slob of a son, and saddened by the fact her husband has left her for a younger woman, Edith takes refuge in the world of her imagination as expressed in her diary. The novel, she wrote on 1 September, would, through its central character of Edith, express an overwhelming sense of lost hope – 'Disappointment in husband, son, career (journalism), politics, her beautiful dream of America.'[12]

The book charts the life of Edith Howland, a writer, stretching over a period of twenty years, from 1955 – when, together with her journalist husband, Brett, and son, Cliffie, she moves from an apartment building in Grove Street, Manhattan, to a house in Brunswick Corner, a small town modelled on New Hope, in Pennsylvania – until after the Watergate scandal of 1974. In narrative terms, the novel is a simple one: it is the tale of the family's transition from town to country; the introduction of Brett's bedridden, invalided uncle, George, into the household; the breakdown of the marriage between Edith and Brett; Cliffie's spiritual and intellectual paucity; the suggestion that Cliffie has murdered George with an overdose of codeine; Edith's creation of a parallel, fictionalised life for herself and her family, her gradual mental disintegration and eventual accidental death. At the centre of the book is the repository of Edith's fantasies – her diary – and just as the heroine uses the journal as a channel for her suppressed desires, a tool by which she can reshape and reconfigure her life, so Highsmith self-consciously exploits the novelistic form to explore the contradictions inherent in the written representation of reality. The idea of writing a novel told through diaries had first occurred to Highsmith in 1942 – 'no form so fertile in introspective devices, in human interest in reading, in variation of reaction to one event', she wrote[13] – and, as a compulsive recorder of her own life, she had firsthand knowledge of the process of transforming the chaos of experience into the ordered world of the written word. It is this gap – the black hole that stretches between empirical existence and its representation on the printed page – that Highsmith analysed in *Edith's Diary*.

Highsmith highlights the theme on the first page, as Edith is introduced, wondering where to pack her diary. Her mind drifts back to the time when Brett and she had first spotted the house in Brunswick Corner, a date which she realises she never recorded in her journal, suggestive of the arbitrary nature of the recording process. Although Edith is thirty-five when the novel opens, the diary, which she had been given fifteen years before while a student at Bryn Mawr, is more than half empty. 'She was rather glad she hadn't filled the diary with trivia all these years,' Highsmith writes.[14] Edith seldom glanced through its pages yet she felt comforted by the fact of its existence simply because the diary functioned as an ordered, edited version of her reality. 'Isn't it safer, even wiser, to believe that life has no meaning at all?' runs one of Edith's diary entries, a sentiment reflective of Highsmith's own view. 'She'd felt better after getting that down on paper.'[15] Edith's subversive rewriting of her own biography begins after she discovers Cliffie – whom she hoped would go to Princeton – has been caught cheating in his college entrance exams. Instead of writing about her feelings of humiliation and disappointment, Edith takes hold of her Esterbrook pen and writes in her diary of his academic success. 'The entry was a lie. But after all who was going to see it? And she felt better, having written it, felt less melancholic, almost cheerful, in fact.'[16]

Like many of Highsmith's characters, Edith is invested with a writerly imagination, able to invent detailed lives for her cast of characters, her make-believe dramatis personae; in her diary, Cliffie is an engineer specialising in hydraulics, splitting his time between Kuwait and his comfortable home near his old college, Princeton; he has a girlfriend, later his wife, Debbie; and a family. Elements of her existence which do not please her – Brett leaving her for another woman, his subsequent marriage and the birth of a child – are simply edited out of her alternative, and increasingly convincing, reality. 'In her diary, Brett's little daughter had no place, had not been mentioned . . . Brett had vanished like a shadow that never was, never had been.'[17] Eventually, in 1969, Edith decides to kill Brett off, by imagining he had died in 1966, choosing to ignore the fact that he had been present at George's funeral earlier that year – after all, she says to herself, her diary is nothing but a way of entertaining herself, and surely one was allowed a little poetic licence? When fantasy and reality clash – for instance when Edith is about to tell her aunt that she intended to use her savings to send Cliffie to Princeton – Edith experiences a psychological crisis, a warping of her perception, as if she had a few drinks too many. By the end of the novel, Edith is no longer sure what is real and what is fiction, amazed as she is to find an entry in her diary describing the sweaters she had knitted for Cliffie's and Debbie's imaginary children, an observation she could not remember having written. 'And the curious thing was that the two sweaters existed, done in her spare time, and they lay in the bottom drawer of the chest of drawers in her bedroom. Now that was strange!'[18]

As Highsmith planned the novel, she wrote how she would like Edith's situation to suggest the poetry of T. S. Eliot, particularly 'The Waste Land' and 'The Hollow Men', expressive as it was of the spiritual drought of modern existence and the hell that exists between dream and reality. The poet's influence also shows itself in one of Edith's verses, a poem which was distributed at Highsmith's own memorial service in March 1995. It opens with a description of the dawn, a few hours after her demise, the sunlight casting light upon the trees in her garden, 'Unweeping for me on the morning of my death'; a poignant reminder of the indifference of nature to the passing away of an individual.

Edith's Diary, indeed a great deal of Highsmith's writing, owes much to her reading of the German psychoanalyst Erich Fromm. In the novel, Edith borrows one of Fromm's books from the lending library and, in a conversation with a psychiatrist, she voices her preference for Fromm over the Austrian ethologist Lorenz. Highsmith had read and owned at least two of Fromm's works, *The Art of Loving*, (selected as a birthday present by her mother and stepfather and inscribed with the words, 'To Pat, Jan 19 '67 from Mother and Stanley'; in retrospect perhaps an ironic choice given its title and their difficult relationship) and *The Anatomy of Human Destructiveness*. In the early stages of planning the novel, Highsmith wrote in her notebook: 'Sadism for son . . . "Attempt to dominate" according to Fromm . . . Overstimulation due to TV . . .'[19] Fromm, in *The Art of Loving*, defined a sadist as a man or woman who experiences a desperate need to escape his or her feeling of aloneness by 'making another person part and parcel of himself',[20] behaviour manifested by many of Highsmith's characters, including Ripley. Fromm believed, like Highsmith, that the source of anxiety was a sense of separateness, the realisation that one cannot escape the prison of the self. 'The *absolute* failure to achieve this aim means insanity, because the panic of complete isolation can be overcome only by such a radical withdrawal from the world outside that the feeling of separation disappears – because the world outside, from which one is separated, has disappeared.'[21] Each of Highsmith's books captures the terrifyingly claustrophobic collapse of such a character, articulating the agonies of separation anxiety and the inevitable ensuing psychological crises.

For *Edith's Diary*, Highsmith originally planned having Cliffie torture the family's fox terrier, behaviour Edith witnesses by spying through a keyhole, but changed this to his attempts to smother the pet cat. 'In most social systems, including ours, even those on lower social levels can have control over somebody who is subject to their power,' writes Fromm. 'There are always children, wives or dogs available.'[22] Cliffie's sadism later manifests itself in his brutal treatment of his great uncle George – the suspected administration of an overdose – and his violent sexual fantasies, imagining having intercourse with a girl while he masturbates into a sock. 'Cliffie made her scream, first with shock and pain, then with delight.'[23] However, when presented with a real girl, Ruthie, a victim of a gang rape by ten boys, he had been unable to perform – he is impotent and after the collapse of his tentative relationship with Luce, he toys with the possibility of creating a lifesize doll of her for his own private enjoyment. Although he is forced to reject the idea – his mother would see it, he reasons, and it would be too difficult to make – he spins a fantasy image of the recently married Luce, whom he makes love to like David Kelsey did with his own living doll, Annabelle. 'Her bastard husband could never give her the pleasure that he could. And Luce knew that.'[24] Fromm argues that sadists are afraid of life and of love – they can only 'love' when they feel in a position of control, when they can control the object of their affections. 'The core of sadism, common to all its manifestations, is the passion to have absolute and unrestricted control over a living being, whether an animal, a child, a man or a woman . . . The person who has complete control over another living being makes this being into his thing, his property, while he becomes the other being's god.'[25]

Dennis Gabor's sociological and economic analysis, *The Mature Society*, which Highsmith read in September 1973, also shaped the novel. In a letter to Barbara Ker-Seymer, she wrote of her fascination for the work, 'which I am reading like a Bible', convinced as she was that it would influence her future work and her thinking.[26] A sequel to Gabor's 1963 book, *Inventing the Future*, *The Mature Society* outlines the reasons why post-war society is haunted by a sense of *Unbehagen*, or malaise. 'Till now man has been up against Nature; from now on he will be up against his own nature,' argues Gabor, who won the Nobel Prize for Physics in December 1971.[27] Poverty had, for the most part, been defeated, while advances in medicine had dramatically reduced illness rates. 'There is no enemy left but man,' he said.[28] Science combined with a widespread spirit of nationalism had resulted in a situation where a Third World War could conceivably destroy civilisation, while an atmosphere of fear, brought about by the Soviet invasion of Czechoslovakia in 1968 and the spread of Russian influence in the Middle East, seemed to hang like a black cloud over the globe. 'The conquest of Nature by rational man, who has created science and technology, has brought us face to face with the basic irrationality of man . . .' he adds. 'Irrational Man craves security, he will fight for it, but he despises it as soon as it is won';[29] a neat summary of Highsmith's own beliefs. Gabor believed that the consumer society – suffering as it was from moral erosion – had to grow up and recognise its responsibilities. In order to do this it was worth remembering two simple aphorisms: 'Man is wonderful in adversity, weak in comfort, affluence and security', and 'Man does not appreciate what he gets without an effort'.[30]

Edith's Diary can be read as a fictional reworking of Gabor's analysis, an indictment of the immature society that is modern America. In the opening chapter, Edith dreams of a better life for her family, a calm existence away from the big city, where her son would have the space to ride a bicycle and the opportunity to grow up in a more 'traditional' America. But then she questions her views, realising that even these most basic of assumptions could no longer be relied upon. 'Or was that true? Edith thought for a few seconds and decided it wasn't necessarily true.'[31] Edith positions herself as a left-leaning liberal, a woman who feels betrayed by her country and the mass media, someone for whom, unlike the unthinking majority, politics still matters. The American government, she believes, fosters an attitude of apathy so the public never question the political doublethink of the establishment system. The news media are so biased, Edith is convinced, that their hidden agenda, particularly when it comes to coverage of communism, results in nothing less than mass brainwashing. '*Reader's Digest* has never failed to print one article per issue about the inefficiency of anything socialized, such as medicine,' runs an entry from her diary.[32]

It's obvious Highsmith turned to her own notebooks as a direct source for some of Edith's political views. In one of her cahiers for 1954, Highsmith wrote on the issue of propaganda and mind control, observing how only the Russians gave true reports of the Spanish Civil War; next to the entry is a scribbled note, in red pen, 'Edith's Diary?'[33], and indeed the comment finds expression in the novel. 'It is still true from 1936 to 1939 the Communists (Russians) were the only people giving the correct interpretation of the Spanish Civil War . . .'[34] Although others in Edith's immediate circle concur with her belief that the Pentagon, by ordering the increasingly brutal and futile war in Vietnam, is nothing more than a 'war-making and war-loving machine',[35] as she ages, Edith feels increasingly isolated by what her friends regard as her extreme views. Her article entitled 'Why Not Recognize Red China?' is rejected by *New Republic*, her editorials for her own newspaper, *The Bugle*, have to be censored and rewritten, while the only publications willing to publish her work are fringe titles such as *Shove It* and *Rolling Stone*. Even her close friend, Gert, finally distances herself from Edith because of what she believes are her authoritarian beliefs – Edith proposes to solve ' "this damned backwardness of the blacks" ' by placing young black children in white, middle-class homes, a view Gert labels as 'Aryan crap'.[36]

Highsmith was quite clear in her intentions – as she told Ian Hamilton, she was interested in the 'phoniness, some people would say half-assedness, of American foreign policy, leading to many mistakes.'[37] In an interview with Susan Smith for the *International Herald Tribune*, Highsmith spoke of how she wanted to explore the souring of the American political dream. 'A lot happened in those years in America that shook up even housewives. McCarthy is mentioned, Vietnam, Nixon. Edith's ideas are partly mine.'[38] Edith's insanity is not only caused by her own familial disappointments, but by the fact she is living in a mad world. How is it possible, Highsmith asks, to live in a media-obsessed country where the Arab-Israeli War is reduced to the same level as a beauty contest in Florida; where Robert Kennedy is shot at the Democratic Nomination Convention; where Jackie Kennedy, once a symbol of hope, ends up marrying a shipping tycoon? America is no longer the idealistic nation of Thomas Paine, whose framed quotation from *The American Crisis* hangs over Edith's desk, 'These are the times that try men's souls,' it begins, the words which were read to General Washington's troops on a wintry night in December 1776 before they launched themselves across the Delaware River. Instead it is a country soiled by the empty rhetoric of Nixon, the Watergate debacle and the shadow of the Vietnam War. 'What a world! What an America!' thinks Edith.[39] Ultimately, Edith, in a spirit of defiance, resists attempts by her ex-husband and a psychiatrist to conform to society's repressive pressures, accidentally falling to her death on her stairs by catching the heel of her shoe. Her death, Highsmith suggests, is symbolic of the death of America.

She thought of injustice, felt her personal sense of injustice combined now with the crazy, complex injustice of the Viet Nam situation – a country in which corruption, as everyone knew, was a way of life, normal. Tom Paine. The summer soldier and the sunshine patriot . . . Her head struck hard, yet gracefully (she believed) on one of the bottom steps or the floor, and the light went out for her.[40]

Surely part of what drives Edith mad is the terror of the domestic, the horror of the banal. Objects crowd the novel with a sinister excess, suggestive of a slow stifling of the female spirit. As Highsmith later told a journalist, Edith's 'profession as housewife slowly and dreadfully kills her', while her intention was to describe with 'absolute realism, every moment in the daily routine of a housewife'.[41] Although she strives for intellectual and metaphysical stimulation, Edith is forever anchored to the home by the sheer drudgery of existence – the household work, the cooking, the cleaning, her caring for George. 'Breakfast time was chores, George's tray with boiled egg and tea and orange juice before Edith could get at the more serious business of breakfast for four downstairs with the toaster popping up as often as possible . . . More soft boiled eggs and excellent cherry preserves.'[42] Highsmith felt no need for the women's movement – she thought the idea unbelievably patronising – yet the novel can be read as a feminist document focusing on the reductive effects of the traditional female domestic role.

No doubt Highsmith also wrote the book as a hypothetical investigation, an extended fantasy of how her own life might have turned out had she married. Just as Ripley was, to a certain extent, an expression of Highsmith's intellectual and cultural aspirations – her sense of freedom – so Edith can be seen as an embodiment of her greatest fears, a symbol of mental and spiritual suffocation. 'Men can leave the house,' she told Bettina Berch. 'Ripley leaves the house . . . I don't see women leaving the house . . . Edith leaves the house? What the hell, where's she going? She can't do anything except be a shop seller . . . I can't really understand a woman getting stuck with marriage to begin with. Getting stuck with childbirth . . . I can't imagine putting myself into a servant's position. You have to marry a man who has quite a bit of money or you turn into a servant.'[43]

In June 1976, soon after sending the manuscript of *Edith's Diary* to Knopf, Highsmith heard that it had been rejected. The publishers told her that the novel – which, according to Kingsley, 'she considered . . . of all her books, a masterpiece'[44] – did not fit into either the crime genre or work as a piece of straight fiction. Bob Gottlieb, according to High-smith, wrote to her agent saying that 'he could not see it as mystery or suspense, and that they could not sell it well as a straight novel.'[45] Although the rejection must have hurt, she decided to show a brave face to the world. When asked by the broadcaster Robert Robinson about the book's uncertain state – whether the novel should be marketed as a suspense or as a serious novel – Highsmith replied, 'frankly I don't care because I think it's rather a nice book, I like it . . . I think it's the publisher's problem, not my problem.'[46] (Highsmith would face an-other blow early in 1977 when a further attempt at television drama – a two-hour, four-episode screenplay commissioned by Thames Televi-sion – was rejected. 'It's just one of those things,' she said, 'just as some people can't swim for some mysterious reason.'[47])

Yet when *Edith's Diary* was finally published – in May 1977 by Heinemann in Britain and later that year by Simon & Schuster in America – the reviews were, on the whole, glowing, commending her for her imaginative power and her vision of a disintegrating America. Neil Hepburn, writing in the *Listener*, observed how 'her characters and their circumstances are transparently emblematic of the state of the Union, as well as of the union, in the horrible Vietnam years . . . the inheritance by the rootless and thoughtless of America the once-beautiful, the irrevocable passing of the patrician strain that, for all its shortcomings, carried within it the ideals of 1776. It is a very pessimistic view of America and, in Miss Highsmith's wonderfully insinuating prose, a very convincing one.'[48] Emma Tennant, in the *Times Literary Supplement*, called the novel a 'masterpiece', – it was, she believed, 'much more frightening, and more extraordinary, than Miss Highsmith's other books' – and praised the writer for her unsettling representation of the everyday. Highsmith, she said, 'nails the phantoms of our present anxieties and unease: the feeling that life has no point, the bright television jargon which teaches us to pray to gods we do not want, the fear of friends who are as quickly gone as the foam on the detergent, the loss of faith in caring', and concluded that the novel was a sharp 'indictment of modern society'.[49] A reviewer in *The New Yorker* thought the book was Highsmith's 'strongest, her most imaginative, and by far her most substantial . . . *Edith's Diary* is a work of extraordinary force and feeling'.[50] Yet Michael Wood, in the *New York Review of Books*, argued that the novel was flawed because of its clumsy attempts to signpost historical events. 'But the main fault of the book is really its ambition, its desire to be a portrait of Our Times.'[51] The problem, he added, was that the novel 'only names political events . . . paints a sort of political border to this essentially private story'.[52]

The dedication at the beginning of *Edith's Diary* reads 'To Marion,' a reference to Dominique Marion Aboudaram, Highsmith's lover from 1975 until 1978. Marion, a Paris-based writer and translator, contacted Highsmith in December 1974, with the proposal of interviewing her for French *Cosmopolitan*, a piece which was not commissioned and never published. After the two women met, thirty-five-year-old Marion became obsessed with the novelist and one night in January 1975, after meeting her at a Tomi Ungerer exhibition, she followed the novelist to the Gare du Lyon and then back to her house in Moncourt.

'She was not happy that I followed her,' says Marion, 'and she told me to give her a break. She was very nervous, hated to see people and liked to be alone in the world. But she took me into her house, where we talked about murder. That night she was wearing a red coat and I later called her my little red riding hood. I wanted to make love to her, but she told me to go back home. "I could be your mother," she said, "I'm too old." I went back home but later I phoned her and told her that I wanted her so badly. I travelled back to her house, but before we went to bed, she summoned me to the bathroom where I had to have a bath to wash off my perfume. It was Chanel, very elegant, but she said the smell made her sick.

'Before I met her I had read all her books and found the novels fascinating. From reading her work I expected that she would be a cruel and lonely person and that was what I found. I'm a masochist, a real one, and she made me feel very ill at ease, ill at ease all the time. I was attracted to her because of her work, not because of the way she looked. In fact, I found her very ugly, terribly ugly. I know she had been lovely, I saw photographs of her when she was younger when she had a dark beauty, but when I met her the alcohol had spoilt everything. She was puffy, she was a mess, but I was crazy about her.

'She was never unkind to me, she was never cold, but she was distant; I was passionately in love with her. I don't think she loved me, although she said she did. I think she appreciated me as a person, she told me I had some very good qualities, but I was not at all her type of woman – she liked blondes.'[53]

Highsmith informed Charles Latimer of the existence of her new lover in a letter she wrote on 15 February 1975, and described her in another note she sent him on 28 February, as '35 (meaning much too young for me), a bit nervous, plump, Jewish (with a mom in Paris who likes gambling and is an art dealer), impulsive, changeable.'[54] The following month, Highsmith had started to compose poems for her, verses which Marion says illustrated the writer's attitude towards romantic love.

'I remember once when I told her I would not be able to see her for a month,' says Marion, 'she replied, "That's marvellous, you're going to turn us into poets." She liked to think and write about people, but she did not particularly want to see them. Pat liked the idea of wanting somebody, writing poetry about someone. She used people to write. She'd change lovers for each book.

'Almost every time before we started to make love, Pat held my hand and would say to me, "Tell me about your mother." My mother was a very beautiful, elegant woman, with good legs, and I always wondered if Pat was more attracted to my mother than to me. I remember Pat made friends with this ugly girl who sold beer at the Gare du Lyon, and she invited her to her house. She liked people who were strangers, anonymous people, those whom she knew nothing about. She needed the idea of love and she liked falling in love but when it became slightly routine she destroyed it.

'She did not eat much – only milk, oranges, popcorn and a little spoon of spaghetti – and because she refused to heat the house, she was always very cold. We made love a lot – the best love we made was at my place in Montmartre, where there were a lot of prostitutes on the streets and I think the proximity of prostitutes excited her. But we also used to make love in a little shack in her garden, where she had placed a little bed. She was obsessed by taxes and domestic problems and in her big house she was very boring, but when she came to the shack she was happy. Her garden was charming and she was like a child there, giving food to a frog and to the birds. She was like a little tomboy.'[55]

For Marion's thirty-sixth birthday on 21 July, Highsmith bought her lover a broom and on another occasion she gave her a vacuum cleaner. 'She was obsessive about cleaning and would take several showers a day,' says Marion. 'As soon as she would come to my small apartment she would start sweeping and cleaning and every time I arrived at her country house she started to wash my clothes. She would give me a dressing gown and put all my clothes into the bath. My raincoat had been washed so many times it was ruined. She was also very stingy. Once, in the winter, when I asked for a radiator, she said, "Put a hot water bottle between your knees. I'm not going to pay for that."

'She was very strange. I remember once when we were invited around to Mary McCarthy's apartment in Paris, Pat was so furious because

Mary did not know who Tom Ripley was – McCarthy thought he was a rock star. When we left the house, Pat was so offended that she banged her forehead on a wall. After that incident, I did not want her to go home in such a state, so she came back to my apartment. I made some warm milk for her with bread and she went home the next day.

'She loved gin, which she mixed with water, Scotch, and beer, which she would swig from the bottle like a tram driver. She would start drinking before breakfast and then with breakfast she would have a small glass of whisky. I told Pat never to hide it from me, but I was very worried. She always said to me, "Poor darling, married to a drunk." '[56]

Drink did not, however, prevent Highsmith from writing. Throughout 1975, she worked on *Edith's Diary* together with a number of short stories. Even the news of her father's death from cancer on 14 May – she chose not to attend Jay B's funeral – failed to interrupt her creative flow. The only thing that did interrupt her routine was the intrusion into her life of journalists and television crews. Being interviewed, she said, was like stepping into the dentist's chair, and afterwards she felt 'shattered and exhausted', unable even to write a short story.[57]

In September, Highsmith – along with novelists Stanley Middleton, the winner of the 1974 Booker Prize, and Michael Frayn – was invited by the Swiss Association of Teachers of English to a hostel in the mountains near Hostein, Switzerland, to participate in a week-long series of seminars. Her task was to talk about *The Glass Cell*, its origins and problems. It was there that she met Peter Huber, one of the students on the course, who later became one of her close friends. 'My first memory of her is of her being very shy,' says Peter, a retired teacher. 'She stood there at the front of the classroom, with her head slightly to one side, with very square shoulders and very strong-looking hands. As she spoke she had this punching movement which she did to emphasise a certain point.

'I had read other novels by her, such as *Those Who Walk Away*, and I think she liked that. She really picked me out of the group and I think I was her favourite. Pat was much more interested in men, in general, and so our friendship was rather instant. On our one free afternoon we went into Basel, where we had tea at my aunt's and went to see a Marx Brothers' film, *A Night at the Opera*. After that we started to correspond and she answered, as they say, as the post turned.

'I was, I must admit, rather flattered that she was famous and she seemed to be interested in me. But I genuinely did like her a great deal. We would talk for hours and later when I went to her house in Moncourt, and then when she bought the plot of land next to our house in Tegna, we would spend long evenings together sitting and talking by the fire.'[58]

One of the other students attending the masterclass was English teacher Frieda Sommer, who Highsmith named as one of the executors of her will and who enjoyed a close friendship with the writer until her death. 'Pat would shift her affection between Frieda and me,' says Peter, 'and usually only one was in favour at any one time. Pat could say very snide or really nasty things about the one who was out of favour. The more I got to know her the more I realised that she could really only get rid of her nightmares by writing.'[59]

Pat returned from Switzerland feeling a little more confident, knowing that she wasn't the only person to feel crippled by shyness. 'Maybe a realization that other people can suffer as much,' she wrote in her notebook. 'It really makes me happier.'[60] During the last months of 1975, Highsmith also made short trips to London, Stockholm and Copenhagen, from where she wrote a short note to Marion, 'saying that she missed her cat, milk and me'.[61]

The relationship continued to be a passionate and loving one – in a letter Marion wrote to Pat on 29 December, the younger woman pledged her fidelity and for the writer's fifty-fifth birthday on 21 January 1976, she gave her four presents, including a Bach harpsichord recording, a gift she knew would be appreciated. However, only four days later, Marion wrote to Pat once again, referring to Highsmith's recent dip in spirits. Pat, it seems, was downcast because of her lover's behaviour – Marion had been haunted by a series of dreams predicting the end of their affair. Most recently, she had been disturbed by one nightmare in which she had watched Highsmith fall in love with a young blonde woman. When Marion, in the dream, questioned Pat about why she was breaking her vow – she had, after all, pledged to stay with her for ever – Highsmith replied that she wasn't to blame and, after all, such promises were often made in the midst of love's madness. Marion's dream would prove to be strangely prescient.

28

Your kisses fill me with terror

1976–1978

In the first few months of 1976, Highsmith's thoughts turned to the issue of inheritance. She was particularly keen to sort out her affairs in the event of her death – she was only fifty-five, but the loss of her stepfather and father, and the continuing mental deterioration of her mother, forced her to think about a matter which, she said, although difficult to write about, she knew had to be addressed. In February she drew up her will, leaving all her stocks and shares to Yaddo, while pledging her literary papers – including her notebooks and copyright – to Kingsley. 'You would be free to make an arrangement with someone else, to do a biography, or some such, assuming I warrant that signal honor,' she wrote to her friend.[1] Not only had Highsmith decided to leave her mother out of her will, but she went to the trouble of listing and naming nine first cousins 'for purposes of elimination'.[2]

Fascinated by the theme of legacy – financial, emotional and familial – in August, she wrote to Kingsley again about her plans for another Ripley novel, a book which, she said, would focus on the story of a sixteen-year-old boy who pushes his rich grandfather over a cliff so as to avoid benefiting from his will. She continued to plot the novel, which she thought of calling 'Ripley and the Inheritor' or 'Ripley and the Money Boy', and which was published, in 1980, as *The Boy who Followed Ripley*, in her notebook during September, October and November. But instead of embarking on writing the book straightaway, she let the ideas swim around in her head for months; it would be a further two and a half years before she was ready to send off the manuscript to the publishers.

Although the narrative would change over time – Highsmith played with the possibility of the boy murdering his grandfather or uncle before settling on his disabled father as the victim – the central premise of the negative psychological effects of inheritance remained a constant. In one of her first notes on the book, in September 1976, Highsmith wrote of how the boy, whom she finally named Frank Pierson, would have a 'mystical and unrealistic attitude toward money', at once fascinated by it and yet terrified of its power.[3] 'I like the idea because the boy is afraid of the responsibility of having money,' Highsmith told Ian Hamilton. 'He doesn't want it and he sort of hates his family for pushing it on him.'[4] Money has liberated Tom, providing him with enough to afford the running of 'Belle Ombre', a well-stocked wine cellar (one bottle of which, a good Margaux, he used to murder the overly curious Murchison in *Ripley Under Ground*), twice-weekly private harpsichord lessons, regular flights around Europe and a stylish wardrobe, yet Frank finds its influence corrupting. The boy functions as a mirror image of Ripley, committing murder not to inherit a fortune – as did Tom after his murder of Dickie Greenleaf – but so as to free himself from its burden. Frank journeys to Europe where he seeks out Ripley, whose dubious reputation he has read of in the American press, and who he sees as a man 'free in spirit'.[5]

At this stage in her life, Highsmith was an unabashed individualist: she thought that, for the most part, people shaped their own lives and refused to subscribe to the notion that society was to blame for their ills. In 1971, she asked herself would she be prepared to sacrifice some of her income to improve the fortunes and lives of those who were less well off? After considering the various options, she had to conclude that she wouldn't – not only did she think she had a right to enjoy her hard-earned money, but she felt frustrated with 'lack of endeavour in other people, and peoples, their stupid resistance to outside help in the form of money, policing, efforts at birth control'.[6] As she wrote to Arthur Koestler in June 1978, she believed that individuals needed to take responsibility for their own actions. '(I say this as an American, bored by those who say the individual is a victim of his environment or society.)'[7]

Yet in *The Boy who Followed Ripley*, Highsmith seems to suggest that a lavish lifestyle funded by crime – as illustrated by Ripley's aestheticism – is vastly superior to the grubby spoils of capitalism, embodied by the Pierson dynasty, with their enormous seaside house in Maine, the flat in Manhattan and their helicopter. Before the book starts, Frank's father, a food millionaire, is shot by a killer hired by a rival company and left with an injury that confines him to a wheelchair.

'"All business, charming business,"' Frank says cynically, as he explains to Ripley.[8]

Tom, one presumes, is left of centre. He cares about the international political arena (like Highsmith herself he is a regular reader of the *International Herald Tribune*); he differentiates himself from Georges and Marie, working-class owners of the local *tabac*, who support Jacques Chirac ('the so-called Fascist'[9] Prime Minister of France between 1974 and 1976); and he loathes the puritanical right-wing opinions of his architect acquaintance, Antoine Grais, who looks down on him for his leisurely existence.

Although he cannot bear the noise of a lobster boiling in a pot, Ripley can easily kill a man without it affecting his conscience. Frank may have aspirations of amorality, but the murder of his father and subsequent loss of faith in his girlfriend, Teresa, leaves him feeling suicidal. '"The fact that I killed this man – It's not going to change my life,"' Ripley tells Frank,[10] but he fails to convince the boy. As the novel is confined to Ripley's perspective – apart from a brief letter which Frank writes to Tom telling him of the murder of his father – the reader never fully understands the boy's motivation. After pushing his father over the cliff why did Frank travel to France to seek out Ripley? Why is he so obsessed with the sophisticated older man? What binds the two together?

Homoeroticism runs through most of Highsmith's novels – it is implicit in the warped power relations which exist between the male figures who frequently shadow and haunt one another – yet in *The Boy who Followed Ripley* the writer chose to wrench it out of the realm of the subtextual and establish it as one of the dominant themes of the book. The boy who follows Ripley is Tom's shadow, his secret self, an embodiment of desires which he has been forced to repress. Ripley may deny to Heloise that Frank is a *tapette*, but the implied sexual attraction between man and boy runs through the book just as Lou Reed's 'Transformer', with its woozy lyrics of self-transformation and sexual transgressiveness, echo through its pages. Frank was at first drawn to Ripley at the age of fourteen, after seeing accounts of the Derwatt picture mystery in the American press; he was attracted by the possibility that the older man could have killed somebody, his cosmopolitan air and his good looks. Even before the couple make their trip to Berlin – where they frequent the notorious gay bars of the city – questions of Ripley's ambiguous sexuality arise. When Antoine questions Tom, whose night-time reading consists of Christopher Isherwood's *Christopher and his Kind*, about the identity of his visiting friend, he asks, rather nastily, '"Male or female?"' to which Ripley replies, '"Guess"'.[11] Frank insists on sleeping on Tom's unchanged bed sheets, is keen to polish Ripley's shoes, and looks at the older man with an expression, 'sometimes radiant, as if he were looking at the girl Teresa with whom he was in love.'[12] Lovemaking between Ripley and Heloise is infrequent, something which Tom is thankful for as a woman who demanded sex several times a week would have turned him off, perhaps even permanently.

Ripley may have chosen Berlin for purely practical reasons – all its inhabitants seemed to be in disguise or playing some kind of role making it the perfect place for he and Frank to disappear – yet the couple certainly don't hesitate when offered the chance to explore the wilder side of life, at the Glad Ass, a gay bar. 'He [Ripley] saw the boy dancing with even more abandon than with the girl in Romy Haag's,' Highsmith writes.[13] Before the two journey out to the forest of Grunewald, Frank tells Ripley that he would never forget their last day together in Berlin – 'The words of a lover, Tom thought,'[14] – and when the boy is kidnapped in the woods, Ripley views the act as a 'rape'.[15] Ripley appreciates the '"crazy fantasy"'[16] of the gay bars, the fluidity of sexual identities, and experiences a frisson of delight when he dresses up in drag, complete with curly auburn-coloured wig and make-up. 'The transformation in Tom's lips amazed him. His upperlip had become thinner, the underlip fuller. He would hardly have recognized himself!'[17] The freedom of it all is exhilarating.

No doubt one of the reasons why Frank feels compelled to commit suicide is the thought of having to part from Ripley, a man whom he believes 'hung the *moon*'.[18] Although Frank's behaviour could be seen as nothing more than hero worship, the frequent allusions to a more intimate relationship suggest that the real source of attraction which underlies the union is indisputably sexual. Ripley, said *New Statesman* reviewer Mark Todd, is clearly 'impelled by a fascination with and desire to help the boy, and in this relationship the author's romantic fascination is caught up, its sexual implication not openly stated but hinted at in small details'.[19] Craig Brown, in the *Times Literary Supplement*, commented on how Ripley felt responsibility and affection for his charge, while the 'boy's admiration borders on love . . . Here, past suggestions that they are two sides of the same character are made stronger by their shared history, their lack of antagonism.'[20] The novel is far from a platform for Ripley's coming out – after all, Tom is still married and there are no explicit suggestions of physical contact between him and Frank. Highsmith denied that the character was gay, but she did acknowledge the fact that he may have had latent homosexual longings. 'I know what you mean,' she told an interviewer in 1986 when she raised the question of Ripley's homosexuality. 'But he represses it all . . . most murderers have something odd about their sex lives . . . I think a man who's happy with his partner sexually is simply not a murderer'.[21] The novel does seem to suggest a greater willingness on Highsmith's part to address the issue of homosexuality in a less tangential manner than she had done in the past and as such it prefigures her later novels, *Found in the Street* and *Small g: A Summer Idyll*.

During the early stages of planning *The Boy who Followed Ripley*, Highsmith realised that she needed to find another strong location for the novel, part of which she wanted to set abroad. She flew to Berlin at the end of September 1976, finding the city a perfect geographical embodiment of Ripley's ambiguous personality: artificial, self-reinventing, its identity constantly in flux, a place split by the splintering of capitalist-communist ideology after the erection of the Wall in 1961. As Tom informs Frank in *The Boy who Followed Ripley*, Berlin was situated only twenty miles away from 93,000 Soviet soldiers and occupied by American, French and English troops. 'The city of Berlin was bizarre enough, artificial enough – at least in its political status – and so maybe its citizens attempted to outdo it sometimes in their dress and behaviour. It was also a way for Berliners to say, "*We exist!*"'[22]

On 22 September, Highsmith travelled into East Berlin by train, an excursion she described in her notebook – and one which she would rework into *The Boy who Followed Ripley* – observing that while the clothes appeared to be somewhat smarter than her trip three years before, the people themselves were 'coarser, heavier, more working class'.[23] In the evenings she attended readings by Allen Ginsberg and Susan Sontag and also saw two films made by the German experimental film-makers Ulrike Ottinger and Tabea Blumenschein. After dark, she and Tabea toured the nightclubs, including the transvestite disco bar 'Romy Haag', which would feature in *The Boy who Followed Ripley*.

In Berlin, Highsmith shared a hotel with her old friend Lil Picard. Yet within hours of meeting, the two women had started to argue about politics. Lil informed the writer that she must not persist in calling the communists 'bastards', and then proceeded to attack her for being, in her view, a racist and a fascist. One of their arguments centred around Highsmith's problems with Wim Wenders' script for his 1977 film, *Der amerikanische Freund*, starring Dennis Hopper and Bruno Ganz, based on her novel, *Ripley's Game*. Highsmith believed Wenders had transformed Ripley into a 'hoodlum', a word that Lil Picard objected to, believing that, ' "They don't exist. They are made hoodlums by society".'[24] In fact, Highsmith was so angry with Wenders' treatment, that she even proposed returning the money from the film rights to the production company. 'What have they done to my Ripley, is my wail,' she wrote to Ronald Blythe.[25]

Wenders had initially tried to secure the rights to *Cry of the Owl* and *The Tremor of Forgery*, only to be told that each of them had already been optioned. Yet after visiting Pat, accompanied by the Austrian writer Peter Handke, in June 1974, he finally secured the rights to *Ripley's Game*. 'She was unbelievably gentle and observing,' says Wenders. 'I felt she could see right through me. You could have no secrets in front of her. Total honesty was the only way to deal with her.'[26] His first impression of her was a sense of shyness. 'In my memory I see her as somebody who was constantly trying to be invisible. She was also one of those people who are obviously used to being alone and have no problem with that. Solitude was around her like a halo. What I liked about her work was that I saw her in a straight line going from Dashiell Hammett over Raymond Chandler and Ross MacDonald into contemporary "crime fiction", only that she was a woman and ventured far deeper into the souls of men than any of her male predecessors. Her novels are really all about truth, in a more existential way than just "right or wrong". They are about little lies that lead to big disasters. As I am really obsessed with the idea of "truth" and "beauty" being identical notions, you can imagine I was attracted by Highsmith's own preoccupations.'[27]

The relationship between director and author was not an easy one, however. Highsmith believed Wenders had made her favourite hero 'a little more common'.[28] 'When she saw the film [for] the first time, she . . . was unhappy . . .' says Wim. 'She objected [to] my cast of Dennis Hopper, almost physically . . . We sat down for a while and just talked. Not that I could have convinced her. I left with a sad feeling, as I was very proud of the film, and so much in awe of Patricia Highsmith. The fact that she didn't appreciate it, bugged me a lot.'[29] A few months later, Highsmith wrote to Wenders to tell him that she had seen the film again and that she had changed her mind, informing the director, who subsequently framed the letter and hung it above his desk, that he had 'come closer to the spirit of the book than any of the previous adaptations'.[30] Yet she never could understand why the stetson-wearing Hopper had been chosen for Ripley. 'Hopper,' she grumbled to one interviewer in 1992, 'is not my idea of Ripley.'[31]

In Berlin, Highsmith had been impressed by Susan Sontag's speech in which she outlined how she 'personally did not belong to any group of writers nor would care to',[32] an opinion she shared and one which is reflected in her work. When Highsmith returned home she embarked on a process of self-analysis, assessing the sum of her achievements. Her goal was not the acquisition of wealth, neither was it the pursuit of fame. What was it then, she asked? 'Just an abstract excellence really,' she said.[33] Another depression clouded her thoughts, caused, as she told Charles Latimer, by the niggling 'loose ends in my life'.[34] She was made anxious by her inability to start writing the new Ripley novel; by the question mark over a synopsis for a one-hour television drama, *The Adventuress*, which she was working on for Joseph Losey, a project which was never completed; by interruptions such as trips abroad to publicise her novels and interviews with journalists; and by commissions like the one she received from the *Radio Times* for a travel piece on Vienna, which she visited in February. (Interestingly, Highsmith chose to provide readers with only the sketchiest of details regarding Vienna, preferring instead to devote a substantial section of the feature to a description of the city's Institute of Medical History, complete with its gory waxwork displays such as Siamese twins with misshapen faces and torsos, and the flayed bodies of women, some pregnant, some opened so as to show the workings of the internal organs. Her enthusiasm for the bloody spectacle of a blonde-haired woman lying in a glass case, the flesh of her stomach peeled back to reveal her insides, is unmistakable; she notes the 'yards and yards of intestines [that] lie around the edge of the opening like ruffles'.[35] As Highsmith wandered around the exhibits, she paused to sketch what she described as the 'monsters', before imagining what it would be like to walk into a room and discover a friend had been butchered. 'Murderers often leave their victims thus, a fact not often reported in the newspapers,' she said.[36]) Such journalistic commissions, however, left her fatigued and on returning from Vienna she wrote to Ronald Blythe, telling him that what she needed was a period of 'repose, or at least concentration' so she could achieve the all-important 'mental poise' necessary for writing.[37]

During the summer of 1977, Highsmith travelled to the Ticino – the Italian part of Switzerland which she would make her permanent home from 1982 – to see Ellen Hill, who lived in Cavigliano. No doubt inspired by Ellen, on 17 August she wrote dismissively in her notebook of the essential differences between the novelistic and the sociological approaches to life. 'It is the very illogicity of people that interests me – out of which stories and plots are made,' she wrote.[38] Yet when Joan Juliet Buck interviewed her over the course of seven hours for a lengthy piece in the *Observer Magazine*, the journalist commented that their conversation seemed peppered with the sociologist's views on economics and politics. In the piece, Buck observed that the 56-year-old Highsmith, 'has the figure of an adolescent who has taken against food; standing slightly hunched in a striped sweater and cotton jeans, her dark hair cut in a blunt pageboy, she reminds me of a college girl. A college girl who would have chosen her future way of life in a fit of asceticism tempered only by cigarettes and a love for animals, and stuck to that choice.'[39]

After the interview, in which Highsmith cleverly avoided disclosing information about any aspect of her inner life, the two women met for a screening of Claude Miller's *Dites-lui que je l'aime* ('Tell Him I Love Him'), an adaptation of Highsmith's *This Sweet Sickness*, starring Gérard Dépardieu and Miou-Miou, which the author thought was 'Kinda crappy'.[40] (The same year saw the release of another film adaptation, Hans W. Geissendörfer's *Die Gläserne Zelle*, starring Helmut Griem and Brigitte Fossey, based on Highsmith's *The Glass Cell*.) At the screening of *Dites-lui que je l'aime*, Highsmith confessed that she was suffering from Buerger's disease, a narrowing of arteries and veins, in her right leg, while at the same time continuing to chain smoke. The following evening, on 21 September, Buck accompanied Highsmith to a performance of *Belle Ombre*, a dramatisation by Francis Lacombrade of two of the author's short stories – 'When the Fleet Was In at Mobile' and 'The Terrapin' – at the Théâtre de l'Épicerie in Paris. At the theatre, Buck noticed how Highsmith was 'hesitant, shy, with an expression of inner doggedness: no different, in fact, from the way she is at home',[41] observing that during the press conference she became increasingly non-communicative. One reporter had to repeat his question three times before Highsmith grasped it, but even then she did not respond. 'The question is dismissed,' wrote Buck. 'That is her answer.'[42] A clue to Highsmith's state of mind can be found in a letter she wrote to Kingsley, in which she confessed that after the performance of *Belle Ombre* she felt so exhausted and overwhelmed that she simply 'collapsed'.[43] Her spirits did not improve when she read a 'horrendous'[44] gossip item in the *Evening Standard* in which Sam White wrote, 'Her French remains primitive and she has difficulty adjusting herself to French ways, especially French food . . . She is in every respect a lonely woman, apparently indifferent to acclaim. Markedly masculine in appearance, she is something of a man-hater, a kind of female chauvinist.'[45] Highsmith was so furious that she dashed off a letter to Simon Jenkins, then the editor of the *Evening Standard*, complaining of the fact that White called her sixty-three, instead of fifty-six, together with his 'snide remarks'[46] about her sexuality and appearance.

Highsmith's self-analysis continued throughout the summer and on 28 September she sat down at her typewriter and composed a short article for the German newspaper, *Welt am Sonntag*, on the subject of her political and religious beliefs. In the piece, published on 9 October, Highsmith argued that whatever one's opinions one should be allowed to express them freely, revealing that she had written to President Carter on a number of issues. In the same article, Highsmith declared she no longer believed in God, either as an abstract power or as a divine presence within the human soul, 'as I used to when I was seventeen or so'.[47] God, she said, caused more wars than any real human conflict and she wished that a belief in the existence of a higher power bred not hatred of one's fellow man, but kindness instead. 'I believe as little in God,' she said, 'as I do in luck.'[48]

In November 1977 Highsmith travelled to Berlin to do some more research for *The Boy who Followed Ripley*. While there she had a taste of what it would be like to be a writer of celebrity status when a married woman, in the presence of her husband, declared her love for her. 'She meant my books,' added Highsmith in a letter to Barbara Ker-Seymer.[49] On 16 November, accompanied by Tabea Blumenschein and a couple of friends, she spent the night drinking at a gay bar, followed by a late-night whisky session back at her hotel. 'I heard so many amazing things in Berlin,' she wrote to Charles Latimer, 'I was busy making notes.'[50] She enjoyed the evening so much that she pasted the label from the bottle of Bell's whisky they were drinking into one of her notebooks. 'Berlin Nov. 17 1977 Hotel Franke – 5:30AM!', she scribbled on to the label;[51] next to the printed words, 'EXTRA SPE-CIAL', describing the age of the whisky, Highsmith added, 'Indeed!'[52]

Two months later, Highsmith was back, to serve on the jury of the Berlin Film Festival. She arrived on 22 February and was at once whisked off to the Pregnant Oyster for a meeting of the committee, where she was elected president of the jury – a decision she was not at all happy with. 'I who am not capable of judging films really, because I do not see enough films . . .' she admitted. 'I had tried to push the office of president onto Angelopoulos, or Sergio Leone, but without success.'[53] The film writer Christa Maerker, who worked for the festival and who later became a friend, remembers how she met Highsmith off the plane.

'I hugged her before handing over the flowers, but she disliked that, stiffening and pushing a little,' says Christa. 'Then she whispered, "I would like to meet Christa Maerker." I had two options – I could tell her that I was Christa Maerker, but she would be embarrassed, or I could lie but then there would be no escape. We walked to the car, and inside the vehicle I shook her hand again and said, "Christa Maerker." "Of course," she said, "I hadn't looked." She was terribly insecure and incredibly shy. She would always cover her face with a curtain of hair, which meant that she didn't see anybody – a bit like a child hiding behind its hands.'[54]

The jury had to squeeze in twenty-three films in ten or eleven days and Highsmith found the process exhausting and frustrating. 'My simplest suggestions were thwarted . . . I was no good as "president",' she said.[55] It was more an honest admission than a statement of false modesty. 'She was chosen as president because she was perhaps the most famous of the group,' says Christa, 'but they were terribly unhappy with her, and she was not happy with the festival.'[56] Highsmith often asked her friend Anne Morneweg, a Berlin-based film subtitler and translator, to accompany her to screenings. 'She asked me, "Can you come along with me in case I miss some of the film,"' remembers Anne.[57] Highsmith also loathed having to watch sex on screen. 'For the first time in my life, I had to sit through and look at a lot of sexual intercourse, which I usually shut my eyes to,' she commented.[58] Yet she was intrigued by the boy and girl prostitutes of Kreuzberg – 'Turks, all made up and in curious period costumes'[59] – which she marvelled at with her friend, the documentary film-maker Julian Jebb, who was in Berlin to make a BBC feature about her. 'We worked for two afternoons at the Tiergarten among the fish tanks in the basement aquarium there,' she said. 'Alas, nothing came of all this.'[60]

This was Highsmith's fourth visit to Berlin and her initial confusion had been replaced by a curious fascination for the city. In the evenings, exhausted after her day at the festival, she would return to her hotel, change into more comfortable clothes and then run outside into the darkness. 'Berlin is bizarre, producing a desperate desire in individuals to be more bizarre, in a curious effort to be "stronger" than what is left of the city,' she said. 'The individual feels he must count for something, prove to himself that he is worth something, that he exists.'[61]

Highsmith was, at fifty-seven, still a striking, if unusual, looking woman, but it was perhaps this urge – to reaffirm her existence as an alluring presence – which accelerated her towards what many of her friends regard as one of her greatest, and ultimately most self-destructive, passions. She had known Tabea Blumenschein, the twenty-five-year-old star and producer of the lesbian avant-garde pirate adventure, 'Madame X' for nearly two years and had had feelings for her since her last trip to Berlin, but, during the 1978 film festival, the relationship between the two women became more intimate. 'I thought Pat was a little bit tough but so handsome, she was a bit like Gertrude Stein,' says Tabea, now a painter. 'I liked the fact that she was a writer – I found her books amusing – but the age difference did not bother me. She was passionate and romantic and she had a good body. She kept herself in good shape, she dressed elegantly but she never ate much and she drank a lot of whisky.'[62]

To the outside world they may have looked an odd couple – the cranky-looking Highsmith, with her wrinkled face and mannish clothes, and the young German, all spiky blonde hair, outlandish make-up and punk-inspired outfits – but the two women shared many tender moments in Berlin. One day they visited the zoo to see the crocodiles and in her notebook, Highsmith wrote of how she would always remember the sight of Tabea pointing at the creatures' wounds, a detail she incorporated into The Boy who Followed Ripley.

'Pat fell in love with Tabea, she was completely infatuated by her,' says Anne Morneweg. 'She was fascinated by Tabea's appearance and although the two women were so physically different, in those times Berlin was such a funny, queer place, it had a special insular existence and this kind of relationship was nothing special. In fact it was almost a must.'[63]

After her trip to Berlin, Highsmith was left 'spinning'[64] by the experience and she returned home to Moncourt on 7 April full of longing for the younger woman. As she repeatedly played records she had bought in Berlin and stared at the bath mat she had stolen from her hotel, Highsmith became increasingly fixated on Tabea, or rather, like David Kelsey from This Sweet Sickness, compulsively attached to a fantasy image of her. On 9 April, she wrote a poem, addressed to Tabea, in which she describes falling in love not with a real person but with 'a picture'. She is anxious that if she touches the object of her affections her image will disappear into the ether: 'I don't want to destroy you./I want to keep you in my eyes.'[65]

As soon as Pat arrived home in Moncourt, Marion Aboudaram realised that their relationship was doomed. 'She showed me a photograph of the German girl in a film looking lovely and as she did so Pat had very dreamy eyes,' remembers Marion. 'From that dreamy look I understood at once that she was in love. Her affair with Tabea was a very passionate and physical one. Pat talked to me all the time about her and I was very jealous of her.'[66]

It was, as Highsmith claimed in a letter to Barbara Ker-Seymer, the first time in her life that she had met a girl 'who combines a strong sexual attraction (for me) with talent'.[67] Tabea also reminded her somewhat of Lynn Roth: both women, wrote Highsmith, had the 'same power to hold', while they shared similar 'juvenile qualities, need a master, a boss', and were attracted to glamour, 'a considerable interest in appearance, moreso [sic] in TB.'[68]

During April, Highsmith continued to write poems to Tabea, including one which described her strange impulse to throw herself into a pool of deep water and drown. 'This isn't blackmail,' she said. 'I'd do it with a smile.'[69] As she tried to organise for her German girlfriend to join her on a trip to London, Pat became so anxious that she refused to leave the house to get her lawnmower repaired in case Tabea phoned.

Yet the six days Pat spent with Tabea in London at the beginning of May – in the Pelham Crescent flat of Julian Jebb, who was on holiday in Greece – were some of the happiest of her life. They took a number 19 bus up the King's Road to a pub in Bramerton Street, Chelsea, where they met a visiting French woman, Linda Ladurner. 'I recognised Highsmith because she had such a distinctive face,' recalls Linda, 'but she and Tabea were a strange-looking couple. When I moved to Paris, I phoned Pat and although we became friends, I never felt completely comfortable with her.'[70] While in London Pat and Tabea browsed in record shops – 'Pat bought me the *Stiff Little Fingers* record and an English-German dictionary,' says Tabea, 'I had a happy time with her,'[71] – and enjoyed cocktails with Arthur and Cynthia Koestler. Before they went for drinks at the Koestlers' house in Montpelier Square, Tabea said that she was apprehensive because she had not read any works by the famous novelist and intellectual. 'Never mind, my dear,' replied Highsmith, 'the last thing writers want to talk about is their work.'[72] It was true: 'Koestler talked about 1968 and the student riots, black magic and Russian politics,' says Tabea.[73]

On their third evening together Highsmith almost spoilt the blissful atmosphere by asking Tabea whether she played games with people. 'It was not easy for me to come here,' responded the young German.

Highsmith went on to write a poem about the experience, which begins, 'Your kisses fill me with terror', a stanza which charts the intensity of the relationship.[74] After Tabea's return to Berlin, Highsmith flew back to France in a state of desperate lovesickness. In this dangerously heightened frame of mind, she turned to poetry to explore her contradictory emotions, emotions which found expression in another suicidal image – blowing her brains out with a gun in front of her new lover. On 1 June she heard that Tabea couldn't make it to Moncourt later in the month, as she had planned, and over the next few weeks Pat went quietly mad. She asked her friends what she should do about Tabea and even asked Alex Szogyi to analyse her lover's handwriting for any clues to her girlfriend's personality and their future together.

'She has a "big" personality,' wrote Alex of Tabea, 'is used to a great deal of lebensraum. She knows herself and is very well adjusted to her life . . . Her mind is highly precise, razor-sharp, and I imagine she doesn't suffer fools gladly. She is very exigent, possessive, and wonderfully open and spontaneous intellectually. She is naturally impatient, but brilliantly cool and collected. A superior lady, indeed . . .'[75]

The days between the 5 and 19 June Highsmith classified as 'awful', and as her depression worsened, she wrote herself an action plan to prevent herself from slipping further into insanity. She told herself to breathe deeply, eat frequently, keep busy and maintain her self-esteem. Yet she also realised that her unhappiness was caused, once again, by an old, familiar source. As she wrote,

> I realize that any sorrow I may know
> Will come from 'wanting',
> Desiring what I cannot have . . .[76]

There was a suggestion that Tabea might join her in the Lot – where Pat was staying with Charles Latimer and Michel Block, who were soon due to leave Europe for America – but the visit never happened. Although Highsmith knew her tenuous relationship with Tabea was making her unhappy, she preferred it to some of her past liaisons. As she wrote to Charles, 'I am such a romantic . . . I am hopeless, maybe, but I'd rather have a dream than some hysterical reality.'[77] Another visit by Tabea was planned to Moncourt in July and while she tried, on the advice of her friends, to play it cool, inside she was a nervous wreck. 'I live on thin air, maybe,' she wrote to Barbara Ker-Seymer. 'So be it. My style.'[78]

The affair came to a climax when Highsmith wrote Tabea a letter asking whether she wanted to end it all. The uncertainty of the situation was not only placing a strain on her mental health, but it was interfering with her work. Tabea wrote back, a kind but brutally honest letter, informing Pat that she was sorry but her affairs never lasted longer than four weeks. 'I think relationships last as long as they last,' says Tabea.[79] The news plunged Highsmith into 'an abyss of misery'[80] for four days; the after-shocks continued to unsettle her for months, if not years, later.

29

A girl who allows me to dream

1978–1980

Highsmith's obsession with Tabea – and the subsequent collapse of their relationship – had an immediate effect on her writing. By 1 January 1978, she had written fifty-two pages of *The Boy who Followed Ripley*, but ever since June, as she admitted in a letter to Barbara Ker-Seymer, she found that she simply could not concentrate and as a result she was making 'slow progress' on the novel.[1] Yet Highsmith's spirits were soon boosted by the entry into her life of a twenty-seven-year-old French woman, Monique Buffet, a teacher of English, who like the young German actress, was blonde and boyish-looking. The two women met in early August, through an English fan and pen-pal and by the end of the month – after a date in Paris – they were lovers.

'I found her very attractive,' says Monique. 'She had a real charm. She was extremely shy, had these incredibly piercing eyes, black hair streaked with grey, and a very soft voice, a lovely voice. I don't know why she was attracted to me, but I think she always seemed to be drawn to women who were a little androgynous. My friends always told me I looked more like a gay boy than a lesbian woman. The thirty-year gap did not bother me at all, in fact I preferred older women. Pat told me that she felt physically attracted to me, which she said was quite rare. Pat was so tender towards me and very attentive. She wanted to offer me everything – a flat in Paris, a car, trips around the world – but I never accepted anything from her. Every time I had a problem, I could go to her and she was always very forgiving – she loved me in spite of my faults.

'She would never eat – she would cook *lapin à la crème* for her two

Siamese cats, but would not touch it herself. She was, of course, crazy about her cats. I remember once, when I was staying over at her house, I heard this strange noise in the night. It was Pat shouting in a bizarre language, one I couldn't understand. The next morning she said, "I'm sorry, maybe you heard me in the night. But I was angry that the cats had scratched the leather sofa in the living room." Apparently she would speak to her cats in a special language.

'I have extremely fond memories of the time we spent together at her house in Moncourt. Pat always worked in her bedroom, in which there was a single bed and a desk. That was her private room and nobody was really allowed in there. But she told me she'd always had working bedrooms in which her bed had to be near her desk.

'She kept thanking me all the time because she had been left devastated by the collapse of her relationship with Tabea. She told me that I was the one who helped her get over that and start writing again. She told me twice that she loved me and it was entirely down to me that she was able to write *The Boy who Followed Ripley*. While she was working on that novel she told me she was looking for a certain type of music for a particular scene and so I lent her a Lou Reed album, which she loved and which she incorporated into the book. Looking at that novel, I'm convinced there are aspects of me in the character of Frank. That is one of the reasons why she dedicated that novel to me.'[2]

From the eighty pages she had written in August 1978, the book swelled to 200 pages by October and by 9 November she had completed the first draft. Her next task was to retype the book which, she said, had been 'so badly interrupted, one solid year, Aug-to-Aug of this year'[3] and check the accuracy of scenes set in the gay men's bars of Berlin with her friend Walther Busch. She put the finishing touches to the manuscript in early 1979 and sent it off to her publishers on 3 April. She asked Calmann-Lévy whether they could increase her advance to 30,000 francs, as Mary Kling, whom she was considering appointing as her new French agent, promised she could secure one of 50,000 francs. 'I know this is advance against royalty, so I never see any big advantage to a high advance,' Highsmith wrote to Alain Oulman, who agreed to the sum, 'except that it forces the publisher to advertise, etc.'[4] On 8 May she heard that Simon & Schuster had rejected the book and exactly a month later she learnt that it had been turned down by Putnam's, because it was 'not enough of a thriller'.[5] The same day, however, Pat Schartle Myer wrote to her to tell her that the Ripley novel had been accepted by Larry Ashmead at Lippincott & Cromwell.

Highsmith was grateful to Monique, whom, as she wrote on the back of a scrap of typing paper, she thanked for being 'a girl who allows me to dream',[6] but although she did her best to forget Tabea Blumenschein, Pat continued to be haunted by memories of her. She described the actress in glowing terms in her letters to friends and at the end of the year she bought a curious mirror crafted from a bicycle gear which she posted to Tabea in Germany. In September she sent Hachette – the French publishing house, which was gathering together material for a planned anthology of work from 'great contemporary writers'[7] – a selection of poems she had written during the short, intense, relationship. 'They requested poems from me, after seeing two in my novels,' she wrote to Alain Oulman. 'I have never considered myself a poet.'[8]

The connections between her personal life and her work would have to be discussed in any future biography, Highsmith believed. In the spring of 1979, she entrusted Kingsley and Charles Latimer, the latter whom she had suggested as a possible assistant to her old friend in her role as literary executor, with the task of 'steering off the wrong biographers when I am dead'.[9] Despite her promises of post-mortem openness – she believed that, after her death, pretending she was anything other than homosexual would be hypocritical – while still alive she remained terribly guarded about her private life. If she went out in public with Monique Buffet she told people that her new lover was her agent and on 21 April, during a broadcast of the BBC's *Desert Island Discs*, she refused to discuss the reason why she had published her second novel, *The Price of Salt*, under a pseudonym. 'No particular reason,' she told Roy Plomley, 'I thought it was outside of the mystery genre.'[10] Her choice of music was varied: the first movement of the Mozart Piano Concerto No. 23; the opening of Rachmaninov's Second Piano Concerto; Bach's 'Coffee Cantata' and his St Matthew Passion; 'In Our Little Den of Iniquity', from the musical *Pal Joey*; Mahler's Symphony No 6; Rondena from the Iberia suite by Albeniz, played by Michel Block, a record also favoured by Ripley; and George Shearing's 'Lullaby of Birdland'. She chose writing materials as her luxury item and her book, in addition to the Bible and the works of Shakespeare, was Melville's *Moby-Dick*. Could she endure loneliness on the fictional desert island, Plomley asked her? 'I think I could, better than most people probably,' she said.[11]

Highsmith's interview on *Desert Island Discs* coincided with the publication of *Slowly, Slowly in the Wind*, a short-story collection which she had dedicated to Natica Waterbury, who had died in March

1978. The stories were originally published between 1972 and 1977, mostly in *Ellery Queen's Mystery Magazine*; two had first appeared in *New Review* and *Winter Crimes* and one, 'Please Don't Shoot the Trees', Highsmith had written for an anthology of twentieth-century nightmare edited by Giles Gordon. The collection articulates familiar Highsmithian themes – the power of the unconscious and the allure of fantasy – illustrating her belief, as voiced by Ripley, in *The Boy who Followed Ripley*, that 'every strong emotion such as love, hatred, or jealousy eventually showed itself in some gesture, and not always in the form of a clear illustration of that emotion, not always what the person himself, or the public, might have expected.'[12]

In 'The Baby Spoon' a respectable professor of English marries a stupid, childish woman because she reminds him of his mother, and is murdered by one of his ex-students, whom he believes has formed a homosexual emotional attachment to him. A doctor in 'A Curious Suicide' murders his old love rival and then, after getting away with the crime, decides that, at some point in the future, he will kill himself. The hero of 'The Man who Wrote Books in his Head' goes to his grave thinking that he has written numerous novels, without having put anything down on paper, a story which Lorna Sage, writing in the *Observer* believed to the best in the collection. 'In it, she [Highsmith] produces a dizzying and very funny illusion within illusion, a casual reminder of the skills behind the blacker magic.'[13] Blake Morrison, reviewing the anthology in the *New Statesman*, observed that Highsmith was 'at her most macabre when most mundane'.[14]

The final story in the collection, 'Please Don't Shoot the Trees', which foreshadows her last short-story collection, *Tales of Natural and Unnatural Catastrophes*, is set in the America of the future, in 2049, at a time when once-great cities had become 'unsupervised prisons of the poor and the black, and New York and San Francisco were dirty words'.[15] Repeated underground nuclear testing has resulted in the growth of strange protuberances on the state's trees – cancerous growths which shoot out a nasty acid-like substance – which the authorities then try to destroy by further underground bombing. The result proves apocalyptic: the trees send out jets of deadly poison and the nuclear bombing sets off a massive earthquake. As Elsie, the heroine of the story, tends her dead husband – a man, she realises, more faithful to the authorities than to her and ultimately a victim of the tree acid – she acknowledges she has to take a moral stand. Although she could escape in her helicopter, as she hears the tremendous roar of the Golden Gate bridge slamming into the Pacific Ocean, she chooses to make one last heroic gesture. The story ends with the logical conclusion to the story of America – its death. 'It was right, Elsie felt, right to go like this, conquered by the trees and by nature . . . A land mass, big as a continent, it seemed, big as she could see, was dropping – slowly for land but fast for her – into the dark blue waters.'[16]

Highsmith's social conscience – her environmentalism, distrust of big business and loathing of war – sits oddly with her support of Margaret Thatcher, leader of the Conservative party from 1975, and following the 1979 general election, Britain's first female Prime Minister. What appealed was Thatcher's rampant economic individualism – in August Pat wrote a letter to Barbara Ker-Seymer voicing her support for the new Prime Minister's tax-cutting policies – and, no doubt, the fact that she was a strong woman who had risen through the political system due to her own efforts, with no help from the feminist movement. 'Pat and I had commented from time to time on how curious it was that Asian and Mideast countries could elevate women to positions of statesmanship, while the opposite was true in Western nations . . .' says Kingsley. 'Thatcher's leadership of the Conservative party was a great boost for women in the West and the possibility of her becoming prime minister would have counted for more, with Pat, at the time than any political differences thereafter.'[17] 'I could never work out Pat's politics,' says the actor and director Jonathan Kent, 'but I suppose they were libertarian right wing.'[18] 'Pat's political sense was quirky, almost as if she didn't want her views to be pigeon-holed,' says Bettina Berch. 'Although she was, later, very anti-Bush, she could just as well come out thinking some right-wing ideologue was cool too because he happened to say something that struck her fancy.'[19]

In September 1979, Highsmith thought about the possibility of buying a property in Switzerland so she could avoid paying French income tax; she could take advantage of this financial loophole if she could guarantee that she lived outside France for 181 days of the year. Another option she had considered was to buy a condominium in New York so she could reduce what she considered was the preposterously high sum of money she paid to the American government – $32,827, in addition to the $14,000 she had given the French authorities. She was, as she confessed to Barbara Ker-Seymer, in the 96 per cent tax bracket for the year, 'as French have access to what I tell USA Income Tax people (48 per cent), and will want the same,' she wrote. 'This has made it imperative I do not earn more money, as I'd then be dipping into USA savings just to exist.'[20]

Carl Laszlo, the writer and art collector, recalls Highsmith's obsession with money. 'Her favourite topic of conversation was to talk about
how expensive things were,' he says. 'For instance, I remember once she
drove sixty miles to a place where she knew spaghetti was cheaper. I
liked her a great deal, she could be very sweet and warm, but at the
same time she never let herself be really free. She had a very closed
nature; she was a strange mind in a strange body.'[21] Hedli MacNeice,
the singer and second wife of Louis MacNeice, who lived in one of the
houses around the common courtyard of the Rue de la Boissiere,
Moncourt, told Barbara Skelton that Highsmith was, 'a lonely, unhappy woman who would have been less so if she had been more
generous with her money . . . She [Pat] told me that practically every
object in her house had come from a dump on the outskirts of Grez.'[22]
Hedli also told Skelton – who met Highsmith in 1982 – that Pat had
once tried to proposition her, but 'Hedli had no lesbian tendencies, so it
had not worked out,' commented Skelton. 'Pat was no beauty. She had
a rather louche overhanging underlip. Her dark hair was her best
feature, worn in a pageboy. She dressed in stylish trouser suits that
came from a fashionable men's shop in downtown Manhattan . . . She
was very skilful with her hands. She painted her own watercolours, and
constructed several of the tables and chairs in her house. She enjoyed
gardening and had created a lovely apple orchard sloping down toward
the river. I rarely found her very easy to talk to.'[23] Anne Morneweg was
fond of Highsmith despite her occasional miserly behaviour. 'Although
she had a reputation of being a bit stingy, that did not bother me,' says
Anne. 'She was generous with her mind, that was all that mattered to
me. She had a lot of unpleasant racist views, and all her friends,
although shocked, chose not to say anything. We were cowards in a
way, but I'm sure those views came with old age. She was, what you
would say in French, *sauvage* – wild and yet afraid of people. But I felt
very honoured that she did not feel like that with me.'[24]

Highsmith's near-obsessive interest in managing her financial affairs
was also behind her decision to split from her American and London
agents, McIntosh & Otis and A.M. Heath. The problem, as she saw it,
was the fact that 'the latter two agents take 5% each on German,
Italian, Scandinavian, Italian, etc. sales, causing me to lose 20% instead
of 10%,' she told Alain Oulman in August 1979. 'With double taxation
arriving or creeping, I cannot afford this.'[25] She wrote to Patricia
Schartle Myer informing her of her refusal to sign any contracts with
A.M. Heath which involved money passing through New York and
London, adding that Heinemann would handle her affairs in Britain,

leaving McIntosh & Otis to concentrate only on her American sales. Schartle Myrer promptly responded with a letter in which she expressed her surprise and anger. 'As you know, I have faithfully represented your work as your primary agent for nearly 20 years . . .' she wrote. 'Heath, as has been pointed out before, is the hub of a wheel that controls the Continent on your behalf. Through Heath and other sub-agents, the entire McIntosh & Otis list is offered around the world . . . Since you clearly feel that you have been cheated in commissions by two of the world's most reputable agents, I am not willing to continue to represent your work . . . It has, of course, come to my attention from many sources that you have reported the downright libel that McIntosh & Otis and Heath charge you an unfair commission. This does sadden me very much indeed.'[26] The row left her with no American agent and no one to handle her film and television sales. Highsmith had been thinking about appointing a single world agent for some time: in July 1979, she had written to Rainer Heumann in Zurich asking him about the possibility of representing her, a request he turned down; in August she contacted Diogenes Verlag with the same proposal. The negotiations surrounding the author-agent percentage split and exactly which territories Diogenes should control – Highsmith was particularly keen to carry on dealing with Calmann-Lévy directly – continued during late 1979 and early 1980 before both parties were happy with the deal, which was finalised in March. 'As you may imagine, it was pretty tough with Diogenes,' Highsmith wrote to Alain Oulman.[27]

At the very end of 1979, Highsmith heard that the French authorities had started to investigate her tax affairs, combing through her records for any irregularities. On 15 January 1980 the writer was sitting at her typewriter, tapping out a sheet of figures detailing her 1979 American income, when a drop of blood fell from her nostrils. A few minutes later the drops had turned into an arterial gush. Highsmith ran to ask one of her neighbours, an elderly woman, if she would come inside her house to phone the doctor as blood was streaming from her nose at such a rate that she could not read the telephone number. When the woman said she couldn't venture outside as she had fallen only the day before, Highsmith ran back into her house, grabbed a tea towel from the kitchen and rushed outside again, where she stopped a passer-by who agreed to telephone for her. After a doctor refused to help, the fire brigade was called, who promptly sped her towards Nemours, where she was admitted to hospital. As she lay in her hospital bed she thought about the sheet of paper left in her typewriter, the rows of figures

Highsmith with one of her adored cats. They provided, she said, 'something for writers that humans cannot: companionship that makes no demands or intrusions'.

Ellen Hill, with whom Highsmith had a torturous four-year relationship in the early 1950s.

Lynn Roth (left) and Ann Clark; ex-lovers who continued to haunt Highsmi throughout her life.

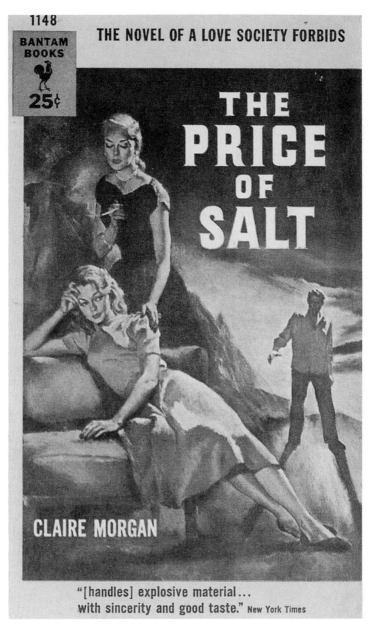

The cover of the first mass-market paperback edition of *The Price of Salt*, published in 1952 under the pseudonym Claire Morgan.

Highsmith's house in Sneden's Landing, Palisades, New York, where she lived between 1956 and 1958.

Mary Ronin, the 'inspiration' for *This Sweet Sickness*. Without her, as Highsmith admitted, 'it would have been quite a different book'.

Pat outside Bridge
Cottage, Earl Soham,
Suffolk, which she
bought in April 1964.

Bridge Cottage, as it is today.

The village of Montmachoux, France, where Highsmith lived between 1968 and 1970 and which she jokingly called 'Mount My Shoes'.

Highsmith's house in Moncourt, France, as it is today.

Highsmith with her friend Arthur Koestler at his chalet in Alpnach, where the two writers watched the moon landings, July 1969.

Marion Aboudaram, Pat's lover from 1975 until 1978.

The many faces of Ripley . . . Alain Delon in Clément's 1959 film, *Plein Soleil*, which Highsmith found 'very beautiful to the eye and interesting for the intellect'.

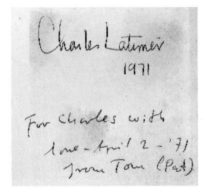

Highsmith's inscription in a copy of *Ripley Under Ground* that she gave to Charles Latimer.

Dennis Hopper in Wim Wenders' 1977 film *Der amerikanische Freund* (*The American Friend*). 'Hopper is not my idea of Ripley,' Highsmith said.

Matt Damon as Tom Ripley in Anthony Minghella's 1999 film *The Talented Mr Ripley*, which also starred Jude Law, Gwyneth Paltrow and Cate Blanchett.

Jonathan Kent and Highsmith – character and creator were brought together for a 1982 *South Bank Show*. Highsmith said that Kent was 'the best Ripley I have seen since Alain Delon'.

The actress Tabea Blumenschein, who Highsmith met in Berlin. 'I thought Pat was a little bit tough but so handsome, she was a bit like Gertrude Stein,' says Tabea.

'Pat fell in love with Tabea, she was completely infatuated by her,' says one of Highsmith's friends. 'She was fascinated by Tabea's appearance and although the two women were so physically different, in those times Berlin was such a funny, queer place, it had a special insular existence and this kind of relationship was nothing special. In fact it was almost a must.'

Highsmith with
Monique Buffet,
'a girl who allows
me to dream'.

Highsmith lived in France for thirteen years, but eventually grew to dislike what she saw as a 'country which assumes everyone is a slight crook'.

Pat's house in Aurigeno, Switzerland, which she bought in 1980.

Highsmith's last house in Tegna, designed for her by Tobias Ammann.

Highsmith in mischievous mood. 'Pat had a raucous, earthy and quite unsophisticated sense of humour,' says Charles Latimer.

Highsmith with her friends Jeanne Moreau and Bee Loggenberg, November 1994.

The church in Tegna, Switzerland, where Highsmith's memorial service was held in March 1995.

Memorial plaque, the church at Tegna, behind which Highsmith's ashes were sealed.

Highsmith in the summer of 1994.

documenting her income tax. 'How appropriate,' she observed, 'to be bleeding in two places.'[28]

Unfortunately the haemorrhaging did not stop and every two hours for the next five days she had to endure the sudden gushes of blood which poured from her nose. The nurses told her to lie back and relax, but if she did alter her position the blood ran down the back of her throat like lukewarm tea. 'Raising myself, at least I can spit, and at the same time the stuffing eases out of my blacked nostrils into the bandage that is taped to my face,' she wrote. 'Bandage is sopping & hangs over upper lip. Down my throat they have poked – with aid of stiffish plastic tube down nose – a thread that bears a tampon of cotton that hangs. Thread is taped to right cheek. This is nauseating, blocks air to some extent and I have to breathe entirely by mouth for five days.'[29]

For six weeks previously Highsmith had been taking drugs to expand the blood vessels in her right leg, and as a result the bleeding was taking longer to control. On her third and fourth days in hospital, Highsmith realised that there was a very real possibility that she might die as she was losing more blood than she was being given. Worried, she asked that the door to her room be left open, but her request was refused as the nursing staff were concerned that the children in the ward might be frightened by the sight of so much blood. 'This made me angry, also ashamed of my fear of dying alone, since I've always known death is an individual act anyway,' she wrote. 'I swear to myself next time I'll be better prepared.'[30]

After being discharged from hospital, she wrote a poem about the banality of death and the fleeting images which pass through one's mind in the final moments of life. The experience had left her with a feeling of joy that she was alive, together with a determination to build up her strength, but also a lingering depression. The illness had forced her to confront an uncomfortable reality. 'I feel happy and secure of myself only when I am daydreaming and creating a story or a book,' she wrote.[31]

In early March, after a brief trip to London, she was admitted to hospital once again, in Paris, for tests to determine the efficiency of her blood circulation. For this, Highsmith had to undergo a general anaesthetic, after which she felt like the doctors had 'rammed an ironing board into one's torso'.[32] The examination revealed that she had a blocked right femoral artery, a condition which would necessitate an operation in the summer. Although she felt in pain and weak after the tests, she travelled to Switzerland in mid-March, where she decided to buy an old house, which needed renovation, in Aurigeno, twelve

kilometres outside Locarno, near Ellen Hill's house in Cavigliano. She
planned to move into the house, which cost $90,000 including refurb-
ishment, later in the year after it had been finished, splitting her time
between France and Switzerland so as to resolve her tax problems.
Then, on 26 March, two officers of the *douane*, French tax officials,
plus a policeman, staged an impromptu raid on her house in Moncourt,
seizing all her papers and documents and informing her, as a French
resident, she was forbidden to have a foreign bank account. The three-
hour search resulted in the removal of all her cheque books, business
papers and accounts. It was, as she said to Christa Maerker, done in a
'real old Nazi style . . . You may imagine my mental state, as I potter
about, trying to convince myself I'm still leading a constructive life.'[33]
Highsmith was so enraged by what she saw as this insulting invasion of
her privacy that she set about removing her entry from the French
edition of *Who's Who* and she blamed the raid for her subsequent lack
of concentration. 'My work is down to about 20% of normal,' she
wrote to her accountant and lawyer.[34] In October 1980, the matter was
finally settled with the payment of a 10,000 franc fine. Her relationship
with France, already rather tentative, was now over. And although she
would keep her Moncourt house for another three years, Highsmith
had had just about enough of a 'country which assumes everyone is a
slight crook'.[35]

In April 1980, Highsmith flew to London to publicise *The Boy who
Followed Ripley*. The journalist Sally Vincent, who interviewed Highsmith over lunch for a profile in the *Observer*, described her as a
woman 'clenched over herself, closed into herself'.[36] The interview
almost did not happen as there was a mix-up over the arrangements,
and Vincent, nearly twenty minutes late, walked into the restaurant to
find Highsmith nursing a paper bag from Boots containing a bottle of
Dettol, one of many curious details scattered throughout the piece
which contributed towards the journalist's view of the author as an
eccentric oddity. At lunch, during which Highsmith drank gin and
water and ate a dish of grilled trout, she talked about how much she
hated the human race, citing Ellen Hill's favourite statistic that 98 per
cent of the population were stupid, a figure she thought a trifle too high;
her love of ironing; her fascination with Ripley; and her flirtation with a
possible move to West Germany. She even took out her shabby-looking
wallet to show the journalist the reason for the move: a Polaroid image
of a heavily costumed, elaborately made-up figure, presumably Tabea.
(In June 1979, while in Munich, Highsmith had told Tabea that she had

loved her for the past eighteen months, a confession which had failed to elicit a response. She had likened her emotional attachment to an illness and she returned home feeling confused and upset. Carl Laszlo recalls Highsmith sitting with a group of people in a restaurant who were all talking about the nature of love when suddenly she said, 'Love is not a passion, love is a sickness.'[37] If so, it was an affliction which continued to plague her.)

While in London Highsmith also took the trouble to consult doctors about her various physical problems. She had been experiencing pains in her right calf for nearly seven years and on examination by a Harley Street doctor, it was discovered that Highsmith was suffering from an occlusion of her right external iliac artery, together with atheromatous disease in the right superficial femoral artery. On 23 May, Highsmith underwent bypass surgery at the Fitzroy Nuffield Nursing Trust in Bryanston Square, where she stayed until 1 June.

'I saw Pat just after she came out of hospital and she made me feel that it was an absolute nothing of an operation,' says Patricia Losey, the widow of film director Joseph Losey. 'Since then I've realised it was a big thing to go through, but she showed no self pity, none whatsoever. She was tremendously brave.'[38]

Joseph Losey had expressed interest in adapting Highsmith's novel *The Tremor of Forgery* in 1974, but although nothing had come of the project, the trio became friends. 'When I first met her, which must have been in the seventies, while we were living in Paris, I was actually a touch scared of her,' adds Patricia. 'But then I remember when she came to our very tiny flat she brought with her some home-made jam. She was in some ways very practical and loved making jam, gardening, looking after her cats.

'I also remember the note she wrote to me about Joe's film, *King and Country* – telling me that she had to look away when the Dirk Bogarde character put the gun in his mouth. I thought that was quite interesting that she couldn't look at that – she of all people. I have a feeling that maybe she would have looked if it had been real life rather than fiction. Although I never thought she was a happy person, she found her equilibrium, where she was able to live and function, and most importantly, write.'[39]

30

People who knock on the door

1980–1982

That delicate equilibrium was threatened in July 1980, when, soon after returning home to Moncourt, Highsmith felt like she was about to suffer another nervous breakdown. 'How can you lead a healthy life if it is dominated by an emotion of hatred and resentment?' she asked herself.[1] She was terrified that if she was forced to abandon her work, she would be left with nothing. 'First and slowly comes the abandonment of the only thing that counts, work,' she said. 'This is the hell, the only potential cause of breakdown. Nervous breakdown is the same as flying a white flag of defeat.'[2] The following month she wrote a poem entitled 'Ending It', in which she imagined what it would be like to face death, and also had the idea for a story called 'The Black House' about a sinister, abandoned building which she said in her notebook was a 'symbol of both death and sex'.[3] Steadfastly refusing to let herself collapse, Highsmith was determined to carry on writing, working on a new edition of *Plotting and Writing Suspense Fiction* and a number of short stories which would be published in 1981 as *The Black House*, a collection of eleven tales exploring the perils of psychological aspiration.

Whereas Timothy, the central character of 'The Black House', is punished for striving to prove the hollow truth which underlies a symbolic fantasy, the protagonists of the other ten stories in the collection, which Highsmith dedicated to Charles Latimer, suffer for their various reality-avoiding tactics. Highsmith documents a world in which people search for meaning in an essentially meaningless universe. Lacking the tools with which they can interpret experience, and devoid of belief systems which might help impose a structure on their lives, her protagonists grapple to find glimpses of significance in whatever comes to hand. Often external objects have the power to precipitate internal disruption. In 'The Terrors of Basket-Weaving', Diane, a thirty-eight-year-old press relations officer, finds an old basket on the beach near her weekend home in Massachusetts. Her ability to mend the basket – an activity which is usually considered therapeutic – disturbs her and she grows to feel that the object has unleashed some terrible force within her, a realisation that perhaps her identity is not quite so stable as she had once thought. 'She felt rather that she was living with a great many people from the past, that they were in her brain or mind.'[4] Finally, Diane burns the basket, but its destruction does nothing to ease her anxiety.

The hero of 'The Kite', a little boy named Walter, whose sister Elsie has recently died from pneumonia, invests his model kite with such intense emotion that it becomes a symbol for his yearning and his grief. His wish to write a poem about a kite which lifts him off the ground and carries him high up into the sky becomes a reality, his kite, emblazoned with Elsie's name, functioning as a metonymical representation of the boy's feelings for his sister. His imagination – literally – takes flight, but after enjoying a few moments of freedom, a helicopter entangles itself in the kite's strings and Walter comes crashing back down to earth, cracking his skull as he lands. The style of the last sentence of the story mirrors the action, its rhythm imitating the cadence of falling. 'Upside down, he struck a heavy branch that cracked his skull, then he slid the last few yards to the ground, limp.'[5]

Just as Highsmith dramatises the conflict between Walter's creativity and the rather more pedestrian mind of his father in 'The Kite', so the other stories in the collection explore the dangerous dynamic that can exist when different value systems collide, an idea she would analyse in greater depth in her next novel, *People who Knock on the Door*. In 'Not One of Us' a closed circle of friends inflict a number of small cruelties on a man, Edmund Quasthoff, who is no longer considered part of the group. After losing his job and his wife, one night Edmund knocks back too many pills with too much booze and dies, a loss which prompts the group to realise the enormity of their actions. In 'I Despise Your Life', Ralph, a twenty-year-old, drug-taking Cornell drop-out and his respectable, wealthy father are forced to confront their differences after the son invites the older man to a raucous party.

The stories in *The Black House* were, said Tom Sutcliffe, writing in the *Times Literary Supplement*, closer in theme to her novels than the 'horrid frivolity' of *The Animal-Lover's Book of Beastly Murder* or the 'sparse and hateful case histories' in *Little Tales of Misogyny*.[6] The best tales in the collection, such as 'Not One of Us', which Highsmith thought a 'good *New Yorker* bet'.[7] and 'Something the Cat Dragged in', which was originally published in Faber & Faber's 1979 anthology *Verdict of Thirteen*, were 'brilliant essays on the moral concerns of the longer works: fear and loathing, moral absolutism and culpability. They are located too in the same bleak territory of dissatisfied satiety and doubt, suburbs with swimming pools but no churches. It's significant, in fact, that the nearest thing to virtue in the entire book is the expression of guilt. In such a world crime becomes a matter of personal taste.'[8] Although the collection was published in 1981 in Britain, readers in America had to wait a further seven years for *The Black House*. Writing in the *New York Times* in March 1988, John Gross explored Highsmith's appeal: although only four or five of the stories featured a crime, the others were located, he said, 'in a border zone of the macabre, the disturbing, the not quite accidental. What almost all of them have in common is a high degree of tension, and a seemingly impassive style that in fact plays insidiously on the reader's nerves. As so often with Miss Highsmith, situations have a way of revealing the dark potentialities that normally stay suppressed.'[9]

In October 1980, Highsmith started to work on *People who Knock on the Door*, which would be published in 1983 in the UK and 1985 in America. Her original plot focused on the conflict between a middle-aged man working as an advertising copywriter in Manhattan, who becomes a Born-Again Christian, and his seventeen-year-old son who impregnates his teenage girlfriend. Although Highsmith would change the profession of the father and the location of the action, the shape of the narrative would remain the same, a story which would explore the ensuing conflict between the fundamentalist and liberal belief systems. When she voiced the idea of analysing the rise of Christian fundamentalism, her friends were delighted. 'I do hope you will persevere with the "born again" idea,' wrote Charles Latimer to her in November. 'It's a great theme, and one that is timely, what with the last president [Jimmy Carter] (alas, still in the White House until January) professing to have been born again.'[10]

Christian fundamentalism in America has a long history, with some commentators tracing its roots back to seventeenth-century New England, when Cotton Mather articulated the belief that the New Englanders were God's chosen people, taking over the land from what was once 'the Devil's territories'.[11] The connections between Christian worship and capitalism had been well and truly forged by the mid-nineteenth century, when, in 1846, William Gilpin, governor of Colorado Territory, declared that the ultimate aim of America was the 'industrial conquest of the world', an ambition which could be attained through the twinned goals of the Christian religion and the generation of profit. Just over a century later – after the fundamentalists had successfully tapped into a spirit of American nationalism, associating communism with Satan and capitalism with God – the process reached its apotheosis in the televangelist movement. 'Maybe your financial situation seems impossible,' said fundamentalist broadcaster and author Jerry Falwell. 'Put Jesus first in your stewardship and allow him to bless you financially.'¹² It's no coincidence that Highsmith chose to make the fundamentalist father in *People who Knock on the Door* a salesman of insurance and retirement plan financial products; in her view both his religion and his profession were guilty of selling empty dreams.

Highsmith felt so compelled by this idea that in January 1981 she travelled to America to research the phenomenon. After a stay in New York, where she had lunch with her editor Larry Ashmead – who had moved from Doubleday first to Simon & Schuster, which published *Edith's Diary* and then Lippincott & Cromwell, American publisher of *The Boy who Followed Ripley* – Highsmith flew to Indianapolis. Over the course of the next week, while staying with Charles Latimer and Michel Block in Bloomington, Highsmith immersed herself in Born-Again propaganda. 'Pat became fascinated by the revivalist preachers who were on American television, so she came over specially to do research, and that formed the basis of the book,' says Charles. 'She couldn't get enough of those awful revivalist programmes. Pat was really riveted by them.'¹³ Highsmith described the TV evangelists in her notebook as, 'these people are all insane, smiling, saying words they surely don't believe, or in order to advertise some product.'¹⁴ While in Bloomington, Pat also met Charles' next-door neighbour, sixty-four-year-old Marge, manageress of a university cafeteria, whom she would use as the basis for the character of Norma Keer in *People who Knock on the Door*. 'I remember we used to go over to Marge's house and have drinks before dinner,' says Charles. 'I was pleased that my crazy alcoholic neighbour Marge got a little role in that book.'¹⁵

Highsmith enjoyed her three weeks in the States, and, after Bloomington, she travelled on to Texas and Los Angeles, before flying back to France. At the end of February, she moved into her new home in Aurigeno, where she started work on the book. By 21 April she wrote to

Charles Latimer again to tell him that she had decided to model the fictional town of Chalmerston on Bloomington, Indiana, and by June she had written 215 pages. By April of the following year, she had finished it, complaining that she thought the novel was peppered with too much dialogue and not enough straight prose, a stylistic imbalance which she thought 'Horrid'.[16]

The novel opens with seventeen-year-old high school student Arthur Alderman reflecting on how an afternoon of lovemaking with his new girlfriend, Maggie Brewster, had changed his perception of the world. After throwing stones into a pond, he cycles home to his father, Richard, a life insurance and pension salesman, his mother, Lois, and his younger brother, Robbie, who subsequently develops a bad case of tonsillitis and a life-threatening fever. After Richard prays for Robbie, he believes that his son's recovery is due, not to modern medicine's techniques and drugs, but because of Christ's miraculous intervention. 'So that Sunday became, in Arthur's mind, the day his father found God, or was "reborn" as his father put it.'[17] As Richard becomes increasingly obsessed with Christian fundamentalism – he subscribes to a number of creationist magazines – so the gulf between him and Arthur, who wants to study biology or microbiology at college, deepens. The crisis occurs when Maggie tells Arthur she is pregnant. The couple, together with her parents, rationalise the situation, deciding that an abortion would be the best solution, but Richard thinks otherwise and does everything in his power to convince his son and her girlfriend about the sinfulness of their actions. The abortion is arranged, Richard throws his elder son out of his family home and brainwashes Robbie into believing that sex outside marriage is a sin. While away at college, Maggie falls for another student, and although Arthur is initially distraught, he attempts to get on with his life, the minutiae of which Highsmith details with a near-documentary preciseness. When violence erupts towards the end of the novel – Robbie shoots and kills his father after discovering that Richard has impregnated a fellow church member, Irene, a mentally unbalanced ex-prostitute – Highsmith describes the horrific act in the same clinical, quotidian tone. 'His jaw and neck were red with blood, as was the top part of his striped shirt . . . The front part of his father's throat looked torn away and also part of his jaw. Blood flowed into the green carpet. Spatters of blood on his father's desk caught Arthur's eye as he straightened . . . Now Arthur noticed that his father's blue trousers were damp between the legs.'[18]

The murder, instead of acting as an agent of familial destruction, invests the Aldermans with a renewed sense of vitality and the book ends on a happy note. Immediately after Richard's death, Lois and Arthur visit their next-door neighbour Norma, where they have something of a jolly party, complete with a delicious spread of food, iced tea and beer. Arthur fulfils his ambition of studying at Columbia, his relationship with Maggie looks set for a revival and the family sell their house and move to the east coast. Yet the future is not so bright for all the characters. Although the surviving members of the Alderman family escape the town, which for them has become something of a prison, there is the suggestion that Irene's daughter – presumably Richard's child, who is born at the end of the novel – will be brought up by the fundamentalist church, an organisation which Highsmith portrays as hypocritical, self-serving, in fact downright evil, an institution which has more in common with a Jim Jones-like cult than a religious order.

What particularly alarmed Highsmith was the unsettling union between the Born-Again movement and right-wing politics in America. 'I think the religious fundamentalism in America now is frightening because it's now attached itself to Reaganite politics,' Highsmith told one interviewer in 1986.[19] Throughout the book, Highsmith makes references to this unholy alliance, one which she believed resulted in a corruption of the democratic process. The narrow-minded and bigoted Richard Alderman used to be a Democrat, but now he is a Republican and like most of the congregation of his church, a supporter of Ronald Reagan, elected President in 1981, a leader known for his cuts in education, increased spending on defence and anti-abortionist views. Highsmith told Bettina Berch that she couldn't bear Reagan, adding, in another letter that he was 'abysmally stupid'.[20] Later in the eighties, Highsmith would satirise Reagan in 'President Buck Jones Rallies and Waves the Flag', one of the stories in her 1987 collection *Tales of Natural and Unnatural Catastrophes*, which culminates in not only his death but an apocalyptic nightmare. The spectre of far-right religion, Highsmith suggests, would continue to haunt the civilised world for decades to come. Highsmith could neither bear 'people who believe in an after-life and try to persuade other people to believe in it',[21] nor those who were driven by profit alone. For her, moral absolutism was just as distasteful as moral blankness.

When *People who Knock on the Door*, a novel which occupies similar territory to *Edith's Diary*, was published in Britain it received good reviews. 'With her usual skill Highsmith produces an apparently clinical, though in fact richly imagined, study of human frailty,' wrote Holly Eley in the *Times Literary Supplement*,[22] while H.R.F. Keating, in *The Times*, highlighted the rancid air of apprehension, an unsettling vagueness, which seemed to cloud its pages. Keating picked out one of the final sentences of the novel, uttered by Arthur: ' "There really is more money in streetwalking," ' noting that it was, 'perhaps the only explicit statement of what the book is about – and they're [the words] not that explicit. But they do say to us, a hard saying, that life is like the casualness of streetwalking, its dangers, its dubious pleasures, its never-ending uncertainties. This is what the whole novel says too . . . Miss Highsmith builds up her large portrait of a world at the mercy of the irrational, the casual. It is not a nice view of things. It will not please every reader. Not those of us who want there to be happy endings, as in Barbara Cartland. Or Mozart. But it has its truth, and truth makes you free.'[23]

Despite the praise it received in Britain, the novel was rejected – as was her short-story collection, *The Black House* – by her American editor Larry Ashmead, who had recently moved from Lippincott & Cromwell to Harper & Row. The rebuff left her with no publisher in the US. 'That was the one book I didn't like,' says Ashmead of *People who Knock on the Door*. 'I don't think her sales ever got up to more than seven or eight thousand copies in America; I think I would have continued publishing her if sales hadn't have been so bad. I had just moved here from Lippincott and it seemed like an apt time to stop publishing her. We just didn't continue a relationship after that – I'd send her a book or ring up for a quote and I don't think she ever responded.'[24] Highsmith tried to adopt an indifferent approach to the news. 'I really don't care much if my books are published in USA or not,' she wrote in 1982. 'I've never lost or changed a publisher because of my demanding a big advance, it's that the USA publishers do not take chances, there's no loyalty – and maybe not much loyalty among readers in USA.'[25]

The village of Aurigeno, which when Highsmith lived there had a population of only 105, lies in the Maggia valley under the shadow of the Dunzio mountain. It is, as she said, a place full of 'old houses, simple people, some tourists in summer'.[26] Highsmith's new home was a two-storey grey granite structure built in 1680 as a summer vacation house, with one-metre thick walls and two cellars, one of which, with its arched ceiling of old stone, she thought looked like 'a dungeon out of *The Count of Monte Christo* or something'.[27] Barbara Skelton de-scribed the house as 'small and dark with tiny windows', noting the fact that it did not have a garden, while from the upstairs room one could see 'snow-capped mountains and a church with a clock that chimed on the hour'.[28] After being redesigned, the house, which had been left empty for twenty years, comprised of a large living room, which was dark but cool, a kitchen and spare room on the ground floor and two bedrooms and a bathroom upstairs, a plan devised by the Swiss architect Tobias Ammann. 'I was contacted by Ellen Hill, who asked me to find a house in the area for her friend Patricia Highsmith,' says Ammann. 'Before I met Highsmith, Ellen told me that she was very closed and she didn't like to have too much contact with people. Yet generally I found it a pleasant experience to work with her. Although we never had problems, sometimes she would have trouble with various workmen and how much they charged and she would quibble over the bills.'[29]

Ena Kendall, who interviewed Highsmith for 'A Room of My Own' in the *Observer* noted her tasteful, but slightly quirky stylistic touches: the fireplace with its chestnut surround; the candlesticks fashioned out of branding irons; a stool and a polished pine coffee table, both products of her woodworking; and a 'surreal-looking owl she made from a scrap of wood and old nails'.[30]

Although life in Aurigeno was quiet, Highsmith did not feel lonely and on 14 June 1981, she invited nine people to her house for a drinks party, where her guests enjoyed devilled eggs and canapés. As Ellen Hill lived only ten kilometres away, the two women started to see a great deal more of one another, but their relationship was far from smooth. 'There were problems with Ellen Hill because she was always coming around to boss Pat – when Pat was with her she was like a little mouse,' says Anne Morneweg.[31] 'Ellen behaved like a governess around Pat, always telling her what to do,' says Christa Maerker. 'I remember once at the train station, Pat said, "Let's have some coffee," and proceeded to order a beer. Ellen, who happened to be in the same café, shouted in a stentorian voice across the room, "But Pat, not in the morning!" After that, the famous writer did not touch a drop of her beer, but simply retreated behind the curtain of her hair.'[32] Peter Huber, who with his wife Anita split his time between Zurich and the Ticino, remembers how Ellen gave him a copy of *The Tremor of Forgery*, inscribed with the words, 'For Ellen – Maybe you will like this one better than most – Love, Pat'.[33] 'But Ellen didn't care for Pat's work at all and she gave me the book, saying, "Since you like all this rubbish, you may as well have it."'[34] The pattern of dominance and submission which had in the past defined, and yet ultimately destroyed their love for one another, would eventually bring about the collapse of their friendship. 'Pat knew it would be hell on earth living near Ellen Hill,' says Monique Buffet, 'but she went ahead and did it anyway.'[35]

After spending the summer in Aurigeno, and making a visit to the Locarno Film Festival, where she met the director Kathryn Bigelow, Highsmith returned to her house in Moncourt, where she planned on staying six months. Yet, as she worked on *People who Knock on the Door*, she realised that she would have to return to America for another research trip. In October she visited Bloomington once more, where she stayed with Charles Latimer and Michel Block. During a trip with Charles and Michel to East Hampton, one of the many places she imagined living, the group stopped off in a small town in Pennsylvania. 'After some junk food we went to fill up the tank,' recalls Michel. 'Looking at the view from that petrol station [of] mountains, white farms and churches dotting the wooded landscape, I commented on how archetypal of the US that view was. We got into the car and I couldn't help but notice how she silently wept for quite some time while Charles and I chatted together in surprised consternation. I really think Pat sacrificed her "every day" life to her reputation as an artist . . . Be that as it may, I think she would have been much happier living in the States.'[36]

Back in Moncourt, she took the trouble to answer a questionnaire sent by *Ellery Queen's Mystery Magazine*, one of the questions of which focused on her wanderlust. What did she look for in the place where she lived? 'I need grass under my feet, silence, and a few friendly birds flying around,' she replied.[37] Highsmith spent that Christmas in London with Kingsley, then working as a television news producer with CBS in London. Despite an enjoyable break, she felt 'wretchedly unhappy',[38] because of her dissatisfaction with her work, and on her return to France in January she suffered another depression. 'This present world for me is hell,' she wrote in her notebook, 'and like a prison.'[39] Her only escape, her one solace, was the recreation of a parallel world through her literary imagination. Her friends were only too aware of how difficult she seemed to find life. 'She was not an easy going person. She would hide her feelings all the time,' says Linda Ladurner. 'I found her interesting, but, to be honest, if I had not known she was a good writer, probably I would not have found her so nice. She was not at peace with herself. She was often uneasy and she used this to write about uneasy people. She was so inhibited after a while it was catching.'[40]

Feeling increasingly annoyed by the bureaucracy of living in France, unable to forget the invasion of her house by the customs officials and frustrated by the endless hopping about between Ticino and France, in March 1982, Highsmith decided once and for all to sell her house in Moncourt and move permanently to Switzerland. It was, she said, something she regretted, as she adored 'that comfortable, homey house, not to mention the garden never-quite-in-order'.[41] However, she did not, as she saw it, have a choice. 'It's the French law that I can't be in Moncourt more than 6 months without incurring French residence status, with its attendant restricting laws against any foreign bank accounts, etc. which I prefer not to live with.'[42] In addition, as she wrote to Barbara Ker-Seymer, Mitterrand, the French socialist president, was 'going to make life increasingly difficult for anyone who earns more than a postman'.[43] She did not, however, feel it necessary to talk to Monique Buffet about how leaving France might affect their relationship. 'Pat and I didn't talk about the end of our relationship,' says Monique Buffet, 'as it seemed like a natural step. It ended when she left for Switzerland, but we remained friends until she died.'[44]

31

A strange interior world

1982–1983

The tall, dark-haired man followed her like her shadow. He brushed past her at the airport, stared at her on the train towards London and then watched as the novelist, dressed in a Burberry trench coat, walked through the foyer of the swish London hotel. Signing the registration book, Highsmith, who was ambidextrous, took hold of the pen first with her left hand and then with her right. A few moments after stepping into the lift, the man was by her side once more. That man was Ripley.

Creator and character were brought together in 1982 for the London Weekend Television arts programme, *The South Bank Show*, a fifty-minute film entitled 'Patricia Highsmith: A Gift For Murder', comprising of an interview with Highsmith by Melvyn Bragg and dramatised scenes from *Ripley Under Ground*, starring Jonathan Kent as Ripley. Wearing a crisp white shirt, black leather waistcoat and black skirt, Highsmith looked distinctly uncomfortable as she was quizzed by Bragg. Why did she like the character of Ripley? 'He's rather free in spirit and audacious and occasionally amusing, to me,' Highsmith replied.[1] What was Ripley like when she first created him and how had he developed? 'In the first Ripley he was quite green and young . . . just learning about Europe, about what he thought was culture and sightseeing and then he became envious of the richer young man . . . He decided to lift himself in his own eyes . . . The one murder that bothers him sometimes is the Dickie murder because the motive was very very sordid and Dickie had been a good friend to him.'[2] Would she call Ripley insane? 'I think in certain areas he could be called psychotic . . . a bit sick in certain areas. But I would not call him insane because his actions are rational . . . He's not so psychopathic that he has to kill somebody. I consider him a rather civilised person who now kills when he absolutely has to. He kills reluctantly.'³ Did she admire him? 'I'm not sure I could find qualities that could be admired in Ripley. He might have a little generosity but not much to be admired. But he's not entirely to be censured, I think.'⁴ How would she describe Ripley's sexual nature? 'He's rather shy of it, not very strong emotions and a little bit homosexual I would say, not that he has ever done anything about that. Very lukewarm.'⁵

Immediately before shooting was due to start in September 1982, for broadcast that November, Jack Bond, producer and director of the film, received a telephone call from Highsmith's French editor, Alain Oulman, asking whether Highsmith knew whom he had cast as Ripley.

'Oulman said to me, "If you have cast someone as Ripley, whom she cares so deeply about, whom she sees so clearly in her mind, without her permission, God knows what will happen,"' remembers Bond. 'Of course, I had cast Jonathan Kent in the role, but had not informed Highsmith. We were due to start shooting at Gatwick airport, filming a scene showing Highsmith arriving in the country, closely followed by Ripley. I told Jonathan to get behind her as she was moving down the travelator, hopeful that I could resolve the situation as we went along. However, the cameraman was not happy with the first, second or third tracking shots and finally Pat stormed up to me and said, "I don't know whether I should mention this or not but there's a young man who keeps following me everywhere I go." I still did not tell her the truth and simply said that he must be a fan of hers. Anyway, at some point during the next shot, Pat must have cottoned on what was happening, because I looked around to see that she had literally pinned Jonathan, by the lapels, against the wall. A moment later, she stomped over to me and said, "I have just questioned this young man and he admits that he is playing the part of Tom Ripley. Is this your idea of Tom Ripley?" After I had admitted that well, yes it was, she said, "You're God damn fucking lucky – he's perfect."'⁶ In fact, as Highsmith wrote to Alain Oulman, Kent was the 'best Ripley I have seen since Alain Delon'.⁷

Jack Bond first met Highsmith at her house in Moncourt. Unable to find Rue de la Boissiere, Bond walked into a café to ask for directions, where he met a postman who not only gave him precise instructions about how to find Highsmith's home but her post as well. 'I banged on the door, the door flew open, Pat took the mail, said thank you and then slammed it in my face,' he says. 'However, after knocking again, I went inside and recall liking her immediately. She was difficult, a bit inaccessible and quite hesitant, but I liked her incredible bitchiness. She slagged people off as though by doing so she would actually remove them from the face of the earth. She was very nice to people in life who were doing "normal things" like delivering the mail or the milk, but she could be very tetchy in restaurants. She was a great slab of a figure – not in size, as she was incredibly slender – but in personality. You can't help but adore people who stand four square to the wind and who live life on their terms, with no compromises. When you met her it was clear who she was and who you were with. She was always bitching about Hitchcock, about how cheaply he had bought the rights to *Strangers on a Train*, and of course she could drink and swear with the best of them. Although I would never inquire her about her personal affairs, she would always ask me, "How's the fucking?" or "Who you fucking?" I remember her with a kind of joy.'[8]

While filming *The South Bank Show*, Jonathan Kent and Highsmith – whose appearance on the programme was later described by Frank Rich as an 'unsmiling figure . . . with a pugnacious, pouchy face framed by thick, parted black hair; she looks rather like her favorite bird, the owl'[9] – stayed in adjoining suites at the Savoy. 'Pat talked about Ripley as though he was real,' says Kent. 'And one of the reasons she liked me was because I was playing Ripley and she thought I *was* Ripley. She was so curious about me, really liked me, in a way that had nothing to do with me; it had more to do with her vision of Ripley.

'I had an enormous affection for her. I liked her independence, her toughness, her slyness. She would hide behind her hair, peering out from under her fringe with a mixture of amusement, shyness and curiosity. She had a great influence on me because when I was twelve or thirteen, growing up in South Africa, I went to see *Plein Soleil*. I had never heard of Highsmith before then, but I saw the film twice and then went out and read my way through her novels. So in a funny way she formed me – I knew so much about her work I could have gone on to *Mastermind* to answer questions about her – and I felt unnaturally linked to her from then on. All her books are about men and their shadows and Ripley was, I believe, an expression of what she wanted to be, an expression of her shadow. Maybe she was incomplete, maybe she never really accommodated her shadow.'[10]

A few weeks after filming *The South Bank Show*, Highsmith was back in Britain again to address a group of Eton schoolboys, a talk organised by seventeen-year-old pupil Roger Clarke, who had written to her in June. On 27 October she travelled by train from London to Slough, where she was met by Clarke and taken to the housemaster's dining room for supper. Yet, according to Clarke, now a writer and journalist, it soon became apparent that Highsmith had started to clam up. After introducing her to the audience of boys, she sat in uncomfortable silence, not knowing what to say, forcing Clarke to step in as interviewer.

'She looked like a cantankerous Texan librarian, fearsome, but at the same time she had this watchful and amused air about her,' he says. 'I got the feeling that she was dealing with things on a number of different levels, and that she had several personalities in play. When the talk was over, we took her back to Slough and a few days later I received the first of many letters from her, one of her usual gnomic three-liners. She told me how she had found this purple comb on the train back to London, how she took it home, washed it and used it. She drew a picture of it. It was then that I began to have an inkling of the depth of her strangeness. From then on we corresponded and became friends of sorts. But I couldn't work her out. Each time we met she would become more mysterious, more peculiar, rather than less. The mystery of her never seemed to end.

'One of the rare times I ever got a reaction from her was when I described, in a letter to her, a male brothel run by a friend of a friend in Chelsea. I went round there on several occasions and kind of hung out; it was intriguing, a den of secrets. One Monday night a punter came in and chose me instead of one of the boys. I didn't accept his proposition and he stormed off. When I told Pat, she thought this was terribly funny; she loved the ambiguities of the situation, the slightly sleazy element, the idea of shifting identities, of amoral opportunities. She had this mischievous, atavistic streak. She was one of the great misanthropists, and there was something almost Swiftian about her. I could imagine her committing unspeakable crimes if she had no outlet, the outlet of her writing.'[11]

In October, Highsmith conceived the idea for the short story, 'The Button', about a couple with a Down's Syndrome child. 'The husband kills maybe a stranger on the street,' she wrote in her notebook, 'because he has so often been tempted to kill the child.'[12] After writing the story, which would be published in the 1985 collection, *Mermaids on the Golf Course*, Highsmith sent it to Vivien De Bernardi, who was then an educational therapist friend of Ellen Hill's and a fellow resident of Ticino. When Vivien read the tale with what she thought of as its unrealistic portrayal of the child, Bertie – with his swollen tongue hanging out of his mouth, his eyes lolling about in his head and his incessant drooling – she felt outraged. She voiced her concerns about the story – that, in her experience, no Down's Syndrome child would ever make such horrific, guttural sounds – and after that initial meeting the two became close friends. Vivien's first impression of Highsmith was of an oddly dressed figure wearing ill-fitting clothes, khakis, a men's trenchcoat and a badly tied scarf around her neck.

'But what I loved from the very beginning was a softness, a peace, a tranquillity about her,' she says. 'Although she wrote about violence she was a very gentle person. I loved being with her, because there was this sense of quiet. One thing that interested me was that she chose me as a friend, not the other way around. She wrote to me, called me, encouraged me to come and see her when I was working part-time and raising two small children. It wasn't as if I had an empty space to fill. But I would meet her and return refreshed – seeing her was like diving into a pool of cool water – and I would come home, my thoughts clearer, able to see things in a new light. However, I didn't like to be with her when other people were around because she behaved like an unruly child, saying the first thing that popped into her head. It was as if she didn't seem to have any inner control mechanisms. She was incapable of not saying what was in her mind. For instance, one day I introduced Pat to a friend of mine who was overweight. A few minutes into the conversation, Pat suddenly said that being fat was like going into a supermarket with a bag with "Eat everything you can see" written on it. As soon as she said this, there was a stunned silence. I couldn't believe it. But Pat didn't even realise she had been rude, she just spat out the first thing that came into her mind.

'In hindsight, I think Pat could have had a form of high-functioning Asperger's Syndrome. She had a lot of typical traits. She had a terrible sense of direction, she would always get lost and whenever she went to the hairdresser's she would have trouble parking even though she had been with me lots of times. She was hypersensitive to sound and had these communication difficulties. Most of us screen certain things, but she would spit out everything she thought. She was not aware of the nuances of conversation and she didn't realise when she had hurt other people. That was probably why her love affairs never lasted very long, because she couldn't overcome these difficulties in communicating. Although she didn't really understand other people – she had such a strange interior world – she was a fantastic observer. She would see things that an average person would never experience.'[13]

It was this seemingly endless capacity to surprise – Highsmith's startling originality of perspective – which fascinated her new friend Jonathan Kent, who came to stay at her Aurigeno house in December. 'I assumed that we would buy some lovely Italian or Swiss delicacies, but after picking me up from the station, we stopped off at Kentucky Fried Chicken for some chicken nuggets, which we ate back at her house,' he says. 'I remember the house was in the shadow of the mountain and the central heating was turned on high. Her cats were completely punch-drunk from the heat, and one cat had sucked all its fur from its tail, like it was suffering from some kind of heat dementia. I remember that she slept in her workroom and would write at night. I woke up at four or five in the morning to hear the World Service playing in her room. One day she took me to see Ellen Hill – a neat, bourgeois woman with reddish-brown hair – and we went out for a pizza. I got the impression that Pat fell out with people – she could be quite difficult and surly – but nevertheless I thought that she was a marvellous, fascinating woman.

'I adored her instinct for the subversive and her dark sense of humour. I remember telling her this story about my grandmother who was suffering from Alzheimer's disease. My mother had taken her a bunch of daffodils, but my grandmother thought the flowers were an advancing army and ate them. I thought it was quite sad but Pat could not stop laughing – she was screaming with laughter. She made me retell the story and each time she would be doubled up with laughter. I kept expecting it to be used in a short story or a book.'[14]

Highsmith had very definite ideas of what she did and did not like. On the list of favoured objects and pursuits she composed for Diogenes Verlag in March 1983 she included Bach's St Matthew Passion; old clothes; sneakers; the absence of noise; Mexican food; fountain pens; Swiss army knives; weekends with no social commitments; Kafka and being alone. Things she disliked, which she detailed on another list for her Swiss publishers, ranged from the music of Sibelius to the art of Léger; live concerts; four-course meals; television sets; the Begin-Sharon regime; loud-mouthed people and those who borrow money; being recognised by strangers in the street; fascists and burglars. To this list, she could have added suicide, an act she regarded as cowardly. Those who threatened to kill themselves should, she wrote in a letter to Barbara Ker-Seymer, 'carry their coffins along with them, and crawl into them by ways of illustrating to the public – what martyrs they are.'[15]

The last person Highsmith would have expected to commit suicide was Arthur Koestler. She was shocked to discover that, on the evening of 1 March, Koestler, who was suffering from leukaemia and Parkinson's disease, and his wife Cynthia, killed themselves at their house in Montpelier Square, London. Highsmith heard the news when she was in Zurich. 'I know that "sitting-room" so well, and can fully imagine it,' she told Alain Oulman.[16] 'My first thought was that he had gently persuaded her; my emotion plain anger,' she wrote to Kingsley.[17] 'I do remember when Arthur died, Pat was inconsolable in a way that I had never seen before,' recalls Kingsley. 'She was absolutely distraught.'[18] 'The only time I ever saw Pat morally outraged was when she talked about the deaths of Arthur and Cynthia Koestler,' says Jonathan Kent. 'She felt that Koestler had persuaded Cynthia to kill herself and that was immoral. As she talked about it her face blackened, she was very angry. She said that she would never forgive him.'[19]

In April, Highsmith travelled from Aurigeno to Paris, where she endured a round of interviews to publicise the French edition of *People who Knock on the Door*. Although she found the city 'poorer and dirtier',[20] she did enjoy an evening with Mary McCarthy and her fourth husband James West at their apartment in Rue de Rennes. On her return to Aurigeno, she was visited by Christa Maerker. 'She picked me up from the station, but driving with Pat was like a kamikaze mission,' she says. 'She didn't know where the key was and when she found it she didn't know where to put it. As we set off, the window wipers would come on and during the journey she pointed out the spot where her car had once been hit by a train. Whether she was joking or not, I don't know.'[21] Highsmith had not been joking. One night, at ten o'clock in the evening, she was driving near her home in Aurigeno when she crossed into the path of a slow-moving train, wrecking the front of the car, but escaping injury herself.

From June, Highsmith started to correspond with Bettina Berch, author of *The Endless Day: The Political Economy of Women and Work* and then professor of economics at Barnard College. Berch initially wrote to her about her time at Barnard for an article she was writing for the alumnae magazine. Was it true, Berch asked her, that Highsmith had written a book under the name of Claire Morgan? 'The less said about Claire Morgan the better, esp. in print,' Highsmith replied.[22] Indeed, when Naiad Press bought the rights to reissue *The Price of Salt* later that year, Highsmith was determined for the book to be published under her pseudonym rather than her own name.

'Pat was worried that being known as a lesbian would damage her reputation as writer of mystery novels,' says Barbara Grier, the publisher of Naiad Press. 'She suffered from internalised homophobia. She lived a very isolated life, shunned contact and I got the impression that it was agony for her to have even a brief conversation. We did everything we could to please her – each time we reprinted the book she would change a word here or a comma there and there must be five feet of files documenting all of that. Talking with her was like pulling teeth. She was not comfortable in her own skin, she was not happy with herself and, of course, this was reflected in her work.'[23]

In late 1983, Highsmith was promised a $5,000 advance for *The Price of Salt* on condition that she agree for the novel to be released under her own name and a mere $2,000 if she insisted on using a pseudonym, an offer she politely turned down. Although she wasn't overly keen for the book to be published in Europe, one advantage of doing so would be to prevent piracy and, in April 1984, she signed a contract with Calmann-Lévy, maintaining that the novel go out under the guise of Claire Morgan. However, when the novel was published, as *Les Eaux dérobées*, in May 1985, and despite the fact that Calmann-Lévy did everything they could to keep her identity a secret, the French critics rumbled her, having 'found a Highsmith touch'.[24] Some critics, quite bizarrely, 'thought the book was by Enid Blyton', while others believed it to be the work of Françoise Mallet-Joris, but, as Alain Oulman wrote to Highsmith, 'the majority by you'.[25]

Highsmith started plotting her next novel, *Found in the Street*, in June 1983. The book, which she dedicated to Kingsley, centres around two men, a 'New York eccentric'[26] – security guard Ralph Linderman, an atheist who lives with his dog, God, in a sordid apartment on Bleecker Street – and Jack Sutherland, a wealthy Princeton graduate, freelance artist and illustrator, who lives with his wife Natalia, and their five-year-old daughter, Amelia, on the more gentrified Grove Street, the Greenwich Village street where Highsmith herself had lived over forty years before. ('The doorway was just the same and the mail boxes were in the same place,' observed Highsmith after revisiting the street while on a research trip to New York.[27]) One night, while out walking his dog, Ralph finds a wallet, which he returns to Jack, complete with $263 in cash, photographs and cards. Coincidences such as finding a wallet in the street, Highsmith knew, were frowned upon by some novelists, but as she believed strange, irrational events were actually part of life, she saw no reason why they should not be reflected in fiction. 'I am very fond of coincidences in plots and situations that are almost but not quite incredible,' she said.[28] 'I always had the idea of someone finding a wallet and returning it,' she said. 'I never did, but I'd like to, it would be *such* a pleasure.'[29]

When planning the novel, Highsmith said that she wanted the book to be suffused by a 'Faustian atmosphere of virginity and lust – equally

male and female'.[30] Certainly, Highsmith does seem to be attempting a
more direct analysis of relationships which sit outside the strict para-
meters of traditional heterosexuality and in September 1984, while still
in the process of writing the book, she told Barbara Ker-Seymer that,
'Half the characters in it [the novel], are gay or half-gay.'[31]

For all his attempts at behaving like a thoroughly modern man –
allowing his wife an extraordinarily free rein, encouraging her independence, enduring her affairs – Jack ultimately finds himself occupy-
ing a similar psychological position to the moralistic, sexually
frustrated Ralph. Both men reconfigure Elsie, the twenty-year-old
waitress and model, in their imaginations according to their own
desires, shaping her personality to fit the blueprint which exists only
in their fantasies. For Ralph, Elsie represents innocence and virginity, a
girl who has to be protected from the sordidness of New York City and
its squalid inhabitants. 'He's a prudish kind of fellow and not terribly
intelligent, he hasn't a real insight on himself,' said Highsmith of Ralph.
'He means well, he's certainly honest and he is very puritanical, he's
worried about the girl's morals and he doesn't want her to meet the
wrong kind of people. There's something comical about him, I think,
because . . . he gets the wrong signals, he mistakes what he sees.'[32] Jack
is intelligent and sophisticated enough to realise that Linderman had
fashioned Elsie into 'an abstract, a symbol of all women',[33] yet he does
not possess sufficient self-awareness to deconstruct his own misreading.
When he first sees Elsie he sees in her not a real woman, but a perfect
embodiment of an imaginative character; she has similar features to
Suzuki, 'the fantasy girlfriend of the adolescent boy',[34] featured in the
book *Half-Understood Dreams*, which he is illustrating. After drawing
Elsie, Jack feels creatively invigorated, almost in love, yet his feelings
seem to relate to the image of her he has fashioned on paper, rather than
the girl herself. For both men, Elsie becomes a 'dream girl'[35] and when
Jack finally manages to declare his love for her, he does so when she is
asleep, in the dim light looking like a fantastical character, 'flying in
space'.[36] As he stares at the photographic shots of Elsie culled from
stylish magazines he realises that the vision he has of her in his head is
much more real than the external image, yet ultimately Jack 'had loved
to admire Elsie from a distance, as if she were a good painting or a
drawing'.[37] The novel ends with both Ralph and Jack imagining
catching a glimpse of the enigmatic Elsie, before finally, and painfully,
realising the truth – that the girl spun from their imaginations is dead.

The characters in the novel behave like the protagonists in Jack's
illustrated book, *Half-Understood Dreams*: a New York couple with

two children, 'all of whom had dreams and expectations that they could not and maybe did not want to disclose to the rest of the family or to anyone else. So the dreams and fantasies were half-understood by the dreamers, and half-enacted in real life, and were misunderstood or unnoticed by the others.'[38] The self-referential sentence could serve as a neat summary of the imaginative territory which Highsmith made her own: the unsettling nexus between mind and matter, the treacherous interplay between the allure of fantasy and the inevitable undercurrent of reality.

The summer of 1983 was an oppressive one in the Ticino as the area suffered from a stifling heatwave. In August, Highsmith said that she had found the last couple of months 'shattering'.[39] Although her reserves of energy were low, she refused to countenance cancelling her public engagements, such as an invitation to the Locarno Film Festival. During the festival, she enjoyed an evening out with its director, David Streiff, whom she had first met in 1982. 'She seemed to enjoy the evening at the Grand Hotel,' says Streiff, now director of the Swiss Federal Office of Culture, 'but not the rather sophisticated menu. She asked for a pizza, which I guess had been deep frozen because it was not on the menu, but she only ate the topping not the dough. I will never forget her wonderful cat-like way of looking at you, nor her simplicity, modesty and shyness.'[40]

That summer, her busy schedule included a few days in London to attend an advance screening of Hans Geissendörfer's *Edith Tagebuch*. based on her novel *Edith's Diary* – the German director simplified the story into a 'neat Freudian mother-son love relationship',[41] and she thought the film, starring Angela Winkler, was 'obvious and a bit vulgar'[42] – and trips to Zurich, Venice, San Sebastian, Barcelona and Madrid. While in the Spanish capital, in September, Highsmith was quizzed by a student writing a dissertation about her work. As she tried to explain her process of writing she felt frustrated that she could not come up with more a concrete explanation for the foundations of her fiction. 'These thesis students,' she wrote in her notebook, 'try to make an organised discipline or science out of my writing, and I feel they are disappointed when I tell them my ideas, therefore my thoughts and thought processes, even, come out of nowhere.'[43]

Occasionally, however, her ideas were rooted in reality. Highsmith conceived the idea for the story, 'The Mysterious Cemetery', about the sinister growth of mushroom-shaped excrescences in a graveyard used to bury cancer victims, in August, soon after hearing about the experiences of Anne Morneweg, who in 1981 had been diagnosed with breast cancer. Anne remembers telling Highsmith the story of how, after having a mastectomy, she had been walking in the gardens of the hospital with a fellow patient when she saw a chimney with smoke streaming out of it. 'I told Pat the smoke was all that was left of our burnt breasts, adding the resulting energy was used to wash our sheets,' recalls Anne. 'Pat, who appreciated black humour, of course found this very funny – she was not at all sentimental. I told her this before she wrote the story about the remains growing from the graves.'[44]

Highsmith conceived 'The Mysterious Cemetery' as the first in a series of stories exploring the various environmental, political and social horrors of the modern world – apocalyptic nightmares including the threat of global extinction, the third world war, atomic destruction and pollution; described by the critic Peter Kemp as 'Greenpeace Gothic'.[45] Within a few days of setting down the idea for the first story, she had thought of another one. 'Moby Dick II,' she wrote in her notebook on 27 August. 'He bounces off missiles . . . he is a dangerous missile himself.' Or 'The Missile Whale'.[46] Highsmith scanned her favourite newspaper, the *International Herald Tribune*, together with *Time* magazine, looking for appropriately grotesque reports. Friends such as Charles Latimer also supplied her with scandalous titbits, such as the allegation that the American government had paid for a football stadium to be built in a university town in the Midwest, under which was stored secret nuclear waste; an idea which she used as the basis for 'Operation Balsam; Or Touch-Me-Not'. The stories in the collection, which she wrote between 1983 and 1987, reminded her, she said, 'of the spoofs I wrote of school subjects at ten and eleven, then again at fourteen for my classmates' amusement. But I trust the content here is more important. I found an *embarras de richesses* of "catastrophes" that the human race has, almost, learned to live with at the end of the twentieth century.'[47]

In November 1983, just before Highsmith planned to fly to New York on a research trip for *Found in the Street*, she contracted the flu and had to postpone the visit by one week. Before she travelled, she was also needled by a sense of anxiety, a feeling that she had simply too much to do before her departure. She arrived in New York on 25 November and stayed in America until 12 December, a trip which comprised of a stay at Charles Latimer's house in East Hampton and two 'jaunts'[48] to New York. Her Manhattan hotel, she observed, housed two cockroaches which lived in the medicine cabinet in her bathroom, 'but that's normal in New York,'[49]; perhaps they inspired her second cockroach story, the truly grotesque 'Trouble at the Jade Towers', one of the *Tales of Natural and Unnatural Catastrophes.*

She walked around the streets of Greenwich Village, the setting for *Found in the Street*, noting how Morton Street was still as shabby as it was when she lived there more than forty years before. The rubbish problem in Manhattan was shocking, she thought; such a contrast to the gleaming spotlessness of Zurich streets. 'It is impossible to imagine someone dropping a Kleenex on a Swiss street,' she wrote to Barbara Ker-Seymer, on her return from America.[50] 'Without a doubt, Pat was very orderly and could, at times, be very critical,' says Kingsley. 'She didn't like the fact that sometimes I ate standing up – it always had to be sitting down with knife and fork. And if you moved an ashtray in one of her houses, she would immediately put it back in the same place.'[51]

While in Manhattan, she also met Anne Elisabeth Suter, who had formerly worked for Diogenes Verlag and continued to represent many of the Swiss publishers' clients in America. 'One always felt that Pat surrounded herself by a camouflage of shyness, of retreat,' she says. 'Yet our relationship, when I was based in New York, was not without storm. She told me where to place her stories and grew angry when that didn't happen. But she didn't know that I protected her from the rejections.'[52] One possibility Highsmith investigated during her stay in New York was the sale of her books through The Mysterious Press, a small publishing house run by Otto Penzler, owner of The Mysterious Bookshop in Manhattan. After attending a book signing at the store on West 56th Street, Penzler presented her with a copy of Stanley Ellin's, *The Dark Fantastic*, a novel published by his company and one she said she liked. 'As I gave her the book, I told her that I would love to do something like this for her, as it was beautifully produced novel by a wonderful writer,' says Otto. 'Highsmith was not a terribly successful writer commercially in America – she moved from publishing house to publishing house and companies dropped her because she did not sell. But I really admired her work.'[53] Although Penzler would publish, for the first time in America, six of her books – one novel, *People who Knock on the Door*, and five collections of short stories, all between 1985 and 1988 – the relationship between publisher and author would soon break down, degenerating into barbed attacks and accusations of betrayal.

32

Work is more fun than play

1983–1986

In 1983, Highsmith had been contacted by an English movie producer about the possibility of filming her novel, *The Blunderer*. The project would be financed by Goldcrest and Home Box Office and would star John Hurt as Walter Stackhouse and Mario Adorf as Melchior Kimmel. Highsmith had signed the contract in December while she was in New York and by February 1984, the film producers had started to look around for a writer. Had she any thoughts who could adapt her novel for the screen? The name Highsmith put forward – that of Marc Brandel – was, perhaps, a surprising one, as the relationship between the two writers had imploded more than thirty years before. Highsmith and Brandel, who in addition to his novels had established himself as a television scriptwriter, even adapting *The Talented Mr Ripley* for US broadcast for Studio One in January 1956, had started to correspond in late 1979, after he had paid a visit to her house in Moncourt. Within a few months of their reunion they had become close friends once more. Highsmith signed her letters to him, 'With much love, Pat', and Marc, in turn, was touched by Pat's kindness. 'It was terribly sweet of you to recommend me for the adaptation of *The Blunderer*,' he wrote to her on 29 March.[1]

Although Brandel was initially passed over in favour of another writer, in May 1985 he and his second wife, Edith, visited Highsmith at her house in Aurigeno to discuss the project further. Edith remembers meeting Highsmith for the first time. 'When I met Pat I was surprised by her looks,' says Edith. 'Marc had always told me how stunning she had been, but when I saw her she was no longer beautiful. She looked very skinny and drawn, considering she wasn't that old. I never had the impression that she was a happy person – I think she was always dissatisfied with herself.'[2] The following month, Highsmith learned from HBO that they had rejected the draft version of the first screenplay, prompting the novelist to ask Brandel if he could take it on.

'I'd love you to do the script . . .' Highsmith wrote to Brandel once more. 'Please tell me if you could do, because I think I could arrange this.'[3] The deal between Highsmith and Goldcrest/HBO collapsed at the end of June, but, despite this, Highsmith was still keen for Marc to write the film. In November 1985, contrary to her somewhat miserly reputation, she sent Brandel a cheque for $8,000 as a retainer on *The Blunderer*, money she paid out of her own bank account as 'Diogenes decided Friday last that it would be "very unusual" to advance a writer money on a property not sold.'[4] Marc was moved by the gesture, writing in a letter of 22 November, 'It gave me a wonderful feeling about you and your friendship.'[5] Brandel started work on the script in January 1986; another producer was found and the film was still under discussion in 1988, yet nothing came of the project. Highsmith, however, did not ask for the money back.

Another dream. Highsmith's mother, consumed with anger and murderous thoughts, cuts off the head of Tabea Blumenschein. 'You will have to help me get rid of the body,' says Mary to her daughter, before coating the head with transparent wax. Highsmith is left feeling shocked and utterly paralysed with horror; on awakening she wrote in her notebook, 'I do not know what happened to head and body.'[6]

On 15 June 1984, Bettina Berch arrived at Highsmith's house in Aurigeno to interview her for a feature she hoped to place in a magazine or journal. Before the interview, Highsmith took her guest out for a pizza, accompanied by the indomitable Ellen Hill, whose poodle sat on her lap throughout the meal. 'It was awkward because I think Ellen, who looked very ladylike, was annoyed that I was there and she was kind of snappy,' says Bettina. 'There was, however, one sweet moment which passed between them, when Ellen called Pat "teacup". I thought that was very sweet. Pat struck me as a very imposing character. She was wearing black loafers, like men's shoes, which I thought was kind of odd, and a man's jacket. It was probably the best look for her because it was comfortable and she wasn't a femme sort at all.'[7]

After supper, Ellen drove back to Cavigliano and Pat and Bettina retired to Highsmith's house for the interview. At midnight, the two women started talking, Highsmith fuelled by a bottle of beer and a packet of Gauloises. Their conversation was wide-ranging, covering the motivation of her characters, particularly Ripley; the source of her ideas: 'They just pop into my head – how else do you say it?'[8], the vulgarity of women's magazines, which she described as 'unrealistic, it's fantasy, it's Prince Charming, or it's how to wash out your vagina,'[9]; and the nature of love and desire: 'There's always one person who loves more than the other, and very often *one* cannot *get* the other.'[10]

The women's movement, remembers Bettina, was one subject she expressed quite vociferous opinions about. 'She talked about women almost as if she was something other, like she wasn't one. It was always women are incapable because they have been foot-bound over the centuries, their minds are worthless and they don't have ambition.

'The other thing that really turned her off the women's movement was what she saw as the lack of privacy that went with talking about one's body and bodily symptoms. That completely offended her. I think she would have rather spent time with the most crude male chauvinist than sit with some woman who wanted to talk about her secretions. And yet I don't think she was a misogynist. I think she loved women too much maybe.'[11]

Highsmith's view of the feminist movement was, as Bettina Berch discovered, completely divorced from the reality. 'It was as if she had decided in her head what the women's movement was all about,' she says, 'and this was symptomatic of the fact that she lived in her own closed, self-created world. I remember spending about an hour with her trying to explain how to use an ATM card. She did not own one but wanted to feature one in *Found in the Street*. I took out my plastic card and showed her what you did, took her through the whole process step by step. I think the last time she had really been in the world was probably back in the fifties.

'Yet I liked her a great deal, I thought she was a wonderful person, and we became friends. After that visit we corresponded regularly and she really cared about what happened in my life. She made me feel that my news was of interest to her and that she was on my side. Although I was keen to write her biography, she was resistant to the idea and told me, "Not while I'm alive, thank you." I respected that. She didn't want to come out because she thought she would become even more obscure. She also believed in the concept of ambiguity – she didn't see any point in clarifying one's sexual orientation. The whole fun was in the ambiguity.'[12]

For all of Highsmith's obsession with order, when she arrived in Istanbul, to write a travel piece for a German magazine, on 5 October

1984, she was immediately charmed by the chaotic sensory delights of the city. Peering out of the window of her taxi as she journeyed from the airport to her hotel, she was thrilled to see the towering minarets, remains of ancient fortresses and majestic watchtowers which rose above the Bosporus. She spent two days in Istanbul, staying at the Hilton hotel, which seemed devoid of personality compared to the vibrancy of the surrounding city. Her one regret, she said, was not being able to see the slums before embarking on the next stage of her journey, a three-day trip on the Orient Express, stopping in Budapest and Vienna, where she attended a dinner and ball at the Palais Schwarzenberg Hotel, finally arriving in Zurich on 11 October. 'I wonder what kind of people can afford 5,500 SF for these six days?' she wrote to Marc Brandel.[13]

Highsmith's relationship with money was an unpredictable and contradictory one. On the one hand she parted easily with the $8,000 retainer she sent to Brandel and yet she made a special effort to drive across the border into Italy with her reading-glasses prescription to have her spectacles made because it was 20 per cent cheaper than in Switzerland. 'Her attitude towards money was nutty,' says Vivien De Bernardi. 'She had all this money, but who knew it? I remember she went to have the snow tyres on her car changed, but refused to pay the bill because she decided it was too high. She wore the same clothes she had worn when she was eighteen and after her death I found the swimsuit she had had ever since she was a teenager – and it was her only swimsuit.'[14] Frieda Sommer told Joan Dupont, 'She must have had deep fears: the way she lived, never allowing herself any luxury because she was afraid she might be a pauper.'[15]

Peter Huber, her friend, and from 1988, her neighbour in Tegna, remembers how Pat closely guarded a heap of old timber, covered with cement and rusty nails, transporting it from her house in Moncourt, to Aurigeno and then on to Tegna. 'One afternoon Pat called my wife Anita and me and asked us if we would like a cup of tea and a look at the fire,' he says. 'We went over to her house where there were two pieces of this building wood on the fire, from where a small flame flickered. After asking us to sit down, she went to the fire and knocked it so as to make it go out. I said, "Pat, Pat, don't do that, that will make the fire go out." But she looked at me in a very queer way, and I realised then that was the reason why she had knocked it – she wanted it out so as not to waste it. After all, this wood had come a long way. It was just extraordinary.'[16] Jack Bond, however, does not believe Highsmith was motivated by stinginess. 'I would have thought she was conserving rather than mean,' he says. 'Maybe she figured that her money had been very hard won, and it could go easily, so she had better save up for rainy days.'[17]

In November, Highsmith typed out a tally of how much it cost to keep her mother in her Fort Worth nursing home. A total of $15,300 was needed each year, $7,486 of which was met by Mary Highsmith's pension. This left a shortfall of $7,814 a year which would have to come from her savings. The idea did not please her. 'If I can get some "tax relief" from a retroactive claim,' she wrote to her cousin, Dan Coates, two years later, 'it will be a tremendous help. My mother's bills now cost me more than my ordinary expenses such as food and clothing.'[18]

Although Highsmith had, in the past, admired right-wing figures such as Margaret Thatcher, in the November 1984 US Presidential election she voted for Democrat Walter Mondale, who campaigned for a nuclear freeze and attacked Reagan for an alleged lack of 'fairness' in his economic policies. Mondale was, however, defeated, losing to the incumbent President. American foreign policy disgusted Highsmith and she even went so far as to say, in a letter to Marc Brandel, that 'I begin to be ashamed of my USA passport, considering what the USA is backing now.'[19]

In early December, Highsmith returned to the USA on another research trip. She spent six days with Charles Latimer in East Hampton and another six in New York, staying at the Royalton. 'I went to the Village three times, much to the benefit of the book I am writing',[20] she wrote to Bettina Berch, referring to *Found in the Street*. In Manhattan, she had lunch with Otto Penzler, whose imprint, Penzler Books, she had chosen as her US publisher and in her hotel room, Highsmith signed 180 sheets of paper which would form the title pages of a special edition of *Slowly, Slowly in the Wind*. Although Highsmith, in a letter to Marc Brandel, professed to liking Penzler, the publisher has no fond memories of her. In fact, in a review in the *Wall Street Journal* in August 2001, to coincide with the publication of W. W. Norton's *The Selected Stories of Patricia Highsmith*, Penzler wrote, 'Two points should immediately be stated about Patricia Highsmith: She may have been one of the dozen best short-story writers of the 20th century, and she may have been one of the dozen most disagreeable and mean-spirited as well . . . The photograph on the cover of this handsome tome shows the hard, harsh face of an unloving and unlovable woman.'[21]

He expanded his views in an interview. 'Besides her writing – which I thought was fabulous and original – there was not one thing I liked about her,' he says. 'There was an unredeemable ugliness to her. I never witnessed a kind thought, a kind word, a kind gesture in all the time we spent together. I took her around some of the publicity interviews and between appointments we'd sometimes have an hour to kill when we'd go and have a beer but most of that time we spent in silence. I could never be at ease with her.

'She was pretty good-looking when she was younger, she was a really attractive woman, but she was ugly later in life. I think a lot of that ugliness – that anger and that hatred, hatred of almost everything and everyone – came from the inside. It might have had something to do with the fact that she wasn't accepted in America and she felt bitter because she thought she was more talented than a lot of other people making more money than her.

'I'm an enthusiast by nature, an optimist and a generally upbeat sort of person, but she was one of the most odious people I've ever met. She was a totally horrible woman. She was mean, unkind, unfriendly and cold and never missed an opportunity to be nasty. I remember once, during a dinner with my then wife, and a publicity director, at one of my favourite New York Italian restaurants, she behaved appallingly. The publicity director arrived with two roses, one for my wife and one for Pat, but when he presented her with it, she just dropped it to the floor without acknowledgement or thanks. She was endlessly strange and I never knew what to make of her.'[22]

In December 1984, Highsmith returned home to find the Ticino in the grip of an unusually cold spell, with temperatures dropping to their lowest in a hundred years. Winter sunlight was rare in Aurigeno, as the village lay on the side of the valley shadowed by the mountains. In fact, the sight of the sun easing its way through the snow-capped peaks was such a novelty it prompted Highsmith to take her cats out to witness the event, while if snow fell in December it was quite common for it to still cover the ground a couple of months later. 'I've been walking through shoulder-high trenches in the snow for [the] past six weeks, now it's knee-high, but the paths are treacherous with ice,' she wrote to Bettina Berch, in early February 1985.[23]

Highsmith busied herself by writing a number of short essays, including a piece about books which she had enjoyed or which had influenced her. She included old favourites such as works by Bram Stoker, Edgar Allan Poe, Joseph Conrad, Hermann Melville, Djuna Barnes and Cyril Connolly, as well as more modern works by Ronald Blythe and Tom Sharpe, particularly *Porterhouse Blue* and *Blott on the*

Landscape. 'If you have to put a Tom Sharpe book down for a few minutes,' she wrote, 'you will want to get back to it as soon as possible, regardless of pressing matters.'[24] In February, she sent off a piece to *Libération* on the subject of why she wrote. She did so, she said, in order to exorcise emotion; to entertain herself; to order experience, and because she was, quite frankly, hooked on it. 'The reward of art is not fame or success but intoxication,' she said, quoting Cyril Connolly in *The Unquiet Grave*, 'that is why so many bad artists are unable to give it up.'[25] She also agreed to answer the famous 'Proust' questionnaire – a 37-question Q & A interview whose subjects in the past had included Karl Marx, Georges Simenon and Eugene Ionesco – for *Frankfurter Allgemeine Zeitung*. Her idea of perfect earthly happiness was visiting the Jeu de Paume in Paris. Her favourite painters were Munch and Balthus; her preferred composers, Mozart and Stravinsky. She admired the ability to stick to principles in men, intelligence in women, and, in friends, honesty and dependability, while her own best quality was, she said, perseverance. She despised selfishness and deception. Her greatest fault was her inability to decide quickly or easily. Asked about her dream of happiness, she responded, 'I don't dream about happiness.' Her favourite colour, flower, and bird were, respectively, yellow, carnation and robin redbreast. Her favourite writer was Dostoevsky, while her choice of poet, W.H. Auden. From history she admired, Horatio Nelson and Lady Mary Wortley Montagu, while she loathed Savonarola, the fifteenth-century Italian religious reformer, and the majority of Popes. The one piece of reform which she most admired was women getting the vote. How would she like to die, she was asked. 'Suddenly,' she said. And her motto? 'Work is more fun than play,' she replied, quoting Noel Coward.[26]

During the spring she finished typing the final draft of *Found in the Street* and by 23 May the finished manuscript was ready to send off to the publishers. Alain Oulman enjoyed it tremendously, but had one major problem: he didn't quite understand the relationship between Jack and Natalia. 'When they are together, they don't speak or act as if they were husband and wife, as if there existed a closeness, an intimacy between them, specially on her part in relation to him,' he wrote. 'Is that deliberate, and if so, why?'[27] One of Highsmith's Swiss friends had also remarked on the distance between the couple, but as Pat replied to Oulman, 'That is the way I see Natalia, however. She would not show her emotions; and if anybody tried to get a tighter hold on her, she would run away.'[28]

The novel had taken sixteen months of steady work and she felt in need of a break. In June she took a four-day trip to Amsterdam, but much of her time was taken up with publicity and on her return to Aurigeno, she took it upon herself to 'relax' by clearing out her library, culling sixty volumes from the mass of books in her upstairs reading room. 'I'm still "on vacation" since end of May,' she wrote to Marc Brandel in July, which she described as 'a dazzling experience'.[29]

Yet Highsmith was never completely at ease when not working, and she always strove for self-improvement, especially in her writing. In November 1984 she had heard that her friend Julian Jebb had committed suicide by taking an overdose. The news unnerved her; on reading the obituaries, Highsmith learnt that the director and producer had most likely died because of a deep dissatisfaction with his achievements. 'Having reaching fifty,' Highsmith wrote in a piece for the book, *A Dedicated Fan: Julian Jebb 1934–1984,* Jebb 'had longed to do more important work, to be taken more seriously as a television director or producer, or both.'[30] Perhaps, she surmised, Jebb had never been able to live up to the early success he found on graduating from Cambridge and working on a satirical show which had played in the West End. Exposure to success at such a precocious age was, she suggested, often a progenitor to tragedy. 'Talent becomes not a gift to work on and develop,' she concluded, 'but a comet that has gone up and then falls to earth fast.'[31] In a letter to Francis Wyndham she voiced the possibility that Jebb was a victim of 'self-torture, as are a lot of us'.[32]

There is little doubt that Highsmith was proud of her own achievements – a result, she believed, of discipline, hard work and sheer perseverance – but at the same time, like Jebb, she felt constantly dissatisfied. 'The only thing that makes one feel happy and alive is trying for something that one cannot get,' she wrote in her notebook in 1985.[33]

Highsmith heard the good news that Heinemann liked *Found in the Street* early in August 1985 and that her advance was to be upped from £3,000 to £5,000. Despite this, Diogenes Verlag believed that Highsmith deserved better and, after Heinemann had had the novel's book jacket designed and printed, they sent out the manuscript to other London publishers for higher bids. Hamish Hamilton quickly offered an £8,000 advance, but Heinemann, distressed at the prospect of losing one of their star writers, served an injunction on Diogenes and Highsmith, 'with a 3-day ultimatum – to stop trying to take my book away'.[34] Two executives were dispatched from London to Highsmith's home in Switzerland to try and persuade her not to change publishers, but she was left feeling unsettled by the whole affair. 'All this makes me nervous,' she wrote to Marc Brandel, 'though it should not; and I'm sorry it's so long drawn out.'[35] By November, the affair had been sorted out, with Heinemann agreeing to Diogenes' terms – a £12,000 advance, a £10,000 advertising campaign and no option on her next book. Although Heinemann had, in September, just published another collection of her short stories, *Mermaids on the Golf Course*, Diogenes took the attitude that she should have another English publisher for her next novel, 'though I'll keep in mind the fact that Heinemann would keep my books in print'.[36]

Just before Christmas, Highsmith came down with what she thought was a bad case of intestinal flu – a cold combined with 'nausea and all that',[37] a condition which lingered for five weeks. She had promised Heinemann to spend a week in London in early February 1986, promoting *Found in the Street*. Although Highsmith still felt ill she did not want to let down her British publishers. She arrived in London on 1 February, enduring a seemingly endless rounds of interviews; 'they really laid it on,' she said of the Heinemann publicity department. 'Four a day, anyway.'[38]

On 6 February, Heinemann hosted a celebratory dinner at the Chelsea Arts Club for the writer they had almost lost a few months before. Highsmith, described as a 'small, hunched figure'[39] by Craig Brown, also a guest at the dinner, sat between Gordon Burn, author of *Somebody's Husband, Somebody's Son* about Peter Sutcliffe, the 'Yorkshire Ripper', a book which Highsmith had reviewed for the *Times Literary Supplement*, and Julian Symons, the novelist and doyen of British crime writers. 'The three could be seen chatting away about Sutcliffe, with Highsmith in the middle looking intense and alert,' remembers Brown, 'but as the evening wore on, the dining-room grew fuller and fuller of louder and louder people . . . As the noise of drunken braying grew, Highsmith . . . grew ever more silent, curling up like a snail. By the time the pudding came, she had stopped talking about Sutcliffe or about anything and her hands were placed firmly over her ears.'[40]

Highsmith returned home to find her car encased in icy snow and, instead of employing someone to dig it out for her, proceeded to try and do it herself, 'clad in Levis without heavy underwear'.[41] She caught a cold, which developed into bronchitis, necessitating a course of antibiotics, but after she had recovered, the doctor advised her to have an X-ray of her chest at the hospital in Locarno. She had a shadow on her right lung. A diagnosis required further tests – more X-rays and a needle biopsy – which had to be sent off for analysis. While waiting for the results, Highsmith travelled to Paris to publicise *Found in the Street*, but she kept her anxieties to herself. 'I said nothing of my troubles and angst to business colleagues or to friends while in France,' she said.[42]

On her return to Switzerland on 26 March, she made an appointment with her local doctor, who had arranged for the test results to be sent to him. 'Pat asked me to take her along to get the results because she was afraid that if it was bad news she wouldn't be able to drive, she would be too upset,' recalls Vivien De Bernardi. 'It was a Saturday morning and I picked her up at 10 a.m. After a hour we were called in to the doctor's office and he told us that there would have to be an operation. The question was whether to have it in Locarno or London. Then the doctor's phone rang and he disappeared for an hour and a half, dealing with an emergency. Meanwhile Pat took a flask out of her purse and there in the doctor's office, drank down her whisky.'[43]

The future looked bleak, but she took some comfort from the love and support of her friends – Vivien De Bernardi invited her to sleep at her house and Ellen Hill advised Highsmith to bypass doctors in Locarno in favour of seeking medical attention in London. Within a couple of days she had secured a private consultation at the Brompton Hospital. On 3 April, Highsmith was examined by John Batten – who observed her grey complexion in his notes – after which she underwent more tests, including X-rays and another biopsy. The results were rushed through and on 5 April, Batten approached the writer in hospital and asked her to sit down. The tests had, he said, revealed that there was a cancerous tumour in her right lung and that it would have to be removed. 'This sounds like a death sentence to me, taken out or not,' she wrote in her notebook, 'as I've never heard of anyone surviving such, or anyway, not for long.'[44]

On 10 April, Highsmith underwent surgery to remove the growth and she was left with a fourteen-inch scar running along her fifth rib and ending just under her right breast. It was, as she wrote to Marc Brandel, 'One hell of an operation and I was scared, I don't mind admitting.'[45] Vivien De Bernardi, whom Highsmith described as a 'gem'[46], sent flowers to the hospital, as did Daniel Keel and Roland Gant, her publisher at Heinemann, while Kingsley organised for a bottle of champagne to be delivered to her sick friend. She stayed in London for thirty-one days, returning home to Switzerland on 1 May, with orders to report back to the doctors in three months time. The waiting was interminable and she found it impossible to concentrate on her work. 'The mental fear needs a thousand words to describe,' she wrote in her notebook. 'It is as though death is right there – suddenly – and yet one feels no pain.'[47]

Highsmith, a smoker since the age of sixteen, had enjoyed what she was determined to be her last cigarette, just before she had stepped on to a plane in Zurich, bound for London. Although she loved smoking she knew that if she were to have any chance at all of surviving the cancer she would have to quit. 'I was so impressed when she gave up smoking,' says Jack Bond. 'She was a chain smoker and she had to stop after her illness. But she did it.'[48]

Although she did not feel like working on her novels or short stories, Highsmith bashed off letter after letter to her friends. 'You must not think I had to use any discipline to stop smoking . . . it was fear alone that made me stop,' she wrote to Patricia Losey. 'Plain terror at being told I had to have an operation. I never wish to go through that again, so it is easy for me not to take a single puff, even though I like the smell, as I do of espresso, too.'[49]

In the same letter, she also told Patricia how much she admired Gore Vidal with whom she had started to correspond. Although the two authors never met, he liked what he describes as 'her fierce clarity'.[50] They also shared a mistrust of Israel. On 22 May, Highsmith read a piece in the *International Herald Tribune*, reprinted from the *New York Times*, in which the commentator William Safire launched an assault on Vidal for opinions he had expressed in an essay for *The Nation*. 'To make sure that nearly a third of the federal budget goes to the Pentagon and Israel it is necessary for the pro-Israel lobbyists to make common cause with the lunatic right,' Vidal had written.[51] Vidal, whose article also attacked Norman Podhoretz, the pro-Israeli editor of the neo-conservative magazine *Commentary*, went on to charge American citizens who supported Israel with dual loyalty, concluding, 'I've got to tell you I don't much like your country, which is Israel.'[52] Highsmith agreed wholeheartedly and that night sat down to compose a letter to the *Tribune* outlining her support for Vidal. On 9 June, Highsmith wrote to Vidal to tell him that the letter published in that day's *International Herald Tribune* under the name of Edgar S. Sallich of Brione, Switzerland, was, in fact, written by her. She took issue with Safire for calling Israel a democracy when, in her view, she thought it more of a theocracy, as it defined its borders by Old Testament names. 'Therefore, the loyalty of U.S. citizens who are Jewish will be forever argued, to little avail,' she wrote. 'An American can be loyal to any religion, but CANNOT be loyal to a country other than America if he or she expects to continue being an American.'[53] As to why she used a pseudonym, she wrote to Vidal, 'I don't care to use my own name too often, so I invent names. I could've said that many Jews in USA seem to like America as a safe berth and as a source of money for Israel. But would such a letter get printed?'[54]

Ever since the operation to remove the cancer from her lung, Highsmith had been dreading the return of the disease. On 11 July – three months after the lobectomy – she turned up at the Brompton Hospital in London for an X-ray. As she waited for the results, she consumed the contents of her hip flask, thinking the worst, but was relieved to hear that the cancer had not returned. During the consultation she was also told that the tumour was the glandular type, one which could have grown even if she had never smoked. 'It is like a reprieve from death,' she noted.[55]

33

No end in sight

1986–1988

'Pat was frightened that this may be the end of her life and she wasn't planning to live in that summer vacation house in Aurigeno for ever,' says Vivien De Bernardi. 'If she was going to have a new home, now was the time.'[1] Highsmith knew living in the adumbrated gloom of the mountains was no good for her health – 'the climate here doesn't suit me at all', she said[2] – and her friends were appalled by the conditions she lived in. 'She took me down to the cellar, which had mushrooms growing from the ceiling,' says Christa Maerker. 'It was really spooky.'[3] 'I couldn't believe that she was living in that house in Aurigeno,' says Jack Bond, 'When I went to see her there it was damp, cold and dark, just awful.'[4]

Although she knew she wanted to move, she could not decide on a location. In February 1986, she flirted with relocating to Santa Fe or Mexico, but then, in June of that year she suddenly tried to pull out of selling her Moncourt house so she could move back to her old French village. The house by the canal, she remembered, was 'very healthful to me',[5] but even though she offered an extra 125,000 francs, her bid to buy out the purchaser failed. 'This leaves me undecided about where to live,' she wrote to Gore Vidal. 'I find the Swiss winters tough to take and not good for me.'[6] In August, after attending the Locarno Film Festival – where she saw Stephen Frears' *My Beautiful Launderette*, which she described as 'a brilliant comment on today's London social picture'[7] – she travelled to Moncourt and spent five days house-hunting in the area, but did not find the light, airy property of her dreams. She knew she could never live in a city as she found modern urban life too stressful. She thought Frankfurt, which she visited for the book fair in

October, a ghost town, 'all new chrome and glass . . . everyone was run ragged with voices, people and TV cameras in your face',[8] while her trips to Washington DC, on 17 October, where she was invited to sit on a panel to discuss film noir, and New York later that month, left her feeling debilitated.

On her return to Switzerland, architect Tobias Ammann contacted Highsmith to inform her that there was a plot of land available in Tegna, a small village seven kilometres from Locarno. As soon as she saw the site, a gloriously open and sunny spot overlooking the Centovalli, in November she knew it was for her. Building a house would be an expensive project – the land alone would cost her 490,000 SF – but she was passionate about creating a home tailored to suit her specific needs. She completed the deal to buy the land in April 1987 and worked closely with Ammann on the designs of 'Casa Highsmith' throughout the year.

'The design of the house reflected her personality in some respects,' says Ammann. 'From the outside it looked quite stark and forbidding, but at the back it was glass and opened out over a beautiful valley. Similarly, she was always very distant and did not like to shake hands – she was fearful of the world and of people – but I'm sure once you got to know her she could be charming in her own way. After the house was built, she kept ringing me up complaining about little things that had to be done – this went on two years after it had been finished – but eventually I realised that she wanted the company. I always spoke to her in German, sometimes in Italian, which was not so good, and I would go over to the house about once a month, to drink whisky. I remember she always had a very good whisky for her guests, but she drank a cheaper one.'[9]

'She lies now, certainly a hundred and ninety, some say two hundred and ten, and with no end in sight,'[10] runs the opening sentence of Highsmith's short story, 'No End in Sight', published as one of the *Tales of Natural and Unnatural Catastrophes*. The story, which focuses on the life of Naomi Barton Markham, an unnaturally aged resident of the Old Homestead Nursing and Rest Home in southern Oklahoma, is a caustic character sketch of her senile mother, a resident of Fireside Lodge, Fort Worth. 'What does it think about?' Highsmith writes. 'Does it go *gubbah-gubbah-gubbah* with toothless gums, as it did in babyhood, when it was also swathed at the loins in a diaper?'[11] Naomi is spoon-fed three times a day (she flushed her false teeth down the toilet at least a century ago), has to have her diapers changed at least ten times every day and babbles on about imaginary characters.

The story was written in September and October 1986, but its gestation had a long history. Highsmith remembered how, in 1961, she told her stepfather that her mother was slowly going insane, but he reacted with indifference. 'My own mother goes on forever, thanks to antibiotics, blood transfusions and the paraphernalia that keeps the old alive these days,' she wrote to Kingsley in February 1976. 'Not that she is at all ill. Only cracked.'[12] While in the Fireside Lodge, Mary Highsmith was confined to a high chair during meal-times – otherwise she would wander around aimlessly swapping other residents' false teeth and drinking all the orange juice – and used eight dozen diapers each month, an extra expense Highsmith resented. 'She wants attention like an actress,' Highsmith scribbled down the side of a letter from her cousin, Dan Coates, in February 1974. 'There is no end and no hope.'[13]

The year before Highsmith wrote 'No End in Sight' she observed how her mother's mental illness was inexorably connected with her own existence. 'My mother would not have become semi-insane,' she wrote in her notebook, 'if I had not existed.'[14] Highsmith believed the source of her mother's insanity was the painful realisation that she was a professional, marital and maternal failure; the same reasons which contributed to Naomi's descent into madness.

The parallels between the fictional and real-life stories are striking. Like Mary, the young Naomi was 'blonde, slender, pert, not much intellectually, because she hadn't gone to school after her mediocre highschool'.[15] In her early twenties, she marries a slightly older man, Eugene, who like Bernard Plangman, suggests she have an abortion so she can concentrate on her career – not as an artist, like Mary Highsmith, but as a dancer in vaudeville theatre. 'Naomi tried hot baths plus gin,' Highsmith writes in the story, 'resulting in a red face for herself, much sweating, but no ensuing period.'[16] After his wife fails to miscarry, Eugene pledges his love to her and suggests taking six months out from her career, but Naomi is adamant that she would rather seek a divorce. Naomi gives birth to their child – in the story Highsmith changes her sex, naming the child Stevey – but after only a few weeks she leaves the home of her parents to resume her career. When the child is nearly four years old, Naomi marries Doug, a man like Stanley Highsmith, 'a simple but decent fellow'[17], whom she then continually berates, 'making their home life worse than rocky'.[18] Her child, Stevey, like Highsmith herself, is initially close to his grandmother, Sarah, who 'raised him from birth to the age of four'[19] but, at ten, finds himself 'in love with his mother'.[20] Subsequently he grows up to realise that he 'needed a mother, or a motherly type, according to Freud.'[21] After the death of his stepfather, Stevey discovers that his mother simply cannot cope with life and is forced to place her in a home, from where Naomi dashes off increasingly vituperative letters to her son – 'Stevey knew his mother well enough to realise that she wanted to start an epistolary argument, back and forth.'[22] In the story, Highsmith writes how the grotesquely old Naomi, kept alive by antibiotics and vitamins, will outlive everyone around her including her son. Stevey dies at the age of seventy-four – the same age Highsmith would be when she died in early February 1995. On the last night of his life, Stevey's thoughts turn once again to his mother, who had been 'a trial and tribulation to all around her, had made good men weep . . . And she lived on.'[23]

In December 1990, Highsmith thought of a sequel to the story, provisionally entitled 'The Tube'. The tale, which she outlined in her notebook but which she never wrote, would focus on an elderly, brain-dead woman who has been reduced to a tube, with food given at one end and expelled at the other. Although Mary Highsmith did not live so long as to fully realise the gerontological nightmare that is Naomi Barton Markham, she died only four years before her daughter. At 8.30 p.m. on 12 March 1991, Mary Highsmith 'faded away'.[24] She was ninety-five and had, noted Highsmith, 'outlived all her friends'.[25]

Throughout 1987, Highsmith continued to jot down her dreams, visions which can be interpreted as fantasies of death and renewal: being stabbed in the street; 'fathering' a son with Lynn Roth, whom she had married and settled down with in Italy; observing the deep, self-inflicted razor-blade slashes on the wrists of a friend; watching her doctor take hold of a metal drill and extract a sample of bone marrow from her left fibula.

Ever since the operation to remove the cancer from her lung, High-smith, despite the twice-yearly check-ups declaring her fit and healthy, had become increasingly conscious that she might not have that long to live. As a result, she was determined to try and squeeze in as much experience as possible into the time left and, perhaps, reveal a little more of herself to those close to her. 'Although she was not into verbal self-analysis, towards the end of her life, Pat did do a certain amount of reflection and talked a little bit about the past,' says Vivien De Bernardi. 'What amazes me, having known her in her last decade of her life, was how happy she seemed to have been in her twenties and thirties – or rather she had enjoyed periods of happiness, as you would never really call her happy. She suffered from depression all her life and my feeling is that she must always have been a difficult person. I don't think people become difficult when they are seventy.'[26]

In January and February, she worked on the last of the *Tales of Natural and Unnatural Catastrophes*. 'President Buck Jones Rallies and Waves the Flag' ends with the death of the leader of the free world and his first lady in a car accident, followed by total global apocalypse. 'The rotating Earth had become entirely too saturated by radioactive atmosphere,' Highsmith wrote, 'which its gravitational force held fast. There seemed less wind or winds than normal, the last curse of all.'[27]

In April, during a publicity tour for her Spanish publishers, Highsmith gave a speech in Lleida, Catalunya, where she talked about her career, outlining the reasons why she wrote, after which she placed herself open to the audience for questions. Did she read accounts of true-life crime? 'I must say I'm attracted to the sinister aspects of many of the stories,' she replied. How did her interest in painting influence her writing? Her favourite painters, she said, were Kokoschka, Munch, and Manet and, in her writing, she strove after visual realism in the description of certain scenes. 'I do try to make my scenes, or the interior of houses, visually clear to a reader,' she said. Should writers have political and social commitments outside their literary work? 'If a writer (or painter) starts preaching, consciously, in his work, it is no longer a piece of art,' Highsmith said. Yet, nevertheless, she had a range of political opinions and was willing to 'boycott, and to be boycotted in return'. Was the dedication in the European editions of *People who Knock on the Door*, which reads, 'To the courage of the Palestinian people and their leaders in the struggle to regain a part of their homeland. This book has nothing to do with their problem,'[28] aimed at the PLO? 'Yes, it is addressed to the leaders, singular or plural, of the Palestinian people, who must choose their own leaders,' she replied. 'If they choose the PLO, as 96 per cent seem to do at the time that I write this, then my dedication is to the PLO. It could be to another organisation next week – if the Palestinian people choose another leader.'[29]

The dedication, however, further alienated her American market and brought about the collapse of her relationship with yet another US publisher. When Otto Penzler saw the line he called Highsmith's agent and asked if he could replace the dedication or drop it altogether. 'I said this is really not going to go down very well in America – the publishing and the reviewing worlds are very heavily populated with Jews and that is just part of New York culture,' says Penzler. 'But I didn't hear back, it got closer and closer to publication date and finally I called the agent again and I said, "Listen we have to have an answer – yes or no," and she said, "OK just drop it," which I did. Years later Pat was being interviewed by a journalist and she told the writer that she wasn't speaking to me because I had dropped the dedication from one of her books. She thought I had done it without her agent's permission, something I would never have done even though I thought it was suicidal for her literary career. At the time, I didn't even know I had had a fall out with Pat as she was always so unfriendly and openly hostile.'[30]

Annoyed with what she thought of as her rather shabby treatment at the hands of Penzler Books, in April 1987 Highsmith signed a contract with the Atlantic Monthly Press to publish her books in America. The following month, her agents also negotiated a new UK deal for her, finally dropping Heinemann in favour of Bloomsbury, who offered an advance of £25,000 for *Tales of Natural and Unnatural Catastrophes*. 'I got annoyed with Heinemann because they seemed to be falling asleep in the office . . .' she later told *Publishers Weekly*. 'They took my work for granted. There was no particular effort to push a book.'[31]

During the summer of 1987, Highsmith also became increasingly agitated by the battle to secure the film rights to her Ripley novels. The previous year, the film producer Joseph Janni had approached her with the idea to adapt *The Boy who Followed Ripley*. She met Janni and the scriptwriter David Sherwin while in London in July 1986 to discuss the project but she was not overly impressed by Sherwin's eight-page treatment, which she described as 'so-so'.[32] But then in March 1987, the BBC sent word of a proposal to film all four Ripley novels, an eight-part series to be directed by Jonathan Powell. Highsmith was attracted by the idea, especially since it would net her $100,000 plus a possible 5 per cent fee from any sales. 'I have been in a quandary for six days over a choice of film versus BBC mini-series,' she wrote to Patricia Losey.[33] 'Well, I can't have the BBC and Janni both, it's either or,' she wrote, again to Patricia Losey, in May.[34] The matter, however, was decided for her when, in September, while in Deauville, she met Robert Hakim, one of the producers of *Plein Soleil*. 'Did I tell you that in Deauville I ran briefly into M. Hakim . . . who fairly attacked me verbally in the lobby,' she wrote to Marc Brandel, 'saying that he had the rights to The Talented Mr Ripley and not I . . . Diogenes can't as yet do anything to dispute this fellow.'[35]

Highsmith had been invited to Deauville – the elegant resort on the French Atlantic coast and home to the Festival of American Film – to collect the 'Prix Littéraire' in recognition of her literary contribution to the movie industry. By 1987, it was clear to film-makers that High-smith's work – for all its ambiguity of characterisation and subtlety of narrative – was highly cinematic and that year saw the release of Chabrol's *Le Cri du Hibou* starring Christophe Malavoy and Mathilda May. Although Joseph Janni's adaptation of *The Boy who Followed Ripley* was squashed by problems with finance, Highsmith's novels continue to be adapted into films.

While in Deauville, accompanied by Alain Oulman, Highsmith met the actors Douglas Fairbanks Jr and Bette Davis. Highsmith described her audience with Davis, which took place in the film star's hotel suite, in a letter to Christa Maerker. The actress was, she said, 'very thin, but nervous and active. She was standing up, black dress and little round black hat, saying hello, but with the air of the sooner you leave, the better. She tells you to leave, by zooming a hand forward and shaking your own hand, which you've of course extended.'[36]

Although she had been in Deauville for only two nights – 8 and 9 September – when she returned home she felt on edge and exhausted. She was due to travel to Mallorca on 14 September to write a 3,000-word travel piece for the *Sunday Times* but knew that if she did not cancel the trip she would be left feeling wretched. 'For the 6th day now I suffer from diarrhoea after the French trip,' she wrote in her diary on 15 September, 'and I did neither eat nor drink unwisely. I can't account for it. Really weakening.'[37] Travelling always upset her constitution and yet she was aware that the next couple of months she would have to fly to Toronto, New York and London to fulfil her various publishing obligations. 'Medical news: intestinal complaints all gone,' she noted on 10 October, a week before her flight to Canada. 'But it takes 5 days of calm to set me right instead of one or two in my youth. What a bore!'[38]

On 20 October she read from *Found in the Street* at the Harbour-front in Toronto – she was one of the star guests of the Toronto International Festival of Authors – and the day after she was driven to Niagara, where, after another reading from the novel, she donned a blue waterproof for a Maid of the Mist tour of the spectacular Falls, accompanied by the author William Trevor. 'I liked her books a great deal and thought that she was one of the best writers of her generation,' he says. 'When I met her in Toronto I had that feeling that this was indeed the woman who had written those novels. One night, after dinner, I was looking for her to go for a drink and came across her in the car park of the hotel, a dark and dingy place, where she was snooping around, probably to gather information or atmosphere for her writing. From the beginning I liked her a great deal – she was, like many novelists, a very private person and she did not push herself forward or promote herself at all. She liked to keep a little bit in the shadows.'[39] On her return to Toronto, she was delighted to receive an invitation to take tea with the Canadian author Margaret Atwood. Highsmith adored Canada – its cleanliness and orderliness no doubt reminded her of Switzerland – but when she flew to New York, she was, as usual, disgusted by what she regarded as the vulgarity and brashness of modern America. She flirted with the idea of Swiss citizenship – something she never actually received; she died a US citizen – as she knew that a return to live in the country of her birth was highly unlikely. 'The very thought of the news reports – now called 'bites', depresses me,' she said.[40]

In New York she met her new US editor Gary Fisketjon of the Atlantic Monthly Press. 'It's strange because for all the time that she spent in Europe, Pat always seemed to me basically an American character,' says Fisketjon. 'She was a Civil War buff and I always used to send her a lot of books on the subject. We hit it off straight away – we both liked to take a drink – and I remember we held a little party for her at a French joint downtown. She has always been very much in favour with a bunch of writers over here and so there was no problem in getting people to come along. I recall that she had this way of letting her hair fall down over her face, which I thought was interesting. She was extremely direct, you knew exactly who you were dealing with; she was an intriguing woman with very good instincts about people. She was also very sweet, because after my son was born, in January 1989, she always remembered his birthday and would send cards over. Although we didn't know each other well, I certainly liked her a hell of a lot. But I didn't know that she was ill; that was something she never talked to me about.'[41]

Considering that Highsmith had been forced to confront her own mortality only the year before, her decision to accept a commission from the *New York Times* to write a detailed piece about Green-Wood cemetery in Brooklyn was a brave one. Highsmith was far from sentimental about death, yet before she died she voiced her fears to Vivien De Bernardi. 'She said she was afraid of dying,' recalls Vivien. 'I asked why and she said, "I guess it's the unknown."'[42]

She made the trip on 26 October, with Phyllis Nagy, then a researcher at the *New York Times*, who picked her up from her hotel in Gramercy Park. 'It was a completely silent, miserable journey to the cemetery except for the three occasions when Pat spoke to me,' says Phyllis. 'First, she asked whether it was true I wanted to be a writer.

"Yes," I said, followed by silence. Then, "What do you think of Eugene O'Neill?" "Not much," I replied. "Good," she said and then there was more silence. Twenty minutes later, "What about Tennessee Williams?" I told her that I liked him and she replied, "Good" once again. We took our tour of the cemetery in silence and every once in a while Pat would use a stick that she was carrying to poke at certain features. Finally we were taken to the ovens used to burn the bodies and we were asked by the guide to place our hands inside. The ovens were still warm and you could hear the bones being grated in this huge blender. It was pretty gruesome. After the tour, which finished at about eleven in the morning, we stood outside and I remember she took out her flask and said in the American accent she never lost, "I don't know about you but I need a drink." After she had had a drink, I took a sip of the Scotch and I think I must have passed some kind of test because she invited me back to her hotel for lunch.'[43]

Highsmith's piece for the *New York Times* – written at the end of 1987 and which she entitled 'Green-Wood: Listening to the Talking Dead' – was never published, but it makes for powerful reading. While travelling in the car with Phyllis towards the cemetery, Highsmith noticed that a garbage truck, edging its way slowly beside them in the slow-moving Manhattan traffic, was overflowing with rotting food, a chlorophyllic leak spilling down its side. 'Its apparently inexhaustible drip of squashed vegetable matter or leftover orange juice reminds me of human mortality with its attendant ugliness, stench and inevitability,' Highsmith wrote.[44] She was keen to learn about the gravestones bearing the names of soldiers killed in the American Civil War and see the statue of twelve-year-old drummer boy Clarence McKenzie, a Brooklyn-born victim who had died at Annapolis. After walking around some of the cemetery's twenty miles of footpaths, Highsmith took an elevator down to the crematorium's ovens, or retorts. Each coffin, she learned, is pushed into one of the five ovens, a gas fire is then switched on and two hours later the contents are reduced to two pounds of ashes.

'I stuck my hand and forearm a little ways into the open retort, and was a bit surprised to find the interior quite warm, perhaps from a cremation of yesterday, perhaps even of that morning . . .' she wrote. 'The warmth of that retort, even though it may have come from a pilot flame, brought home death to me as none of the stone monuments above ground had.'[45]

From New York, Highsmith flew to London to promote *Tales of Natural and Unnatural Catastrophes*, arriving in Britain on 30 October. After only a weekend's rest, she ploughed herself into the punishing round of interviews, including a television appearance on BBC2's *Cover to Cover*, recorded on 3 November for transmission two days later. Her fellow guests included the actor Jack Klaff, the biographer and writer Victoria Glendinning and the actor Kenneth Williams, whom Highsmith described as 'screaming gay, v. pleasant, however'.[46] Williams, a fan of Highsmith's work, took the trouble to record the meeting in his diary: 'Patricia came right across the hospitality room to me with outstretched hand. "You *are* Kenneth Williams? I *so* wanted to meet you." I could hardly believe it . . . I was amazed that she'd even *heard* of me: she's always lived in France or Switzerland . . . Tried to be reasonable about [the] Highsmith [book] but made it clear I found it disappointing. She said, "Kenneth obviously thinks I've written a moral tract instead of the usual thriller," but I quickly interjected, "No, it is entertaining reading . . . just not what I expected." '[47] During the discussion, Highsmith outlined her intention, 'I meant . . . to talk about certain problems of our time'[48] – a point which was taken up by Glendinning, who said that the stories articulated the 'psychopathology of the whole world' and that they were 'politically important, as well as being funny, in the same way that something like *Animal Farm* is politically important because there is hardly anything that's going wrong which she does not treat in these stories.'[49]

In London, Highsmith also had to endure a grilling by the writer and journalist Duncan Fallowell, who quizzed her about her personal life. Had she ever fallen in love, he asked. 'Yes, I think so,' she replied after a long pause. When was the last time she was in love? 'Nine years ago. In Germany,' she said, a veiled reference to Tabea Blumenschein. How would she define love? 'It's . . . a kind of madness,' was her response.[50] In the interview – which wasn't published until after her death – Fallowell described the writer, who was wearing black trousers, white socks, black patent-leather loafers and a purple silk cravat, as 'in-turning, as if hugging an awful secret; and when a low-key humour plays about her, which it quite often does, it lends her personality a creepy fascination which may be unjustified and is perhaps simply a combination of painful vulnerability and iron will'.[51] Her face was free of make-up, her thick lips quite sensual, adding that her 'soft brown eyes' were 'wary'. Obviously Highsmith loathed the experience. 'Her manner has returned to its slow, taciturn, lizard-like self, giving only enough to dispatch the question and no more,' wrote Fallowell. 'I have been told that she doesn't like to talk about her writing. And she likes to talk about her personal life even less. There is a sense of cramp about her personality, a lack of spiritual generosity, a parsimoniousness, as though every little thing must be hoarded up, reserved, meted out only in work.'[52]

She also took the opportunity to see her friends Jonathan Kent; Roger Clarke; Patricia Losey; Phyllis Nagy, who coincidentally happened to be in Britain; her new editor at Bloomsbury, Liz Calder; and the literary agent Tanja Howarth, who represented Diogenes Verlag in the UK. 'Before I met her I was terrified because I assumed that she must have a very dark side,' says Tanja. 'But as I got to know her I found that she was a caring and warm-hearted person. She would write to my son, always wanting to know how he was and encouraging him professionally, and because she did not really have a family, I hoped that she would regard my son Peter and me as "surrogate relations". Every Friday I would ring her – knowing that at that point she had done her work and would have drunk some whisky – and after years of being her London link, we became friends. What I remember most about her was her *Ausstrahlung*, her physical presence, which was both strong and strange; it was incredibly powerful. If she was to walk into a room, you would never forget her. I think she was a genius who has yet to be fully appreciated.'[53] 'She was one of the most sensitive, vulnerable, and insecure people I've ever met,' says Phyllis. 'After meeting her in London, she wrote to me in New York saying, "I trust you weren't in the King's Cross tube fire." And that was it – she wrote to me every week from then on.'[54] Highsmith's generosity was 'unstinting,' says Phyllis.[55] 'Pat strove to help me in any way she could when I moved to London.' Highsmith also took great pride in Nagy's progress as a writer, 'in the last two years of her life, she commented on how much pleasure she had taken in watching me become a playwright . . . sending me newspaper cuttings from foreign papers about me and other young writers she'd felt connected to or proud of'.[56]

Back in Switzerland, Highsmith wrote an essay on Jack the Ripper for Alan Hollinghurst at the *Times Literary Supplement* and the piece on Green-Wood Cemetery. Death obviously preyed on her mind – just before the close of the year she dreamt that an unidentified corpse was being passed around between a group of neighbours who were using the body to fertilise their gardens – and in order to prepare her estate, she invited Kingsley over to Aurigeno for a six-day stay to sort through some of her papers.

'There I go in a few years, I thought,' she wrote in her feature on Green-Wood cemetery, referring to the ovens in which the bodies are burned, 'as cremation is my preferred way, ashes to be scattered any old where that is permitted.'[57]

34

A face accustomed to its ghosts

1988

'Ripley touches madness,' Highsmith scribbled in her notebook on 1 January 1988.[1] She had been thinking about writing a fifth Ripley novel for some time; at the end of 1986 she had noted down a scenario featuring art dealers or collectors and in April 1987 she had announced to her audience in Lleida that she was sure she would write another book about the amoral, but charming, killer. Her new idea, outlined in her cahier in January 1988, focused on Ripley's breakdown, a mental collapse brought about by the stress of maintaining two separate identities – his comfortable, gentlemanly home life, painting water-colours and playing the harpsichord, and his enjoyment of the darker aspects of his existence such as forgery and murder. Yet the day after sketching these bare details in her notebook, she wrote to Marc Brandel and told him she didn't think she was quite up to writing another book. 'I am not enough collected as yet, unfortunately,' she said. 'Very uncomfortable feeling.'[2]

She let the Ripley idea sit at the back of her mind for a couple of months, taking up her notebook again in March to explore the theme of the balance between man's aspirations towards beauty and nobleness and the concomitant desire to take pleasure in violence and degrada-tion. The delicate equation is one of the themes she would explore in the final version of the new Ripley novel, *Ripley Under Water*, published in 1991 in the UK and a year later in America. The book starts, five years after the Murchison affair detailed in *Ripley Under Ground*, with the entry into Tom's life of a strange American couple, David and Janice Pritchard, whom he initially nicknames the 'Odd pair'.[3] The Pritchards proceed to shadow Tom – they take photographs of the house and, as

Ripley correctly surmises, telephone him, pretending to be Dickie Greenleaf. After questioning Janice, Ripley discovers that David takes pleasure in torturing those around him and that he is his latest victim. Pritchard follows Ripley, his wife, Heloise, and her friend, Noelle, to Tangier, where he continues to haunt them. While the two men are enjoying a cup of refreshing mint tea at the cliff-top café, La Haffa, Tom roughs Pritchard up a little, kicking him in the crotch and leaving him prostrate on the ground. Ripley manages to free himself from Pritchard and he flies back to France without his stalker's knowledge. He travels on to London where he discovers the reason why Pritchard knows so much about him: information received from Cynthia Gradnor, the one-time girlfriend of Bernard Tufts, a woman who is certain that Tom killed Murchison and that he was responsible for Bernard's suicide. On returning to 'Belle Ombre', Tom is sickened to learn that Pritchard has been dredging the local rivers and canals in search, he presumes, of Murchison's corpse. Fearing exposure of his past crimes, Ripley invites journalist Ed Banbury – one of the benefactors of the Derwatt art fraud – over to his house to help, but then, early one morning, he opens the front door to see a bundle of tarpaulin containing Murchison's headless skeleton lying outside. In revenge, Ripley and Ed deposit the bones in the Pritchards' pond, but, after hearing a noise, the couple come out of their house into the dark garden. David tries to reach into the pond to retrieve the mysterious object floating before him, but he falls in and, as Janice tries to help him out, she too slips into the murky water, where they both drown. Their bodies are found the next day, along with an unidentified skeleton. Ripley is questioned by the police, but once again, he escapes punishment.

The novel has its faults – Julian Symons, usually a fan, thought that the book ended with a 'distinctly undramatic climax' and that the writing was occasionally 'bad and clumsy'[4] – yet the work can be read as an exploration of the aesthetics of taste and an analysis of the relationship between the noble pursuits of the mind and spirit and the baser animalistic desires of the flesh. At first sight, it appears that the dualistic dynamic is split, quite neatly, between the characters of Tom Ripley and David Pritchard. Ripley, sophisticated, wealthy, and cultured, lives within the exquisite surroundings of 'Belle Ombre', with its harpsichord, rich art collection, antique furniture and well-stocked wine cellar, its reassuring aromas of freshly brewed coffee, rose petals and *cirage de lavande*. Pritchard, the son of a lumber merchant from Washington state, meanwhile, leads a somewhat shabbier existence. When Tom pays a visit to his rented house he looks down on the ugly wooden fireplace, painted white with 'an unfortunate dubonnet trim' and the 'false rusticity' of their furniture.[5] He is similarly appalled by the dining-room table and chairs – which he describes as 'horrid made-yesterday antique'[6] – and the cheap floral paintings on the walls, the kind one sees in hotel bedrooms. David is literally not one of us, a judgement with which the reader is forced to concur as we align ourselves with Ripley's point of view.

Highsmith forces us to identify with Ripley by using her favoured technique of imprisoning the reader within his narrative perspective and by portraying the Pritchards as even more psychopathic than Tom. Not only are David and Janice 'phoney',[7] 'Weirdos'[8] and *'Mentally sick'*,[9] but the couple are obviously involved in some strange sado-masochistic relationship. While researching the novel, Highsmith turned to the works of Menninger and Fromm for psychological insights into sado-masochism and she asked her friends for any titbits about the phenomenon. Originally, Highsmith planned to bring the S/M dynamic to the fore, imagining a scenario in which David and Janice ask Ripley to kill someone so they can watch and another possible plotline which involved them tormenting one another. As she started to write the book at the end of May 1989, however, she decided to tone this down, suggesting the true nature of the relationship through details such as Janice's bruising and the rumoured discovery of a whip and chain after the police search the Pritchards' house.

Despite this narrative trickery – the subtle conjuring by which Highsmith seduces the reader into believing Ripley's point of view is perfectly normal and respectable – Tom's perspective is seriously warped. Originally, Highsmith wanted to explore Ripley's descent into madness. Perhaps, she mused, walking around an empty house for sale could precipitate a crisis of identity? Or maybe the breakdown could be brought about by an honest reassessment of his past behaviour? 'He escapes into another person,' she wrote in her notebook. 'A form of schizophrenia.'[10] Although Highsmith decided against exploring this idea in detail, it's clear from a close reading of the book that Ripley, for all his surface charms, is not far from insanity. He often feels paranoid and loses himself in dream-like states – 'Sometimes his imagination was as clear as a remembered experience'[11] – and at one point he refers to himself in the third person, a symptom suggesting a degree of deper-sonalisation. But what, Highsmith asks, prevents him from slipping over the edge? He had a 'screen' that separated reality from memory – 'it was self-preservation'.[12] Ripley may like to think that he is better than Pritchard, but both men are reificators, judging people by their clothes, accessories and the objects which surround them. Tom cannot bear David's receding hair-line, his supermarket furniture, his white basket-weave shoes and his watch, with its gold stretchable strap. Ripley preferred his Patek Philippe watch with its brown leather strap. In turn, Pritchard is drawn towards Ripley, and feels compelled to torture him not because of any personal motive – the two men are, after all, strangers – but because he spotted Tom at an airport wearing an expensive leather and fur coat, an object which incited envy in him. Pritchard's mission, he declares to Ripley, is 'The pleasure of seeing a snob crook like yourself go belly up.'[13]

In Pritchard, Ripley sees a variation on his own theme, a fragment of his personality taken to the extreme and that is one of the reasons why he wants to 'disembarrass'[14] himself of him. In truth, Ripley is just as much a sadist as Pritchard. He may not beat up his charming wife, but he still has the capacity to relish the infliction of pain – only when he thinks it is well-deserved, of course. 'Never kick a man when he's down,' Tom thought, and gave Pritchard another kick, hard, in the midriff.'[15] And the sight of the couple falling to their deaths in the pond elicits a joyous response, a feeling of relief and merriment. He may well laugh – after all, Ripley had long harboured an irrational fear of deep water. His parents had drowned in the sea off Boston and, ever since he was a small boy, the sight of water had made Tom feel sick. In *The Boy who Followed Ripley*, he looks at a postcard of a cruise ship sailing across a fjord, an image which is enough to unsettle him, as he 'often thought that somehow his end might be watery'.[16] Yet, of course, Tom remains safely on *terra firma*. The last time we see Ripley – for this was Highsmith's final novel in the series – he is standing on a bridge in Moret holding the one piece of incriminatory evidence, Murchison's ring, which he knows links him to his past murders. A policeman approaches him. Has he been caught? No, he is simply asked to move his white station-wagon. He swings his arm back and hurls the ring into the river. Now that his past is safely under water, the man with the most fluid identity in modern literature is free once more.

In January 1988, after years of commercial and critical neglect in America, Highsmith finally received the kind of attention she deserved when Terrence Rafferty wrote a serious analysis of her work in *The New Yorker* to coincide with the US publication of *Found in the Street*. 'These novels fill our heads with unsavory images, clammy bad dreams, unflattering reflections, confirmation of our direst fears, the annihilation of our comforts,' wrote Rafferty. 'And then – final humiliation –

we discover that we've accepted, and felt weirdly stimulated by, this stripping of our identity, these awful desert hallucinations.'[17] For all of Highsmith's previous protestations of not caring about her reception in the States, she could not contain her joy at what she finally saw as an open-armed acceptance by the American literary community. 'Did you happen to see the very good critique of my work in 4th Jan New Yorker?' Highsmith wrote to Kingsley. 'You can be sure my editors (and I) are quite happy with this.'[18] But while a literary analysis such as Rafferty's did great things for her reputation, it failed to bump up her sales: *Found in the Street* sold 40,000 copies in Germany, compared to a paltry 4,000 in the US.[19] 'In Germany, she has been famous for so long, she is stopped in the street in Munich for autographs,' Daniel Keel told the journalist Joan Dupont in 1988. 'And when she goes to Spain, the Prime Minister invites her to dine. But in the U.S., her sales have been the worst in the world.'[20]

Joan Dupont arrived in Aurigeno on 15 March and immediately noticed how Highsmith looked less haunted – but more cautious – than she did when she last interviewed her eleven years before. Dressed in jeans, open-necked shirt, lavender bandana, and white sneakers, the author's face, observed Dupont, appeared 'accustomed to its ghosts, more assured, but also more wary'.[21] Dupont, in an attempt to address the question of Highsmith's relative unpopularity in America, conjec-tured that readers in the United States were left cold by the writer's amoral investigations into perverse behaviour and quoted Gary Fisketjon as saying that, although she was on the verge of a revival, 'She's had to wait 35 years for acceptance here.'[22] Yet Dupont chose not to examine one of the main factors which skewed her reception in America – her controversial attitude towards the Middle East. 'I do think her attitudes pro PLO did her in with a lot of Americans, including Gary Fisketjon who worried about it,' says Joan. 'She sounded off about it a lot, hated the Israelis, and maybe some Jews, thought Begin was the most evil man in the world. I chose not to repeat the ranting because it would have done her no good.'[23]

Highsmith felt passionate about the complex issues surrounding the Arab-Israeli conflict and genuinely traumatised by the uprising in the Gaza Strip and West Bank which broke out in December 1987 and which continued to dominate the news in 1988. 'I spent a lot of time composing letters I think may be useful to peace and stopping the deaths,' she wrote in her diary on 28 February, '72 Palestinians so far dead, no Jews.'[24] She felt motivated by a genuine sense of injustice and, as a member of Amnesty International, she felt compelled to 'speak up and speak out'. She viewed the conflict as a David and Goliath battle, with her sympathies firmly on the side of the underdog. Yet the methods she chose to articulate her particular point of view were far from subtle. For instance, in February 1989, while on a publicity trip to Milan, she insisted on wearing her, ' "Palestine PLO check" sweater' for the photo-shoots. 'I was able in perhaps 4 out of 12 interviews, to express genuine USA opinion on Israeli atrocities in Gaza & West Bank,' she wrote in her notebook,[25] while the dedication in *Ripley Under Water* reads, 'To the dead and the dying among the Intefada and the Kurds, to those who fight oppression in whatever land, and stand up not only to be counted but to be shot.'[26] In addition she sent money to the Jewish Committee on the Middle East, an organisation which represented American Jews who supported Palestinian self-determination.

In an unpublished essay Highsmith wrote about the Middle East conflict in August 1992, she outlined the historical background that had formulated her position. When Israel was created – in May 1948, while Highsmith was at Yaddo, writing *Strangers on the Train* – following the withdrawal of the British, she remembers feeling optimistic about its future. 'How happy and cheerful we all were then, gentiles and Jews alike!' she wrote. 'A new state had been born, and was therefore to be welcomed into the community of democracies.'[27] Yet soon after the state was formed – initially an area comprising of Jewish and Arab land, together with an internationally administered zone around Jerusalem – it was invaded by Arab forces, a move which in turn prompted Israeli troops to seize and gain control of three-quarters of Palestine. Highsmith was appalled at what she saw as Israeli brutality and insensitivity, remembering how some of her Palestinian friends were forced to flee their homeland. Since then, of course, the area has been the site of a series of complex, and increasingly violent, power struggles, yet from the beginning Highsmith aligned herself with other writers such as Gore Vidal, Alexander Cockburn, Noam Chomsky and Edward W. Said, who believed in Palestinian self-determination. In December 1994, Highsmith nominated a collection of Said's essays and talks, *The Politics of Dispossession: The Struggle for Palestinian Self-Determination 1969–1994*, as her book of the year for the *Times Literary Supplement*, commenting that she thought him 'both famous and ignored. His eloquence on the real issues makes America's silence seem all the louder.'[28] Highsmith agreed with Said's opinion that the alliance between Zionism and the United States had resulted in the continued displacement of Palestinians. As a result, she felt forced to take a stand, no matter how small. After the election of Menachem

Begin as Prime Minister in 1977, Highsmith would not allow her books
to be published in Israel. 'I'm sure the world couldn't care less, but it
shows that not every American refuses to see what's happening,' she
said.[29] In interviews she told journalists that she loathed Ariel Sharon
and the Likud party, and that she found America's support of the Israeli
regime to be despicable.

'Americans and the world know that America gives so lavishly to
Israel,' she wrote, 'because the United States wanted Israel as a strong
military bulwark against Soviet Russia during the Cold War. Now that
the Cold War is over, America has cut none of its aid . . . What is an
American tax-payer to make of the fact that the USA gives thirteen
million dollars a day, still, to Israel without any request for repayment?
. . . I blame my own country for the majority of injustices now being
inflicted by the Israelis in what they consider Greater Israel . . . I blame
[the] American government for the bad press permitted about the Arabs
in the United States.'[30]

Although the piece is an attempt by Highsmith to argue rationally
about the Middle East conflict, in conversation her views were far from
logical and coherent. 'I agreed with her that the Palestinians should
have a state of their own, but felt that her disparagement of Israel was
sometimes unduly harsh,' says Kingsley.[31] Friends remember how
Highsmith would recommend certain books on the subject. One of
these was Douglas Reed's *The Controversy of Zion*, which she first read
in 1988. The book, published in 1978, is the work of a former London
Times correspondent in central Europe, who died in South Africa in
1976 at the age of eighty-two. After leaving full-time employment in
1938 he turned to writing books, including a number of non-fiction
bestsellers such as *Insanity Fair* and *Disgrace Abounding*. Yet there was
one issue he wanted to address – the subject of Zionist nationalism –
which he suspected would never be properly analysed in the British or
American press, a media which, for the most part, censored any
unfavourable comment. In his 1951 book, *Far and Wide*, Reed questioned the number of Jews who had perished in the Holocaust, believing
the generally accepted figure of six million to be too high, but after its
publication he was effectively silenced by the mainstream publishing
industry and the manuscript of *The Controversy of Zion* was discovered sitting on the top of his wardrobe after his death. In it, Reed
attempted to trace the links between fundamentalist Zionism and the
modern political landscape, illustrating how the Jewish massacre at the
Arab village of Deir Yasin on 9 April 1948 was motivated by a literal
reading of ' "the Law" laid down in Deuteronomy . . . This was the

most significant day in the history of Zionism.'[32] Reed believed that a fundamentalist interpretation of the ancient texts of the Talmud and the Torah, a movement he described as 'Talmudic chauvinism', would result in catastrophe. 'In our time, I judge, a barbaric superstition born in antiquity and nurtured through the ages by a semi-secret priesthood, has returned to plague us in the form of a political movement supported by great wealth in all capitals of the world.'[33]

Highsmith wrote to Gore Vidal about Reed's book in December 1989, telling him how she had recently bought three copies to send to friends. The Israelis did not ever want peace because, she believed, they were yearning for the next Holocaust and that they 'love to be hated'.[34] Yet, in her essay on the Middle East, she said that she still harboured a hope for peace. Although some of her views on the subject were, quite frankly, objectionable, ultimately all Highsmith was striving for was a more honest and balanced analysis of the situation. It was the responsibility of each individual, she said, to make his or her mind up on such a subject, a process which involved wrestling with a complex matrix of historical and cultural questions. 'The important thing is to express one's view, not to be a sheep, not to feel like a sheep,' she had once said, 'and not to allow one's government (presumably elected) to believe that the people it is governing are a herd of sheep.'[35]

On 18 June 1988, Highsmith was given another opportunity to air her views – this time on murder – when she was invited to appear on Channel 4's *After Dark*, a live and informal late-night show starting at 11.30 p.m. and which often stretched into the early hours. The subject under discussion was how to survive a murder, and the guests, in addition to Highsmith, included Lord Longford, the author and penal reformer; Georgina Lawton, the daughter of Ruth Ellis; June Patient, co-founder of Parents of Murdered Children, whose daughter was killed in 1976; David Howden, whose daughter was murdered in 1986; James Nelson, a minister in the Church of Scotland who had served nine years of a life sentence for the murder of his mother in 1969; Peter Whent, a detective superintendent with Essex police; and Sarah Boyle, a social worker and wife of the reformed criminal Jimmy Boyle. The debate was chaired by Professor Anthony Clare.

Dressed in a blue suit and a red blouse, her neck covered by a cravat, Highsmith took special interest in the case of David Howden's daughter who was discovered strangled in the family home in January 1986. Sitting next to Howden, Highsmith questioned the bereaved father in a near-clinical fashion. What kind of man was the murderer? Had he been watching the daughter? Was robbery part of the motive? Had she been raped? When Howden told of how he and a friend had had to go and clean up the room in which his daughter had been murdered, Highsmith was quick to respond. Just exactly what kind of stains had been left on the carpet? Throughout the programme, it's obvious Highsmith found herself more comfortable in the role of the interviewer than interviewee. When asked direct questions, she tended either not to answer or she addressed the issue in such an oblique way as to shroud the essence of her thoughts in an impenetrable mist of vagueness. Yet Professor Clare did his best to pin her down. Had she met any real murderers? 'You can meet them in Texas or Marseille . . . oh yes,' she said nonchalantly. What was sin? 'Sin is what somebody says it is,' she said. Could she imagine the horror of murder? 'The evil, yes . . .' What did evil mean to her? 'Abstractly – something bad or anti-social or wrong or also unhealthy.' How would she describe an evil person? If they were 'malicious or small-minded or back-biting,' she replied. What about murderers? 'Frankly, I'd call them sick if they were murderers, mentally sick.' Central to the debate was the question of absolution – was it possible to forgive a murderer? Highsmith's atheistic attitude stood in stark contrast to the strong Christianity of the Reverend James Nelson, who took the attitude that, ultimately, only God could forgive. 'I'm not in such good touch with God as you,' she said spikily. 'When you say to me, "It's only God [who can forgive]," how do I know God is going to even tell me?'[36]

Highsmith had no faith in the after-life, loathed organised religion, and thought life was fundamentally meaningless. Throughout the year she did everything she could to put her affairs in order in the event of her death. In May, she sent a copy of her will, dated 19 April, to Kingsley, in which she bequeathed her clothes, furniture, household items, personal effects, and insurance policies to her old friend, whom she also appointed literary executor. She empowered Kingsley to sell her papers to the University of Texas and for the profits of such a sale to go directly to Yaddo, to which she also left the bulk of her property. In June, while in London for *After Dark*, Highsmith once again visited John Batten, who carried out a number of tests, including another lung X-ray and an ECG. Although the results showed that she was free of lung cancer, Highsmith obviously felt she should prepare herself for the worst as, later in the year, she joined EXIT, stipulating that if she developed a hopelessly terminal illness she should not be kept alive by drugs. She did not want to be resuscitated in the event of a heart attack, while if she entered a senile state she demanded that she be given, at most, nutritional fluid. 'If and when my condition is diagnosed as hopeless, I am to be given any amount of analgesics, although their effect could be lethal.'[37]

In whatever time she had left, Highsmith was determined to squeeze every last drop of experience out of life and in July, she accepted an invitation from Buffie Johnson to visit her in Tangier. The trip would give her a good opportunity to catch up with her old friend but it was not entirely driven by the pursuit of pleasure – she travelled there with a commission from the *Sunday Times* and she would also use the location in *Ripley Under Water*. She arrived in the north Moroccan port overlooking the Strait of Gibraltar on 17 August and took a taxi from the airport to Buffie's flat, 15 Immeuble Itesa – the apartment situated below that of Paul Bowles, which had once belonged to his wife Jane. Buffie, however, was not at home and so Pat announced herself to Bowles, who although she found him eating in bed from a tray, made her feel welcome. 'By the time I got home she was ensconced in Paul's apartment drinking his Scotch,' says Buffie.[38] Highsmith delighted in the exoticism of Tangier, noting that the view of the old town from her window looked like a Braque or Klee composition; enjoyed drinks at the famous 1930s Hotel El Minzah, whose guests had included Cecil Beaton and which is featured in *Ripley Under Water*; and took a tour around the house of Woolworth's heiress Barbara Hutton, who, it was rumoured, outbid General Franco for the palace. Yet the visit was not wholly successful, as Pat and Buffie, once close friends, felt distinctly uncomfortable with one another. 'Because the guest room was in fact my studio, for the next week I had to sacrifice my work to entertain Pat . . .' says Buffie, who was in the final stages of proofing her book, *Lady of the Beasts: Ancient Images of the Goddess and her Sacred Animals*. 'She had by then the look of someone no longer enjoying life.'[39] For her part, Highsmith found Buffie to be strangely distant and on her return to Switzerland at the end of the month, she wrote a letter to Christa Maerker telling her that the experience had left her feeling disconnected. 'I felt like someone transported me to the moon,' she said.[40] After sending off her thirteen-page piece to the *Sunday Times*, she heard back that it had been rejected, but she did manage to place a 500-word feature on Paul Bowles with *Le Monde*.

After a couple of weeks at home, Highsmith was off on her travels again, this time to Hamburg where she was due to read from *Plotting and Writing Suspense Fiction* and *Little Tales of Misogyny* – she in English, the actress Angela Winkler in German – at the Festival der Frauen. Accompanying Highsmith to the festival was her Ticino friend,

Gudrun Mueller, who met Pat at the airport and travelled with her by taxi to the Intercontinental Hotel. 'At the hotel there was a bottle of champagne waiting for her in the suite, but she didn't drink it,' says Gudrun, a painter. 'Instead, she took from her handbag a bottle of whisky, a cheap one, fetched a glass from the bathroom and poured herself a large measure. She glugged down a few glasses, each time pacing around the room. I said to her that she must rest and not drink too much. Eventually she forced herself to go down to the lobby of the hotel, where lots of photographers and newspaper people were waiting for her. Journalists asked her questions, and although she'd had a lot to drink, she answered in a clear and professional manner. She was not at all drunk.'[41]

Gudrun remembers Pat with a mixture of affection, frustration, wonder and puzzlement. During their fifteen-year friendship, Gudrun only caught an occasional glimpse of the essence of Highsmith's personality. 'It was so difficult to talk to her. Often if I asked her questions she would get angry and tell me that I was just like one of the journalists who bothered her. I said, "I'm not a journalist, I'm your *friend*." I would cry out, "who are you?" but she would never answer. She never showed her feelings and I never knew what she thought of me. If someone reached out to touch or greet her she would always take one or two steps back. Yet her face was full of life and everything she thought or felt you could see in her eyes.'[42]

35

Art is not always healthy and why should it be?

1988–1992

On 13 December 1988 – after a ten-day trip to America – Highsmith moved into her new house in Tegna. Although Semyon, her Siamese, howled non-stop for ten days and nights, Charlotte, her ginger barn cat, and Pat settled in quite comfortably. From the front, 'Casa Highsmith' looked quite forbidding – the windows were nothing but minimal slashes in the anonymous grey cladding – but at the back French doors opened on to the large garden overlooking the valley. The view of the mountains was sublime, although Pat would joke how the Alpine peaks were mere youngsters in comparison to the grand old men of the American Rockies.

The house was a U-shaped structure, with its two wings arranged around a central courtyard. Highsmith's bedroom and bathroom were situated at one end, the guest bedroom and bathroom in the other wing, the areas separated by a large living room. It was a single-storey building, apart from a terrace above the sitting room, and a cellar below, an underground nuclear shelter, a prerequisite for all newly built houses in Switzerland. 'As I recall, Pat's shelter was for eight to ten people subsidized by the community of Tegna,' says Vivien De Bernardi. 'I always thought God help both Pat and anyone that might be required to live in that confined space with her.'[1]

At first glance, visitors compared the structure to a 'bunker',[2] a 'municipal bath'[3] and a 'fortress',[4] but the light and spacious interior of the house, with its terracotta-tiled floor, its eclectic mix of new and old furniture and the occasional decorative touch, often surprised. 'At one end of the sitting-room sits a sculpture of a hand holding a bright blue eyeball through which a length of wire has been placed, but her own paintings are unexpectedly cheery,' observed Craig Brown.[5] Janet Watts, during an interview with the writer in 1990, described her bedroom: 'A single bed is in one corner. Her imposing French roll-top desk bears a small Olympia typewriter, covered with a printed handkerchief. Above it is a tiny painting of a monk gazing at a crucifix and a skull.'[6] Mavis Guinard, who interviewed the writer for the *International Herald Tribune*, observed that the open-plan rooms were 'spacious and cool',[7] while its patio was nothing but a 'patch of parched grass' dotted with the occasional marigold. 'The long dining table is stacked with papers and books,' she said. 'At the far end, there's barely space for a bamboo place mat for one, an open pack of Gauloise cigarettes beside the plate.'[8]

During the six years she lived in Tegna, Highsmith enjoyed close friendships with a number of her neighbours. Irma Andina, who lives in a small house near the village's railway station, remembers Highsmith as a modest, kind woman, but someone who felt distinctly ill at ease with the world. 'To me she wasn't a genius, or a writer; to me she was a simple person, someone who was not at all stuck up,' she says. 'I used to weed her garden for her and one day she turned up with a huge bucket of roses for me. The only thing I didn't like about her was the fact that when you went to greet her, she never held your hand. She didn't know how to react; she didn't like to breathe other people's air.'[9] Ingeborg Lüscher first remembers seeing Highsmith shopping in the village. Although she wanted to approach her and introduce herself, Ingeborg held back, which in retrospect was a fortunate move as she knew Highsmith would have hated such an invasion. Over time, the neighbours became good friends. 'She was a fascinating writer, but for a long time we had extremely boring conversations,' says Ingeborg, an artist. 'She spoke to me about the cost of bills and health insurance, very practical things. But then, we started to speak about other things, such as Gertrude Stein and Oscar Wilde. It was never possible to analyse a subject in depth, but she had this ability of saying something that another person would take an hour to express. So, after five sentences the whole discussion was over and then we started speaking about bills or whatever again. She had a very delicate personality and I felt like I wanted to help her. But she was also very witty. She made the most curious jokes, she imitated people – at times she could be quite theatrical and she was a performer. She loved to make me laugh.'[10]

Soon after moving into the house, Highsmith's long, tortuous relationship with Ellen Hill – who Ingeborg Lüscher remembers as a woman 'not only full of poison for Pat, but full of poison for the whole world'[11] – finally came to an end. Highsmith was, as she told Kingsley in a letter on 6 February, 'sick of her scolding and all round domineering'.[12] 'When the Tegna house was finished, Pat didn't allow Ellen to enter,' says Peter Huber, 'but one day Ellen arrived and dashed in like a rugby player. She walked around and had a look, but Pat told her to leave. She did not want anything to do with her.'[13] Vivien De Bernardi recalls Highsmith telling her that her friendship with Ellen was over. 'Pat told me she was angry with her because Ellen had insulted her, which I can believe because Ellen insulted me too,' she says. 'She continually told her she was stupid, and one day Pat had had enough.'[14]

Unsurprisingly, Highsmith did not invite Ellen to a drinks party at the Tegna house, which she hosted for twenty-five people on 25 February. Immediately before the housewarming, Highsmith turned to Vivien De Bernardi for help as it was obvious she did not have a clue how to organise or plan the event. 'She was inept when it came to basic, simple things,' says Vivien. 'She was a really good writer and that was it – period.'[15] During a shopping trip at a local supermarket, Vivien witnessed her friend panic and fall apart. 'Pat was overwhelmed by sensory stimulation – there were too many people and too much noise and she just could not handle the supermarket,' she says. 'She continually jumped, afraid that someone might recognise or touch her. She could not make the simplest of decisions – which type of bread did she want, or what kind of salami? I tried to do the shopping as quickly as possible, but at the check-out she started to panic. She took out her wallet, knocked off her glasses, dropped the money on the floor, stuff was going all over the place.'[16] The next day, Vivien arrived at the party, but as she walked into the hallway she was met by a floor full of wet newspaper – it was raining outside – and a yellow bucket full of long-stem red roses. 'Daniel [Keel] had sent her something like fifty red roses, but she had stuck them in this plastic bucket. It was hysterical. Earlier in the day, one of my colleagues who had helped her move, rang Pat and asked about her favourite colours. She replied that she liked orange and yellow and so he went out and bought this most gorgeous bouquet of flowers in those colours. He gave her the flowers, arranged very artistically with lots of greenery, but the next thing I knew she started to yank out all the green. "Pat, it's supposed to be like that," I said. She just didn't have a clue. She'd stick newspapers on her floor and put the roses in a plastic bucket and whip out all the greenery from a 200 franc bouquet of flowers.'[17]

The party was a success, but after an hour and a half Vivien decided it was probably best if she and her husband left, as she knew of Pat's limited endurance when it came to socialising in groups. She looked around for her friend, but she was nowhere to be seen. Finally, after walking through the length of the house, she found Pat locked in the bathroom. 'She just couldn't stand it – there were too many people, too much talking, she did not know what to say, how to act, what to do. It was just overwhelming for her.'[18]

During the spring, Highsmith wrote a number of essays and features: 'Scene of the Crime', about her inspiration for Ripley, for *Granta*; 'Pleasures of the Wandering Mind', for *Die Welt*; a piece about Cézanne for a Swiss publication and a new preface for *The Price of Salt*, for Naiad Press. At the end of May she started to write *Ripley Under Water* – the first draft would take her a year to complete – and she devoted time to overseeing the dramatisation of twelve of her short stories for television, a French-English venture produced by Vamp in Paris and Crossbow and HTV in Britain. In June, she travelled to London and Cardiff, where she met the actor Anthony Perkins who had been employed to introduce the unsettling tales, stories which included 'Under a Dark Angel's Eye', starring Ian Richardson and Anna Massey; 'Sauce for the Goose', with Ian McShane and Gwen Taylor; 'The Birds Poised to Fly', with Paul Rhys; Jane Lapotaire in 'A Curious Suicide'; and Edward Fox, Michael Horden and Bill Nighy in 'The Cat Brought It In', a reworking of 'Something the Cat Dragged in'. The series was broadcast as *Les Cadavres Exquis de Patricia Highsmith* in France, starting in April 1990, and *Mistress of Suspense* in the UK, in May 1990 and at intervals throughout 1992.

Although travel disturbed her health – when she returned from Britain she felt sick and was plagued by digestive problems – after finishing another batch of essays and book reviews, in September she flew to America for fifteen days, during which time she visited her cousin Dan and his wife Florine in Texas. 'Now I should be working on a novel, but am not,' she wrote to Christa Maerker, referring to the break in her writing of *Ripley Under Water*.[19] On returning from the States, she considered writing a short story entitled 'The Pits', about a town in Nevada which houses America's misfits and losers, the ill, the mad and the disabled. Tourists are so intrigued by the modern-day freak show that they take regular helicopter rides over the area to look at the ever-increasing number of unfortunates, but eventually the city swells to such an extent that it spills out into the whole of America. The USA, in Highsmith's apocalyptic imagination, had been transformed into one large, disease-ridden pit. Just as she had collected newspaper and magazine stories for *Tales of Natural and Unnatural Catastrophes*, so she continued to cut out snippets of news about political cover-ups, nuclear accidents and environmental disasters, gathering all the pieces of paper into a folder entitled 'The Pits'. Another story which might have formed part of the collection was entitled, 'Adventures of an Unwanted Fertilized Egg', which she thought of in 1992. A fertilised egg in an artificial insemination laboratory is washed down the sink or toilet, but it survives in the sewer, feeding on the nutrients from human excrement, sick and blood, eventually growing limbs and body parts. Although the authorities try to shoot it, bullets make no discernible difference and the monster stalks the sewers, emerging to wreak havoc on towns and cities.

Both stories, although only in note form, can be seen as powerful metaphors for the threat posed by those that have been marginalised and repressed by modern America. It's also tempting to see them as representative of Highsmith's anger against her own country, symbolic of the rage she felt towards an America whose foreign policy she abhorred and whose publishing industry had all but ignored and exiled her. 'My publishers, Calmann-Lévy in France, and Bloomsbury and Heinemann [in London], they would stick with me through thick and thin,' she told the writer Neil Gordon while on a publicity tour in 1992. 'Here in America they say get out, we're not interested in the story, we don't care about the quality, we're looking at what the last books sold.'[20]

At the beginning of February 1990, Highsmith scribbled in her cahier the outline of a story about death. The unwritten tale, which she provisionally entitled 'Mr D' or 'Mr Death', centres on a dying man, Joe, who, like the writer herself, belongs to EXIT. After meeting the figure whom he has appointed to administer the fatal sedative, Joe tells a friend that he doesn't like the stranger. He finds another man, but again Joe feels uncomfortable and finally chooses the original figure. Highsmith envisaged the story as an expression of the struggle between the basic, animalistic drive for life and, when illness and old age has stripped an individual of all dignity, the logical desire for death, what Joe described as 'the long sleep'.[21]

It was to be an ominous tale. In the middle of the month her cat Semyon had to be put down because of kidney failure, while at the end of March, Alain Oulman, her French editor and head of Calmann-Lévy, died from a heart attack at the age of sixty-one. The news, she said, 'stunned' her for several hours.[22] She had last seen Oulman on 5

March, in Paris, as he had accompanied her to La Cinemathèque Française, where Highsmith received the honour of Officier dans l'ordre des Arts et des Lettres. As ever, Highsmith was self-effacingly modest about her own success and in an obituary of Oulman which she wrote for the *Guardian*, she took the trouble to praise her editor for his skill, patience and observation to detail, stressing that, at the award ceremony, it was 'Alain who shaped my clumsy sentences into something graceful in French, which I read out to the Minister of Culture'.[23]

While trying to finish the first draft of *Ripley Under Water*, which she wrote in intensive bouts over Christmas and Easter, she read Richard Ellmann's biography of Oscar Wilde, a book which Ripley enjoys in the novel. On 21 April she wrote in her notebook words which would appear, in a slightly different form, in *Ripley Under Water*: 'Something about Oscar's life, reading it, was like a purge, man's fate encapsulated; a man of goodwill, of talent, whose gifts to human pleasure remained considerable, had been attacked and brought low by the vindictiveness of *hoi polloi*, who had taken sadistic pleasure in watching Oscar brought low.'[24] The following month Highsmith observed how Wilde produced some of his best work while with Lord Alfred Douglas, a man who was, for all intents and purposes, bad for him. Later in life, alone in Paris, Wilde tried to work, but with 'not the same kind of pep and enthusiasm'.[25] She was reminded, she said, of Proust's remark on the joy which comes from falling back into the arms of someone who is bad for us. 'Art is not always healthy,' she said, 'and why should it be?'[26] Now that she was without a lover, did Highsmith look back to the times when she felt, by turns, tortured and inspired by her various muses?

She was certainly forced to address the question when, in mid-June, she travelled to London to publicise *Carol*, the renamed *The Price of Salt*, which Bloomsbury was bringing out that October, after its publication in German by Diogenes. For years, Daniel Keel had asked Highsmith whether he could reissue the novel in German, as it had already been found pirated in Holland and, although she would have preferred it to be published under her old pseudonym, she was eventually persuaded to embrace it as her own. That did not mean, however, that Highsmith felt comfortable enough to talk about her sexuality in public. 'Pat sent me a copy of the book and, I mean, nobody could have any doubts, could they?' says Patricia Losey. 'So she had a kind of coming out, didn't she, even though she didn't want to talk about it.'[27] David Sexton of the *Sunday Correspondent* asked why she never returned to the subject of lesbianism after *The Price of Salt*? 'An idea never came to me to do another such book,' she replied.[28] Had she had relationships with women, asked Janet Watts of the *Observer Maga-zine*? She refused to answer. Highsmith loathed such close questioning, but surely, with the release of *Carol*, she must have expected it? When Sarah Dunant travelled to Tegna to interview Highsmith for BBC2's *The Late Show*, she put the question to her – why was she surprised by inquiries of a personal nature when the publication of *Carol* actually seemed to invite it? Highsmith did not understand. Surely the book functioned as a literary coming out, Dunant persisted? 'I'll pass that one to Mrs Grundy,' Highsmith said, looking distinctly ruffled.²⁹ 'As a fellow writer, I thought she handled it perfectly,' says Dunant. 'She chose to say only what she wanted to say and I had tremendous respect for that. However, I was torn because as a television presenter I thought she could deliver a bit more. She was incredibly tense and prickly and did not want to talk about what this book might have meant for her. I was struck by her house, which seemed, architecturally, to be like a fortress – I thought it was fascinating that she had come to live in Switzerland, a place of security and beauty, and chose to look in rather than out. I was also intrigued by the portrait of her as a young woman in the living room [the one painted by Allela Cornell], which was dazzling, yet also poignant as it contrasted so sharply with the stooped, elderly woman who seemed to guard herself so profoundly.'³⁰

Highsmith was dreading the reviews of *Carol* as she thought, nearly forty years after its original publication, people would find the novel soppy and sentimental. Critics, however, relished the concept of a 'forgotten' Highsmith novel, especially one which had lesbian romance at its core. Victoria Glendinning thought it was 'intense and accom-plished . . . It is a Cinderella story, written with verve and some neat malice.'³¹ Craig Brown, writing in the *Sunday Times*, thought that the book was 'as much part of the Highsmith vision as *Edith's Diary* or *Deep Water*, and almost as chilling'.³² Susannah Clapp, writing in the *London Review of Books*, compared the book to a Highsmith novel of suspense, as it featured 'pages of uneasy eventlessness punctuated by sudden alarm'.³³ She praised Highsmith for her strong sense of place, the Hopper-like feel of certain locations, 'at once sharp-edged and one-dimensional',³⁴ and the use of unsettling visual descriptions and me-taphors. Clapp also positioned *Carol* in the larger context of High-smith's oeuvre, concluding, the novel 'has the compulsion of a thriller; Highsmith's thrillers have the lure of romance.'³⁵

In August, Christa Maerker came to stay with Highsmith for a week. 'Pat had agreed to write one of the "Impossible Interviews" for the radio station, Südwestfunk, which was running a series of short radio plays in which an author interviewed a person of their choice, but Pat misunderstood the assignment. The "impossible interview" had to be with somebody deceased, but Pat had chosen a living politician and she gladly accepted my proposal to help with the rewrite.'[36] Once arriving at the house, Christa insisted on stocking up the fridge so that she felt free to be able to help herself to food and drinks. But while out shopping for groceries, Highsmith filled up the trolley with whisky and beer; the only food she picked out were a few oranges and a bunch of bananas. 'Even though I had paid for the shopping, somehow the kitchen seemed to be off limits and so I went out and bought some biscuits,' says Christa.[37] One night, at two in the morning, Highsmith announced dinner. 'She eventually came back from the kitchen with a small plate with what I thought was goulash, some brown sauce and some burnt pepperoni. I started to put a fork into a piece of meat and watched as it flew off the plate – it was a bone. The cat, Charlotte, must have had the meat and I was left with four pieces of bone. I wasn't sure if Pat had done this so as to test me or that she simply did not know what she had cooked. Whenever she was invited out, Pat ordered and then only played with her food; after she died, one of her friends said that Pat had starved to death.'[38]

During the week, Christa felt increasingly uncomfortable. 'Opium is a terrific perfume, but after Highsmith announced that Charlotte couldn't stand it, I decided to have a shower, after which she reminded me, "We have to save water,"' says Christa. 'That indicated to me that whatever I did was wrong for her and the mere mention of the radio play and the rewrite stopped all conversation. Pat vanished into the garden or tried to find Charlotte. Needless to say, the "impossible interview" was never written. Leaving was a relief, I must say. When I drove away from the house, I thought this could easily be the end of our friendship, but soon after Pat wrote to me to tell me that she had had a fantastic time, and that I was one of her best visitors.'[39]

The following month, Barbara Skelton and Mary Ryan, Pat's old neighbour from Moncourt, came to visit. Highsmith had been a hardened drinker for years – according to Skelton as soon as she got out of bed, Pat would reach for the vodka bottle, marking it so as she knew her limit for that day – but she could not bear boorish drunken behaviour, especially in public. When Mary, obviously the worse for wear, fell as she was trying to ease herself out of the car, Highsmith shouted, ' "What will the neighbours think! People just don't behave like that here. This is a very puritanical country! Suppose one of the neighbours saw you lying in my drive drunk! I risk having my Swiss citizenship annulled." '⁴⁰ According to Skelton, Highsmith said this 'with sadistic contempt, and set the tone of the visit.'⁴¹

Highsmith sent off the manuscript of *Ripley Under Water* at the end of October 1990. On 10 December, she wrote in her diary that Liz Calder of Bloomsbury liked the book enormously and at the beginning of 1991, Highsmith was offered a £60,000 advance for the novel, the largest of her career. 'I was quite surprised,' she said. 'I would have been content with one-third of that.'⁴² She was faced with an 'horrendous' Swiss tax bill,⁴³ and she had had to ask Diogenes for a substantial amount of the previous year's earnings in advance in order to cover it. 'Easy come, easy go,' she concluded.⁴⁴

The new year also brought news of a less pleasing nature: the threat of an American bombing campaign on Iraq following the invasion of Kuwait, a threat which was realised on 17 January. Highsmith was appalled by President Bush's bully-boy tactics, writing to Patricia Losey that the Gulf War was 'the most revolting Exercise in Political Hypocrisy in a long while'.⁴⁵ Highsmith was also left depressed by the deaths of Graham Greene, Max Frisch, and Martha Graham, all of whom died in late March or early April. She had never met Greene, but the two writers had corresponded and after hearing the news, which she confessed made her feel 'shaken',⁴⁶ she visited her local doctor for another chest X-ray. To her relief she was given the all clear.

She boosted her spirits by taking up oil painting. Daniel Keel had given her a set of oils for her seventieth birthday and she intended to take regular painting lessons from her friend Gudrun Mueller. The two women were supposed to meet up each week, but in fact Pat only had two lessons. 'I don't know why,' says Gudrun. 'It was very difficult to teach her, to tell her anything. She was shy, hard-headed, and she had her own ideas.'⁴⁷ Then, at the end of July, together with Charles Latimer and one of her neighbours, she organised a visit by car to Bayreuth to see Wagner's *Der Ring des Nibelungen*. When Highsmith told Ingeborg Lüscher of her forthcoming visit to Bayreuth, her friend advised her on the rather formal dress code – if she attended the opera wearing her trademark blue jeans, man's shirt and necktie, then she would stand out, and surely, Ingeborg asked, she wouldn't want that? Pat told her that she had a wonderful skirt which she had worn to receive the honour, Officier dans l'ordre des Arts et des Lettres. 'But when she brought it out it was a thick woollen item with an elasticated waist,' says Ingeborg. 'And the shoes she intended to wear were ones fit for only a teenager, light blue shoes with little flowers.'[48] Highsmith, however, chose not to wear this ensemble, opting instead for a black, pleated skirt which she bought in Locarno. In Bayreuth, she enjoyed a meeting with Wolfgang Wagner and his wife and wrote in a letter to Kingsley of how the highlight of the event was the Rhinemaidens' river scene. On her return journey, in early August, her female neighbour who was driving the car tried to take a sharp bend in top gear as they were passing down the Albula Pass. '*Nicht schnell!*' shouted Highsmith from the front seat. The road was wet, the speed too high and a split second later the passengers were thrown forwards as the car slammed into an abutment. 'Thank goodness Pat and her friend were wearing their seatbelts,' says Charles. 'Although I wasn't wearing mine, I was in the back and was thrown forwards hitting the front seats. But it was a miracle we weren't killed. I think the accident really shook Pat up. It was another intimation of mortality.'[49]

She travelled to London in September for publication of *Ripley Under Water* and stayed in Hazlitt's Hotel on Frith Street, where the famous essayist had died in 1830. 'I collected her there for an evening on the town,' says Liz Calder, 'and she had discovered that so crooked were the floors that her whisky bottle slid of its own accord down the top of her chest of drawers and she was catching it with glee as it flew off the edge. She kept repeating this trick a bit like Pooh and his balloon. She had a childlike pleasure in simple things.'[50]

Although critics did not rave about the book, those who were fans thanked her for another chance to encounter Tom Ripley. James Campbell, writing in the *Times Literary Supplement*, said that he welcomed the novel, but judged it to be 'a less complex novel than *The Talented Mr Ripley* or *Ripley Under Ground*, and slighter than all the previous four – rather like a one-hour television drama next to a feature film'.[51] Hugo Barnacle, in the *Independent*, observed, 'Highsmith's plots have always had an impoverished air, but with the woollier psychology as well the effect is more awkward than usual. The reader falls back on the agreeable unpretentiousness of the writing and the irresistible brand of dark escapism, which more or less defy critical approach, let alone reproach.'[52]

After nine days in Tegna, Highsmith was off again, this time on a publicity tour of Germany, accompanied by Kingsley. They took in Frankfurt, Hamburg and Berlin, spending two days in each. She returned home to further red tape – taxes, the worry of death duties, doctors' appointments and details about her will. She toyed with the idea of turning her Tegna house into a Swiss-style Yaddo foundation for writers and artists so as to avoid the 48 per cent estate tax. Looking back on the year, she told Marc Brandel that it had been 'rough' and 'boring'; she had 'accomplished little, despite effort. Rotten atmosphere for working, alas.'[53]

Pat was still troubled by the blocked artery in her left leg. She had suffered pain for months, particularly when walking. When she made an appointment to see her doctor in London, in December, she wrote in her diary of her fears that she might have to undergo a bypass, but after the examination, in mid-January, the doctor was doubtful whether she should have any invasive treatment whatsoever. The risks of surgery might prove too much for her, he said, and advised that she might have to live with the pain. Further tests, however, were scheduled for 20 January at the Royal Free Hospital, Hampstead. The day before, Heather Chasen hosted a birthday tea party for her at her mews house in central London. 'I think she enjoyed herself and she was pleased that I'd made the effort to entertain her,' says Heather. 'I remember we talked about the nature of consciousness, something she was very interested in. She was ill, but she didn't talk about that. Some people are very keen on talking about their operations and ailments, but she wasn't like that at all.'[54] On the morning of the operation, Pat recorded in her notebook that she had enjoyed a cup of Nescafé at Hazlitt's before being driven to the hospital where she spent two hours on the operating table. It was decided to perform an angioplasty, or what Highsmith called 'ye olde pipe-cleaner method'.[55] Under a local anaesthetic, surgeons widened the left femoral artery from a diameter of one to six millimetres, an operation doctors considered successful. 'Well, you're lucky,' said the doctor a few days later, following a check-up. 'I feel lucky,' Highsmith replied.[56]

36

I hesitate to make promises

1992–1995

'Now I've an idea for a novel set in Zuerich, if I can pull it together,' Highsmith wrote to Liz Calder on 19 March 1992. 'Zuerich can be a violent town.'[1] Initially, Highsmith plotted out the bare bones of what she envisaged as a novel of suspense – the discovery of a young gay man lying dead in his boyfriend's bed; the search by police of the Zurich apartment and the supposition that the killer entered through a balcony window; and the investigation of the two prime suspects, both homosexual men. Yet, soon after outlining these details, Highsmith changed tack, deciding instead to relegate crime to the fringes of the novel. It may open with a shocking description of the stabbing and murder of Petey Ritter, the twenty-year-old boyfriend of Rickie Markwalder, but the book, if it can be classified at all, is essentially a romance, as is suggested by its title, *Small g: a Summer Idyll*. Most of the action is centred around a Zurich bar, Jakob's Bierstube-Restaurant, categorised in guidebooks 'with a "small g" – meaning a partially gay clientele but not entirely'.[2] Highsmith plucked the term from a diary in her possession, 'Metro Man '92', a pocket-sized volume marketed at gay men. The book contained graphic photographs of naked men and featured a guide to the gay scene in a number of cities, including Zurich. Under the heading, 'Codes in this book', the diary lists 'G' as, 'Gay: male homosexuals mainly or only' and 'g' as, 'Partly gay'.

Highsmith's description of Jakob's was based on a bar near the home of her friend Frieda Sommer, who lived in Dorfstrasse, Zurich. 'It was low-ceilinged and dark, with a bar/drinking section in the front and a few tables for eating in the back,' remembers Vivien De Bernardi.[3] Pat took the central character of Rickie Markwalder, a forty-six-year-old graphic designer who is told by his doctor that he is HIV-positive so as to scare him into practising safe sex, from a fifty-two year-old acquaintance who lived near Frieda, describing the real-life commercial artist as 'well-meaning, generous, popular at the pub'.[4] Although the storyline of Rickie's fake HIV status strikes an unconvincing note, apparently Highsmith based the deliberate misdiagnosis on the experience of Frieda's friend. 'I remember Frieda telling me about him [her friend] when we went for lunch to the little restaurant that was small g in the novel,' says Vivien De Bernardi. 'I was astounded by the fact that his doctor gave him a misdiagnosis just to scare him.'[5]

After the opening chapter in which Petey Ritter's murder is described, Highsmith fast-forwards six months to the summer. Rickie Markwalder is getting on with his life, working on his designs, and socialising at Jakob's, the regular haunt of Renate Hagnauer, a club-footed couturier, her young apprentice and tenant, Luisa Zimmermann, and the 'mentally retarded'[6] Willi Biber, whom Renate uses as her henchman. Rickie and Luisa grow closer after the graphic designer gives her a scarf which once belonged to Petey, whom Luisa loved, yet the platonic relationship is derided by Renate, who is at once fascinated and repelled by homosexuals. Both Rickie and Luisa also find themselves attracted to the figure of Teddie Stevenson, a young aspiring writer whom they both meet at Jakob's. Yet Renate, growing increasingly possessive of her young charge, orders Willi to beat up Teddie, whom she thinks is gay, and one night the hulking giant follows the boy out of the bar and attacks him with a piece of metal, leaving him injured. Teddie and Luisa enjoy a couple of dates together, but Luisa also finds herself feeling a strong attraction for Dorrie Wyss, a young freelance window dresser. As Luisa tries to assert her independence, her friends dream up a plot to free her from her tyrannical employer and landlady, a plan outlined by Rickie: ' "She finds Dorrie in bed with you one night . . . Opens your room door, for instance. A shriek of horror. Renate – she's bound to fire you. Or she may have a real heart attack!" '[7] Renate duly discovers Luisa and Dorrie in bed together, but as Dorrie rushes towards the door the club-footed couturier falls down the stairs to her death. Finally, it is revealed Luisa is the sole beneficiary of Renate's will; she continues to sleep with both Teddie and Dorrie and the novel ends with a plea for greater sexual fluidity.

If one reads *Small g* like other Highsmith novels one is bound to be left feeling disappointed – after all, there is little suspense, the characters are thinly drawn, and, for the most part, it is thematically barren. There is, it has to be said, an air of insubstantiality about the book. Yet if one approaches it as the extended fairy tale it so obviously is, one can reap greater rewards. Willi is compared to a 'sinister figure in a fairy-tale';[8] Renate is described as an 'old witch',[9] and Luisa, a 'fairy-tale queen, all beauty and shining eyes'.[10] When Luisa looks at a black and white drawing of a castle with a spire, the image transports her back to her innocent childhood, 'looking into picture books when she could believe in them'.[11]

In previous novels, Highsmith had investigated the negative effects of fantasy – its power to distort the mind, a psychological warping which often resulted in delusion, violence and ultimately murder – but in *Small g*, she seems to be suggesting that life as experienced within the boundaries of the imagination is not so harmless after all. The characters in *Small g* may inhabit a fantasy world of their own creation, but apart from the gullible and simple-minded Willi and the mean-spirited, repressed Renate, most of them come to no harm. Indeed, the fantasies actually help them survive. Luisa's love for Petey, whom she knew to be a gay man, was nothing but a 'dream',[12] but perhaps such a non-threatening relationship enabled her to come to terms with the sexual abuse she had suffered at the hands of her stepfather? Similarly, Rickie's infatuation with Teddie, who is described as 'a creature of dream',[13] may have helped him recover from losing Petey. Teddie sometimes goes by the name of Georg, so as to 'feel like another person'; the descriptions of his recent experiences that he writes for a newspaper under a pseudonym tell of encounters such as 'his first date with a pretty girl, who, like Cinderella . . . had to be brought back *before* eleven.'[14] His columns have a certain 'naivety',[15] and, like *Small g* itself, are invested with a quaint, unreal quality. Just as Petey's murder gives way to the romantic attachments of Jakob's clientele, so tragedy is displaced by comedy and the action is bathed in a gentle summer glow, a celebration of life reminiscent of a late play by Shakespeare. It can hardly be a coincidence that Highsmith, albeit in a rather bathetic manner, alludes to *A Winter's Tale* in the scene when Lulu, Rickie's dog, dances with her owner at Jakob's. As Rickie glides across the dance floor, with his dog on his shoulders, people point at the creature thinking it to be a statue, before realising that it is, in fact, alive. 'Lulu was still as a white statue, however, her expression calm. She was doing her work.'[16]

The novel ends on an optimistic note. Luisa, once a prisoner, is freed from her bondage; neither Rickie nor his policeman lover, Freddie, are HIV-positive; Freddie's wife, Gertrud, accepts her husband's unconventional relationship, while Teddie seems happy to share Luisa with

Dorrie. Sexual ambiguity triumphs, yet one is reminded that the summer idyll cannot last for ever. Happiness is precarious and, Highsmith suggests, romance should be embraced, experienced and enjoyed to the full. Love, as she knew all too well, was not so much the meeting of minds as the intermeshing and entanglement of fantasies. The point was far from a new one – as we have seen, this idea underpinned all her fiction from the very beginning of her writing career – yet it is the form and tone of the novel which is striking. As Highsmith wrote, she was conscious that she did not have much time left and, at the end of her life, she chose to switch genres, from crime to something approaching romance or the pastoral. 'With *Small g* one got the feeling that, while it is not a very good novel,' says Craig Brown, 'she had reached a point where she experienced something like happiness.'[17] *Small g*, for all its limitations, stands as an intriguing insight into a writer trying to make peace with herself. 'If it can be read as a final utterance, Patricia Highsmith died having made peace with her demons,' wrote James Campbell in the *Times Literary Supplement*. 'Good triumphed over bad. Too bad for her readers.'[18]

From the very beginning Highsmith had doubts about the novel. She started writing it in the spring of 1992, completing ninety-two pages by 22 May. However, she felt dissatisfied, describing what she had written as, 'Slow, unfocused,'[19] something which would necessitate a 're-think'.[20] The problem, as she saw it, was that the basic story was not 'easily believable' and she would only pull it off if she wrote it well.[21] While researching the book, she turned to Julia Diethelm for information about the couture business. 'I remember her asking me all these questions on apprenticeship,' says Julia, who once owned a dressmaking business. 'She was extremely good on details and although most of her research was done very seriously, often you hardly noticed. She would ask you something in a conversation, "Oh, by the way, what happens when a person dies in Zurich? Can an apprentice inherit a business?" She was very grateful for these details because she wanted authenticity; she didn't want to make believe.'[22] She dedicated the novel to her friend Frieda Sommer whom she asked about the Zurich gay scene.

While working on the novel, Pat also found time to write pieces for *The Oldie* – a feature on Venice, complete with a set of her illustrations, and another on Greta Garbo, 'Thank you for your films, your style, your beauty', she wrote[23] – and a review of Patrick Marnham's biography of Simenon for the *Times Literary Supplement*, which she also nominated as her book of the year in a *TLS* round-up. On 23 April, a chauffeur drove her from Tegna to Peter Ustinov's house in Rolle, near Geneva, where the two writers were due to meet for a question and answer interview for German *Vogue*. Highsmith admired the oil paintings on the walls and made a note in her diary of Ustinov's informality and friendliness. ' "He is a very appealing, warm-hearted man, Ustinov," ' she told Liz Calder.[24] After lunch, Highsmith left for Geneva, where she had made an appointment to meet the accountant Marylin Scowden, who had agreed to help with her US tax return. Over time the two women became friendly.

'She was such an odd character, she was so reserved. I suppose I felt she was a typical artist, in that she was eccentric. I went to see her for the occasional weekends, but she wouldn't let you get close to her. I got the impression that she was very unhappy and that's why she drank so much. She started drinking beer from when she got up in the morning and then she moved on to Scotch in the evening, but she never slurred her words or anything, as she developed such an immunity to alcohol. She tried to be very hospitable and, as she often worked in the evenings, she worried that I would be bored. She ordered a couple of videos, one of which was *The Importance of Being Earnest*, but she didn't watch it with me. Sometimes she would cook, but because she didn't eat, she would let things sit in the refrigerator and they would go bad; she would only ever have a couple of bites. There were so many things we didn't talk about – I tried to ask questions, but she wouldn't respond. She was so secretive.'[25]

Back in Tegna, Highsmith was appalled to learn of the Los Angeles riots, in which more than fifty people died and 2,000 were injured, following the acquittal of the police officers accused of the Rodney King beating. In the forthcoming presidential election she said she intended to vote for Ross Perot, the Texan-born billionaire and founder of the Reform Party, as opposed to the mainstream candidates George Bush and Bill Clinton; such a move was, she said, a protest. In the last election, she had voted for Bush; even though she loathed him – all he cared about was, she said, 'the rich, plus his golf games'[26] – she hoped he 'would take a more realistic stand about the situation in Palestine'.[27] She had been proved wrong. 'Instead of that they keep issuing more money to those people there, the Israelis.'[28] Even though Perot was defeated in the election – he received 19 per cent of the votes – she admitted to feeling pleased when Clinton became President later that year.

In October, Highsmith travelled to America on a publicity tour for *Ripley Under Water*, published by Knopf. In New York, where she spent nine days, she read an extract from her new Ripley novel at Rizzoli's in Soho, and met Donald Rice, chairman of Yaddo's board of directors. Highsmith wanted to bequeath her Tegna home to the writers' and artists' colony, so the corporation could use it as a little Yaddo in Switzerland. Rice knew of the impracticalities of such an arrangement – the house, with its two bedrooms and bathrooms was simply not large enough – but did not discourage her as he hoped she might think of another way in which Yaddo could benefit from her generosity. 'She had this wonderful, gruff, chain-smoking, tough-guy way of speaking, and she was someone who I took to immediately,' says Rice. 'I'm a tax lawyer and one thing I find with people who have money is that they generally like to control other people. I think Pat was quite expert in being manipulative. I am not saying that critically, I think it was something that she took great delight in.'[29] Rice remembers the intrigue which surrounded his dealings with Highsmith – the 'telephone calls from phone booths, cryptic correspondence, continually changing documents, hiring and firing of professional advisers, cock-a-mamey schemes . . . How I miss that husky voice, and the scent of a smoldering Gauloise cigarette mingled with a whiff of Scotch whiskey.'[30] Rice's patience certainly paid off: in July 1994, Highsmith sent Yaddo – anonymously – a cheque for $27,500; in December of the same year she ordered her bank to dispatch another contribution for $300,000, and in her will she named the corporation as her sole beneficiary. 'Pat Highsmith's bequest is an expression of everything she stood for,' says Rice. 'She was an artist to the core, whose work was her life and vice versa.'[31]

While in New York, Highsmith also met the author Neil Gordon, who was writing a critique of her work for the literary journal, the *Threepenny Review*. The two writers met in the lobby of her midtown hotel. 'Highsmith showed up late and rushed, just back from a signing,' says Gordon. 'She was a shortish and very plain woman, gracious and very unpretentious. Perhaps my overwhelming impression was a kind of cognitive dissonance on three levels: that this mild and polite woman was the author of some of the grisliest murder I'd ever encountered; that this rather bigoted woman was the author of what I consider one of the most politically radical bodies of contemporary fiction; and finally that such an amazing distance existed between the complexity of her work and the simplicity of her own view of it. She denied, for example, any suggestion that Ripley was homosexual – suggesting that he was 'lukewarm toward women'. But the question of Ripley's homosexuality is so key to unlocking the radical complexity of those books, and even if you don't want to get all psychoanalytic about it, you just have to watch the movies made about Ripley to see how hard directors have worked to come to terms with his elusive sexuality, and how much it has affected their efforts to adapt those books to the screen.

'None of this was without meaning to me: to me, Ripley's homosexuality is key simply because these are books about the adaptation to the unbearable reality of bigotry. To me, the same psychotic split that allows Ripley to kill so easily is clearly articulated by Highsmith as the same necessary adaptation that allowed him to exist in the horrendous homophobia of '50s America. Just as Ripley consistently denies, in the context of '50s America, the unbearable reality of his homosexuality, he denies the fact of being guilty of murder. It was, therefore, fascinating to see a very similar psychotic split in Highsmith herself, where she in effect denied the central thematics of her own work, as well as its key radicalism.'[32]

From New York, Pat travelled to Texas, where she stayed with her cousin Dan Coates at his ranch in Weatherford and where she was interviewed by a journalist from *People* magazine. Although she was fond of her cousin and his wife, she felt depressed by the crass materialism, the vulgar philistinism and the pro-Republican opinions she encountered in Texas. After six days in the state where she was born but where she no longer felt at home, she flew to Toronto for a reading at the Harbourfront Festival on 18 October and a party with guests that included Margaret Atwood and Michael Ondaatje. She was relieved to fly home at the end of the month. 'On visiting Texas – something is missing: it's Europe, it's the world missing,' she wrote in her notebook.[33]

The reporter from *People* magazine, in an effort to try and capture Highsmith's ethereal quality, described the writer as 'reclusive',[34] a notion she rejected. 'To say I'm a recluse is journalistic nonsense . . .' she told Naim Attallah. 'I like talking to people on the phone, I like people to drop by for a coffee. I do not consider myself a recluse.'[35] One who can testify to the truth of Highsmith's statement is Bee Loggenberg, whom the writer met in late 1992. She may have been private, but that did not mean she did not still enjoy getting to know new people. 'Pat and I seemed to get on very well together instantly,' says Bee. 'She always used to say that I was so exuberant and full of life and it was quite a treat for her to come and chatter about things, as she was broody. We talked about sexuality – I'm homosexual, and she was homosexual. She was quite a tough bird in many ways – she felt quite comfortable with gay men, but she didn't particularly like lesbians. She was quite masculine in outlook and, for me, spending time with Pat was like being with a mate, like being with another boy. She talked about Ripley quite a lot and identified with him very strongly.'[36] Loggenberg laughs as he recalls a conversation in which Highsmith complained of the cost of maintaining her Tegna garden; she simply could not afford to get someone in to help, she said, neither did she want to spend money on the mowing of her lawn. Bee – who employed a full-time gardener at his house in Monte Bré, near Locarno – kindly offered to help. Just before she died, Pat was discussing her will with Bee, when she mentioned casually that she had a substantial amount of money in one of her accounts. 'That's when I realised that she probably had as much money as I had and I had been cutting her fucking lawn,' he says. 'My garden costs something like two thousand quid a month [to maintain], but I was spending a day weeding her garden!'[37]

It started with a cold, accompanied by a series of nosebleeds. As she battled to finish the first draft of *Small g*, which she did in mid-March 1993, she felt increasingly wretched. Yet Highsmith refused to let the illness get the better of her. On 14 July, she finally saw a doctor about the problem. He told her she was badly anaemic – after a blood test, it was discovered that she had only 40,000 as opposed to the 150,000 platelets of a healthy person. In order to find out exactly what was wrong, the doctor ordered more tests at the hospital in Locarno; she was also ordered to give up drinking for three weeks. 'I thought she wouldn't be able to do that, but she did, she went cold turkey for three weeks,' says Vivien. 'Yet her behaviour didn't change. I think by this time she would be what you call a classic alcoholic. Pat would just feel halfway decent when she drank alcohol because by that time the alcoholism had progressed to such a point that she was depressed whether she drank or not. It wasn't that she got real cheerful when she drank or anything. By the end she was basically living on beer. She would carry jars of peanut butter around in her handbag, as that's all she could eat.'[38]

That summer, Highsmith said, was 'rough'.[39] On 14 September she underwent surgery in Locarno's Caritas hospital for removal of a non-cancerous tumour in her lower intestine and then on 10 October she was admitted to Basel's Kantonspital, a modern hospital specialising in blood disorders. There she was given daily injections of Neupogen, a drug designed to treat neutropenia, the shortage of neutrophils (cells which surround and destroy bacteria in the body). 'I am said to be

stable now,' she wrote to Barbara Skelton. 'To me that means I may not
die in the next months, which I certainly thought I would do last year
and most of this year. I've lost about 15 kilos in a year, have far less
strength, but now I'm not losing more, and have managed to learn to
stuff myself with calories – hoping to gain an ounce or two.'[40] Finally, it
was discovered that she was suffering from aplastic anaemia, failure of
the bone marrow to produce sufficient blood cells, and multiple small
tumours in the lung and the adrenal gland. Treatment proved proble-
matic – the cancers could not be removed by surgery because they were
too minute, while radiotherapy and chemotherapy could not be administered until the blood marrow had recovered. Doctors prescribed a
drug which inhibited the auto-immune attack of the bone marrow; a
high dose of intravenous immunoglobulins for three days and another
medication to help stimulate the production of blood cells. After the
initial treatment, Highsmith's blood had to be tested twice a week and
she had to go for transfusions of haemoglobin and thrombocytes once
every nine days. This made her feel, as she told Bettina Berch, as though
she were 'a dog on a leash'.[41]

Highsmith tried to be optimistic about the future – she continued to
hope that the aplastic anaemia would right itself, as it sometimes did, and
even voiced the possibility of having a bone marrow transplant – but,
feeling weak and continually fatigued, she knew that her time was
limited. In September 1993, Diogenes Verlag bought the world rights
of Highsmith's complete works and in January 1994, she gave Frieda
Sommer the power of attorney. In May 1994, she appointed Bruno
Sager, who had spent time in the monastery at Einsiedeln, as her carer.
'She was small, thin, almost transparent, with these very fine hands she
didn't want you to touch,' remembers Sager, who lived with Highsmith
from June until December. 'I liked her – she was intelligent and sensitive,
had very good taste in literature and art. But she did not talk a lot. To
begin with, she wanted somebody in the house in case of an emergency
and a driver who could take her to hospital. But when I arrived, I started
to help organise the house and clear the garden. She loved her roses, and
she showed me exactly how to cut them, but she hadn't the strength to do
any real gardening. She told me that she could be difficult to live with,
but we occupied separate parts of the house, sharing the big living room.
She would get up at around eight in the morning, and we would take
breakfast separately. She worked in the mornings, we had lunch at about
one, she slept a little in the afternoon and then read or wrote. I did a lot of
the cooking as she didn't have the energy. Sometimes she said, "I would
love to have some cornbread," and I would make it. She loved American

food, things like beans with bacon, but only very small portions. After supper, we would sometimes watch television – she would look at her watch and say, "Oh, it's time for *EastEnders*", which she liked – or videos of films made from her books. She would go to bed around ten or eleven. Her bedroom was also her workroom – it contained a single bed, a little table and her desk.

'She was very clean and she liked to have everything in order; for instance, the laundry had to be done in a certain way. I think one can also say she saw that money was not spent too easily. I did the shopping and she would look at what I'd bought, saying, "Why did you buy this, this is much too expensive." She paid me a very small amount, I think 400 SF a month, but I didn't do it for the money. Although at the beginning it was difficult, as I really didn't know what she wanted, I'll never forget the experience and I'll never forget her. She was a real character.'[42]

Highsmith appreciated Bruno's efforts – she told Kingsley that 'life is better' with him[43] – and Vivien De Bernardi witnessed an improvement in her friend's spirits. 'She had a reflowering,' says Vivien. 'He took over the day-to-day work; she ate a little; she had a wonderful six months.'[44] Photographs taken by Ingeborg Lüscher in the summer of 1994 show Pat, her slight frame enveloped by a mannish sweater, her neck swathed in an elegant cravat, sporting an enormous grin, her dark eyes sparkling with mischief, looking like she had just heard a dirty limerick. Despite her desperate lack of energy, she carried on working, writing book reviews for the *Times Literary Supplement* and *The Oldie*, a piece about O.J. Simpson for the *Washington Post*, and in September and October she oversaw the editing of *Small g*, a novel which netted her a £20,000 advance from Bloomsbury. Jean-Etienne Cohen-Séat, president of Calmann-Lévy, wrote to her expressing his admiration for the book: 'No doubt many a reader will be delighted by this modern approach to everlasting issues such as human compulsion for pleasure and suffering through sexuality, love, friendship and social life.'[45]

However, when the manuscript was shown to her American publishers, Knopf, they felt they had no choice but to turn it down. 'It's a very sweet and baffling book,' says Gary Fisketjon. 'In the best of all possible worlds it would be published as a young title, but the lunatic right-wing fringe that's running this country wouldn't have that.'[46] If Knopf had gone ahead and published the book, 'it would have undone whatever good had been done over the years,' says Fisketjon. 'But she wrote back, saying that she didn't take the rejection personally. I think she probably knew it wasn't quite up to snuff.'[47] The rejection left her with no

American publisher at the end of her life, a final symbolic gesture summing up the uneasy relationship between the displaced writer and the country of her birth. Highsmith's marginalisation in the US, believes Neil Gordon, is symptomatic of the country's failure to grapple with the power of her writing. America has, for the most part, 'denied her insight – her painful and complicated insight into guilt and denial – much as her characters deny their guilt. That leaves her, so to speak, denied in the unconscious of our literature much like guilt is denied in her characters: always present, never cured, never acknowledged and never understood.'[48]

In November, she travelled to Paris with Bee Loggenberg, where she met her friend, the actress Jeanne Moreau. The occasion was the celebration of *Le Nouvel Observateur*'s thirtieth anniversary. 'She went to Paris even though she was feeling very weak at the time – sort of a Last Hurrah,' says Kingsley.[49] Snapshots taken by Bee in a restaurant show her looking frail, although smartly dressed in a white shirt, cobalt-blue cowboy pendant and Mexican-style waistcoat. 'When we went to Paris she was already very ill and weak,' says Bee, 'but we had a lot of fun.'[50] She did everything she could to fulfil her obligations, but she had to admit that she couldn't possibly commit herself to future engagements. 'I hesitate to make promises about next March,' Highsmith wrote to Jean-Etienne Cohen-Séat after he asked whether she would be free to travel to Paris in March 1995 for the launch of *Small g*. 'I wish I could . . . I haven't the strength that I had a year ago.'[51]

Back home, Highsmith took up, once again, the task of settling the details of her estate. On 15 November, she wrote to Daniel Keel asking him to act as a mediator in the sale of her papers to the Swiss Literary Archives, in Berne. There had been some discussion about whether to sell her literary remains to the Harry Ransom Humanities Research Center, the University of Texas at Austin. At the end of September, Highsmith had written a letter to Tom Staley, the director of the Center, in which she tried to outline, in as modest a way as possible, her status amongst world writers, dropping in the fact that in 1991 she had been nominated for the Nobel Prize for Literature, an honour which that year went to Nadime Gordimer. But although Texas had bid $26,000 for the documents, Highsmith thought this amount 'insulting and so she decided she would leave her papers to Switzerland,' according to Vivien De Bernardi. 'The Swiss Archive paid 150,000 SF which was nearly four times as much.'[52]

Vivien had assumed that Highsmith had finalised the deal. However, when Vivien visited Pat at home six weeks before she died, Pat called her into her bedroom. 'She had back pain, was lying down on the bed and as she got up to go to the bathroom, she said to me, "While I'm gone, look at that will on the desk,"' says Vivien. 'She said she was afraid that she wouldn't have the energy to rewrite it. I asked her why she wanted to change it and she told me that she had decided to leave her papers to the Swiss Archives. I said, "Are you kidding? Are you telling me you haven't done that?" She said, "No – because it would take so much time to write it all out by hand." I said, "You don't write it out by hand – you go to a lawyer and the lawyer does it." But she didn't want to pay the lawyer – that was why. I told her I would take it home and type it out, which I did. We went through the will together and she showed me the paragraphs – there were two – which had to be changed about the executors and the archives. If she was going to leave her literary papers to an institution in the United States she would have chosen Kingsley, but as it was Switzerland she decided on Daniel Keel.'[53] Feeling weak and tired, on 12 January Highsmith wrote to Kingsley for the last time to tell her friend of her change of plans and the fact that Daniel Keel, whom she described as being 'very helpful . . . He's my "Vermittler" or go-between (not agent) on all this,'[54] had, with her permission, taken away a number of her drawings and paintings which he promised to gather together to form a book; the handsome volume, *Zeichnungen*, was duly published by Diogenes after her death.

After the departure of Bruno Sager, Highsmith was cared for by a twenty-year-old girl who left after only a month. Her friends visited regularly and Ingeborg Lüscher gave Pat soothing massages, which she enjoyed, remarkable for a woman who did not usually like to be touched. 'I was very gentle because she was only bones in the end,' says Ingeborg. 'She did not want to talk about dying with me, but in the last two weeks of her life, we became especially close. She had this way of looking at me, something which went beyond words. For me it was important not to look away, but to maintain eye contact. She was telling me, "Look, I'm dying, maybe this is the last time that I will see you. I'm dying, I'm dying." She wanted support, but a wordless support.'[55] During the last weeks of her life she started vomiting blood and her skin turned yellow – the latter a sign that she needed to have another transfusion – but she said she felt little pain. 'I would have expected her to be more afraid,' says Vivien. 'In the six weeks before she died, Pat didn't seem that depressed. It was funny – she was so often in an emotional turmoil over something that happened halfway around the world, but she was calm before she died. There was a tranquillity about her. She seemed to be quite peaceful, and as lucid as could be.'[56]

On 1 February, she made her final will, nominating Daniel Keel as her literary executor, whom she also named, together with Vivien De Bernardi and Frieda Sommer, as one of the testamentary executors. She instructed that if her literary papers were sold to the Swiss Literary Archives, the proceeds of the sale should go to Yaddo, the beneficiary of the rest of her estate. The next evening, she felt so drained of energy she could no longer get out of bed to go to the bathroom. She called Bert and Julia Diethelm, telling them, ' "I'm completely hopeless and I'm in a very bad way." '[57] The couple arrived to find Highsmith in bed, 'which she had never done before as she had always received us fully dressed,' says Bert. 'Now she really was at the end, I thought.'[58] Bert and Julia led her gently into their car, where Highsmith gave Julia a hug, and then drove her to hospital in Locarno.

That day, Highsmith had been due to meet Marylin Scowden to sort out her financial affairs, but, feeling unwell, she had cancelled the meeting. 'We knew that she wasn't going to live that much longer, and I told her that we really had to meet,' says Marylin, who visited her in hospital on 3 February, and who was the last person amongst her friends to see Highsmith alive. 'It was terrible. She was just nothing. Her legs were hurting so badly and she asked me to rub her leg, which was amazing because normally she wouldn't let anybody touch her. When I did touch her I realised there was nothing there – it was just bone. Although I tried to stay, she wouldn't let me. I believed what the doctors said, that she would be home soon, and so I left.'[59] Vivien phoned and asked Pat if she would like her to visit, but she refused saying that the day would be taken up by tests. At 6.30 on the morning of 4 February 1995, Highsmith died, alone. 'I regret leaving her very much,' says Marylin, 'but I wonder whether she knew what was coming; maybe she wanted to be alone.'[60] Vivien was shocked when she heard the news, early on that Saturday morning, as Marylin had told her how bright she had seemed the night before. 'It's no fun dying or being sick,' says Vivien, 'but all things considered I would say it was one of the lesser traumas of her life.'[61]

Epilogue

On the morning of 6 February, in accordance with her wishes, High-smith was cremated. Her friends chose a simple white blouse for her from which the lace had been removed. A dozen mourners gathered at the hospital in the mortuary room where Pat lay in an open casket, before driving to the cemetery in Bellinzona. There, Highsmith's friends followed the funeral car on foot as it made its way slowly to the crematorium. 'It was a cold day and sad, but also very simple and I remember thinking Pat would have been pleased by this and pleased by the small number of mourners, all people who had known and loved her,' says Vivien De Bernardi, who spoke briefly at the service. 'I felt it was exactly the way Pat would have wanted it.'[1]

As is the custom in Switzerland, Highsmith's house in Tegna was sealed, but as Marylin Scowden was staying in the property, the authorities decided to place what they thought might be of value into one room, which was then declared off-limits. Their choice of items was bizarre – the dining-room table, complete with the mess of objects sitting on its surface, including a tiny promotional box of Lindt chocolates and a fruit cake, and a leather-bound set of the Encyclo-paedia Britannica. After the authorities had disappeared, Marilyn opened the closet door and found a literary treasure trove – a cupboard full of Highsmith's manuscripts. 'When I heard that story I realised how much I missed her, as that was exactly the kind of thing I would have called to have told her about,' says Vivien. 'I would loved to have phoned her and said, "You know what they've sealed – they've sealed your Encyclopaedia Britannica." Pat would have loved it.'[2] Before its contents were cleared, Diogenes authorised film-maker Philippe Kohly to enter the house so as to make a documentary about Highsmith's life and work, after which Daniel Keel and Anna von Planta began the task of sorting through the literary remains. The files, says von Planta, Highsmith's editor at Diogenes since 1985, 'are so massive that when spread out they are 150 feet in length.'[3] In addition to the standard obituaries which traced the course of Highsmith's life, *The Times* devoted one of its leaders to her. 'Crime need not be a second-class genre of literature,' ran the headline. The piece called for a reassessment of her work, tracing how she reinvented the crime novel as a 'whydunit, in which an interest in the criminal and criminal psychology replaces the puzzle.'[4] This was far from her only achievement. She would be remembered for the creation of Ripley, one of the most intriguing characters in modern literature; for her kinship with Nietzsche, Dostoevsky and the masters of existentialism and for the unsettling moral uncertainty which permeated her novels. The director and novelist Michael Tolkin, writing in the *Los Angeles Times*, said that Highsmith was America's 'best expatriate since Henry James',[5] and later articulated his debt to her, a legacy inherited by a number of contemporary writers and film-makers. 'She was one of the best writers in the world . . . she was . . . the last turn of the dial to unlock my novels. I don't think I could have written *The Player* without her.'[6]

The week after her death, final copies of *Small g* arrived at Bloomsbury's office in Soho, and it was published at the beginning of March. 'I wished she could have seen it, but she had said she liked the cover,' says Liz Calder.[7] Grey Gowrie, in the *Daily Telegraph*, wrote that the book was a 'delight', classifying it as a fascinating coda to Highsmith's main body of work;[8] Geoffrey Elborn, in the *Guardian* thought that the novel possessed a 'serenity rarely found in Highsmith's world'[9]; and William Trevor in the *Independent on Sunday* analysed it as a transgressive fairy tale – 'there's no living happily ever after. That was never the Highsmith style. Truth was her business.'[10] Lorna Sage, in the *Observer*, enjoyed the novel for a similar reason to William Trevor, noting how Highsmith disturbed the sterile, ordered environment of Switzerland by the introduction of ambiguity. 'In this latest novel she imagined a new generation of golden boys and girls who would escape the gingerbread house of either/or.'[11]

Yet some critics regarded the publication as a mistake. The reviewer from the *Sunday Times* commented on how the novel seemed to lack 'the author's usual trademark, the undercurrent of menace, of fear, of cruelty,'[12] and Rose Wild, in *The Times*, felt frustrated by the decision of the 'high priestess of the nasty' to turn soft. 'Highsmith's homosexuality has only been obliquely present in her previous fiction,' she wrote. 'It is hard to put aside the suspicion that she finally decided to let rip with a real message here. It is disappointing that it is such a starry-eyed view.'[13] There were those who went even further. Michael Dobbs, in the *Sunday Telegraph* believed that the book 'makes a sad epitaph for such a renowned writer'[14] and Brian Glanville, one of Highsmith's friends, classified the novel as 'an oyster without grit . . . *Small g* . . . is a dreary piece of book-making. I wish it had not appeared.'[15]

Highsmith's memorial service was held in Tegna's small church, with its 'pastel frescoes and flying cherubs'[16] on the afternoon of Saturday 11 March, carnival day in the village. The building was packed with a German television camera crew; 'black-clad villagers' and fans;[17] and a number of close friends, including Kingsley and Frieda Sommer, although Ellen Hill decided not to attend, saying, ' "I had difficulties with Miss Highsmith at the end." '[18] Her publishers – from Britain, France, Spain, Italy and Germany, but none from America – addressed themselves to the question of Highsmith's extraordinary abilities as a writer and Vivien De Bernardi stood up and spoke of what Pat meant to her as a friend. 'Because of her isolation, her mind was not contaminated by fashion, convention or inhibition,' she said. 'She was like a wild horse that no one could tame . . . Visits with Pat were like cleaning one's glasses . . . Referring to some of the saccharine phrases used to describe her after her death, my son said, "She had a *caratteraccio* and that's why we liked her!" It's true. She was sometimes a difficult friend, fascinating, wild and wonderful. And her loss has left a gaping hole in the middle of the lives of those of us who cared deeply about her.'[19] At the end of the service, on a cloudless early spring day, Kingsley carried the urn containing her friend's ashes out of the church; she walked through the small cemetery and placed it in a recess within a wall of remembrance, where it was sealed. 'Then a man placed a picture of Highsmith and her cat in front of the recess,' recalls Tanja Howarth. 'As he was in tears, I asked him whether he was a relation. "No," he said. "I just read all her books." '[20]

As Daniel Keel walked out of the church into the graveyard, the publisher told the journalist Joan Dupont that Highsmith was ' "going to get bigger and bigger; she's going to become a classic." '[21] Keel passed out two poems written by Highsmith – one from *Edith's Diary*, in which Edith imagines the trees in her garden, teeming with life, indifferent to her death only hours before, and one written in 1979 entitled 'A Toast', which celebrates the ennobling pursuit of human aspiration and the quest towards achievement: 'A toast to optimism and to courage!/A glass to daring!/And a laurel to the one who leaps!'[22] At the end of the service, as Tanja was standing in the churchyard, she heard a thunderous noise. 'After the emotionally charged silence, we turned around and saw this train coming towards us, travelling on the lines which ran past the church,' she says. 'We were waved to and cheered at by a group of young people travelling on a passing train, a stone's throw away from Pat's resting place. 'Strangers on a train indeed.'[23]

Throughout her career, Highsmith had written in her notebooks about death – wondering about her fears, her final thoughts and the changing nature of consciousness as her body grew weaker until she breathed no more. In a way, death was something she always aspired to, as she viewed it as a state of pure thought, a transcendent perfection. In 1973, Highsmith imagined the last words she would ever speak – 'It was all so predictable', she surmised.[24] On this occasion, Highsmith was wrong; far from following a clear, well-trodden path, the writer veered off into the margins, exploring dark aspects of the psyche which are usually hidden in the shadows. Her perspective, for all its distortions and fantastical illusions, was unique and, ironically, it is only now, after her death – thanks, in part, to the release of Anthony Minghella's 1999 film *The Talented Mr Ripley* and the reissuing of her novels – that the power of her work is finally being appreciated, especially in America. In October 2002, W.W. Norton published *Nothing That Meets the Eye*, a collection of twenty-eight mostly unpublished stories, described by James Campbell as consisting of 'completed pieces by a natural storyteller . . . Her settings and characterizations, established with a few deft strokes, and her endless fund of seemingly simple situations, put one in mind of another laureate of everyday life, Guy de Maupassant.'[25]

To a degree, a cultural change is also responsible for the Highsmith renaissance as the mass market is now much more comfortable with literature and film that subverts genre expectations and disturbs popular notions of morality. 'I think Pat was born a little too early for her work to be properly understood,' says Tanja Howarth. 'Yet in many ways she can be seen as an example of the twentieth century itself – she was so way ahead with her sexual ideas and with her sense of freedom.'[26] Some critics have even gone so far as to link Highsmith's renewed relevance with the recent changes in American society. Whereas America in the past was perhaps too complacent to appreciate Highsmith, a 'post-Oklahoma City, post-Columbine United States . . .

may just now be catching up to her,' says Margaret Caldwell Thomas.[27] Ed Siegel, writing in the *Boston Globe*, believes that Highsmith's work has significant lessons to teach us. 'In the wake of September 11, Highsmith's world is not only more like ours, where crime and punishment or cause and effect don't necessarily go hand in hand, she seems a more important writer than ever,' he writes.[28]

Just as Highsmith, as she wrote, began to see the world through the skewed vision of her characters, so I, as I worked on her biography, felt my self slipping away, finding my perspective transformed. At times, sitting alone in my study, looking at a small copy of Allela Cornell's haunting portrait of the young Highsmith, tinged as it is with a strange, terrible beauty, I felt what it might be like to view the world through my subject's eyes. I understood, for a moment, how she must have found life difficult; why she chose relationships she knew would end bitterly, why she needed to dull her senses with alcohol and why she, albeit unconsciously, chose to transform herself from a beauty into something approaching the grotesque, projecting her psychological pain onto the thickly lined contour map of her face. Writing, as we have seen, helped her survive; what she would have done without it is a frightening thought.

   In the middle of researching the book, during one of my many interviews with Kingsley at her New York apartment, Highsmith's closest friend presented me with a gift – Pat's old dressing gown. It was a touching gesture, both a sign of trust and a symbol of the biographical task that lay ahead of me – the dangerous job of literally inhabiting another's life, slipping under their skin to find out how they experienced the world. Back home in London, I examined the garment. Made from thick, dark blue wool, with black, blue and beige stripes on its cuffs and its lining and a rather fine twill, tasselled waist-cord, the dressing gown, purchased from Harrods, still bore traces of its owner – strands of grey hair nestling around the neck. Although a dry-cleaning ticket was safety-pinned to its collar, there was something musty about it, as if its wearer steadfastly refused to relinquish it for good, an air of otherworldliness that suggested Highsmith was nearby.

   Gingerly, I took hold of it and placed it around my shoulders, easing my arms through the same soft, dark spaces once occupied by her slight frame. I tied the waist-cord around me and sat at my desk, looking down at my hands which I knew would one day write these words. I had read all her work, her diaries, her letters, and listened to her most intimate thoughts. I had repeatedly dreamt about her and, in all seriousness, probably knew more about her than anyone alive. Now I was inhabiting her private space, slipping on an item of clothing which once would have brushed against her bare skin. Like Highsmith, who compared new fictional ideas to birds that she saw at the corner of her eye, I'm convinced I recognised a dark form at the periphery of my imaginative vision, a shape which was unmistakable. I caught a glimpse of her and then she was gone.

Notes

Abbreviations used in the Notes

AK: Alfred A. Knopf Archive, Harry Ransom Humanities Research Center, the University of Texas at Austin

BCA: Barnard College Archive, New York

CLA: Calmann-Lévy Archive, Paris

CM: Private collection of Christa Maerker

DS: Donald L. Swaim Collection, MSS Collection # 177, Archives & Special Collections, Ohio University Libraries

EB: Private collection of Edith Brandel

FW: Private collection of Francis Wyndham

GV: Gore Vidal Collection, Wisconsin Center for Film and Theater Research, Madison, Wisconsin, now held by the Houghton Library, Harvard University

HA: Harper Archive, Harry Ransom Humanities Research Center, the University of Texas at Austin

HRA: Harper & Row Archives, Rare Book and Manuscript Library, Columbia University, New York

JR: Private collection of Janice Robertson

KA: Koestler Archive, Edinburgh University Library

NY: *The New Yorker* Records, Manuscripts and Archives Division, The New York Public Library, Astor, Lenox and Tilden Foundations

PH: Patricia Highsmith

PL: Private collection of Peggy Lewis

RB: Private collection of Ronald Blythe
SLA: Swiss Literary Archives, Berne
TU: Temple University, Paley Library, Urban Archives, Philadelphia
WBA: William A. Bradley Literary Agency Archive, Harry Ransom Humanities Research Center, The University of Texas at Austin
YA: Yaddo Archive, Saratoga Springs, New York

Highsmith dated her cahier entries using the American dating system unless otherwise indicated.

Introduction

1 Søren Kierkegaard, 'Repetition', quoted in Walter Lowrie, *A Short Life of Kierkegaard*, Princeton University Press, 1942, quoted by PH, Cahier 19, SLA.
2 PH, Afterword, *Carol*, Bloomsbury, London, 1990, p. 260.
3 Ibid.
4 PH, Cahier 19, 7/1/50, SLA.
5 PH, Diary 10, 21 January 1951, SLA.
6 Susannah Clapp, 'The Simple Art of Murder', *The New Yorker*, 20 December 1999.
7 PH, Diary 2, 24 May 1942, SLA.
8 PH, Cahier 20, 9/14/51, SLA.
9 Craig Brown, 'Too Busy Writing to be a Writer', *Daily Telegraph*, 29 January 2000.
10 Janet Watts, 'Love and Highsmith', *Observer Magazine*, 9 September 1990.
11 Ibid.
12 Interview with Daniel Keel, 27 October 1999.
13 Interview with Carl Laszlo, 22 August 1999.
14 Interview with Barbara Roett, 5 May 1999.
15 Interview with Vivien De Bernardi, 23 July 1999.
16 John Wakeman, ed., *World Authors 1950–1970, A Companion Volume to Twentieth-Century Authors*, The H.W. Wilson Company, New York, 1975, p. 642.
17 PH, Cahier 18, inside cover, undated, SLA.
18 PH, *Plotting and Writing Suspense Fiction*, The Writer Inc., Boston, 1966, p. 50.
19 PH, Cahier 15, 3/18/47, SLA.
20 *Harper's Bazaar*, February 1989.
21 Terrence Rafferty, 'Fear and Trembling', *The New Yorker*, 4 January 1988.
22 Ibid.
23 *The Late Show*, BBC2, 7 February 1995.
24 Interview with Daniel Keel.
25 W.H. Auden, 'The Guilty Vicarage', 1948, *The Dyer's Hand and Other Essays*, Random House, New York, 1962, p. 147.
26 Diana Cooper-Clark, 'Patricia Highsmith – Interview', *The Armchair Detective*, Vol. 14, No. 4, 1981, p. 320.
27 Ibid., p.316.
28 Graham Greene, Foreword, *Eleven*, Heinemann, London, 1970, p. x.
29 Ibid., p. ix.
30 Ibid.
31 PH, Cahier 6, 2/14/42, SLA.
32 Interview with Julia Diethelm, 27 March 1999.

33 Interview with Bert Diethelm, 27 March 1999.
34 PH, Diary 8, 21 September 1949, SLA.
35 Interview with Daniel Keel.
36 Interview with Larry Ashmead, 20 May 1999.
37 Craig Brown, 'No Ordinary Crime', *Homes & Gardens*, March 1981.
38 PH, Cahier 15, 3/25/47, SLA.
39 PH, Diary 2, 1942, SLA.
40 PH, Letter to Charles Latimer, 22 March 1979, SLA.
41 PH, Letter to Charles Latimer, 20 July 1978, SLA.
42 PH, Cahier 2, 7/18/40, SLA.
43 PH, Cahier 22, 10/9/53, SLA.
44 PH, *The Blunderer*, Cresset Press, London, 1956, p. 140.
45 PH, Cahier 6, 5/10/42, SLA.
46 Ibid.

1 The forever seeking 1921 and before

1 PH, Cahier 8, 11/18/42, SLA.
2 PH, Cahier 16, 11/13/47, SLA.
3 PH, Cahier 4, 8/7/40, SLA.
4 Interview with Phyllis Nagy, 7 October 1999.
5 PH, *Strangers on a Train*, Cresset Press, London, 1950, p. 36.
6 Duncan Fallowell, 'The Talented Miss Highsmith', *Sunday Telegraph Magazine*, 20 February 2000.
7 PH, Letter to Calmann-Lévy, 6 November 1951, CLA.
8 T.R. Fehrenbach, *Lone Star: A History of Texas and the Texans*, American Legacy Press, New York, 1983, p. 257.
9 Ibid.
10 Ibid., p. 717.
11 Ibid., p. 304.
12 J'Nell L. Pate, *Livestock Legacy: The Fort Worth Stockyards 1887–1987*, Texas A & M University Press, 1988.
13 Tarrant County Historic Resources Survey, Phase III, Fort Worth's Southside, 1986.
14 PH, *Strangers on a Train*, p. 5.
15 Ibid, p. 35.
16 Joan Dupont, 'The Mysterious Patricia Highsmith', *Paris Metro*, 9 November 1977.
17 Rub Kneasel, Letter to PH, 9 November 1967, SLA.
18 Samuel Smith Stewart, Family History, 1935, SLA.
19 Interview with Don Coates, 26 November 1999.
20 Interview with Dan Coates, 20 November 1999.
21 John Wakeman, ed., *World Authors 1950–1970, A Companion Volume to Twentieth-Century Authors*, The H.W. Wilson Company, New York, 1975, p. 641.
22 PH, Cahier 8, 8/23/42, SLA.
23 Interview with Dan Coates.
24 Dan Coates, Letter to PH, 20 April 1990, SLA.
25 PH, Cahier 13, 9/20/45, SLA.
26 Dan Coates, Letter to PH, 20 April 1990, SLA.
27 Joan Juliet Buck, 'A Terrifying Talent', *Observer Magazine*, 20 November 1977.
28 Sarah Jane Deutsch, 'From Ballots To Breadlines 1920–1940', from Nancy F. Cott, ed., *No Small Change: A History of Women in the United States*, Oxford University Press, Oxford, 2000, p. 440.
29 Mary Highsmith, Letter to PH, undated, SLA.

30 Interview with Don Coates.
31 Interview with Dan Coates.
32 Walter Plangman, Letter to PH, 28 September 1973, SLA.
33 Jay Bernard Plangman, Letter to PH, 4 January 1971, SLA.
34 PH, Letter to Marc Brandel, 11 November 1985, EB.
35 Ibid.
36 Walter Plangman, Letter to PH, 22 August 1971, SLA.
37 Pat Patrick, 'Plangman Gave Them Brush With Life', *Fort Worth Star-Telegram*, 19 January 1975.
38 Ibid.
39 Joan Dupont, 'Criminal Pursuits', *New York Times Magazine*, 12 June 1988.
40 PH, Letter to Jay Bernard Plangman, 15 July 1971, SLA.
41 Jay Bernard Plangman, Letter to PH, 30 July 1971, SLA.
42 Dan Coates, Letter to PH, 6 August 1988, SLA.
43 Deutsch, 'From Ballots to Breadlines' in *No Small Change*, p. 441.
44 Ibid., p. 413.
45 Frederick Lewis Allen, *Only Yesterday: An Informal History of the Nineteen-twenties*, Harper & Brothers, New York, London, 1931, p. 108.
46 Jay Bernard Plangman, Letter to PH, 30 July 1971, SLA.
47 Dan Coates, Letter to PH, 6 August 1988, SLA.
48 Interview with Dan Coates.
49 PH, Letter to Mary Highsmith, undated, SLA.

2 Born under a sickly star 1921–1927

1   Michael E. Parrish, *Anxious Decades: America in Prosperity and Depression* 1920–1941, W.W. Norton & Company, New York, London, 1992, p. 75.
2   Harold Stearns, *Civilization in the United States*, quoted in Michael E. Parrish, *Anxious Decades*, p. 191.
3   Parrish, *Anxious Decades*, p. 154.
4   F. Scott Fitzgerald, *This Side of Paradise*, W. Collins & Sons & Co., London, 1921, p. 292.
5   PH, Cahier 5, 9/1/41, SLA.
6   PH, 'Daran glaube ich', *Welt am Sonntag*, 9 October 1977.
7   Diana Cooper-Clark, 'Patricia Highsmith – Interview', *The Armchair Detective*, Volume 14, No. 4, 1981, p. 317.
8   PH, Cahier 6, 4/11/42 , SLA.
9   Bettina Berch, 'A Talk with Patricia Highsmith', 15 June 1984, unpublished interview, SLA.
10 PH, 'An American Book Bag', 1974, SLA.
11 PH, Cahier 3, 1/30/41, SLA.
12 Ibid.
13 PH, Letter to Bettina Berch, 2 July 1983, SLA.
14 Duncan Fallowell, 'The Talented Miss Highsmith', *Sunday Telegraph Magazine*, 20 February 2000.
15 Berch, 'A Talk with Patricia Highsmith'.
16 PH, 'An Weihnachten gewöhnt man sich' ('Some Christmases – Mine or Anybody's'), *Frankfurter Allgemeine Magazin*, 20 January 1991.
17 Ibid.
18 PH, 'An American Book Bag', 1974, SLA.
19 Duncan Fallowell, 'The Talented Miss Highsmith'.
20 John Wakeman, ed., *World Authors* 1950–1970, A Companion Volume to Twentieth Century Authors, The H.W. Wilson Company, New York, 1975, p. 642.
21 William Trevor, *Independent on Sunday*, 26 March 1995.

22 Susannah Clapp, 'The Simple Art of Murder', *New Yorker*, 20 December 1999.
23 PH, Cahier 17, 3/8/48, SLA.
24 PH, Cahier 6, 4/12/42, SLA.
25 Interview with Vivien De Bernardi, 23 July 1999.
26 PH, Letter to Anita Bryant, 13 May 1978, SLA.
27 PH, 'Between Jane Austen and Philby', written for *Vogue*, September 1968, SLA.
28 PH, Cahier 2, 7/8/40, SLA.
29 PH, 'An American Book Bag', 1974, SLA.
30 PH, Letter to Stanley Highsmith, 29 August 1970, SLA.
31 PH, Cahier 27, 12/28/64, SLA.
32 PH, Cahier 23, 10/16/54, SLA.
33 PH, Diary 2, 11 June 1942, SLA.
34 PH, Cahier 31, 1/12/70, SLA.
35 Hannah Carter, 'Queens of Crime', *Guardian*, 1 May 1968.

3 A house divided 1927–1933

1 Robert A.M. Stern, Gregory Gilmartin, Thomas Mellins, *New York 1930: Architecture and Urbanism Between the Two World Wars*, Rizzoli International Publications Inc., New York, 1987, p. 29.
2 St John Ervine, 'New York – The City of Beauty', *Vanity Fair*, March 1921.
3 William Bristol Shaw, quoted in Stern et al, *New York 1930*, p. 35.
4 Works Progress Administration, *New York City Guide*, Guilds' Committee for Federal Writers' Publications Inc., Random House, New York, 1939, p. 52.
5 Ann Douglas, *Terrible Honesty: Mongrel Manhattan in the 1920s*, Picador, London, 1995, p. 17.
6 PH, 'The World's Champion Ball-Bouncer', *Woman's Home Companion*, April 1947.
7 Ibid.
8 Walter Lippmann, *A Preface to Morals*, quoted in Douglas, *Terrible Honesty*, p. 17.
9 F. Scott Fitzgerald, 'My Lost City', in *The Crack-Up*, ed. Edmund Wilson, New Directions, New York, 1945, p. 25.
10 Ibid.
11 Jane Mushabac, Angela Wigan, *A Short and Remarkable History of New York City*, Fordham University Press, New York, 1999.
12 Ford Maddox Ford, *New York is Not America*, Albert & Charles Boni, New York, 1927.
13 Peter Marcus, *New York: The Nation's Metropolis*, Brentano's, New York, 1921.
14 *Book Beat*, Interview with Donald Swaim, CBS Radio, 29 October 1987, DS.
15 In her unpublished essay, 'A Try At Freedom', PH locates the school on West 99th Street, but after checking with the New York Historical Society no such school can be found. Most likely the school Highsmith attended in 1927 was PS 166 on West 89th Street, built by C.B.J. Snyder in 1898.
16 PH, 'A Try At Freedom', SLA.
17 PH, Cahier 26, 5/3/62, SLA.
18 PH, 'Sherlock Holmes From Home', *Queen*, November 1969.
19 PH, *Plotting and Writing Suspense Fiction*, The Writer Inc., Boston, 1966, p. 75.
20 PH, Cahier 7, 6/23/42, SLA.
21 PH, Cahier 11, 5/29/44, SLA.
22 Pupil Records, PS 122 Queens, Astoria, New York list her address as 2418 28th St.; Queens Phone Directory, Summer 1932, consulted at the Queens Borough Public Library, lists it as 2482 28th St.
23 Vincent F. Seyfried, William Asadorian, *Old Queens, N.Y. in Early Photographs*, Dover Publications Inc., New York, 1991.
24 Arleigh Homes advertisement, *New York Herald*, 10 June 1923.

25 Lewis Mumford, 'The Sky Line: Bridges and Beaches', *The New Yorker*, 17 July 1937.

26 *The New Yorker*, 13 November 1929, quoted in Douglas, *Terrible Honesty*, p. 17.

27 PH, Cahier 13, 2/8/46, SLA.

28 Pupil Records, PS 122 Queens, Astoria, New York.

29 PH, Cahier 26, 9/6/62, SLA.

30 PH, 'A Try At Freedom', SLA.

31 Sydney Smith, ed., *The Human Mind Revisited, Essays in Honor of Karl A. Menninger*, International Universities Press Inc., New York, 1978, p. 14.

32 Karl Menninger, *The Human Mind*, Knopf, New York, 1930, p. 3.

33 PH, Letter to Karl Menninger, 8 April 1989, SLA.

34 Menninger, *The Human Mind*, p. ix.

35 Janet Watts, 'Love and Highsmith', *Observer Magazine*, 9 September 1990.

36 PH, Letter to Diogenes Verlag, corrections to Notes on *Highsmith Chronik zu Leben Und Werk*, SLA.

37 Ian Hamilton, 'Patricia Highsmith', *New Review*, August 1977.

38 Craig Brown, 'The Hitman and Her', *The Times*, Saturday Review, 28 September 1991.

39 'Patricia Highsmith: A Gift for Murder', *The South Bank Show*, LWT, 14 November 1982.

40 PH, Letter to Willie Mae Coates, undated, SLA.

41 PH, 'A Try At Freedom', SLA.

42 Ibid.

43 Ibid.

44 Interview with Vivien De Bernardi, 23 July 1999.

45 PH, Letter to Stanley Highsmith, 1 September 1970, SLA.

46 PH, Letter to Mary Highsmith, 16 March 1973, SLA.

47 PH, 'Girl Campers', *Woman's World*, July 1935.

48 Ibid.

49 Ibid.

50 Ibid.

51 PH, Letter to Mary Highsmith, 16 March 1973, SLA.

52 Interview with Vivien De Bernardi.

53 PH, Letter to Stanley Highsmith, 29 August 1970, SLA.

54 PH, Letter to Jay Bernard Plangman, 8 August 1970, SLA.

55 PH, Letter to Nini Wells, 29 March 1972, SLA.

4 Suppressions 1933–1938

1 PH, Cahier 36, 31/10/83, SLA.

2 PH, Cahier 19, 7/22/50, SLA.

3 PH, Diary 8, 2 April 1948, SLA.

4 PH, Letter to Dan Coates, 26 December 1968, SLA.

5 PH Cahier 4, 8/24/40, SLA.

6 Naim Attallah, 'The Oldie Interview, Patricia Highsmith', *The Oldie*, 3 September 1993.

7 PH, Letter to Nini Wells, 29 March 1972, SLA.

8 Ibid.

9 PH, Cahier 36, 3/9/83, SLA.

10 Interview with Bert Diethelm, 27 March 1999.

11 PH, Letter to Alex Szogyi, 18 February 1969, SLA.

12 PH, Cahier 10, 5/22/43, SLA.

13 George J. Lankevich, *American Metropolis: A History of New York City*, New York University Press, New York & London, 1998, p. 163.

14 Michael E. Parrish, *Anxious Decades: America in Prosperity and Depression 1920–1941*, W.W. Norton & Company, New York, London, 1992, p. 289.

15 PH, *Strangers on a Train*, Cresset Press, London, 1950, p. 212.
16 Works Progress Administration, *New York City Guide*, Guilds' Committee for Federal Writers' Publications Inc., Random House, New York, 1939, p. 124.
17 Caroline F. Ware, *Greenwich Village, 1920–30*, Houghton Mifflin & Co., 1935, quoted in George Chauncey, *Gay New York: The Making of the Gay Male World 1890–1940*, Flamingo, HarperCollins, 1995, p. 233.
18 Bruce Rogers, 'Degenerates of Greenwich Village, Current Psychology and Psychoanalysis', December 1936, p. 29ff, quoted in Chauncey, *Gay New York*, p. 234.
19 Selma Berrol, *The Empire City: New York and its People*, 1624–1996, Praeger Publishers, Westport, Connecticut & London, 1997, p. 117.
20 *New York City School Buildings 1806-1956*, Board of Education, quoted in Robert A.M. Stern, Gregory Gilmartin, Thomas Mellins, *New York 1930: Architecture and Urbanism Between the Two World Wars*, Rizzoli International Publications Inc., New York, 1987, p. 120.
21 PH, 'A Try At Freedom', SLA.
22 Ibid.
23 Julia Richman, Isabel Richman Wallach, *Good Citizenship*, American Book Company, 1908, p. 70.
24 Diana Cooper-Clark, 'Patricia Highsmith – Interview', *The Armchair Detective*, Vol. 14, No. 4, 1981, p. 318.
25 PH, 'A Try At Freedom', SLA.
26 PH, 'Books in Childhood', January 1986, SLA.
27 PH, Answers to Q&A for *Ellery Queen's Mystery Magazine*, sent 18 November 1981, SLA.
28 PH, 'Books in Childhood', SLA.
29 PH, *Strangers on a Train*, p. 238.
30 PH, Cahier 9, transcription of 1935 diary, SLA.
31 PH, Letter to Stanley Highsmith, 1 September 1970, SLA.
32 Ibid.
33 PH, Cahier 26, 2/3/62 , SLA.
34 PH, Letter to Mary Highsmith, 12 April 1966, SLA.
35 Ibid.
36 PH, Cahier 26, 2/3/62, SLA.
37 Interview with Muriel Mandelbaum, 10 February 2000.
38 PH, Cahier 9, transcription of 1935 diary, SLA.
39 Edna McKnight, 'Jobs – For Men Only? Shall We Send Women Workers Home?', *Outlook and Independent*, 2 September 1931, quoted in Lillian Faderman, *Odd Girls and Twilight Lovers, A History of Lesbian Life in Twentieth-Century America*, Penguin Books, London, 1992, p. 96.
40 Karl Menninger, *The Human Mind*, Knopf, 1930, p. 252.
41 'Women's Personalities Changed by Adrenal Gland Operations', *New York Times*, 28 October 1935, quoted in Faderman, *Odd Girls*, p. 100.
42 Sheila Donisthorpe, *Loveliest of Friends*, Charles Kendall, New York, 1931, quoted in Faderman, *Odd Girls*, p. 101.
43 New York Evening Graphic, 1931, 'Lesbian Herstory Archives', quoted in Faderman, *Odd Girls*, p. 107.
44 Faderman, *Odd Girls*, p. 119.
45 PH, 'First Love', *Sunday Times Magazine*, 20 January 1974.
46 Bettina Berch, 'A Talk with Patricia Highsmith', 15 June 1984, SLA.
47 PH, Cahier 20, 10/20/50, SLA.
48 PH, Cahier 9, transcription of 1935 diary, SLA.
49 Ibid.
50 PH, 'Between Jane Austen and Philby', written for *Vogue*, September 1968 , SLA.
51 Ibid.
52 Eugene Wood, 'What the Public Wants to Read', *Atlantic Monthly*, October 1901, quoted in Stuart E. Knee, 'Christian Science in the Age of Mary Baker Eddy', *Contributions in American History*, No. 154, Greenwood Press, Westport, Connecticut & London, 1994, pp. 117,118.

53 Diana Cooper-Clark, 'Patricia Highsmith – Interview', *The Armchair Detective*, Vol. 14, No. 4, 1981, p. 320.
54 PH, Diary 8, 24 March 1948, SLA.
55 PH, Cahier 9, transcription of 1935 diary, SLA.
56 Mary Baker Eddy, *Science and Health with Key to the Scriptures*, The First Church of Christ, Scientist, Boston, Massachusetts, 1991, p. xi.
57 *Kaleidoscope*, BBC Radio, 17 March 1975.
58 'Patricia Highsmith: A Gift for Murder', *The South Bank Show*, LWT, 14 November 1982.
59 PH, 'Primroses Are Pink', *The Bluebird*, Fall 1937, Vol. 25, No. 1, p. 57, Julia Richman High School archives, Julia Richman Educational Complex, New York.
60 PH, 'Primroses Are Pink', manuscript, SLA.
61 Ibid.
62 'Why I Write', sent to *Libération*, Paris, 22 February 1985, published March, SLA.
63 PH, Cahier 30, SLA.
64 PH, Cahier 23, 10/16/54, SLA.
65 PH, Cahier 7, 6/7/42, SLA.
66 PH, Letter to Stanley Highsmith, 1 September 1970, SLA.
67 Ibid.
68 Interview with Vivien De Bernardi, 23 July 1999.
69 PH, Diary 5, 18 October 1943, translated from the German by Ulrich Weber, SLA.
70 Gary Carey, Judy Holliday, *An Intimate Life Story*, Robson Books, London, 1983, p. 12.
71 PH, 'A Try At Freedom', SLA.
72 PH, Letter to Stanley Highsmith, 29 August 1970, SLA.
73 Cahier 9, transcription of 1938 diary, SLA.
74 PH, *Plotting and Writing Suspense Fiction*, The Writer Inc., Boston, 1966, p. 20.
75 PH, Cahier 13, 12/23/45, SLA.
76 'The Book Programme', *BBC2*, 11 November 1976.
77 Cahier 9, transcription of 1938 diary, SLA.
78 Ibid.

5 The taste of freedom 1938–1940

1 PH, 'A Try At Freedom', SLA.
2 Donald Glassman, Letter to the author, 12 May 2000.
3 Joan Dupont, 'The Mysterious Patricia Highsmith', *Paris Metro*, 9 November 1977.
4 PH, *Plotting and Writing Suspense Fiction*, The Writer Inc., Boston, 1966, p. 73.
5 Kate Kingsley Skattebol, Letter to the author, 6 May 2001.
6 Virginia Gildersleeve, 'The Dean's Report, 1926', p. 7, quoted in Marian Churchill White, *A History of Barnard College*, Columbia University Press, New York, 1954, p. 124.
7 Ibid.
8 Julia Treacy Wintjen, 'An Interview with Miss Sturtevant', *Barnard College Alumnae Monthly*, January 1939, p. 12, BCA.
9 Professor Cabell Greet, *A Minute on the Death of Miss Ethel G. Sturtevant*, 28 October 1968, BCA.
10 PH, Diary 10, 23 May 1950, SLA.
11 PH, Cahier 1, 1938, SLA.
12 PH, 'Quiet Night', *Barnard Quarterly*, XIV: 1, Fall 1939.
13 PH, Cahier 4, 9/19/40, SLA.
14 PH, Cahier 2, dated February 1940, SLA.
15 PH, Cahier 2, 5/27/40, SLA.
16 PH, Letter to Arthur Koestler, 21 March 1966, KA, MS 2385/3.

17 Ibid.
18 Frederick R. Benson, *Writers in Arms: The Literary Impact of the Spanish Civil War*, New York University Press, New York, 1967, University of London Press, London, 1968, p. 52.
19 W.H. Auden, quoted in Hugh Thomas, *The Spanish Civil War*, Eyre & Spottiswoode, London, 1961, p. 222.
20 C.S. Lewis, 'The Nabara', *Overtures to Death and Other Poems*, Jonathan Cape, London, 1938.
21 PH, Letter to Patricia Losey, 20 May 1992, SLA.
22 Benson, *Writers in Arms*, p. 276.
23 Auriol Stevens, 'Private Highsmith', *Guardian*, 29 January 1969.
24 PH, Cahier 9, dated August 1939, SLA.
25 Interview with Rita Semel, 6 April 2000.
26 Joseph R. Starobin, *American Communism in Crisis, 1943–1957*, Harvard University Press, Cambridge, Massachusetts, 1972, p. 23.
27 Lewis Miller, quoted in James Oneal & G.A. Werner, *American Communism: A Critical Analysis of Its Origins, Development and Programs*, E.P. Dutton & Co. Inc., 1947, p. 248.
28 Earl Browder, 'The Way Out of the Imperialist War', 13 January 1941, published in his book of collected speeches, *The Way Out*, International Publishers Co. Inc., New York, 1941, p. 199.
29 Browder, *The Way Out*, p. 208.
30 PH, Diary 1, 8 September 1941, SLA.
31 Arthur Koestler, *The Invisible Writing*, Collins with Hamish Hamilton, London, 1954, p. 15.
32 PH, Cahier 2, 7/7/40, SLA.
33 PH, Cahier 4, 1940, undated, SLA.
34 PH, Cahier 10, 7/18/43, SLA.
35 *Mortarboard*, 1942, BCA.
36 PH, 'A Mighty Nice Man', *Barnard Quarterly*, XIV:3, Spring 1940.
37 William Leith, 'Mighty Nice, Really Tasty', *Independent on Sunday*, 7 October 1990.
38 PH, 'The Legend of The Convent of Saint Fotheringay', *Barnard Quarterly*, XV:3, Spring 1941.
39 PH, Cahier 16, 10/24/47, SLA.
40 PH, Cahier 3, 1940, undated, SLA.
41 Interview with Deborah Karp, 9 February 2000.
42 Interview with Rita Semel.
43 Interview with Mary Cable, 1 February 2000.
44 PH, Cahier 1, 1938, undated, SLA.
45 PH, Cahier 4, 10/26/40, SLA.
46 PH, Letter to Arthur Koestler, 20 January 1965 , KA, MS 2385/2.
47 PH, Letter to Alex Szogyi, 10 July 1967, SLA.
48 PH, Cahier 2, 7/9/40, SLA.
49 PH, Cahier 2, 6/6/40, SLA.
50 Interview with Kate Kingsley Skattebol, 19 May 1999.
51 Greek Games programme, 13 April 1940, Barnard College, SLA.
52 Interview with Rita Semel.
53 Interview with Deborah Karp.
54 PH, Cahier 1, undated, SLA.
55 PH, Cahier 4, 8/12/40, SLA.
56 PH, Cahier 3, 4/16/40, SLA.
57 PH, Cahier 2, dated December 1939, SLA.
58 PH, Cahier 2, 6/19/40, SLA.
59 PH, Cahier 9, 3/3/39, SLA
60 PH, Cahier 9, 12/9/39, SLA

6 A trail of unmade beds 1940–1942

1 Marian Churchill White, *A History of Barnard College*, Columbia University Press, New York, 1954, p. 142.
2 Thomas Wolfe, quoted by David Herbert Donald, *Look Homeward: A Life of Thomas Wolfe*, Bloomsbury, London, 1987, p. 280.
3 PH, Diary 1, 20 June 1941, SLA.
4 PH, Letter to Charles Latimer, 3 March 1974, SLA.
5 PH, Diary 1, 23 June 1941, SLA.
6 PH, Diary 1, 1941, undated, SLA.
7 PH, Cahier 5, 9/25/41, SLA.
8 PH, Diary 1, 1 September 1941, SLA.
9 Marcel Proust, *Remembrance of Things Past*, Vol. 1, *Swann's Way, Swann in Love*, trans. C.K. Scott Moncrieff, Chatto & Windus, London, 1941, p. 271.
10 Proust, *Remembrance of Things Past*, Vol. 4, *Within a Budding Grove*, Part Two, p. 346.
11 Proust, *Remembrance of Things Past*, Vol. 3, *Within a Budding Grove*, Part One, p. 219.
12 Interview with Rita Semel, 6 April 2000.
13 Interview with Kate Kingsley Skattebol, 14 May 1999.
14 PH, Diary 1, 27 June 1941, SLA.
15 PH, Diary 1, 7 July 1941, SLA.
16 Interview with Buffie Johnson, 18 May 1999.
17 Buffie Johnson, *Patricia Highsmith*, unpublished, undated, courtesy of Buffie Johnson.
18 Ibid.
19 'Between the Lines', *New York*, 16 December 1968.
20 Interview with Kate Kingsley Skattebol.
21 PH, Diary 1, 22 July 1941, SLA.
22 PH, Diary 1, 1 August 1941, SLA.
23 PH, Diary 1, 23 August 1941, SLA.
24 'Between the Lines'.
25 PH, Cahier 5, 7/16/41, SLA.
26 PH, Diary 2, 11 April 1942, SLA.
27 PH, Diary 1, 11 September 1941, SLA.
28 PH, Cahier 5, 9/29/41, SLA.
29 Interview with Kate Kingsley Skattebol.
30 Mary Highsmith, Letter to PH, undated, SLA.
31 PH, Letter to Stanley Highsmith, 29 August 1970, SLA.
32 PH, Diary 2, 3 January 1942, SLA.
33 PH, Diary 2, 10 January 1942, SLA.
34 PH, Diary 2, 15 January 1942, SLA.
35 PH, Diary 2, 29 March 1942, SLA.
36 PH, Diary 2, 11 June 1942, SLA.
37 PH, Diary 2, 21 June 1942, SLA.
38 Ibid.
39 PH, 'The Heroine', *Eleven*, Heinemann, London, 1970, p. 135.
40 PH, Cahier 7, 7/8/42, SLA.
41 PH, Cahier 6, 12/19/41, SLA.
42 PH, Cahier 6, 12/17/41, SLA.
43 Virginia C. Gildersleeve, 'Educating Girls for the War and the Postwar World', quoted in Marian Churchill White, *A History of Barnard College*, Columbia University Press, New York, 1954, p. 148.
44 PH, Diary 1, 1 November 1941, SLA.
45 PH, Diary 1, 18 December 1941, SLA.
46 PH, Cahier 6, 12/17/41, SLA.
47 PH, Diary 2, 29 April 1942, SLA.

48 PH, Cahier 6, 5/13/42, SLA.
49 PH, Cahier 6, 3/2/42, SLA.
50 Ibid.
51 PH, Diary 2, 2 March 1942, SLA.
52 PH, Cahier 6, 4/14/42, SLA.
53 PH, Cahier 6, 3/26/42, SLA.
54 PH, Diary 2, 22 February 1942, SLA.
55 PH, Cahier 7, 6/27/42, SLA.

7 The dungeon of thy self 1942–1943

1   PH, Diary 6, 15 December 1944, translated by Ulrich Weber, SLA
2   Julian Green, quoted in Glenn S. Burne, *Julian Green*, Twayne Publishers Inc., New York, 1972, p. 29.
3   Julian Green, 17 September 1928, *Diary, 1928–1957*, selected by Kurt Wolff, trans. by Anne Green, A Helen and Kurt Wolff Book, Collins & Harvill Press, London, 1961, p 3; English translation, Harcourt, Brace & World Inc. & Harvill Press, 1964.
4   PH, Diary 4, 21 July 1943, translated by Ulrich Weber, SLA.
5   Green, 31 December 1931, *Diary*, p. 21.
6   Green, February 1938, *Diary*, p. 78.
7   Green, 1 October 1940, *Diary*, p. 102.
8   Green, 20 August 1948, *Diary*, p. 201.
9   Julian Green, *If I Were You*, translated by J.H.F. McEwen, Eyre & Spottiswoode, London, 1950 p. v.
10 Ibid., p. 22.
11 Ibid., p. v–vi.
12 Green, 6 December 1952, *Diary*, p. 306.
13 Burne, *Julian Green*, p. 45.
14 PH, Cahier 10, 2/20/43, SLA.
15 *Book Beat*, Interview with Donald Swaim, CBS Radio, 29 October 1987, DS.
16 PH, Diary 2, 17 June 1942, SLA.
17 Ibid.
18 PH, Letter to William Shawn, 8 July 1942, NY.
19 PH, Diary 2, 25 June 1942, SLA.
20 Kate Kingsley Skattebol, Letter to the author, 5 May 2000.
21 PH, 'Uncertain Treasure', *Home & Food*, August 1943.
22 PH, 'My First Job', *The Oldie*, 14 May 1993.
23 *Book Beat*, Interview with Donald Swaim, CBS Radio, 29 October 1987, DS.
24 PH, Foreword to *New York Stories*, Librarie A Hatier, SLA.
25 PH, Letter to Winifer Skattebol, 9 January 1983, SLA.
26 Works Progress Administration, *New York City Guide*, Guilds' Committee for Federal Writers' Publications Inc., Random House, New York, 1939, p. 226.
27 PH, Diary 3, 7 September 1942, SLA.
28 PH, Lleida speech, 26 April 1987, SLA.
29 Susannah Clapp, 'The Simple Art of Murder', *The New Yorker*, 20 December 1999.
30 *The Book Programme*, BBC2, 11 November 1976.
31 PH, *Plotting and Writing Suspense Fiction*, The Writer Inc., Boston, 1966, p. 47.
32 PH, Cahier 7, 6/21/42, SLA.
33 Anonymous memo, attached to letter from William Shawn to PH, 24 September 1942, NY.
34 PH, Cahier 6, 2/23/42, SLA.
35 PH, Cahier 9, 12/5/42, SLA.
36 Interview with Peter Huber, 14 March 1999.

37 PH, Cahier 8, 9/27/42, SLA.
38 PH, Cahier 9, 10/25/42, SLA.
39 PH, Cahier 8, August 1942, SLA.
40 PH, Cahier 8, 9/27/42, SLA.
41 PH, Cahier 8, 10/10/42, SLA.
42 PH, Diary 3, 13 September 1942, SLA.
43 Ibid.
44 PH, Cahier 9, 12/2/43, SLA.
45 PH, Cahier 9, 12/29/42, SLA.
46 PH, Cahier 8, 9/27/42, SLA.
47 PH, Cahier 9, 1942, SLA.
48 PH, Cahier 8, 11/18/42, SLA.
49 Interview with Ruth Bernhard, 9 June 2000.
50 PH, Diary 3, 9 August 1942, SLA.
51 Ibid.
52 PH, Diary 3, 11 August 1942, SLA.
53 PH, 'An American Book Bag', 1974, SLA.
54 Dorothy Edson, Letter to the author, 29 February 2000.
55 PH, Diary 3, 13 August 1942, SLA.
56 PH, Diary 3, 21 August 1942, SLA.
57 PH, Diary 3, 16 August 1942, SLA.
58 PH, Diary 3, 18 September 1942, SLA.
59 Ibid.
60 PH, Diary 3, 20 September 1942, SLA.
61 Interview with David Diamond, 17 August 2000.
62 Interview with Kate Kingsley Skattebol, 31 August 1999.
63 PH, Diary 5, 15 October 1943, translated by Ulrich Weber, SLA.
64 PH, List of Lovers, undated, SLA.
65 PH, Diary 4, 10 September 1943, SLA.
66 Ibid.
67 PH, Diary 5, 21 October 1943, translated by Ulrich Weber, SLA.
68 PH, Diary 5, 8 November 1943, translated by Ulrich Weber, SLA.

8 A carefully nurtured bohemianism 1943–1945

1 PH, *A Game for the Living*, Heinemann, London, 1959, p. 58.
2 PH, Cahier 9, 1/10/43, SLA.
3 PH, Letter to Kate Kingsley Skattebol, 22 March 1952, SLA.
4 Katherine Anne Porter, 'A Country and Some People I Love', interview by Hank Lopez, *Harper's*, September 1965, quoted in John Unterecker, *Voyager: A Life of Hart Crane*, Anthony Blond, London, 1970, p. 658.
5 Edith Mackie, Sheldon Dick, *Mexican Journey: An Intimate Guide To Mexico*, Dodge Publishing Company, New York, 1935, p. xi.
6 Malcolm Lowry, *La Mordida*, quoted in Gordon Bowker, *Pursued by Furies: A Life of Malcolm Lowry*, HarperCollins, London, 1993, p. 205.
7 PH, Letter to Kate Kingsley Skattebol, 12 May 1944, SLA.
8 PH, 'An Weihnachten gewöhnt man sich' ('Some Christmases – Mine or Anybody's'), *Frankfurter Allgemeine Magazin*, 20 January 1991, SLA.
9 PH, Diary 6, 25 December 1944, translated by Ulrich Weber, SLA.
10 PH, Cahier 11, 1/6/44, SLA.
11 Aldous Huxley, *Beyond The Mexique Bay*, Chatto & Windus, London, 1934, p. 309.
12 Malcolm Lowry, Letter to Jonathan Cape, 2 January 1946, *Sursum Corda! The Collected*

Letters of Malcolm Lowry, Vol. 1, 1926–1946, edited with an introduction and annotations by Sherill E. Grace, Jonathan Cape, London, 1995, p. 502.

13 Paul Bowles, Foreword to *O My Land, My Friends: The Selected Letters of Hart Crane*, ed. Langdon Hammer and Brom Weber, Four Walls Eight Windows, New York, London, 1997, p. vii.

14 Paul Bowles, quoted in Millicent Dillon, *A Little Original Sin: The Life and Work of Jane Bowles*, 1st ed. 1981, University of California Press, Berkeley, Los Angeles, London, 1998, p. 88.

15 Aldous Huxley, *Beyond The Mexique Bay*, p. 309.

16 Paul Bowles, Letter to Virgil Thomson, 27 July 1941, Virgil Thomson Archive, Music Library, Yale University, quoted by Dillon, *A Little Original Sin*, p. 97.

17 William Spratling, *A Small Mexican World*, Little, Brown & Co., Boston, Toronto, 1964, originally published as Little Mexico, 1932, pp. 6, 12.

18 PH, Mexico Diary, 25 April 1944, SLA.

19 PH, Cahier 11, 4/16/44, SLA.

20 PH, Cahier 11, 2/10/44, SLA.

21 PH, Mexico Diary, 9 April 1944, SLA.

22 PH, Mexico Diary, 17 April 1944, SLA.

23 PH, Cahier 11, 4/2/44, SLA.

24 PH, Mexico Diary, 19 March 1944, translated by Anna von Planta, SLA.

25 PH, *A Game for the Living*, p. 241.

26 PH, Cahier 11, 4/14/44, SLA.

27 PH, Mexico Diary, 30 March 1944, translated by Anna von Planta, SLA.

28 PH, Lleida speech, 26 April 1987, SLA.

29 PH, Cahier 12, 11/24/44, SLA.

30 PH, *The Click of the Shutting*, p. 1, SLA.

31 Ibid., p. 5.

32 Ibid., p. 113.

33 Ibid., p. 145.

34 Ibid.

35 PH, Mexico Diary, 6 April 1944, SLA.

36 PH, Cahier 8, 9/25/42, SLA.

37 Andre Gide, *The Counterfeiters*, translated by Dorothy Bussy, Alfred Knopf, London, 1928, p. 63.

38 Ibid., p. 311.

39 Graham Greene, Foreword, *Eleven*, Heinemann, London, 1970, p. x.

40 PH, Cahier 11, 4/16/44, SLA.

41 PH, Mexico Diary, 13 April 1944, SLA.

42 PH, Cahier 11, 10/16/44, SLA.

43 PH, *Strangers on a Train*, Cresset Press, London, p. 56.

44 PH, Letter to Kate Kingsley Skattebol, 12 May 1944, SLA.

45 Ibid.

46 Ibid.

47 Kate Kingsley Skattebol, Letter to the author, 13 July 2001.

48 PH, Cahier 11, 6/11/44, SLA.

49 PH, Cahier 11, 6/22/44, SLA.

50 PH, Cahier 11, 6/25/44.

51 Lucretia Stewart, 'Animal Lover's Beastly Murders', *Sunday Telegraph*, 8 September 1991.

52 PH, Cahier 16, 12/4/47, SLA.

53 PH, Cahier 14, 12/18/46, SLA.

54 PH, Diary 9, 30 June 1947, SLA.

55 Vivien De Bernardi, Letter to the author, 9 August 2001.

56 Interview with Janice Robertson, 10 October 2002.

57 Kate Kingsley Skattebol, Letters to the author, 23 July 2001, 28 July 2001, 1 August 2001.

58 PH writing as Claire Morgan, *The Price of Salt*, Coward-McCann Inc., New York, 1952, p. 67.

59 PH, *Ripley Under Ground*, Heinemann, London, 1971, p. 15.
60 PH, *The Price of Salt*, p. 7.
61 Ibid., p. 207.
62 PH, *The Blunderer*, Cresset Press, London, p. 77.
63 PH, Cahier 11, 9/29/44, SLA.
64 PH, Cahier 12, 11/26/44, SLA.
65 PH, Cahier 12, 3/20/45, SLA.

9 The strange, subtle pluckings of terror 1945–1948

1   Anatole Broyard, *Kafka was the Rage: A Greenwich Village Memoir*, Carol Southern Books, New York, 1993, p. 80.
2   Ibid., p. 29.
3   Ibid., p. 3.
4   Ibid., p. 31.
5   Charles Neider, *New York Times Book Review*, 5 August 1945.
6   Ibid.
7   Edwin Berry Burgum, *The Novel and the World's Dilemma*, Oxford University Press, New York, 1947, p. 93.
8   PH, Cahier 17, 2/16/48, SLA.
9   PH, Diary 9, 22 February 1948, translated by Ulrich Weber, SLA.
10 PH, Cahier 13, 10/31/45, SLA.
11 PH, Cahier 13, 8/16/45, SLA.
12 PH, Cahier 13, 9/8/45, SLA.
13 PH, Cahier 12, 4/11/45, SLA.
14 PH, Cahier 13, 10/19/45, SLA.
15 Emily M. Morison, Letter to PH, 8 August 1945, AK.
16 PH, Cahier 13, 8/21/45, SLA.
17 Janet Flanner, *Paris Journal*, Vol. 1, 1944–1965, Atheneum, New York, 1965, p. 49.
18 Jean Wahl, 'Existentialism: A Preface', *New Republic*, 1 October 1945, p. 442.
19 *Time*, 28 January 1946, p. 16.
20 John Patrick Diggins, *The Proud Decades: America in War and Peace, 1941–1960*, W.W. Norton & Company, New York, London, 1988, p. 51.
21 PH, Cahier 13, 5/8/46, SLA.
22 Jean-Paul Sartre, 'Camus' *The Outsider*', February 1943, anthologised in *Literary and Philosophical Essays*, translated by Annette Michelson, Rider and Company, London, 1955, p. 24.
23 Albert Camus, *The Outsider*, translated by Stuart Gilbert, Hamish Hamilton, London, 1946, p. 9; published under the title *The Stranger*, Alfred A. Knopf Inc., New York, 1946.
24 Ibid., p. 81.
25 Albert Camus, preface, *The Outsider*, American University Edition, Appleton-Century-Crofts Inc., 1955.
26 PH, Cahier 13, 5/3/46, SLA.
27 PH, Cahier 13, 11/25/45, SLA.
28 PH, Cahier 14, 12/26/46, SLA.
29 PH, Cahier 13, 12/16/45, SLA.
30 PH, Cahier 16, 8/28/47, SLA.
31 PH, *Plotting and Writing Suspense Fiction*, The Writer Inc., Boston, 1966, p. 47.
32 PH, Diary 9, 23 June 1947, translated by Ulrich Weber, SLA.
33 PH, Diary 9, 30 August 1947, translated by Ulrich Weber, SLA.
34 PH, *Plotting and Writing Suspense Fiction*, p. 145.
35 PH, Diary 9, 3 August 1947, translated by Ulrich Weber, SLA.

36 PH, Cahier 16, 11/22/47, SLA.
37 PH, Diary 21, undated, SLA.
38 Marion Chamberlain, Letter to Margot Johnson, 15 January 1948, SLA.
39 PH, Diary 9, 20 January 1948, translated by Ulrich Weber, SLA.
40 Marion Chamberlain, Letter to Margot Johnson, 15 January 1948, SLA.

10 How I adore my Virginias 1945–1948

1 PH, Answers to Q&A for *Ellery Queen's Mystery Magazine*, sent 18 November 1981, SLA.
2 Fyodor Dostoevsky quoted by PH, Cahier 13, undated, SLA.
3 Thomas Mann, Introduction, *The Short Novels of Dostoevsky*, Dial Press, New York, 1946.
4 Fyodor Dostoevsky, *Crime and Punishment*, translated by Frederick Whishaw, Everyman, J.M. Dent, London, E.P. Dutton, New York, 1911, p. 8.
5 PH, *Strangers on a Train*, Cresset Press, London, 1950, p. 149.
6 Ibid., p. 7.
7 Dostoevsky, *Crime and Punishment*, p. 392.
8 PH, *Strangers on a Train*, p. 158.
9 PH, Cahier 15, undated, SLA.
10 Dostoevsky, *Crime and Punishment*, p. 167.
11 PH, *Strangers on a Train*, p. 193.
12 Ibid., p. 194.
13 PH, Cahier 33, 8/30/75 SLA.
14 PH, *Strangers on a Train*, p. 20.
15 Ibid., p. 307.
16 Dostoevsky, *Crime and Punishment*, p. 343.
17 Dostoevsky, quoted in Sven Linner, *Dostoevsky on Realism*, Almqvist & Wiksell, Stockholm, 1967, p. 35.
18 Dostoevsky, quoted in Linner, *Dostoevsky on Realism*, p. 178.
19 Jean-Paul Sartre, 'Aminadab or the fantastic considered as a language', *Literary and Philosophical Essays*, translated by Annette Michelson, Rider and Company, London, 1955, p. 62.
20 Tzvetan Todorov, *The Fantastic: A Structural Approach to a Literary Genre*, originally published in 1970, translated by Richard Howard, Cornell University Press, Ithaca, New York, 1975, p. 120.
21 Mikhail Bakhtin, *Problems of Dostoevsky's Poetics*, translated by R. W. Rotsel, Ardis Publishers, New York, 1973, p. 122.
22 Sartre, 'Aminadab', *Literary and Philosophical Essays*, p. 65.
23 PH, Cahier 25, 2/18/59, SLA.
24 PH, Cahier 19, 7/22/50, SLA.
25 PH, Cahier 15, 4/16/47, SLA.
26 Ibid.
27 Adoption Papers, Surrogate's Court, Westchester County, New York, November 1946, SLA.
28 Ibid.
29 'Cholly Knickerbocker Says', 21 December 1933, unknown newspaper, TU.
30 *Philadelphia Evening Bulletin*, 24 April 1935, TU.
31 Ann Clark (formerly Ann Smith), Letter to the author, 5 February 2000.
32 PH, Diary 10, 11 October 1950, SLA.
33 PH, Diary 15, 9 February 1968, SLA.
34 PH, Cahier 15, 4/29/47, SLA.
35 PH, Cahier 16, 9/1/47, SLA.
36 Interview with Maggie Eversol, 13 March 2000.
37 Maggie Eversol, Letter to the author, 4 April 2000.

38 Interview with David Diamond, 17 August 2000.
39 PH, Cahier 14, October 1946, SLA.
40 PH, *Strangers on a Train*, p. 242.
41 PH, Cahier 16, 9/4/47, SLA.
42 PH, Cahier 16, 10/23/47, SLA.
43 PH, Diary 11, 28 July 1951, SLA.
44 PH, Cahier 16, 11/13/47, SLA.
45 PH, Diary 9, 4 January 1948, translated by Ulrich Weber, SLA.
46 PH, Cahier 16, 9/24/47, SLA.
47 *Woman's Hour*, BBC Radio, 29 June 1965.
48 PH, Letter to Kate Kingsley Skattebol, 2 June 1948, SLA.
49 Graham Greene, Foreword, *Eleven*, Heinemann, London, 1970, p. xi.
50 PH, Letter to Millicent Dillon, 5 June 1977, SLA.
51 Kate Kingsley Skattebol, Letter to the author, 28 July 2001.
52 PH, Diary 9, December 1947, translated by Ulrich Weber, SLA.
53 PH, Diary 9, 11 December 1947, translated by Ulrich Weber, SLA.
54 PH, Diary 9, 11 March 1948, translated by Ulrich Weber, SLA.
55 Ibid.
56 Susan Smith, 'A painter of psychological portraits', *Fort Worth Star-Telegram*, 15 June 1976.
57 Craig Brown, 'The Hitman and Her', *The Times,* Saturday Review, 28 September 1991.
58 PH, Yaddo application, 2 March 1948, YA.
59 PH, Yaddo application, 15 March 1948,YA.
60 Margot Johnson, Letter to Elizabeth Ames, 11 March 1948, YA.
61 Anon., Letter to Elizabeth Ames, 9 April 1948, YA.
62 PH, Diary 8, 19 April 1948, SLA.
63 Ibid.
64 PH, Analysis of relationships, undated, SLA.

11 Yaddo, shadow – shadow, Yaddo! 1948

1 PH, Inscription, *Strangers on a Train*, 1950, YA.
2 Marjorie Peabody Waite, *Yaddo Yesterday and Today*, 1933, reprinted Argus Press, Albany, New York, 1995, p. 22.
3 Katrina Trask, *Yaddo Chronicles of 1888*, quoted in Waite, *Yaddo Yesterday*, p. 22.
4 Katrina Trask, *Yaddo*, written 1917–1918, published in 1923, quoted in Waite, *Yaddo Yesterday*, p. 26.
5 Gerald Clarke, *Capote: A Biography*, Hamish Hamilton, London, 1988, p. 100.
6 PH, Diary 8, 5 July 1948, SLA.
7 Chester Himes, *The Quality of Hurt, The Autobiography of Chester Himes, Volume 1*, Michael Joseph, London, 1971, p. 104.
8 PH, Letter to Ronald Blythe, 3 September 1967, RB.
9 PH, Letter to Kate Kingsley Skattebol, 2 June 1948, SLA.
10 PH, Diary 8, 11 May 1948, SLA.
11 Ian Hamilton, 'Patricia Highsmith', *New Review*, August 1977.
12 PH, Diary 8, 17 June 1948, SLA.
13 PH, *Strangers on a Train*, Cresset Press, London, 1950, p. 194.
14 Clifford Wright, Letter to PH, 13 December 1976, EB.
15 *Kaleidoscope*, BBC Radio, 17 March 1975.
16 PH, Diary 8, 17 June 1948, SLA.
17 PH, Diary 8, 5 July 1948, SLA.
18 Ibid.
19 PH, Diary 8, 24 June 1948, SLA.

20 J.H. Jackson, *San Francisco Chronicle*, 14 February 1947.

21 PH, Diary 8, 5 July 1948, SLA.

22 PH, Diary 8, 26 August 1948, translated by Ulrich Weber, SLA.

23 Interview with Edith Brandel, 7 September 1999.

24 Ann Clark, Letter to the author, 12 April 2000.

25 Ibid.

26 PH, Cahier 25, 10/8/58, SLA.

27 Ann Clark, Letter to the author.

28 Ibid.

29 Anatole Broyard, *Kafka was the Rage: A Greenwich Village Memoir*, Carol Southern Books, New York, 1993, p. 45.

30 Lillian Faderman, *Odds Girls and Twilight Lovers: A History of Lesbian Life in Twentieth-Century America*, Penguin Books, London, 1992, p. 132.

31 Dr Richard Robertiello, *Voyage From Lesbos: The Psychoanalysis of a Female Homosexual*, Citadel Press, New York, 1959.

32 PH, Letter to Stanley Highsmith, 1 September 1970, SLA.

33 Ibid.

34 PH, Diary 8, Therapy Diary, First visit, translated by Ulrich Weber, SLA.

35 Ibid.

36 PH, Diary 8, Therapy Diary, Sixth visit, translated by Ulrich Weber, SLA.

37 PH, Diary 8, Therapy Diary, Fourteenth visit, translated by Ulrich Weber, SLA.

38 PH, Diary 8, 18 May 1949, SLA.

39 PH, Diary 8, 6 May 1949, SLA.

12 Instantly, I love her 1948–1949

1 PH, Afterword, *Carol*, Bloomsbury, London, 1990, p. 260.

2 *The Late Show*, BBC2, 3 October 1990.

3 Interview with Priscilla Kennedy, 19 April 2000.

4 PH, Cahier 18, 12/9/48, SLA.

5 Ibid.

6 PH, Diary 8, 22 December 1948, SLA.

7 PH, Letter to Barbara Ker-Seymer, 5 March 1969, SLA.

8 PH, Letter to Stanley Highsmith, 29 August 1970, SLA.

9 Interview with Ann Clark, 18 February 2000.

10 PH, Diary 8, 30 March 1949, SLA.

11 PH, Diary 8, 8 May 1949, SLA.

12 PH, Diary 8, 24 May 1949, SLA.

13 PH, Cahier 16, 11/20/47, SLA.

14 PH, Cahier 22, 10/27/53, SLA.

15 Kate Kingsley Skattebol, Letter to the author, 13 August 2001.

16 PH, Diary 8, 20 May 1949, SLA.

17 PH, Diary 8, 4 June 1949, SLA.

18 PH, Diary 8, 26 June 1949, SLA.

19 PH, Cahier 18, undated, SLA.

20 PH, Diary 8, 1 July 1949, SLA.

21 PH, writing as Claire Morgan, *The Price of Salt*, Coward-McCann Inc., New York, 1952, p. 169.

22 PH, Diary 8, 7 September 1949, SLA.

23 PH, Diary 8, 8 September 1949, SLA.

24 PH, Cahier 18, 7/29/49, SLA.

25 PH, Diary 8, 3 October 1949, SLA.

26 Søren Kierkegaard, *A Kierkegaard Anthology*, ed. Robert Bretall, Princeton University Press, Princeton, New Jersey, 1946, p. 353.
27 Robert Bretall, Introduction, *A Kierkegaard Anthology*, p. xvii.
28 Kierkegaard, *A Kierkegaard Anthology*, p. 107.
29 Ibid., p. 217.
30 PH, Cahier 20, 11/2/50, SLA.
31 Kierkegaard, *A Kierkegaard Anthology*, p. 296.

13 Carol, in a thousand cities 1949–1951

1 PH, Diary 8, 22 October 1949, SLA.
2 PH, 'The Birds Poised to Fly', *Eleven*, Heinemann, London, 1970, p. 13.
3 PH, Diary 10, 15 November 1949, SLA.
4 PH, Diary 8, 9 October 1949, SLA.
5 PH, writing as Claire Morgan, *The Price of Salt*, Coward-McCann Inc., New York, 1952, p. 67.
6 PH, Cahier 8, 9/22/42, SLA.
7 PH, *The Price of Salt*, p. 60.
8 Ibid., p. 51.
9 PH, Diary 10, 5 May 1950, SLA.
10 PH, Diary 10, 19 November 1949, SLA.
11 PH, Afterword, *Carol*, Bloomsbury, London, 1990, p. 261.
12 PH, Diary 10, 12 October 1950, SLA.
13 Lillian Faderman, *Odd Girls and Twilight Lovers, A History of Lesbian Life in Twentieth-Century America*, Penguin Books, London, 1992, p. 141.
14 Ibid.
15 Rosie G. Waldeck, 'Homosexual International', *Human Events*, New York Lesbian Herstory Archives, 1950s file, quoted in Faderman, *Odd Girls*, p. 146.
16 PH, *The Price of Salt*, p. 221.
17 Ibid., p. 244.
18 Ibid., p. 276.
19 PH, Afterword, *Carol*, p. 261.
20 *Forbidden Love: The Unashamed Stories of Lesbian Lives*, National Film Board of Canada, 1992, quoted in Jaye Zimet, *Strange Sisters: The Art of Lesbian Pulp Fiction 1949–1969*, Viking Studio, Penguin, New York, 1999, p. 20.
21 Ibid.
22 Zimet, *Strange Sisters*, p. 27.
23 PH, Cahier 19, 8/7/50, SLA.
24 PH, Diary 10, 1 January 1950, SLA.
25 PH, Cahier 19, 1/26/50, SLA.
26 PH, Cahier 19, 1/19/50, SLA.
27 PH, Diary 10, 19 April 1950, SLA.
28 PH, Diary 10, 23 May 1950, SLA.
29 PH, Diary 10, 31 May 1950, SLA.
30 PH, Cahier 19, 6/6/50, SLA.
31 PH, Diary 10, 30 June 1950, SLA.
32 PH, Cahier 19, 6/30/50, SLA.
33 PH, Cahier 19, 7/2/50, SLA.
34 *Book Beat*, Interview with Donald Swaim, CBS Radio, 29 October 1987, DS.
35 PH, Letter to Ronald Blythe, 30 August 1971, RB.
36 *The New Yorker*, 18 March 1950, p. 114.
37 *New York Herald Tribune Book Review*, 16 April, 1950, p. 26.

38 Alfred Hitchcock, Letter to Ramona Herdman, 17 May 1950, SLA.

39 PH, Letter to Robert Calmann-Lévy, 21 January 1967, CLA.

40 Gerald Peary, 'Highsmith', *Sight & Sound*, Spring 1988.

41 Ann Clark, Letter to the author, 12 April 2000.

42 Brian Glanville, 'Sad finale to a literary life's work', *European Magazine*, 10–16 March 1995.

43 Raymond Chandler, Letter to Bernice Baumgarten, 13 September 1950, *The Raymond Chandler Papers, Selected Letters and Non-Fiction, 1909–1959*, ed. Tom Hiney and Frank MacShane, Hamish Hamilton, London, 2000, p. 135.

44 Raymond Chandler, Letter to Alfred Hitchcock (unsent), 6 December 1950, *Selected Letters of Raymond Chandler*, ed. Frank MacShane, Jonathan Cape, London, 1981, p. 244.

45 Tom Hiney, *Raymond Chandler: A Biography*, Chatto & Windus, London, 1997, p. 193.

46 Raymond Chandler, Letter to Carl Brandt, 11 December 1950, *Selected Letters*, p. 247.

47 PH, Introduction, *The World of Raymond Chandler*, ed. Miriam Gross, Weidenfeld and Nicholson, London, 1977, p. 5–6.

48 Gerald Peary, 'Highsmith', *Sight & Sound*, Spring 1988.

49 PH, Diary 10, 24 November 1950, SLA.

50 Marc Brandel, *The Choice*, Harper & Brothers, New York, 1950; Eyre & Spottiswoode, London, 1952, p. 34.

51 Ibid., p. 123.

52 Ibid., p. 124.

53 Ann Clark, Letter to the author, 12 April 2000.

54 Ibid.

55 PH, Diary 10, 29 October 1950, SLA.

56 PH, Diary 10, 6 January 1951, SLA.

57 Ibid.

58 Charles J. Rolo, 'Carol and Therese', *New York Times Book Review*, 18 May 1952, p. 23.

59 Ann Clark, Letter to the author, 27 April 2000.

14 Two identities: the victim and the murderer 1951–1953

1   PH, Cahier 21, 11/30/52, SLA.

2   PH, Letter to Kate Kingsley Skattebol, 14 June 1952, SLA.

3   *Evening News*, 16 February 1951.

4   PH, Cahier 20, 2/16/51, SLA.

5   PH, Cahier 20, 11/2/50, SLA.

6   PH, Diary 11, 25 February 1951, SLA.

7   PH, Diary 11, 20 April 1951, SLA.

8   PH, Diary 11, 17 May 1951, SLA.

9   PH, Cahier 20, 5/5/51, SLA.

10 PH, Diary 11, 11 August 1951, SLA.

11 Ian Hamilton, 'Patricia Highsmith', *New Review*, August 1977.

12 PH, Letter to Kate Kingsley Skattebol, 23 March 1953, SLA.

13 Interview with Kate Kingsley Skattebol, 14 May 1999.

14 PH, *The Traffic of Jacob's Ladder*, SLA.

15 PH, Cahier 20, 8/15/51, SLA.

16 Interview with Kate Kingsley Skattebol.

17 Interview with Peggy Lewis, 14 December 1999.

18 Interview with Peter Huber, 14 March 1999.

19 PH, Diary 11, 2 September 1951, SLA.

20 PH, Diary 11, 4 September 1951, SLA.

21 Interview with Kate Kingsley Skattebol.

22 PH, Diary 11, 14 October 1951, SLA.

23 PH, Cahier 20, undated, SLA.
24 Diana Cooper-Clark, 'Patricia Highsmith – Interview', *The Armchair Detective*, Vol. 14, No. 4, 1981, p. 313.
25 PH, Diary 11, 29 December 1951, SLA.
26 PH, Diary 11, 21 May 1952, SLA.
27 PH, Diary 11, 22 May 1952, SLA.
28 PH, Cahier 22, 6/18/52, SLA.
29 PH, 'Scene of the Crime', *Granta*, Vol. 29, Winter 1989; published in German as 'Tom Ripleys Geburt', *Frankfurter Allgemeine Zeitung*, 24 August 1991.
30 PH, Diary 11, 4 July 1952, SLA.
31 PH, *The Blunderer*, Cresset Press, London, 1956, p. 18.
32 Ibid., p. 24.
33 PH, Diary 11, 15 August 1952, SLA.
34 PH, Letter to Kate Kingsley Skattebol, 5 January 1967, SLA.
35 PH, Diary 11, 10 September 1952, SLA.
36 PH, Letter to Kate Kingsley Skattebol, 26 October 1952, SLA.
37 PH, Diary 11, 6 November 1952, SLA.
38 PH, Diary 11, 11 November 1952, SLA.
39 Brian Glanville, 'Sad finale to a literary life's work', *European Magazine*, 10–16 March 1995.
40 Ibid.
41 Interview with Brian Glanville, 12 September 1999.
42 PH, Diary 12, 24 May 1953, SLA.
43 PH, Diary 12, 3 July 1953, SLA.
44 PH, Diary 12, 4 July 1953, SLA.
45 PH, *The Blunderer*, p. 60.
46 PH, Diary 12, 14 August 1953, SLA.
47 PH, Diary 12, 7 August 1953, SLA.

15 Pat H, alias Ripley 1953–1955

1 PH, Cahier 20, 9/10/50, SLA.
2 PH, Diary 12, 16 June 1953, SLA.
3 John Patrick Diggins, *The Proud Decades: America in War and Peace, 1941–1960*, W.W. Norton & Company, New York, London, 1988, p. 181.
4 Ibid., p. 178.
5 David Riesman, with Nathan Glazer 38; Reuel Denney, *The Lonely Crowd: A Study of the Changing American Character*, Yale University Press, New Haven, 1950, p. 22.
6 Diggins, *The Proud Decades*, p. 187.
7 PH, *The Blunderer*, Cresset Press, London, 1956, p. 25.
8 Ibid., p. 15.
9 Ibid., p. 26.
10 Ibid., p. 15.
11 Ibid., p. 278.
12 PH, Letter to Kate Kingsley Skattebol, 27 October 1953, SLA.
13 'Plenty of Quiet and Afternoon Beer One Author's Recipe for Success', *Fort Worth Star-Telegram*, dated by PH as September or October 1953, SLA.
14 PH, Letter to Kate Kingsley Skattebol, 24 December 1953, SLA.
15 PH, Letter to Kate Kingsley Skattebol, 27 October 1953, SLA
16 PH, Cahier 22, 10/7/53, SLA.
17 Diary 12, 9 November 1953, translated by Anna von Planta, SLA.
18 Diary 12, 16 March 1954, SLA.
19 Ibid.

20 PH, Cf. LR, TB, undated, SLA.

21 PH, Cahier 23, 5/8/54, SLA.

22 PH, Cahier 23, 4/22/54, SLA.

23 PH, Cahier 23, 7/30/54, SLA.

24 'Patricia Highsmith: A Gift for Murder', *The South Bank Show*, LWT, 14 November 1982.

25 PH, Cahier 18, 4/19/49, SLA.

26 PH, Cahier 18, 9/26/49, SLA.

27 PH, Cahier 23, 3/28/54, SLA.

28 PH, Cahier 23, 6/15/54, SLA.

29 PH, *Plotting and Writing Suspense Fiction*, The Writer Inc., Boston, 1966, p. 68.

30 PH, *The Talented Mr Ripley*, Cresset Press, London, 1957, p. 83.

31 PH, *Plotting and Writing Suspense Fiction*, p. 69.

32 Ibid.

33 PH, personal dedication to Charles Latimer, *Ripley Under Ground*, 2 April 1971, Charles Latimer Collection, The University of British Columbia.

34 Interview with Charles Latimer, 2 November 1998.

35 Interview with Bettina Berch, 18 May 1999.

36 PH, Letter to Barbara Ker-Seymer, 24 May 1969.

37 Interview with Peter Thomson, 16 May 2000.

38 PH, Cahier 23, 10/1/54, SLA.

39 PH, *The Talented Mr Ripley*, p. 232.

40 Ibid., p. 35.

41 Ibid., p. 73.

42 Ibid., p. 112.

43 Ibid., p. 167.

44 Ibid., p. 175.

45 PH, Cahier 18, 10/1/49, SLA.

46 PH, Cahier 23, 10/1/54, SLA.

47 'Patricia Highsmith: A Gift for Murder', *The South Bank Show*.

48 PH, Letter to Alex Szogyi,8 January 1969, SLA.

49 PH, Cahier 23, 11/19/54, SLA.

50 Interview with Peggy Lewis, 14 December 1999.

51 Interview with Dan Coates, 20 November 1999.

52 Interview with Kate Kingsley Skattebol, 14 May 1999.

53 Craig Brown, 'The Hitman and Her', *The Times,* Saturday Review, 28 September 1991.

54 *The New Yorker*, 7 January 1956.

55 Ibid.

56 Anthony Boucher, *New York Times Book Review*, 25 December 1955.

57 PH, *Plotting and Writing Suspense Fiction*, p. 69.

16 Each Man is in His Spectres power 1955–1958

1 PH, Cahier 23, 2/14/55, SLA.

2 PH, Cahier 23, 3/21/55, SLA.

3 PH, Diary 14, 7 June 1962, SLA.

4 PH, Cahier 23, 4/30/55, SLA.

5 PH, Cahier 23, 7/12/55, SLA.

6 PH, *Deep Water*, Heinemann, London, 1958, p. 1–2.

7 Ibid., p. 2.

8 PH, Cahier 23, 4/6/55, SLA.

9 PH, *Deep Water*, p. 91.

10 Anthony Boucher, *New York Times Book Review*, 6 October 1957.

11 PH, *Deep Water*, p. 170.
12 Ibid.
13 Ibid., p. 40.
14 Russell Harrison, *Patricia Highsmith,* Twayne Publishers, New York, 1997, Preface, p. x.
15 PH, Cahier 24, 1/13/56, SLA.
16 Ibid.
17 PH, *Plotting and Writing Suspense Fiction*, The Writer Inc., Boston, 1966, p. 17.
18 PH, 'The Barbarians', *Eleven*, Heinemann, London, 1970, p. 168.
19 PH, Cahier 24, 6/8/56, SLA.
20 PH, Cahier 24, 7/31/56, SLA.
21 PH, Cahier 24, 10/21/56, SLA.
22 Ibid.
23 PH, Cahier 24, 5/22/57, SLA.
24 PH, *A Game for the Living*, Heinemann, London, 1959, p. 5.
25 PH, Cahier 24, 2/20/57, SLA.
26 PH, Cahier 24, 1/18/57, SLA.
27 PH, Cahier 24, 5/1/57, SLA.
28 PH, Letter to Joan Kahn, 27 July 1957, HA.
29 PH, Letter to Joan Kahn, 5 October 1957, HA.
30 PH, Cahier 24, 9/29/57, SLA.
31 PH, Cahier 24, 9/30/57, SLA.
32 Quoted in Colin Wilson, *The Outsider*, Victor Gollanz, London, 1956, p. 12.
33 Quoted in ibid., p. 15.
34 Quoted in ibid., p. 79.
35 Quoted in ibid., p. 23.
36 William Blake, '"Each Man is in His Spectres power", Notebook Poems c. 1800–1806', *The Complete Poems*, edited by Alicia Ostriker, Penguin Books, London, p. 494.
37 Carl Jung, 'Conscious, Unconscious, and Individuation', 1939, quoted in *The Essential Jung*, Selected and Introduced by Anthony Storr, Fontana Press, London, 1998, p. 221.
38 Francis Wyndham, 'Sick of Psychopaths', *Sunday Times*, 11 April 1965.
39 PH, *The Straightforward Lie*, unpublished manuscript, p. 240, SLA.
40 PH, *A Game for the Living*, p. 122.
41 PH, Cahier 24, 1/3/58, SLA.
42 Joan Kahn, Letter to PH, 14 February 1958, HRA.
43 PH, Letter to Joan Kahn, 19 February 1958, HRA.
44 Dorothy B. Hughes, Letter to Joan Kahn, 9 November 1958, HRA.
45 Joan Kahn, Letter to Dorothy B. Hughes, 12 November 1958, HRA.
46 PH, *Plotting and Writing Suspense Fiction*, revised edition, Poplar Press, London, 1983, p. 139.
47 Ibid.
48 PH, *Plotting and Writing Suspense Fiction*, 1966, p. 140.
49 PH, Cahier 25, 6/3/58, SLA.

17 This sweet sickness 1958–1959

1 PH, *This Sweet Sickness*, Heinemann, London, 1961, p. 19.
2 PH, Cahier 2, undated entry but the notebook covers the period 1939/1940, SLA.
3 Friedrich Nietzsche, 'Assorted Opinions and Maxims', *A Nietzsche Reader*, Selected and Translated by R.J. Hollingdale, Penguin Books, London, 1977, p. 232.
4 PH, *This Sweet Sickness*, p. 15.
5 Nietzsche, 'Daybreak', *A Nietzsche Reader*, p. 221.
6 Nietzsche, 'Human, All Too Human', *A Nietzsche Reader*, p. 215.

7 PH, *This Sweet Sickness*, p. 14.
8 Ibid., p. 16.
9 Ibid.
10 Nietzsche, 'Thus Spoke Zarathustra', *A Nietzsche Reader*, p. 243.
11 PH, *This Sweet Sickness*, p. 23.
12 Ibid., p. 172.
13 Ibid., p. 197.
14 Ibid., p. 167.
15 Ibid., p. 239.
16 Ibid., p. 240.
17 Nietzsche, 'Daybreak', *A Nietzsche Reader*, p. 234.
18 PH, Cahier 25, 6/13/58, SLA.
19 PH, Cahier 25, 11/5/58, SLA.
20 'Meet Your Instructor . . . Mary Ronin', Famous Artists School, Westport, Connecticut, undated.
21 Ibid.
22 Letter to PH, signed M and dated by Highsmith October or November 1958, SLA.
23 Ibid.
24 Ibid.
25 PH, Cahier 25, 12/30/58, SLA.
26 PH, Cahier 25, 11/5/58, SLA.
27 Ibid.
28 PH, Letter to Kate Kingsley Skattebol, 12 February 1959, SLA.
29 Joan Kahn, Letter to PH, 8 May 1959, HRA.
30 Ibid.
31 PH, Cahier 25, 2/18/59, SLA.
32 PH, Cahier 25, 2/15/59, SLA.
33 PH, Cahier 25, 5/24/59, SLA.
34 PH, Cahier 25, 6/11/59, SLA.
35 PH, Cahier 25, 10/21/59, SLA.
36 Duncan Fallowell, 'The Talented Miss Highsmith', *Sunday Telegraph Magazine*, 20 February 2000.
37 PH, Letter to Jenny Bradley, 29 December 1958, WBA.
38 Patricia S. Myrer, Letter to the author, 1 October 2000.
39 Patricia S. Myrer, Letter to the author, 24 February 2001.
40 Patricia S. Myrer, Letter to the author, 1 October 2000.
41 Ibid.
42 Patricia S. Myrer, Letter to the author, 3 September 2000.

18 A lurking liking for those that flout the law 1959–1960

1 PH, Cahier 25, 11/14/59, SLA.
2 David M. Potter, *People of Plenty: Economic Abundance and the American Character*, University of Chicago Press, Chicago, 1954, p. 71.
3 C. Wright Mills, *White Collar: The American Middle Classes*, Oxford University Press, New York, 1951, p. xx.
4 Ibid., p. ix.
5 Daniel Bell, *The End of Ideology: On the Exhaustion of Political Ideas in the Fifties*, The Free Press of Glencoe, Illinois, 1960, p. 116.
6 Chris Matthew, 'Writing the wrong-doers', *Radio Times*, 2 December 1972.
7 Neil Gordon, Letter to the author, 9 November 2001.
8 PH, *The Blunderer*, Cresset Press, London, 1956, p. 178.

9 *Current Biography Yearbook*, 1990, p. 302.

10 Craig Brown, 'Too Busy Writing to be a Writer', *Daily Telegraph*, 29 January 2000.

11 Interview with Otto Penzler, 21 May 1999.

12 Interview with H.R.F. Keating, 20 June 2000.

13 Julian Symons, *Bloody Murder, From the Detective Story to the Crime Novel: A History*, Faber & Faber, London, 1972, p. 91.

14 Julian Symons, 'Life with a Likeable Killer', *New York Times Book Review*, 18 October 1992.

15 Julian Symons, *The Modern Crime Story*, The Tragara Press, Edinburgh, 1980, p. 14.

16 PH, *Plotting and Writing Suspense Fiction*, The Writer Inc., Boston, 1966, p. 51.

17 Diana Cooper-Clark, 'Patricia Highsmith – Interview', *The Armchair Detective*, Vol. 14, No. 4, 1981.

18 Ibid.

19 Hannah Carter, 'Queens of Crime', *Guardian*, 1 May 1968.

20 PH, Letter to Jenny Bradley, 30 September 1961, WBA .

21 Margaret Pringle, 'The Criminal Not The Crime', *Nova*, May 1971.

22 Francis Wyndham, 'Sick of Psychopaths', *Sunday Times*, 11 April 1965.

23 Louise Roddon, 'View to a kill', *Today*, 6 April 1986.

24 Interview with Roger Clarke, 15 January 2001.

25 Interview with Vivien De Bernardi, 23 July 1999.

26 Interview with Kate Kingsley Skattebol, 12 December 2001.

27 PH, Cahier 23, 4/2/54, SLA.

28 PH, Diary 10, 27 October 1950, SLA.

29 PH, *A Game for the Living*, Heinemann, London, 1959, p. 87.

30 PH, Cahier 25, 2/7/59, SLA.

31 Ibid.

32 Ibid.

33 PH, Letter to Dan Coates, 12 December 1974, SLA.

34 Ibid.

35 PH, Diary 8, 23 May 1949, SLA.

36 PH, Cahier 25, 9/28/59, SLA.

37 PH, Cahier 25, 11/20/59, SLA.

38 PH, Letter to Joan Kahn, 17 November 1959, HRA.

39 PH, Cahier 25, 2/3/60, SLA.

40 PH, Cahier 25, 2/11/60, SLA.

19 The ultra neurotic 1960–1962

1 James Sandoe, *New York Herald Tribune Book Review*, 7 February 1960, p. 11.

2 PH, *Plotting and Writing Suspense Fiction*, The Writer Inc., Boston, 1966, p. 9.

3 PH, Cahier 25, 5/3/60, SLA.

4 PH, Letter to Joan Kahn, 6 September 1960, HRA.

5 PH, Letter to Jenny Bradley, 13 October 1960, WBA.

6 PH, Cahier 26, 10/14/60, SLA.

7 PH, *Plotting and Writing Suspense Fiction*, p. 121.

8 Joan Kahn, Letter to Patricia Schartle, 21 February 1961, HRA.

9 Ibid.

10 PH, Letter to Joan Kahn, 29 February 1961, HRA.

11 Joan Kahn, Letter to PH, 3 May 1961, HRA.

12 PH, Letter to Joan Kahn, 10 May 1961, HRA.

13 PH, Letter to Jenny Bradley, 31 May 1961, WBA .

14 Anonymous reader report sent to Joan Kahn, 28 May 1962, HRA.

15 Joan Kahn, Letter to PH, 6 June 1962, HRA.

16 Brigid Brophy, *Don't Never Forget, Collected Views and Reviews*, Jonathan Cape, London, 1966, p. 155.
17 Brigid Brophy, 'Swindler and Son', *New Statesman*, 28 February 1964.
18 Julian Symons, 'Terror all the way', *Sunday Times*, 23 February 1964.
19 PH, *Plotting and Writing Suspense Fiction*, p. 122.
20 PH, Cahier 26, 3/3/61, SLA.
21 PH, *The Two Faces of January*, Heinemann, London, 1964, p. 204.
22 Ibid., p. 259.
23 Fyodor Dostoevsky, *Notes from Underground*, translated by Richard Pevear and Larissa Volokhonsky, Vintage, Random House, London, 1993, p. 8.
24 Colin Wilson, *The Outsider*, Victor Gollanz, London, 1956, p. 157.
25 PH, Cahier 15, 3/18/47, SLA.
26 PH, *The Two Faces of January*, p. 30.
27 Ibid., p. 118.
28 Ibid., p. 19.
29 Ibid., p. 244.
30 Ibid., p. 63.
31 Dostoevsky, *Notes from Underground*, p. 6.
32 Ibid., p. 129.
33 Interview with Peggy Lewis, 25 August 2000.
34 Dorothy Herrmann, *The Genius Belt: The Story of the Arts in Bucks County, Pennsylvania*, James A. Michener Art Museum, Doylestown, Pennsylvania, 1996, p. 46.
35 PH, Cahier 26, 12/16/60, SLA.
36 PH, *First Person Novel*, unpublished, c. 1961, SLA.
37 Ibid.
38 Ibid.
39 PH, Cahier 26, 2/9/61, SLA.
40 PH, Cahier 26, 2/4/61, SLA.
41 Ibid.
42 PH, Cahier 26, 2/9/61, SLA.
43 PH, *The Cry of the Owl*, Heinemann, London, 1963, pp. 5–7.
44 PH, Letter to Kate Kingsley Skattebol, 30 May 1961, SLA.
45 PH, Cahier 26, 8/31/61, SLA.
46 PH, 'Suspense: Rules and Non-Rules', *Writer Magazine*, November 1964.
47 Brophy, *Don't Never Forget*, p. 154.
48 Phyllis Meras, 'A Talk with Brigid Brophy', *New York Times Book Review*, 21 May 1967.
49 PH, *The Cry of the Owl*, p. 5.
50 Ibid., p. 3.
51 Ibid., p. 27.
52 Ibid., p. 7–8.
53 Ibid., p. 116.
54 Ibid., p. 17.
55 Ibid., p. 165.
56 Ibid., p. 270.
57 Ibid., p. 271.
58 Joan Kahn, Letter to PH, 8 February 1962, HRA.
59 Ibid.
60 PH, Cahier 26, 6/1/61, SLA.
61 Ibid.
62 Interview with Peggy Lewis, 25 August 2000.
63 Interview with Phillip Powell, 25 August 2000.
64 PH, Cahier 26, 8/8/61, SLA.
65 Daisy Winston, Letter to PH, 28 December 1991, SLA.
66 Ibid.
67 PH, Letter to Kate Kingsley Skattebol, 29 April 1967, SLA.

68 PH, Cahier 26, 12/22/61, SLA.
69 Interview with Alex Szogyi, 16 May 1999.
70 PH, Cahier 26, 6/8/62, SLA.
71 Oscar Wilde, 'Letter to H.C. Marillier', *The Letters of Oscar Wilde*, ed. Rupert Hart-Davis, Rupert Hart-Davis Ltd, London, 1962, p. 185, quoted by PH, Cahier 26, 2/7/62.

20 A freedom from responsibility 1962–1964

1   PH, 'First Love', *Sunday Times Magazine*, 20 January 1974.
2   PH, Diary, SLA.
3   PH, Diary, SLA.
4   PH, Diary, SLA.
5   Lucretia Stewart, 'Animal Lover's Beastly Murders', *Sunday Telegraph*, 8 September 1991.
6   PH, *Plotting and Writing Suspense Fiction*, The Writer Inc., Boston, 1966, p. 102.
7   Ibid., p. 103.
8   Ibid.
9   John Bartlow Martin, *Break Down The Walls – American Prisons: Present, Past, and Future*, Ballantine Books, New York, 1954, Foreword.
10 Ibid., p. 268.
11 PH, *Plotting and Writing Suspense Fiction*, pp. 103–104.
12 Ibid., p. 103.
13 PH, Diary, SLA.
14 PH, Diary, SLA.
15 PH, Diary, SLA.
16 Interview with Francis Wyndham, 1 March 2000.
17 Francis Wyndham, 'Miss Highsmith', *New Statesman*, 31 May 1963.
18 Ibid.
19 Ibid.
20 PH, Diary, SLA.
21 PH, Diary, SLA.
22 PH, Diary 15, 3 May 1963, SLA.
23 PH, Diary 15, 5 June 1963, SLA.
24 Interview with Peter Thomson, 16 May 2000.
25 PH, Cahier 27, 7/14/63, SLA.
26 PH, Diary 15, 8 August 1963, SLA.
27 Joan Kahn, Letter to Patricia Schartle, 15 October 1963, HRA.
28 Joan Kahn, Letter to PH, 13 November 1963, HRA.
29 PH, Diary 15, 26 October 1963, SLA.
30 Richard Ingham, Letter to the author, undated but received 14 May 2002.
31 PH, *Plotting and Writing Suspense Fiction*, revised edition, Poplar Press, London, 1983, p. 130.
32 Ibid., p. 131.
33 'Worse and Worse', *Times Literary Supplement*, 25 February 1965.
34 Ibid.
35 PH, Cahier 9, transcription of teenage diary, undated entry, SLA.
36 PH, Cahier 32, 7/30/73, SLA.
37 John Wakeman, ed., *World Authors 1950–1970, A Companion Volume to Twentieth-Century Authors*, H.H. Wilson Company, New York, 1975, p. 642.
38 Julian Symons, *The Modern Crime Story*, The Tragara Press, Edinburgh, 1980, p. 14.
39 PH, Letter to Arthur Koestler, KA, MS 2385/1.
40 PH, Letter to Kate Kingsley Skattebol, 19 April 1964, SLA.
41 Interview with Ronald Blythe, 15 January 2002.

42 PH, *Plotting and Writing Suspense Fiction*, rev. ed., p. 36.
43 PH, *A Suspension of Mercy*, Heinemann, London, 1965, p. 1.
44 In Highsmith's story, 'It's a Deal', published in *Nothing That Meets the Eye: The Uncollected Stories of Patricia Highsmith*, W.W. Norton, New York, 2002, the name is given as Vanderholt.
45 Richard Ingham, *It's a Deal*, Richard Ingham collection, p. 51.
46 Richard Ingham, Letter to the author, undated but received 14 May 2002.
47 PH, Letter to Ronald Blythe, 15 September 1969, RB.
48 PH, *Plotting and Writing Suspense Fiction*, p. 6.
49 PH, Letter to Kate Kingsley Skattebol, 27 July 1964, SLA.
50 PH, *Plotting and Writing Suspense Fiction*, p. 37.
51 Diana Cooper-Clark, 'Patricia Highsmith – Interview', *The Armchair Detective*, Vol. 14, No. 4, 1981.
52 Ibid.
53 Bettina Berch, 'A Talk With Patricia Highsmith', 15 June 1984, unpublished, SLA.
54 PH, Cahier 27, 8/1/64, SLA.
55 Charles Latimer, Letter to the author, 17 December 2001.
56 Interview with Charles Latimer, 2 November 1998.
57 Interview with Ronald Blythe.
58 PH, Letter to Ronald Blythe, 26 November 1966, RB.
59 Interview with Ronald Blythe.
60 PH, Cahier 25, 12/30/58.
61 Bettina Berch, 'A Talk With Patricia Highsmith'.
62 PH, *A Suspension of Mercy*, pp. 33–34.
63 Ibid., p. 180.
64 Ibid., p. 239.
65 Ibid., p. 251.
66 PH, Letter to Peggy Lewis, 16 October 1964, PL.
67 PH, Cahier 27, 12/15/64, SLA.

21 Love was an outgoing thing 1964–1967

1   PH, Cahier 27, 12/16/64, SLA.
2   PH, Letter to Arthur Koestler, 28 January 1966, KA, MS 2385/3.
3   PH, Letter to Arthur Koestler, 20 January 1965, KA, MS 2385/2.
4   PH, Letter to Kate Kingsley Skattebol, 8 January 1965, SLA.
5   PH, *Plotting and Writing Suspense Fiction*, The Writer Inc., Boston, 1966, p. 6.
6   Ibid., p. 7.
7   PH, *Plotting and Writing Suspense Fiction*, revised edition, Poplar Press, London, 1983, p. ix.
8   PH, 'Not-Thinking with the Dishes', *Whodunit? A Guide to Crime, Suspense and Spy Fiction*, ed. H.R.F. Keating, Winward, London, 1982, p. 92.
9   Ibid.
10 Ibid.
11 Interview with Ronald Blythe, 15 January 2002.
12 PH, Diary 13, 16 November 1962, SLA.
13 PH, Letter to Robert Calmann-Lévy, 16 March 1965, CLA.
14 Manès Sperber, Letter to PH, 27 March 1965, CLA.
15 PH, Letter to Manès Sperber, 30 March 1965, CLA.
16 Ibid.
17 Manès Sperber, Letter to PH, 5 April 1965, CLA.
18 PH, Letter to Peggy Lewis, 29 July 1964, PL.
19 PH, Letter to Stanley Highsmith, 1 September 1970, SLA.

20 PH, Letter to Jenny Bradley, 18 May 1965, WBA.
21 *The Arts This Week*, BBC Radio, 21 January 1971.
22 Pooter, *The Times*, 25 January 1969.
23 PH, Cahier 34, 3/13/77, SLA.
24 PH, Letter to Dan Coates, 31 August 1976, SLA.
25 PH, Letter to Alex Szogyi, 12 May 1965, SLA.
26 PH, Diary, SLA.
27 Ibid.
28 Mary Highsmith, Letter to PH, undated, SLA.
29 Ibid.
30 PH, Diary, SLA.
31 PH, Cahier 27, SLA.
32 PH, Cahier 27, SLA.
33 PH, Letter to Alex Szogyi, SLA.
34 Ibid.
35 PH, Letter to Alex Szogyi, SLA.
36 PH, Letter to Kate Kingsley Skattebol, 26 June 1965, SLA.
37 Sir Michael Levey, Letter to the author, 8 February 2002.
38 PH, Cahier 28, SLA.
39 PH, Cahier 28, 9/12/65, SLA.
40 PH, Cahier 28, 8/19/65, SLA.
41 PH, Cahier 28, 12/23/65, SLA.
42 Ibid.
43 PH, 'The Snail-Watcher', *Eleven*, Heinemann, London, 1970, p. 10.
44 Graham Greene, Foreword, *Eleven*, p. xi.
45 Interview with Peter Thomson, 16 May 2000.
46 Interview with Larry Ashmead, 20 May 1999.
47 PH, Cahier 28, 2/7/66, SLA.
48 PH, 'The Quest for Blank Claveringi', *Eleven*, p. 87.
49 PH, Letter to Mary Highsmith, 12 April 1966, SLA.
50 PH, Cahier 28, 6/30/66, SLA.
51 Ibid.
52 Auriol Stevens, 'Private Highsmith', *Guardian*, 29 January 1969.
53 PH, Letter to Alex Szogyi, SLA.
54 PH, Cahier 28, 1/2/67, SLA.
55 Interview with Barbara Roett, 5 May 1999.
56 PH, Cahier 28, SLA.
57 Ibid.
58 PH, Cahier 28, 11/3/66, SLA.
59 Julian Symons, *Bloody Murder, From the Detective Story to the Crime Novel: A History*, Faber & Faber, London, 1972, p. 178.
60 PH, *Those Who Walk Away*, Heinemann, London, 1967, p. 10.
61 Ibid., p. 46.
62 Ibid., p. 56.
63 Anthony Boucher, *New York Times Book Review*, 30 April 1967.
64 J.M. Edelstein, 'Cat and Mouse', *New Republic*, 20 May 1967.
65 *Times Literary Supplement*, 1 June 1967.
66 Symons, *Bloody Murder*, p. 179.
67 PH, *Those Who Walk Away*, p. 23.
68 Ibid., p. 42.
69 Ibid., p. 87.
70 Ibid., p. 86.
71 Ibid., p. 224.

22 This shimmery void 1967–1968

1 Edmund Pilon, *The Country Round Paris (Île-de-France)*, The Medici Society, London, 1929, p. 15.
2 Ibid., p. 11.
3 Ibid., p. 214.
4 PH, Cahier 29, 1/27/67, SLA.
5 Ibid.
6 PH, Letter to Alex Szogyi, SLA.
7 PH, Letter to Alex Szogyi, SLA.
8 PH, Letter to Alex Szogyi, SLA.
9 Ibid.
10 Ibid.
11 PH, Dedication, *The Tremor of Forgery*, Heinemann, London, 1969.
12 PH, Cahier 29, 12/12/67, SLA.
13 Graham Greene, Foreword, *Eleven*, Heinemann, London, 1970, p. x.
14 PH, *The Tremor of Forgery*, p. 10.
15 Ibid., p. 66.
16 PH, Cahier 28, 1/1/67, SLA.
17 PH, *The Tremor of Forgery*, p. 230.
18 Ibid., p. 229.
19 Ibid.
20 Ian Hamilton, 'Patricia Highsmith', *New Review*, August 1977.
21 PH, *The Tremor of Forgery*, p. 88–89.
22 PH, *The Tremor of Forgery*, p. 104.
23 PH, Cahier 29, 2/11/68, SLA.
24 PH, Cahier 29, 3/12/67, SLA.
25 Ian Hamilton, 'Patricia Highsmith', *New Review*, August 1977.
26 PH, *The Tremor of Forgery*, p. 24.
27 Ibid., p. 72.
28 PH, Letter to Barbara Ker-Seymer, 12 November 1967, SLA.
29 PH, Cahier 29, 1/26/68, SLA.
30 Interview with Larry Ashmead, 20 May 1999.
31 PH, Letter to Alain Oulman, 2 July 1968, CLA.
32 PH, Cahier 29, 1/18/68, SLA.
33 PH, Letter to Alain Oulman, 28 August 1974, CLA.
34 PH, Letter to Alain Oulman, 20 July 1968, CLA.
35 Julian Symons, 'Patricia Highsmith: Criminals in Society', *London Magazine*, June 1969.
36 Ibid.
37 Janice Elliott, *New Statesman*, 24 January 1969.
38 Terrence Rafferty, 'Fear and Trembling', *The New Yorker*, 4 January 1988.
39 PH, Cahier 29, 1/28/67, SLA.
40 PH, Cahier 29, 2/3/68, SLA.
41 PH, Cahier 29, 3/11/68, SLA.
42 PH, Cahier 29, 11/1/67, SLA .
43 PH, Diary 15, 14 December 1967, SLA.
44 PH, Diary 15, 2 January 1968, SLA.
45 PH, Cahier 30, 8/7/68, SLA.
46 PH, Letter to Barbara Ker-Seymer, 17 February 1968, SLA.
47 PH, Letter to Kate Kingsley Skattebol, 14 March 1968, SLA.
48 Interview with Madeleine Harmsworth, 23 August 2000.
49 PH, Diary 15, 17 March 1968, SLA.
50 Ibid.
51 PH, Letter to Barbara Ker-Seymer, 17 May 1968, SLA.

52 PH, Letter to Alex Szogyi, 8 January 1969, SLA.
53 PH, Letter to Barbara Ker-Seymer, 17 May 1968, SLA.
54 Tariq Ali, Susan Watkins, *1968: Marching in the Streets*, Bloomsbury, London, 1998, p. 86.
55 PH, Cahier 29, 6/5/68, SLA.
56 PH, Diary 15, 15 June 1968, SLA.
57 PH, Letter to Arthur Koestler, 2 June 1968, KA, MS 2386/1.
58 Auriol Stevens, 'Private Highsmith', *Guardian*, 29 January 1969.
59 PH, Cahier 29, 7/17/68, SLA.
60 Interview with Madeleine Harmsworth.
61 PH, Letter to Barbara Ker-Seymer, 20 July 1968, SLA.
62 Interview with Heather Chasen, 6 October 1999.
63 Interview with Madeleine Harmsworth.
64 PH, Letter to Alex Szogyi, 1 February 1969, SLA.
65 Ibid.
66 Interview with Madeleine Harmsworth.

23 The false, the fake and the counterfeit 1968–1969

1 PH, Cahier 28, 7/22/65, SLA.
2 PH, Cahier 29, 2/23/66, SLA.
3 PH, Cahier 30, 10/3/68, SLA.
4 PH, Cahier 30, 11/20/68, SLA.
5 PH, Cahier 30, 11/5/68, SLA.
6 PH, Cahier 30, 10/11/68, SLA.
7 PH, Letter to Alex Szogyi, 26 December 1968, SLA.
8 PH, Letter to Barbara Ker-Seymer, 29-30 November 1968, SLA.
9 PH, Cahier 30, 11/15/68, SLA.
10 PH, 'The Hand', *Little Tales of Misogyny*, Heinemann, London, 1977, p. 3; first published as *Kleine Geschichten für Weiberfeinde*, Diogenes Verlag, Zurich, 1975.
11 PH, Letter to Barbara Ker-Seymer, 18 December 1968, SLA.
12 PH, Letter to Barbara Ker-Seymer, 4 January 1969, SLA.
13 Auriol Stevens, 'Private Highsmith', *Guardian*, 29 January 1969.
14 PH, Letter to Barbara Ker-Seymer, 10 February 1969, SLA.
15 Cynthia Koestler, 21 January 1969, Diary December 1968 – December 1969, KA.
16 Ibid.
17 PH, 'Togetherness', Cahier 30, 1/6/69, SLA.
18 PH, Letter to Alex Szogyi, 25 June 1969, SLA.
19 Cynthia Koestler, 20 July 1969, Diary December 1968 – December 1969, KA.
20 Ibid.
21 PH, Diary 16, 20 August 1969, SLA.
22 PH, Dedication, *Ripley Under Ground*, Heinemann, London, 1971.
23 Interview with Hester Green, 16 November 2000.
24 PH, *Ripley Under Ground*, p. 5.
25 Chris Matthew, 'Writing the wrong-doers', *Radio Times*, 2 December 1972.
26 PH, *Ripley Under Ground*, p. 183.
27 'The Talented Miss Highsmith', *Times Literary Supplement*, 24 September 1971.
28 PH, *Ripley Under Ground*, p. 163.
29 Michiko Kakutani, 'The Kinship of Macabre and Banal', *New York Times*, 19 November 1999.
30 PH, *Ripley Under Ground*, p. 10.
31 Ibid., p. 265.
32 Ibid., p. 269.

33 Ibid., p. 276.
34 Ibid., p. 298.
35 *The Times*, 21 January 1971.
36 Pooter, *The Times*, 25 January 1969.
37 Ibid.
38 PH, *Ripley Under Ground*, p. 65.
39 Ibid., p. 210.
40 Ibid., p. 169.
41 Ibid., p. 280.
42 Oscar Wilde, quoted in Richard Ellmann, *Oscar Wilde*, Hamish Hamilton, London, 1987, p. 529.
43 Wilde, *The Picture of Dorian Gray*, Penguin Books, London, 1949, p. 164.
44 Ibid., p. 201.
45 PH, *Ripley Under Ground*, p. 69.
46 Wilde, *The Picture of Dorian Gray*, p. 92.
47 Bettina Berch, 'A Talk With Patricia Highsmith', 15 June 1984, unpublished interview, SLA.
48 Wilde, *The Picture of Dorian Gray*, p. 164.
49 Wilde, 'Pen, Pencil and Poison', *Fortnightly Review*, January 1889, *Intentions*, James Osgood, London, 1891, p. 65.
50 Wilde, 'Lecture on Thomas Chatterton', quoted in Ellmann, *Oscar Wilde*, p. 269.
51 Wilde, 'The Decay of Lying', *Nineteenth Century*, January 1889, *Intentions*, p. 54.
52 PH, *Ripley Under Ground*, p. 148.

24 An equal opportunity offender 1969–1970

1   Tom Paulin, 'Mortem Virumque Cano', *New Statesman*, 25 November 1977.
2   Ibid.
3   PH, Letter to Kate Kingsley Skattebol, 20 March 1969, SLA.
4   Kathleen Gregory Klein, *And Then There Were Nine...More Women of Mystery*, ed. Jane S. Bakerman, Bowling Green State University Popular Press, Bowling Green, Ohio, 1985, p. 174.
5   Philippa Burton, 'Patricia Highsmith: Male Perspective and Little Tales of Misogyny', *Quarto* 11, 1999, adapted from a speech given at the Research School for Literature, University of Leiden, the Netherlands, 15 December 1998.
6   Interview with Barbara Roett, 5 May 1999.
7   Interview with Heather Chasen, 6 October 1999.
8   PH, Letter to Ronald Blythe, 26 November 1966, RB.
9   Bettina Berch, 'A Talk with Patricia Highsmith', 15 June 1984, unpublished interview, SLA.
10 Ibid.
11 Ibid.
12 Interview with Michael Kerr, 10 April 2002.
13 PH, Cahier 6, 2/27/42, SLA.
14 PH, Cahier 8, 11/17/42, SLA.
15 PH, Cahier 27, SLA.
16 Interview with Vivien De Bernardi, 23 July 1999.
17 PH, Letter to Alex Szogyi, 10–11 March 1969, SLA.
18 PH, Letter to Barbara Ker-Seymer, SLA.
19 Ibid.
20 PH, Letter to Barbara Ker-Seymer, 15 March 1969, SLA.
21 Ibid.
22 PH, Letter to Alex Szogyi, 10–11 March 1969, SLA.
23 PH, Letter to Alex Szogyi, 31 March 1969, SLA.
24 PH, Cahier 28, 12/19/64, SLA.

25 PH, Letter to Barbara Ker-Seymer, 15 April 1969, SLA.
26 Interview with Charles Latimer, 2 November 1998.
27 PH, Cahier 30, 5/27/69, SLA.
28 PH, Letter to Alex Szogyi, 20 May 1969, SLA.
29 PH, Cahier 30, 12/30/69, SLA.
30 Ibid.
31 PH, Cahier 30, 6/23/69, SLA.
32 PH, Letter to Alex Szogyi, 14 November 1969, SLA.
33 PH, Cahier 30, 11/14/69, SLA.
34 Interview with Barbara Roett.
35 PH, Letter to Alex Szogyi, 17 December 1969, SLA.
36 Mary Highsmith, Letter to PH, 3 March 1970, SLA.
37 PH, Letter to Stanley Highsmith, 11 June 1970, SLA.
38 Mary Highsmith, Letter to PH, 3 March 1970, SLA.
39 Ibid.
40 PH, Letter to Ronald Blythe, 17 March 1970, RB.
41 PH, 'Must We Always Write for Money', 1974, SLA.
42 PH, Letter to Arthur Koestler, 26 April 1970, KA, MS 2386/5.
43 Ibid.
44 PH, Letter to Alex Szogyi, 23 August 1970, SLA.
45 Ibid.
46 PH, Letter to Kate Kingsley Skattebol, 30 July 1978, SLA.
47 Stanley Highsmith, Letter to PH, 23 August 1970, SLA.
48 Ibid.
49 Ibid.
50 Ibid.
51 Ibid.
52 PH, Letter to Stanley Highsmith, 1 September 1970, SLA.
53 PH, Letter to Stanley Highsmith, 10 November 1970, SLA.
54 PH, Letter to Kate Kingsley Skattebol, 29 November 1970, SLA.
55 PH, Cahier 31, 12/20/71, SLA.
56 Mary Highsmith, Letter to PH, 6 February 1971, SLA.
57 Mary Highsmith, Letter to PH, 3 February 1971, SLA.

25 Name: Ishmael 1970–1971

1 PH, Letter to Alex Szogyi, 3 January 1970, SLA.
2 PH, Letter to Ronald Blythe, 24 May 1970, RB.
3 Ibid.
4 PH, Cahier 31, 5/5/70, SLA.
5 PH, Letter to Alex Szogyi, 29 July 1970, SLA.
6 PH, Letter to Alex Szogyi, 18 August 1970, SLA.
7 PH, Letter to Ronald Blythe, 18 February 1971, RB.
8 PH, Letter to Ronald Blythe, 16 August 1970, RB.
9 Ibid.
10 PH, *A Dog's Ransom*, Heinemann, London, 1972, p. 105.
11 Ibid., p. 110.
12 Ibid., p. 32.
13 Ibid., p. 127.
14 PH, Letter to Ronald Blythe, 18 February 1971, RB.
15 PH, *A Dog's Ransom*, p. 281.
16 Ibid., p. 115.

17 Ibid., p. 15.
18 PH, Cahier 31, 1/26/70, SLA.
19 Gore Vidal, Letter to the author, undated but received January 2000.
20 PH, 'My Favorite writer(s)', sent to *Konkret Sonderhefte*, Hamburg, 20 July 1987, SLA.
21 Ibid.
22 PH, 'The Novel', written for *New Review*, unpublished, SLA.
23 Saul Bellow, *Mr Sammler's Planet*, Weidenfeld & Nicolson, London, 1970, p. 205.
24 Bellow, *Mr Sammler's Planet*, p. 43.
25 PH, Cahier 31, undated.
26 PH, *My Favorite writer(s)*.
27 PH, Letter to Janice Robertson, 14 April 1973, JR.
28 PH, 'Tradition in American Literature', Barnard essay, 23 April 1942, SLA. Highsmith received an A-grade for the essay, along with the comment, from Professor Thornbury, 'Interesting, but some of the generalizations are questionable'.
29 PH, Cahier 23, 6/28/54, SLA.
30 Frank Rich, 'American Pseudo', *New York Times Magazine*, 12 December 1999.
31 Lucretia Stewart, 'Animal Lover's Beastly Murders', *Sunday Telegraph*, 8 September 1991.
32 *Kaleidoscope*, BBC Radio, 17 March 1975.
33 PH, 'The Novel'.
34 PH, Letter to Alain Oulman, 6 August 1979, CLA.
35 James Campbell, 'Murder, She (Usually) Wrote', *New York Times*, 27 October 2002.
36 PH, Letter to Alain Oulman, 26 July 1979, CLA.
37 PH, Letter to Alain Oulman, 10 September 1979, CLA.
38 Kate Kingsley Skattebol, Letter to the author, 21 May 2002; PH's story 'The Trouble with Mrs Blynn, The Trouble with the World', *The New Yorker*, 27 May 2002.
39 Joan Dupont, 'Criminal Pursuits', *New York Times Magazine*, 12 June 1988.
40 Ian Hamilton, 'Patricia Highsmith', *New Review*, August 1977.
41 Craig Brown, 'Too Busy Writing to be a Writer', *Daily Telegraph*, 29 January 2000 .
42 Larry Ashmead, Letter to the author, 7 November 2002.
43 Janice Robertson, Letter to the author, 10 October 2002.
44 PH, Letter to Janice Robertson, 15 February 1973, JR.
45 Interview with Janice Robertson, 10 October 2002.
46 Interview with Roger Smith, 14 October 2002.
47 Publishing Proposal, *A Dog's Ransom*, Heinemann, JR; figures quoted include home and export.
48 Interview with Gary Fisketjon, 21 May 1999.
49 Ibid.
50 Larry Ashmead, Letter to the author, 7 November 2002.
51 Rosemarie Pfluger, *Of Books and their Makers: Diogenes, Portrait of a Publishing House*, September 1998, SF DRS and 3sat.
52 Ibid.
53 Ibid.
54 PH, Letter to Barbara Ker-Seymer, 7 November 1970, SLA.
55 PH, Letter to Barbara Ker-Seymer, 5 October 1972, SLA.
56 Interview with Kate Kingsley Skattebol, 14 May 1999.
57 Pfluger, *Of Books and their Makers*.
58 PH, Cahier 31, 1/5/70, SLA.
59 Lucretia Stewart, 'Animal Lover's Beastly Murders', *Sunday Telegraph*, 8 September 1991.
60 PH, Letter to Alex Szogyi, 25 June 1969, SLA.
61 PH, Letter to Ronald Blythe, 16 August 1970, RB.
62 PH, *A Dog's Ransom*, p. 161.
63 Alain Oulman, Letter to PH, 28 September 1971, CLA.
64 PH, Letter to Alain Oulman, 1 October 1971, CLA.
65 PH, Letter to Barbara Ker-Seymer, 9 May 1971, SLA.
66 PH, Cahier 31, 6/5/71, SLA.

67 PH, Cahier 31, 7/14/71, SLA.
68 PH, Cahier 31, 8/25/71, SLA.
69 PH, Letter to Barbara Ker-Seymer, 24–25 October 1970, SLA.
70 Interview with Daniel Keel, 27 October 1999.
71 Interview with Vivien De Bernardi, 23 July 1999.
72 PH, Letter to Ronald Blythe, 24 May 1970, RB.
73 Joan Juliet Buck, 'A Terrifying Talent', *Observer Magazine*, 20 November 1977.
74 Interview with Winifer Skattebol, 18 May 1999.
75 Interview with Barbara Roett, 5 May 1999.
76 PH, Cahier 31, 8/25/71, SLA.
77 PH, Cahier 31, 10/17/71, SLA.
78 Interview with Tristram Powell, 25 March 2002.
79 PH, Letter to Arthur Koestler, 20 June 1971, KA, MS 2387/2.
80 PH, Letter to Barbara Ker-Seymer, 2 December 1971, SLA.
81 Alain Oulman, Letter to PH, 28 September 1971, CLA.
82 Mary Borg, 'Violent Rations', *New Statesman*, 28 April 1972.
83 'Man Hunts Dog', *Times Literary Supplement*, 12 May 1972.
84 Graham Greene, Letter to PH, 5 May 1972, quoted by PH, Letter to Alain Oulman, 6 June 1972, CLA.
85 Diane LeClercq, *Books and Bookmen*, August 1972.
86 'A need to go to the very edge', *The Times*, 27 April 1972.
87 Reg Gadney, 'Criminal Tendencies', *London Magazine*, June–July 1972.
88 Brigid Brophy, 'Poodle', *Listener*, 11 May 1972.

26 What are the odds of cat versus person? 1971–1973

1 PH, Cahier 32, 11/2/71, SLA.
2 PH, Cahier 32, 11/24/71, SLA.
3 PH, Letter to Barbara Ker-Seymer, 8 December 1971, SLA.
4 PH, *Ripley's Game*, Heinemann, London, 1974, p. 1.
5 PH, Cahier 31, 7/20/71, SLA.
6 PH, *Ripley's Game*, p. 165.
7 Ibid., p. 124.
8 Ibid., p. 211.
9 Ibid., p. 263.
10 PH, Cahier 32, 11/26/71, SLA.
11 PH, Cahier 32, 11/20/71, SLA.
12 PH, *Ripley's Game*, p. 174.
13 Ibid., p. 270.
14 Ibid.
15 *Spectator*, 23 March 1974.
16 Tony Henderson, *Books and Bookmen*, May, 1974, p. 84.
17 Ibid.
18 PH, 'Ming's Biggest Prey', *The Animal-Lover's Book of Beastly Murder*, Heinemann, London, 1975, p. 65.
19 PH, Letter to Barbara Ker-Seymer, 15-16 March 1972, SLA.
20 Marghanita Laski, 'Long Crimes, Short Crimes', *Listener*, 20 November 1975.
21 PH, 'The Cat Complex', *Murderess Ink: The Better Half of the Mystery*, ed. Dilys Winn, Bell Publishing Company, New York, 1981, p. 37.
22 Kate Kingsley Skattebol, Letter to the author, 13 February 2002.
23 Interview with Janice Robertson, 10 October 2002.
24 Interview with Bruno Sager, 25 September 1999.

25 PH, Cahier 13, 6/3/46, SLA.
26 PH, Letter to Alex Szogyi, 12 September 1967, SLA.
27 PH, Letter to Arthur Koestler, 10 April 1968, KA, MS 2386/1.
28 PH, 'The Day of Reckoning', *The Animal-Lover's Book of Beastly Murder*, p. 142.
29 PH, Cahier 31, 13/8/70, SLA.
30 Interview with Gudrun Mueller, 25 July 1999.
31 Neil Gordon, Letter to the author, 9 November 2001.
32 PH, 'Notes from a Respectable Cockroach', *The Animal-Lover's Book of Beastly Murder*, p. 147.
33 Ibid., p. 146.
34 PH, Letter to Barbara Ker-Seymer, 20–21 January 1972, SLA.
35 PH, 'The Man who Wrote Books in his Head', in *Slowly, Slowly in the Wind*, Heinemann, London, 1979, p. 5.
36 PH, 'The Pond', *Slowly, Slowly in the Wind*, p. 41.
37 PH, Cahier 32, 4/4/72, SLA.
38 PH, Letter to Ronald Blythe, 28 May 1972, RB.
39 Ibid.
40 PH, Letter to Barbara Ker-Seymer, 3 June 1972, SLA.
41 Interview with Hester Green, 16 November 2000.
42 Jay Bernard Plangman, Letter to PH, 26 May 1972, SLA.
43 Mary Highsmith, Letter to PH, 27 June 1972, SLA.
44 Ibid.
45 PH, Letter to Barbara Ker-Seymer, 5 October 1972, SLA.
46 PH, Letter to Ronald Blythe, 6 October 1972, RB.
47 PH, Letter to Barbara Ker-Seymer, 14 February 1973, SLA.
48 PH, Letter to Alex Szogyi, 1 March 1973, SLA.
49 Charles Latimer, Letters to the author, 20 March 2001, 31 March 2001.
50 Vivien De Bernardi, Letter to the author, 27 March 2001.
51 Sir Michael Levey, Letter to the author, 8 February 2002.
52 PH, Postcard to Arthur Koestler, 24 August 1973, KA, MS 2388/3.
53 PH, *Jahrbuch Film 78/79*, Herausgegeben von Hans Günther Pflaum, Berichte, Kritiken, Daten, Carl Hanser Verlag, Munich.
54 PH, Cahier 32, 7/19/73, SLA.
55 PH, Cahier 32, 7/27/73, SLA.
56 Interview with Heather Chasen, 6 October 1999.
57 Daisy Winston, Letter to PH, 22 March 1974, SLA.
58 PH, Letter to Barbara Ker-Seymer, 31 August 1973, SLA.
59 PH, 'First Love', *Sunday Times Magazine*, 20 January 1974.
60 Ibid.

27 The summer soldier and the sunshine patriot 1973–1976

1 Michel Block, Letter to the author, 7 May 2002.
2 Patrick Cosgrave, *Spectator*, 23 March 1974.
3 Ibid.
4 Hugh Hebert, 'Maid a'killing', *Guardian*, 18 March 1974.
5 PH, Cahier 33, 7/12/74, SLA.
6 Interview with Don Coates, 26 November 1999.
7 Interview with Dan Coates, 20 November 1999.
8 Mary Highsmith, Letter to PH, 31 September 1974, SLA.
9 Interview with Phyllis Nagy, 7 October 1999.
10 PH, Letter to Ronald Blythe, 26 February 1977, RB.

11 PH, Cahier 33, 8/2/74, SLA.
12 PH, Cahier 33, 9/1/74, SLA.
13 PH, Cahier 6, 4/19/42, SLA.
14 PH, *Edith's Diary*, Heinemann, London, 1977, p. 4.
15 Ibid., p. 5.
16 Ibid., p. 56.
17 Ibid., p. 182.
18 Ibid., p. 284.
19 PH, Cahier 33, 11/21/74, SLA.
20 Erich Fromm, *The Art of Loving*, World Perspectives, Harper & Brothers, New York, 1956, p. 20.
21 Fromm, *The Art of Loving*, pp. 8–9.
22 Fromm, *The Anatomy of Human Destructiveness*, Jonathan Cape, London, 1974, p. 289.
23 PH, *Edith's Diary*, p. 76.
24 Ibid., p. 303.
25 Fromm, *The Anatomy of Human Destructiveness*, p. 289.
26 PH, Letter to Barbara Ker-Seymer, 9 September 1973, SLA.
27 Dennis Gabor, *The Mature Society*, Secker & Warburg, London, 1972, p. 1.
28 Ibid.
29 Gabor, *The Mature Society*, p. 4.
30 Ibid., p. 47.
31 PH, *Edith's Diary*, p. 2.
32 Ibid., p. 13.
33 PH, Cahier 23, 7/11/54, SLA.
34 PH, *Edith's Diary*, p. 13.
35 Ibid., p. 68.
36 Ibid., p. 238.
37 Ian Hamilton, 'Patricia Highsmith', *New Review*, August 1977.
38 Susan Smith, 'Trouble With Patricia Highsmith: No Label', *International Herald Tribune*, 3 August 1977.
39 PH, *Edith's Diary*, p. 154.
40 Ibid., p. 310.
41 Noelle Loriot, 'Trois Jours Avec Patricia Highsmith', *L'Express*, 2–8 June 1979, quoted in Russell Harrison, *Patricia Highsmith*, Twayne Publishers, New York, 1997, pp. 82, 145.
42 PH, *Edith's Diary*, p. 64.
43 Bettina Berch, 'A Talk with Patricia Highsmith', 15 June 1984, unpublished interview, SLA.
44 Interview with Kate Kingsley Skattebol, 14 May 1999.
45 PH, Letter to Alain Oulman, 26 June 1976, CLA.
46 *The Book Programme*, BBC2, 11 November 1976.
47 Ian Hamilton, 'Patricia Highsmith', *New Review*, August 1977.
48 Neil Hepburn, 'Nuclear Reactions', *Listener*, 26 May 1977.
49 Emma Tennant, 'Frighteningly normal', *Times Literary Supplement*, 20 May 1977.
50 *New Yorker*, 29 August 1977.
51 Michael Wood, 'A Heavy Legacy', *New York Review of Books*, 15 October 1977.
52 Ibid.
53 Interview with Marion Aboudaram, 17 July 1999.
54 PH, Letter to Charles Latimer, 28 February 1975, SLA.
55 Interview with Marion Aboudaram.
56 Ibid.
57 PH, Cahier 33, 6/6/75, SLA.
58 Interview with Peter Huber, 14 March 1999.
59 Ibid.
60 PH, Cahier 33, 11/11/75, SLA.
61 Interview with Marion Aboudaram.

28 Your kisses fill me with terror 1976–1978

 1 PH, Letter to Kate Kingsley Skattebol, 11 February 1976, SLA.
 2 Ibid.
 3 PH, Cahier 34, 9/1/76, SLA.
 4 Ian Hamilton, 'Patricia Highsmith', *New Review*, August 1977.
 5 PH, *The Boy who Followed Ripley*, Heinemann, London, 1980, p. 69.
 6 Cahier 32, 10/20/71, SLA.
 7 PH, Letter to Arthur Koestler, 25 June 1978, KA, MS 2391/3.
 8 PH, *The Boy who Followed Ripley*, p. 29.
 9 Ibid., p. 4.
10 Ibid., p. 220.
11 Ibid., p. 74.
12 Ibid., p. 86.
13 Ibid., p. 122.
14 Ibid., p. 123.
15 Ibid., p. 130.
16 Ibid., p. 160.
17 Ibid., p. 177.
18 Ibid., p. 275.
19 Mark Todd, 'Silhouettes', *New Statesman*, 9 May 1980.
20 Craig Brown, 'Perspectives of Guilt', *Times Literary Supplement*, 25 April 1980.
21 Helen Birch, 'Patricia Highsmith', *City Limits*, 20–27 March 1986.
22 PH, *The Boy who Followed Ripley*, p. 112.
23 PH, Cahier 34, 9/22/76, SLA.
24 PH, Cahier 34, 9/23/76, SLA.
25 PH, Letter to Ronald Blythe, 28 April 1977, RB.
26 Wim Wenders, Letter to the author, 22 February 2002.
27 Ibid.
28 PH, Cahier 34, 9/23/76, SLA.
29 Wim Wenders, Letter to the author.
30 Ibid.
31 Craig Little, 'Patricia Highsmith', *Publishers Weekly*, 2 November 1992.
32 PH, Cahier 34, 9/23/76, SLA.
33 PH, Cahier 34, 1/31/77, SLA.
34 PH, Letter to Charles Latimer, 10 February 1977, SLA.
35 PH, 'Vienna revisited', *Radio Times*, 30 April–6 May 1977.
36 Ibid.
37 PH, Letter to Ronald Blythe, 26 February 1977, RB.
38 PH, Cahier 34, 8/17/77, SLA.
39 Joan Juliet Buck, 'A Terrifying Talent', *Observer Magazine*, 20 November 1977.
40 Ibid.
41 Ibid.
42 Ibid.
43 PH, Letter to Kate Kingsley Skattebol, 22 September 1977, SLA.
44 PH, Letter to Barbara Ker-Seymer, 5 October 1977, SLA.
45 Sam White, 'That Lady from Texas', *Evening Standard*, 30 September 1977.
46 PH, Letter to Barbara Ker-Seymer, 5 October 1977, SLA.
47 PH, 'Daran glaube ich', *Welt am Sonntag*, 9 October 1977, SLA.
48 Ibid.
49 PH, Letter to Barbara Ker-Seymer, 29 November 1977, SLA.
50 PH, Letter to Charles Latimer, 21 November 1977, SLA.
51 PH, annotations to Bell's whisky label, Cahier 34, SLA.
52 Ibid.

53 PH, *Jahrbuch Film 78/79*, Herausgegeben von Hans Günther Pflaum, Berichte, Kritiken, Daten, Carl Hanser Verlag, Munich.
54 Interview with Christa Maerker, 13 January 2000.
55 PH, Jahrbuch Film 78/79.
56 Interview with Christa Maerker.
57 Interview with Anne Morneweg, 14 January 2000.
58 PH, Jahrbuch Film 78/79.
59 PH, 'Berlin and After', *A Dedicated Fan, Julian Jebb 1934–1984*, ed. Tristram and Georgia Powell, Peralta Press, London, 1993.
60 Ibid.
61 PH, *Jahrbuch Film 78/79*.
62 Interview with Tabea Blumenschein, 13 January 2000.
63 Interview with Anne Morneweg.
64 PH, Cahier 34, 3/22/78, SLA.
65 PH, 'Poem for T, Written Not on Horseback But on the Typewriter', Cahier 34, dated 9 April 1978, SLA.
66 Interview with Marion Aboudaram.
67 PH, Letter to Barbara Ker-Seymer, 18 May 1978, SLA.
68 PH, Cf. LR, TB, undated, SLA.
69 PH, 'April 11, '78', Cahier 34, SLA.
70 Interview with Linda Ladurner, 8 January 2001.
71 Interview with Tabea Blumenschein.
72 PH, Letter to Kate Kingsley Skattebol, 15 May 1978, SLA.
73 Interview with Tabea Blumenschein.
74 PH, '10 May 1978', Cahier 34, SLA.
75 Alex Szogyi, Letter to PH, 19 June 1978, SLA.
76 PH, '2 June '78', Cahier 34, SLA.
77 PH, Letter to Charles Latimer, 19 June 1978, SLA.
78 PH, Letter to Barbara Ker-Seymer, 3 July 1978, SLA.
79 Interview with Tabea Blumenschein.
80 PH, Letter to Barbara Ker-Seymer, 10 September 1978, SLA.

29 A girl who allows me to dream 1978–1980

1 PH, Letter to Barbara Ker-Seymer, 19 August 1978, SLA.
2 Interview with Monique Buffet, 27 January 2001.
3 PH, Letter to Carl Laszlo, 17 December 1978, SLA.
4 PH, Letter to Alain Oulman, 6 May 1979, CLA.
5 PH, Letter to Alain Oulman, 8 June 1979, CLA.
6 PH, Note to Monique Buffet, 29 October 1978, SLA.
7 PH, Letter to Barbara Ker-Seymer, 19 August 1978, SLA.
8 PH, Letter to Alain Oulman, 14 December 1978, CLA.
9 PH, Letter to Kate Kingsley Skattebol, 28 April 1979, SLA.
10 *Desert Island Discs*, BBC Radio, 21 April 1979.
11 Ibid.
12 PH, *The Boy who Followed Ripley*, Heinemann, London, 1980, p. 59.
13 Lorna Sage, 'Black Mischief', *Observer*, 1 April 1979.
14 Blake Morrison, 'Hot Stuff', *New Statesman*, 30 March 1979.
15 PH, 'Please Don't Shoot the Trees', *Slowly, Slowly in the Wind*, Heinemann, London, 1979, p. 166.
16 Ibid., p. 178.
17 Kate Kingsley Skattebol, Letter to the author, 19 March 2002.

18 Interview with Jonathan Kent, 19 January 2000.
19 Interview with Bettina Berch, 18 May 1999.
20 PH, Letter to Barbara Ker-Seymer, 3 November 1979, SLA.
21 Interview with Carl Laszlo, 22 August 1999.
22 Barbara Skelton, 'Patricia Highsmith at Home', *London Magazine*, August/September 1995.
23 Ibid.
24 Interview with Anne Morneweg, 14 January 2000.
25 PH, Letter to Alain Oulman, 2 August 1979, CLA.
26 Patricia S. Myrer (née Schartle), Letter to PH, 21 August 1979, CLA.
27 PH, Letter to Alain Oulman, 10 February 1980, CLA.
28 PH, Cahier 35, 15/1/80, SLA.
29 Ibid.
30 Ibid.
31 PH, Cahier 35, 2/24/80, SLA.
32 PH, Letter to Barbara Ker-Seymer, 21 March 1980, SLA.
33 PH, Letter to Christa Maerker, 14 April 1980, CM.
34 PH, Letter to Mr Okoshken, 27 June 1980, CLA.
35 PH, Cahier 35, 6/1/83, SLA.
36 Sally Vincent, 'Wave from afar', *Observer*, 27 April 1980.
37 Interview with Carl Laszlo, 22 August 1999.
38 Interview with Patricia Losey, 6 October 1999.
39 Ibid.

30 People who knock on the door 1980–1982

1 PH, Cahier 35, 7/10/80, SLA.
2 Ibid.
3 PH, Cahier 35, 13/7/80, SLA.
4 PH, 'The Terrors of Basket-Weaving', *The Black House*, Heinemann, London, 1981, p. 52.
5 PH, 'The Kite', *The Black House*, p. 234.
6 Thomas Sutcliffe, 'Graphs of Innocence and Guilt', *Times Literary Supplement*, 2 October 1981.
7 PH, Letter to Alain Oulman, 13 September 1979, CLA.
8 Thomas Sutcliffe, 'Graphs of Innocence and Guilt'.
9 John Gross, '3 Mystery Books Offer Crimes High and Low', *New York Times*, 18 March 1988.
10 Charles Latimer, Letter to PH, November 1980, SLA.
11 Steve Brouwer, Paul Gifford, Susan D. Rose, *Exploring the American Gospel: Global Christian Fundamentalism*, Routledge, New York, London, 1996, p. 15.
12 Ibid., p. 28.
13 Interview with Charles Latimer, 2 November 1998.
14 PH, Cahier 35, 1/16/81, SLA.
15 Interview with Charles Latimer.
16 PH, Letter to Marc Brandel, 22 April 1982, EB.
17 PH, *People who Knock on the Door*, Heinemann, London, 1983, p. 20.
18 Ibid., pp. 243–244.
19 Helen Birch, 'Patricia Highsmith', *City Limits*, 20–27 March 1986.
20 PH, Letter to Marc Brandel, 18 April 1986, EB.
21 PH, *Twenty Things that I Do Not Like*, 20 March 1983.
22 Holly Eley, 'The Landscape of Unease', *Times Literary Supplement*, 4 February 1983.
23 H.R.F. Keating, 'The vaguest of dooms ahead', *The Times*, 24 February 1983.
24 Interview with Larry Ashmead, 20 May 1999.

25 PH, Letter to Marc Brandel, 23 April 1982, EB.
26 PH, Letter to Ronald Blythe, 21 October 1988, RB.
27 *Book Beat*, Interview with Donald Swaim, CBS Radio, 29 October 1987, DS.
28 Barbara Skelton, 'Patricia Highsmith at Home', *London Magazine*, August/September 1995.
29 Interview with Tobias Ammann, 24 July 1999.
30 Ena Kendall, 'Patricia Highsmith, 'A Room of My Own', *Observer*, 15 June 1986.
31 Interview with Anne Morneweg, 14 January 2000.
32 Interview with Christa Maerker, 13 January 2000.
33 PH, Inscription, *The Tremor of Forgery*, 23 July 1975, the collection of Peter Huber.
34 Interview with Peter Huber, 24 July 1999.
35 Interview with Monique Buffet, 27 January 2001.
36 Michel Block, Letter to the author, 7 May 2002.
37 PH, Answers to Q&A for *Ellery Queen's Mystery Magazine*, sent 18 November 1981, SLA.
38 PH, Letter to Barbara Ker-Seymer, 30 January 1982, SLA.
39 PH, Cahier 35, 1/26/82, SLA.
40 Interview with Linda Ladurner, 8 January 2001.
41 PH, Letter to Marc Brandel, 22 April 1982, EB.
42 PH, Letter to Marc Brandel, 23 April 1982, EB.
43 PH, Letter to Barbara Ker-Seymer, 18 March 1982, SLA.
44 Interview with Monique Buffet.

31 A strange interior world 1982–1983

1 'Patricia Highsmith: A Gift for Murder', *The South Bank Show*, LWT, 14 November 1982.
2 Ibid.
3 Ibid.
4 Ibid.
5 Ibid.
6 Interview with Jack Bond, 13 March 2001.
7 PH, Letter to Alain Oulman, 18 September 1982, CLA.
8 Interview with Jack Bond.
9 Frank Rich, 'American Pseudo', *New York Times Magazine*, 12 December 1999.
10 Interview with Jonathan Kent, 19 January 2000.
11 Interview with Roger Clarke, 15 January 2001.
12 PH, Cahier 35, 10/11/82, SLA.
13 Interview with Vivien De Bernardi, 23 July 1999.
14 Interview with Jonathan Kent.
15 PH, Letter to Barbara Ker-Seymer, 14 September 1973, SLA.
16 PH, Letter to Alain Oulman, 4 March 1983, CLA.
17 PH, Letter to Kate Kingsley Skattebol, 14 May 1983, SLA.
18 Interview with Kate Kingsley Skattebol, 14 May 1999.
19 Interview with Jonathan Kent.
20 PH, Letter to Marc Brandel, 15 May 1983, EB.
21 Interview with Christa Maerker, 13 January 2000.
22 PH, Letter to Bettina Berch, 23 August 1983, SLA.
23 Interview with Barbara Grier, 11 October 1999.
24 Alain Oulman, Letter to PH, 23 May 1985, CLA.
25 Alain Oulman, Letter to PH, 25 September 1985, CLA.
26 PH, Cahier 35, 17/6/83 (European dating), SLA.
27 Tim Bouquet, 'Sweet Smell of Cyanide', *Midweek*, 10 April 1986.
28 PH, *Plotting and Writing Suspense Fiction*, The Writer Inc., Boston, 1966, p. 51.

29 Helen Birch, 'Patricia Highsmith', *City Limits*, 20–27 March 1986.
30 PH, Cahier 35, 20/7/83 (European dating), SLA.
31 PH, Letter to Barbara Ker-Seymer, 16 September 1984, SLA.
32 *Book Beat*, Interview with Donald Swaim, CBS Radio, 29 October 1987, DS.
33 PH, *Found in the Street*, Heinemann, London, 1986, p. 97.
34 Ibid., p. 49.
35 Ibid., p. 92.
36 Ibid., p. 168.
37 Ibid., p. 266.
38 Ibid., p. 6.
39 PH, Letter to Barbara Ker-Seymer, 7 August 1983, SLA.
40 David Streiff, Letter to the author, 20 January 2001.
41 PH, Letter to Barbara Ker-Seymer, 13 September 1983, SLA.
42 PH, Letter to Patricia Losey, 16 April 1984, SLA.
43 PH, Cahier 36, 18/9/83 (European dating), SLA.
44 Interview with Anne Morneweg, 14 January 2000.
45 Peter Kemp, 'Led down murky, twisted ways', *Sunday Times*, 8 November 1987.
46 PH, Cahier 36, 8/27/83, SLA.
47 PH, Jacket blurb, *Tales of Natural and Unnatural Catastrophes*, Bloomsbury, London, 1987.
48 PH, Letter to Marc Brandel, 11 January 1984, EB.
49 Ibid.
50 PH, Letter to Barbara Ker-Seymer, 13 January 1984, SLA.
51 Interview with Kate Kingsley Skattebol.
52 Interview with Anne Elisabeth Suter, 8 January 2001.
53 Interview with Otto Penzler, 21 May 1999.

32 Work is more fun than play 1983–1986

1 Marc Brandel, Letter to PH, 29 March 1984, SLA.
2 Interview with Edith Brandel, 7 September 1999.
3 PH, Letter to Marc Brandel, 12 June 1985, EB.
4 PH, Letter to Marc Brandel, 11 November 1985, EB.
5 Marc Brandel, Letter to PH, 22 November 1985, SLA.
6 PH, Cahier 36, 4/3/84, SLA.
7 Interview with Bettina Berch, 18 May 1999.
8 Bettina Berch, 'A Talk with Patricia Highsmith,' 15 June 1984, unpublished interview, SLA.
9 Ibid.
10 Ibid.
11 Interview with Bettina Berch.
12 Ibid.
13 PH, Letter to Marc Brandel, 1 October 1984, EB.
14 Interview with Vivien De Bernardi, 23 July 1999.
15 Joan Dupont, 'The Poet of Apprehension', *Village Voice*, 30 May 1995.
16 Interview with Peter Huber, 14 March 1999.
17 Interview with Jack Bond, 13 March 2001.
18 PH, Letter to Dan Coates, 11 November 1986, SLA.
19 PH, Letter to Marc Brandel, 1 October 1984, EB.
20 PH, Letter to Bettina Berch, 16 December 1984, SLA.
21 Otto Penzler, *Wall Street Journal*, 31 August 2001.
22 Interview with Otto Penzler, 21 May 1999.
23 PH, Letter to Bettina Berch, 7 February 1985, SLA.
24 PH, 'Good Books', written 6 January 1985, SLA.

25 PH, 'Why I Write', SLA.
26 PH, 'Fragebogen', *Frankfurter Allgemeine Magazin*, 10 May 1985.
27 Alain Oulman, Letter to PH, 19 August 1985, CLA.
28 PH, Letter to Alain Oulman, 23 August 1985, CLA.
29 PH, Letter to Marc Brandel, 3 July 1985, EB.
30 PH, 'Berlin and After', *A Dedicated Fan: Julian Jebb 1934–1984*, edited by Tristram and Georgia Powell, Peralta Press, London, 1993, p. 160.
31 Ibid.
32 PH, Letter to Francis Wyndham, 7 November 1984, FW.
33 PH, Cahier 36, 5/8/85, SLA.
34 PH, Letter to Francis Wyndham, 25 October 1985, FW.
35 PH, Letter to Marc Brandel, 11 October 1985, EB.
36 PH, Letter to Marc Brandel, 11 December 1985, EB.
37 PH, Letter to Marc Brandel, 24 January 1986, EB.
38 PH, Letter to Marc Brandel, 25 February 1986, EB.
39 Craig Brown, 'The Hitman and Her', *The Times*, Saturday Review, 28 September 1991.
40 Ibid.
41 PH, Cahier 36, 30/8/86, SLA.
42 Ibid.
43 Interview with Vivien De Bernardi.
44 PH, Cahier 36, 30/8/86 (European dating), SLA.
45 PH, Letter to Marc Brandel, 18 April 1986, EB.
46 PH, Cahier 36, 30/8/86, SLA.
47 Ibid.
48 Interview with Jack Bond.
49 PH, Letter to Patricia Losey, 12 June 1986, SLA.
50 Gore Vidal, Letter to the author, undated but received April 2000.
51 Gore Vidal, quoted in William Safire, 'Vidal's Injurious Equation: Friends of Israel = Traitors', *International Herald Tribune*, 22 May 1986.
52 Ibid.
53 PH writing as Edgar S. Sallich, Letters page, *International Herald Tribune*, 9 June 1986.
54 PH, Letter to Gore Vidal, 9 June 1986, GV.
55 PH, Cahier 36, 30/8/86 (European dating), SLA.

33 No end in sight 1986–1988

1 Interview with Vivien De Bernardi, 23 July 1999.
2 PH, Letter to Alain Oulman, 10 June 1986, CLA.
3 Interview with Christa Maerker, 13 January 2000.
4 Interview with Jack Bond, 13 March 2001.
5 PH, Letter to Marc Brandel, 25 February 1986, EB.
6 PH, Letter to Gore Vidal, 25 June 1986, GV.
7 PH, Letter to Marc Brandel, 12 October 1986, EB.
8 Ibid.
9 Interview with Tobias Ammann, 24 July 1999.
10 PH, 'No End in Sight', *Tales of Natural and Unnatural Catastrophes*, Bloomsbury, London, 1987, p. 127.
11 Ibid., p. 139.
12 PH, Letter to Kate Kingsley Skattebol, 11 February 1976, SLA.
13 PH, annotation to a letter from Dan Coates, 28 February 1974, SLA.
14 PH, Cahier 36, 28/5/85 (European dating), SLA.
15 PH, 'No End in Sight', *Tales of Natural and Unnatural Catastrophes*, p. 132.

16 Ibid., p. 133.
17 Ibid., p. 134.
18 Ibid., p. 136.
19 Ibid., p. 134.
20 Ibid.
21 Ibid., p. 135.
22 Ibid., pp. 135–6.
23 Ibid., p. 136.
24 PH, Diary 17, 14 March 1991, SLA.
25 Ibid.
26 Interview with Vivien De Bernardi.
27 PH, 'President Buck Jones Rallies and Waves the Flag', *Tales of Natural and Unnatural Catastrophes*, p. 189.
28 PH, Dedication, *People who Knock on the Door*, Heinemann, London, 1983.
29 PH, Lleida speech, 26 April 1987, SLA.
30 Interview with Otto Penzler, 21 May 1999.
31 Craig Little, 'Patricia Highsmith', *Publishers Weekly*, 2 November 1992.
32 PH, Letter to Marc Brandel, 3 August 1986, EB.
33 PH, Letter to Patricia Losey, 22 March 1987, SLA.
34 PH, Letter to Patricia Losey, 19 May 1987, SLA.
35 PH, Letter to Marc Brandel, 2 January 1988, EB.
36 PH, Letter to Christa Maerker, 28 September 1987, CM.
37 PH, Diary 17, 15 September 1987, SLA.
38 PH, Diary 17, 10 October 1987, SLA.
39 Interview with William Trevor, 22 April 2002.
40 PH, Diary 17, 10 October 1987, SLA.
41 Interview with Gary Fisketjon, 21 May 1999.
42 Interview with Vivien De Bernardi.
43 Interview with Phyllis Nagy, 7 October 1999.
44 PH, 'Green-Wood: Listening to the Talking Dead', unpublished, SLA.
45 Ibid.
46 PH, Diary 17, November 1987, SLA.
47 *The Kenneth Williams Diaries*, Edited by Russell Davies, HarperCollins Publishers, London, 1993, p. 773.
48 *Cover to Cover*, BBC2, 5 November 1987.
49 Ibid.
50 Duncan Fallowell, 'The Talented Miss Highsmith', *Sunday Telegraph Magazine*, 20 February 2000.
51 Ibid.
52 Ibid.
53 Interview with Tanja Howarth, 13 December 1999.
54 Interview with Phyllis Nagy.
55 Phyllis Nagy, Letter to the author, 18 August 2002.
56 Ibid.
57 PH, 'Green-Wood: Listening to the Talking Dead', unpublished, SLA.

34 A face accustomed to its ghosts 1988

1 PH, Cahier 36, 1/1/88, SLA.
2 PH, Letter to Marc Brandel, 2 January 1988, EB.
3 PH, *Ripley Under Water*, Bloomsbury, London, 1991, p. 2.
4 Julian Symons, 'Life with a Likable Killer, *New York Times Book Review*, 18 October 1992.

5 PH, *Ripley Under Water*, p. 27.
6 Ibid., p. 28.
7 Ibid., p. 4.
8 Ibid., p. 34.
9 Ibid., p. 11.
10 PH, Cahier 36, 12/6/88, SLA.
11 PH, *Ripley Under Water*, p. 96.
12 Ibid.
13 Ibid., p. 83.
14 Ibid., p. 111.
15 Ibid., p. 84.
16 PH, *The Boy who Followed Ripley*, Heinemann, London, 1980, p. 13.
17 Terrence Rafferty, 'Fear and Trembling', *The New Yorker*, 4 January 1988.
18 PH, Letter to Kate Kingsley Skattebol, 3 January 1988, SLA.
19 Joan Dupont, 'The Poet of Apprehension, *Village Voice*, 30 May 1995.
20 Joan Dupont, 'Criminal Pursuits', *New York Times Magazine*, 12 June 1988.
21 Ibid.
22 Ibid.
23 Joan Dupont, Letter to the author, 10 April 2001.
24 PH, Diary 17, 28 February 1988, SLA.
25 PH, Cahier 37, 15–17/2/89 (European dating), SLA.
26 Dedication, *Ripley Under Water*, Bloomsbury, London, 1991.
27 PH, 'Peace in the Middle East', August 1992, unpublished, SLA.
28 PH, 'International Book of the Year', *Times Literary Supplement*, 2 December 1994.
29 Naim Attallah, 'The Oldie Interview, Patricia Highsmith', *The Oldie*, 3 September 1993.
30 PH, 'Peace in the Middle East', August 1992, unpublished, SLA.
31 Kate Kingsley Skattebol, Letter to the author, 12 April 2002.
32 Douglas Reed, *The Controversy of Zion*, Bloomfield Books, Sudbury, Suffolk, 1978, p. 448.
33 Ibid., p. 568.
34 PH, Letter to Gore Vidal, 12 December 1989, GV.
35 PH, 'Daran glaube ich', *Welt am Sonntag*, 9 October 1977, SLA.
36 *After Dark*, Open Media, Channel 4, 18 June 1988.
37 EXIT membership card, dated June 1990, SLA.
38 Buffie Johnson, 'Patricia Highsmith', unpublished, undated.
39 Ibid.
40 PH, Letter to Christa Maerker, 2 September 1988, CM.
41 Interview with Gudrun Mueller, 25 July 1999.
42 Ibid.

35 Art is not always healthy and why should it be? 1988–1992

1 Vivien De Bernardi, Letter to the author, 28 April 2002.
2 Craig Brown, 'The Hitman and Her', *The Times*, Saturday Review, 28 September 1991.
3 Interview with Kate Kingsley Skattebol, 25 May 1999.
4 Janet Watts, 'Love and Highsmith', *Observer Magazine*, 9 September 1990.
5 Craig Brown, 'The Hitman and Her'.
6 Janet Watts, 'Love and Highsmith'.
7 Mavis Guinard, 'Patricia Highsmith: Alone With Ripley', *International Herald Tribune*, 17–18 August 1991.
8 Ibid.
9 Interview with Irma Andina, 24 July 1999.

10　Interview with Ingeborg Lüscher, 24 July 1999.

11　Ibid.

12　PH, Letter to Kate Kingsley Skattebol, 6 February 1989, SLA.

13　Interview with Peter Huber, 14 March 1999.

14　Interview with Vivien De Bernardi, 23 July 1999.

15　Ibid.

16　Ibid.

17　Ibid.

18　Ibid.

19　PH, Letter to Christa Maerker, 11 October 1989, CM.

20　Neil Gordon, Letter to the author, 9 November 2001.

21　PH, Cahier 37, 2/2/90, SLA.

22　PH, Alain Oulman obituary, *Guardian*, 12 April 1990.

23　Ibid.

24　PH, *Ripley Under Water*, Bloomsbury, London, 1991, p. 169.

25　PH, Cahier 37, 20/5/90 (European dating), SLA.

26　Ibid.

27　Interview with Patricia Losey, 6 October 1999.

28　David Sexton, 'Forbidden love story', *Sunday Correspondent*, 30 September 1990.

29　*The Late Show*, BBC2, 3 October 1990.

30　Interview with Sarah Dunant, 2 May 2002.

31　Victoria Glendinning, 'Forbidden love story comes out', *The Times*, 11 October 1990.

32　Craig Brown, 'Packing a Sapphic punch', *Sunday Times*, 14 October 1990.

33　Susannah Clapp, 'Lovers on a Train', *London Review of Books*, 10 January 1991.

34　Ibid.

35　Ibid.

36　Interview with Christa Maerker, 13 January 2000.

37　Ibid.

38　Ibid.

39　Ibid.

40　Barbara Skelton, 'Patricia Highsmith at Home', *London Magazine*, August/September 1995.

41　Ibid.

42　Craig Little, 'Patricia Highsmith', *Publishers Weekly*, 2 November 1992.

43　PH, Diary 17, 14 January 1991, SLA.

44　Ibid.

45　PH, Letter to Patricia Losey, 23 February 1991, SLA.

46　PH, Letter to Patricia Losey, 4 April 1991, SLA.

47　Interview with Gudrun Mueller, 25 July 1999.

48　Interview with Ingeborg Lüscher.

49　Interview with Charles Latimer, 2 November 1998.

50　Liz Calder, 'Patricia Highsmith', *The Oldie*, March 1995.

51　James Campbell, 'How pleasant to meet Mr Tom', *Times Literary Supplement*, 4 October 1991.

52　Hugo Barnacle, 'The gentle art, or how to get away with murder', *Independent*, 12 October 1991.

53　PH, Letter to Marc Brandel, 6 January 1992, EB.

54　Interview with Heather Chasen, 6 October 1999.

55　PH, Letter to Bettina Berch, 26 January 1992, SLA.

56　PH, Cahier 37, 8/2/92 (European dating), SLA.

36 I hesitate to make promises 1992–1995

1 PH, Letter to Liz Calder, Bloomsbury Publishing, 19 March 1992.
2 PH, *Small g: a Summer Idyll*, Bloomsbury, London, 1995, p. 4.
3 Vivien De Bernardi, Letter to the author, 30 April 2002.
4 PH, Cahier 37, 14/3/92 (European dating), SLA.
5 Vivien De Bernardi, Letter to the author, 29 April 2002.
6 PH, *Small g: a Summer Idyll*, p. 9.
7 Ibid., p. 219.
8 Ibid., p. 9.
9 Ibid., p. 230.
10 Ibid., p. 155.
11 Ibid., p. 45.
12 Ibid., p. 48.
13 Ibid., p. 73.
14 Ibid., p. 151.
15 Ibid.
16 Ibid., p. 186.
17 Interview with Craig Brown, 30 April 2001.
18 James Campbell, 'Criminal negligence', *Times Literary Supplement*, 24 February 1995.
19 PH, Diary 17, 22 May 1992, SLA.
20 PH, Diary 17, 23 May 1992, SLA.
21 PH, Letter to Charles Latimer, 30 May 1992, SLA.
22 Interview with Julia Diethelm, 27 March 1999.
23 PH, 'My Life with Greta Garbo', *The Oldie*, 3 April 1992.
24 Liz Calder, 'Patricia Highsmith', *The Oldie*, March 1995.
25 Interview with Marilyn Scowden, 28 March 1999.
26 Lucretia Stewart, 'Animal Lover's Beastly Murders', *Sunday Telegraph*, 8 September 1991.
27 Ibid.
28 Ibid.
29 Interview with Donald S. Rice, 17 November 1999.
30 Donald S. Rice, 'A Personal Remembrance from Our Chairman', *Yaddo News*, Special Edition, Spring 1998, p. 2.
31 Ibid.
32 Neil Gordon, Letter to the author, 9 November 2001.
33 PH, Cahier 37, 27/11/92 (European dating), SLA.
34 Paula Chin, Michael Haederle, 'Through A Mind, Darkly', *People*, 11 January 1993.
35 Naim Attallah, 'The Oldie Interview, Patricia Highsmith', *The Oldie*, 3 September 1993.
36 Interview with Bee Loggenberg, 31 August 1999.
37 Ibid.
38 Interview with Vivien De Bernardi, 23 July 1999.
39 PH, Letter to Dan Coates, 31 October 1993, SLA.
40 Barbara Skelton, 'Patricia Highsmith at Home', *London Magazine*, August/September 1995.
41 PH, Letter to Bettina Berch, 19 March 1994, SLA.
42 Interview with Bruno Sager, 25 September 1999.
43 PH, Letter to Kate Kingsley Skattebol, 20 August 1994, SLA
44 Interview with Vivien De Bernardi
45 Jean-Etienne Cohen-Séat, Letter to PH, 25 May 1994, CLA.
46 Joan Dupont, 'The Poet of Apprehension', *Village Voice*, 30 May 1995.
47 Interview with Gary Fisketjon, 21 May 1999.
48 Neil Gordon, 'Murder of the Middle Class', *Nation*, 1 October 2001.
49 Kate Kingsley Skattebol, Letter to the author, 27 August 2002.
50 Interview with Bee Loggenberg.
51 PH, Letter to Jean-Etienne Cohen-Séat, 27 October 1994, CLA.

52 Interview with Vivien De Bernardi
53 Ibid.
54 PH, Letter to Kate Kingsley Skattebol, 12 January 1995, SLA.
55 Interview with Ingeborg Lüscher, 24 July 1999.
56 Interview with Vivien De Bernardi.
57 Interview with Bert Diethelm, 27 March 1999.
58 Ibid.
59 Interview with Marilyn Scowden.
60 Ibid.
61 Interview with Vivien De Bernardi.

Epilogue

1 Vivien De Bernardi, Letter to the author, 8 May 2002.
2 Interview with Vivien De Bernardi, 23 July 1999.
3 Anna von Planta, 'Notes on the Stories', *Nothing That Meets the Eye: The Uncollected Stories of Patricia Highsmith*, W.W. Norton, New York, 2002, p. 451.
4 'Crime need not be a second-class genre of literature', *The Times*, 6 February 1995.
5 Michael Tolkin, 'In Memory of Patricia Highsmith', *Los Angeles Times Book Review*, 12 February 1995.
6 Brooks Peters, 'Stranger Than Fiction', *Out*, June 1995.
7 Liz Calder, 'Patricia Highsmith', *The Oldie*, March 1995.
8 Grey Gowrie, 'Why her place is secure', *Daily Telegraph*, 11 March 1995.
9 Geoffrey Elborn, 'Mellow at the last', *Guardian*, 7 March 1995.
10 William Trevor, *Independent on Sunday*, 26 March 1995.
11 Lorna Sage, 'Savage Swiss-army knife', *Observer*, 12 March 1995.
12 T.J. Binyon, 'Murder Most Fair', *Sunday Times*, 12 March 1995.
13 Rose Wild, 'Ms Nasty turns out nice', *The Times*, 25 March 1995.
14 Michael Dobbs, 'A dark and oppressive world', *Sunday Telegraph*, 5 March 1995.
15 Brian Glanville, 'Sad finale to a literary life's work', *European Magazine*, 10–16 March 1995.
16 Joan Dupont, 'The Poet of Apprehension', *Village Voice*, 30 May 1995.
17 Ibid.
18 Ibid.
19 Vivien De Bernardi, Memorial address, 11 March 1995.
20 Interview with Tanja Howarth, 13 December 1999.
21 Joan Dupont, 'The Poet of Apprehension'.
22 PH, Cahier 34, A Toast, 1979, SLA.
23 Interview with Tanja Howarth.
24 PH, Cahier 32, 7/30/73, SLA.
25 James Campbell, 'Murder, She (Usually) Wrote', *New York Times*, 27 October 2002.
26 Interview with Tanja Howarth.
27 Margaret Caldwell Thomas, *Women of Mystery*, ed. Martha Hailey DuBose, quoted in Ed Siegel, 'Killer Instinct', *Boston Globe*, 27 January 2002.
28 Ed Siegel, 'Killer Instinct'.

List of Illustrations

Acknowledgements

This book could not have been written without the help of Highsmith's literary executor, Daniel Keel, president of Diogenes Verlag, Zurich, and his trusted editor, Anna von Planta. They gave me unrestricted access to Highsmith's most personal of journals – her diaries – and permission to quote from both her unpublished and published works. I cannot thank them enough for this and for their continued support while researching and writing the book.

The bulk of Highsmith's papers – diaries, notebooks, letters, essays and sketches – are held at the Swiss Literary Archives (SLA), Berne, which gave me permission to publish material from their vast collection. I owe a deep debt of gratitude to all the staff at the SLA, but in particular Dr Thomas Feitknecht, Ulrich Weber, Stéphanie Cudré-Mauroux and Lucienne Schwery. In addition to their first-rate curatorial skills and utmost professionalism I would also like to thank them for their friendliness and hospitality. They made my frequent visits to the Swiss capital even more enjoyable.

I also consulted archival material in a number of private collections. Thank you to Ronald Blythe, Edith Brandel, Peggy Lewis, Christa Maerker, Janice Robertson, and Francis Wyndham for making their correspondence available to me.

Acknowledgement is also due to the following for the use and publication of other archival material: Barnard College, New York; Bloomsbury Publishing, London; Calmann-Lévy, Paris; Rare Book and Manuscript Library, Columbia University, New York, (the Harper & Row archives); Edinburgh University Library (Koestler Archive); Harry Ransom Humanities Research Center, the University of Texas at

Austin, (which holds the Alfred A. Knopf, Harper, and William A. Bradley Literary Agency collections); the New York Public Library, (*The New Yorker* records); Temple University, Paley Library, Urban Archives, Philadelphia; Wisconsin Center for Film and Theater Research, Madison, Wisconsin, for access to the Gore Vidal Collection (now held at Houghton Library, Harvard University); and Yaddo, Saratoga Springs, New York. In particular I would like to thank Donald Glassman, archivist at Barnard College; Elisabeth Laye at Calmann-Lévy; Jean Ashton at the Rare Book and Manuscript Library, Columbia University, New York; Tara Wenger at the Harry Ransom Humanities Research Center, the University of Texas at Austin; Wayne Furman, Office of Special Collections, the New York Public Library; Brenda Wright and Sarah Sherman, Temple University, Urban Archives; Benjamin Brewster, Wisconsin Center for Film and Theater Research, Madison, Wisconsin; and Lesley Leduc at Yaddo.

Other curators, libraries and institutions which have provided invaluable help include: Douglas Anderson and Tammy Hiltz at the Ashtabula Reference Library, Ohio; Blaine County Court Records Library, Idaho; National Library, British Film Institute, London; Dr Christopher Fletcher, the British Library, London; British Library Newspaper Library; Fort Worth Public Library, Texas; Fort Worth Independent School District, Texas; Walt Reed at Illustration House, New York; Julia Richman High School, New York; New Hope Public Library, Pennsylvania; New York Historical Society; Birgitta H. Bond at the James Michener Arts Museum, Doylestown, Pennsylvania; PS 122 Queens, Astoria, New York; the Queens Borough Public Library, New York; Ridgewood Public Library, New Jersey; Tarrant County Records Library, Fort Worth, Texas.

For permission to quote further copyright material, I would like to thank the following: Jean-Etienne Cohen-Séat, president of Calmann-Lévy; Richard Ovenden, Edinburgh University for the unpublished letters and diaries of Arthur and Cynthia Koestler; and Olivia Kahn, the sister of the late Joan Kahn.

I must also acknowledge the help of Anna von Planta, Ulrich Weber and Lucienne Schwery, who rendered sections of Highsmith's diaries written in idiosyncratic French, German, Spanish and Italian into clear, concise English.

A large number of people agreed to talk to me about their memories of Patricia Highsmith and I would like to thank each of them for their time, honesty and insight. Every one of them made a special contribution to this book. Interviews have been conducted with the following:

Marion Aboudaram, Tobias Ammann, Irma Andina, Larry Ashmead, Bettina Berch, Vivien De Bernardi, Ruth Bernhard, Ronald Blythe, Tabea Blumenschein, Jack Bond, Edith Brandel, Craig Brown, Susan Brynteson, Monique Buffet, Peter Burton, Mary Cable, Frederique Chambrelent, Heather Chasen, Ann Clark, Roger Clarke, Dan Coates, Don Coates, Betty Curry, David Diamond, Burt Diethelm, Julia Diethelm, Sarah Dunant, Joan Dupont, Maggie Eversol, Gary Fisket-jon, Brian Glanville, Hester Green, Barbara Grier, Madeleine Harms-worth, Tanja Howarth, Anita Huber, Peter Huber, Richard Ingham, Buffie Johnson, Deborah Karp, H.R.F. Keating, Daniel Keel, Priscilla Kennedy, Jonathan Kent, Michael Kerr, Linda Ladurner, Carl Laszlo, Charles Latimer, Peggy Lewis, Bee Loggenberg, Patricia Losey, Ingeborg Lüscher, Christa Maerker, Muriel Mandelbaum, Anne Morneweg, Gudrun Mueller, Phyllis Nagy, Ulrike Ottinger, Otto Penzler, Phillip Powell, Tristram Powell, Donald S. Rice, Janice Robertson, Barbara Roett, Bruno Sager, Marilyn Scowden, Rita Semel, Kate Kingsley Skattebol, Roger Smith, Anne Elisabeth Suter, Alex Szogyi, Peter Thomson, William Trevor, David Williams and Francis Wyndham.

I would also like to thank the following for their letters to me: Pamela Anderson, Larry Ashmead, Thomas Beckman, Vivien De Bernardi, Michel Block, Ann Clark, Philip Davis, Jennifer Dewey, Joan Dupont, Dorothy Edson, Maggie Eversol, Donald Glassman, Neil Gordon, Charles Latimer, Henry Lea, Sir Michael Levey, Marijane Meaker, Patricia Schartle Myrer, Janice Robertson, Kate Kingsley Skattebol, Winifer Skattebol, David Streiff, Gore Vidal, and Wim Wenders.

Throughout the book I have quoted from a number of newspapers, magazines and critical journals. I would like thank the following writers: Naim Attallah, Hugo Barnacle, Helen Birch, the late Brigid Brophy, Craig Brown, Joan Juliet Buck, James Campbell, Susannah Clapp, Diana Cooper-Clark, Michael Dobbs, Joan Dupont, Geoffrey Elborn, Duncan Fallowell, Victoria Glendinning, Grey Gowrie, the late Ian Hamilton, Ena Kendall, William Leith, Craig Little, Blake Morrison, Gerald Peary, Margaret Pringle, Terrence Rafferty, Frank Rich, the late Lorna Sage, David Sexton, the late Barbara Skelton, Lucretia Stewart, the late Julian Symons, William Trevor, Sally Vincent, Janet Watts, Francis Wyndham. I would also like to thank Bettina Berch for her permission to quote at length from the transcript of her unpublished interview 'A Talk With Patricia Highsmith', 15 June 1984; Natasha De Bernardi for sending me 'The Eye Reflecting the Whole', her thesis on Highsmith; and Lucienne Schwery for 'Der Nachlass Patricia Highsmith'.

Acknowledgement is also due to a number of broadcast sources including the BBC Information and Archives; LWT; Sebastian Cody at Open Media, London; Donald L. Swaim's interview for *Book Beat* (CBS Radio), Archives & Special Collections, Ohio University Libraries; and the National Sound Archive, London.

For use of the photographs in the book I am grateful to the following: Associated Newspapers; Bantam Press; Naomi Brandel; the British Film Institute; Canal +; Ann Clark; Alberto Flammer; Priscilla Kennedy and her family; the Kobal collection; Bee Loggenberg; London Weekend Television; Ingeborg Lüscher; Miramax Films; Road Movies Filmproducktion GmbH; Kate Kingsley Skattebol; Jacques-Eric Strauss; Temple University, Urban Archives, Philadelphia; and, of course, the Swiss Literary Archives.

At Bloomsbury I would like to thank Liz Calder, who commissioned the book and who remained enthusiastic from the outset, as well as my copy-editor Victoria Millar, assistant editor Katherine Greenwood and rights director Ruth Logan. My agent Clare Alexander at Gillon Aitken not only helped get the project off the ground, but she continued to act as a constant source of support and friendship. I must also thank Fanny Blake and Deborah Singmaster for the important roles they played in the gestation of this book.

I would like to express my gratitude and love to those who have had to share me with the shadow of Patricia Highsmith over the last few years. Thank you to my family, close friends, everyone at Alpeneggstrasse, 10, Berne and Marcus Field.

This book is dedicated to Kate Kingsley Skattebol and the late Charles Latimer, friends Highsmith entrusted with the job of 'steering off the wrong biographers' after her death. I hope I haven't disappointed.

Index

Works by Patricia Highsmith (PH) appear directly under title; works by others under authors' names

A NOTE ON THE AUTHOR

Andrew Wilson is a journalist who has written for most of Britain's national newspapers, including the *Observer*, the *Daily Telegraph*, the *Guardian*, the *Independent on Sunday* and the *Daily Mail*. This is his first book.

A NOTE ON THE TYPE

The text of this book is set in Linotype Sabon, named after the type
founder, Jacques Sabon. It was designed by Jan Tschichold and
jointly developed by Linotype, Monotype and Stempel, in response
to a need for a typeface to be available in identical form for
mechanical hot metal composition and hand composition using
foundry type.

Tschichold based his design for Sabon roman on a fount engraved
by Garamond, and Sabon italic on a fount by Granjon. It was first
used in 1966 and has proved an enduring modern classic.